"Joseph Gordon offers a sophisticated, creative, and compelling account of the human-divine character of Scripture, and of Scripture's instrumental role in the divine economy of human transformation for participation in the life of the Triune God. Gordon's treatments of the rule of faith as hermeneutical necessity, the soul (reinterpreted for our context) as the subject of transformation, and the theological significance of the Bible's concrete, diverse instantiations inform his overall project in fresh ways. This is an important volume that deserves the careful attention of both biblical scholars and theologians."

—Michael J. Gorman, Raymond E. Brown Professor of
Biblical Studies and Theology, St. Mary's Seminary & University

"God may not have a context, but Scripture—God's inscripturated word—certainly does, and the major contribution of Gordon's study lies in its careful unpacking of the role that various historical contexts have on its authors' and readers' categories of understanding. As an added bonus, *Divine Scripture in Human Understanding* contains one of the clearest descriptions of Bernard Lonergan's unique approach to theology's task of faith seeking textual and traditioned understanding for today that I have yet come across."

—Kevin J. Vanhoozer, Research Professor of Systematic Theology,
Trinity Evangelical Divinity School

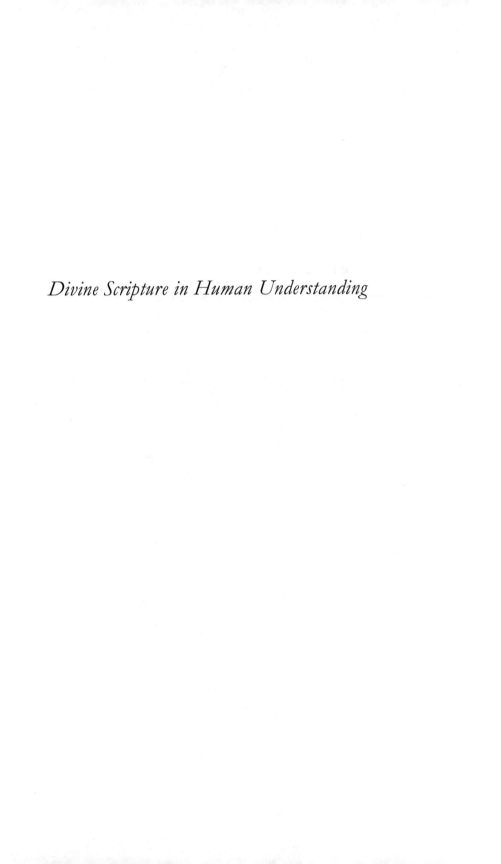

Divine Scripture in Human Understanding

READING THE SCRIPTURES

Gary A. Anderson, Matthew Levering, and Robert Louis Wilken

series editors

Divine Scripture in Human Understanding

A SYSTEMATIC THEOLOGY OF THE CHRISTIAN BIBLE

JOSEPH K. GORDON

UNIVERSITY OF NOTRE DAME PRESS

NOTRE DAME, INDIANA

University of Notre Dame Press
Notre Dame, Indiana 46556
www.undpress.nd.edu

Published © 2019 by the University of Notre Dame

Published in the United States of America

Library of Congress Cataloging-in-Publication Data

Names: Gordon, Joseph K., 1985– author.
Title: Divine scripture in human understanding : a systematic theology
    of the Christian Bible / Joseph K. Gordon.
Description: Notre Dame : University of Notre Dame Press, 2019. |
    Series: Reading the Scriptures | Includes bibliographical references and index. |
    Identifiers: LCCN 2019003978 (print) | LCCN 2019004374 (ebook) |
    ISBN 9780268105198 (pdf) | ISBN 9780268105204 (epub) |
    ISBN 9780268105174 (hardback) | ISBN 0268105170 (hardback)
Subjects: LCSH: Bible—Criticism, interpretation, etc.
Classification: LCC BS511.3 (ebook) | LCC BS511.3 .G667 2019 (print) |
    DDC 230/.041—dc23
LC record available at https://lccn.loc.gov/2019003978

° *This book is printed on acid-free paper.*

CONTENTS

ACKNOWLEDGMENTS

I am overwhelmed when I recall all of the help and encouragement I have received while working on this project. I must first acknowledge my gratitude to the God who is Father, Son, and Holy Spirit for sustaining me during this work. As I have reflected and written, I have regularly felt the weight of responsibility that comes from writing and teaching about divine things (James 3.1) and have prayed countless times that these words would be relatively adequate to the reality of God's economic work in and through Christian Scripture. My prayer is that this work will be useful and edifying for those who hope to read and understand the treasures of the written Word of God. Anything valuable in this work I owe ultimately to God. I am eternally grateful to the communities of St. John's, Abbottsford Hall, Real Life, and St. Luke and St. Peter's, and for my friends in the Ekklesia Project for prayer and for spiritual and emotional support through the process of writing this work.

"We can become transformed vicariously," David Burrell writes in *Friendship and Ways to Truth*, "in the transformation of those whose lives have become entwined with ours" (17). My life has been entwined with—and so transformed by—countless others as I worked on this project, which began its formal life as my doctoral dissertation at Marquette University. I owe many thanks to friends and colleagues in the Department of Theology at Marquette, and to their significant others, for stimulating conversations and for the joy of their company. There are too many to name, but I must single out Stephen and Katie Waers and Ryan and Kate Hemmer for special mention. Thanks are also due to Jeremy Blackwood, Christopher Brenna, Anne Carpenter, Nick Elder, Jen Fenton, Kirsten Guidero, Jon Heaps, Geoff Holsclaw, Karen Keen, Samantha Miller, Jakob Rinderknecht, Gene Schlesinger, Tyler Stewart, Eric Vanden Eykel, and Juli Vasquez for their encouragement and feedback regarding specific aspects of this project. Thanks are also due to numerous members of the theology faculty at Marquette who taught me in seminars or took the time to discuss theology, Scripture, and professional matters with me. I owe thanks to Michel Barnes, Josh Burns, Michael Cover, Ralph Del Colle (†), Deirdre Dempsey, Julian Hills, Mark Johnson, Therese Lysaught, Joseph Mueller, Joseph Ogbonnaya, Andrei Orlov, David Schultenover, Susan Wood, and Wanda Zemler-Cizewski. I owe a great deal to professors and mentors at Johnson University and Lincoln Christian Seminary, especially John Castelein, Steve Cone, Steve Cook, Bob Kurka (†), Bob Rea, and Chris Simpson. Thanks are also due to John Barton, Adam Bean, Cynthia Crysdale, Steve Fowl, Ben Fulford, Michael Gorman, David Bentley Hart, Stephen Lawson, Matthew Levering, Eric Mabry, David Mahfood, Peter Martens, Dan McClain, Neil Ormerod, Randy Rosenberg, Matt Tapie, Roy Terry, and Jeremy Wilkins, who took time to discuss aspects of this work with me or offered encouragement. I owe special thanks to Neil Ormerod and Kevin Vanhoozer for their vital critical and constructive feedback and reassurance during the formal review process. I could not have asked for, or imagined, having better mentors and dissertation codirectors than Bob Doran and Steve Long. Those I have mentioned have undoubtedly contributed to whatever strengths this work has. They cannot, and should not, be blamed for any of its shortcomings, for which I take full responsibility.

I am thankful for and humbled by the financial support I received from the Department of Theology at Marquette during my doctoral studies; I am especially grateful for the dissertation fellowship I received during the 2014–15 school year and for nominations for two university-wide fellowships. I am also thankful to the Lonergan Research Institute for receipt of the Crowe Bursary in 2015, awarded as support for my research on this project. I also owe special thanks to Sheila Berg, Susan Berger, Stephen Little, Wendy McMillen, and the rest of the staff at the University of Notre Dame Press, who answered every question I asked promptly and with exceptional professionalism; their efforts have made the review and publication process go incredibly smoothly.

I am extremely grateful to the administration and faculty of Johnson University for entrusting me with the lofty work of forming students for theological reflection and for financial, emotional, and spiritual support since July 2015. I owe special thanks to Nealy and Jeff Brown, Mike Chambers, Lora Erickson, Heather and Jamey Gorman, Les Hardin, Kendi Howells-Douglas, Rafael Rodriguez, Tommy Smith, Gary Stratton, Jon Weatherly, Gary Weedman, Mark Weedman, and Mark Ziese for their encouraging words and patience as I finished this project. Thanks are also due to Marla Black in the Johnson University Florida library for exceptionally prompt help with acquiring resources and to Taylor Wells, Angel Domenech, Elijah Mize, and Brian Cook for their capable work as teaching assistants. I owe special thanks to my parents, David and Marie, for their constant care, words of encouragement, and prayers. Thanks are also due to my in-laws, Neal and Miriam Windham; to my siblings, Renee, Ben, Luke, and Sarah; and to those others in my family, especially Grandma Gordon, who prayed for me and encouraged me during this process. Final thanks are reserved for Charis, to whom I dedicate this work, and Stephen David, who arrived in our lives as this project neared its completion. I cannot imagine a lovelier and more thoughtful and patient partner in ministry and life than Charis. Thank you for walking alongside me with so much grace and encouragement, both in this work and in our life together.

Abbreviations for the books of the Bible and other common terms generally follow the guidelines in *The SBL Handbook of Style: For Biblical Studies and Related Disciplines*, 2nd edition (2014).

1 Apol.	*Apologia i*
1 Clem.	1 Clement
2 Clem.	2 Clement
An. post.	*Analytica posteriora*
ASC	Bernard Lonergan, *A Second Collection*
ATC	Bernard Lonergan, *A Third Collection*
Autol.	*Ad Autolycum*
B. Bat.	Baba Batra
Barn.	Barnabus
C. Ap.	Josephus, *Contra Apionem*
CD	Karl Barth, *Church Dogmatics*
Cels.	Origen, *Contra Celsum*
Civ.	Augustine, *De civitate Dei*
Comm. Jo.	Origen, *Commentarii in evagelium Joannis*
Comm. Matt.	Origen, *Commentarium in evangelium Matthaei*
Comm. Rom.	Origen, *Commentarii in Romanos*
Common.	Vincent of Lérins, *Commonitorium*
Conf.	Augustine, *Confessionum librii XIII*
CWL	Collected Works of Bernard Lonergan
De an.	Aristotle, *De anima*
De pud.	Tertullian, *De pudicitia*
Decr.	Athanasius, *De decretis*
Dial.	Justin Martyr, *Dialogus cum Tryphone*

Did.	Didache
Doctr. chr.	Augustine, *De doctrina christiana*
DSS	Dead Sea Scrolls
EM (ME)	Henri de Lubac, *Exégèse médiévale/Medieval Exegesis*
Ep.	*Epistle*
Epid.	Irenaeus, *Epideixis tou apostolikou kērygmatos*
Faust.	Augustine, *Contra Faustum Manichaeum*
Fr. 1 Cor.	Origen, *Fragmenta ex commentariis in epistulam i ad Corinthios*
Gen. Man.	Augustine, *De Genesi contra Manichaeos*
Gos. Thom.	Gospel of Thomas
Haer.	Irenaeus, *Adversus Haereses (Elenchos)*
HE (HS)	Henri de Lubac, *Histoire et esprit/History and Spirit*
Hom. Exod.	Origen, *Homiliae in Exodum*
Hom. Gen.	Origen (or John Chrysostum), *Homiliae in Genesim*
Hom. Jes. Nav.	Origen, *In Jesu Nave homiliae xxvi*
Hom. Judic.	Origen, *Homiliae in Judices*
Hom. Matt.	John Chrysostum, *Homiliae in Matthaeum*
Ign. *Eph.*	Ignatius, *To the Ephesians*
Ign. *Phld.*	Ignatius, *To the Philadephians*
Inc.	Athanasius, *De incarnatione*
Inst.	Cicero, *Institutio oratoria*
Jub.	Jubilees
Let. Aris.	Letter of Aristeas
LXX	Septuagint
Metaph.	Aristotle, *Metaphysica*
MIT	Bernard Lonergan, *Method in Theology*
Mor. Manich.	Augustine, *De moribus Manichaeorum*
MT	Masoretic Text
NT	New Testament
OT	Old Testament
Philoc.	Origen, *Philocalia*
Pol. *Phil.*	Polycarp, *To the Philippians*
Praep. ev.	Augustine, *Praeparatio evangelica*
Praescr.	Tertullian, *De praescriptione haereticorum*
Prax.	Tertullian, *Adversus Praxean*

Princ.	Origen, *De principiis*
ProEccl	*Pro Ecclesia*
SC	Sources chrétiennes
Sof.	*Soferim*
Somn.	Philo, *De somniis*
ST	Thomas Aquinas, *Summa Theologiae*
Strom.	Clement of Alexandria, *Stromateis*
Tr. Ps.	Hilary of Portiers, *Tratatus super Psalmos*
Util. cred.	Augustine, *De utilitate credenda*
Virg.	Tertullian, *De virginibus velandis*

CHAPTER ONE

Scripture at the Level of Our Times

Situation, Exigencies, and Thesis

> The problem of reading the Holy Book—if you have faith that it is the
> Word of God—is the most difficult problem in the whole field of reading.
> There have been more books written about how to read Scripture than
> about all other aspects of the art of reading together. The Word of God is
> obviously the most difficult writing men can read; but it is also, if you
> believe it is the Word of God, the most important to read.
> —Mortimer Adler and Charles Van Doren, *How to Read a Book*

Determining the function and role of Scripture in Christian life and
thought and articulating the precise parameters of interpretation of the
Bible have been perennial challenges for the Christian community.[1] Contemporary Christians must face such challenges head-on, though, if they
are to maintain the conviction that Scripture is indeed the written Word
of God. The challenges are especially acute today, when there are dozens
of competing approaches to Scripture in academic, ecclesial, and secular
settings. As Robert Sokolowski declares, our present postmodern situation provides "an embarrassment of riches" for understanding the Bible.[2]
Popular and technical literature devoted to promoting the meaning and

1

use of Christian Scripture has proliferated in recent years. Within academic or scholarly study of the Christian Bible, this literature can be divided roughly into three major families of approaches: historical-critical, contextual, and primarily theological. This tripartite typology is admittedly imprecise.[3] Even given its imprecision, though, it is useful to the extent that it identifies family resemblances characteristic of contemporary scholarly interpretive approaches to the study of the Christian Bible.

I discuss each of the three approaches briefly below, but it is important to first note that these approaches have emerged as scholars interested in the Christian scriptures have engaged and appropriated recent developments in philosophical reflection on textual interpretation and on the general conditions and possibilities of human understanding. The most pressing challenge of our contemporary situation is to measure up to the significance of the fact that all human understanding is tied to specific times and places and to think through how this judgment should affect Christian engagement with Scripture.[4] "Historical consciousness" names this dimension of contemporary reflection; contemporary readers and hearers of texts have become acutely mindful that all human meanings are nested in historical, cultural, social, and linguistic contexts.[5] The texts of Scripture bear the marks of their specific times and places. And the human readers of these texts always interpret them from somewhere and never from nowhere.[6] The judgment of the need to attend to the locatedness of all human expressions and interpretations has received helpful exposition in the work of the later Ludwig Wittgenstein, Hans Georg Gadamer, Paul Ricoeur, and various postmodern philosophers such as Stanley Fish and Jacques Derrida.[7] Any full account of reading and understanding a text well must attend to the insights of such seminal figures.[8] Human understanding of the world and of texts that precede us is inescapably shaped, if not determined, by our cultural and linguistic formation in communities of understanding. As the product of human understanding in distinct cultural settings, "concepts have dates."[9]

While early Christian interpreters were not entirely naive regarding the historical and cultural differences between their own worlds of meaning and the worlds they encountered in Scripture, the recent emphasis on historical consciousness has instigated a much more thoroughgoing investigation of the diverse ancient historical, social, and cultural worlds reflected in Scripture than took place in premodern engagement with Scripture. The relatively recent major discoveries of the Dead Sea Scrolls, the Oxyrhynchus papyri, the Nag Hammadi texts, the Codex Sinaiticus, and countless other ancient artifacts and texts from antiquity, coupled with the fruition of such historical consciousness, have made possible the concerted and disciplined consideration of the Bible as a historical anthology of texts that reflect multiple different ancient social, cultural, and linguistic worlds of meaning.[10] Focus on the original historical settings of Christian Scripture and the concern to avoid anachronism are the characteristic features of the family of contemporary hermeneutical approaches designated by the label "historical criticism."[11] Given that human beings who produced, edited, and passed on the scriptures are situated within and bear the marks of their distinct times and places, historical critics ask what we can understand and what judgments we can make about the authors of these texts and the functions of these texts in the ancient "worlds" from which such documents emerged. Practitioners of historical criticism concern themselves with the tasks of understanding the texts within their hypothetically reconstructed original settings of composition, redaction, interpretation, and use. They raise and answer questions concerning what we can know about the worlds of meaning "behind" the texts and the relationship of the texts themselves to these backgrounds. Historical-critical work has borne much fruit in helping contemporary readers understand the biblical texts in their own contexts.[12] It is not, however, without its problems.

Though the analysis of the historical uniqueness of the cultures attested in Scripture has its own intrinsic value, its processes and results build "an impenetrable wall" between the texts and contemporary people.[13] Historical scholarship makes demands upon readers and interpreters that can only be met through the study of ancient languages and cultures; as such, it threatens to take Scripture out of the hands of everyday Christian believers. Even within the confines of the guilds of biblical scholarship, narrative criticism and the applications of structuralism and semiotics to biblical texts have emerged to remedy some atomizing tendencies common within historical criticism and to address the perceived failure of historical criticism to edify religious communities.[14] Narrative approaches give direct attention not to the worlds of meaning "behind the texts" but instead to those worlds of meanings and values projected or "created by" the texts of Scripture themselves. Such literary approaches have frequently emphasized the usefulness of the texts as they stand for challenging readers to ascend to new and fuller horizons of understanding and acting in the world.

In recent years a number of so-called contextual approaches to the study of Scripture have emerged and gained influence in academic biblical scholarship. Though all reading, as I have noted above, is necessarily contextual, the aforementioned "contextual" approaches attend not primarily to the worlds in which ancient texts were produced or to the worlds that they depict but instead focus on "the worlds in front of the texts." Such reading strategies focus on the concerns that culturally and socially located readers—especially those who have suffered from disenfranchisement and marginalization—bring to the texts from their own horizons of experience and meaning. As noted above, the commitments, values, beliefs, and practices of readers themselves inevitably affect reading and interpretation.[15] Practitioners of contextual reading approaches have also challenged the hegemony of historical criticism within the guild of academic biblical scholarship by drawing attention to the fact that practitioners of the latter approach have frequently been insufficiently attentive to their own social and cultural locations and the effects of their situatedness upon their interpretive work. Because they have not been sufficiently attentive to their own social and cultural locations, historical critics have often unreflectively endorsed androcentric and narrowly Western perspectives. The pretension of historical criticism to total neutrality has revealed itself as a farce. The claim that neutral, bias-free study of Scripture is possible and that historical criticism is its embodiment dissemblingly masks the commitments necessarily involved in historical-critical engagement with Scripture.[16]

In addition to the development of historical criticism and contextual approaches, a rapidly growing number of historical and constructive studies on the explicitly theological nature of the task of Christian interpretation of Christian Scripture have appeared during the past twenty years.[17] These efforts stem, in part, from an ecumenical groundswell of interest in both academic and ecclesial contexts in drawing on the riches of the Christian past in order to aid the task of reuniting scriptural exegesis and theology. These new theological approaches promote an emphasis on the need for Christians to identify the constitutively *Christian* dimensions of

Christian scriptural interpretation. In *Engaging Scripture*, Stephen Fowl captures the emphases of these new theological approaches well. *Christian interpretation of Scripture*, he writes, at least in order to be distinctively Christian, "needs to involve a complex interaction in which Christian convictions, practices, and concerns are brought to bear on scriptural interpretation in ways that both shape that interpretation and are shaped by it."[18]

Many of these theologically focused studies have attempted to recover aspects of premodern approaches to the function and role of Scripture in the day-to-day lives of Christian communities.[19] Other recent studies have laudably sought to recover and present the achievements of premodern figures and movements in order to address contemporary questions about the nature and interpretation of Scripture.[20] The relationship of these three families of approaches to one another is unclear, even to those who affirm the relative legitimacy of each. A multifaceted question arises: How should these various approaches—historical critical, contextual, and theological—be related to one another, and how should they inform contemporary engagement with and use of Scripture in Christian communities today?[21]

The problem of knowing precisely what to do with Scripture and how to interpret it is not restricted, of course, to the academy. The various approaches that have recently emerged in the academic study of Scripture have trickled down to various ecclesial communities with varying effects.[22] A significant number of studies have appeared in recent years that examine the ecclesial dimensions of Christian reading and the place of Christian Scripture in Christian community. This literature includes constructive studies, works that attempt to retrieve and employ aspects of premodern understandings of the relationship between Scripture and church, congresses of specific ecclesial traditions, and ecumenically inclined dialogues between different ecclesial communities.[23] New interfaith initiatives, such as Scriptural Reasoning groups, have also brought individuals and groups from different religious traditions together—particularly from the three Abrahamic traditions—to read the respective holy books of represented participants.[24]

While the Bible is perhaps not as "strange[ly] silent" in many mainline Protestant churches as it was forty years ago, there is often still confusion about how to integrate the ongoing, and so changeable, achievements of historical approaches to Scripture with traditional practices of reverence for Scripture as the written Word of God.[25] As the New Testament scholar Dale Martin has recently argued, the historical-critical training that many clerical leaders received in seminary has proven impotent as an aid for effective preaching.[26] Contemporary evangelical groups in America, particularly communities that hold to "high views" of the authority of Scripture, are aptly characterized by what Christian Smith has called "pervasive interpretive pluralism."[27] Despite the fact that these Christian groups universally agree that Scripture should be authoritative, they exhibit a great deal of diversity in their understandings of its content and application.[28]

The problem of interpretive plurality, of course, is not restricted to evangelical groups.[29] Nor is it the only problem that contemporary Christian communities face regarding the use and interpretation of Scripture. Stephen Prothero's *Religious Literacy: What Every American Needs to Know—And Doesn't* draws attention to the widespread phenomenon of biblical illiteracy characteristic of American Christianity.[30] Despite the fact that significant percentages of Americans—whether evangelical, mainline Protestant, Catholic, Orthodox, or other—affirm the authority and centrality of Scripture for their faith, knowledge of its contents is low and is decreasing across the ecclesial spectrum.[31]

When contemporary readers, whether scholars, laypeople, exegetes, or theologians, do engage Scripture, they are frequently perplexed by the "strange new world[s]" that they encounter depicted within it.[32] The historical, moral, and even religious distance that has opened up between the worlds of meaning mediated by the texts of Scripture—to the extent that we can understand them and make correct judgments about them—and the worlds of meaning that most contemporary readers inhabit have proven stupefying to countless Christian believers.[33] The most pressing concerns are moral in nature. What are Christians to do with an authoritative Scripture that seems to depict God as not only condoning, but even sanctioning slavery, wanton violence, genocide, patriarchy, and racism?[34] That such difficult "texts of terror" have been invoked to justify atrocities in history requires attention and a response from anyone who would seek to understand and articulate the authority of Christian Scripture in the contemporary world.[35] Given not only the distance and strangeness of the worlds of the Bible, but its witness to and ostensible approval of moral atrocities, one historical critic has suggested that the discipline of historical criticism should have the task of completely dismantling the cultural ca-chet of the Christian Bible as its only end.[36] To accept such a proposal is not an option for contemporary Christians committed to Scripture and its au-thority. But how are they to understand it? What are they to do with it?

The sheer plurality of approaches to the interpretation of the Bible and the speed at which they have emerged and developed in recent years are dizzying. At this time there is nothing even remotely close to consen-sus on the relationship between these extremely different approaches to the Christian Bible. They pose unique theological problems for Chris-tians committed to the authority of Scripture and its central place in Christian faith. Recognizing the moral difficulties involved in reading Scripture today muddles the problem even more. Given the cacophony of competing approaches to Scripture, and the seemingly irreconcilable claims the different groups are making of it, is it still possible for contem-porary Christians to believe in the inspiration, unity, and authority of the Christian Bible? If so, how? What should Christians expect of the Bible? How should they read it? The situation of Christian Scripture in our own times calls for a response.

The starting point for reading Scripture well, whether one's focus is explicitly theological or religious in nature, is *an adequate understanding of what the Bible actually is.* As Martin has written, "The first step in learning how to interpret the Bible . . . is to make explicit what one thinks Scripture *is.* How one interprets Scripture depends a great deal on what one thinks the Bible is."[37] "What it is," Scott Swain writes, "must determine how we ap-proach and use it."[38] But Scripture is not separable from its contexts of use and meaning. Besides clearly identifying what Scripture *is,* we must also "locate" Scripture relative to the other realities, divine and human, that surround it. Context, as contemporary philosophers of interpretation from various backgrounds regularly note, determines meaning. Anthony Thiselton argues that "only the context (and perhaps agreed training) will limit pluralism against unmeant or irrelevant possibilities."[39]

A number of scholars have recognized and responded to the prob-lems that our contemporary situation presents for understanding the na-ture and purpose of Scripture and have suggested fruitful ways to move forward. This project appropriates aspects of some of these suggestions but ultimately proposes a unique way of addressing the difficulties. The present work proposes a systematic theology of the Christian Bible at the level of our own times as a means of addressing the present challenges and opportunities.[40] Such a systematic theology will provide a resource for both responsibly locating Scripture in its divine and human contexts and identifying Scripture in those surroundings. The only way to responsibly evaluate the various approaches to Scripture explained above is through having a responsible understanding of what Scripture has been and is and through situating Scripture responsibly and faithfully in its natural and supernatural contexts.

What follows, then, provides a constructive systematic account of the nature and purpose of Christian Scripture that articulates the intelligibility of Scripture and locates it within the work of the Triune God in history and within human cultural history.[41] I assume that the purpose and function of systematic theology is the articulation of the intelligibility of Christian doctrines affirmed in the present at the level of one's own time.[42] Because I have taken a systematic approach in the present work, what follows is not structured through an exegetical appropriation of insights from premodern or contemporary figures.[43] Instead, specific questions and judgments about the Triune God, about the economy of God's creative and redemptive work, about the intelligibility of human persons in history, about the material history of Scripture, and finally about traditional Christian beliefs concerning Scripture itself organize the work.[44] The remainder of this introduction therefore introduces the primary figures whose work I utilize, provides an explanation of the notion of systematic theology adopted here, and gives a justification for the rationale behind the structural organization of the following chapters.

It is important for me to draw attention to and comment on the subtitle of this project, *A Systematic Theology of the Christian Bible*. The presence of the indefinite article *A* is significant. While the scope of this work is ambitious, it cannot provide an exhaustive treatment of the objects of its inquiry and investigation. Such an account would require more research and reflection than any one person could perform over a lifetime. The present work does aspire to provide *one* relatively adequate account of divine Scripture in human understanding as an answer to the following questions: What is the nature and purpose of the Christian Bible, and what is its location in the contexts of the economic work of the Triune God and the cultural history of humanity?

THE PRIMARY INTERLOCUTORS OF THE PROJECT

Though this is a constructive project, it depends upon engagement with and appropriation of the contributions of a number of theologians and exegetes of the present day, the recent past, and the distant past. Prior to outlining the intelligibility of the structure of the work, then, I want to introduce my two primary interlocutors, Bernard Lonergan and Henri de Lubac, to clarify precisely how I appropriate their insights.

On any account Bernard Lonergan is among the giants of philosophy and theology of the twentieth century.[45] At first glance, however, he would appear to be a strange interlocutor for a study on the nature and purpose of Christian Scripture. What help can Lonergan offer for the task at hand? While Lonergan was not himself a biblical scholar, he did have an extensive knowledge of the contents of the Christian Bible. He was also well read in the historical-critical scholarship of his day.[46] A significant number of biblical scholars have explicitly employed insights from Lonergan's work to address difficulties in the current situation of Scripture in our time.[47] In addition, a number of other theologians have utilized Lonergan's work to clarify the place of Scripture in contemporary theological reflection.[48] This work builds on much of their previous work but attempts to go further by providing a wide-ranging heuristic account of the location of Scripture within history and the work of the Triune God, the location of Scripture relative to human nature and human cultural history, and, finally, the history, nature, and purpose of Christian Scripture itself. The first key contribution that Lonergan provides is his articulation of the functions and goals of systematic theology.[49] I provide an overview of his position on systematics below. But his work offers other key insights for the present systematic theology of Christian Scripture.

Lonergan's most salient observation for the present work, to which I regularly return, is insistence on the need to pay attention to "the fact that theologies are produced by theologians, that theologians have minds and use them, that their doing so should not be ignored or passed over but explicitly acknowledged in itself and in its implications."[50] The same thing must be said about biblical scholarship, whether it is historical critical, literary, contextual, or explicitly theological; it is produced by human persons, and those human persons have minds and use them, and this fact should be acknowledged in itself and in its implications. It can, and must, also be said about all humans, whether scholars or not, who engage Scripture. In his monumental work, *Insight*, Lonergan explains the subjective involvement intrinsic to the human quest for truth and clearly distinguishes its components. By exploring and interrogating the achievements of the philosophical traditions of rationalism and empiricism, modern scientific method, and the development and functioning of common sense, Lonergan is able to provide a relatively comprehensive and compelling account of the constants of consciousness in human nature that undergird all human understanding. Through his investigation of the dynamics of human consciousness, Lonergan demonstrates that objectivity, or the correspondence of one's judgments with the way things are, results from the cultivation and practice of authentic subjectivity.[51] *This is true in every distinct field of human inquiry.* We are successful as human knowers when we are attentive in our experiencing; intelligent in our questioning, conceptualizing, and imagining; rational in our judging; and responsible in our deciding.[52] Lonergan's phenomenological explanation of the invariant structure of human cognition is an account of the bedrock of human knowledge. It helpfully articulates the very means through which all advances in understanding and judgment are possible.[53] Lonergan's achievement embraces the legitimate emphases on the linguistic nestedness, historicity, and fallibility of human knowing and yet rightly shows how the *relativity* and *subjectivity* of human knowledge does not entail a vicious *relativism* or *subjectivism*.[54] The present project can be fruitfully understood as an attempt to think through the implications of Lonergan's axiom with reference to the nature and purpose of Christian Scripture.

Readers who are familiar with Lonergan's work will likely more easily get the import of what I am trying to do here and elsewhere. To those who are not, I must offer an apology, in both senses of the word, for my dependence upon and use of Lonergan. Lonergan is not without his critics.[55] His work is admittedly prohibitively dense and idiosyncratic. His later work, especially *Method in Theology*, is extremely terse.[56] It also bears witness to Lonergan's own intellectual development from the beginning to the end of his career.[57] His mind was a mind in motion and his manner of expression moved from what could be considered a scholastic idiom to an existential idiom.

Lonergan himself admits the difficulty of his work. In *Method in Theology* he suggests that readers will likely not be able to understand *Method* unless they have already wrestled their way through *Insight*.[58] The present systematic theology of Christian Scripture builds not just on Lonergan's achievements in both of those works, but on the work of a number of others who have appropriated and extended it, including Ben F. Meyer, Seán McEvenue, David B. Burrell, David Tracy, Frederick E. Crowe, and Robert M. Doran.[59] As I proceed I define key terms and relate positions developed by Lonergan and his students to other strands of theological reflection. The heuristics for understanding the human subject, the structure of history, and the relationship between grace and human action that Lonergan and some of his students have provided have proven extremely useful for many later theologians. I have found them indispensable. I cannot promise that my readers will share this judgment but ask that they read my own work with charity. One of the great merits of Lonergan's work was the generosity with which he engaged the work of other theologians, philosophers, and scholars. He also insisted that theology was necessarily a collaborative effort.[60] While I have utilized Lonergan's methodological work to structure this book, I draw on the work of many other exegetes, theologians, philosophers, and historians in what follows. Henri de Lubac, in particular, serves as another major influence.

With Lonergan I understand the task of systematic theology *not* as the pursuit of an understanding of past documents or theologians but instead as the pursuit of an understanding of the doctrinal judgments presently held by theologians and their communities at the levels of their own times. The task of Christian systematic theology does, however, necessarily depend upon a critical appropriation of the authentic achievements in understanding and judgment of past Christian communities.[61] What, then, are these achievements? With regard to the present project I must ask the question, What are the constitutive, and so necessary, Christian doctrinal judgments about the nature and purpose of Christian Scripture itself, and where can one go to find these judgments?

While modern theological historical scholarship has frequently emphasized the distance between modern and premodern forms of thought, a current in twentieth-century Roman Catholic thought centered in France and known ironically as the Nouvelle théologie was characterized by its quest for a critical recovery of the genius of the Christian tradition in the past.[62] The theologians associated with this movement sought a *ressourcement* of Christian thought in its intensity and fecundity in the early centuries of its existence.[63] The present renewal of interest in premodern use and interpretation of Scripture that has greatly enhanced contemporary discussions of the theology of Scripture has the work of the theologians of the Nouvelle théologie as its clearest major influence. Henri Cardinal de Lubac, another giant of twentieth-century theology, has had a particularly important role in retrieving the achievements of premodern Christian thought on the nature and purposes of Christian Scripture.[64]

As I have noted elsewhere, de Lubac wrote more on the history and theology of the interpretation of Scripture than on any other theological topic.[65] He was convinced that ancient Christian exegesis could serve as a resource for helping the Christians of his day understand and act in a Christian manner within the existing social, political, and spiritual circumstances.[66] In the years that have elapsed since de Lubac's pioneering work, a number of extremely useful studies have been published that examine and expound de Lubac's works on the history of Christian scriptural exegesis.[67] In the present work, I depend upon de Lubac's insights, both directly and indirectly, to identify and explain some of the key constitutive Christian doctrines concerning the nature and purpose of Christian Scripture. Such doctrines are the starting point for systematic theological reflection on the nature and purpose of Scripture.[68]

In his memoirs de Lubac declares that he had no disdain for systematics; he saw his own purpose, however, as the recovery of the vitality of the Christian tradition for the edification of the church of his day.[69] It is my contention that de Lubac does recover vital developments in the Christian tradition on the nature and purpose of Scripture that have relevance for contemporary theological reflection on Scripture. Contemporary systematic theology must build on the genuine achievements of past reflection.[70] De Lubac's major works on traditional Christian understandings of the nature and purpose of Scripture provide tremendous resources for contemporary theological reflection. Beyond depending upon de Lubac's achievements, however, I intend to build upon his work in new ways. I also consider and incorporate questions and data to which de Lubac did not, and could not, have had access. My debt to de Lubac's recovery of traditional Christian reflection on the doctrines of the inspiration of Scripture and the relationship between the written word of Scripture and the living Word, Jesus Christ, in particular, will be clear in what follows.

Despite my obvious dependence on the work of both de Lubac and Lonergan, my primary intention is not to offer an interpretation of the work of either figure but to responsibly build on their achievements to offer a systematic theology of Christian Scripture for contemporary Christian believers.[71] The exigency of responsibility requires theologians to distinguish our efforts to understand and articulate past positions from our efforts to speak and write in direct discourse about the God with "whom we have to do" (Heb 4.13) today. We must also measure up to what we can learn about Scripture itself from recent historical discoveries and the achievements in understanding of each of the major approaches to Scripture listed above. The present work is my attempt to articulate a systematic theology of the nature and purpose of Christian Scripture at the level of our own time that addresses both exigencies.[72] Whatever advances, if any, the present account makes no doubt depend upon previous achievements. And those advances will themselves instigate further questions and insights that would take subsequent readers beyond the horizons limned in what follows. Whatever mistakes the present account contains, I hope, will invite readers to overturn said errors and so help to advance Christian understandings of the nature of Scripture, its meaning, and its use by providing a negative example. I trust that attentive, intelligent, reasonable, responsible, and loving readers will propose advances and reversals where needed.

THE APPROACH OF THE PROJECT

The systematic intention of the present work is shared with Telford Work's excellent monograph on the nature and interpretation of Scripture, *Living and Active: Scripture in the Economy of Salvation*.[73] *Living and Active*, as Work states, "develops a fully Trinitarian account of Scripture, establishing and exploring its divine and human character and its salvific purpose in its Church setting and beyond."[74] Work calls his account a "systematic bibliology," but he never precisely defines what he means by "systematic." He does note that such an account must relate Scripture to the various loci of systematic theology.[75] While I think that Work achieves a penetrating and relatively comprehensive account of the nature and purpose of Scripture, the structure and contents of *Living and Active* differ in significant ways from what follows.[76] The present work adopts a specific notion of systematic theology, and that notion provides the rationale for the work's organization.

Systematic theology is arguably in need of defense at the present time.[77] For many contemporary scholars, theologians, and philosophers interested in Christian thought in the past and the present, to even attempt a systematic theology is a mistake.[78] For some, system and systematics are *necessarily* violent; systematics trades in explanations, and explanations are thought to be colonizing and totalizing and are to be avoided at all costs. Any system, hypothetical postmodern interlocutors might argue, violently imposes an artificial and inadequate conceptual straightjacket on the particularities of history and the particularities characteristic of specific groups and persons.[79] Wittgensteinians, emphasizing the linguisticality of all human understanding and the natural history of human language use, would perhaps suggest that we restrict ourselves to theological "description" instead of aspiring to theological "explanation."[80] In response to Hegel's voracious and all-consuming dialectic, subsequent continental philosophies have urged that contemporary scholars or philosophers eschew "system" in favor of highlighting and reveling in the difference and particularity of histories, communities, cultures, and religious traditions.[81]

Systematic theology does not necessarily, by its very nature, run roughshod over the particularities of histories, languages, cultures, and peoples. Systematic theologians have been guilty of such faults in the past and may even be prone to such irresponsibility in the future, but their fault does not lie in having adopted a methodology that necessarily leads to domination and colonization. To modify a phrase from Stephen Fowl, methodologies do not have ideologies.[82] It is possible to understand systematic theology not as the pursuit of a totalizing discourse but instead, with Lonergan, as the effort to understand and articulate the intelligibility of the mysteries of Christian faith at the level of the systematic theologian's own time.[83] For Lonergan, the systematic theologian affirms and appropriates the mysteries of Christian faith in doctrinal judgments that she has received within her Christian community from antecedent Christian tradition.[84] The systematic theologian does not remain content with mere repetition of those doctrines or with mere description of those doctrines; she pursues an explanation of the mysteries identified by such doctrines. Such an explanation, however, is and must remain "imperfect, analogical, obscure, and gradually developing."[85] The systematic theologian holds that it is nevertheless still highly fruitful to pursue such an explanatory understanding of the true judgments about reality expressed in the doctrines of Christian faith.[86] Instead of merely describing how realities appear to her, she seeks to understand and express the intelligible, objective interrelationships of realities to one another.

I should note that I use the terms "understanding" and "judgment," both here and elsewhere, in a technical sense. Because of the structural exigencies of systematic theology, which I explain below, I do not provide explicit definitions of those terms until chapter 4. I hope the reasons for this postponement will be clear in what follows, but I owe potentially perplexed readers at least a brief rationale for doing so. In an important sense, the theological and philosophical anthropology of chapter 4 *is* foundational for the whole work.[87] As a systematic theology of Christian Scripture, this work provides an understanding of the judgments of Christian doctrine. As thoughtful and informed readers will recognize, however, there is no theological or philosophical consensus on what these understandings and judgments actually are. The present project presupposes and builds upon a certain understanding of understanding itself and a certain understanding of judgments themselves.[88] In systematic theology, following Lonergan, however, the theologian is not preeminently preoccupied with the dialectical work of sorting out the coherence or truth of competing epistemologies. That is important work, but it deserves its own treatment, and others have done such work elsewhere. I leave it aside in the present project. I am not preoccupied with those foundational and dialectical concerns in a direct way, but this project does presuppose their fruit.

Near the end of his chapter on systematics in *Method in Theology*, Lonergan addresses a number of accusations made against systematic theology. Detractors have argued that it is "speculative, irreligious, fruitless, elitist, [and] irrelevant."[89] To the first charge, Lonergan argues that systematics can and has been speculative, but what he advocates "is really quite a homely affair. It aims at understanding the truths of faith, a *Glaubensverständnis*. The truths envisaged are church confessions."[90] My present approach attempts to offer an understanding of Scripture in its relationship to the foundational confessions of the Christian community, particularly the Nicene Creed.[91] Lonergan takes the utmost care to ward off the charge that systematics is irreligious. His account of systematics, in fact, presupposes that the theologian will have personally experienced religious conversion and that such conversion will ground her theological work.[92] And, he writes:

> when conversion is the basis of the whole theology, when religious conversion is the event that gives the name, God, its primary and fundamental meaning, when systematic theology does not believe it can exhaust or even do justice to that meaning, not a little has been done to keep systematic theology in harmony with its religious origins and aims.[93]

Systematics is ultimately concerned with providing an understanding of the transformative religious realities—that is, the Triune God who makes Godself available—experienced by the theologian and her community. It has as its object the intelligibility of the redemptive work of the Triune God in history. To the charge that systematics is fruitless, Lonergan argues that the criteria he gives for dialectic provide a means for pruning fruitless systematic endeavors. He admits that systematics is difficult, but that admission does not constitute a reason for rejecting its legitimacy; like other difficult subjects such as mathematics, science, scholarship, and philosophy, when done well systematic theology produces good fruit.[94] The difficulty is worth meeting. Finally, Lonergan argues that systematics is only irrelevant if it does not serve as the basis for communication of the truths understood by the theologian. She cannot effectively communicate these truths, of course, if she has not understood them. Ultimately, systematics is sublated by the greater good of the propagation and dissemination of the good news of the redemptive work of the Triune God in history.

The present work, as noted above, adopts Lonergan's approach to systematics.[95] The systematic theologian undertakes the tasks of systematics as one seeking to advance the understanding of the Christian community and through doing so to edify it. As a teacher, she must take the admonition of the author of the epistle of James to heart: "Not many of you should become teachers, my brothers and sisters, for you know that we who teach will be judged with greater strictness. For all of us make many mistakes" (3.1–2a). The systematic theologian is ultimately responsible for the positions she takes. She should certainly not undertake systematics lightly or thoughtlessly. Systematics is not without its risks.

As I noted above, the systematic theologian can and must draw from the riches of Christian tradition in seeking to articulate the intelligibility of the doctrinal beliefs of Christian faith within her present situation.[96] She is accountable to that tradition. Her responsibility to Christian tradition requires that she attend carefully to the judgments and understandings she encounters in the tradition. In faith, however, she seeks to understand not past figures and texts but instead the work of the Triune God itself, past, present, and future. She seeks to understand the work of the Triune God in her own time and the place of humanity in that work; in faith she trusts that the Triune God is continually acting, and she affirms that the people called by the Triune God have as much responsibility as ever to recognize and participate in that work.

While Lonergan uncontroversially argued that historical investigation of the Christian tradition was essential for contemporary theological reflection, he simultaneously insisted that the dictates of human authenticity required Christians to give an account of the intelligibility of their faith at the level of their own time as well. They cannot merely parrot sources. Such sources have their integrity and intelligibility in their own times and places. The process of identifying, understanding, and determining the truths mediated by such sources has its own value and norms. But that work, while essential, is not all that is needed. In *Method in Theology* Lonergan differentiates the tasks of historical retrieval from the tasks of appropriation, understanding, and proclamation of the faith at the level of one's own time. By adverting to the subjective involvement that theological sources reflect—their authors, redactors, and preservers are, after all, experiencers, understanders, judgers, and deciders acting in history—and to the subjective involvement inescapably constitutive of the investigation of premodern sources required of contemporary theologians, Lonergan is able to articulate a basis for continuity between past articulations of Christian faith and present reflection on its meaning.

Contemporary believers share the same subjective constitution with premodern believers.[97] Our objects of inquiry, namely, the Triune God in God's redemptive action and the writings that witness to that action, are also the same. The mysteries that the Triune God has revealed once and for all may be better understood, but forward movement in human understanding of these mysteries will still have the same mysteries of the work of the Triune God in history as its objects whether that understanding takes place in the first or the twenty-first century. Lonergan's articulation of the normative structures of human cognition and understanding throughout history provides a means for identifying and affirming actual historical developments within Christian theological reflection that should be retrieved, appropriated, and, if necessary, reframed in contemporary theological reflection.[98]

This work's understanding of systematics must be located in its context in Lonergan's broader account of the nature of theological method at the level of our time. For him, contemporary Christian theology is a communal enterprise in which a theologian mediates the truth of her religious faith to her culture.[99] Lonergan differentiates the process of this mediation into eight different and interrelated functions, operations, or activities, which he labels "functional specialties."[100] As Lonergan stated shortly before *Method in Theology* was published, "The eight functional specialties are a set of self-regulative, ongoing, interdependent processes. They're not stages such that you do one and then you do the next. Rather you have different people at all eight and interacting. And the interaction is not logical. It's attentive, intelligent, reasonable, responsible, and religious."[101]

"Systematics" or "systematic theology" is just one of the eight "functional specialties." It cannot be undertaken apart from the others. It is intimately related to the others, because each functional specialty emerges within and depends upon the self-transcending capacities of the human persons who employ them. Lonergan's account of the functional specialties is isomorphic, or structurally parallel, with the structure of human consciousness that he begins to lay out in *Insight* and further specifies in *Method in Theology*. In brief, Lonergan argues that because humans are experiencers, understanders, judgers, and deciders, the structure of contemporary theology ought to parallel these differentiations of our conscious constitution. Because humans do their experiencing, understanding, judging, and deciding in human cultures that themselves develop and because they are inescapably beholden to past tradition, the theological task can accordingly be differentiated into two phases. The first phase details tasks undertaken when theologians engage the resources of Christian tradition in the past to understand such sources in their particularity.[102] The second phase details tasks theologians undertake when they attempt to understand and articulate the truth of Christian faith at the level of their own time.[103]

In the first phase, "the mediated phase," Lonergan differentiates four functionally distinct sets of operations that theologians and theological communities engage in when they study past traditions (whether written, spoken, or otherwise created). The first functional specialization, "research," refers to the tasks involved in concentrated and concerted engagement with the written or spoken resources of the theologian's tradition(s).[104] In research, theologians assemble the data of past tradition. The process of seeking to understand instantiations of past tradition, not surprisingly, corresponds to the transcendental human drive to understand and falls under the functional specialty of "interpretation."[105] In this functional specialty theologians attempt to grasp the meaning of some instantiation of past tradition. They do not rest content with an understanding of a single document or artifact, however, but instead seek to understand the place of that document or artifact within an ongoing history. They want to know what was going forward. The functional specialty of "history" corresponds to the transcendental drive to make judgments about what actually has been the case. In historical investigation, theologians attempt to understand texts and figures in their contexts, without importing foreign or anachronistic perspectives, to grasp precisely "what was going forward" at certain specific times in history.

Lonergan argues that critical history that pursues, in Leopold von Ranke's famous words, *wie es eigentlich gewesen*, is desirable and possible.[106] The difficulties involved in doing critical history are, of course, manifold. The critical historian must have fluency in the requisite languages of the time period she studies. She must take care to assess the documents and artifacts of this time period and the historical narratives that have emerged regarding their diachronic relationships with assiduous scrutiny. She must become thoroughly habituated to the time period under consideration.[107]

She must not fear overturning received paradigms, and she must not set out to make a name for herself by manufacturing sensational "discoveries." Her only concern can be to assess all of the extant evidence and the secondary and tertiary accounts of the evidence attentively and intelligently, making only the probabilistic judgments about what was going forward that she can make reasonably and responsibly.

Many who hold to characteristic "postmodern" emphasis on the relativity and perspectival nature of all frames of reference would likely find such a pursuit hopelessly and naively modern. As noted above, Lonergan shares a concern for the perspectival nature of all human inquiry and learning, but his position on objectivity, namely, that it results from the exercise of authentic subjectivity, provides a means of both affirming the necessary emphasis on the perspectival nature of all inquiry and reversing the counterposition of a hopeless relativism.[108] While true judgments about what was going forward in history require a great deal of work and remain probabilistic, they are still possible and desirable.[109] I presume that such historical understanding is both possible and invaluable, even necessary, for responsible and faithful contemporary theological reflection.

Dialectic is the final functional specialty of the mediated phase of the functional specialties and involves the theologian in the tasks of adjudicating ethical, metaphysical, epistemological, and cognitional conflicts between traditions or even such conflicts present within her own tradition.[110] Dialectic corresponds to the level of decision and value. Dialectic "has to add to the interpretation that understands a further interpretation that appreciates. It has to add to the history that grasps what was going forward a history that evaluates achievements, that discerns good and evil."[111] The extant literary heritage of Christianity contains countless authentic achievements and advances in understanding and judgment that Christians must carry forward to be authentically Christian; it also witnesses to a great variety of perspectives and positions, some of which are in tension with one another or are even directly contradictory. In dialectics the theologian attempts to untangle the conflicts she encounters in her examination of her tradition to carry forward what is authentic.[112]

Besides the process of encountering and seeking to understand and critically appropriate past Christian tradition, the exigencies of the theological task require that Christian theologians understand and communicate the intelligibility of Christian faith in their own time. As I stated above, theology mediates the meaning of Christian faith for the contemporary world at the level of the theologian's own time. The second phase of the functional specialties, the mediating phase, distinguishes four distinct sets of functional operations in which this contemporary mediation takes place. In the first, the theologian affirms and appropriates the truth not only of the Christian horizon, but the metaphysical, moral, and religious convictions and dispositions that characterize it. This first mediating phase functional specialty is known as foundations.[113] Lonergan includes a discussion of the intellectual, moral, and religious conversions that are the theologian's basis for doing contemporary theological work and a discussion of the development of "general categories" and "special categories" in his treatment of this functional specialty.[114]

In foundations the theologian adverts to the reality that she is an experiencer, understander, judger, and decider. She understands the different sets of operations involved in each of these levels and their interrelations; she judges that these levels and operations constitute her conscious, intellectual, and existential being; and she decides that she will take responsibility for these operations. The theologian comes to understand her own horizon and to objectify and articulate her self-understanding in terms of her transcendental commitments to attentiveness, intelligence, reasonableness, responsibility, and Christian charity as determined by the law of the cross.[115] As one who has received the love of God "which has flooded her heart" (Rom 5.5), the love that is fully manifested in Christ's sacrificial death on the cross, she has received a disposition of universal antecedent willingness. Through this love she can begin to look on all she sees with love; she recognizes that this disposition is fleeting and that she can resist it but that this love is a gift, which, when operating in her, represents the fulfillment of her being. This disposition of love is the imitation of the God who loves the world (John 3.16); it is even a created participation in God's very knowledge and being.

The objectification of the aforementioned personal horizon of being and willing serves as the basis from which the theologian derives "general categories" and "special categories." "General categories" are sets of terms and relations that are shared with other disciplines besides theology; they are derived from the theologian's judgment that she is—just as all human beings are—an experiencer, understander, judger, decider, and lover. The "special categories" are sets of terms and relations derived from her acknowledgment that she has received the love of God poured into her heart. As a Christian she utilizes the specific categories Christian tradition has utilized to refer to, and so objectify, the human experience of transcendent reality. She professes that the meaning and scope of the love of God for the world is manifested in the life, teaching, death, and resurrection of Jesus Christ. *This* is the love of God that the Spirit of God has poured into her heart. *This* love of God is redemptive. In acknowledging herself as one who experiences, understands, judges, and decides, she recognizes that she has not always measured up to the reach of these capacities. She affirms that human history is rife with such failure. She recognizes the universal human impotence to resist such failure. She affirms that only the redemptive work of Christ, head and members, which is mediated through the work of the Holy Spirit in individuals and communities, can stem the tide of decline, reverse it, and bring good out of evil on the way to the consummation of all things in Christ's eschatological return.

The theologian articulates her horizon in terms of specific concrete judgments that clearly objectify her affirmations about the salvific work of the Son of God and the Spirit of God in history. Lonergan treats these judgments under the functional specialty of "doctrines."[116] The doctrines the theologian holds are the judgments of the Christian tradition about the redemptive work of the Triune God in history. These are articulated most concisely and famously in the early ecumenical creeds such as the Apostle's Creed, the Niceno-Constantinopolitan Creed, and the Athanasian Creed.[117] Such creeds objectify the Christian horizon; they concretize Christian judgments about the features of the redemptive work of the Triune God that Christian communities have come to understand and in which they participate.

As Robert Doran writes, however, "Affirming Christian doctrine as true is one thing, while understanding what one has affirmed to be true is something else."[118] The theologian does not simply affirm the judgments constitutive of Christian tradition in Christian confessions; she seeks an understanding of them at the level of her own time. The functional specialty of systematics details the pursuit of such understanding.[119] As hinted at above, the principal function of systematic theology is the pursuit of an understanding of the mysteries of Christian faith at the level of the theologian's own time. "The aim of systematics," Lonergan writes, "is not to increase certitude but to promote understanding. It does not seek to establish facts. It strives for some inkling of how it could possibly be that the facts are what they are. Its task is to take over the facts, established in doctrines, and to attempt to work them into an assimilable whole."[120] Systematics gives an account of the intelligibility of the truth of Christianity in history. It mediates a Christian understanding of the creative work of the Triune God, the history of human progress and decline, and the redemptive work of the Son of God and the Spirit of God in that history.

The articulation of the intelligibility of the mysteries of Christian faith in history has its own relevance and use. For the committed Christian theologian, however, it is the service of a greater goal. Systematic theology has as its final end the proclamation of the gospel. It is in "communications," the final functional specialty, that "theological reflection bears fruit."[121] In communications, the theologian communicates the cognitive, constitutive, and effective meaning of Christian faith. Christian faith "is cognitive inasmuch as the message tells what is to be believed. It is constitutive inasmuch as it crystallizes the hidden inner gift of love into overt Christian fellowship. It is effective inasmuch as it directs Christian service to human society to bring about the kingdom of God."[122] What is understood and affirmed in past history and in the present is located within and put to the service of the transformative work of the Triune God taking place in the theologian's own day. All Christian theological reflection, for Lonergan, is in the service of the communication of the good news of the Christian gospel.[123] Because of its close proximity to communications and its concern for explanation at the level of the times, systematic theology has a special place in this process. For the good news to be good news, it must be understood and communicated. Systematics helps to provide an understanding of the good news for the sake of its effective communication.

THE STRUCTURE OF THE PROJECT

Given Lonergan's account of the exigencies of systematic theology, we are faced with the following questions: What would a systematic theology of the Christian Bible entail? And what should its order be? Since systematics does not mediate the history of doctrinal or historical development in

Christian thought but instead offers an understanding of Christian faith at the level of the theologian's time, it does not follow the same order or presentation of the theological specialties of the mediated phase.[124] Lonergan illustrates this difference with reference to the periodic table of chemistry.[125] The atomic weights of the elements in the periodic table represent the cumulative achievements of a community of chemists that were worked out through decades of research. Contemporary chemists, however, do not need to repeat the experiments that led to the discoveries that the periodic table summarizes. Chemistry textbooks appropriately begin with the periodic table and do not rehearse the history of discoveries that it represents. The generalized achievements of the periodic table are assumed and become the basis for future discoveries. As Lonergan writes, "Inquiring, investigating, and demonstrating begin with what is obvious, while teaching begins from those concepts that can be understood without understanding other elements."[126]

The analogy, of course, limps. The periodic table presents the intelligibility of the atomic weights of elements. Systematic theology, on the other hand, attempts to present or manifest the intelligibility of the being and work of the Triune God whose "ways are not [our] ways and [whose] thoughts are not [our] thoughts" (Isa 55.8). Systematic theology has as its object divine mystery. Even so, systematic theology begins with what is most general and proceeds to an explanation of what is more specific. The present systematic theology of Christian Scripture begins, therefore, with an articulation of the general theological and anthropological and cultural contexts of Christian Scripture and then proceeds from these contexts to identify and explain the human and divine characteristics of Scripture itself.

Chapters 3 and 4, then, provide accounts respectively of the specific intelligibility and ends of the providential work of the Triune God in history in the creative work of the Father and the mission of Jesus Christ the Son of God and the mission of the Holy Spirit (ch. 3), and the specific intelligibility of the human persons in which and through which this work takes place (ch. 4). The former gives an account of the broadest and most general context in which Scripture is located — the creative and redemptive work of the Triune God in history. The latter identifies the conditions under which all human action, including experience, understanding, judgment, decision, and action, with regard to Christian Scripture are possible. These two heuristics serve as necessary contexts for locating Christian Scripture in divine and human history.

Though chapters 3 and 4 articulate the two general "locations" of Christian Scripture within the economic work of the Triune God and within human cultural history, it is impossible to understand the nature and purpose of Christian Scripture without an understanding of *what Christian Scripture actually is and has been in that history*. Chapter 5, then, offers an account of the concrete material *realia* of Christian Scripture. It draws on studies of the technology, media, language, and scope of Christian Scripture to provide a thorough, though of course not exhaustive, account of some of the key characteristics of the actual material history of Christian Scripture. Finally, chapter 6 provides an account of the relationship of Scripture to the Triune God by providing explanations of three key Christian doctrinal beliefs concerning Scripture.[127] First, Christian Scripture is inspired by the Holy Spirit. Second, Christian Scripture is the written Word of God that mediates the meaning of Jesus Christ as its referent. And third, Christian Scripture is a preeminently useful (2 Tim 3.16) instrument within the redemptive pedagogy of the Triune God in history.

Astute readers, especially Protestants, will recognize that I do not directly treat much of the technical language developed since the Reformation, especially in bibliocentric and evangelical traditions, for articulating the intelligibility of Christian Scripture. In the following pages I refer only sparingly, or not at all in some cases, to the language of "inerrancy," "infallibility," "plenary inspiration," "perspicuity," and, of course, "sola scriptura." I do not doubt the possible usefulness of such language and do not deny the truthfulness of the judgments its adherents hold.[128] I have chosen not to utilize it extensively, however, for four primary reasons. First, responsible use of such language would require me to take historical detours that would distract from my overall goals as stated above. Second, it is possible to faithfully understand and articulate the intelligibility of Christian Scripture without delving into the distinctively Protestant controversies in which such technical language developed. Third, I have often witnessed the use of such language in arguments characterized by more heat than light. Fourth, the avoidance of such language allows me to treat some of the key issues and questions concerning the doctrines of Scripture considered in chapter 6 in fresh ways.[129]

Chapter 6, then, provides a fresh examination of the aforementioned three key doctrinal judgments in light of the previous chapters. Lonergan notes that systematics pursues an account of the "interconnection of the mysteries [of Christian faith] with one another and with our last end."[130] For this reason, I have located the doctrinal judgment that Scripture is inspired by the Holy Spirit in a broader account of the economic mission of the Holy Spirit. In like fashion, I have located the doctrinal confession that Scripture is the Word of God in its broader context of the mission of the Son of God, who is the living Word of God, as well. Finally, I locate the doctrinal judgment that Scripture is a useful instrument of divine pedagogy relative to the account of human nature and human community—created, fallen, and redeemed—in chapter 4. That section explains how Scripture functions within the processes of our transformation and sanctification on the way to seeing God face-to-face. Each traditional doctrine finds its place and intelligibility in the fundamental context of the mystery of the Triune God's economic work in the missions of the Son and Holy Spirit.

Chapters 3 through 6 purposely have the structure of an inclusio, with each of the outer chapters focused on the divine "dimensions" of Christian Scripture and each of the inner chapters focused on the human "dimensions" of Christian Scripture. While chapters 3 and 4 move from the broad generality of the divine context of Christian Scripture in the economic work of the Triune God to the more specific location of Christian Scripture in the possibilities and actuality of human history, chapters 5 and 6 are ordered differently. While I affirm the unity of Scripture in chapter 6, I have taken care in chapter 5 to give special attention to its historical diversity and materiality. Though a number of recent studies have acknowledged and affirmed the human history of the texts of Scripture, I have been dissatisfied with how little scholarly achievements concerning the actual material history of Scripture have figured in theological accounts of the nature and purpose of Scripture. To write about Scripture at the level of our times, it is necessary to give attention to the theological significance of recent historical discoveries concerning the material histories of Christian Scripture. I therefore give a great deal of space to the histories of Scripture in chapter 5. Following that work on the diversity of Scripture in chapter 5, chapter 6 provides a hypothetical articulation of the unity of Scripture within the work of the Triune God at the level of our time. That final chapter provides an explanation of how Christian Scripture has been and remains useful within the work of the Triune God in a way that can account for and incorporate the insights of the history of Christian Scripture articulated in chapter 5.

I have not yet explained the purpose of chapter 2. It functions as a historical interlude prior to the work in chapters 3 and 4. Chapter 2 is not systematic in nature; it has an apologetic purpose. It provides a historically focused account of early Christian articulations of the rule of faith as the appropriate Christian context for engaging Scripture. Readers may be perplexed by that starting location. The following excursus provides the rationale for why the historical work of chapter 2 must come next in this project.

Excursus: What Does the Bible "Say"?

I wholeheartedly affirm the work of biblical scholarship, and the biblical scholars who accomplish and promote it, to measure up to the very words, and to the extent possible, the minds of their human authors—whether individual or communal—to the best of our human abilities. Such careful and bold exegetical work is necessary, as Eugene Peterson notes, "because exegesis respects the words enough to use every means we have to get the words right."[131] But while such work is necessary as a matter of responsibility, I hold that it is not the whole or even most important reason for engaging Scripture for a Christian reader or hearer. Such work, often called positive theology or historical theology, takes place on the mediating side of theology in the functional specialties of research, interpretation, history, and even dialectic. The present work depends upon my own appropriation of the achievements of scholars operating in those phases, and in some cases even on my own practice of such work.[132] Again, though, the present project has as its goal not the understanding of one particular isolated text or author—whether of Scripture itself or from the history of Christian exegesis—but instead an understanding of Scripture itself within the work of God in history and within human cultural history. Systematic theology moves beyond the indirect discourse of reporting on what an ancient person or community said about reality at the level of his or her own time to the direct discourse of articulating hypothetical understandings and judgments about reality at the level of our own time. It is not opposed to historical and positive work, and even depends on them, but it has a different purpose and function.

I presume that Scripture is inspired and that it mediates divine revelation in the very particularity of its words. I take such judgments to be essential or constitutive for a Christian understanding of the nature and purpose of Christian Scripture. Given the fact that I affirm that a "high view" of Scripture is necessary within Christian faith, it would seem appropriate to begin an explanation of the nature and purpose of Scripture by investigating the "internal" testimony of Scripture in order to let the Bible "speak for itself."[133] The judgment that it is possible to "let Scripture speak for itself," however, is hermeneutically naive at best and obfuscating at worst. *Scripture is not a speaking and acting agent.*[134] "Texts do not think or suppose," Charles Hefling elaborates; they do not "consider or decide or feel."[135] It is impossible, in fact, to *take a good look* at the Bible *to simply see* what it "says" about itself. Dale Martin declares, "The text of the Bible does not 'say' anything. It must be interpreted."[136] Lonergan states about reading in general:

> The plain fact is that there is nothing 'out there' except spatially ordered marks; to appeal to dictionaries and grammars, to linguistic and stylistic studies, is to appeal to more marks. . . . If the criterion of objectivity is the 'obviously out there,' then there is no objective interpretation whatever; there is only gaping at ordered marks, and the only order is spatial.[137]

While there is no doubt that the marks on the pages of Scripture are objectively other than us, *all* engagement with the textual otherness of Scripture *depends upon the subjective constitution of the individuals or communities* engaging those marks. The marks, of course, are there because of intentional efforts of subjects as well. Any reading or interpretation of Scripture based on the objective marks of Scripture, as reading or interpretation, will necessarily involve and depend upon the subjectivity of those who produced and subsequently engage the text. While the desire to allow Scripture "to speak for itself" seems noble, the attempt to do so could easily divert our attention from the divine and human agents who have worked in the historic production, redaction, dissemination, canonization, and understanding of Scripture; such an approach to Scripture risks "de-peopling" the pursuit of its meaning.[138] Any thorough account of Christian Scripture must give attention to the intentionality of the historical agents or persons—human and divine—at work in the aforementioned dynamic processes. Christian Scripture does not fall from heaven ready-made. The histories of the texts that human agents have brought together, edited, and translated in our modern versions are rife with the mysterious, the intriguing, and the banal. It is necessary to understand and to account for both the human and divine agencies at work in this process.

Casual use of the common catchphrase "the Bible says" can easily hide from hearers and readers a myriad of assumptions about the nature and function of divine authority which are inadequate as understandings of how God has actually providentially brought about and used Scripture in human history.[139] We must critically interrogate such language to keep ourselves from misunderstanding what we and others are doing when we use it. The Bible, despite its "self-testimony," is not an agent that speaks, commands, admonishes, or rebukes. There are, to be sure, ubiquitous references both in Scripture itself (see John 7.38; 7.42; 19.24; 19.37; Rom 4.3; 9.8; 9.17; 10.11; 11.2; Gal 3.8; 4.30; 1 Tim 5.18; Jas 2.23; 4.5) and in the history of its interpretation (for early references, see 1 Clem. 23.3; 34.6; 35.7; 42.5; 2 Clem. 2.4; 14.2; Barn. 4.7; 4.11; 5.4; 6.12; 13.2; 16.5; *Haer.* 1.22.1; 3.6.1; *Epid.* 44) that suggest that Scripture "speaks" or "says" (ἡ γραφὴ λέγει).[140] Such examples, however, certainly do not authorize haphazard or irresponsible usage of such language.[141] There is, of course, ample evidence within both Christian Scripture and the early history of its interpretation for identifying the "speaker" of Scripture as God (for a few examples, see Matt 19.4–6; Acts 4.24–25; 13.34–35; Rom 9.15; 9.25; Heb 3.7; 4.7; 10.15–17 and Barn. 6.8; *Dial.* 65.6; *Haer.* 1.10.3).[142] That evidence also does not authorize us to irresponsibly wield the words of Scripture as direct and univocal divine address at all times and all places. The primary purpose of engaging Scripture for people of Christian faith is to understand the will of the Triune God and to participate in the work of the Triune God. But the Triune God does not speak and act in the exact same ways at distinct times and in distinct places (see, e.g., Heb 1.1–4).

Scripture's authority, of course, is derived; any authentic authority it "possesses" or "wields" comes from and must be aligned with the authority of Jesus Christ, the one to whom the Father has given "all authority in heaven and on earth" (Matt 28.19). It is for this reason that we must locate Scripture within and relative to the missions of the Son of God and the Holy Spirit in history. We must ask and answer the questions, What has the Triune God done? What is the Triune God doing? What will the Triune God do in history? Scripture is an instrument and means of this doing, past, present, and future.

As I noted above, we always interpret and understand from somewhere and never from nowhere. The perspectival nature of all inquiry makes it impossible, then, for anyone to set her understandings of the meaning and direction of human history and her understandings of God's work within that history—or the impossibility of divine work in history—aside to simply "take a look" at Scripture to see "what it says" about any particular historical event or doctrinal teaching.[143] Unless we can recognize the colloquial nature of the expression "The Bible says . . . ," we risk greatly obfuscating what is going on when we make appeals to the authority of Scripture by invoking this language.

It is my conviction that the exigencies of our own situation, particularly our awareness of the drastic historical differences between our own situation and the situations out of which the texts of Scripture emerged and our awareness of the subjectivity involved in all appeals to authority, make it necessary for contemporary Christians to be cautious in our use of language concerning the "speaking" of Christian Scripture. Ultimately, I will argue that Scripture serves as a useful and virtually indispensable instrument through which the Triune God accomplishes God's work in history, both in presenting and testifying to that work and through effecting that work in its readers and hearers.[144] Such a thesis requires justification, but for now I will only suggest that it is necessary to take caution in utilizing phrases such as "The Bible says X, Y, or Z." Are we not actually claiming that the Triune God "says X, Y, or Z"?

How can we understand, unless we are first taught to read within a Christian horizon? As Robert Jenson notes, citing the example of the interaction between Philip and the Ethiopian Eunuch recorded in Acts 8, "It is not a novel late modern insight that texts by themselves do not necessarily flaunt the sense they harbor."[145] Christians need to learn how to read, hear, and meditate on Scripture in a Christian manner. Instead of giving an account of what the Bible "says" about itself, then, we can put ourselves in better theological company by articulating a Christian horizon in which all Christian engagement with Scripture takes place.[146] To do so is to follow a precedent set at the beginnings of Christian history. Historically, Christian faith in the extratextual actions of the God of Israel in Jesus Christ and through the Holy Spirit has served as the orienting context for early Christian engagement with Scripture. This is evident in the work of Irenaeus, Origen, and Augustine, who each summarize the content of Christian faith in the "rule of faith" and appealed to that "rule"as a foundational hermeneutical criterion for engaging Scripture.[147] Chapter 2 provides an examination of the ways in which these three major Christian thinkers engaged and interpreted Christian Scripture from within "the rule of faith." The inclination to articulate the judgments of Christian faith in the rule of faith represents an authentic Christian strategy that must be retained and appropriated in a contemporary Christian understanding of the nature and purpose of Christian Scripture. Again, we cannot understand what Scripture is unless we know where it is located.

CHAPTER TWO

Historical Precedents

The Rule of Faith in Irenaeus, Origen, and Augustine

> But when the fullness of time had come, God sent his Son, born of a woman, born under the law, in order to redeem those who were under the law, so that we might receive adoption as children. And because you are children, God has sent the Spirit of his Son into our hearts, crying, 'Abba! Father!' So you are no longer a slave but a child, and if a child then also an heir, through God.
>
> —Galatians 4.4–7

> Now I should remind you, brothers and sisters, of the good news that I proclaimed to you, which you in turn received, in which also you stand, through which also you are being saved. . . . For I handed on to you as of first importance what I in turn had received.
>
> —1 Corinthians 15.1–3a

The canonical shape of Christian Scripture, beginning with a narrative of the creation of the world in Genesis and ending with a depiction of the eschaton in the book of Revelation, reflects a theological understanding of history. The general order of the books in Christian Bibles, however, did not fall from heaven.[1] That order is the product of judgments by specific historical individuals and communities.[2] Before pandects, or complete manuscript copies of Christian Scripture, became relatively common in the Middle Ages, the distinct books and manuscripts of the Bible were more a library than a single book.[3] The theology of history from creation to consummation reflected in the order of the Christian Scriptures actually reflects precanonical Christian convictions about the unity of the creative and redemptive work of the Triune God in history.[4] Christians have characteristically affirmed some version of this theological depiction of history to be divinely revealed and truthful, but such understandings and articulations of the economic work of the Triune God are no less a product of human subjects and communities acting in history for that fact.

Historical critics have demonstrated, however, that there is not just one theology of history attested in Christian Scripture. Biblical scholarship of the past couple hundred years has forced us to advert to the diversity of horizonal perspectives attested within not just the canon, but in different books in each Testament and even in individual books that still bear marks of their not quite seamless redaction. Some obvious examples of differences of perspective in close literary proximity are the two accounts of creation in Genesis (1.1–2.4a; 2.4b–3.24), the differing accounts of the activities of the kings of Israel and Judah in 1 Kings and 2 Kings and 1 and 2 Chronicles, respectively, the chronological and geographic differences of the four canonical gospels, the contrasting depictions of Paul's life and teaching in Acts and what can be gleaned about his life from his letters, and the literary and conceptual relationships between Colossians and Ephesians and Jude and 2 Peter respectively.[5] If we can recognize and acknowledge the presence of multiple perspectives among the diverse books of the canon of Scripture and if we can acknowledge the pervasive interpretive plurality characteristic of groups committed to the authority and truthfulness of Scripture, we must admit the insufficiency of Scripture alone for comprehensively establishing the content of Christian faith.[6] Scripture itself does not reign in its constitutive plurality and particularity. As I emphasized earlier, it is not an agent capable of doing such work.

Such an admission does not require us to abandon judgments about the sufficiency and authority of Scripture full stop. We must, however, find an adequate way to understand its usefulness and authority that can recognize the differences of perspective of its human writers, redactors, canonizers, and interpreters. An adequate theological account of the nature and purpose of Christian Scripture must provide an answer to the following questions: how can we articulate a Christian theology of history, or "horizon," in which these various details can find their correct place, and how can we articulate this understanding of history in a way that is adequate to traditional Christian claims about the economic work of the Triune God, to the post-Enlightenment recognition of the historicity of human meaning, and to recent discoveries concerning the material history of Christian Scripture?

I use the word *horizon* in a metaphorical sense to refer to the bounded scope of understandings, judgments, and interests constitutive of an individual or group. As Lonergan writes:

> As our field of vision, so too the scope of our knowledge, and the range of our interests are bounded. As fields of vision vary with one's standpoint, so too the scope of one's knowledge and the range of one's interests vary with the period in which one lives, one's social background and milieu, one's education and personal development. . . . In this sense what lies beyond one's horizon is simply outside the range of one's knowledge and interests: one neither knows nor cares. But what lies within one's horizon is in some measure, great or small, an object of interest and of knowledge.[7]

The question to which this chapter begins to respond is the following: What are adequate understandings, judgments, and interests that constitute a Christian horizon for engaging and understanding Christian Scripture today?

When we search for evidence of explicit reflection on something like a "Christian horizon" in the history of theological reflection in Christianity, an obvious candidate that presents itself for examination is the "rule of faith" or "rule of truth." The rule of faith or truth provided early Christians with an articulation of a Christian horizon. And that horizon served to identify the content of Scripture and normed its use and interpretation in Christian communities.

From the vantage of historical development, believers in Christ, and thus the Christian faith, are antecedent to the historical recognition of the two Testament Christian Bible.[8] The scriptures that the church has come to know as the Old Testament were, of course, present from the very beginnings of the Christian faith, but the recognition of a two-Testament Bible itself took place only gradually.[9] Even if most of the books that would become the New Testament were functionally authoritative as early as the beginning of the second century AD, Athanasius's festal letter, dated to AD 367, represents the first extant list of all twenty-seven books of the New Testament without any additions or subtractions. Later lists and manuscripts do not uniformly agree with Athanasius's list either.[10] But Christian faith preceded these processes of discernment and recognition by centuries. As Rudolf Voderholzer has strikingly put it, "The earliest Christian martyrs of the Church died for their faith in Jesus Christ without ever having held a New Testament in their hands."[11] While gaps in the extant evidence—especially our lack of access to the actual oral transmission of Christian tradition in the early centuries—preclude us from having a comprehensive and finally definitive historical account of the development of Christian faith and theological reflection prior to the recognition and stabilization of the later recognition of the "complete" Christian biblical canon, it is possible, and desirable, to examine the development of Christian reflection on and understanding of the Christian message antecedent to the emergence of the two Testament canon.[12] Attention to the earliest extant works of Christian writing shows that canons/rules of faith/truth emerge in Christian history before any of our recognizable canons of Christian Scripture do.[13]

Recent scholarship on patristic hermeneutics and exegesis has drawn attention to how the rule of faith or truth formed a heuristic theological framework that circumscribed the ways that the early Christians used and interpreted the texts they held to be sacred.[14] The rule expressed constitutive Christian beliefs about the creative and providential work of the God of the ancient scriptures and the culmination and fulfillment of that work in the actions of Jesus Christ and the new community established by him through the Holy Spirit. A number of theologians have recently argued that contemporary Christians seeking to understand and faithfully utilize Scripture today should follow the patristic practice of using the rule of faith as a hermeneutical guide for exegetical praxis.[15]

This chapter examines historical employments of the "rule(s)" in the works of Irenaeus, Origen, and Augustine, three of the most influential scriptural exegetes of the early Christian centuries, to show how the historical rule(s) of faith articulated in the early church represent objectifications of early Christian beliefs in the redemptive work of the Triune God in history, expressed in narrative form, which affirm the unity and actuality of the economic work of the Father, Son, and Holy Spirit and which also admit of and even invite technical development and specification.

Objectifications of the creative and redemptive work of God, of course, are already present in the texts that would become the New Testament. Such objectifications arguably witness to the presence of all the major core convictions of the later rule(s) in the earliest Christian communities. The early Christians committed their beliefs about their experiences, understandings, and judgments concerning the work and activity of God in Jesus Christ and the Holy Spirit to language. They *expressed* these convictions. Such expressions are objectifications. As Ben Meyer notes, the "lapidary form" of such expressions has ensured the preservation of their fundamental perspectives.[16] The two scriptural epigraphs at the beginning of this chapter represent such objectifications. The artistry and intentional structure of such confessions is striking; a number of scholars have argued that they may be liturgical forms that antedate the texts of the New Testament.[17]

Though it is likely impossible to trace the precise geographic and temporal development of the rule(s) of faith and later creeds and their exact relationships to earlier confessions, the kerygmatic passages of the New Testament texts themselves, and to pre–New Testament confessions, they undoubtedly have some relationship to these earlier expressions of faith.[18] Even so, while the rule(s) distill the content of Scripture in some way, they are ultimately antecedent to Scripture and are themselves expressions of judgments not primarily about what Scripture contains—as if Scripture were a plastic Tupperware full of "meanings," to emphasize the ineptitude of the metaphor—but instead objectify and so mediate understandings and judgments about what is the case.[19] The rules are objectifications of the actuality of the "mystery and economy of the existent God" (*Haer.* 2.28.1).

After brief historical investigations of the rules and their significance and functions in the work of Irenaeus, Origen, and Augustine, the next chapter expounds the following normative judgment: the practice of clearly articulating the unified work of the Triune God in history is an authentic practice of the early church, and the articulation of a rule of faith at the level of our own times is a desideratum for contemporary engagement with Christian Scripture. What are the criteria for the judgment that the development of rule(s) is an authentic one that we should emulate in the present? The practice of articulating rules of faith emerged as Christian communities both spontaneously and of necessity began to organize their core convictions about the tradition they had received and their experience of the work of the Holy Spirit and Christ in their worship and life. The converted Christian communities held and passed on the judgment that God was reconciling the world to God's self via the work of Jesus Christ and the Holy Spirit. This judgment is a judgment about history and reality and articulates the *res* to which the texts of Scripture themselves refer. To reiterate, the rule(s), then, do not only predate the recognition of the Christian scriptural canon(s), they emerge both organically from Christian worship and practice and of necessity in response to criticisms and misunderstandings of the beliefs of Christian communities by outsiders and in response to the need for clear catechetical materials for discipleship.

The same motivations—catechetical clarification of worship and defense of the faith—exist today for the rule(s). There is also a phenomenological reason for articulating a rule of faith at the level of our times. A Christian understanding of the Christian scriptures will both inform and be located in the Christian community's or individual's judgments concerning the meaning and purpose of the history that is and the work of the Triune God in that history. While our understanding of the work of the Triune God in history undoubtedly must be informed by our engagement with and understandings of the meaning(s) of Scripture, that antecedent understanding, our horizon, or *Begrifflichkeit*, will inevitably and inescapably influence subsequent encounters with Scripture. Exegesis without presuppositions is impossible.[20] As D. Stephen Long states, "We can only read, hear, and interpret any text when it is placed in a proper sequence that renders the text intelligible. Such a proper sequence inevitably functions as a 'canon' by which the interpreter sets forth a 'right' reading. This is not optional; it is a necessary condition for reading, speaking, hearing, interpreting. . . . The question then is not if we have a canon, but which one do we have."[21] The horizon of understanding one had prior to one's encounter with the Triune God was ultimately a means through which one understood her first encounter with God, but that encounter dilated, overturned, and reoriented that previous horizon.[22] We must ask, What kind of horizon of understandings and judgments is necessary to read the Christian Bible in a way that is distinctively Christian and that is accountable to the exigencies of subjective authenticity, the historical development of Christian understanding, and the material and ideational realities of the texts of Scripture themselves?[23]

But why should we start with an articulation of a Christian horizon and not with Scripture?[24] It will perhaps strike many readers as odd that this systematic theology of the nature and purpose of Scripture does not begin with an articulation of what the Bible "says about itself." Should we not simply carefully read Scripture in order to let it confront us with its own testimony? Such an approach risks a mistaken understanding of the relationships between written human language and human understanding. The written text as written, and even as recited from memory, does not "speak." As noted in the previous chapter, this metaphorical way of talking about written or recited text involves us in the risk of "depeopling" the pursuit of meaning. Subjects produced, edited, redacted, and transmitted Scripture purposely, whether or not they were fully conscious of their intentions, and subsequent readers and hearers can seek to understand how Scripture has been used by God and human persons and will be used in the future. Even the judgments that Scripture is inspired and that it is the written Word of God are judgments about the relationship of Scripture to the divine subjects of the Holy Spirit and Son of God.

As noted above, we cannot temporarily suspend our judgments about what Christian faith entails or what Scripture is in order to "take a good look at it" to see what it "says about itself." As Angus Paddison rightly asserts, "An account of what Scripture 'is' is inseparable from the series of divine and human actions in which it is a participant. Scripture is not a text in pursuit of a location—it is *already* located within the reconciling action of God and the practices of the Church."[25] To fail to inquire into the intelligible structures and orders of these "locations" would be irresponsible. To state things concisely, then, in a systematic theology of Christian interpretation of Christian Scripture, a Christian understanding of the being and work of the Triune God and the intrinsic intelligibility of the creation and redemption, including an account of the structures of human nature that make such understanding possible, must come prior to and serve as the context for subsequent accounts of what Christian Scripture is and what its purpose is.

The history of the created economy, as a history of progress, decline, and redemption, is the history in which the Triune God acts. Whatever the Christian scriptures are, human engagement with them will take place within the history that is. *But our understanding of the history that is will inescapably influence subsequent engagement with and assessment of that history.* By "the history that is," I refer not to history as written but to the history written about. Bernard Lonergan distinguishes these two understandings of the word *history*: "There is history (1) that is written about, and there is history (2) that is written. History (2) aims at expressing knowledge of history (1)."[26] We understand—with relative adequacy—and misunderstand the history that is. This point is almost so obvious as to not mention, but it has great significance for the present project. A Christian approach to Scripture will necessarily take its point of departure from a Christian theology of history.[27] A *fully* responsible Christian exegesis of Scripture will be impossible without a critically articulated Christian understanding of what has happened in the history that is. Such an account of history, in order to be adequate to Christian proclamation about the activity of the Triune God in the world, cannot be positivist or historicist. It must be able to acknowledge the historicity of human activity represented in Scripture but must also take a stand on history as the arena of divine activity. As such it requires an articulation of salvation history that sublates "secular" history.[28] As Robert Jenson has recently argued, contemporary engagement with Scripture cannot but be critical.[29] Christian scriptural interpretation has arguably been critical from the very beginning.[30] What Jenson specifically means, I think, is that those engaging Scripture today must give an account of their own historicity, locatedness, and fundamental operative commitments with respect to their engagement with Scripture.[31] For Christians this means we can and must allow Christian convictions to affect our engagement with Scripture.[32] Authentic Christian engagement with Scripture requires the interpreter (or interpreting community) to conscientiously and critically self-appropriate her Christian horizon, expressing or objectifying it in something like a contemporary rule of faith.

The ways that Irenaeus, Origen, and Augustine articulated their faith in judgments about the work of the Triune God in history provide resources for the constructive "rule" provided in the next chapter and elaborated throughout the rest of this book. The constructive rule of the next chapter is neither the repetition of premodern rules explored in the present chapter nor a comprehensive exposition of the theological context of Christian engagement with Scripture. It merely represents *one* heuristic objectification of a Christian horizon that draws on the ecclesial tradition of the early church exemplified in the rule(s) I examine that also appropriates later historical, theoretical, and theological developments. The heuristic so constructed will provide a broad theological conception of the work of the Triune God in history, the broadest and most significant context in which Christian engagement with Scripture will take place. Following that constructive rule in chapter 3, the next chapter provides a theological and philosophical anthropology as a further complementary heuristics for locating Scripture. Chapters 3 and 4, then, draw on the work of the present chapter and on other insights from premodern and contemporary theological reflection to affirm the providential and redemptive work of the Triune God who creates, sustains, and redeems God's creation, and to articulate an account of the intelligibility of human persons—with reference to their interior and social capacities for self-transcendence—as the primary arena of God's redemptive work.[33] First, however, it is necessary to explore the precedents for the present work in the historical developments of the rule of faith as a hermeneutical criterion in the early church.

Given the overall purpose of the present work, I need to offer some comments about the relationship between such "rules" and systematic theology. The rules represent flexible objectifications of specific doctrinal beliefs of the early Christians.[34] When invoked, they often provided occasions for quasi-systematic reflection on the part of the early Christians. None of the rules is systematic in the precise and technical sense of systematic theology that I explained in the previous chapter. But the decision to articulate such rules reflects subjective exigencies of Christian communities and individuals towards understanding and judgment that are not unrelated to systematics as I have described it. I will therefore comment on the relationship between the various uses of the rule and systematic theology in what follows. The rules of faith are located within a broader set of developments in the early church whereby the earliest Christians began to articulate the judgments—that is, doctrines—and intelligibility of their faith in a differentiated manner. A full account of such differentiation is not possible at this point, but it is necessary to note that such differentiation has its place in what Lonergan has called "the origins of Christian realism."[35] Others have customarily referred to this process as the development of doctrine or dogma. In this process, the early Christians appropriated and significantly transformed the linguistic resources from Greek culture—and even invented new linguistic resources—to understand and communicate the truths of Christian faith with greater and greater nuance and precision.

Contemporary literature on the rules of faith has raised a number of fascinating historical and theological questions concerning the rules, including the following: What precisely are they? How are they related to one another historically and conceptually? What are their settings and functions in early Christian faith and life? How are they related to earlier Christian summaries of faith and confessions? What is their precise historical relationship to the Christian scriptures? What is their relationship to the relatively fixed formulas of later creeds? What is going forward in the early church's use of these rules? What is the relationship between early expressions of the rule of faith/truth and present attempts to invoke the rule to provide boundaries for contemporary Christian engagement with Scripture? While the following exposition responds to such questions at a number of points, my more specific goal is to inquire into the purposes and intentions of such rules and to ask about how their *functional purposes* in early Christian thought might provide directives for contemporary engagement with Scripture. I am not asking questions primarily about the historical development of the rules but instead raising a question of performance. *What were these early Christians doing by articulating and employing such rules of faith/truth in catechesis and polemics and especially with regard to scriptural exegesis and hermeneutics?*

FROM THE NEW TESTAMENT TO IRENAEUS

As the epigraphs to this chapter attest—and they are only two examples among many others—the Christians who lived during the time in which the texts of the New Testament were produced regularly expressed their beliefs in short, straightforward, and dense confessions that reflected their convictions concerning the definitive work of the God of Israel in Jesus Christ and God's work in the new community that carried forward Christ's work in the Holy Spirit.[36] In *The Making of the Creeds,* Frances Young has detailed how the judgments contained in such early Christian writings represented summative accounts of the stories of specific local Christian communities: "From the very beginning, the Christian communities developed stereotyped in-language to summarize their fundamental teaching to tell their particular story. . . . From such stereotyped material, selection was made to confront challenges to the 'over-arching story' that enabled Christians to make sense of the world."[37]

The presence of such summaries in the texts of the New Testament is unsurprising given the fact that these communities were originally communities of Jewish believers. "Such Jewish confessions [as Deut 5.4 and 26.5]," Young notes, "were embedded in worship, and so at first were the Christian confessions that replaced them. Creeds have their genesis in doxology, and they are not to that extent a surprising or uncharacteristic development from Christianity's Jewish background."[38] The earliest Jewish Christians thus inherited the practice of objectifying their judgments about the work of God in history from their Jewish ancestors. While such objectification is, of course, not the objectification that takes place in technical or scientific language, the earliest Christians were already spontaneously developing confessions that were constitutive of their horizon for understanding the world.[39] As the context of the second epigraph above (see 1 Cor 15.3–4) indicates, convictions about "the scriptures" figured into these Christian confessional statements from the very beginning.[40] Confessions and exclamations concerning the work of the God of Israel who had raised Jesus Christ from the dead had their origins in worship. Lonergan, probably alluding to Paul's words in 1 Corinthians 15, refers to these early summaries of Christian beliefs as the "the original message."[41] As noted above, this message, and the process of its expression—that is, its linguistic objectification—is historically antecedent to the "close" of any extant canons of Christian Scripture.

The summaries of faith in the writings that would become the Christian New Testament are probably organically related to the confessions referred to in the second century as the *regula fidei* (or *regula veritatis*)

or κανών τῆς πίστεως (or κανών τῆς ἀληθείας).[42] Most secondary literature conventionally refers to such later confessions as simply the "rule
of faith."[43] These quasi-confessional summaries of Christian belief that
emerged in the second century, as Tomas Bokedal writes, were "used from
early on to designate the basic theology of the church."[44] Prior to the Christian era Greek philosophers and rhetors had borrowed the term κανών
from the linguistic tool kit of Greek carpentry, where it signified a ruler or
level, to refer to a critically and clearly delineated set of teachings.[45] Aristotle defined κανών as a straight measuring stick utilized in carpentry work
(*De an.* 1.5).[46] In its pre-Christian usage κανών characteristically designated the principles and boundaries of philosophical reason.[47] κανών
appears infrequently in the texts of the New Testament, with extant occurrences only in Paul's letter to the Galatians (6.16) and 2 Corinthians
(10.13, 15, 16).[48] In Galatians 2.14 Paul makes reference to "the truth of the
gospel" (τὴν ἀλήθειαν τοῦ εὐαγγελίου); further along in the letter he would
write of the need for his readers or hearers to follow "this rule" he has laid
down for them in 6.16 (καὶ ὅσοι τῷ κανόνι τούτῳ στοιχήσουσιν).[49] The
next extant Christian mention of such a "rule" occurs in 1 Clement, probably written in the last two decades of the first century AD.

In 1 Clement 7.1–2, Clement explains the purpose of his letter to the
Corinthians: "We write these things, dear friends, not only to admonish
you but also to remind ourselves. For we are in the same arena, and the
same contest awaits us. Therefore let us abandon empty and futile
thoughts, and let us conform to the glorious and holy rule (κανόνι) of our
tradition." Clement proceeds to exhort his readers to attend to the salvific
work of Christ and its universal and cosmic significance (7.3–4) and gives
examples from Scripture of the repentance necessary for participating in
the work of God (7.5–8.5). Despite his use of the Greek word, Clement of
Rome does not employ it in order to indicate a set of judgments about the
Father, Son, and Holy Spirit. For this reason Prosper Grech judges that
Clement's use of κανών is not yet "technical."[50] As William Farmer has argued, however, all of the elements of the later trinitarian "rule" are already
present in doxological and doctrinal statements elsewhere in 1 Clement.[51]

All of the constitutive components of the rule, in fact, are at the very
least consonant with the judgments found in New Testament confessions.[52] Other trinitarian confessions of faith occur in second-century

Christian literature and do not explicitly bear the label "rules of faith" or "rules of truth."[53] What happens between Clement's time and the time of Irenaeus that brings about the emergence of the "technical" trinitarian rule? Farmer plausibly suggests that Marcion's conviction of the radical heterogeneity of the creator God of the Jewish scriptures and the God of Jesus Christ—a distinction he shared with various gnostic groups—provided the impetus for the second- and third-century fathers to express the "rule" in its more customary trinitarian—three-clause—and binitarian—two-clause—forms; these forms allowed them to emphasize that there were not two Gods (contra Marcion) but one.[54] Such confessions that tied the work of the Father and Son together intimately served the purpose of expressing the unity of the economic work of God in creation and salvation and of reiterating the early Christian emphasis on the goodness of creation.[55] The apostle Paul had already set a precedent for such two-clause confessions in 1 Corinthians 8.5–6: "for us there is one God, the Father, from whom are all things and for whom we exist, and one Lord, Jesus Christ, through whom are all things and through whom we exist."

Even where scholars have identified instances of the technical usage of the rule of faith, it has a notable flexibility in the second and third centuries.[56] Its flexibility may result from the primarily oral function of such early Christian forms and from differences of emphasis in traditions of specific distinct geographic regions.[57] As Young notes, the various iterations of the rule of faith "were not 'Articles of Belief' or a system of doctrine, but rather 'confessions' summarizing the Christian story, or affirmations of the three 'characters' [Father, Son, and Holy Spirit] in the story. They tell who God is and what he has done." Such confessions, she continues, "invite the convert to make that story and the affirmation his or her own: the word for 'confess' means also 'acknowledge' and even 'praise.'"[58] Paul Blowers has shown how these confessions had a distinctive and irreducible narrative character.

> The Rule of Faith . . . served the primitive Christian hope of articulating and authenticating a world-encompassing story or metanarrative of creation, incarnation, redemption, and consummation. . . . [T]he Rule, being a narrative construction, set forth the basic "dramatic" structure of a Christian vision of the world, posing as an hermeneutical

frame of reference for the interpretation of Christian Scripture and Christian experience, and educing the first principles of Christian theological discourse and of a doctrinal substantiation of Christian faith.[59]

Though the rule was wielded in and refined by polemics, it was likely not originally born of conflict.[60] The striking resemblance of the rule to known baptismal confessions suggests that it was closely related to or even emerged from the liturgical and confessional praxis of the early Christian communities.[61] Such confessions gained their characteristic tripartite structure very early, and this feature is probably dependent on the trinitarian baptismal formula in Matthew 28, where the risen Christ commissions his followers to baptize in the name of the Father, the Son, and the Holy Spirit.[62] Young elsewhere suggests that the rule may have emerged as an aid in worship "because the lectionary passages were virtually unintelligible without an overall perspective."[63] As I explain below, the rule frequently had a vitally important hermeneutical purpose.

While these summaries emerged in distinct local communities and were marshaled at specific times for specific purposes, my contention is that the practice of developing such summaries represents an authentic and inevitable objectification of early Christian experiences of, understandings of, and judgments concerning the work of the Triune God in history. Such objectifications obviously do not antedate the use and interpretation of the Old Testament scriptures by early Christians, but they do antedate the final recognition of any extant canonical collections used by contemporary Christian communities. Such rules are historically antecedent to the recognition of any contemporary canonical collections of Christian Scripture.

For the second-century church fathers, such rules provided the boundaries of proper Christian interpretation of the authoritative scriptures received by the early Christian communities. As Frances Young writes in *Biblical Exegesis and the Formation of Christian Culture*:

Long before the formation of the canon of two Testaments, Old and New, or the listing of authorized books that belonged to it, the unity of the Bible and its witness to Christ was the assumption underlying its "reception" by readers and hearers in the "public" assembly of the community.[64]

She goes on to articulate the hermeneutical significance of the rule:

> [The Rule of Faith] provided ... the proper reading of the beginning and ending [of the biblical narrative], the focus of the plot and the relations of the principal characters, so enabling the "middle" to be heard in bits as meaningful. They provided the "closure" which contemporary theory prefers to leave open. They articulated the essential hermeneutical key without which texts and community would disintegrate in incoherence.[65]

As Young demonstrates in *The Making of the Creeds*, the flexibility of various local rules eventually gave way to the more stable fixity of specific creeds that followed the same basic structure of the rule.[66]

The time between the emergence of Christianity and the development of more fixed creeds provides a unique window on how Christian understandings of Christian faith developed and how Christians understood the authority of Scripture before the "close" of the canon. Though, as noted above, it is impossible to ignore the diversity of perspectives in particular books of the Christian Bible, and while it is impossible to trace out the direct historical connections between specific historical instantiations of the proclamation about Christ and its implications in the early church, we must also note the earliest Christians both received and passed on Scripture within a distinctive, largely integral, and developing set of related horizons that provided the context for their reception of these books in the first place. The most famous employments of the "rule" with reference to scriptural exegesis are found in the works of Irenaeus of Lyons (ca. AD 125–202), Origen of Alexandria (ca. AD 185/186–253/254), and Augustine of Hippo (ca. AD 354–420).[67] While these early witnesses to the rule demonstrate its constitutive flexibility and indeterminacy, each shares an emphasis on its usefulness as a hermeneutical criterion for scriptural exegesis.

What follows is a critical examination of the ways Irenaeus, Origen, and Augustine invoke the rule in their reflections on the purpose of Scripture, their understandings of its authoritative function, and their understandings of how it provided and circumscribed the legitimate boundaries of scriptural interpretation. I have chosen these specific figures because of their significance and unmistakable influence on subsequent

Christian engagement with Scripture.[68] The investigation of the stated origins and functions of the rule for these figures provides a touchstone for the argument of how an articulation of the rule at the level of our own times is not only merely a desideratum for contemporary Christian use and interpretation of Scripture, but is absolutely essential from a historical, theological, and phenomenological standpoint.

IRENAEUS OF LYONS AND THE RULE OF FAITH

Irenaeus's *Adversus Haereses* (ca. AD 175–80; hereafter *Haer.*) represents the earliest extant witness to the "technical" use of the rule.[69] In *Haer.*, Irenaeus refers to the rule—in this work most often designated as the κανών τῆς ἀληθείας—explicitly in 1.8.1–1.10.1; 2.27.1; 2.28.1; 3.2.1; 3.4.2; 3.11.1; 3.12.6; 3.15.1; and 4.35.4.[70] In the preface, Irenaeus states that he intends to give his reader, probably a bishop of another Christian community, "a concise and clear report on the doctrine of . . . the disciples of Ptolemaeus, an offshoot of the Valentinian school." "We will also offer suggestions, to the best of our limited capacity," he continues, "for refuting this doctrine, by showing how utterly absurd, inconsistent, and incongruous with the Truth their statements are" (*Haer.* 1.pref).[71] Because Irenaeus notes that he hopes to present and refute the teachings of Ptolemaeus and the Valentinians, it is unsurprising that *Haer.* is polemical in its tone. In order to use the truth of Christian faith against aberrant teachings, however, Irenaeus must first report and explain that truth. Irenaeus's citations of the rule in *Haer.* represent our earliest extant witnesses to the historical innovation of the objectification of the Christian community's horizon in terms of judgments about reality structured in a "trinitarian" fashion.[72] As Young has argued, Irenaeus makes the Christian communities' "emerging sense of identity" explicit in his reflections on the rule of faith in *Haer.*[73] Despite the polemical purpose and tone of *Haer.*, a number of scholars have drawn attention to its quasi-"systematic" dimensions.[74] While *Haer.* clearly does not exhibit all of the characteristics of systematic theology enumerated in the previous chapter, Irenaeus's frequent appeals to the rule and his regular appeals to the interconnectedness of Christian beliefs demonstrate his concern for orderliness and his concern to clearly articulate the fundamental beliefs of

Christian faith. His recurrent emphasis on the unity and interrelatedness of the work of the Son and the Spirit in the recapitulative work of the Father exhibits the synthetic thrust of *Haer*. Ultimately, however, Irenaeus's work is not organized by technical considerations.[75]

Irenaeus also makes reference to the rule in a later catechetical work, the Ἐπίδειξις του αποστολικού κηρύγματος 3 and 6 (hereafter referred to as *Epid*.).[76] Irenaeus's appeal to the rule in this later work shows that the rule had a catechetical function as well as a polemical function in his time.[77] Irenaeus states that he wrote the *Epid*. as a "summary memorandum" to one Marcianus, in order to strengthen its recipient's faith (*Epid*. pref). In this later work, Irenaeus uses the language of the "κανών τῆς πίστεως" instead of the "κανών τῆς ἀληθείας." As Eric Osborn has helpfully noticed, the differences in vocabulary ("of faith" vs. "of truth") correspond to the distinct purposes of each work. The former was presumably more appropriate for catechesis and the latter more fitting for polemics.[78] In general the content and emphases, however, are almost identical.

When Irenaeus invokes the rule in *Haer*., he does not provide a uniform exposition of its components. His longest expositions of the content of the rule are in *Haer*. 1.10.1 and 1.22.1. The former passage is his most extensive extant exposition of the rule. "The Church, indeed," he writes,

> though disseminated throughout the world, even to the ends of the earth, received from the apostles and their disciples the faith in one God the Father Almighty, the Creator of heaven and earth and the seas and all things that are in them; and in the one Jesus Christ, the Son of God, who was enfleshed for our salvation; and in the Holy Spirit, who through the prophets preached the Economies, the coming, the birth from a Virgin, the passion, the resurrection from the dead, and the bodily ascension into heaven of the beloved Son, Christ Jesus our Lord, and His coming from heaven in the glory of the Father to recapitulate all things, and to raise up all flesh of the whole human race, in order that to Christ Jesus, our Lord and God, Savior and King, according to the invisible Father's good pleasure, Every knee should bow [of those] in heaven and on earth and under the earth, and every tongue confess Him, and that He would exercise just judgment toward all; and that, on the other hand, He would send into eternal fire

the spiritual forces of wickedness, and the angels who transgressed and became rebels, and the godless, wicked, lawless, and blasphemous people; but, on the other hand, by bestowing life on the righteous and holy and those who kept His commandments and who have persevered in His love—both those who did so from the beginning and those who did so after repentance—He would bestow on them as a grace the gift of incorruption and clothe them with everlasting glory. The Church, as we have said before, though disseminated throughout the whole world, carefully guards this preaching and this faith which she has received, as if she dwelt in one house. She likewise believes these things as if she had but one soul and one and the same heart; she preaches, teaches, and hands them down harmoniously, as if she possessed but one mouth. (1.10.1)

In the latter passage, Irenaeus writes the following:

The Rule of the Truth that we hold is this: There is one God Almighty, who created all things through His Word; He both prepared and made all things out of nothing, just as Scripture says: "For by the word of the Lord the heavens were made, and all their host by the breath of His mouth" [Ps 33.6]. And again: "All things were made through Him and without Him was made not a thing" (John 1.3). From this all nothing is exempt. Now, it is the Father who made all things through Him, whether visible or invisible, whether sensible or intelligible, whether temporal for the sake of some dispensation or eternal. These He did not make through Angels or some Powers that were separated from His thought. For the God of all things needs nothing. No, He made all things by His Word and Spirit, disposing and governing them and giving all of them existence. This is the one who made the world, which indeed is made up of all things. This is the one who fashioned man. This is the God of Abraham and Isaac and Jacob, above whom there is no other God, nor a Beginning, nor a Power, nor a Fullness. This is the Father of our Lord Jesus Christ, as we shall demonstrate. (1.22.1)

A number of features of the rule as Irenaeus presents it in these two forms deserve special comment. Almost every time that Irenaeus invokes the rule he specifies that he has received it from the church; his use in these two loci is no exception. In the first passage (*Haer.* 1.10.1), Irenaeus states that he has received the rule from the apostles and their disciples. As Young summarizes, for Irenaeus "it is the tradition of the truth which is to be esteemed, and if there are any doubts about it, enquiry should be made from the oldest churches in which the apostles lived."[79]

Prior to the advent of modern critical scholarship many ecclesiastical writers held that Irenaeus was referring to the Apostle's Creed when he invoked the rule of truth/rule of faith.[80] In book 3 of *Haer.* Irenaeus provides his famous account and defense of apostolic succession (see 3.1–5). Given the fragmentary nature of the documentary evidence of the earliest Christian centuries, and our lack of access to oral tradition qua oral, a complete answer to the question of the historicity of Irenaeus's claim that he has received the rule from the apostles, or the precise nature of the transmission of the faith, is not possible. The modern recognition of the historicity of doctrinal development forces us to temper if not abandon the high rhetoric of the uniformity and universality of Christian teaching emphasized by Irenaeus and other fathers.[81] Christian thought is not static; it is not dependent on, or the explication of, a univocal "already back then real" deposit of faith entrusted to the saints (Jude 3).[82]

While responsible recognition of the historicity of the rule means we cannot accept Irenaeus's judgment of its temporal and geographic catholicity, it is not necessary to abandon his judgment of its truthfulness. The antiquity of the distinct faith judgments it preserves is also probable.[83] While the meanings of the Christological confessions of the New Testament are by no means univocal and absolutely perspicuous, Irenaeus's account of the rule arguably recycles various clauses from each of them.[84] It could be understood, without much stretching, as a reorganization and elaboration of understandings and judgments of the first two epigraphs in this chapter.

Irenaeus's invocation of "the truth" in the preface to book 1 of *Haer.* indicates the *realist* or *referential* nature of the rule. The defining genitive that Irenaeus employs when he makes reference to the rule, in 1.9.4 as Tomas Bokedal notes, "indicates that the *faith* or *the truth itself* is the rule or norm for Christian belief and practice."[85] While the rule clearly has an irreducible narrative and linguistic character for Irenaeus, its realist or referential implications are no less evident.[86] Affirmation of the rule was more than a matter of mere narrative recital. As he writes in the preface to the *Epid.*:

> We must keep the rule of faith unswervingly, and perform the commandments of God, believing in God and fearing Him, for He is Lord, and loving Him, for He is Father. Action, then, comes by faith, as "if you do not believe," Isaias says, "you will not understand"; and the truth brings about faith, for faith is established upon things truly real, that we may believe what really is, as it is, and <believing> what really is, as it is, we may always keep our conviction of it firm. Since, then, the conserver of our salvation is faith, it is necessary to take great care of it, that we may have a true comprehension of *what is*. (*Epid.* 3; emphasis mine)[87]

He insists on the realist nature of the rule in *Haer.* as well:

> Since, then, we possess the Rule of Truth itself and the manifest testimony about God, we ought not to cast out the solid and true knowledge about God by running from one solution to another. No, it is proper to direct the solution of difficulties toward that standard [the Rule], and *to discipline ourselves by investigating the mystery and economy of the existent God,* and to grow in the love of him who has done and does so much for our sakes. (*Haer.* 2.28.1; emphasis mine)

I utilize the etic language of "realism" simply to point out that Irenaeus does not *merely* insist that Christians must confess certain things in a certain way or follow an explicit grammar of Christian faith that he has received as the authoritative tradition of the church; he certainly does insist on regulating speech about God and on the need to adhere to the tradition of the church. This received language and grammar, however, is no less essentially *referential.* Irenaeus does not marshal the rule to discipline Christian speech only. He does so in order to both *declare* and *indicate* the unity of the work of the Father, Son, and Spirit *in history.* The rule is an articulation of the actuality of the work of the Father, Son, and Spirit in the history that is.[88] The judgment of the realist, referential nature of the rule will prove significant for our own constructive articulation of a rule of faith adequate to contemporary engagement with Scripture in the next chapter.

Irenaeus not only objectifies the horizon of his Christian community (in terms of specific doctrinal judgments about the Father, the Son, the Holy Spirit, the economy of their work, etc.), but he also presents understandings of that horizon by relating judgments about the primary actors to one another in the unity of their work. Later theologians, such as Thomas Aquinas, will state this axiomatically by insisting that the work of the Triune God *ad extra* is one, even while the persons of the Trinity, by appropriation, are consistently described as effecting and bringing about specific actions.[89] For Irenaeus, the Son and the Holy Spirit are the two hands by which the Father has accomplished and continues to accomplish the work of "recapitulation" in creation.[90] Irenaeus states this "recapitulation" is the explicit purpose of God's action in Christ and the Holy Spirit.[91] The later debates and arguments through which orthodox or creedal trinitarian theology are forged also focus explicitly on the identities of and relationships between the various divine actors of the rule/creeds. The irreducible narratival nature of the rule in its trinitarian forms mediates the unity of the work of Father, Son, and Spirit in the economy of creation.[92] The second iteration of the rule quoted above (1.22.1), following the precedent set by the apostle Paul (1 Cor 8.6), unequivocally indicates the unity of the work of the Father, Son, and Spirit in the act of creation.

While the rule represents an authoritative inheritance from Irenaeus's community, it has its organic roots in the liturgical praxis of the church. Just prior to the first passage (1.10.1), Irenaeus notes that the rule of truth was "received through baptism" (1.9.4). Irenaeus probably alludes to a trinitarian confession that accompanied baptism.[93] As Young notes, the practice of reading from the various texts of Scripture in the ecclesial assembly, a custom dating to the first century (see Acts 13.5; 1 Tim 4.13), would have made the articulation of something like the rule absolutely necessary when the church was composed largely of gentile believers.[94] Those unfamiliar with the precise meanings of these not always perspicuous texts, not unlike the Ethiopian eunuch of Acts 8, needed some perspective by which they could rightly understand their referents and intelligible interconnections.

As already noted, the rule served as a hermeneutic delimiting the boundaries of appropriate Christian scriptural exegesis. This is explicit in Irenaeus's *Haer.* from the outset. "[For Irenaeus] there has to be," Young writes, "some overarching sense of what the scriptures are about, some framework which allows the interpreter to fit the pieces of the mosaic together in the appropriate way."[95] That the rule predates our extant scriptural canon(s) is significant. A number of scholars insist that the rule of faith is derived from Scripture itself; this point is true but only in a qualified sense.[96] While functional canons of New Testament scriptures already may exist during Irenaeus's time, it is important to keep in mind the fact that the rule, for Irenaeus, cannot be understood exclusively as a digest of a completely fixed two-Testament canon—which did not yet exist—nor can it be understood as the perspicuous meaning of the Old Testament scriptures.[97] Even so, while Irenaeus did not possess a collection of scriptures directly identifiable with any of the extant canons utilized by contemporary Christian communities, his functional New Testament canon is close to that found in contemporary Christian Bibles.[98] The very presence of rival interpretations of Scripture by Jews and Gnostics, however, clearly demonstrated that shared scriptures were not self-interpreting.[99]

Irenaeus makes the hermeneutical import of the rule explicit in the first book of *Haer.* In 1.8.1, he uses the metaphor of a mosaic to famously contrast his own approach to the exegesis of Scripture with that of the Valentinians:

> Suppose someone would take the beautiful image of a king, carefully made out of precious stones by a skillful artist, and would destroy the features of the man on it and change around and rearrange the jewels, and make the form of a dog, or a fox, out of them, and that a rather bad piece of work. Suppose he would then say with determination that this is the beautiful image of the king that the skillful artist had made, at the same time pointing out the jewels which had been beautifully fitted together by the first artist into the image of the king, but which had been badly changed by the second into the form of the dog. (*Haer.* 1.8.1)

Irenaeus notes that the Valentinians both draw on writings that are not accepted in the churches and refuse to acknowledge the authority of certain writings that are held in esteem by the Christian communities. Their greater error, however, is misreading the texts that both Irenaeus and his opponents agree are authoritative. In their misreading, the Valentinians "braid ropes of sand" and fabricate systems that anyone familiar with the scriptures would recognize to be mere fancy:

> They gather together sayings and names from scattered places and transfer them, as we have already said, from their natural meaning to an unnatural one. They act like those who would propose themes which they chance upon and then try to put them to verse from Homeric poems, so that the inexperienced think that Homer composed the poems with that theme, which in reality are of recent composition. (*Haer.* 1.9.4)

While Irenaeus insists on the actuality of the rule, he also insists that it is a subjective disposition in the interpreter. "Anyone," he writes, "who keeps unchangeable *in himself* the Rule of the Truth . . . will recognize the names and sayings and parables from the Scriptures" (*Haer.* 1.9.4).[100] In contradistinction to what he deemed the esoteric revelry of gnostic speculation, Irenaeus insists that he has received a clear and definitive account of the unity of the work of the Father, Son, and Spirit handed down from the earliest Christian communities. The unity of the economic work of the Father, Son, and Spirit provided the hermeneutical key for the interpreter intent on discerning the unity of the nascent two-Testament Bible. Irenaeus's articulation of the rule provided the pertinent details of the work of the Father, Son, and Spirit in history. As Denis Farkasfalvy has rightly noted, Irenaeus's focus on the unity and salvific purpose of the economic work of the Triune God has had a profound impact on subsequent Christian reflection: "Irenaeus' vision of salvation history persisted—and does so up to our day—as a lasting source of inspiration and a paradigmatic ideal."[101] What he had received reflected the complementarity and unity of the work of the Triune God in history, and for Irenaeus the rule, as expressed, articulated Christian adherence to and confession of the reality of this work. Origen would adopt many of the achievements also present in Irenaeus's work but would extend the usefulness of the rule of faith further yet.

ORIGEN OF ALEXANDRIA AND THE RULE OF FAITH

As Henri de Lubac has shown, Origen's influence on subsequent Christian exegesis and hermeneutics is as definitive as it is ubiquitous.[102] In his chapter on the patristic origins of the fourfold sense of Scripture in *Medieval Exegesis*, de Lubac concludes that "more than any other figure in the fields of hermeneutics, exegesis, and spirituality, [Origen] would be the grand master."[103] Much of Origen's influence was due to his major treatise *Peri Archōn/De Principiis* (hereafter referred to as *Princ.*).[104] While Origen makes reference to the rule of faith at a number of locations in his work, the locus classicus occurs in his own preface to *Princ.*[105] Origen employs the rule of faith for hermeneutical purposes in a way not dissimilar to Irenaeus.

Origen wrote *Princ.* in Alexandria sometime between AD 216 and 231, around the same time he was working on his commentaries on John, Genesis, and the Psalms.[106] A number of scholars have explored the question of the motivations that led Origen to write it and the precise genre of the work, and a few have drawn specific attention to the systematic nature of the work.[107] Origen's *Princ.* does not meet all of the precise canons for systematic theology that I made explicit in the introduction, but it does have a more systematic tenor than Irenaeus's works. As Ronald Heine notes, the fact that Origen does not mention his patron Ambrose in *Princ.* suggests that he wrote the work on his own initiative and with general intentions.[108] Unlike Irenaeus's *Haer.*, which is primarily polemical and only secondarily systematic, and his *Epid.*, which is catechetical, Origen's *Princ.* is a constructive and creative work. Origen begins by laying out specific doctrinal beliefs and then proceeds to raise questions about their meaning and to provide accounts of their intelligibility.[109] Origen utilizes the rule to move from the ecclesiastically received positions towards better understandings of how such beliefs could be true.

Western Christianity received *Princ.* in Latin from the pen of one of Origen's apologists, Rufinus (AD 345–410). As a number of scholars have rightly pointed out, the extant Latin translations of Origen's works, including that of *Princ.*, are not completely faithful to his original writings.[110] The posthumous fights over Origen's orthodoxy, especially after his condemnation in 553 at the second council of Constantinople, had significant consequences for his works. Most were destroyed, and what remains has been modified by his apologists and perhaps by his detractors as well. In the preface to his translation of *Princ.*, Rufinus admits that he corrects Origen, "taking care not to reproduce such passages from the books of Origen as are found to be inconsistent with and contrary to his true teaching" (Rufinus, pref. 2).[111] Origen's discussions of the natures of the Son and the Spirit are frequently censored or modified by his later apologists.[112] The originality of Origen's trinitarian theology and the fact that some later fathers edited his works should give us caution when we examine the rule of faith in *Princ.* As Albert Outler has demonstrated, however, the iteration of the rule of faith that Origen provides in the preface to *Princ.* is entirely consonant with Origen's invocation of the rule in his extant Greek works and does not veer decisively from traditional articulations of the rule by other ancient Christian witnesses.[113]

In the preface to this work, Origen notes that the presence of so many competing perspectives of self-proclaimed followers of Christ regarding God, Jesus Christ, and the Holy Spirit requires that he "lay down a definite line and unmistakable rule in regard to each of these, and to postpone the inquiry into other matters until afterwards" (*Princ.* pref. 1). As William Farmer has rightly noted, the account of the rule of faith that Origen proceeds to give "is a truly traditional summary of the essential doctrine of the apostolic church of 1 Clement, Ignatius, Polycarp, Irenaeus, Clement of Alexandria, and Tertullian. There is little new in it."[114] While its precise content is mostly unremarkable, the scope of Origen's articulation of the rule is much more extensive than what we find in Irenaeus's works. Origen's account of the rule in *Princ.* extends beyond the traditional trinitarian clauses to include judgments about anthropology, demonology, angelology, cosmology, and, finally, the inspiration of Scripture itself (see *Princ.* pref. 4–8). The rule he lays out in the preface to *Princ.* provides a comprehensive framework for the rest of his theological reflection in the work. It serves as "the ground of his theology and metaphysics."[115] Origen, as Outler rightly judges, "turned to these summaries of belief as starting points for his own exercise in rational speculation. He was moving from faith to philosophy, and as a part of that process he was undertaking to transform statements born out of religious experience, statements suited to moments of worship, into extremely comprehensive and general conclusions about God, the world, and man."[116]

Just as Irenaeus before him, Origen makes explicit the ecclesial origins of the rule.[117] As Outler notes, "In Origen's thought the faith of the church holds a primary place; it is *sine qua non* to the wider development of theological speculation."[118] Origen sounds much like Irenaeus in his insistence on the apostolicity, antiquity, and catholicity of the rule. "The teaching of the church," he writes, "handed down in unbroken succession from the apostles, is still preserved and continues to exist in the churches up to the present day, we maintain that that only is to be believed as the truth which in no way conflicts with the tradition of the church and the apostles" (*Princ.* pref. 2).[119]

Origen follows Irenaeus in insisting God has created the world ex nihilo. That judgment belongs in the rule for Origen, and he mentions it at the very beginning of his articulation of the rule in *Princ.* Origen unsurprisingly shares Irenaeus's emphasis on the unity of the work of the Father as described in the ancient Jewish Scriptures with the work of the Son:

> The kind of doctrines which are believed in plain terms through the apostolic teaching are the following: First, that God is one, who created and set in order all things, and who, when nothing existed, caused the universe to be. He is God of all righteous men, of Adam, Abel, Seth, Enos, Enoch, Noah, Shem, Abraham, Isaac, Jacob, of the twelve patriarchs, of Moses and the prophets. This God, in these last days (cf. Heb 1.1), according to the previous announcements made through his prophets, sent the Lord Jesus Christ, first for the purpose of calling Israel, and secondly, after the unbelief of the people of Israel, of calling the Gentiles also. This just and good God, the Father of our Lord Jesus Christ, himself gave the law, the prophets and the gospels, and he is God both of the apostles and also of the Old and New Testaments. (*Princ.* pref. 4)

Heine has pointed out that Origen's emphasis on *creatio ex nihilo* and on the unity of God's work as recorded in the prophets and patriarchs with his work in Christ and the apostles are representative of his anti-Gnostic and anti-Marcionite convictions.[120] For now, however, we must treat two other significant aspects of Origen's presentation of the rule in the preface to *Princ.*

As noted above, however, Origen does include new judgments in his articulation of the rule in *Princ*. His inclusion of judgments about the freedom of the soul, its struggle against demonic powers, and its future judgment (*Princ.* pref. 5), unique to his presentation of the rule, also bear witness to his preoccupation with presenting an adequate Christian response to the unorthodox positions of elitist determinism of "gnostic" thinkers.[121] "The soul," he writes,

> having a substance and life of its own, will be rewarded according to its deserts after its departure from this world; for it will either obtain an inheritance of eternal life and blessedness, if its deeds shall warrant this, or it must be given over to eternal fire and torments, if the guilt of its crimes shall so determine. . . . This is also laid down in the Church's teaching, that every rational soul is possessed of free will and choice; and also, that it is engaged in a struggle against the devil and his angels and the opposing powers; for these strive to weigh the soul down with sins, whereas we, if we lead a wise and upright life, endeavor to free ourselves from such a burden. There follows from this the conviction that we are not subject to necessity, so as to be compelled by every means, even against our will, to do either good or evil. For if we are possessed of free will, some spiritual powers may very likely be able to urge us on to sin and others to assist us to salvation; we are not, however, compelled by necessity to act either rightly or wrongly, as is thought to be the case by those who say that human events are due to the course and motion of the stars, not only those events which fall outside the sphere of our freedom of will but even those that lie within our own power. (*Princ.* pref. 5)

As Peter Martens has demonstrated comprehensively in *Origen and Scripture*, Origen frequently identifies serious Christian engagement with Scripture as a unique and necessary task in the process of the formation of the Christian soul.[122] Engagement with Scripture, for him, has a central and indispensable place in Christian formation and discipleship. Even philology plays a role in Christian discipleship in Origen's understanding.[123] Scholarly engagement with the written words of Scripture, however, must be contextualized in an understanding of the purpose and usefulness of Scripture as an instrument of the Holy Spirit for transforming Christian believers.[124]

While extant articulations of the rule frequently mention the role of the Holy Spirit in speaking through the prophets or apostles, Origen innovatively locates the judgment of the inspiration of Christian Scripture in the rule itself in the preface to *Princ.*

> The scriptures were composed through the Spirit of God and . . . they have not only that meaning which is obvious, but also another which is hidden from the majority of readers. For the contents of scripture are the outward forms of certain mysteries and the images of divine things. On this point the entire Church is unanimous, that while the whole law is spiritual, the inspired meaning is not recognized by all, but only by those who are gifted with the grace of the Holy Spirit in the word of wisdom and knowledge. (*Princ.* pref. 8)

Origen frequently cites Paul's words in 1 Corinthians 10.9 and Romans 15.4 to argue that the scriptures are given to believers for spiritual instruction. They are distinctly "useful" for this purpose (2 Tim 3.16–17).[125] In one of his homilies on Exodus Origen states explicitly that Paul's practice of identifying the rock that followed the Israelites in Sinai with Christ (1 Cor 10.3–4) provides a "rule of interpretation" that Christians are to follow (*Hom. Exod.* 5.1–2).[126] Christians must receive the law—that is, the Old Testament—in a spiritual manner (cf. 2 Cor 3.1–18). Origen's understanding of the spiritual interpretation of Scripture has received conflicting evaluations in recent scholarship, and a full treatment of his "allegorism" is beyond the scope of the present work.[127] Nevertheless, his understanding of the nature of the rule of faith and its hermeneutical implications for scriptural exegesis propose interesting heuristics for locating scriptural interpretation within the work of the Triune God in history and the formation of Christian believers. As with Irenaeus, the rule functions for Origen as a synthetic set of judgments about the work of God in history that provides the context for Christian engagement with the biblical texts.

Origin's judgments about the freedom of the soul and the inspiration of Scripture provide the heuristic for his reflection on the "contours of the exegetical life."[128] Even if we should not or cannot follow Origen's precise understanding of the relationship between human freedom and sanctification and the place of scriptural study in this process, his articulation of the received Christian judgments about human freedom and destiny and the inspiration of Scripture—located in his account of the rule of faith—provides us with a potential invitation for addressing the precise role of scriptural interpretation in contemporary Christian thought and praxis. "The challenge Origen presents to Christian theologians and biblical scholars today," Martens concludes, "is whether they wish to join him in contextualizing the project of biblical scholarship within the Christian drama of salvation."[129] Augustine's detailed theological account of the purposes of Scripture and its interpretation and use in preaching poses a similar challenge.

AUGUSTINE OF HIPPO AND THE RULE OF FAITH

While Origen's *Princ.* has undoubtedly had an extensive influence on subsequent Christian exegesis of Scripture and theoretical reflection on the nature and purpose of Scripture, its influence in the history of Christian interpretation is more subtle and subterranean than that of Augustine's famous *De doctrina christiana* (hereafter *Doctr. chr.*).[130] While Augustine's own legacy is far from unproblematic, *Doctr. chr.* has justly received almost universal acclaim in Western Christianity.[131] Like both Irenaeus and Origen before him, Augustine employs the rule of faith as a criterion for Christian exegesis. In the beginning of *Doctr. chr.* Augustine follows a precedent set by Irenaeus and followed by Origen—whether consciously or not—of framing adequate faithful Christian engagement with Scripture within an account of the truths of the rule of faith.

It is likely that Augustine began writing *Doctr. chr.* sometime in AD 395 or 396, around the time he succeeded Valerius as bishop of Hippo.[132] He completed everything in *Doctr. chr.* through 3.24.35 and then abruptly stopped writing in 397, only to return to the unfinished work and complete the end of book 3 and all of book 4 in 427 or 428.[133] Charles Kannengieser adduces three primary reasons why the writing of the work would have been a valuable—or perhaps even necessary—endeavor for Augustine at this particular time in his career. As the newly ordained bishop of Hippo, Augustine likely found it desirable to establish his exegetical competency.[134] From the time of his conversion, Augustine was also continually assessing how his conversion and new pastoral responsibilities should modify or transform his training in the liberal arts and philosophy as he utilized his training to understand the scriptures.[135] Finally, the vicissitudes of Augustine's local setting may have demanded such a work; Augustine needed to offer a robust Catholic hermeneutics as a rejoinder to the sectarian hermeneutics of the Donatists.[136] The work shows the fruit of Augustine's early engagement with and reflection on Scripture and bears the marks of his training in the liberal arts and exposure to the philosophical schools of his day.[137] His engagement with Manichaean and Donatist thought is also faintly evident in the work.[138] That being said, *Doctr. chr.* is not a polemical work. Karla Pollmann makes a strong argument that Augustine's own comments in the prologue, among other things, indicate that he intended *Doctr. chr.* to function as a universal guidebook for the interpretation of Scripture.[139] Augustine opens the work by stating:

> There are some rules for dealing with the scriptures, which I consider can be not inappropriately passed on to students, enabling them to make progress not only by reading others who have opened up the hidden secrets of the divine literature, but also by themselves opening them up to yet others again. I have undertaken to pass these rules on to those who are both willing and well qualified to learn. (*Doctr. chr.* prol. 1)

The fact that he found *Doctr. chr.* significant enough to complete later in life also may suggest that he thought the work had general and universal relevance.[140] As we will see presently, the rule of faith has an indispensable place in Augustine's account of scriptural interpretation in *Doctr. chr.* Before we examine what Augustine says about the rule in his work on scriptural interpretation, however, we should note some of the key features of Augustine's employment of the rule of faith in his other works.[141]

Augustine, like Origen and Irenaeus before him, frequently includes clauses on the Father, the Son, and the Holy Spirit, respectively, in his articulations of the rule of faith.[142] In a number of locations he practically identifies the rule with a baptismal creed.[143] Augustine, just as Irenaeus and Origen, insists on the apostolicity and catholicity of the rule.[144] Like Irenaeus and Origen, Augustine also maintains the realist dimension of the rule. The rule provides judgments about realities affirmed in Christian faith; its content is the actual work of the Triune God in history.[145] The transcendence of God from creation is also a key feature of the rule for Augustine.[146] The rule thus provides a set of judgments relating the taxis of the Triune God's economic work.[147] His account of the rule in *Doctr. chr.*, however, lacks a number of the generic features of the rule as it is attested in the works of the other fathers and elsewhere in his own writings.

In the preface to the work, Augustine explicitly states that *Doctr. chr.* has a twofold purpose. In it he intends to expound both "a way to discover what needs to be understood" (*modus inviendi quae intellegenda sunt*) in divine Scripture and "a way to put across what has been understood" (*modus proferendi quae intellect sunt*).[148] The sections of *Doctr. chr.* that Augustine completed through the year 397, books 1–3, treat the first purpose of *inventio*—discovery—by moving respectively from a discussion of things and the love of God and neighbor as the end of scriptural interpretation in book 1 to strategies for understanding unknown signs and a discussion of the nature of Scripture itself in book 2 and finally to rules for sorting out the ambiguous signs of Scripture in book 3.[149] Near the beginning of book 3 on ambiguous signs, Augustine explicitly states that the *res* discussed in book 1 are to be understood as the rule of faith: "When ... you still see that it is uncertain how something is to be phrased, or how to be pronounced, you should refer it to the rule of faith, which you have received from the plainer passages of Scripture and from the authority of the Church, about which we dealt sufficiently when we were talking in the first book about *things*" (*Doctr. chr.* 3.2.2; emphasis mine). What are the precise "things," then, that Augustine identifies with the rule of faith, and what does he say about them?

Augustine begins *Doctr. chr.* by making a distinction between things (*res*) and signs (*signa*): "All teaching is either about things or signs; but things are learned about through signs" (1.2.2). Augustine then distinguishes between things to be enjoyed—*frui*—and things to be used—*uti* (1.3.3). Ultimately, for Augustine, *only* the Triune God is to be enjoyed:

The things therefore that are to be enjoyed are the Father and the Son and the Holy Spirit, in fact the Trinity, one supreme thing, and one which is shared in common by all who enjoy it; if, that is to say, it is a thing, and not the cause of all things; if indeed it is a cause. It is not easy, after all, to find any name that will really fit such transcendent majesty. In fact it is better just to say that this Trinity is the one God "from whom are all things, through whom are all things, in whom are all things" (Rom 11.36). Thus Father and Son and Holy Spirit are both each one of them singly God and all together one God; and each one of them singly is the complete divine substance, and all together are one substance. (1.5.5; see also 1.6.6–1.7.7)

All other things, *including the signs of Scripture,* are to be used in the enjoyment of God. Augustine proceeds to argue that the divine life of the Trinity is not bodily but spiritual and intelligible; it is living wisdom (1.8.8–1.9.9). Human persons are to participate in this wisdom, however, and so God has provided a means of their purification through the incarnation of the Son and the preaching of the Son (1.10.10–1.14.13). Augustine proceeds to give an account of God's economic pedagogy through the example of Christ, the indwelling presence of the Holy Spirit, the institution of the church, repentance, and the resurrection (1.15.14–1.21.19). He reiterates that only God is to be enjoyed (1.22.20–1.22.21) and then discusses the purposes of self-love and the love of others, including angels, and the proper ordering of these loves (1.23.22–1.33). He next locates the proper order of human loves within the providential use of all things by the Triune God (1.31.34–1.34.38). Ultimately, his whole discourse provides an account of how various realities function and relate to one another within the purposes of the Triune God in history. Augustine then summarizes his discussion of "things":

> So what all that has been said amounts to, while we have been dealing with things, is that "the fulfillment and the end of the law is" and of the divine scriptures is "love" (Rom 13.8; 1 Tim 1.5); love of the thing which is to be enjoyed, and of the thing which is able to enjoy that thing together with us, because there is no need for a commandment that we should love ourselves. So in order that we might know how to do

this and be able to, the whole ordering of time was arranged by divine providence for our salvation. . . . So if it seems to you that you have understood the divine scriptures, or any part of them, in such a way that by this understanding you do not build up this twin love of God and neighbor, then you have not yet understood them. (1.35.39–1.36.40)

While Augustine's reflections in 1.5.5–1.22.20 do follow the general structure of the tripartite rule(s) and creeds, he does not employ a typical, trinitarian clausal formulation of the rule.[150] He instead gives an interpretive account of the intelligibility of some of the referents of the rule. While he reiterates the content of the rule that is to be believed, his more significant purpose is to provide an account of the purposes of the Triune God and the means God has provided for accomplishing those goals. Like Origen, Augustine understands engagement with Scripture to play an indispensable role in the formation and transformation of Christian readers. As Lewis Ayres summarizes, for Augustine "the fullness of the rule of faith includes not only the narrative of God's action in Christ, and the doctrinal propositions embedded in the telling of that story, but also the movement and ascent that Christ accomplishes in Christians, the transference of attention from things of this world to the divine mystery."[151] Like Origen, Augustine holds that Scripture is an instrument of divine pedagogy that God has given for effecting the transformation of its readers and interpretive communities.

SUMMARY AND CONCLUSION

Irenaeus, Origen, and Augustine exhibit both continuity and development in their respective articulations of the contents and function of the rule of faith for engagement with Scripture. Irenaeus calls the rule "the manifest testimony about God" and the standard towards which all theological reflection should tend (*Haer.* 2.28.1). For him it represents a quasi- or proto-systematic account of the realities to which Scripture refers. The rule provides an account of the Christian understanding of reality in which Scripture can be rightly engaged and understood. Irenaeus's employment of the rule, and the nature of *Haer.* itself, is piecemeal and pragmatic. In

Epid. he employs the rule in a more general context, articulating it as a context for catechesis, but does not utilize it as an occasion for setting up a systematic explication of Christian faith. While Origen engages in various polemics in *Princ.*, his intentions in that work are more general than Irenaeus's. For Origen, as for Irenaeus, the rule is constituted by received Christian judgments about reality. Origen, however, utilizes this ecclesially received, structured set of judgments about reality to speculate on as yet undefined aspects of the faith (see *Princ.* pref. 2). While Origen does not leave polemics aside completely in *Princ.*, the generality of the work is sui generis in early Christian literature. Augustine's presentation of principles for engaging Scripture in *Doctr. chr.* represents a further advance in generality and universality because of his almost exclusive focus on scriptural hermeneutics. For Augustine, the rule likewise provides the *res* to which Scripture bears witness. The *res* to which both Scripture and the rule refer includes the work of the Triune God in the souls of interpreters of Scripture. The redemptive work of the Triune God sets the finis of the development of the Christian soul. For Augustine, Scripture and all other things in this economy serve as instruments through which the Son and the Spirit transform Christian readers so that they can participate in the wisdom that is God's own.

The present constructive work follows the precedent set by Origen in *Princ.* and Augustine in *Doctr. chr.* by articulating a rule of faith about the work of the Triune God in history *prior* to discussing the nature, purpose, and interpretation of Scripture.[152] As such the present systematic theology of Scripture has a genetic relationship to these earlier texts. Our problems, however, are not exactly the same as those faced by Origen, Augustine, or Irenaeus. The heterodox speculations of Valentinus, Basilides, Marcion, Arius, Donatus, and Pelagius do not represent real historical threats to the church today.[153]

Besides, the present account is not polemical but systematic in its intentions. A systematic theology of the nature and purpose of Scripture—in order to be truly systematic—must pursue the generalist impulses in the rule of faith especially evident in Origen's *Princ.* and Augustine's *Doctr. chr.* It maintains, with Irenaeus as well as with Origen and Augustine, that an adequate statement of the economic work of the Triune God provides the broadest necessary context for responsible and faithful Christian engagement with Scripture. Our own time does necessitate that we give ample attention to the questions of the inescapable subjectivity of all textual interpretation and to the historicity of human understanding and meaning, including the historicity of Scripture itself, but those particular concerns are not my primary concerns at the moment.[154] In the following chapter, I take up the task of articulating such a generalist rule in a way that draws on the achievements of Irenaeus, Origen, and Augustine, and on other achievements in theological reflection, but simultaneously rises to meet contemporary challenges that must be addressed.

CHAPTER THREE

The Location of Scripture I

The Economic Work of the Triune God

With all wisdom and insight he has made known to us the mystery
of his will, according to his good pleasure that he set forth in Christ,
as a plan for the fullness of time, to gather up all things in him, things
in heaven and things on earth.

—Ephesians 1.8b–10

Since, then, we possess the Rule of Truth itself and the manifest testimony
about God, we ought not cast out the solid and true knowledge about
God by running from one solution to another. No, it is proper to direct the
solution of difficulties toward that standard [the Rule], and to discipline
ourselves by investigating the mystery and economy of the existent God, and
to grow in the love of him who has done and does so much for our sakes.

—Irenaeus, *Haer.* 2.28.1

A number of studies in recent years not only note the role of the rule of
faith for early Christian interpretation of Scripture but also suggest its
relevance for guiding contemporary theological and historical engagement with the Bible.[1] What precisely are these studies proposing? No one,

to my knowledge, has argued that it is necessary to repeat the rule(s) in the explicit forms that Irenaeus, Origen, Augustine or any other father give to it. We cannot simply and uncritically reproduce one of these ancient rules of faith as a guide for Christian engagement with the biblical text today. While there is a great deal of overlap in their respective presentations of the rule, each of the figures I have examined articulates the rule in distinct ways and each bears witness to distinct historical developments in the presentation of the rule. Although the antiquarian route of appropriating premodern iterations of the rule is closed to us, we can nevertheless carry forward key foci that appear in these various expressions of the rule. Each of the figures discussed invoked the rule, with its unique developments, in order to address challenges his Christian community faced. Use of the rule in our own time would require that we do what they did for our own time; we must provide a rule of faith that is in continuity with the authentic developments we have discovered in past iterations of the rule— and which can appropriate other authentic theological developments—in a way that is adequate to the exigencies of our own time.

What precisely must we carry forward and appropriate from these premodern attempts to locate Christian engagement with Scripture within the work of the Triune God in creation and redemption in the rule of faith? I suggest that the following features and functions of the rule are necessary for a contemporary rule of faith: (1) a contemporary rule must be attentive to the ecclesiastical base of the rule by faithfully appropriating the authentic understandings and judgments of the historical Christian communities; (2) a contemporary rule must appropriate the narrative, sequential, and synthetic character of the rule in its emphasis on the saving work of the Triune God in history; (3) a contemporary rule must maintain the referential or realist nature of the historical rule(s); and (4) a contemporary rule must both maintain the openness of the rule to further development and to technical specification and appropriate such advances when they have occurred in the history of Christian theological reflection.[2]

A contemporary account of the rule would need to be drawn from the best of Christian—and so necessarily ecclesial—reflection on the economic work of the Triune God; would relate judgments about the actuality of the history of God's salvific action in Israel, Christ, and the church; and would both reflect and appropriate authentic developments in theological reflection on the work of the Triune God in such a way that it could simultaneously affirm authentic developments in human knowledge in other disciplines. Just as Irenaeus, Origen, and Augustine propounded accounts of Christian faith at the levels of their own times, a contemporary account of the rule must meet the exigencies of our current situation. What follows, then, provides further exposition of the ecclesial, realist, synthetic, and advancing dimensions of the rule of faith with reference to the distinct challenges faced by Christians living in the twenty-first-century globalized world. Following that exposition, utilizing the judgments of the Nicene Creed and some key judgments from Scripture and the historical investigation of the previous chapter, I propose a set of linked understandings and judgments concerning the economic work of the Triune God as a heuristic account of the most general divine contexts out of which Christian Scripture emerges and in which it has served and will continue to serve as an instrument.

APPROPRIATING CHRISTIAN UNDERSTANDINGS AND JUDGMENTS

While Irenaeus, Origen, and Augustine, among other church fathers, insist on the apostolicity, uniformity, and universality of the rule of faith, their unique and distinct iterations of the rule demonstrate its flexibility and its openness to development and elaboration. Just as we cannot responsibly treat Scripture as a static deposit of already-back-there-then/out-there-now-real completely perspicuous revealed propositions about reality, we cannot responsibly treat the rule as an already-back-there-then account of a static deposit of Christian truth. Our recognition of the historicity of meaning militates against uncritical acceptance of certain church fathers' statements about the antiquity, immutability, and comprehensive coherence of a single timeless rule of faith. We cannot accept without qualification, for instance, a facile understanding of Vincent of Lérins's famous statement that "we hold that faith which has been believed everywhere, always, by all" (*Common.* 2.6) as an adequate way of expressing the continuity of Christian thought given our awareness of the reality that Christian understanding and expression is not absolutely univocal and unchanging at all times and in all places.[3] The words, concepts, understandings, and judgments of specific Christian thinkers and communities have dates. Because of our awareness that changes in language represent changes in constitutive meaning, we must propose another way of discerning the unity of Christian faith through the vicissitudes of progress, decline, and redemption in history.[4] We can, however, identify and carry forward some of the major emphases evident in the employment of the rule of faith by Irenaeus, Origen, and Augustine. In what follows I identify four specific dimensions of the rule that a contemporary heuristic of the divine context of Christian Scripture must maintain. These four dimensions are inseparable from one another.

Ecclesial Dimensions of the Rule

The rule represents the relatively stable results of Christian reflection upon and discernment of the lineaments of the work of God in Jesus Christ and the Holy Spirit, even though such judgments and understandings are always the judgments and understandings of specific communities and individuals in specific times and places. These understandings and judgments are on the move; the Christian community grows in its understandings of the truths of the mystery of faith.[5] A contemporary formulation of a rule of faith must, however, emerge from familiarity with the actual historical evidence of the rule. Failure to attend to the extant evidence of the rule(s) in the context of early Christian thought, and especially in its ecclesial dimensions, will put us at risk of distorting the faith. At the very least we will miss out on real advances in Christian understanding of the reality of the Triune God's redemptive work on our behalf due to our ignorance of history. As Lewis Ayres notes, "Suggestion about the contemporary formulation and articulation of doctrine is inseparable from . . . historical investigation."[6] We are thus beholden to the achievements of our forebears, and we cannot pass judgment on what we have not yet understood. In order to represent these achievements well, the present account will maintain the judgments of the Niceno-Constantinopolitan Creed as an apt summary of the historical achievements of the Christian community as it has sought to clearly articulate its constitutive meaning in the early centuries after Christ. While we ought not understand the rule(s) as any sort of direct linear precursors to the later creeds—the creeds do not necessarily and inevitably follow the rule(s)—both rule(s) and creed(s) emerge from the same dynamic impulse shared by specific Christian thinkers and specific Christian communities—that of clearly articulating the received constitutive judgments of Christian faith.[7]

"Narrative" Character of the Rule

Paul Blowers has provided a formidable argument for the irreducible narrative character of the rule of faith in early Christianity.[8] "At bottom," he writes,

> the Rule of Faith (which was always story or associated with Scripture itself) served the primitive Christian hope of articulating and authenticating a world-encompassing story or metanarrative of creation, incarnation, redemption, and consummation. . . . [I]n the crucial "proto-canonical" era in the history of Christianity, the Rule, being a narrative construction, set forth the basic "dramatic" structure of a Christian vision of the world, posing as an hermeneutical frame of reference for the interpretation of Christian Scripture and Christian experience, and educing the first principles of Christian theological discourse and of a doctrinal substantiation of Christian faith.[9]

Elsewhere in the same article Blowers writes that the rule presents Scripture as "a grand story, with God himself as the primary narrator. It was drama gradually unfolded with a coherent plot, climaxing in the coming of Jesus."[10]

The rule of faith and the faith that the rule articulates both antedate the two-Testament canon of the Christian scriptures. The rule serves as a concise designation of the constitutive content of Christian faith and so provides points of reference for understanding Scripture itself. The rule, like the later creedal confessions, however, does not provide a Cliff Notes version of the plot of Scripture. Though the rule does depict key features of the narrative plot of the work of the Triune God in history, it would be anachronistic to insist that the rule exhibits a highly developed narrative character in terms of modern literary theory.[11] Blowers locates the genesis of the rule in the antecedent process of self-definition of the earliest Christian communities. The rule is thus experientially and phenomenologically prior to polemics. The rule does not merely provide the boundaries of scriptural exegesis, then, but instead represents a set of necessary judgments for articulating *a coherent or synthetic account of the intelligibility of God's action in the world in which the Christian community participates.* The rule, then, provided an account of the intelligible sequence of the Triune God's activity in creation, redemption, and consummation. As such, it represents an objectification of the horizon of Christian being in the world with reference to the action of the Triune God in the world. It also characteristically emphasizes the synthetic unity of the economic work of the Triune God. A contemporary rule of faith would need to maintain these key sequential and synthetic functions.

Referential/Realist Nature of the Rule

The fathers examined in the previous chapter insist upon the referential nature of the rule of faith. The rule is composed of judgments about the actuality of God's work in history and so proper adherence to the rule was not merely a matter of regurgitating judgments about God's actions in a specific order or simply retelling the story. In his essay "On Understanding Salvation History," Charles Hefling points out the limitations of endorsing such a "theology of recital." In such an approach

> scripture is an ongoing, cumulative recounting of *magnalia Dei.* . . .
> [W]hat theologians write today should likewise be a theology of recital. It should not, that is, be an explanation of what scripture narrates, but itself a sort of continuation or extension of that narrative. The strength of this view is its recognition that for speaking to *Existenz* nothing is so effective as a story. . . . Its weakness appears as soon as . . . the systematic, critical, and methodical exigencies begin to operate, generating further questions which no theology of recital can answer without going beyond narrative as the carrier of meaning— and thus becoming a theology of some other kind.[12]

Mere recital invites further questions. It is not enough to simply repeat the language of the rule of faith in its original order. We must raise further systematic, critical, and existential questions about it. The rule itself was not a mere recital of a synthetic or sequential unity for its adherents. It served as an objectification of their judgments about the history that is and the work of the Triune God in that history. This qualification should not diminish the importance of attending to the narrative or dramatic sequential dimensions of the rule of faith or to the narratival nature of much of Scripture itself. As Doran notes, certain doctrinal teachings of constitutive truths of Christian faith, given their character as mysteries, can only be adequately expressed, at least in the limit, in narrative, dramatic, or symbolic forms.[13] Mere recital, however, whether of the narratives of Scripture or of the salvation-historical account of reality in the rule of faith, does not rule out and in fact invites further systematic and critical questions regarding the *actuality* or *reality* of history itself. A rule of faith at the level of our own times would not only recognize the historical development of such critical insights, but would appropriate them where it is fitting and would address contemporary critical, systematic, and methodical exigencies. Such exigencies would impel us to develop the rule in precision, nuance, and scope. While we have observed a number of elements of continuity in the respective articulations of the dimensions and functions of the rule in Irenaeus, Origen, and Augustine, the works of the latter two fathers, as I noted, evince developments and innovations as well. Each, given his circumstances, was able to apply the rule in new ways; among other thinkers, these fathers proposed useful developments for the rules.

Openness of the Rule to Development and Specification

As we have already noted, the rule(s) that these early theologians invoked in controversies and catechesis bear striking similarities with the later Apostles' Creed and Niceno-Constantinopolitan Creed in their trinitarian structure and in their focus on the intelligibility of the economic narrative work of the Triune God in history. The Niceno-Constantinopolitan Creed, however, bears witness to a significant development of the language of the rule(s). The inclusion of the clause on the *homoousios* in the latter creed is a decisive and necessary novelty. *Homoousios* is a technical term that identifies the unity of nature of the Father and Son expressed in the Athanasian canon: the Son is of the same nature with the Father, and thus like the Father in all things except that the Son is not the Father and the Father is not the Son. Arius's judgment that "there was when the Son was not" precipitated a crisis for the Christians of his day.[14] The church faced the difficulty of maintaining their faith in the full efficacy of Christ's recapitulative saving work. If Christ was not with the Father from eternity, and thus was merely a creation of the Father who was lesser in deity, he could not effectively save humanity in his incarnation, death, resurrection, and ascension. Athanasius was disappointed that he had to employ the nonscriptural term *homoousios* in order to insist on this unity but recognized the necessity of using the term or something like it to maintain the salvific work of the Son (see *Decr.* 5.18–19).

Young has detailed the exegetical contours of the battle between Arius and Athanasius in *Biblical Exegesis and the Formation of Christian Culture*. As she astutely notes, however, the battle could not remain merely exegetical. Arius and his followers utilized the scriptures in an ingenious way to argue their case that the Son was merely a creature. As she states, the "debate made questions of meaning explicit."[15] By insisting on the mere creaturehood of the Son, Arius rent the fabric of the Christian belief in the recapitulative redemptive work of the Son of God in history. In response to Arius, Athanasius insisted that the Son had taken on flesh in the incarnation in order to deify humanity.[16] In doing so he repeated a judgment already found in Irenaeus, who had declared that it was anathema to hold the belief that Christ was merely a man.[17] For Athanasius as for Irenaeus, an adequate understanding of God's work in history, and Scripture's mediation of this work, required one to grasp and adhere to the *hypothesis* or the *dianoia* of the redemptive work of God in history that entailed belief in the divine identity of Jesus Christ.

Young has demonstrated that these early fathers insisted that this *hypothesis* or *dianoia* was in fact the "the mind of Scripture."[18] "Discernment of the mind of scripture," she writes, "meant discernment of its underlying coherence, its unitive testimony to the one true Son of God."[19] The distinct rules of faith represent objectifications of the mind of Scripture. It is important to note again, however, that such discernment was going on before the terminus of the canonization of Christian Scripture.[20] The results of such earlier discernment conditioned Christian engagement with Scripture *as the Christian canon(s) of Scripture* emerged. This discernment was therefore not primarily the determination of the meaning of a text with clearly defined borders but the discernment of the intelligibility and actuality of the work of the God of Israel in the person of Jesus Christ and in the Holy Spirit in the new Christian community.

Young points out that such "discernment involved what we might call a critical stance towards a literalizing view of religious language."[21] The vocabulary used by the authors of Scripture is largely untechnical; its human authors communicated through the commonsense, symbolic, and artistic linguistic resources of their own traditions and communities.[22] They certainly used those traditional linguistic resources to striking effect. The language and thought patterns of their religious and cultural traditions were in some measure completely sufficient to indicate their judgments about reality. They were certainly sufficient—as their residual impact on Western culture for thousands of years indicates—for moving their audiences. Lonergan writes, however, that though "symbols [and, he would also affirm, art] have a particularly effective, and quite necessary, role in penetrating our sensibility and moving our affectivity, they are fairly unreliable in communicating truth."[23] Common sense has its uses as well, but it is not generalizable. It has no guaranteed traction outside of the particularity of its time and place.

But common sense, symbols, and art, of course, are not the only ways to speak about reality. "Being is spoken in many ways" (Aristotle, *Metaph.* Γ.2). Technical or theoretical language can allow one to speak or write about reality with greater precision of thought and expression. The developments that led to the church's employment of technical language for speaking about the Oneness and Threeness of the Father, Son, and Holy Spirit and the incarnation of the Son of God exhibit the Christian drive to understand Christian confession of and worship of the Father, Son, and Holy Spirit. Technical language proved invaluable for facilitating that understanding. Lonergan calls this process, as it takes place in the early Christian reflection on the Trinity and the incarnation, the development of "Christian realism."[24] The employment of *homoousios* as a technical term is an achievement that eventually allowed the early Christians to express intelligently the mystery of the Triune God they confessed and worshipped.

When consciousness constructs its world symbolically, it advances by reinterpreting traditional materials. When it leans towards philosophy, a Xenophanes or a Clement of Alexandria will rule anthropomorphism out of humanity's apprehension of the divine. The resulting purely spiritual apprehension of God will create tension between biblical and later Christology, and the technical means available in a post-systematic culture may be employed to clarify the faith.[25]

To ensure the intelligibility of the Christian horizon of understanding in which the Son and Spirit, both with the Father from the beginning, were sent into the world to save the world, Athanasius and subsequent pro-Nicene theologians must employ nonscriptural language. Athanasius, as I noted above, regretted that necessity. Such an approach to Scripture, Lonergan argues, had already become necessary almost two hundred years earlier when gnostic groups proposed different referents for the symbolic language of Scripture:

> If the only interpretation of scripture were symbolic, then you could never settle what the symbols are symbols of. *If you are going to say that the symbols are not just symbols of more symbols, then you have to have some idea of reality.* And if Clement [of Alexandria] was to contribute to defeating the Gnostic exegesis of scripture (which reduced it to nonsense, really) he had to appeal to some reality, and he had to appeal to some method that settled just what the real was. You have, in the exegetic problem, the implicit philosophic problem, What do you mean by reality?[26]

Providing an adequate answer to the question, "What do you mean by reality?," requires one to move beyond symbolic or commonsense language to develop technical or systematic terms and expressions. The judgment that the Father and the Son are *homoousios* stands to the narrative and symbolic framework of the rule—and of much of Scripture—as the Kelvin, Celsius, and Fahrenheit temperature scales stand to the relative descriptive terms "hot" and "cold." The judgment of the simplicity of God and God's creation ex nihilo have a similar function with reference to the anthropomorphic and anthropopathic language used to portray God's action in Scripture.[27] The technical term *homoousios* directly names and locates the judgment of the full divinity of Christ from eternity. Such a judgment, while it certainly represents a technical advance in understanding, simultaneously preserves the narrative character of the antecedent rule(s). The technical, systematic meaning achieved in the *homoousios* was in the service of the church's faith in Christ's saving work; while it has a value all its own, as an insight it was arrived at by attending to the necessary questions concerning how Christ actually could save. It is a judgment about reality arrived at in order to ensure the continuity of Christian faith in Christ's salvific work.[28]

As already noted, from a historical perspective, Christian confessions such as the rule(s) of faith articulated by Irenaeus, Origen, and Augustine antedate any "close" of the Christian scriptural canon. The early Christians received and read Scripture within a horizon of preunderstanding and experience they received through the practices of catechesis, baptism, the eucharist, communal reading, preaching, and Christian worship. Christian confessions of the constitutive judgments about reality reflect the Christian desire to objectify that horizon and are evident in and probably antedate the New Testament.

Something, however, happened before these confessions. Ultimately, the action of God in Jesus Christ and the Holy Spirit is the *res* that was historically prior to those confessions. The early Christians engaged the scriptures of Israel in order to adequately understand the work of the Triune God *in history*. Early Christians did not seek to simply take a look at Scripture (for most of them, primarily the Old Testament) to "see what it said," they read it diligently in order to understand God's activity in the world, in the midst of human communities, and in their own selves. The meaning of Scripture was not an already-out-there-now-real that they sought to get from out there "into" their minds. They read and recited and so were transformed, their subjective horizons expanded to be capacious enough to become isomorphic with the structure of God's redemptive work in history. Because they affirmed that God was recapitulating all things in Christ (Eph 1.10), they sought to plumb the depths of this mystery (Eph 1.3) by investigating the meanings and resonances of the event of Christ with the ancient Jewish scriptures. They advanced in their understanding as well. The technical formulations of the simplicity of the Triune God and the consubstantiality of the Father, Son, and Holy Spirit represent technical achievements of systematic meaning. Such achievements preserved the symbolic and narrative character of the rule(s) with respect to the judgments it mediated about reality, but they simultaneously provided further resources for clearly expressing the intelligibility of the realities so affirmed.

As we recall from Lonergan's differentiation of the functional specialties, "history" has as its goal the discernment of what was developing or
going forward in a particular time period. For the earliest Christians,
what was going forward was God's work in Jesus Christ of Nazareth, raising him from the dead and conferring the Holy Spirit on the Christian
community, recapitulating all things into Christ on the way to the consummation of all things in union with the Father (see 1 Cor 15.20–28; 2
Cor 5.21; Eph 1.3–14). What is going forward in the early church is development in understanding these specific judgments about the actuality of
that divine work in Jesus Christ and the Holy Spirit. A contemporary rule
of faith must retain the advances in understanding and judgment achieved
in the early church concerning the economic work of the Triune God. It
will supplement those understandings and judgments with the requisite
systematic and technical resources to clarify their meaning. That is my
present task. Below I provide a contemporary heuristic of the economic
work of the Triune God—a rule of faith plus technical specifications—as
an articulation of the divine location of Christian Scripture.

THE WORK OF THE TRINITY IN HISTORY

In systematic theology it is necessary to start with that which is most general and then proceed to discuss the particular.[29] The most general topic
of exploration for a systematic theology of Christian Scripture is the actual creative and redemptive work of the Triune God. As Angus Paddison
rightly avers, "The diverse contexts (intra *and* extra-ecclesial) in which
Scripture's authority is construed cannot be more decisive than the ultimate context for construing Scripture's authority—God's saving economy."[30] A number of recent studies have helpfully reoriented the question
of the precise authority that Scripture bears in the more comprehensive
context of the question of the effective authority of the Triune God in history.[31] The artifacts of Scripture emerge from and are engaged within the
time and space of the economic work of the Triune God. Whatever humans might do with Scripture, however they might understand it, the
present account of its nature and purpose holds that an understanding of
the work of the Triune God in history provides a generalized and orienting context for locating Scripture. The purposes of the Triune God in his-

tory, and the exercise of divine authority in that history, set the norms against which human use and interpretation of Christian Scripture can be judged. Authoritative Christian use and interpretation of Christian Scripture does not depend upon readers successfully determining the univocal intentions of texts, human authors, or even communities of interpretation. It instead depends upon the adequacy of that use and interpretation for the creative and redemptive work of the Triune God in human history. Scripture finds its rightful place within the divine economy.

There is not, of course, some objective conception of the work of the Triune God in history out there in the world. Any perspective that locates engagement with Scripture within the work and authority of the Triune God will inescapably consist of *human* understandings and judgments concerning the contours of that divine work. Those *human* understandings and judgments will necessarily receive their distinct communicative shape in the conventions of *human* communication, whether intersubjective, linguistic, symbolic, or artistic. We cannot escape from this subjective mediation.[32] The rule(s) of faith and creeds are unique instantiations of these subjective apprehensions of God's work. Such understandings and judgments start from the fundamental judgment that the Triune God has revealed Godself in history. But such understandings and judgments, as engagement with patristic theological reflection reveals, are on the move. What follows is an account of the rule of faith, supplemented with hypothetical technical proposals for understanding aspects of the judgments of the rule, that attempts to remain faithful to and in continuity with the achievements of the historic rules and creeds but simultaneously goes beyond them to address unique questions and concerns that have arisen in recent times.

The traditional confession of the Niceno-Constantinopolitan Creed will stand as the ecclesially received rule of faith for the present account of the nature and purpose of Christian Scripture. Systematic theology, after all, does not propose new doctrines that must be believed but instead attempts to provide an *understanding* of received doctrines at the level of the theologian's own time. The creed, which is almost universally accepted among Christian communities, serves as an extremely useful summary of those doctrines.

We believe in one God, the Father, the almighty, creator of heaven and earth, of all things visible and invisible.

And in one Lord, Jesus Christ, the only begotten Son of God, born of the Father before all ages, God from God, Light from Light, true God from true God, begotten, not made, consubstantial with the Father; through whom all things were made. For us men and for our salvation he came down from heaven and by the power of the Holy Spirit was incarnate from the Virgin Mary, and was made man; he was also crucified for us under Pontius Pilate, suffered, and was buried; and on the third day he rose again according to the Scriptures and ascended into heaven; he is seated at the right hand of the Father and will come again in glory to judge the living and the dead; and his kingdom will have no end.

And in the Holy Spirit, the Lord and Giver of life, who proceeds from the Father [and the Son], who together with the Father and the Son is likewise worshipped and glorified. He has spoken through the Prophets. And in one, holy, catholic, and apostolic Church. I acknowledge one baptism for the forgiveness of sins. And I await the resurrection of the dead, and the life of the world to come. Amen.[33]

This confession, like the rule(s) of faith, enumerates constitutive Christian judgments about the order and actuality of the work of the Triune God. As such, it fulfills both the narratival and realist exigencies that I identified above. It is one thing to make such judgments, however, and another thing to understand them. *That* the Triune God has acted in such ways, through creation, through the incarnation, crucifixion, resurrection, and ascension of the Son, and through the work of the Holy Spirit in the prophets and Christian communities, is not in question. *How* the Triune God has acted and *why* the Triune God has acted in such ways, however, are questions that have arisen spontaneously in the history of Christian reflection on these acts of God. They are questions that have received historical answers in Christian faith and that still call out for answers today. In keeping with the paradigmatic practice of the ancient Christian communities, and represented in the Niceno-Constantinopolitan Creed above, the rule expounded in the present work begins with an account of the intelligibility of the creative work of the Triune God.

I must make one final qualification before proceeding. I consider the creed to be a set of doctrines, that is, judgments, about reality. My employment below of further hypotheses and judgments not explicit in the creed obviously goes beyond the language of the creed. I am not equating or iden-tifying those hypotheses and judgments with either the rule of faith or with the creed in any explicit way. The further hypotheses and judgments that I propose serve as technical tools that I hold to be useful for understanding the referents and intelligibility of the creed. By supplying such hypotheses and judgments, I am following the final exigency of the rule of faith I noted above. The judgments and language of the church invite further questions and so found subsequent developments in Christian understanding.

The creed begins with the affirmation that God the Father has created all things. The present account of the work of the Triune God in history requires an adequate articulation of the creative work of the Triune God and the relationship of that free work to the free creatures that have been created. As Blowers has recently demonstrated, discussions of "creation" in patristic thought covered a number of different theological topics. They frequently included reflection on the actual beginnings of the created world, creation itself in its concrete existence, the "ontological chasm," or *diastēma*, between created and uncreated natures, and the work of God in maintaining and redeeming creation.[34] Such topics and terms have their place in what Kathryn Tanner has called a coherent "grammar" that un-dergirded and held together these affirmations in premodern Christian theological reflection.[35] The church fathers attended to each of the theo-logical topoi enumerated by Blowers in their varied attempts to under-stand and articulate their judgments of the transcendence, sovereignty, and freedom of the Triune God and the freedom and responsibility of human persons as actors within creation. Such understandings, of course, have their own histories. Brief attention to some facets of the historical developments of theologies of creation and the relationship between cre-ator and creation will help us to highlight some constitutive Christian judgments regarding these topics.

Young has argued that Irenaeus's theology of creation represents a major milestone in Christian understanding of the relationship between the Triune creator and creation itself. As she summarizes:

> The doctrines of God's transcendent infinity and of *creatio ex nihilo* are not spelt out in so many words in scripture any more than the doctrine of the Trinity is. The recognition of their coherence with one

another, their importance for clarifying the apostolic tradition over against philosophical theory and Gnostic revelation alike, and their essential place in the framework which alone allows scripture to be interpreted appropriately, we owe largely to the work of Irenaeus.[36]

As we have seen above, the extant ancient versions of the rule of faith, like the major creeds, frequently begin with the profession that God has created all things. Irenaeus invokes this judgment in *Adversus Haereses* as "the first and greatest principle" in his demonstration of the nonsensical nature of Valentinus's and his followers' mistaken cosmology:

> The Creator God . . . made heaven and earth and all things in them, . . . there is nothing either above him or after him, and . . . he was influenced by no one but, rather, made all things by his own counsel and free will, since he alone is God, and he alone is Lord, and he alone is Creator, and he alone is Father, and he alone contains all things, and he himself gives existence to all things. (*Haer.* 2.1.1)

Irenaeus will later argue that the characteristics of transcendence and simplicity differentiate the Christian God from the anthropomorphic deities of the Valentinian system.

> For the Father of all things is far removed from the actions and passions that men and women experience. He is simple and not composite; with all members of similar nature, being entirely similar and equal to himself. He is all Mind, all Spirit, all Understanding, all Thought, all Word, all Hearing, all Eye, all Light, and the whole Source of all blessings. That is how devout people can speak properly of God. (*Haer.* 2.13.3)[37]

Origen, for his part, also maintains the simplicity of God and the judgment that God creates ex nihilo.[38] As he writes in *Princ.* pref. 4, "God is one, who created and set in order all things, and who, when nothing existed, caused the universe to be." Augustine's adherence to *creatio ex nihilo* is worked out through his extensive engagements with the creation accounts in Genesis in various treatises.[39] While there are certainly differences of perspective and nuance between the positions of these three thinkers, they share the judgments of the absolute transcendence of God, the ontological or qualitative distinction between God and creation, and God's free creation ex nihilo.[40]

Later Christian thinkers, Thomas Aquinas chief among them, would organize and order the various abovementioned theological affirmations— that God is simple, absolutely transcendent, and created the universe ex nihilo and the various apophatic divine attributes such as impassibility and immutability—in their discussions of the nature of God.[41] Many of these affirmations have fallen on hard times in contemporary theological discourse.[42] This is in part because, as Ben Meyer puts it, "we have inherited a cosmology that deadens the sense of divine intervention and election, of a providence that is really operative."[43] Besides getting us closer to the notions of divine action assumed by the authors of Scripture, however, an *aggiornamento* of such judgments could provide contemporary theologians with an extremely useful resource for affirming the simultaneity of divine and created freedom and the gratuitousness of the redemptive grace that the Triune God effects in God's creation. Their recovery and rearticulation represents a significant resource for understanding and speaking precisely about how it can be that both the Triune God and humans act in the writing, production, redaction, canonization, and dissemination of Christian Scripture.[44]

A number of contemporary scholars have noticed the value of affirming the absolute transcendence, free creation, and irresistible efficient causality of the Triune God for understanding and articulating how it is that the Triune God acts in history and reveals Godself in history. As Cynthia Crysdale and Neil Ormerod write with respect to Aquinas, "Not only did [he] hold that God created *ex nihilo* (out of nothing), with no preconditions or constraints, he also held that God's plan for the world was effective. Indeed, these two propositions are inextricably linked. Only a God who creates *ex nihilo* can be the provident Lord of history, for otherwise God, too, is subject to the constraints imposed by the contingency of creation."[45] In *The God of Faith and Reason,* Robert Sokolowski argues that the ontological or qualitative distinction between God and the world provides a resource that can allow us to speak intelligibly about divine and human causation in a noncompetitive, nondualistic way. The claim "that God could be all that he is had the world not existed," he argues, "is needed to determine what occurs in creation, providence and redemption."[46] David B. Burrell corroborates Sokolowski's convictions. As Burrell declares, "Nothing short of a free creation can ground a free revelation, and, with it, a free human response to the One from whom all that is comes forth."[47]

The affirmation of the distinction between God and the world provides a way of understanding the relationship between divine and human activity that allows us to simultaneously maintain that God freely creates and sustains the economy that is and that God brings about the emergence and freedom of created beings within that economy. God's transcendence from the world of creation and God's free decision to bring the world into existence provide key judgments for navigating questions about how God exercises agency before, in, with, and through all created actions, including those involved in the production and dissemination of Christian Scripture. Sokolowski states the significance of the distinction for understanding Scripture when he declares that "the most fundamental intellectual requirement for understanding the Bible is that it be read in the light of the Christian distinction between God and the world."[48] Affirming the distinction allows us a way to affirm that created causes freely participate in the sovereign activity of the Triune creator. The history of created natures itself has a derivative being.[49] Its being is in its participation in divine being through the free creation of the Triune God.

Proving that the distinction is the only or best means of speaking about the paradox of divine and created freedom in the economy of creation and redemption is beyond the scope of the present work. Since this systematics of the Christian Bible is not a dialectical or polemical work, I defer to the arguments of others for the positions herein espoused.[50] Nevertheless, though I cannot provide a definitive demonstration of the necessity of articulating the distinction between God and the world for a systematic theology of Scripture, I must still offer an account of its intelligibility and its appropriateness for the tasks at hand.[51]

What precisely can we glean from these reflections on the relationship of nonreciprocal dependence between God and the world? Sokolowski elaborates:

In Christian faith God is understood not only to have created the world, but to have permitted the distinction between himself and the world to occur. He is not established as God by the distinction.... No distinction made within the horizon of the world is like this, and therefore the act of creation cannot be understood in terms of any action or any relationship that exists in the world. The special sense of sameness in God "before" and "after" creation, and the special sense of otherness between God and the world, impose qualifications on whatever we are to say about God and the world, about creation out of nothing, about God's way of being present and interior to things yet beyond them.[52]

Sokolowski notes, following Aquinas, that "God is not related by a real relation to the world."[53] He continues:

This should not be taken psychologically, it should not be taken in terms of human emotions, and it does not mean that God is unconcerned with the world; it describes how God exists. And the world is not diminished in its own excellence, it is not somehow slighted because God is not related by a real relation to it; rather the world is now understood as not having had to be. If it did not have to be, it is there as a choice. And if the choice was not motivated by any need of completion in the one who let it be, and not even motivated by the need to be "there" to be more perfection and greatness, then the world is there through an incomparable generosity.[54]

Because God has no need of creation and because it is possible for creation not to have been, it is possible, even imperative, for us to understand the economy of creation itself as a first gift. Within the grammar of the distinction between the Triune God and creation, the latter is not something God did at some point in the past but instead names the ongoing dependence of all that exists that is not God upon God. All that is created is God's and depends upon God. God is not a cause within or before or outside of creation but is instead the one "within whom we live and move and have our being" (Acts 17.28). And such life and motion and possession of creaturely being is intrinsically free and, in that very freedom, testifies to the glory of its creator. "The world," writes Sokolowski "exists simply for the glory of God."[55]

The great, but I think as yet unrealized potential, for invoking the distinction between God and the world as a means of understanding divine and human agency in the production of Scripture faces significant difficulties. Sokolowski himself suggests that the "Bible does not say explicitly that God could have been all that he is even if he had not created the world."[56] If it is not biblical, is the "distinction" so necessary to Christian faith then? Is it not an intrusion of an alien Hellenism into biblical faith, as many biblical scholars and theologians, following the work of Adolf von Harnack, have argued?[57] Sokolowski's claim that no biblical author explicitly endorses the distinction is, strictly speaking, accurate. However, a number of scriptural texts exist that appear to reflect judgments about God's nature and being and God's relationship to creation and can be understood *as anticipating* the distinction.[58] Sokolowski argues that assertions of God's transcendence and providential work in creation extant throughout the scriptures contain the distinction without actually articulating it. Christian Scripture, he insists, "contains a narration of events, and these events can contain the Christian distinction without explicitly formulating it."[59] The distinction, he argues, "is lived by Jesus in a more accurate and effective way than it is anywhere formulated."[60] It is possible to reaffirm and reassert the distinction between God and the world as an explanation of the witness of Scripture to the freedom of the God of Israel who acts definitively in Jesus Christ and the Holy Spirit and gives contingent freedom to creatures.[61] The articulation of the distinction between God and creation is a historical achievement of the Christian church in the realm of what Lonergan calls systematic meaning.[62] According to Lonergan, in the achievements of systematic meaning, Christian believers advance to a "purely spiritual apprehension of God."[63] This "purely spiritual apprehension of God" is anticipated in a number of scriptural texts without being explicitly present.

A number of authors and texts in both the Old Testament and the New Testament suggest understandings of God that invite the questions about the precise relationship between God and creation that the distinction expresses. In his speech at the dedication of the temple, for instance, King Solomon affirms that God cannot be contained or located physically; "even heaven and the highest heaven cannot contain you, much less this house that I have built" (2 Kgs 8.27). Solomon arguably anticipates the judgment that God is not a material body located in time and space. A number of New Testament authors suggest this as well. In the narrative of

Jesus's interaction with the Samaritan woman at the well in John 4, Jesus declares that true worship of God is not restricted to only one physical location as if God were constrained by time and space. "The true worshippers will worship the Father in Spirit and truth," he declares, "for the Father seeks such as these to worship him. God is Spirit, and those who worship him must worship in spirit and truth" (John 4.23–24). In his speech in the Areopagus in Athens, Paul insists, "The God who made the world and everything in it, he who is Lord of heaven and earth, does not live in shrines made by human hands, nor is he served by human hands, as though he needed anything, since he himself gives to all mortals life and breath and all things. . . . For 'in him we live and move and have our being'" (Acts 17.24–28). James insists that every created gift comes from the unchanging Father above, "with whom there is no variation or shadow due to change" (Jas 1.17). As Paul declares at the climax of his reflections on the unity and profundity of God's economic work in Israel and Christ in Romans 9–11, "from him, through him, and in him are all things" (Rom 11.33, see also 1 Cor 8.5–6; Eph 4.4).

Language suggesting the exhaustiveness of God's creative activity—and so the aptness of articulating God's creation as ex nihilo—also occurs in a variety of places in both Testaments (see, e.g., Isa 45.7; Pss 33.6–9; 148.4–6; John 1.1–18; Rom 4.17; Heb 11.3).[64] The titular merism that the God of Scripture is creator, redeemer, and judge of "[the] heaven[s] and [the] earth," which recurs in the first clause of the creed and appears throughout both Testaments, implicitly contains the distinction between God and all created things (see Gen 1.1; 14.19; 14.22; 24.3; Ex 20.11; 31.17; 2 Kgs 19.15; 2 Chron 2.12; Ez 5.11; Pss 89.11; 115.15; 121.2; 134.3; 146.6; Isa 37.16; 65.17; 66.22; Jer 10.11–12; 23.24; 32.17; 33.25; 51.48; Hag 2.6; 2.21; Zech 21.1; Matt 11.25; Luke 10.21; 2 Pet 3.7; 3.13; Rev 14.7; see also Gen 2.1; 2.4; 1 Chron 29.11).[65] "God," Burrell writes, practically restating that ubiquitous biblical judgment, "is *not* one of those things whose beginning and end lie in God."[66] The church fathers frequently insisted on the qualitative distinction between God and created human persons by citing the aforementioned passages among others. Numbers 23.19 played an especially significant role in their articulation of the distinction between God and the world: "God is not a human being, that he should lie, or a mortal, that he should change his mind. Has he promised, and will he not do it?

Has he spoken, and will he not fulfill it?"[67] Unlike changing, finite, fallible, and sinful human persons, many early Christian thinkers stated explicitly that God was perfect in simplicity and constancy.

Many texts of Scripture, however, admit of readings suggesting God's mutability (Gen 6; 17; 22; Ex 32.14; 1 Chron 21.15; Jer 26.1; Amos 7.1–3), that God creates out of preexistent matter (Gen 1.1–3; Job 26.12–13; Pss 74.12–14; 89.10–11), and that God does not know future contingent realities (Gen 18.20–21; 22.12). The following questions arise for those who wish to take seriously the panoply of perspectives of various scriptural authors of apparent divine temporality and mutability: Is it possible to satisfactorily resolve the dialectic between texts that attribute temporality and mutability to God and those that appear to portray the opposite judgment that God is immutable? If so, how? What are the grounds for choosing the judgments of one set of texts and rejecting another?[68]

There are a number of ways of addressing these questions. Brian Robinette has helpfully enumerated three.[69] A first option would be to reject the distinction between divine and created nature as an imposition of static and abstract Greek thought upon the largely dynamic "Hebrew mind-set" of the scriptures. A number of contemporary theologians and biblical scholars have taken this route.[70] Such a perspective, however, does not adequately address the prevalence of so-called Hellenic perspectives in the texts of the New Testament. There is, properly speaking, no completely un-Hellenized Judaism in the first century.[71] Besides, the notions of the personal nature of God and of God's creation out of nothing, despite the confusion of some modern thinkers, were repugnant to Greek thinkers.[72] Such judgments cannot be understood as derived from Hellenizing tendencies.[73]

A second approach would be to attempt, anachronistically, to insist that the judgments of the distinction, divine simplicity, and *creatio ex nihilo* are present in Scripture itself. Such an approach is also a dead end. As Soskice notes with respect to *creatio ex nihilo*:

> The books of the Pentateuch show no metaphysical longing for first principles. It would be unreasonable and anachronistic to suppose that they did. But it is not unreasonable to read them as attesting to the disclosure of the revelation of the One who is and was and will always be, a God of loving faithfulness who has created and will re-

deem. This is what subsequent Jewish and Christian reflection has done, and it was in order to secure this distinctive understanding that Abrahamic understandings of divine eternity and of *creatio ex nihilo* were developed.[74]

The sovereignty of the God of Israel is absolute; it is not shared with other deities. The intuition of the personal freedom of YHWH that the authors of the texts of Christian Scripture present is also unique. These two scriptural insights point towards a third way of addressing the aforementioned challenge. The judgment of the distinction between God and the world provides a technical way of maintaining those particular revealed notions of divine and created freedom present in the texts of both Testaments.

The third possibility is not to see the judgment of *creatio ex nihilo* as a foreign imposition upon Scripture or as found in Scripture but instead to recognize it as continuous with Scripture. Gary Anderson calls it a "trajectory internal to the larger canonical witness."[75] The judgment of God's distinction from the world, then, is not a judgment that such a position can "be found" in Scripture in its full form. It is not necessary to locate definitively the distinction between God and the world somewhere "in the scriptures" in order to affirm its *usefulness* for expressing the relationship(s) between God and creation that renders certain narratives and statements about God's action in history and relationship to creation intelligible.[76] The judgment that God is wholly transcendent from God's freely created creation is a judgment that allows one to *understand* the biblical testimony to God's transcendence and intimacy with creation in a powerful way. Such a judgment, however, would require a differentiated understanding of the language of Scripture. If we were to adopt the judgment of the distinction as a means of understanding Scripture, we could no longer accept certain scriptural expressions of God's action and characteristics univocally, even if their human authors and original audiences would have done so.[77] The judgment of God's nonembodied and nontemporal transcendence would force us to approach Scripture from a recognition of its commonsense—and so, pretheoretical or presystematic—idiom.[78] That judgment would also provide a means for recognizing the development of theological reflection on the nature and attributes of the divine within Scripture itself, even if we cannot chart such development definitively.

The present account works from the judgment that the distinction represents a means of articulating the judgment of the absolute sovereign transcendence of God from creation in a formal way that allows one to read the scriptural texts intelligently. Like the doctrine of *creatio ex nihilo* and the judgment that Jesus Christ is *homoousios* with the Father, "the distinction" was a judgment arrived at and articulated in specific historical times and places and articulated in ways apposite for those times and places.[79] But we should not, for all that, consign it to the dustbin of history. Robinette differentiates between the historical and the formal nature of the judgment of creation ex nihilo particularly well:

> If *creatio ex nihilo* reflects a particular logic about the God-world relationship that can be stated in technical language, especially when induced to do so by a particular philosophical and theological dispute, it need not be thought of as divorced from the concrete circumstances that nourish the insight "from below." Of course, it is possible at some later time to declare that *creatio ex nihilo* has always been the biblical view of creation, though such an assessment is clearly mistaken. *But it is no less mistaken to ignore those trends in Scripture that evidence a process of discovery about the God-world relationship that makes those formal terms eminently coherent.*[80]

It is most fruitful, in my estimation, to argue that the developed articulations of the distinction between God and the world, God's creative activity ex nihilo, divine simplicity, and divine concursus bear witness to "differentiations of consciousness" that take place within the persons and communities that formulated them. The persons and communities who formulated and developed them did so by immersing themselves in Christian Scripture. The judgment that God was distinct from the world has a long history as a hermeneutical resource for Christian scriptural interpretation. The judgment of the distinction between God and the world and the judgment that God speaks to humanity in ways that humanity can understand served as principles of exegesis for the church fathers from almost the very beginning of Christian interpretation.[81]

The Triune God stoops down to our level by utilizing human culture and language to speak to us at our own created level, and this principle of divine communication is evident throughout Scripture.[82] Scripture undoubtedly contains anthropomorphic and anthropopathic language for God, outdated cosmologies, and even mythopoetical forms of expression.[83] As Lonergan notes, such symbolic language is extremely important, even essential, for Christian reflection because of its ability to both capture attention and provoke change in hearers. But symbolic language is by its very nature imprecise.[84] The presence of symbolic language in Scripture does not intrinsically forbid attempts to understand the mystery of the activity of the work of the Triune God in systematic fashion. The early church developed such systematic expressions as a means of articulating how it is that Christ and the Father were divine. With respect to creation, their articulation of the distinction between God and the world excluded God from the realm of creaturely causation in a way that allowed them to simultaneously affirm God's transcendence from *and* immanence to creation.[85] Such an approach can be marshaled to emphasize the freedom of creaturely causation.

Lonergan, following Aquinas's understanding of divine providence, declares emphatically that God operates in every economic historical operation whether natural or voluntary.[86] Just as the Nicene affirmation of the *homoousion* does not propose the presence of an ethereal material or conceptual entity—"divinity"—that is shared in some bodily way by both the Father and the Son but is instead a means of affirming the Athanasian rule that the same things are predicated of the Son as of the Father, except that the Son is not the Father, so also the judgments that God creates ex nihilo and operates in every operation whether natural or voluntary are ways of affirming the freedom of the Triune God in bringing creation into existence out of nothing, efficaciously sustaining the contingent universe in all of its emergent freedom, and allowing and enabling the created freedoms of the creatures of this economy.[87]

The present account takes a classical approach to the paradoxical problem of how we can simultaneously understand the Triune God to be transcendent, sovereign, and free and the author of secondary causes that have their own relative freedom and efficacy. Lonergan summarizes this position well in a book review from 1946, "On God and Secondary Causes": "God not only gives being to, and conserves in being, every created cause, but also he uses the universe of causes as his instruments in applying each cause to its operation, and so is the principle cause of each and every event as event. [Humanity] proposes, but God disposes."[88] This position provides a way of understanding expressions in Scripture that maintain both the efficacy of God's sovereignty and the freedom of God's creatures, especially God's rational creatures.[89]

The previous judgment about the relationship between divine and human freedom is illuminating, in my estimation, for understanding precisely how we can meaningfully speak of the freedom of God's action in creation and the freedom that inheres in the action of created causes. Charles Hefling expresses it well: "If anything has in fact occurred, then God is the efficient, exemplary, and final cause of its occurring, whether the occurrence is a chemical reaction or the historical development of chemistry. Otherwise stated, the universe is not deterministic but emergently probable, human history included, and God is its Creator but not one of the agents it includes."[90] The God who is the efficient, exemplary, and final cause of all that is in creation is not a perfect being conjured by philosophers but the Triune God of Scripture. The judgment that the God who has brought creation into being acts concurrently in every created action is a hypothetical explanation of the judgment of the first clause of the Nicene Creed.

As Hefling helpfully notes, for the Christian there are some notable exceptions to the claim that God is not among the causes of creation.[91] The Son of God has been sent into the economy of creation, becoming incarnate in Jesus Christ, and has revealed the love of the Father, has taught and preached, has been crucified, has died, has risen from the grave, and has ascended to "the right hand of the Father" for our salvation. The Holy Spirit has also been sent in the economy to testify to Christ and to bring about our healing and transformation as adopted sons and daughters of God.[92] The work of the Triune God, as noted above, provides the broadest horizon within which human engagement with Scripture takes place.[93] And the doctrinal judgment that Scripture is inspired by the Holy Spirit must be understood relative to the overall mission of the Holy Spirit in history. In like manner, the doctrinal judgment that Scripture is the written Word of God and that all of Scripture leads to and refers to Jesus Christ, the incarnate Word of God, is a judgment about Scripture in its relationship to the overall mission of the Son of God in history. It is thus necessary to provide an initial understanding of God's saving work through the Son and Holy Spirit in history in order to specify the general theological location of Christian Scripture in the economic work of the Triune God. In chapter 6 I explore in greater depth the implications of the judgment that Scripture functions in the missions of the Son and the Holy Spirit.

The number of historical and constructive or creative proposals for reflection on the Trinity that have come forth in recent years is enormous; for our present purposes it is unnecessary to make extensive forays into this literature.[94] The present systematic theology of scriptural interpretation does not require us to give an analogical account of the intelligibility of the immanent Trinity.[95] The present goal is not to provide an analogous understanding of the Triune God in Godself but instead to provide an understanding of the work of the Triune God in history. In order to do so, we will follow Irenaeus's injunction to "discipline ourselves by investigating the mystery and economy of the existent God" (*Haer.* 2.28.1). As Karl Rahner has argued, after all, "the 'economic' Trinity is the 'immanent' Trinity and the 'immanent' Trinity is the 'economic' Trinity."[96] While Rahner's *Grundaxiom* can be understood in multiple ways, I invoke it to simply note that the following account of the Triune God's work in the economy of creation assumes that God does as God is.[97]

Any contemporary account of trinitarian theology, of course, must be conditioned by the exigencies of soteriology. The work of the Son and the Holy Spirit is, as the Niceno-Constantinopolitan Creed testifies, *pro nobis* (for us). The understandings of the immanent life of the Trinity that post–New Testament Christians developed emerged from their reflection on their worship and from their convictions about the saving work of God in their midst in history.[98] The economic work of the Trinity was and is the salvific work that God is doing in history. As Frederick Crowe argues, the missions of the Son and the Spirit, at least from the perspective of Paul in Ephesians, must be understood in their relationship to the overarching plan of the Father, who has "destined us for adoption as his children through Jesus Christ, according to the good pleasure of his will, to the praise of his glorious grace that he freely bestowed on us in the Beloved" (Eph 1.3–6).[99] The Father, in his providential governance of his creation, "with all wisdom and insight ... has made known to us the mystery of his will, according to his good pleasure that he set forth in Christ, as a plan for the fullness of time, to gather up all things in him, things in heaven and things on earth" (Eph 1.9–10). All of the works of the Triune God *ad extra* are one and serve the Father's end of recapitulating all things in Christ through the Holy Spirit.[100]

What is this overarching plan, what is its shape, and how is it for us? The good news of Christianity is that God is redeeming human persons in the history that is. As de Lubac writes in *Catholicism*, "If the salvation offered by God is in fact the salvation of the human race, since this human race lives and develops in time, any account of this salvation will naturally take a historical form—it will be the penetration of humanity by Christ."[101] While all of the work of the Trinity *ad extra* has this recapitulation in Jesus Christ as its end, it is possible to speak, by appropriation, of the distinctive missions of the Holy Spirit and of the Son. The Father accomplishes his purposes through these "two hands."[102] In one of his later essays, "Mission and the Spirit," Lonergan offers a concise and complementary account of the "penetration of humanity by Christ." In his typically terse idiom, Lonergan writes in that essay that "there is a threefold personal self-communication of divinity to humanity, first, when Christ the Word becomes flesh, secondly, when through Christ [persons] become temples of the Spirit and adopted [children] of the Father, thirdly, when in a final consummation the blessed know the Father as they are known by him."[103] This all-encompassing divine work is the broadest context for locating Christian Scripture, and Scripture somehow serves as an instrument within this "threefold personal self-communication."[104]

The uncreated Triune God could not have created uncreated beings by definition.[105] But the Triune God *has* brought created beings into being. While everything created participates in God as One through God's operation in every voluntary and natural operation, the Triune God has acted in our history to make it possible for humans to participate in God's Triune life. Through the economic work of the Son and Holy Spirit, the Triune God has made a way for created beings to "become participants in the divine nature" (2 Pet 1.4).[106] As Herbert McCabe declares, God "could not make man by nature divine, but he has given him divinity as a gift. This is what we call grace. We do share in the divine nature, we do behave like God, but not by nature. We can do what God does, but in God it is natural, in us it is not—we call it supernatural."[107] Our supernatural doing, traditionally described as participation in the theological virtues of faith, hope, and love, is possible because of our participation in a supernatural order. The supernatural order, the order of grace, is an order entitatively disproportionate to the created order.[108] It is completely gratuitous, just as creation is, but it is an elevation of the created nature of human persons beyond what is possible to them on their own in their immanent reaching.[109] This supernatural grace that is the work of the Son and the Holy Spirit in history is the means of our redemption and participation in the life of the Trinity. What the Son and the Spirit do in the economy heals us where we have failed to live up to the exigencies of our nature as human persons and communities, and elevates us to participate in the glorious life of the Triune God as we are transformed, according to the apostle Paul, from "one degree of glory to another" (2 Cor 3.18).[110] Sanctifying grace is thus both *sanans*, or healing, and *elevans*, or elevating.[111] Because the healing and elevating work of the Triune God is God's purpose for us, we should expect that Scripture will have some place within that healing and elevating work in history.

The distinction I have made between systematic theology and historical theology makes a way for us to affirm and directly appropriate the scriptural testimony about the work of the Son and the Holy Spirit from a systematic perspective.[112] To risk an oversimplification, the historical development of Western Christian trinitarian theology began from scriptural judgments about the saving work of the Son, to the conclusion of the consubstantiality of the Son with the Father, to the judgment of the consubstantiality of the Holy Spirit with the Father and Son, finally to imaginative, speculative, and/or analogical reflection on meaningful ways of understanding the relations of the persons in the immanent Trinity by utilizing the technical language of processions, real relations of opposition, and persons.[113] Thomas Aquinas, by beginning his account of the Trinity from *quaestiones* on the technical notion of processions and from there proceeding to explanations of the relations of Paternity, Sonship, and Spiration, then to persons, and finally to the missions of the Son and Holy Spirit in the economy of creation, bears witness to the full scope of these historical developments (*ST* 1 qq. 27–43).

The technical language that Thomas developed does not serve as a replacement for Scripture, and it does not oppose the testimony of Scripture.

It provides a resource for stating with clarity the relationality and intimacy of the Father, Son, and Holy Spirit already expressed but not technically specified by the authors of the New Testament.[114] The systematic theologian holds that the authors of Scripture speak intelligently about divine and created being, even though they do not do so univocally or technically. The recognition that the authors of Scripture must not be forced to conform to the strictures of technical discourse and that such technical discourse is not about the meaning of Scripture itself but about reality frees us to trust and affirm the biblical testimony to the work of the Son and Holy Spirit of the biblical authors, recognizing its diversity, from within a systematic horizon. Thomas's technical understanding of the Trinity is not the understanding of John, Paul, or Peter but presents a technical way of understanding and articulating what the God of Scripture, Father, Son, and Holy Spirit, has revealed about Godself. The commonsense and symbolic idioms of Scripture, and all of the generic conventions of both Testaments, are wholly appropriate for expressing the mystery of the identity and work of the Triune God in history.[115] Systematic theology develops technical and precise language for affirming and understanding the diffuse affirmations of Scripture after further questions for understanding and judgment arise in the histories of specific Christian communities and individual believers. We are accountable to the specific inspired language of the texts of Scripture regarding the Triune God, but such accountability does not prohibit, and in fact even requires, that we recognize that the language of Scripture concerning reality is not identical with the realities—divine and created—that it mediates. It is not only possible, but responsible and faithful, to develop precise language for understanding and speaking truthfully about the God to whom the texts of Scripture bear witness.

While the Holy Spirit *and* the Son bring about our healing and transformation through dwelling in us, our recognition and affirmation of this healing and transformation will always follow on the antecedent *actuality* of the Holy Spirit's work in us. It is the Holy Spirit, after all, who reveals to us the Triunity of God and who makes us participants in the divine nature.[116] Our introduction to God's Triunity begins with "God's love flooding our hearts through the Holy Spirit given to us" (Rom 5.5).[117] It is therefore appropriate to begin my treatment of the missions with an account of the work of the Holy Spirit; such an account, though it comes "second" in this presentation, provides a hypothetical explication of some key elements in the third clause of the historical rules of faith and creeds.

The creed contains few explicit judgments concerning the details of the work of the Holy Spirit in human history. Though the creed is sparse in its testimony to the work of the Holy Spirit, the authors of the New Testament give ample testimony to the work of the Spirit. An exhaustive account of the creedal and biblical testimony to the work of the Holy Spirit, however, would take us far beyond the scope of the present work.[118] My primary goal, as stated above, is to provide enough theological context to locate Scripture within the work of the Triune God in history. Let me start with creedal affirmations and then fill out that account with a presentation of scriptural testimony to the work of the Holy Spirit.

In the creed Christians profess directly that (1) Christ was born of the Virgin Mary through the power of the Holy Spirit, that (2) the Holy Spirit is coequal with the Father and the Son,[119] and that (3) the Holy Spirit spoke through the prophets. De Lubac shows that a number of church fathers thought that the articles that followed the profession of belief in the Holy Spirit specified the dimensions of the Holy Spirit's work.[120] Under such an understanding, the Holy Spirit would play a special role in the establishment and maintenance of the one, holy, apostolic, catholic church, would have some significant role in baptism, would achieve the forgiveness of sins, and would bring about the resurrection of the dead. The works of the Triune God *ad extra*, of course, are one.[121] We could spend equal time investigating the work of the Son in establishing and maintaining the Christian community, or discussing how baptism is a participation in the death of Christ, or explicating the efficacy of Christ's passion for our forgiveness, or, finally, examining how our resurrection will be a participation in Christ's resurrection. Each of these is effected in us directly, however, through the immediate presence of the Holy Spirit to us and in us. Again, it is the Holy Spirit who introduces us to and incorporates us into the mystery of the Trinity.

Theologians have understood the judgment that the Holy Spirit affects the incarnation of the Son from the Virgin Mary in multiple ways. Hans Urs von Balthasar argues that this affirmation provides an insight into the taxis of the temporal missions of the Son and the Holy Spirit.

Though the Son proceeds only from the Father and the Holy Spirit proceeds from the Father and the Son in the immanent Trinity, Balthasar argues that the mission of the Holy Spirit is antecedent to the mission of the
Son in the economy. The Spirit must effect the Son's incarnation and lead
and direct the Son in his incarnate work (see Luke 4.14, 18–19). Following the completion of the Son's incarnate work—which comprises his
teaching, miracles, crucifixion, death, resurrection, and ascent to the right
hand of the Father—the Holy Spirit is then sent to the church. The temporality of the economic missions, then, for Balthasar, reflects an inver-
sion of the taxis of the processions of the Son and the Holy Spirit in the
immanent Trinity.[122]

Robert Doran, following the work of Frederick Crowe, has also argued for the temporal priority of the mission of the Holy Spirit. The judgment of the Spirit's temporal priority provides a way of articulating the
universality of the salvific will of the Triune God (see 2 Pet 3.9). For
Doran, the Holy Spirit is operative invisibly at all times and all places, testifying to and leading people to participate in the redemptive work that
the Triune God is accomplishing in history.[123] Jesus Christ, the incarnate
Son of God, reveals this work in its fullness and completes it in his life,
passion, resurrection, and ascension. At Pentecost the invisible mission of
the Holy Spirit "becomes visible . . . in confirmation of the revelation that
occurs in the visible mission of the Word."[124] Both Balthasar and Doran
share an emphasis on the testimonial nature of the mission of the Holy
Spirit. The Spirit, both invisibly and visibly, points to the redemptive
work of the Triune God in and through Jesus Christ and the Christian
community. This brings us to the creedal judgment of the Holy Spirit's
testimony through the prophets.[125]

The judgment that the Holy Spirit spoke through the prophets
reflects the conviction of the earliest Christians that the Holy Spirit utilized *both* the historic prophets of the Old Testament and the actual texts
of the Old Testament to testify to the coming of Jesus Christ.[126] The conviction that "the prophets" testified to the coming of Jesus Christ, the fullness of the revelation in human history in all of the dimensions of his incarnate life and meaning, occurs throughout the New Testament as a
constitutive Christian conviction (see Matt 2.23; 11.13; 26.56; Mark 1.2;
Luke 1.70; 18.31; 24.25, 27; John 5.39; Acts 3.18–24; 7.52; 10.43; 13.27;
24.14; 26.22; 28.23; Heb 1.1–3).[127]

In Paul's list of what he has received "as of first importance" he emphasizes this judgment, stating that Christ died, was buried, and rose from the dead "in accordance with the scriptures" (1 Cor 15.3–4). A number of New Testament authors state directly that it is the Holy Spirit who achieves this testimonial work, either through the texts themselves or through their authors (see Mark 12.36; Acts 4.25; Eph 3.5; 2 Tim 3.16; esp. 2 Pet 1.21). It is, after all, the Spirit who reveals God's wisdom, "for the Spirit searches everything, even the depths of God" (1 Cor 2.10). In addition to the Spirit's work through the prophets and texts of Scripture, the Spirit provides testimony to the identity of Jesus Christ as the beloved Son of God at Christ's baptism (Matt 3.16; Mark 1.10; Luke 3.22), through Christ's miraculous works (Matt 12.28) at Pentecost and through the miracles of the early church (Acts 2.1–13; 4.31; 10.44; 13.2; 19.6), and in the production of fruit in believers (Gal 5.22–23).

The question still remains *how it is* that the Holy Spirit testifies to, and leads human persons to, Jesus Christ and the intelligibilities of his incarnate, linguistic, symbolic, interpersonal, and theological meanings. All such testimony can only be adequately recognized through the antecedent internal work of the Spirit in the hearts and minds of persons. In Romans and 1 Corinthians Paul testifies that the Spirit of Christ dwells in believers (Romans 8.9, 11; 1 Cor 3.16). In his farewell discourse in John's gospel, Jesus promises the disciples that he will send the Spirit to them as "an advocate" who will "testify on my behalf" (John 14.15–17, 26; 15.26). The Holy Spirit, whom Jesus calls "the Spirit of Truth,"

> will guide you into all the truth; for he will not speak on his own, but will speak whatever he hears, and he will declare to you the things that are to come. He will glorify me, because he will take what is mine and declare it to you. All that the Father has is mine. For this reason I said that he will take what is mine and declare it to you. (John 16.13–15)

The author of the first epistle of John states that the Son will dwell in believers "by the Spirit that he has sent us" (1 John 3.24). In John's gospel Jesus states that the Son *and* the Father will take up residence in believers (see John 14.23). We receive adoption through the redemptive work of the Son, but this takes place through the indwelling of the Holy Spirit

(Gal 4.4–6). The Spirit, then, mediates the meaning, work, and even persons of the Son and the Father in believers through coming and dwelling within them.

The judgment that the Holy Spirit, Son, and Father dwell within believers calls out for a systematic explication. The Spirit's work of illuminating persons so that we recognize the manifest revelation of the Triune God in history comes through our participation in sanctifying grace. In a set of notes used for a course on sanctifying grace at the Jesuit Seminary in Toronto in 1951–52, Lonergan provides a concise and extremely useful summary of the various statements the authors of the New Testament make about the mission, work, effects, and presence of the Holy Spirit in believers in sanctifying grace.

> To those whom God the Father loves [1] as he loves Jesus, his only begotten Son, (2) he gives the uncreated gift of the Holy Spirit, so that (3) into a new life they may be (4) born again and (5) become living members of Christ; therefore as (6) justified, (7) friends of God, (8) adopted children of God, and (9) heirs in hope of eternal life, (10) they enter into a sharing in the divine nature.[128]

Lonergan draws together these various New Testament judgments to provide an exposition of the work of the Holy Spirit under the technical terms of a theology of sanctifying grace. The texts provide evidence of the beliefs of the New Testament authors and communities.[129] The authors of the New Testament testify to these dimensions of the work of the Holy Spirit in their own communities and even their own persons. Attentive and intelligent engagement with the judgments about the work of the Holy Spirit mediated by the authors of the New Testament provides us with an occasion for understanding their own meaning and for understanding what was going forward in their reflection on the Spirit of God as distinct from Jewish or Greco-Roman understandings of spirits and spirituality.

Aside from providing evidence of the beliefs of the earliest Christians, however, we can ask whether or not we can share or have shared in the experiences, understandings, and judgments of these authors and their communities. Have we experienced the love of God flooding our hearts through the Holy Spirit (Rom 5.5)? Have we received the spirit of adoption by which we are children of God (Rom 8.16; Gal 4.5; Eph 1.5)? Lonergan brings together these various New Testament judgments in a synthetic statement of the reality of the Holy Spirit's work in his self and in those participating in his Christian community. The convictions of the authors of the New Testament become Lonergan's own, and he provides a systematic account of their intelligibility through the technical language of sanctifying grace.

Sanctifying grace, for Lonergan, names our participation in the active spiration of the Holy Spirit. As noted above, this grace both heals what has gone awry within our created natures, and so remedies the effects of sin in our lives, and elevates us to participate in the divine life of the Trinity. Such healing and elevation are the means through which we come to recognize and understand—albeit imperfectly—the mysteries of God's revelatory work in history. Sanctifying grace thus produces in us supernatural faith, or belief in the truths revealed about and by the Triune God (1 Cor 12.9),[130] and supernatural hope, or trust in the promise of the consummation of our adoption as daughters and sons who will see God face-to-face (Matt 5.8; 1 Cor 13.13; 2 Cor 3.18).

The Spirit dwelling in us, as Paul writes, bears the fruit of "love, joy, peace, patience, kindness, generosity, faithfulness, gentleness, and self-control. There is no law against such things" (Gal 5.22–23; see also Rom 8.6; 14.17; 15.13; 2 Cor 6.6; 1 Thess 1.6). The fruit of love that we bear makes manifest our direct participation in the passive spiration of the Holy Spirit. "What is breathed forth from sanctifying grace is charity," Doran writes, "the love of God above all things and in all things and the love of neighbor as ourselves, the gift of fidelity to the two greatest commandments."[131] Though the Holy Spirit is properly named gift, we have already seen that the Father and Son come and dwell in us through this gift (John 14.23; 1 John 3.24). We are thus able to participate in and manifest the primordial love of the Father and the judgment of value of the Son. "We love because he first loved us" (1 John 4.19). Such love is most fully expressed in what Lonergan calls the "law of the cross," wherein we, through the grace of the Triune God dwelling in us, are able to love not just our neighbors, but even our enemies, returning good for the evils done to us (Matt 5.44–45).[132] Our deification is thus cruciform.[133] The indwelling of the Trinity empowers us to love our enemies even unto our own deaths, in obedience to the "new commandment" that Jesus Christ gives to his disciples (John 13.34). In this obedience we imitate the Father's love, demonstrated in the economic work of the Son, who reconciled us to the Father "while we were enemies" (Rom 5.10). Through passive spiration, we come to truly imitate our Father, and so can fulfill Jesus's paradoxical command that we "be perfect . . . as [our] heavenly Father is perfect" (Matt 5.48). Such perfection represents the telos of the dwelling of the Triune God in us.

However we understand the work of the Holy Spirit in the manifold historical processes of the production of Christian Scripture, that is, in the doctrine of inspiration, and however we understand the work of the Holy Spirit in leading us into all truth, the fullness of the Triune God's mysterious self-revelation in Jesus Christ, the incarnate Son of God and God's wisdom through our engagement with Scripture, that is, in the doctrine of illumination, both of these understandings must be conditioned by, and located in, the broader contexts of the work of the indwelling of the Holy Spirit in believers and the ends of the Spirit's work that I have just specified. An adequate understanding of the mission of the Holy Spirit provides the proper contextual horizon for orienting responsible, Christian, spiritual reading of Scripture. I return to the context of the Holy Spirit's mission in chapter 6 when I focus on the Spirit's work with reference to Scripture in more detail.

Having offered accounts of the participation of human persons in the mission of the Holy Spirit, I must now briefly offer an explanation of the work of Jesus Christ of Nazareth, one person in two natures, in his mission as the only Son of the Father sent to do the Father's work.[134] We know the meaning and significance of the work of Jesus Christ, as we have already seen, through the internal and external testimony of the Holy Spirit. The Son also bears witness to his meaning in his invisible mission by granting us supernatural faith. We have already seen that the Holy Spirit, by bringing the Father and the Son into us, applies the redemptive work of the Son to us. What is this work of the Son, then, that the Spirit applies to us? Again, it is not possible to provide a comprehensive account of the intelligibility of the creedal and biblical testimony to the mission of the Son in history; what follows, however, is necessary for providing the context necessary for understanding the relationship between the meaning of Jesus Christ and the meaning(s) of Scripture.

In the creed we profess belief in "in one Lord, Jesus Christ." Again, since the focus here is on the economic mission of the Son and because we have already affirmed the Son's consubstantiality with the Father, we need not revisit that judgment. We can therefore proceed to present an explanation of the mission of the Son with reference to the remainder of the clause and the testimony of the authors of the New Testament:

> For us men and for our salvation he came down from heaven and by the power of the Holy Spirit was incarnate from the Virgin Mary, and was made man; he was also crucified for us under Pontius Pilate, suffered, died, and was buried; and on the third day he rose again according to the Scriptures and ascended into heaven; he is seated at the right hand of the Father and will come again in glory to judge the living and the dead; and his kingdom will have no end.

These judgments comprise the totality of what de Lubac has referred to as the "event" or "fact of Christ."[135] The second clause of the creed begins with an assertion of the purpose of Christ's mission. The Son is sent in order to save humanity. The wedding of the Word, who is with the Father and the Holy Spirit from eternity, with humanity, achieves the possibility of human participation in the divine nature. As Athanasius most famously has put it, "He became human that we might become divine" (*Inc.* 54).[136] The Son's assumption of humanity does not entail any changes in the Trinity; neither the incarnation nor Christ's passion brings about suffering or any other change in the divine nature.[137] What changes, then, is not God but humanity's relationship to God.

Given what we have already affirmed above, namely, that the Triune God effects our redemption through the indwelling of the Holy Spirit, how does "God taking part in man's making of man" in Jesus Christ's work change us as well?[138] Our *relationship* with the Triune God changes through Christ's work—and the work of the Holy Spirit—but *human understanding* of the Triune God also changes, and changes drastically, through the revelatory nature of this work.[139] What Jesus Christ accomplishes, especially in his death and resurrection, is both the means of human salvation and the fullest revelation of the love of the Father for all of humanity (John 3.16).[140] Jesus Christ, in his linguistic, symbolic, interpersonal, and incarnate meaning, is the fullness of divine revelation in the economy. The sending of the Son reveals the love of the Triune God (1 John 4.9). In his mission the Son reveals the things of the Father. As Jesus states in Matthew's gospel, "All things have been handed over to me by my Father; and no one knows the Son except the Father, and no one knows the Father except the Son and anyone to whom the Son chooses to reveal him" (Matt 11.27; see also Luke 10.22). In John's gospel Jesus states that he can only do what he sees the Father doing (John 5.19). The Father dwells in him and speaks and works through him (John 14.10). Those who have seen Jesus have therefore seen the Father (John 14.8–9).

Through the work of the Father in him, Jesus, in his humanity, is the definitive economic "site" of divine revelation. Through his human consciousness he discerns how to communicate his ineffable self-understanding of the divine nature—his beatific knowledge of the Father—in human language, in his intersubjectivity, and ultimately in his passion. "The inexpressible intelligibility of divine mystery became expressible in the single human consciousness of Jesus of Nazareth as subject of his earthly life," writes Doran. "He learned how to express it. His earthly life *was* the expression of his grasp of divine mystery."[141] The Son emptied himself (Phil 2.5–11) and became like us in all things save sin (Heb 4.15; see also 2.17), and as such he "grew in wisdom and knowledge and favor with God and man" (Luke 2.52). Jesus's kenotic experience of growth and understanding is strikingly displayed in his willingness to meet with, love, and heal those deemed unlovable according to the social, cultural, and religious values of his time; he submits to, and so learns from, even a Syrophonecian woman (see Mark 7.24–30). The entirety of his life is a mystery of love, exhibited finally and most fully in his faithfulness unto his humiliating death, making manifest the "law of the cross."[142] The Triune God, in providential care, has willed to bring good out of evil (Matt 5.38–48; Luke 6.27–28; Rom 12.17–21; 1 Pet 3.9). Christ's cross and resurrection epitomize this law.

Strictly speaking, in a technical sense at least, the Son's mission in the economy is his own. We only "participate" in it analogously through the work of the Spirit in us, conforming us to the form of the Son's mission. If we are able to have "the mind of Christ" (1 Cor 2.16), this must take place through the indwelling of the Father and the Son subsequent to the Holy Spirit's work in coming and dwelling in us. We can do so by setting our minds on the things of the Spirit (Rom 8.5), because the Spirit mediates to us not what is his own but what belongs to the Son (John 16.14).[143] The redemptive work of the Son and the Spirit, however, includes the work of the Christian community. As Christ and the Spirit were sent, so we also are sent.[144] The Son's work of redemption and revelation are ongoing in his body (1 Cor 12.27; Eph 4.4; 4.12). The mystical body of Christ carries out the work of the head in subsequent history. This does not entail the possibility of "new" doctrinal revelations but does mean that the Spirit, who searches the depths of God (1 Cor 2.10), will lead the body of Christ into fuller understanding of the manifold ramifications of the singular truth of the Son, the one who is the way, the truth, and the life (John 14.1; 16.13; see also 15.26).

The judgments that the Christian scriptures testify on Christ's account (John 5.39), that he came not to abolish but to fulfill the law and the prophets (Matt 5.17–18), that he is the end of the law (Rom 10.4), and that Scripture is written about him (Luke 24.27) and fulfilled in him (Luke 22.37), must be understood within adequate understandings of the redemptive and revelatory mission of the Son of God, Jesus Christ of Nazareth, in human history. "Long ago," the letter to the Hebrews begins, "God spoke to our ancestors in many and various ways by the prophets, but in these last days he has spoken to us by a Son, whom he appointed heir of all things, through whom he also created the worlds. He is the reflection of God's glory and the exact imprint of God's very being, and he sustains all things by his powerful word" (Heb 1.1–2).

An adequate account of Christ's comprehensive revelation of "the mystery kept secret for long ages" (Rom 16.25) in which the Triune God is "gathering up all things in Christ" (Eph 1.9–10) provides the proper context for understanding the nature and purpose of Christian Scripture. What the Son has done through his mission, and the intelligibility of this work, provides the orienting context for reading Scripture in a christologically responsible—and so distinctively Christian—way.

SUMMARY AND CONCLUSION

As noted in chapter 1, a systematic theology of Christian Scripture, conceived on the terms sets out in the present work, would necessarily start with the articulation of what is most general and universal and proceed to what is less general. What is most general is God and God's necessity, what is next in generality is God's economic work. As Karl Barth would caution, we only know the Triune God through God's redemptive activity on our behalf. Any inquiry into the nature of God, whether we are considering God's Triunity or God's character under the scholastic delineation of God's divine characteristics in God's unity, must proceed from and be in accordance with God's self-revelation economically. I have begun, therefore, with an account of the intelligibility of the economic work and purposes of the Triune God.

The present work parallels the approach of John Webster in *Holy Scripture: A Dogmatic Sketch*. Near the beginning of that work, Webster writes that he intends to treat Scripture "in terms of its role in God's self-communication, that is, the acts of Father, Son and Spirit which establish and maintain that saving fellowship with humankind in which God makes himself known to us and by us."[145] But such work is never intelligible or mediated except through human judgments and understandings, even if such judgments and understandings are inspired by and adequately—at least insofar as is possible—express God's revelation of Godself. While all theology must start from God as God has revealed Godself to us, theologians—that is, human subjects—are the ones starting. The mediation of human subjectivity, whether individual or communal, is operative in all theological reflection.

Human understanding of the work of the Triune God in history, as we have seen through our examination of the related yet still varied expressions in the rule of faith, is not a static thing. Human understandings of that work are on the move. Failure to advert to the historicity of advances in the understanding of the mystery of the economy of the Triune God that have actually taken place in Christian reflection will put us at risk of committing anachronisms or failing to advert to eminently intelligent, reasonable, responsible, and useful historic formulations of the faith. This chapter has therefore attempted to provide both a rule of faith—the Nicene Creed—and an understanding of the special theological doctrines of the rule at the level of our times, "objectifying" a Christian framework that affirms and details the parameters and nature of the activity of the Triune God in history. That objectified general theological context is the most general, and so most important, context of Christian Scripture.[146]

Our understandings of divine and human action in history will necessarily influence our understanding of the nature of Scripture, its purpose, and the possibilities of Christian engagement with it. As Young writes, "Not only is a framework necessary for interpretation, but a systematic theology also, and both will need to be at the same time traditional and 'novel' to meet the challenge of performing a text in a situation where its traditional meaning is being subverted."[147] My own account has examined the ecclesiastical, narratival-synthetic-sequential, referential, and technical dimensions of the historical rule(s) of faith and has proposed one contemporary account of Christian doctrines of the rule that attempts to be true to each of its dimensions for the sake of serving as the requisite systematic framework for a faithful and responsible articulation of the nature and purpose of Scripture.

The goal of Christian interpretation of Scripture cannot be the apprehension of an already-out-there-now-real meaning that inheres in the Bible.[148] To reiterate what I have already said, I am not suggesting that there is nothing objective about Christian Scripture. The words on the pages of Christian Bibles are certainly there. They are intelligible, and in some sense their intelligibilities are intransigently other than us and call us to account when readers, hearers, and even communities—as has so frequently and tragically happened in Christian history—ignore the "literal sense," avoid "the way that the words run," or reject "the plain sense."[149] To quote Lonergan again, however, "the plain fact is that there is nothing 'out there' except spatially ordered marks."[150] Our only access to the texts as intelligible is our own subjective constitution made up of our own experiences, our own linguistic apparatus, our own horizons of understandings, judgments, decisions, our own memories, and our own imaginations.[151]

What has occupied our attention from the outset, for historical, theological, and phenomenological reasons, however, is the fact that communal Christian self-understanding is antecedent to and the condition of the recognition of the Christian Bible as Christian Scripture. Christian Scripture, as Christian Scripture, is unintelligible outside of Christian tradition. And Christian tradition results from the achievements in understanding and judgment of historic Christian believers reflecting upon their experience of and worship of the Triune God of creation and redemption. What I have articulated in this chapter is a Christian horizon for understanding divine and human action in history that provides the context in which Christian engagement with Scripture takes place.

The explicitly theological perspective offered in this chapter will not be palatable to those expecting historical demonstrations of the truthfulness of Christian faith. It is impossible to demonstrate the truth of the mysteries affirmed in Christian faith via philological, hermeneutical, historical, or dialectical means.[152] The first four of Lonergan's eight functional specialties provide directives for understanding expressions of Christian faith in the past, for discerning what was going forward in actual historical developments, and for clearly differentiating dialectically opposed perspectives in the history of Christian reflection. Anyone can participate in such work. One must experience conversion, however, not just to examine the works and deeds of historical figures, but to appropriate such words and deeds for one's self. For Lonergan, the functional specialty of foundations entails a "fully conscious decision about one's horizon, one's outlook, one's worldview. It deliberately selects the frame-work, in which doctrines have their meaning, in which systematics reconciles, in which communications are effective."[153] The framework, for Lonergan, however, is not just deliberately selected and appropriated. An authentically Christian framework would acknowledge the communal and individual reception of graces disproportionate to the theologian's natural powers; such graces would include the graces of specific revealed beliefs, which by their very nature, as supernatural, are not demonstrable.

The framework I have provided holds that the prebiblical stance of the early church towards the constitutive meaning of Christian faith, articulated in the rule of faith and later the creeds, is an authentic move, and it is an authentic move that we should understand in its historical unfolding and that we must appropriate at the level of our own times. To cite Young again, our own understanding of the work of the Triune God in history must not only have continuity with what the Church has said is the original message, but must be sufficiently "novel" to meet the challenges of our own day.[154] It is not enough to parrot or even to understand early Christian articulations of being in the world as expressed in the rule of faith or the creeds.

It will not do to simply reconstruct the words of the historical Jesus, the *kerygma*, the content of pre-Pauline hymns and other liturgical texts in the New Testament, the second-century *regulae* or *kanoni*, or the later ecumenical creeds. Work in all of these areas is absolutely necessary—and much remains to be done—but such work will not, in itself, answer the question of how we can move from indirect discourse about what others believed to direct discourse about the truthfulness and intelligibility of Christian faith. Here I have argued that traditional but transposed positions on the relationship of divine and human action and the missions of the Son and the Spirit in history provide an authentic, relatively adequate articulation of the horizon of the Christian interpreter of Christian Scripture at the level of our own time. In my articulations of divine creation, providence, and action and the work of the Triune God in the economy of God's creation, I have attempted to carry forward the advances present within premodern confessions of faith. But it is necessary to appropriate these confessions intelligently, and our own context requires us to give attention to questions that our forebears did not directly address.

The articulation of the structure of human nature and its dynamic openness to transcendence that I articulate in the next chapter provides further useful context for locating Christian Scripture. The universe that the Triune God speaks into being and enters into through the missions of the Son and the Holy Spirit is relatively but not comprehensively intelligible without recourse to special categories. With regard to advances in the hard sciences, few contemporary people doubt that it is not only possible but also desirable to ask questions, formulate hypotheses, and undertake investigations into the intelligibility and actuality of physical, chemical, biological, and neurological processes. Few also doubt the relevance of investigating the histories of such investigations and the histories of human social arrangements and cultures. The present account provides a heuristic for assessing the precise nature of the history that God enters into and is redeeming through the work of the Son and the Holy Spirit. Such an account can affirm the privileged status of Christian Scripture, as an instantiation of not only human cultural values, but a revelation of divine meaning, especially in and through its testimony to the meaning of Jesus Christ, the Son of God and Son of Man.

It is impossible for Christians to read Scripture in a theologically responsible and distinctively Christian way if we cannot recognize its location in the divine activity of the Triune God in the economy of creation and redemption. Christian tradition affirms that the Triune God is at work in the history that is, and in our own histories, through the production of Christian Scripture and Christian engagement with it, to bring about our increasing understanding of the intelligibility of God's work in the history that is, and to transform us for our more comprehensive participation in that work. We cannot read Scripture responsibly, however, if we are ignorant of its human dimensions and human contexts. We must therefore give attention to the dynamics of the subjectivity of the authors and communities of the production, dissemination, transmission, translation, and interpretation of Christian Scripture, and it is to that task that I now turn.

CHAPTER FOUR

The Location of Scripture II

Human Persons and Human Meaning in History

The mystery of Christ is ours also. What was accomplished in the
Head must be accomplished also in the members. Incarnation, death,
and resurrection: that is, taking root, detachment, and transfiguration.
No Christian spirituality is without this rhythm in triple time. We have to
make Christianity penetrate to the deepest human realities, but not let it
be lost or disfigured there. It must not be emptied of its spiritual substance.
It must act in the soul and in society as a leaven raising the whole dough;
it must supernaturalize all. It must put a new principle at the heart of
everything; it must make the exigency and urgency of the call from
above resound everywhere.

—Henri de Lubac, *Paradoxes of Faith*

Inasmuch as encounter with eminent texts enlightens, corrects, and refines,
perseverance in interpretation is the primary schooling of the interpreter.
—Ben F. Meyer, *Critical Realism and the New Testament*

The previous chapter provided the necessary doctrinal framework and
special categories of a systematic theology of the nature and purpose of
Scripture by offering an account of the economic supernatural work of

the Triune God. The present chapter bears the burden of laying out the requisite general categories for the theology of Scripture herein articulated. The ultimate end of human persons is our adoption as daughters and sons of God the Father and participation in the light of glory, which the Triune God will bring to fruition ultimately in the eschaton but which begins in our present experience through our reception of sanctifying grace and through our possession of the habit of charity. The Triune God has created us and holds us in being and, in response to our sinful rebelliousness, has entered into the human community through the incarnation and through the mission of the Holy Spirit to redeem us.

Who are we, though, as the subjects of this redemptive work? "What are human beings that you are mindful of them," the psalmist asks God, "mortals that you care for them?" (Ps 8.4). What is it about us that makes it possible for us to uniquely become "participants in the divine nature" (2 Pet 1.4)? In addition to the accounts of the relationship between divine and created freedom and of the economic work of the Triune God provided in the previous chapter, it is necessary to have an adequate philosophical and theological understanding of what human nature is that it can be transformed, how such transformation is possible, and what its effects are in us.

Contemporary theological anthropology would be impoverished if it did not draw on the distinctive theological achievements of Christian tradition. It must also, however, adequately appropriate key achievements in the understanding of human nature made in recent years. A contemporary philosophical and theological anthropology must therefore have a place for the new and the old. It is also necessary to draw on the resources and real achievements of philosophical anthropology. This is so because theology "has to speak both of the man that grace converts and of the world in which he lives."[1] "An account of man's salvation," Lonergan asserts, "cannot get along without an adequate understanding of man himself."[2] Our understandings of human nature and history—whether articulated or implicit—will have an obvious relevance in a systematic theology of Scripture. While Scripture both results from and serves as an instrument within the revelatory and saving action of the Triune God in history, it is no less "a human activity" for that fact.[3] It is therefore necessary to provide an account of what human beings are that they can serve as the conduits of divine activity in the production, redaction, dissemination, canonization, reading, exegesis, meditation upon, and study of Scripture.

In recent years a number of studies have appeared that draw attention to the premodern judgment, shared by many individuals across geographic and temporal differences, that Christian Scripture has a specific and unique purpose within the redemptive pedagogy of the Triune God.[4] These studies display the early Christian conviction that the Triune God has given Scripture to human persons and communities for the purpose of redeeming and elevating human persons through the transformation of their hearts and minds.[5] In the second chapter I gestured towards how Irenaeus, Origen, and Augustine expounded this judgment in various ways.[6] The present work holds that this judgment is a doctrinal axiom that should have a constitutive place in a systematic theology of Scripture and its interpretation.

Affirming the judgment that the Triune God gives Scripture to human persons as divine pedagogy for our transformation and that Scripture is useful for such work is one thing, however, and understanding that judgment in a reasonable, responsible, and faithfully Christian way at the level of our own time is another. An adequate contemporary understanding of the judgment *that* Scripture is useful for and plays a constitutive role in the transformative work that the Triune God does in believers and communities, to echo suggestions I have made elsewhere, will not and cannot be strictly identical to the understandings of any of our forebears. Our understanding of the judgment that Christian Scripture is divine pedagogy must, of course, have some relationship of continuity with the authentic advances in Christian understanding of the pedagogical function of Scripture that these premodern masters share. It must also, however, address the legitimate questions and appropriate authentic achievements of our own situation. I address the contours of the pedagogical nature of Scripture in chapter 6. Before that can take place, however, it is necessary to have an adequate understanding of what human persons actually are such that their transformation through engagement with Scripture is possible.

The exigencies of our contemporary situation and the need to draw on past Christian reflection on anthropology pose a number of significant problems for philosophical and theological reflection, however. A brief examination of some reflections on Scripture and anthropology by

Lewis Ayres and Krister Stendahl serves to highlight some of the problems, in particular, that arise in appropriating premodern perspectives on anthropology. It is also necessary to consider the most appropriate way to articulate a theological and philosophical anthropology today. Those brief detours will provide points of departure for the following constructive position on human nature. The constructive section of the chapter presents accounts respectively of the structure and normativity of authentic human subjectivity, the inescapable enmeshment of human subjects in culture and tradition mediated by language and other carriers of meaning, the possibility and actuality of human progress in self-transcendence, the historical effects of sin and bias upon human persons and human communities, and the characteristic features of the redemptive work of the Holy Spirit in human persons. That account of human nature and the position on the economic work of the Triune God from the previous chapter provide the requisite contexts for the concentrated examination of Christian Scripture itself in the next two chapters.

SCRIPTURE, ANTHROPOLOGY, AND DEIFICATION

Henri de Lubac unsurprisingly followed the premodern figures who were the subjects of his massive works in promoting a pedagogical understanding of the divine purpose of Scripture. "For de Lubac," Ayres summarizes, "the teaching of Scripture on all 'levels' exists to aid the restoration of the inner person, the soul, and learning to meditate on the scriptures (as far as is possible for each person) is one of the fundamental practices of the Christian life."[7] In a recent article, Ayres has suggested that many modern attempts to appropriate de Lubac's work on premodern exegesis as a resource for contemporary use and interpretation of Scripture have missed out on one of its key features. "De Lubac's understanding of Christian attention to the various senses [of Scripture] united under the label 'spiritual,'" Ayres argues, "depends on a robust notion of the soul, its transformation and purification."[8] Ayres's article demonstrates that De Lubac's work, and the traditions he seeks to represent, maintains the integrality of notions of the soul in premodern scriptural hermeneutics and exegesis.[9] Accordingly, then, Ayres argues, "if we are to make good use of the resources de Lubac offers, we must develop for ourselves something like the deep connections between a doctrine of the soul and an account of exegetical practice that we find in his writing."[10]

What would such a recovery entail? Ayres has provided a number of helpful guidelines, to which I will return. We must recognize, from the outset, however, that such a recovery of "a robust notion of the soul" would face significant difficulties in the contemporary intellectual environs of post-Enlightenment Christian theological reflection.[11] For one, as Ayres notes, the notions of the soul that aided Christian reflection on God's transformative work have long been forgotten. The anthropological "terms and distinctions" employed by the fathers, Ayres writes, are "now very deeply buried in the church's memory."[12] Recovery from our amnesia, though, is only one challenge that we face. Some have suggested that the Christian employment of Greek notions of anthropology represents a key feature in the declension narrative of the "Hellenization" of Christianity. Are not the patristic notions of the soul—those notions that are intrinsically connected to patristic exegetical praxis and reflection on soteriology—the "un-biblical" results of the Hellenization of the pure Hebraic gospel, just like the doctrinal developments of Nicaea, Chalcedon, and the subsequent ecumenical councils? Since I have already discussed the flaws of the Hellenization thesis, I will not revisit them in great detail at this juncture.[13] Even so, a couple of basic observations are in order. The presence of "Hellenistic" notions of anthropology in Jewish texts antecedent to and contemporaneous with the New Testament (see 2 Macc 6.20; 2 Enoch 23.5; Test Job 20.3) undermines the hypothesis that an extraneous Greek influence seeped into and corrupted the faith of the New Testament communities. Hellenistic influence on notions of the nature and purpose of human persons is also present in the earliest Christian texts that would become the New Testament (see Matt 16.26; Jas 1.21, 5.20; 1 Pet 1.22; and most famously 1 Thess 5.23).[14] "The earliest Christian traditions," Ayres writes, "were already familiar with a notion of soul as the inner spiritual core of the human being and gradually adopted and adapted themes from a wide variety of possibilities to shape their own argument about how best to speak of the soul, given their particular theological concerns."[15]

Ayres helpfully draws attention to the fact that early Christian adoption and adaptation of extra-Christian Greek notions of the soul was not a monolithic or unidirectional historical process. An adequate historical narration of the Christian appropriation of language of the soul would be exceedingly complex.[16] Specialists in historical theology have discerned and drawn attention to the influence of Platonic, Neoplatonic, Stoic, and Aristotelian philosophical psychologies in the thought of specific church fathers; each father adopted and adapted various useful elements of the philosophies of his day, in conjunction with intensive study of Scripture, in order to offer an account of how human participation in the divine work of redemption and transformation takes place.[17] The church fathers employed the resources of their philosophical contexts, "plundering the Egyptians," in order to offer explanations of the terms they found in Scripture.[18] They used various Greek accounts of the capacities and features of human persons as means of explaining the contours of the divine work wrought by the indwelling Trinity in human persons.

The very historicity of such understandings of the soul represents another major obstacle to the task of recovering an adequate notion of the soul for the renewal of theological engagement with Scripture. Adverting to the diversity of historical notions of the soul raises an inescapable question: *which* particular notion of the soul should we choose?[19] Should we aim at articulating only a "biblical anthropology," restricted to drawing from the texts of Scripture, or can antecedent and subsequent philosophical and theological reflection on human nature provide resources for our purposes? Even if we accepted as our foundation, for instance, the "tripartite anthropology" of 1 Thessalonians 5.23—that humans are body, soul, and spirit—the apostle Paul offers us precious little further reflection on what such "parts" are, what their functions are, and how they are related.[20] Whose thought should fill in the gaps? That of Plato? Aristotle? The Stoics? Augustine? Aquinas? Descartes? Freud? All of the above? None of the above?

An illustration from one of the great developments in New Testament studies during the twentieth century will serve to sharpen the problem we face. In his famous article "The Apostle Paul and the Introspective Consciousness of the West," Krister Stendahl identifies the anachronism inherent in the judgment that the great reformer Martin Luther's notion of conscience adequately reflects Paul's understanding of conscience in Romans and elsewhere in the apostle's writings.[21] The question Luther brought to the text of Romans—"How can I discover a merciful God?"—was not

Paul's question. Stendahl suggests that the history of Christian reflection on conscience and human interiority moved farther and farther away from Paul's focus in that first-century epistle.[22] The apostle who actually wrote that famous letter, according to Stendahl, was not concerned with assuaging his guilty conscience. Paul did not undertake an articulation of a normative account of internal human consciousness and conscience prior to, during, and subsequent to Christian conversion.[23] In his article Stendahl shows how Paul actually sought to articulate an adequate understanding of the purpose of the Torah after the coming of the Messiah and of the ramifications of the coming of the Messiah for Jewish-Gentile relations in the new-covenant community.[24]

Paul, then, does not give us Augustine's notions of interiority and introspection; he certainly does not give us Luther's.[25] Stendahl cautions that we must avoid anachronism as much as possible in our assessments of Paul's understanding of consciousness and anthropology. Stendahl's article has played an important role in the development of the "New Perspective on Paul," which has undoubtedly enriched our understanding of the Christian faith of the first century by directing scholars more and more to the realities of Jewish thought and practice of Jesus, the disciples, and Paul himself in their contexts in the varieties of Second Temple Jewish faith and praxis.[26]

To reiterate what I have stated elsewhere, concepts and words have dates. Paul's own notion of "conscience" in Romans is no exception. It would be irresponsible to force or impose Reformation-era, modern, or postmodern notions of human consciousness and conscience onto Paul or any other premodern figure who discusses human nature and human interiority.[27] The recognition of the historicity of human understanding and speech requires that we give due attention to the historical nestedness of the discourse of authors in their actual historical contexts to the extent that such investigation is possible and to the best of our abilities. Stendahl's caution against anachronism and Ayres's insistence on the need to recover historical notions of the soul for an adequate theology of scriptural interpretation seem to be in tension with one another. The challenge we face today is that of articulating a Christian notion of the human person that is grounded in the tradition of Christian reflection but that simultaneously has a place for more recent advances in human understanding of the constitution of human nature. We must undertake this task without engaging in irresponsible anachronism or archaism.[28] The exigency of providing an adequate account of what is distinctive of human nature today cannot be met responsibly by appropriating whole cloth any one particular historical notion of the soul, including those adopted and adapted by the early church from Stoic, Platonic, middle Platonic, Aristotelian, or any other philosophical source.

We need not start completely from scratch, however. Despite the clear differences between the notions of the soul developed in these discernibly different philosophical traditions, each represents a relatively attentive, intelligent, reasonable, and responsible attempt to understand, conceptualize, distinguish, identify, and relate the constitutive dimensions of human nature. Each approach presents different hypotheses about the experiences of consciousness, knowledge, and desire and the possibility of epistemological, moral, and even spiritual self-transcendence beyond bodily sensation.[29] Such historical philosophical perspectives have in common the fact that they are the linguistic and conceptual products devised by specific individuals and communities at specific times and places, to mediate understandings and judgments about the intelligible structures constitutive of humans qua human.[30] The various notions of human persons developed with the Western philosophical tradition have at their genesis varieties of the same questions: What is a human person? What is distinctive about human persons that makes them persons? What are the ends for which human persons exist? How are such ends ordered? Those same questions confront us today, and they are the questions that the current account attempts to answer in a modest way.[31]

Cases could be made, no doubt, for the relative merits of each distinctive notion of the soul developed in Christian history. Each notion undoubtedly deserves to be studied in its own right as a key moment in the development of the Western philosophical tradition. Beyond their intrinsic historical interest, however, such notions of human personhood, through their historical strangeness and the relative authenticity of their purveyors, can aptly serve to highlight significant deficiencies in more recent notions of human personhood. Ayres, for instance, highlights the fact that de Lubac's understanding of the soul opposes modern immanentist notions of human persons that would deny that we have an intrinsic orientation towards a transcendent cause.[32] Our need today is for an articulation of the intelligibility of human nature that maintains the advances of understanding in historical philosophical and theological anthropologies and simultaneously addresses the pressing questions about the historical locatedness and cultural diversity of humanity that have arisen in recent years in an adequate way. We face the task of *ressourcement* and *aggiornamento*; we must both recover and update.

Before we can update we must first pursue an answer to the question of what it is that was going forward in Christian utilization of notions of the soul. We must identify and appropriate the key achievements of premodern Christian anthropologies. If we do not draw on the real achievements of this tradition of reflection, our work will lack sufficient grounding as a "Christian" anthropology. We are faced, however, not with a simple task of recovery but instead with the task of responsibly adjudicating the authentic developments in Christian anthropology and expressing them in a way that is adequate to both traditional Christian affirmations about the reality of the human person and its end in God and which simultaneously affirms and appropriates the authentic achievements reached through contemporary discoveries about human nature and culture.[33]

As indicated above, Christians not only participated in and drew from the ongoing reflection on the nature of the soul in Greek philosophical circles; they also decisively adapted the philosophical perspectives they encountered for their own specific theological purposes.[34] Christian thinkers marshaled philosophical notions of the soul to give an account of the intelligible processes whereby human persons could undergo the kind of transformations of desiring, understanding, and willing entailed in Christian discipleship. Ayres has summarized a number of key presuppositions of the premodern theologians that he thinks must be recovered in order for us to profit from our engagement with these earlier perspectives. For these premodern figures, the soul was a constitutive element of the human person, as was the body. The soul's life, Ayres argues, was "inherently mediatorial and poetic."[35] Ayres continues:

> The soul is that in us which lies at the core of our status as *imago Dei*. The soul is the seat of our activities of attention, imagination, judgement and contemplation. The soul's activity constitutes the fundamental desire in and with which we image the divine life of rational, creative and productive love. . . . [The soul is] the spiritual core of

human existence, enabling the human being's dual-focus attention. The soul should both attend to and through the creation and simultaneously do so as it attends to the divine informing light. In other words, true human temporal and material existence is rendered possible *because* we may, as embodied soul, image in time God's own care and love. Thus the character of human desire and the process of imagination (understood as an activity interwoven with the character of human desire) are inseparable from the fundamental orientation or attention of the soul.[36]

Such a summary statement, of course, cannot be found in any historically extant articulation of the soul in patristic reflection. It represents a distillation of key judgments that would inform, for Ayres, for de Lubac, and for those who would affirm their own work of *ressourcement*, a contemporary articulation of some necessary theological and philosophical components of a Christian anthropology.[37] It presents a set of specific judgments that will be elements of any adequate account of the work of the Triune God in human persons. Any such understanding, however, will necessarily take us beyond the implicit and unthematized and even explicit understandings of the human person in Scripture or even in the works of the fathers.

In general, the premodern achievements that a contemporary account of the soul must recover in order to be faithfully Christian can be organized relative to two key judgments. First, a contemporary theological anthropology would affirm that humans have as their supernatural telos the beatific vision.[38] "For now we see in a mirror, dimly," the apostle Paul writes, "but then we will see face to face" (1 Cor 13.12). Contrary to modern positions on human nature that hold that human individuals are autonomous and completely self-constituting, premodern Christians held that human persons had received their specific ends from God; humans do not therefore establish their own *telē*.[39]

Given the qualitative ontological distinction between created and uncreated natures expounded in the previous chapter, we face a significant paradox. Though through the transforming work of the Triune God in us we become "participants in the divine nature" (2 Pet 1.4), such transformation does not *replace* our created nature with divine nature; we *par-*

ticipate in the divine nature in a new way that heals and elevates our created nature. Given that God's nature is infinite, the transformation we experience through sharing in that nature will be interminable in our earthly lives.[40] Human terrestrial development, then, takes place in an inherently "anagogic context."[41] We are always on the way "upward" towards our final resting place in the bosom of the Trinity. Aside from affirming that we are wayfarers constantly changing, this judgment entails concomitant commitments to humility and openness to correction and further development in our understandings and judgments about the Triune God, ourselves, and the world in which we live. Our understandings of the work of the Triune God in us and in the world are thus inescapably conditioned by our createdness and its attendant finitude and fallibility. We must also take care to recognize our propensity for sin and to be on guard against our individual and group egoism and our willful rejection of the good. While true judgments and faithful praxis are possible through our reception of grace and while our end is certain, such admissions do not permit moral or intellectual laxity.

The second key premodern achievement to be recovered is the judgment that humans have distinct, identifiable characteristics, capacities, and abilities that are the means of our transformation on the way to the beatific vision. These characteristics, capacities, and abilities set the conditions under which our transformation is possible. While some earlier accounts of human nature differentiated these features under metaphysical rubrics, the present account attempts to ground even those metaphysical achievements in the intelligibility of the actual performance of self-transcendence that those metaphysics or other conceptualities depend upon and reflect. Lucid perception, relatively and possibly adequate understanding, true yet conditioned judgment, responsible moral decision, and rightly ordered desire are possible—though seemingly rare—in this life. Given our terrestrial status *in via*, however, we can expect that our experiences, understandings, judgments, decisions, and desires will perpetually admit of modification. Because we still "see through a mirror dimly," we are continually subject to the transformative work of the Triune God in this life. The following account of human nature assumes that human persons and communities have their final telos in a unique relationship to the Triune God, made possible by God's conferral of grace upon us and by God's demonstration of the exigencies of such a relationship in Jesus Christ. It also assumes that what have been labeled the properties of our soul, that is, our intellectual, appetitive, and volitional capacities, are the means through which such a relationship, through which our growth, is possible.

The question remains as to how best to articulate a contemporary theological and philosophical anthropology. It is possible to start from a classic position and then proceed to update it, but such work would require significant exegetical labors. We would also risk committing great anachronisms or archaisms if we appropriated any particular premodern account of the soul whole cloth. How, then, should we proceed? While it would be inadequate to promote the psychology of Aristotle as a contemporary theology and philosophy of the soul, a brief examination of Aristotle's articulation of the nature of the soul in *De anima* allows us to contextualize the constructive account of the soul employed in the present work.[42] Aristotle's methodological approach to human nature, while it cannot stand as the foundation for a contemporary account of human nature, nevertheless provides a helpful point of comparison for the subsequent attempt to articulate what is distinctive in human nature.[43]

After commenting on the value of knowledge of the human soul, proposing a framework for its examination, and examining the perspectives of his predecessors in book 1 of *De anima*, Aristotle proposes his famous metaphysical definition of the soul in book 2: "The soul may . . . be defined as the first actuality of a natural body potentially possessing life; and such will be any body which possesses organs" (412a28–412b1).[44] Aristotle proposes this as an *omni et soli*, abstract definition; he intends to determine as precisely as possible that which distinctively characterizes living things independent of specific concrete plants, animals, or human persons.[45] It is significant that the key terms of the definition—"actuality" (*entelecheia*), "natural" (*physikou*), "body" (*sōmatos*), and "life" (*zētein*), respectively—already have precise technical meanings in Aristotle's metaphysics.[46] Aristotle maintains this metaphysical idiom through the remainder of the work, and I discuss its significance at greater length below. In books 2 and 3 Aristotle famously analyzes and distinguishes the nutritive (*threptikon*), sensitive (*aesthetikon*), and rational (*dianoētikon*) powers or faculties (*dynameis*) of living things. The nutritive power names the capacity of living things to eat, grow, and reproduce. The sensitive power names the capacity of living things to touch, taste, smell, see, and/or hear and the accompanying capacities for "desire, inclination, and wish" (414b2–3). It is also closely tied to the sensitive power of locomotion. Finally, the rational power names the distinctively human capacities for understanding, reflection, imagination, and deliberation. Aristotle indicates that living things can have either one, two, or three of these powers in conjunction. Plant life possesses only the nutritive power, whereas animals possess both the nutritive and sensitive powers. Humans, finally, and all other superior beings, possess all three in conjunction. Each set of "lower" powers is required for the actuality of the respective "higher" powers (414a29–414b19). The differentiation of lower and higher powers provides Aristotle with a technical apparatus for clearly distinguishing humans from other animals.

After treating the five senses in book 2.5–book 3.2, Aristotle concludes by providing an account of the various rational capacities possessed by humans and their interrelated relations in book 3.3–3.13. It is this final book in which he explains, among other things, the relation between sense and thought (427a18–427b28), the nature of the imagination relative to the senses (427b29–428b10), the possibility of error in thought (428b11–429a9), the distinction between sensation and thought (429a10–429b22), the activity and passivity of the mind (430a10–430a25), the practical intellect (431a1–431b19), appetite, the mind, and locomotion (432a15–434a22), and finally the dependence of sensation and thought upon nutrition and growth (434a23–435a10).

Throughout the work Aristotle operates with the distinctive notion of science that he articulates in his *Posterior Analytics*. There he proposed that science or understanding (*epistēmē*) occurs when "we believe that we know (i) that the cause from which the fact results is the cause of that fact, and (ii) that the fact cannot be otherwise" (*An. post.* 1.2, 71b 10–12).[47] For Aristotle, then, true or real knowledge "consists in the conclusions that follow necessarily from self-evident, necessary principles."[48] Within the constraints of his notion of scientific understanding, Aristotle's metaphysical account of the soul in *On the Soul* is an immense achievement.[49] Alongside his differentiation of the applications of the powers of the rational soul in habits in the *Nicomachean Ethics*, Aristotle was able to construct an eminently useful theoretical apparatus for naming and relating the distinctive powers characteristic of human beings in their social, political, and cultural contexts.

The Aristotelian scientific ideal of necessary knowledge of first principles, however, sharply contrasts with what modern science proposes as the goal of scientific investigation. Modern scientific investigation proceeds and advances on the basis of the usefulness of its empirical canons for producing a succession of possibly relevant and, in the end, actually verified hypotheses concerning the intelligibility of the given data of the world.[50] In this different methodological context, Aristotle's account could stand only as one possibly relevant hypothesis regarding the intelligibility of human nature. The metaphysical nature of his account harbors significant problems as well. The precision and rigor of mathematics and logic perhaps bewitched Aristotle with an overly abstract and objective epistemological ideal.[51] De anima reflects this ideal in its treatment of life. In this work, Lonergan comments, "Aristotle employed one and the same method for the study of plants, animals, and men. One was to know acts by their objects, habits by acts, potencies by habits, and the essences of souls by their potencies."[52] In such an approach, "the road to science and to philosophy is not straight and narrow but broad and easy."[53]

Lonergan offers a helpful analysis of the potential shortcomings inherent in such a metaphysical account.

> Human nature was studied extensively in a metaphysical psychology, in an enormous and subtle catalogue of virtues and vices, in its native capacities and proneness to evil, in the laws natural, divine, and human to which it was subject, in the great things it could accomplish by God's grace. But such study was not part of some ongoing process; everything essential had been said long ago; the only urgent task was to find the telling mode of expression and illustration that would communicate to the uneducated of today the wisdom of the great men of the past. As the study of man was static, so, too, man was conceived in static fashion. There was no notion that man had existed on earth for hundreds of thousands of years; or that there had been, and still was going forward, an ascent from crude primitive cultures, through the ancient high civilizations, to the effective emergence of critical intelligence in the first millennium B.C., and to the triumph of scientific intelligence in the last few centuries.[54]

The ideal of necessity arguably kept Aristotle, and all of his lesser and greater heirs, from attempting a science of the accidentals of historical change, and so, by extension, from adequately acknowledging the historical locatedness of all human understandings and judgments.[55] By abstracting from the particularity of individual human persons to get to the "core" reality of human nature, Aristotle's abstract metaphysical approach has a built-in predisposition against attending to and understanding human nature with reference to its concrete changes in the processes of human maturation. The abstraction built into Aristotle's approach could not easily accommodate the possibility that humanity's understanding of itself and of the world could develop and advance.[56] Aristotle's own presentation, then, represents a hypothesis about human nature that, despite its explanatory power, could bewitch us away from recognizing the contingency of its own status as an achievement of a concrete—and brilliant—human person who lived in a drastically different social and cultural situation than the present. The understanding of human nature in the present account must be open to the fact that despite the constants of human nature, human understanding of that nature is not static but is ongoing.[57] While we should take care not to shirk the achievements of metaphysical systems, such systems (1) are potentially misleading in their rigorous abstraction and distance from the concrete and (2) require technical idioms no longer easily understood by contemporary theologians and philosophers, let alone laypeople. These judgments do not automatically suggest that it would be better to do "theology without metaphysics," as Kevin Hector has recently argued.[58] The present approach to human nature is no less hypothetical than Aristotle's account of the structured constituents of human nature, and it includes an implicit metaphysics, but in what follows I attempt to stay closer to concrete human experience than is easily possible within a developed metaphysical idiom.[59] It must be evaluated not on the basis of its metaphysical sophistication but instead on its adequacy to the data of sense and consciousness.

It is necessary to appropriate the advances represented by the tradition of theological reflection on the nature of the human person, but in each case of theological reflection, the one theologizing adopted, adapted, or, in rare cases, proposed a remarkably creative new philosophical psychology towards the end of understanding precisely what it is that human persons are. Such achievements, however, are only relatively adequate.

The relative adequacy of each philosophical apparatus depends upon its instrumental value for communicating or conveying the actual intelligibility of the constitution of human persons in their actual concrete capacities, abilities, operations, and processes of growth. Metaphysical accounts of human life such as Aristotle's, or any other premodern philosopher's or theologian's no doubt, have immense heuristic value for advancing our understanding of human nature in the concrete. But the present account holds, with Lonergan, that an adequate contemporary approach to human nature would "without repudiating the analysis of humanity into body and soul . . . [add] the richer and more concrete apprehension of the person as incarnate subject."[60]

The reader will not be surprised to discover that the following constructive position on human nature draws extensively on the work of Bernard Lonergan. Even so, in what follows I am not attempting to present an exegesis of Lonergan's notion of human nature. As Lonergan's major works, *Insight* and *Method in Theology,* demonstrate, his own understanding of human nature developed significantly later in his career. I leave the task of detailing Lonergan's personal development in his understandings of human nature, with its intrinsic interest, to historians of Lonergan's work.[61] My debt to Lonergan's work will be obvious in what follows, but I draw significantly on other resources as well. I have attempted to offer the following position on human nature in conversation with other key figures and emphases. My intention, then, is not exegetical but constructive; what follows represents a hypothetical position on human nature.

Earlier I indicated that historical presentations of human nature resulted from the wonder, questions, insights, and judgments of specific individuals and communities in specific times and places. The following account of human nature takes its primary point of departure from one specific question: What is it in human persons as such that allows us to investigate, understand, and conceptualize human nature, to recognize and understand the difference between earlier and later historical philosophical notions of the human person, and to propose possible genetic or dialectical relationships between concepts or notions of human nature? The very fact that we can recognize and categorize diachronic differences and developments in notions of human nature poses a new question that an adequate notion of the human person must answer. Whatever the constants of human nature are, such constants have paradoxically founded the possibility of change and development in human understanding and human culture. Such constants allow us to raise questions concerning diachronic developments in the notion of human nature; such constants allow us to recognize, identify, and hypothesize about such developments.

These possibilities result from our intrinsic ability to transcend the boundaries of our limited horizons of interest and to grow in our understandings and judgments about ourselves, the worlds in which we live, and the cultural achievements of humanity. Concrete human persons, concrete societies, and concrete cultures are obviously not identical across temporal and spatial differences. Yet something is shared in the human persons who have participated in and created these cultures across time and space that is the condition allowing for the emergence of such differences and such change. Some set of capacities and/or attainable habits allows us to recognize the differences of perspectives of our forebears. Even though we cannot do so definitively, given the nature of the evidence, we can nevertheless make probabilistic judgments about the relationships between earlier perspectives and our own. The immense historical problem and the tasks it entails of identifying, cataloging, and communicating all of those monumental changes is not my present concern, however. Instead, I want to seek out what it is within us that makes such investigation possible. Those self-transcending capabilities and capacities, after all, are the means through which the human authors and transmitters of Scripture were able to produce and pass on Scripture; they are the means through which we are able to engage, understand, and be transformed by those texts.

HUMAN PERSONS I: HUMAN NATURE, CONSCIOUSNESS, AND SELF-TRANSCENDENCE

Aristotle's account of human nature emphasizes the rationality of human animals as *the* distinctive characteristic of human nature. The human capacity for reason and rationality, however, is only one key feature or characteristic of human persons. Our capacities for reason and refined knowledge about reality identify one multifaceted dimension of something more basic and constitutive of our natures: human persons are fundamentally self-transcending animals. The present account maintains the hypothesis that an investigation of this self-transcendence in its dynamic unfolding in our incarnate subjectivity can provide resources for an adequate and comprehensive account of human nature that can both affirm the achievements of premodern accounts of the soul and meet the needs of our contemporary situation with regard to the historical locatedness of human understanding and meaning making.[62] Giving adequate attention to the human capacities for self-transcendence will allow us to identify that which is distinctive of human nature and which is shared by human persons irrespective of their specific times and places.

We reach the apex of human self-transcendence—qua human, at least, in taking responsibility for who we will be at the level of rational self-consciousness when we decide for ourselves what we will make of ourselves.[63] But we are not only responsible; we are also rational, intelligent, and sensate. These other dimensions of our nature, or to borrow a metaphor from Lonergan, "levels of consciousness," will require our attention before we can discuss responsible self-possession.[64] Beyond our natural operations at the conscious levels of experience, understanding, judgment, and decision, the supernatural redemptive and elevating work of the Triune God in us takes us beyond what is natural to us as human persons. The love of God floods our hearts (Rom 5.5) and decisively heals and re-orders our sensation, intelligence, reason, and responsible self-possession.[65] The Triune God meets, heals, and fulfills the "anagogic" reach characteristic of human persons and takes our self-transcendence beyond our immanent capacities.

I discuss this supernatural self-transcendence and its features and exigencies below. For now I focus on the dimensions of self-transcendence that are natural to us as human persons. Before offering the following account of human nature, I must remind my readers why such an account is relevant in a systematic theology of Christian Scripture. While Christians affirm that the texts of Scripture result from and facilitate the divine work of the Triune God in history, as I have already noted, they are no less a product of human action for that fact. As a human work, the biblical text is a product of human self-transcendence in history. The historical development of languages provides evidence of human self-transcendence in history; the extant writings of ancient peoples exhibit this key dimension of human nature. Beyond its resulting from concrete self-transcending human persons, written communication has served as an instrument that helps facilitate such self-transcendence in its subsequent readers and hearers. "To learn to read . . . ," writes Jean-Louis Chrétien, "teaches us also to read ourselves, to decipher ourselves as we decipher, according to a perspective that wasn't ours to begin with. . . . Readers are themselves read by the books they read."[66] Scripture—as written in human language by human persons—is not exempt from this general rule; moreover, its status as a conduit of divine teaching within Christian faith and praxis suggests its supernatural aptitude for facilitating such self-knowledge. I will have regular occasion to return to the ways in which Scripture reflects and facilitates such self-transcendence below and especially in chapter 6.[67]

Instead of articulating a notion of human nature by employing a metaphysical set of first principles, the present account of human nature attempts to name and relate the actual concrete operations of incarnate human subjects through which we achieve self-transcendence.[68] What follows, then, represents a nonreductive explanation of the phenomena—or, to use a technical term nontechnically, a phenomenology—of human consciousness and action. This is, of course, not the only way to go about examining human nature. I invite the reader to fulfill the Socratic imperative, inscribed on the portals of the temple to Apollo, "know thyself" (gnōthi seuton), by considering whether the understanding of human nature herein articulated adequately reflects her or his own experiences of self-transcendence through consciousness, sensation, cognition, emotion, decision, and action. The following account necessarily remains hypothetical, but I hope that it is more than that. I invite readers to identify its oversights and contribute their own corrective and complementary insights to the account.

Concretely, human persons characteristically see, hear, touch, taste, smell, wonder, inquire, imagine, understand, conceive, formulate, believe, reflect, marshal and weigh evidence, judge, deliberate, decide, evaluate, act, speak, listen, write, and read, among many other transitive actions.[69] All recorded reflection on human nature in the theological and philosophical positions of the past resulted from actual theologians, philosophers, and communities engaged in these operations. Aristotle's account of the nature of the soul, to cite a specific example, was the product that resulted from Aristotle undergoing a number of these operations in succession. Aristotle's *De anima* represents his attempts to communicate his understandings and judgments concerning his own sensory experiences and his understandings of his own insights and judgments and the expressed insights and judgments of his forebears. The understandings and judgments of Aristotle came at the end of a long discursive process that began in his own wonder and in his conviction of the value of such an undertaking.[70] We could ask and attempt to answer a number of fascinating different questions about Aristotle's life and times that allowed him to undergo the various operations that he did that made his particular achievement possible. Having adequate answers to those questions would require us to undertake a number of the operations so named. Ultimately, however, the present goal is not to explore Aristotle's development or achievement—or Aquinas's or Lonergan's, for that matter—but rather to develop some account of the notion of human nature that adequately takes account of the recent development of historical mindedness but also provides a means of grasping what human persons are that the Triune God can affect their transformation through their engagement with Scripture.

I take the risk of assuming that my readers have experienced some, if not all, of the abovementioned concrete operations. That assumption stands at the beginning of the following constructive position on human nature. Now again, it is one thing to name these various operations and another to understand them, still another to adequately relate them together. An investigation and objectification of these various operations will provide a means of naming human nature and identifying its norms and exigencies. Some of the operations, however, provide us with unique and significant challenges. While it is possible to observe many of the operations in others, the operations involved in experiencing our conscious operations, that is, actual experiences of understanding, judging, and deciding, because of their "internal" character, "inside" our minds, present specific problems.[71] It is not possible to directly "see" any of them in other persons. We can, however, through introspection of our own consciousness, attend to, understand, make correct judgments about, and take responsibility for our internal operations of consciousness.[72] The word *introspection*, however, is potentially misleading. It is not possible to take an "inner look," inside of one's mind.[73] Instead of thinking of introspection as an inner look, I understand it, with Lonergan, as designating "the process of objectifying the contents of consciousness."[74] Objectification, as stated above, is the utilization of the conventions of language—technical terms and relations—to attempt to identify and interrelate extralinguistic realities in an explanatory way. Doing so is a matter of great difficulty, but it is a worthy endeavor.[75] Carefully considering the functions, purposes, and relations of these operations can provide a means of understanding the constitution of concrete human persons that readers can verify or falsify not on the basis of accepting a metaphysical paradigm but instead on the basis of its adequacy to their own experience, understanding, and practice of these operations. Examining these operations will provide a means for heightening our awareness of what we are already always doing, gaining new purchase into how knowledge of anything—whether of the Triune God, of ourselves, or of Scripture—makes its "bloody entrance" into our lives.[76]

The operations distinguished above do not take place in a totally haphazard manner; they are interrelated, successive, recurrent, and cumulative. When fully awake, adult human persons are typically characterized by their practice of these interrelated and successive operations.[77] The operations unfold on four distinct levels of consciousness.

> There is the *empirical* level on which we sense, perceive, imagine, feel, speak, move. There is an *intellectual* level on which we inquire, come to understand, express what we have understood, work out the presuppositions and implications of our expression. There is the *rational* level on which we reflect, marshal the evidence, pass judgment on the truth or falsity, certainty or probability, of a statement. There is the *responsible* level on which we are concerned with ourselves, our own operations, our goals, and so deliberate about possible courses of action, evaluate them, decide, and carry out our decisions.[78]

Each successive level has its own exigencies and norms and each entails a greater degree of self-transcendence than the former. Adult human persons constantly operate at these levels to engage our physical, social, and cultural environs.[79] Each level characteristically includes a number of specific operations—the concrete operations named above, among others—which intend distinct objects. Despite their differences, the levels of experience, understanding, judgment, and decision "are united by the unfolding of a single transcendental intending of plural, interchangeable objectives."[80] The levels are dually transcendental.[81] They are transcendental first in the sense that they are the a priori means by which our free engagement with the universe of proportionate being, or creation, is possible.[82] They set the conditions of our successful navigation of reality that is other than us. Through meeting the exigencies of each level we come to reach and grasp what is actually other than us. They are also transcendental in the sense that operations at each level intend the respective scholastic transcendentals of being (*ens*), unity (*unum*), the true (*verum*), and the good (*bonum*).[83] The scholastic transcendentals, of course, are convertible; they are isomorphic with the levels of consciousness—of raw existence, intelligibility, actuality, and goodness.[84] From the subjective side of things, we engage proportionate being at each respective level through different but complementary operations and questions. "The many operations come together and cumulatively regard a single identical object," writes Lonergan, "so that what is experienced is to be understood, what is understood is to be affirmed, what is affirmed is to be evaluated."[85] Each level—experience, understanding, judgment, and decision—possesses its own subjective exigencies, so mature human engagement with the world requires distinctive virtues at each level.

Before I can articulate the distinctive levels of human consciousness at which we engage the world, however, it is important to acknowledge the physical and biochemical basis of our consciousness. Human consciousness, as scientific investigation has shown, depends upon the proper and recurrent operation of a number of finely tuned biochemical and neural manifolds. Disruption of these manifolds by physical injury, disease, or the deterioration of old age can have significant impacts upon our capacities for sensation, understanding, memory, speech, and countless other characteristic human actions.[86] Even so, the distinct operations of consciousness, and the distinct levels of consciousness especially, cannot be exhaustively understood by explaining or describing the intelligible relationships of their underlying physical, chemical, and biological manifolds.[87] Recent developments in medical scanning technology have—quite amazingly— offered a means of "locating" emotions, recalled memories, and the processes of understanding, judgment, and decision as they light up in specific neural pathways in the brain, but our ability to map such experiences in their biological and neural manifolds does not provide an exhaustive explanation of consciousness. Consciousness has its own emergent intelligibilities that depend upon but cannot be reduced to such biochemical and neurological manifolds.[88] Consciousness is certainly related to our intelligibilities as sensing, living, functioning embodied beings; but consciousness has its own emergent intelligible structures beyond what behavioral psychologists, biologists, chemists, and physicists can tell us about what human beings are. The following account of human self-transcendence is an attempt to precisely name and relate those structures of consciousness that are the emergent concrete processes and operations constitutive of human nature in its fullest reach. I also assume that the emergence of such conscious operations can only take place concretely for any individual in community. As Alasdair McIntyre has helpfully put it, we are "dependent rational animals."[89] The emergence and sustenance of the levels of conscious self-transcendence enumerated and explained below, whether intellectual or moral, depend upon both the soundness of our embodied health and our participation in relatively nurturing human communities.[90]

Our ability to engage our environment through sensation takes place at the first level of consciousness. When we are awake, our senses make that which is sensed present to us. Through this sensitive experience we engage the world that is intrinsically other than us and so transcend ourselves in a basic sense. What is seen is present to us in the act of seeing, what is smelled is present in the act of smelling, what is heard is present in the act of hearing, and so on. When we are biologically and psychologically in good health, our senses operate with remarkable facility and fluidity. We need only open our eyes or turn our head to see what is within our physical horizon. We need only adequate proximity to the laptop computer to reach out and feel the keys of the keyboard or the heat emanating from the power apparatus. We smell the coffee on the desk, and taste its flavor notes and feel its heat as we drink it. We hear the noises of pages turning and papers shuffling as other library patrons go about their work. We see the black marks on the page or screen. Our conscious experience is not an operation but is instead the flow of waking consciousness itself that inundates us from the moment we awaken until we sleep at night.

Out of this continuous flow, it is possible for us to distinguish between the act of sensation and its content or objects. Waking consciousness has both sensory and cognitional content.[91] The objects of our sensation include the data in the immediacy of our surroundings—what we can see, hear, smell, touch, and taste—and those that we can "picture" or operate upon imaginatively through mediation—that is, spatially distant, temporally absent, or modally imagined objects mediated in our consciousness through language, symbol, and other imaginative expressive media. The unique human ability to engage mediated objects is not completely automatic; it comes about only through the process of adaptation and assimilation that human persons characteristically experience in the transition from infancy (*in fans*—"without speech") to the world of adulthood.[92] Adult human persons live in world(s) "mediated by meaning and motivated by value."[93] I will have more to say about that process of human learning and growth and the adult human world "mediated by meaning and motivated by value" below.

Human self-transcendence at the empirical level results from our attentiveness to what our senses make automatically present to us in our acts of sensation. Human persons share our capacity for sensation, and the fivefold array of sensory powers, with many other living things. In fact, a number of animals have sensory capacities that outstrip our own in both scope and precision. Even so, those animals are not reading these words and cannot read these words. As Ormerod and Crysdale put it, "Only humans can ponder our own heritage."[94] Human self-transcendence extends beyond the boundaries of sensation in our capacities for intelligent questioning and insight, rational reflection and judgment, and moral deliberation and decision. This effort to understand, and the possibility and criterion of success in understanding, represents the next level of consciousness that is constitutive of human nature.

"Our consciousness expands in a new dimension," Lonergan writes, "when from mere experience we turn to the effort to understand what we have experienced."[95] Beyond our mere seeing, hearing, smelling, tasting, and touching, humans wonder, ponder, inquire, and seek. Beyond gaping slack-jawed at that which our nervous system and sensory apparatus make—seemingly automatically—present to us merely through our waking, we focus our attention on objects both within our immediate physical horizon of experience and outside of our physical horizon that language, symbol, and other carriers of meaning mediate to us.[96] Beyond our immediate horizon of sensation, we also engage the interests and knowledge of the fuller horizons of human meaning making that are the products of human history:

> As our field of vision, so too the range of our interests and the scope of our knowledge are bounded. As fields of vision vary with one's standpoint, so too the range of one's interests and the scope of one's knowledge vary with the period in which one lives, with one's social background and milieu, with one's education and personal development. In this fashion, there has arisen a metaphorical or analogous meaning of the word 'horizon.' In this sense, what lies beyond one's horizon is simply outside the range of one's interests and knowledge: one knows nothing about it and one cares less. And what lies within one's horizon is in some measure, great or small, an object of interest and of knowledge.[97]

Our capacity for wonder and questioning is an exceptional aspect of the constitution of human nature. While sensitive self-transcendence allows animals to dwell in a habitat, "we live within a universe, because beyond sensitivity we question, and our questioning is unrestricted."[98] Anyone who has spent extensive time with children has heard the persistent question, Why?, and so knows something of the unrestrictedness of human questioning. The primary interrogatives—Who? What? When? Where? Why? How? How often?—spill out of us spontaneously and draw us out beyond our immediate physical horizon bounded by how far we can see and explore into the much broader human worlds "mediated by meaning and motivated by value."[99] The persistence of our identities through temporal distention allows us to raise questions of development, process, and frequency. We can notice and ponder the reality of change in our world and even in ourselves. The human imagination allows us to raise questions not only about what is the case but also about what is possible and impossible, or what is the case but could be otherwise. Even as infants, though, before we could formulate our questions in spoken and written word, we wondered and learned and grasped the intelligibility of our experienced world.[100]

The object of the intellectual level of understanding is the pursuit of the transcendental of unity, *unum*, in the particulars of human experience. Our questioning and wondering, whether formulated or merely implicit, sets us off on a quest to discover connections, parts and wholes, distinctive features, identities, and so on, in the data of our experience. We seek the intelligible unity of the data of experience—whether of sense or of consciousness—and insights bring us to those unities. We selectively attend to, inquire about, investigate, and ponder our experience, and finally the figural lightbulb appears over our head. The ecstatic "Eureka!" moment comes and brings us temporary satisfaction.[101] Human persons and communities have characteristically conceptualized such insights in hypotheses, theories, schematics, diagrams, propositional language, or other representational media. The flowering of the specialized communal disciplines of knowledge such as theoretical mathematics, physics, chemistry, biology, anthropology, sociology, psychology, economics, political science, philosophy, and theology among others depends upon our capacities for wonder, investigation, unifying insight, and imaginative formulation.[102] Such disciplines result from the ongoing work of cooperative inquiry, insight, formulation, testing, and revision. While certain questions seem unanswerable from our relatively limited current vistas, the ongoing processes of inquiry, insight, hypothesis, and critical reflection continue to yield breakthroughs. Some questions may never receive exhaustively satisfactory answers; they still can be raised, however, and we will still ask and seek to answer them. The aforementioned disciplines of human learning—many of which are rapidly expanding in the reach of their own communal horizons—represent the cooperatively achieved results of such unrestricted questioning writ large.

But not all human persons become specialists, scholars, or scientific theorists. Most people do not undertake the kind of ascetic program necessary to develop the requisite theoretical and linguistic apparatus for understanding and advancing the collective growing fund of human knowledge of ourselves, our history, and the cosmos of proportionate being. Most of us simply need only to know what is necessary "to go on," to borrow a phrase from the later Wittgenstein.[103] "To go on" we need only develop the skills and habits of socialization into our community of birth and home. We need only the bare minimum of ostensive linguistic training to grasp how to use words to meet our needs and wants. We need only to attend to the commonsense language and customs of our familial, societal, and cultural traditions and through trial and error make our way into these commonsense traditions. Such commonsense is ubiquitous. "One meets intelligence in every walk of life," Lonergan writes.

> There are intelligent farmers and craftsmen, intelligent employers and workers, intelligent technicians and mechanics, intelligent doctors and lawyers, intelligent politicians and diplomats. There is intelligence in industry and commerce, in finance and taxation, in journalism and public relations. There is intelligence in the home and in friendship, in conversation and in sport, in the arts and in entertainment. In every case, the man or woman of intelligence is marked by a greater readiness in catching on, in getting the point, in seeing the issue, in grasping implications, in acquiring knowhow. In their speech and action the same characteristics can be discerned as were set forth in describing the act that released Archimedes' "Eureka!" For insight is ever the same, and even its most modest achievements are rendered conspicuous by the contrasting, if reassuring, occurrence of examples of obtuseness and stupidity.[104]

Commonsense knowledge, while it is common, still represents the achievement of intellectual self-transcendence. The trial and error process of question and answer—whether our questions are articulated or not, and even if we cannot yet articulate them—moves us from the nursery into the unique brand of common sense—or "form of life"—of our community of birth and home.[105] Given our ultimate goal of understanding Scripture, an inherently linguistic reality, I must offer a more extensive account of the nature of language below. Human language usage, however, can best be understood relative to its place within a field of other human activities and capacities. While language plays a special role in such questioning and advances it profoundly, the desire to know precedes our acquisition of language and can guide us—however haltingly—into as yet unknown "forms of life" and foreign languages. Lonergan writes, "Language makes [explicit] questions possible. Intelligence makes them fascinating."[106] And, as Hefling states, "However important words may be—and they are extremely important—what they refer to is more important still."[107]

Through the questioning and answering that are constitutive of the discursive and bloody process of learning we can transcend the boundaries not only of our own nursery but also of the boundaries of the common sense of our own people and culture as we encounter the commonsense conventions of other societies and cultures present and past. Through the specializations of the processes of wonder, inquiry, and hypothesis in humane scholarship and the "hard" sciences we can transcend common sense entirely in the asymptotic pursuit of more and more adequate conceptions of space-time reality and the histories of human meaning making. The results of such pursuits do not give us univocal unmediated access to reality in their languages, concepts, symbols, narratives, histories, and theories. Such objectifications are necessarily and inescapably mediations. But human knowing is not therefore inadequate or falsified for being mediated.[108] Despite our propensity to use ocular metaphors when we talk about human understanding—we colloquially say, "I see what you mean," or speak of "the mind's eye"—our intelligence is not reducible to simply "taking a good look" at an "already out there now real."[109] It always involves wonder, questions, insights, formulation, and critical reflection and judgment. We never achieve knowledge in the realm of the humane apart from the mediation of meaning.[110]

While our intellectual consciousness promotes us from "raw" experience to an understanding of the intelligibility of that which is other than us, still our insights and formulations of the way things are in the world are not infallible. "Certainly," Lonergan writes, "insights are a dime a dozen. Any insight, by itself, is quite inadequate. Only the cumulative fruit of the self-correcting process of learning is significant."[111] At a third level of consciousness, that "self-correcting process of learning" takes us beyond the questions and products of the primary interrogatives—who, what, when, where, why, and how—to test the products of our insight against reality. Beyond our insights or intuitions into the synthetic unity and intelligibility of the data of our experience and consciousness, and the formulations of such insights, we can ask the further question, Is it so or not? Beyond insights through which we come to discern unities in the data of sense and consciousness, we have further reflective insights of affirmation or negation. At a further level of self-transcendence, then, the level of rational reflection, we subject the intelligible and intelligent products of our questioning and wonder to scrutiny to discern their relative adequacy for helping us make our way in the world of immediacy and the world mediated by meaning. Often our insights and conceptualizations come up wanting in that process. The inadequacy of so many of our bright ideas, however, does not leave us without footholds in the world. Some insights prove, upon repeated testing, apparently unassailable. Some admit no radical revision. At the very least, they facilitate our "going on" in the world.[112] We are able to answer yes.

We are partially satisfied when we grasp and express the intelligible unities or probabilities of the world around us, but our drive to know unnerves us, and so we raise the question whether our graspings and expressions are actually adequate to reality. When we operate at the rational or critical level of consciousness, we are in pursuit of the *verum*—what is true irrespective of our limited point of reference. Our critical judgments are objective when the products of our intellect—our images, concepts, conventional words and signs derived from insights—correspond to, or are isomorphic with, the intelligible way things really are in the worlds of immediacy and in human world(s) mediated by meaning and motivated by value. We discern such correspondences by inquiring into and investigating the conditions under which the products of our intellect would be true. Our capacity for self-transcendence is not only empirical and rational; it is also critical. We hypothesize, if W, X, and Y are the case, then Z, but W, X, and Y *are* the case, therefore Z. We reach true judgments when we investigate the conditions of affirmation and negation and when we find that such conditions have or have not been met.[113] Human beings cannot function for long without making definite judgments about reality; such judgments are implicit in the ways we go about doing things. Unless afflicted with psychosis, humans are not content with our mere bright ideas about how the world is independent of any investigation and solid evidence. We have a vested interest in having our understanding and judgment correspond to what is actually the case. Our capacity for critical judgment facilitates this getting beyond ourselves.

> For when we say that this or that really and truly is so, we do not mean that this is what appears, or what we imagine, or what we would like, or what we think, or what seems to be so, or what we would be inclined to say. No doubt we frequently have to be content with such lesser statements. . . . [T]he greater statement is not reducible to the

lesser. When we seriously affirm that something really and truly is so, we are making the claim that we have got beyond ourselves in some absolute fashion, somehow have got hold of something that is independent of ourselves, somehow have reached beyond, transcended ourselves.[114]

Our capacity for self-transcendence, though, extends even further yet.

As I indicated above, the fourth level, that of personal and responsible decision, represents the highest level of human self-transcendence. It is at this level that we come to recognize and squarely face the challenge of deciding just who we are and what we will make of ourselves. It is at this level that we deliberate about what is truly good and truly valuable. It is at the level of responsibility that we not only come to recognize that our being in the world is mediated through our sensations, understandings, and judgments, but that we can come to decide whether or not we will take responsibility for allowing the exigencies of attentiveness, intellectual integrity, and reasonableness their freedom to take us beyond our current metaphorical horizon, with its limited ego- or group-centered biases, towards what is actual, intelligible, true, and good. "Besides the world that we know about," writes Lonergan, "there is the further world that we make. . . . It is not enough to mean; one also has to do."[115] The decisions we make concerning who we are and who we will be are the apex of normal human development.

The object of the level of responsibility is the transcendental of the *bonum,* that which is truly good in itself. Our capacities for intelligence and judgment open us up to the world that is other than us, but our capacities for decision and evaluation indicate our further ability to raise and answer questions not merely of what is the case in the universe of proportionate being, but of the concrete good that is actually or possibly existent in this world.

> Though being and the good are coextensive, the subject moves to a further dimension of consciousness as his or her concern shifts from knowing being to realizing the good. Now there emerge freedom and responsibility, encounter and trust, communication and belief, choice and promise and fidelity. On this level subjects both constitute them-

selves and make their world. On this level persons are responsible, individually, for the lives they lead and, collectively, for the world in which they lead them.[116]

While the self-transcendence we achieve through our insights into the intelligibilities and actualities of the world direct our attention to objects, at the level of decision we come to recognize that our own authenticity is at stake. We are here concerned with ourselves as subjects. At this level, we come to recognize that "deeds, decisions, discoveries affect the subject more deeply than they affect the objects with which they are concerned. They accumulate as dispositions or habits of the subject; they determine him or her; they make him or her what they are and what they are to be."[117] So as adults we determine and pursue that which is intrinsically valuable.[118]

Our capacity for self-transcendence is operative before we can even name it, and that capacity allows us to enter into and engage both our immediately physical environment and the vast horizons of the history of human understanding and meaning. That capacity was operative in us at these various levels of experience, understanding, judgment, and decision before we could objectify them in language, and it will continue to operate in us even if we should deny its intelligibility, actuality, or value as an explanation of our nature. Each level has its own respective exigencies, and the exigencies of one level are not the exigencies of another. The actual achievement of self-transcendence requires that we follow the dictates of each level—that we be attentive in our sensation, intelligent and reasonable in our pursuit of the intelligibility and actuality of that which is other than us, and, finally, responsible in our decisions regarding the relative goodness of the concrete universe that is other than us. "Genuine objectivity," then, "is the fruit of authentic subjectivity."[119]

Objectivity is a tightly woven "triple cord." Actual objectivity requires an experiential element in "the givenness of relevant data," a normative element in "the exigencies of intelligence and rationality guiding the process of knowing from data to judging," and finally "an absolute component that is reached when reflective understanding combines the normative and the experiential elements into a virtually unconditioned; i.e., a conditioned whose conditions are fulfilled."[120] This objectivity is not achieved by following a set of instructions mechanically; it is a matter of ongoing virtuous praxis. While the various levels of consciousness have their own respective exigencies and corresponding virtues, those exigencies and virtues exhibit the unfolding of a single unified dynamic drive.[121] As Lonergan writes in *Method in Theology,* "The many levels of consciousness are just successive stages in the unfolding of a single thrust, the *eros* of the human spirit."[122] The self-transcendence of which we are capable and which defines us as humans becomes actual to the extent that we allow "the *eros* of the human spirit," our innate drive towards being, intelligibility, the true, and the good, to have its free rein in us. The value of our beliefs, understandings, judgments, and achievements does not come merely from their intrinsic merit but from how such "products" actually make manifest our own personal growth in virtue and character.[123] There is no way to the truth or the good aside from the authentic exercise of our subjectivity in self-transcendence.

Human persons, irrespective of time, place, and culture, bear witness to the usefulness of this hypothesis on human nature through their concrete operations. Effective and authentic functioning at the structured and interrelated levels of experience, understanding, judgment, and decision is the means through which all human meaning making and meaning understanding has been possible and has actually taken place in history. If the above hypothesis represents an adequate account of human nature in its structures, exigencies, and reach, then it will be especially fruitful for an investigation of the nature and purpose of Scripture. Scripture, after all, is a historical product of human meaning making, and its subsequent readers, hearers, and other interpreters can only engage it and understand it within the constraints of their historically concrete subjectivity.[124]

Besides helping us to recognize the human dimensions of Scripture, the aforementioned account of human nature and self-transcendence is illuminating for considering how Christians can engage Scripture as divine revelation. As I have noted and maintain in the present work, Christians hold that Scripture is inspired by the Holy Spirit and bears witness to the meaning of the living Word of God. But we still experience this Word; we hear the Scriptures read aloud, or we gaze at the written words. We still understand and discern this Word; we seek the intelligibility and actuality of divine revelation as we investigate the scriptures through question and insight, conceptualization and judgment. We still encounter and are confronted by this Word. As de Lubac writes, "Revelation, in fact, is at the same time a call: the call to the Kingdom."[125] The living Word confronts us as we engage the written words that witness to him; he calls upon us to decide and act. "But what about you?," he inquires. "Who do you say that I am?" (Mark 8.29). "Take up your cross and follow me," he commands (Matt 16.24). Our capacities for self-transcendence, which exhibit the form and norms of our nature, are active and at work in all of our engagement with Scripture as we seek to understand and be changed by the Triune God who has providentially shaped it and the human persons and communities who are God's instruments.

The above account of the differentiation of the concrete operations, their various exigencies, and their normative interrelations characteristic of the human person in her self-transcendence is, of course, cached out in human language. I am not arguing that the above account of human nature was shared by the authors of Scripture, or by any of its premodern interpreters, nor am I arguing that they would have agreed to it in all of its details if it was somehow possible to communicate it to them. Nevertheless, I am making the controversial argument that the same structured intentional consciousness, with its exigencies and norms, is shared by all human persons across cultures and across times.[126]

The human authors of the scriptural texts shared these capacities; subsequent human readers and interpreters of these texts share such capacities. The fact that such self-transcendence is transcultural and at the roots of human development of culture requires us to recognize and give special concentrated attention to the cultural and linguistic embeddedness of human understandings, judgments, and decisions mediated by language. Because of its unique manifestation of our capacity for self-transcendence, language deserves special attention in philosophical and theological anthropology. "One might say," Lonergan writes, "that the heavens show forth the glory of God; what can mere words add? . . . [O]ne must answer that, however trifling the uses to which words may be put, still they are the vehicles of meaning, and meaning is the stuff of humanity's making of itself."[127] It is therefore necessary to give a fuller account of the nature and motivations of human language and meaning making.

HUMAN PERSONS II: HUMAN HORIZONS OF MEANING AND VALUE

Human persons, to be sure, are rational and symbolic animals.[128] Our capacity for communicative and creative expression represents a key dimension of our capacity for self-transcendence. Speech, writing, reading, and other differentiated forms of symbolic communication demonstrate our capacity for self-transcendence and so have special significance among the concrete operations characteristic of human beings. The achievements of human language distinguish us from the beasts of the field and the birds of the air.[129] All human understanding, in order for actual communication to occur, must be mediated through the local and communal conventions of speech, writing, diagrams, symbols, and other expressive media available in specific times and places. As such, the extent of one's own and one's community's linguistic development functions as a soft limit on our communication.[130] To cite an example, I personally lack knowledge of the technical vocabularies of linguistics and cognitive science that could potentially enhance my ability to clearly communicate the nuances of the constitution and norms of human *psychē*. Undertaking research and reflecting philosophically on the insights and achievements of contemporary psychology would provide me with tools for more adequately communicating the precise contours of human cognition and action. Such work would undoubtedly greatly enhance the aforementioned heuristic account.[131] Yet at the same time, the above account names, distinguishes, and interrelates *actual concrete operations* that human persons characteristically experience and exhibit—across time and culture—both spontaneously and purposefully. The account is thus an apt means of identifying and differentiating the complex structures of human self-transcendence.[132] Though it is inescapably restricted by human language, it provides a set of terms and relations that are eminently useful for designating the distinctive characteristics and exigencies of human nature. Still, careful attention to the precise nature and function of language and to the processes through which we attain language will help to elaborate upon some specific distinctive dimensions of our self-transcending nature.

Human persons are not born with the tools of human language; we must obtain them through a long and arduous process. All of us learned our "native" languages. Maturing human beings not only are able to inhabit our immediate environments but also, through the mediation of meaning, are able to "inhabit" the social structures and cultures that represent the achievements of human self-transcendence.[133] While Plato describes the process through which we come to grasp the intelligible forms as *anamnesis* and Augustine famously presented his own understanding of language as an infant as if he had already possessed some primitive language, Piaget—and Lonergan following him—explains that language acquisition is a process of trial and error, or of assimilation and adjustment, and grouping.[134] In normal development, infants must first achieve a number of milestone capabilities such as object permanence, refinements in sensation and motor skills, and increasing awareness of the relationship between their bodies and their surroundings before they can learn how to use language.[135] From a very early age most humans learn the physical skills necessary for locomotion and the vocalizations and gestures through which we can express our discomfort or our desires for affection, food, sleep, or toys.

While language at first functioned only as a means to these other ends, its unique capacities eventually allowed us to transcend the immediacy of those basic desires. Before we possessed language, wonder and investigation—buoyed by an increasing repertoire of abilities—allowed us to grow in our awareness of the world. It is doubtless strange to imagine how we could have "wondered" or "questioned" without possessing language, but one who has observed infants and children learning can recognize the process of trial and error, assimilation and adjustment, that allows them to become socialized into the linguistic apparatus and social and cultural norms of their community.[136] Such language learning is inherently intersubjective and communal as well; the infant's acquisition of language is only possible through constant contact with other persons.[137]

As infants, our acquisition of language through that trial and error process of assimilation, adjustment, and grouping moved us out of the world of immediate experience of our surroundings in the nursery and into a much larger world mediated by and constituted by meaning.[138] Our learning was not a process of recalling forms forgotten through our descent to materiality, nor did we discern the meanings of sounds and images on the basis of a preexisting private language. Language acquisition was possible because of our natural built-in aptitude for coming to know "how to go on" unfolding through the trial and error processes characteristic of infant development. Our native language limits but does not straightjacket our development. Besides representing a characteristic achievement in human development, the child's acquisition of language facilitates degrees of personal self-transcendence not possible without it.

Lonergan's distinction between the infant's world of immediacy and adult worlds "mediated by meaning and motivated by value" draws attention to the monumentally important nature of language. Such a distinction is crucially important because it points to the precise character of fully human knowledge and shows how we are not locked within our "native" languages or the distinct brand of common sense of our community of birth. While the immediate operations of our senses allow us to operate on that which is immediate to us via tasting, touching, hearing, smelling, and seeing, our conscious operations associated with intelligence and judgment allow us to "operate immediately with respect to a sign, a symbol, an image, and by the mediation of the sign, the symbol, the image, [we] operate with respect to the referent."[139] This distinction between the immediate and the mediate, Lonergan continues, "leads to a distinction in the development of culture. The infant lives in a world of immediacy. As the child learns to speak, goes to school, goes to work, marries, he moves more and more into a world mediated by meaning and motivated by values."[140] Our early use of language, as I noted above, is almost exclusively instrumental. But it does not remain so. There is no doubt that language molds or shapes our developing consciousness,

> but also it structures the world about the subject. Spatial adverbs and adjectives relate places to the place of the speaker. The tenses of verbs relate times to his present. Moods correspond to his intention to wish, or exhort, or command, or declare. Voices make verbs active and now passive and, at the same time, shift subjects to objects and objects to subjects.[141]

By its capacity for mediation language also liberates our consciousness.[142] While at first language took a backseat in our development as a set of acquired tools, soon it seemed to take on a life of its own. Beyond coming to learn "how to do things with words," the words and symbols of humanity extant in the achievements of our cultures and histories began to work upon us.[143] As we moved out of the immediacy of the nursery we began to encounter, through the mediation of language, "the far larger world revealed through the memories of other men, through the common sense of community, through the pages of literature, through the labors of scholars, through the investigations of scientists, through the experience of saints, through the meditations of philosophers and theologians."[144] Our acquisition of language permitted our entry into the diverse cultural achievements of the human race. Because such cultural achievements depend upon the historical action of specific persons and communities at specific times in specific places, this larger world mediated by meaning is not singular and univocal.[145] The "world mediated by meaning" includes the entirety of the products of human meaning making throughout human history. But the history of meaning making does not contain only human—or at least *merely* human—products. Christians affirm that the Triune God has entered into our history to have a say in humanity's making of itself. Revelation is the name for the entry of divine meaning into history.[146] Christian Scripture mediates the meaning of divine revelation.[147] The rule of faith and the creeds also mediate that divine meaning. The previous two chapters provided a historical assessment of the early Christian development of Christian meaning and a contemporary heuristic of that meaning.

The fact that we each found our way into already made worlds of meaning is not insignificant. Most of our knowledge of the world is not immanently generated. Our own horizons of meaning are constituted by belief and trust even more than they are constituted by our own achievements of understanding and judgment.[148] In normal human development, our personal experiences are supplemented by "an enormous context constituted by reports of the experience of other people at other places and times."[149] Human knowledge in any community or discipline depends upon the achievements of countless antecedent individuals and groups. Meanings, as I have noted frequently, are nested in linguistic and historical contexts. Any particular understanding or judgment depends upon allusions, associations, and other judgments and beliefs. Even modern science depends upon trust and belief. Each chemist does not need to reproduce the experiments that led to development of the periodic table. Instead, she can assume them as a stable foundation for her own subsequent experiments and achievements.[150] No one person in a community or in a specialized discipline understands the entirety of her own context of communal meaning, let alone the entirety of human meanings outside of her own horizon. "Human knowledge," Lonergan declares, " . . . is not some individual possession but rather a common fund, from which each may draw by believing, to which each may contribute in the measure that he performs his cognitional operations properly and reports their results accurately."[151] Biblical scholarship and theological reflection are no exceptions to this rule. While geniuses like Aristotle or even Thomas Aquinas could aspire to and achieve a certain degree of competence in their understanding of the full scope of human knowledge in their time, the flourishing of human understanding that has taken place in the past couple of centuries—and that is accelerating at an unprecedented pace today— precludes that possibility completely in the present. The specialization of human knowledge in our own time requires us to recognize the communal dissemination of knowledge and to defer to experts more frequently than has ever been necessary in the past.[152]

We have also only relatively recently come to recognize the historical locatedness of all human understanding and language in a serious way. Knowledge and language are not static. For better or worse, as I noted in the first chapter, we have become historically conscious, or historically minded; that is, we are acutely aware of differences and developments of human meanings reflected in human cultures across time and geographic differences.[153] "Concepts have dates," as Doran puts it succinctly.[154] Scripture is not exempt from the insights of historical mindedness, as the guild of historical-critical biblical scholarship demonstrates.

The judgments that Scripture either witnesses to a single normative culture or that scriptural interpretation and use could, did, or will found a single normative culture are the kind of judgments concerning meaning that Lonergan identifies as characteristic of a "classicist" notion of culture.[155] The "classicist" notion of culture assumes that there is only one normative culture. The general usage of the adjective *cultured* points to this former notion of culture. To be "cultured" was to have received the appropriate training in said normative culture. "Its classics," writes Lonergan, "were immortal works of art, its philosophy was perennial philosophy, its assumptions were eternal truths, its laws were the depository of the wisdom and prudence of mankind."[156] The ideal of classicist culture was a sort of Renaissance man who was completely competent in his grasp of the arts and sciences.[157] Barbarism was the opposite of culture.[158] Such a notion of culture arguably underwrote the utilization of Christian Scripture in the "formation of Christian Culture" in the early centuries of Christianity.[159]

Attention to the historical developments of human language, and to the intelligibility and integrity of non-Western perspectives, however, Lonergan insists, has made it impossible to continue to maintain the classicist notion that there is a single normative culture. Contemporary scholars and theorists of culture have instead developed an empirical notion of culture.[160] In such a notion, culture is not the sole provenance of high-minded elites; "culture is everywhere human beings are."[161] This contemporary notion of culture carries implicit in itself a built-in recognition of the multiplicity and plasticity of culture. Classical—or classicist—culture has become only one culture among many.[162] An adequate contemporary understanding of the nature and purpose of Scripture must affirm its abiding authority even through the variegated cultural historicity of its contents.[163]

It is also important to draw attention to the fact that culture, because of its dependence upon human persons and communities and because of its existence in conventions of meaning, whether intersubjective, linguistic, symbolic, or artistic, is not only changing, but fragile. The instrumental efficacy of language is not mechanistic or automatic.[164] Human communication—as anyone who has had any practice with it knows—is always precarious. Our experience shows us that we do not always express ourselves clearly; even our best efforts at clarity can be misheard or misunderstood. Lying is not only possible for humans, but is abundant within human communities. We not only deceive others, we can even deceive ourselves. The cultural worlds mediated by meaning are thus insecure, "since besides truth there is error, besides fact there is fiction, besides honesty there is deceit, besides science there is myth."[165] I discuss this insecurity at greater length below. Beyond acknowledging the pitfalls of language use for communication, we can also use language, as all expression, for noninstrumental purposes in symbolism and art.[166] The products of artistic and symbolic expression always exceed linguistic explanation. This is as true of written classics as it is of other visual and tactile material media such as paintings and sculpture.

Human beings are not merely meaning-making or meaning-understanding automatons, of course. Human living is never without motivation. While we are certainly rational animals, we are also feeling, desiring, and loving animals.[167] Our experiences of the world of immediacy and the worlds mediated by meaning are charged with feeling and emotion from the very beginning of our lives. Our feelings and emotions develop and differentiate along with our intellectual capacities. As adults we characteristically experience both nonintentional states—such as tiredness, touchiness, anxiety, excitability, sullenness—and intentional responses—such as hunger and thirst, wonderment, fear, trust—and such feelings have a great deal of significance in our daily living and in our existential self-determination and expression. Our feelings give "mass, momentum, drive, [and] power" to our intentional consciousness.[168] As Lonergan elaborates:

> Because of our feelings, our desires and our fears, our hope or despair, our joys and sorrows, our enthusiasm and indignation, our esteem and contempt, our trust and distrust, our love and hatred, our tenderness and wrath, our admiration, veneration, reverence, our dread, horror, terror, *we are oriented massively and dynamically* in a world mediated by meaning. We have feelings about other persons, we feel for them, we feel with them. We have feelings about our respective situations, about the past, about the future, about evils to be lamented or remedied, about the good that can, might, must be accomplished.[169]

Without such feelings, human understanding and action in the world would be "paper thin."[170] Our feelings, especially our intentional states, play an exceptionally important role when we operate at the level of decision and action. Lonergan highlights a key dialectic operative in and reflective of our motivations in decision and action. Intentional states, he writes, "regard two main classes of objects: on the one hand, the agreeable or disagreeable, the satisfying or dissatisfying; on the other hand, values, whether the ontic value of persons or the qualitative value of beauty, understanding, truth, virtuous acts, noble deeds."[171] When we decide and act on the basis not of personal preference but of ontic value, we operate at our highest level of natural self-transcendence in our estimation of and pursuit of that which is truly good. Action and decision on the basis of preference—the agreeable and the disagreeable—on the other hand, is inherently ambiguous. We may desire that which regards only our own satisfaction or the satisfaction of our community to the detriment of others and the rejection of the common good. On the other hand, we may desire that which is truly good, and our feelings may take us towards it, but sometimes the truly good may be disagreeable for us or for our immediate community.[172]

When our feelings do respond to values, they do so in accord with a scale of preference that may be either implicit or explicit. Lonergan writes:

> We may distinguish vital, social, cultural, personal, and religious values in an ascending order. Vital values, such as health and strength, grace and vigor, normally are preferred to avoiding the work, privations, pains involved in acquiring, maintaining, restoring them. Social values, such as the good of order which conditions the vital values of the whole community, have to be preferred to the vital values of individual members of the community. Cultural values do not exist without the underpinning of vital and social values, but none the less they rank higher. Not on bread alone doth man live. Over and above mere living and operating, men have to find a meaning and value in their living and operating. It is the function of culture to discover, express, validate, criticize, correct, develop, improve such meaning and value. Personal value is the person in his self-transcendence, as loving and being loved, as originator of values in himself and in his milieu, as an inspiration and invitation to others to do likewise. Religious values, finally, are at the heart of the meaning and value of one's living and one's world.[173]

Because feelings arise spontaneously, nonintentional states and intentional responses are not intrinsically praiseworthy or blameworthy. How we respond to such states and intentional responses, however, is a matter of personal and collective responsibility. At the highest level of self-transcendence we come not only to recognize the truly good—actual objective values in their integral relations—but to decide for the good and to make it the basis for our action. It is possible to discipline our feelings towards the end of the good by either reinforcement or curtailment.[174] We are able to repress or reinforce feelings by giving them attention or by withholding attention from them.

Earlier I noted that patristic notions of human nature emphasized the transformative work of the Triune God not only in intelligence, judgment, and willing, but in desire. The indwelling of the Triune God certainly heals and elevates our capacities for understanding and judgment: through the Holy Spirit we can have "the mind of Christ" (1 Cor 2.15). Such transformative work is the foundation for articulating the kind of heuristic account of the divine economy reflected in the rule(s) of faith and creeds. The presence of God in us *also* reorders our desires and heals and elevates our capacities for feeling and emotion; having the mind of Christ and holding the judgments about the work of the Triune God in history bring us to desire heavenly things (Col 3.12). I return to the nature of desire and the notion of value below. For now, however, I must fill out my account of subjectivity by giving further attention to the diachronic/historic unfolding of human development, to its possible truncations and breakdowns, and, finally, to its radical transformation through grace in the processes of conversion.

HUMAN PERSONS III: FINITUDE, FALLENNESS, AND TRANSFORMATION

Even if my readers are prepared to affirm that self-transcendence at the empirical, intellectual, rational, and responsible levels provides an adequate and useful heuristic for understanding human nature, the fact remains that concrete human persons, the author included, only achieve such transcendence in fits and starts. As creatures, we are finite and fallible. "Our creaturely status," writes Stephen Fowl, "needs to circumscribe all notions of autonomy and freedom."[175] In fact, sustained self-transcendence in concrete persons is both rare and fleeting. Our personal histories demonstrate our inability to consistently follow the dictates of our native drives towards what is intelligible, true, and good. Our often inauthentic per-

sonal and social feelings, desires, and dispositions regularly derail our anagogic orientation towards self-transcendence. Given our status as finite,
fallible, and fallen, we are not "fully or substantially present to ourselves,"
Fowl states.[176] As Lonergan puts it, "We do not know ourselves very well; we
cannot chart the future; we cannot control our environment completely
or the influences that work on us; we cannot explore our unconscious and
preconscious mechanisms. Our course is in the night; our control is rough
and approximate."[177]

We need not despair, however, because we can identify the markers
of self-transcendence in our own lives, in our communities, and in our
home cultures. Our capacity for self-transcendence *itself* is what allows us
to identify our own failures and the failures of our community and culture. That capacity also allows us to devise ways of overturning such deficiencies and gives us resources for deciding and acting in accordance with
such planning.

Neither nonhuman animals nor infants can read academic prose, but
all who are reading these words were once infants. The metaphorical distance that humans characteristically traverse from infancy to adulthood
demonstrates not only the possibility of self-transcendence, but its actuality in the history that is. The fact that you are reading the words I have
written and that you understand them indicates the scope of your own
progress and growth in self-transcendence. You have acquired the requisite grasp of the possible and probable meanings of the words I have employed, and you can wonder at and raise questions concerning the adequacy of what I have written to your own experience of being human.
Human lives bear witness to the dramatic process of our development to
maturity.[178] Human being, then, or as Lonergan puts it, "the being of the
subject, is becoming."[179] Our becoming, when in accord with the dictates
of self-transcendence, is a process of progress and development. And "development," Lonergan writes, "is a matter of increasing the number of
things one does for oneself. Parents and teachers and professors and supe-
riors let people do more and more for themselves, decide more and more
for themselves, find out more and more for themselves."[180]

Now such becoming or development has major identifiable land-
marks. While we are largely unaware, at least directly, of our development
through most of our lives, at a certain point we must come to decide what

we will make of ourselves. As noted above, the existential decision concerning what one will make of oneself takes place at the highest level of self-transcendence. It is at this point that the subject of such development recognizes that "deeds, decisions, [and] discoveries affect the subject more deeply than they affect the objects with which they are concerned. They accumulate as dispositions and habits of the subject; they determine him or her; they make him or her what they are and what they are to be."[181]

Even if one's own development brings him or her to this point, deciding to go with the dictates of self-transcendence at the levels of experience, understanding, judgment, and decision requires a great deal of fortitude, courage, and effort. Even when we have made the decision to pursue the good and not merely that which we find most agreeable, we may lack the skills and habits necessary to carry out that pursuit. Even if we recognize that attentiveness, intelligence, reasonableness, and responsibility call us to constant account in our action and decision, we have frequently enough ignored such exigencies.[182] While Socrates may be correct that the unexamined life is not worth living, ignorance of the exigencies of self-examination proves itself blissful. It seems better not to bother ourselves with the kind of dramatic overhaul that self-appropriation—or taking responsibility to abide by the imperatives of attentiveness, intelligence, reasonableness, and responsibility—requires. We may even willfully choose to ignore our own deficiencies or the deficiencies of our communities and culture in the pursuit of that which is not good. We may be completely blind and ignorant of such deficiencies. While we cannot be blamed, at least at first, for inheriting the inauthenticity of our community and culture, our conscience—itself a key feature of our capacity for self-transcendence in its intrinsic orientation to the good—can make us uneasy by raising questions for us that our limited perspectives cannot accommodate.

While it is necessary to take note of our fallibility and the limitations our creatureliness imposes upon us, humans are notoriously adept at not only ignoring but also actively rejecting the exigencies for self-transcendence built into our nature. We are equally adept at turning our skills, capacities, and powers towards ends that are not true values. Our desires and feelings can be bent inwards in our egoism and the group interests of nepotism, classism, nationalism, and racism. While our spontaneous feelings of intentional response can regard what is actually good, or true values, they also regard the agreeable and disagreeable. It is possible, and easy, to reject the built-in exigencies of discerning and acting on what is truly good in preference for that which regards only our personal satisfaction.[183] In egoism, or individual bias, we set up our own notion of the good as ultimate and decide and act in accordance with that truncated notion of the good.[184] Our capacity for self-transcendence does not cease to operate within our egoism; we are remarkably adept at utilizing our skills, including our capacities for truthful understanding and judgment, to take advantage of situations for selfish gain. But one who takes advantage of situations and people for personal gain only partially and selectively follows the built-in dictates of self-transcendence. "Egoism," Lonergan writes in *Insight*, " . . . is an incomplete development of intelligence."[185] It manifests one's stunted moral development.

Beyond personal egoism, whole communities can be inauthentic. While one must overcome one's spontaneous feelings of belonging and responsibility to one's community to operate in accord with the dictates of egoism or individual bias, in group bias one's own community reinforces one's truncated moral and intellectual development.[186] As I noted above, normal human development involves our socialization or enculturation into already existing social orders and contexts of meaning. The "social," Lonergan writes, designates a "way of life, a way in which people live together in some orderly and therefore predictable fashion."[187] The conventional structures of family, state, legal courts, economy, technology, and religious organizations make up distinct discernable wholes oriented and related to one another in the larger whole of the social fabric. Human beings have developed such organizations in both organic and distinctly intentional manners to ensure the stability and recurrence of the vital values of nourishment, living stability, and community. Such social orders, upon their development, recurrently operate and function without regular critical reflection or intervention.[188]

The ordered social structures enumerated above—family, state, economy, and so on—operate successfully by achieving a dialectical balance of practical intelligence and spontaneous intersubjectivity.[189] But the sensitive spontaneity of such social orders does not automatically tend towards the common good of other individuals and groups outside of its boundaries. Groups can put their practical intelligence and talents to work in promoting their own interests and well-being without consideration of other groups and individuals. They can even promote their interests to the direct detriment of those others.[190] Inauthentic communities and social orders produce inauthentic cultures or traditions. While we can become socialized into and follow astutely the conventions of our kith and kin, still that social order is not necessarily intrinsically good. Social orders only imperfectly realize goods of order. So Lonergan helpfully contrasts minor authenticity—the authenticity of an individual relative to his or her own tradition—and major authenticity—the relative authenticity of the tradition itself.[191] Specific social orders can also reject the value of cultural pursuits, or worse yet the importance of responsibility and self-appropriation. To the extent that one is socialized and enculturated into such a social order or tradition, "in that measure he can do no more than authentically realize unauthenticity."[192]

Finally, we can also elevate practical reason and the exigencies of common sense to the point that we disparage or even reject the relevance of theory and long-term concerns. Lonergan labels this truncation of self-transcendence "general bias."[193] At the level of common sense we are concerned only with what is necessary to go on in the here and now. We have no need of abstract or generalized laws, we give no heed to the long-term consequences of our actions, we cannot be bothered to interrogate the relationship between our own values and what is truly good. We not only fail to raise and seek to answer all relevant questions in a situation or problem, but we reject those questions as irrelevant and the pursuit of adequate answers to them as worthless. Specialists in diverse fields, despite their concern with the theoretical, with long-range consequences, and even with ultimate values, can manifest general bias if they fail to recognize and acknowledge the importance and relevance of other fields. "Common sense," though, Lonergan writes, "almost invariably makes that mistake; for it is incapable of analyzing itself, incapable of making the discovery that it too is a specialized development of human knowledge, incapable of coming to grasp that its peculiar danger is to extend its legitimate concern for the concrete and the immediately practical into disregard of larger issues and indifference to long-term results."[194] One may blamelessly inherit such biases from one's communal formation, but sooner or later one's native drive towards the intelligible, the true, and the good will force that individual to confront the realities of the inadequacy of her moral formation and the moral formation of her community.

Such failures of self-transcendence manifest the sinful conditions of human persons and communities in the concrete. Our collusion with such forces is ubiquitous. Scripture witnesses to these human proclivities to sin; various texts depict the moral failings of individuals and communities without sanitization.[195] The realities of individual and group bias especially are manifest in the history of interpretation of Christian Scripture. Christians have unfortunately proven quite resilient in their ability to utilize the scriptural texts to advance their own ends to the detriment and even destruction of others.[196] As Fowl warns, "Christians need to be attentive to their own tendencies to read Scripture in ways that underwrite their sin."[197] Our awareness of these biases and our recognition of our own complicity in such sinful practices should heighten our vigilance against such abuses of Scripture itself and of one another.

We could despair at our personal and collective moral and epistemological impotence, yet we need not. The fact of collective and personal human progress in understanding and action, though faint and infrequent, remains despite the ubiquitous evidence of bias and decline in human societies and cultures. Beyond the evidence of our progress, however, Christians hold that the Triune God has entered into our situation to redeem us from our moral impotence and culpable ignorance. The gospel is not merely a report that God showed up at a specific time and place and then left just as quickly, though. The good news that the Triune God is recapitulating all things in Jesus Christ, while it is true news and while its truth is the actuality of the historical advent and work of Jesus in first-century Palestine, is a truth that has a subsequent history in the work of the Holy Spirit in human societies and cultures since Pentecost.

The truth of the missions of the Son and Holy Spirit in our history is not truth that is so objective as to get on without human subjects. It is, after all, redeeming truth *pro nobis*. It is the reality of the Triune God coming to us, flooding our hearts with the love that is God's own (Rom 5.5), transforming us by the renewing of our minds (Rom 12.1–3) so that we have the mind of Christ (1 Cor 2.16) and think spiritual things through the indwelling and teaching of the Holy Spirit (1 Cor 2.13). It is through this religious conversion that our capacities for desire, intelligence, reflection, and action can be healed and elevated.[198] While self-transcendence is fleeting apart from grace, in grace we are caught up in the love of God, which radically reorients our values, priorities, and understanding and enables the sustained exercise of our capacities for self-transcendence. "That love" which effects such a transformation, Lonergan writes,

> is not this or that act of loving but a radical being-in-love, a first principle of all one's thoughts and words and deeds and omissions, a principle that keeps us out of sin, that moves us to prayer and to penance, that can become the ever so quiet yet passionate center of all our living. It is, whatever its degree, a being-in-love that is without conditions or qualifications or reserves, and so it is other-worldly, a being-in love that occurs within this world but heads beyond it, for no finite object or person can be the object of unqualified, unconditional loving. Such unconditional being-in-love actuates to the full the dynamic potentiality of the human spirit with its unrestricted reach and, as a full actuation, it is fulfilment, deep-set peace, the peace the world cannot give, abiding joy, the joy that remains despite humiliation and failure and privation and pain.[199]

It is not within our ability to achieve such a radical transformation in our own power. It is a gift to us. While our natural inclination towards self-transcendence is what drives and makes possible our progress, the complete fulfillment of that exigency is not in our power. The peak experience of being in love with God unrestrictedly, which religious conversion names, "is the proper fulfilment of that capacity."[200] It is not mere assent to the truth that the Triune God loves us. It is the reception of that love and the beginning of a new relationship not with an abstract reality but with the living God. Such a momentous change in our being has equally momentous implications for our decisions and actions in our social and cultural contexts and in the rest of the world. For "while the basis of the change involves our underlying nature, the result of the change is a revolution in how we live and think."[201] The experience of being in love with God unrestrictedly "dismantles and abolishes the horizon in which our knowing and choosing went on, and it constructs a new horizon in which the love of God transvalues our values and the eyes of that love transform our knowing."[202] In that experience the Triune God transforms our subjectivity, enabling us to more consistently follow the self-transcending dictates of our consciousness at the levels of experience, understanding, judgment, and decision.[203]

While we might, in our own light, periodically recognize the demands that actual values make upon us at the level of decision, and while we might sometimes even choose to pursue that which is good and chart courses of action for pursuing it, we cannot do so habitually in our own power. Fear, uncertainty, and advertence to our own vital well-being keep us from taking moral stands that could imperil us socially or even result in bodily harm or worse. But in grace, we are healed and elevated in our capacity for recognizing that which is actually good, for making true judgments of value, and for deciding and acting in accord with those judgments. Moral conversion—or the transformation we undergo when we come to decisively regard, affirm, and pursue value and not mere satisfaction at the level of decision and action—thus follows upon and is intrinsically connected to religious conversion.[204] Through our reception of the faith, hope, and love present in us through God's own love in us, we can be confident in the trustworthiness of God, the hope of the resurrection, and the power of the love of God for transforming the world. "Because that love [of God] is the proper fulfillment of our capacity [for self-transcendence]," Lonergan writes,

> that fulfillment brings a radical peace, the peace that the world cannot give (John 14.27). That fulfillment bears fruit in a love of one's neighbor that strives mightily to bring about the kingdom of God on this earth. . . . Though not the product of our knowing and choosing, it is a conscious, dynamic state of love, joy, peace, that manifests itself in the harvest of the Spirit, in acts of kindness, goodness, fidelity, gentleness, and self-control (Gal 5.22).[205]

Beyond changing the subject so that she can recognize the demands that true values have upon her, the indwelling presence of the Triune God enables her to follow through on that exigency by efficaciously loving God with all of her heart, soul, mind, and strength and by loving her neighbor as herself (Mark 12.30). That fulfillment leads her, in the limit, to imitate

Christ by following Christ's command to love even her enemies (Matt 5.44), to overcome evil with good (Rom 12.21). She thus comes to affirm the intelligibility, truth, and goodness of the just and mysterious law of the cross, despite its ostensible folly from a more restricted and merely human perspective (1 Cor 1.18), as the only actual remedy for sin and death available in the history that is.[206]

The transformations wrought in us at the level of our fundamental orientation—religious conversion—and the level of decision and action—moral conversion—have further effects on us at the other levels of consciousness. Intellectual conversion can result from moral conversion when we recognize truth and intelligibility for the intrinsic values that they are. In intellectual conversion we recognize, understand, and affirm the distinctions between the levels of experience, understanding, and judgment and take responsibility for following through on—and not confusing—the exigencies of each level. We no longer regard objectivity as a matter of biological extroversion, or "taking a good look," but instead recognize that the only assured path towards the coherence of our thought and its correspondence to reality is through giving free rein to the manifold operations of intelligence and reason; we must let them take us where they will. In recognizing the value of the intelligible and the true, intellectual conversion affords us a disposition of generosity towards the intellectual achievements of humanity. We come to recognize, understand, and affirm the value of the knowledge enshrined in the common sense of distinct communities alongside the different but complementary achievements in understanding that have taken place in scholarship, theory, literature, art, and other fields.

In intellectual conversion we can thus recognize and affirm the value of what Lonergan calls "differentiations of consciousness."[207] In the realm of common sense one is concerned only with understanding and abiding by the conventions of one's community. But questions arise that could take one outside of those confines to consider questions regarding the historical permutations of the common sense of one's own community at a different time. Further questions could bring one to consider the products of common sense of other people in much different times and places. Giving sustained attention to these historical questions would facilitate a scholarly or historical differentiation of one's consciousness.

The scholarly differentiation of consciousness is that of the linguist, the man of letters, the exegete, the historian. It combines the brand of common sense of its own place and time with a commonsense style of understanding that grasps the meanings and intentions in the words and deeds that proceeded from the common sense of another people, another place, or another time. Because scholarship operates in the commonsense style of developing intelligence, it is not trying to reach the universal principles and laws that are the goal of the natural sciences and the generalizing human sciences: Its aim is simply to understand the meaning intended in particular statements and the intentions embodied in particular deeds.[208]

Besides the scholarly differentiation of consciousness, we could just as well undergo the disciplined regime of study required for raising and answering questions of theoretical mathematics or of quantum physics, and these alternative courses would facilitate a theoretical differentiation of our consciousness. We could instead seek to differentiate our consciousness religiously or artistically, becoming sensitive to the questions and pulls of the divine or the beautiful respectively.[209]

Finally, intellectual conversion itself, at least when objectified, exhibits the achievement of interiorly differentiated consciousness. In interiorly differentiated consciousness the subject raises and answers questions concerning the constitution and norms of her internal conscious operations in experience, understanding, judgment, and decision in any differentiated realm. While we are aware that experts, scientists, theorists, scholars, artists, and mystics are not infallible, we can expect to learn much from them by attending to and investigating their achievements because of the ways that they have followed the exigencies of intelligence and reasonableness in their intellectual work. The kind of development and growth that attends the transformation God is working in us is not only "anagogic," then, drawing our attention and priorities to ultimate things; it also facilitates a horizontal openness in us so that we might acknowledge, attend to, understand, and affirm the truth wherever we might find it.

Intellectual conversion has profound implications for our understanding of and expectations of Scripture and for our assessments of the results of scholarship and other reading strategies. Intellectual conversion provides a basis for both affirming and critiquing the differentiated achievements of historical criticism, premodern theological and spiritual interpretation, and contextual or advocacy approaches to Scripture. If one adopts the account of the intelligibility of human nature of the present work, one will expect that the practitioners of these various "approaches" will produce authentic achievements that demand our attention and assent so long as those who apply the canons of their respective approaches to Scripture do so in an authentic way. We can likewise expect to encounter shortcomings in such works so long as those who produce them are affected by the inattention, obtuseness, unreasonableness, and irresponsibility characteristic of concrete human persons. Our ability to judge such works will depend upon our own authenticity.

The final criterion of judgment upon such human accomplishments is ultimately the revelatory and redemptive work of the Triune God in the history that is. But to the extent that readers and interpreters of Scripture, irrespective of their approach to the text, achieve insight into various features of the history that is, we cannot understand the unfolding economic work of the Triune God adequately if we do not incorporate those authentic achievements. Ultimately providence will pass judgment on all such human accomplishments as it has in the past and will continue to do until the consummation of all things in Christ.

The conversions identify key milestones in the concrete unfolding of our lives. Once they arrive, though, assuming that they do, they are not automatic. Our dramatic personal histories are not unidirectional but are subject to possible derailments. Inauthenticity in our social and cultural environments and our own propensity to take shortcuts and settle for half solutions and clichés will always be obstacles to our recognition of and embodiment of the conditions of self-transcendence. Our only recourse now is to strive to follow the imperatives of attentiveness, intelligence, reasonableness, and responsibility, to pray for wisdom and trust that God will grant it freely (James 1.5), and to strive to bear fruit in keeping with repentance (Matt 3.8), the harvest of the Spirit (Heb 12.11; Gal 5.22), a harvest befitting our status as sons and daughters of God (Rom 8.19; Gal 3.26; 4.5; 1 John 1.12). Against such things there is no law.

SUMMARY AND CONCLUSION

This chapter offers an account of human nature that both explains our capacities for self-transcendence and identifies the ways in which such self-transcendence has been frustrated, healed, and even transformed in history. The challenge of authentically living in accordance with our capacities and drives to self-transcendence is monumental and ongoing. As Lonergan writes:

> There is no easy solution. To recognize and acknowledge the authentic, one already must be authentic. If already one is unauthentic, such recognition and acknowledgement is beyond one's effective reach. Such is the moral impotence of the human person, the concrete fact of original sin, not the remote origins of original sin (*peccatum originale originans*), but the present fact (*peccatum originale originatum*).[210]

Still, the articulation of the intelligible structures and constraints of human living and being is a key achievement which reflects such self-transcendence in action. The account of human nature articulated herein delineates the human context of Christian Scripture in the economic work of the Triune God.

As I have repeatedly noted, while I hold as a matter of faith that Christian Scripture results from the divine activity of the Triune God in history, that theological judgment does not negate the judgment that it is also a product of human subjective activity. It is the product of specific human persons and communities acting at all levels of consciousness but primarily at the levels of experience and decision. Its original human authors, moved by the Holy Spirit, acted to communicate their experiences, understandings, and judgments about the work of God in their midst through writing.[211] Subsequent communities and individuals have acted at the levels of experience, understanding, judgment, and decision in preserving, redacting, copying, translating, reading aloud, reading in silence, memorizing, interpreting, describing, canonizing, and explaining the material texts of Scripture.

Divine providence has operated in all of these activities. *Deus operatur in omni operantione naturae et voluntatis.* Beyond acting in the preservation, prolongation, and disintegration of the societies and cultures out of which Christian Scripture emerged and which it reflects, however, divine providence has ordained that the Son of God should become incarnate in order to redeem the persons and communities who are the producers of societies, cultures, economies, and religions. Divine providence has ordained that through the outpouring of the Holy Spirit, human persons can participate in the divine life, resulting in their own healing and transformation and impelling them to recognize and participate in the redemptive economic work of the Triune God in greater and greater measure. I provided understandings of the missions of the Son of God and Holy Spirit in the previous chapter. They constitute an objectification of a horizon of meaning that provides the divine context of Christian Scripture. Divine providence has also willed that the Holy Spirit inspire the authors, redactors, and canonizers of Scripture towards the end of communicating the good news of the revelatory and redemptive entry of divine meaning in history in the person of Jesus Christ, the incarnate Son of the Father. Divine providence has willed that readers of Scripture encounter the living Word of God through the manifold words of the two Testaments and so be transformed and conformed to that living Word "from one degree of glory to another" (2 Cor 3.18).

The present chapter has borne the burden of articulating an account of human persons that provides an explanation of how we can be *capax Dei* in that economy. These two investigations are necessary components of a systematic theology of the nature and purpose of Scripture because they objectify the divine and human contexts out of which Scripture has emerged and in which it is still located. Having offered accounts of these necessary contexts, we can now proceed to examine Scripture itself in the history of human meaning and culture in the next chapter and in the work of the Triune God in chapter 6.

CHAPTER FIVE

Scripture in History I

The Realia *of Christian Scripture*

> Christian tradition and Christian theology give us the Bible, a unified
> whole, these days bound in one volume, in a translation that gives it a
> homogeneous style. History gives us a collection of documents varied in
> language, style, origin, date, authorship, character, genre, purpose, attitude,
> and so on. To do justice to the Bible we have to retain the element of
> 'givenness' while 'unimagining' it and taking account of the somewhat
> messy human business of the canon's formation.
>
> —Frances M. Young, *Virtuoso Theology*

The previous two chapters provided theological doctrines and philosophical judgments—and understandings of those doctrines and judgments—
that serve as heuristic accounts of the intelligibility of the economic work
of the Triune God and the constitution of human persons in that history,
respectively; Christian Scripture emerges historically in those contexts and
continues to serve as an instrument in them. Both this chapter and chapter 6 articulate an answer to the specific question, What is Christian Scripture?, in light of the judgments and hypotheses of the previous two chapters on the respective divine and human contexts of the Christian Bible.

At first glance, the question, What is Christian Scripture?, would seem to have a straightforward answer. One could simply point to one's Bible on the shelf and exclaim, "That is it!" Yet any sustained reflection on the question is bound to lead to immediate and potentially paralyzing perplexity. Is *this* particular translation—the New Revised Standard Version, or the New American Bible, or the English Standard Version, or the New International Version—*the* Christian Bible? Is *this* canonical collection— the listing of books laid down by the Council of Trent, the "Protestant" Bible with its rejection of the deuterocanonical or Apocryphal books, the canon of the Tewahedo Ethiopian Church—the Christian Bible?[1] Is *this* textual family or critical text tradition—the ancient Septuagint (though which recension? and only the Pentateuch?), the Dead Sea Scrolls manuscripts, the Masoretic Text, the Vulgate, the *Textus Receptus*, the UBS 5 or Nestle-Aland 28—the Christian Old Testament or New Testament? The extant material data of Christian Scripture invite all of these questions and others. Any responsible account of the nature and purpose of Christian Scripture *must* adequately address the question of how we can even satisfactorily identify the Bible given the diversity of the extant *realia* of the history of Scripture.

In order to know what Christian Scripture *is*, we must know what it *has been*. What follows is a multifaceted examination of the reality and intelligibility of Scripture. In this chapter and the next I provide answers to the following questions: What are the physical, material texts of Christian Scripture, and what are their characteristics? How and by whom was/is Christian Scripture produced? What is/are the judgments and/or meaning(s) that Christian Scripture mediates? And, finally, what is the purpose of Christian Scripture?[2] What follows depends upon and builds upon material from the previous chapters to identify and locate Scripture within the economic work of the Triune God and within the history of human culture.

While the next chapter addresses the unity of Scripture within the work of the Triune God in history, the present chapter serves as an overview examination of the material *realia* of Christian Scripture. Such evidence is frequently downplayed or ignored in discussions of the nature and purpose of Scripture. Any adequate understanding of the nature and purpose of Christian Scripture, though, must do justice to the *actual ex-*

tant evidence of Christian Scripture. Scripture's material reality has theological significance. Christian communities have preserved and transmitted the texts of Scripture, and even under the most restrictive and exclusivistic understandings of what the boundaries of the church are, the Christian community has not fixed and preserved exactly the same text. Specific communities have utilized specific distinct texts at specific and distinct times in history. The Triune God, though, has spoken to such communities through texts which are not identical to one another. There is no one already-out-there-now-real Bible at which we can point to answer the question, What is Christian Scripture? An illustration from one exegete, Thomas Aquinas, will serve to highlight the complexity of answering this question.

IDENTIFYING CHRISTIAN SCRIPTURE:
THE EXTANT EVIDENCE

Sometime in the spring of 1256, Thomas Aquinas delivered two inception sermons, called *principia*, at the University of Paris to complete the formal requirements for the degree of *magister in sacra pagina*.[3] In the second of these sermons, known as the resumption *principium*, Thomas utilizes his chosen theme verse—"This is the book of the commandments of God, and the law that is forever. All that keep it shall come to life: but they that have forsaken it, to death" (Bar 4.1)—to reflect on the nature, purpose, and structure of Christian Scripture.[4] Following his affirmations of the authority, efficacy, beauty, and usefulness of Scripture, Thomas proceeds to divide and categorize the two Testaments of Scripture and their respective contents.[5]

In his resumption *principium*, Thomas unsurprisingly reflects the "high" classical doctrinal beliefs about Scripture shared almost uniformly by premodern Christian interpreters.[6] It is noteworthy, yet unsurprising, however, that aside from his mention of some of the specific books of Scripture in this work—and he does not name all of them—Thomas nowhere else answers the precise question, *quid est Sacra Scriptura*? This question apparently was not pressing in the setting of medieval Christendom; Thomas nowhere indicates that he is troubled by the fact that the scriptures he possesses are translations of texts that originally appeared in other languages, and he gives only limited attention to textual variants or to matters of textual criticism.[7] Thomas assumes that he can definitively identify his Bible with the *liber* of Baruch 4.1.[8]

It is ironic, however, that Thomas utilizes a passage from Baruch to emphasize the uniformity of Scripture. The canonicity of that book, bearing the name of Jeremiah's friend and scribe (see Jer 39, 43, 50–51), was contested in the early church between the fourth and sixth centuries AD, and many Protestant groups have rejected its canonicity since the Reformation.[9] At the beginning of the fifth century Jerome already rejected the book as inauthentic and did not translate it (see *Comm. Jer.* praef.). A version from the *Vetus Latina* did eventually make it into the medieval Vulgate.[10] I have found no scholarly defense of the antiquity or authorial authenticity of the book.[11] There are no extant manuscripts of it in a Hebrew *Vorlage*, and it has never appeared in the Jewish Tanakh.[12]

There are further ironies in Thomas's citation. In its original literary context in Baruch, Thomas's chosen *prothema* appears near the end of a hymn in praise of Wisdom. While many hymnic or poetic odes to Wisdom in ancient Jewish literature emphasize the universal availability of Wisdom (see Prov 8; Wis 3), Baruch restricts its provenance to Israel and the Torah alone.[13] Thomas, in order to extoll the authority, unity, and usefulness of *Christian Scripture*, repurposed a text that suggested that God's authority, expressed in the Torah exclusively, was the sole possession of Israel. Thomas exploited a peculiarity in the Latin text in order to do so. In the Greek text of Baruch, Wisdom itself (see 3.12 and 3.23 and the feminine pronouns in 3.15, 3.21, 3.22, 3.31, 3.32, and 3.38) is the antecedent of the demonstrative pronoun (αὕτη) in 4.1a.[14] The Latin translator, after rendering the feminine ἡ βίβλος with the masculine *liber*, has rendered the preceding pronoun as *hic* to bring it into agreement with *liber*.[15]

Thomas, while not unaware of the Greek Christians of his day and the existence of the Tanakh in Jewish communities, nevertheless lived in a much more homogeneous culture in the Christendom of thirteenth-century Europe than the historically conscious twenty-first-century world.[16] Thomas, while remarkably astute, did not make the variability, plasticity, and diversity of human cultures a key theme in his thinking.[17] Thomas also antedates the recent discoveries of extremely significant manuscripts of Scripture, the creation of standard critical eclectic texts, and the recent explosion of translations; and, of course, he lived long before the events of the Reformation made the question of the precise canonical limits of Christian Scripture a pressing matter in ecumenical dialogue. Our contemporary awareness that Scripture has such a variegated history impels a theological question that Thomas did not answer. How is Scripture the written Word of God even in and through the apparent messiness of its concrete history? A systematic theology of the Christian Bible cannot proceed without giving adequate attention to the concrete actualizations of Scripture in history. An adequate understanding of what Scripture is must attend to what Scripture has been.

Many contemporary theological treatments of Scripture do not give attention to its material instantiations. Our awareness that Scripture itself has a material history requires us to reexamine the precise question of how it can be held to be authoritative, efficacious, and uniform. We must also evaluate its material history and historicity from a theological perspective. What is the theological significance of the fact that throughout Christian history human persons have had to continually *determine* Christian Scripture at the levels of its material instantiations, its actual words (textual criticism) and their rendering in receptor languages, and finally with respect to the precise boundaries of the canon? We cannot understand the nature and purpose of Christian Scripture systematically if we refuse to countenance these questions.

Many have questioned whether it is responsible, given our awareness of the particularities of the history of the Christian Bible, to speak of its uniformity or authority today in general terms.[18] I maintain that it is possible to understand and articulate the doctrinal judgments that Scripture is inspired by the Spirit of God, uniform in its purposes, and decisively authoritative for Christian believers, but that possibility depends upon our ability to adequately articulate those judgments in such a way that acknowledges the human subjective processes involved in the ongoing determination of Scripture; it especially depends upon our ability to understand and articulate the instrumentality of Scripture within the work of the Triune God in human history. We cannot responsibly locate the uniformity and authority of the Christian Bible in some already-back-there-then uninterpreted set of canonical autographs. The authority of Scripture, then, while objective and discernible in history, is nevertheless exercised or enacted only when its transmitters, translators, readers, and hearers are transformed in accordance with the divine intentions of its author, the Triune God, who has caused it to be written and to whom it testifies. But this is to anticipate a judgment I will expound in the next chapter. For now, I need to offer a few words concerning the instrumentality of Scripture.

The Instrumentality of Scripture and Its Locations in Christian History

I will provide an extensive—though not exhaustive—investigation of the material history of Christian Scripture in a moment, but prior to doing so it is necessary to recognize that Scripture has always been written and copied *to be read aloud, recited, heard, remembered, meditated upon, and understood.* The early Christians put Scripture to use in liturgical worship, in catechesis, in meditative and technical commentary, in theological treatises, in apologetics, in the establishment of ecclesial order, and in paraenesis; the natural setting of Christian Scripture was within the communal and individual life and activity of Christians.[19] They would not have produced, transmitted, adorned, and cherished Scripture apart from their performative judgment, expressed in their use of Scripture for all of these purposes, that it was eminently useful for Christian life in all of its facets (2 Tim 3.16). Contemporary scholars and religious communities, in fact, would not have access to the Jewish and Christian scriptures without the rich histories of their use and transmission in Christian (and, for the Hebrew Bible/Old Testament, Jewish) communities.

The actual concrete writtenness of Scripture has always served instrumental purposes. As determined, then, whether finally or provisionally, the words of Scripture, in all of the precise and imprecise particular configurations in which they are extant, *always point beyond themselves.* Christian Scripture is an instrument of human and divine meaning making in history. The human authors of Scripture, and especially the early Christian communities that received them, all assume the instrumentality of Scripture.[20] To anticipate the final section of the next chapter, I hold that the diverse concrete historical instantiations of the Old Testament and the New Testament have served as useful, divinely ordered instruments that have mediated the meaning and actuality of the economic work of the

Triune God throughout Christian history. They continue to serve as useful instruments for facilitating that work in the Christian individuals and communities who receive them, take them up, and read them today. Having offered this clarification, I now proceed to examine and describe some of the most striking features of Christian Scripture in its material histories.

The Artifacts I: Book Technology in the History of Christian Scripture

It is quite difficult for contemporary people, this side of the technological developments of advanced publishing and printing technology, word processors, and an array of digital options for reading, to appreciate the scope and significance of the technological developments that have taken place since the documents that make up the Christian Bible were originally produced. Such developments have unsurprisingly had profound impacts on the shape, presentation, accessibility, and relative availability of the scriptures. The histories of the employment of such technologies for the transmission and use of Scripture are fascinating and worthy of investigation for their own sake, but a thorough investigation of such considerations would take us far beyond the scope of the present work.[21] Even so, it is necessary to study aspects of this history; to understand Christian Scripture, we must know what it has been. It is imperative to reflect theologically on the fact that the Bible has a unique material history.

Perhaps the most jarring detail of the pre-Reformation history of Christian Scripture is that the texts that we take for granted as the Christian Bible have survived only because they were copied again and again by hand—as the etymology of the word *manuscript* indicates—by innumerable and often nameless individuals and communities.[22] Though the fact that such copying has taken place and that we would not possess the Bible that we now take for granted does not necessarily rule out the judgment that these texts are inspired and unified, as I argue in the next chapter, we cannot ignore the influence and impact of this human activity even in our supposedly "finalized" or stabilized Christian Bible(s) today. Many contemporary versions of the Bible attest to this history by including footnotes that indicate variants in the actual wording of the manuscripts. Even so, few readers of Christian Scripture outside of the academy of biblical scholarship give extensive attention to this fact.[23] I discuss the significance of such variations in wording at greater length below. Prior to doing so, it is necessary to examine and theologically evaluate the distinctive characteristics of the actual physical materials—or artifacts—that have served as the vehicles of the written and copied words of Christian Scripture throughout its history.

The revolutionary invention of the Gutenberg printing press (1440) and more recent inventions of digital printing techniques represent monumental achievements that have made "complete" copies of the Bible, or pandects, easily available in most of the world today.[24] The very possibility of assembling a single-volume Bible, however, is a distinctive historical achievement that depends upon and reflects a number of prior technologically and theologically significant developments. For most of Christian history the Bible was passed on as a collection of separate books or as collections of books. "[It] is, and always has been," writes James Kugel, "a collection of texts, a kind of literary miscellany."[25] In his description of and instructions for interpreting Christian Scripture in his *Institutions*, Cassiodorus (485–585) expressed this traditional judgment when he called Christian Scripture a "sacra bibliotheca" (holy library).[26] For most of Christian history the Bible has existed physically as a multivolume collection.

Pandects were extremely rare in the early church.[27] The massive majuscule manuscripts of Sinaiticus, Vaticanus, and Alexandrinus of the fourth and fifth centuries AD are the exceptions that prove the rule.[28] Portable pandects comparable in size to contemporary Bibles did not become widely available until the thirteenth century, and even then they exhibited a great deal of variability in content and arrangement.[29] As Susan Boynton and Diane Reilly state, "The concept of the Christian Bible as a unit is . . . a medieval invention."[30] Multivolume Bibles, however, remained common even long after the invention of the "modern" Bible in the thirteenth century.[31] I discuss the significance of the unification of the Christian scriptures into one volume below, but there are other key developments that I must treat prior to doing so.

Long before the "unification" of the Bible in the Middle Ages, the earliest Christian communities promoted a technological development in book production that rivals the invention of the printing press in its importance. "The physical form of the book," Anthony Grafton and Megan Williams indicate, "[was] in flux in late antiquity."[32] Prior to the third century AD, most of the written literary works of antiquity were composed as rolls or scrolls of papyrus—a plant-based material used almost exclusively in Egypt—or parchment/vellum made from animal skin.[33] From the second to the fourth century, however, Christians in particular, and then other classical writers, transitioned from the use of rolls/scrolls to the use of the leaf book, or codex.[34] It is hard to overestimate how significant the adoption of the codex has been for Christian reading and use of Scripture.

Modern people are perhaps liable to view this transition as insignificant due to our familiarity with codex books. The almost universal Christian preference for the codex format for the manuscripts of the texts that we recognize as Scripture, however, is quite shocking in its historical context. As Harry Gamble declares, "A codex or leaf book was not recognized in antiquity as a proper book."[35] There are some extant literary codices in Egypt from around the end of the first century AD, but for the most part ancient writers prior to the second century used codices only for the transmission of nonliterary information. Before Christians adopted the codex as their preferred textual medium, simple wood and papyrus codices were used for recording legal transactions, accounting and figures, inventories, and school exercises. The larger codex is the progeny of such pedestrian tablets and notebooks, called πίνακες.[36]

The Jewish communities of the Second Temple Period (538 BC–AD 70) followed the literary conventions of their times by copying their scriptures exclusively on rolls.[37] Undisputedly Jewish codex-form manuscripts of the Hebrew Bible are not extant until well after the Talmudic period.[38] Our earliest undoubtedly Christian works, however, the early manuscripts of the texts that we know as the New Testament, are codices.[39] There are a number of ways to evaluate the Christian preference for the codex for the works that we recognize today as the books of the New Testament. The practicality of the codex format is certainly a significant reason the early Christians chose it. Unlike the content of scrolls/rolls, which could only be read or accessed sequentially, codices allowed for the possibility of "random access."[40] Codices were also slightly less expensive given their ability to accommodate more text.[41] They were more compact and portable than rolls, and small codices could be held in one hand.[42] The compactness of the codex meant it could be more easily utilized in early Christian missionary endeavors.[43]

The early Christian utilization of the codex also likely manifests some significant and unique theological presuppositions of the early church regarding the texts of both the New and Old Testaments. In *Christianity and the Ancient Book*, Grafton and Williams identify a key ideational advantage of the codex format for early Christians. "The codex," they write, "offered possibilities different from those the roll had for the expression of extra-textual meaning."[44] Grafton and Williams demonstrate how the medium of the codex was necessary for complicated textual arrangements of the critical apparatus of Origen's *Hexapla* and Eusebius's *Chronicon* of world history. Codex technology itself allowed its authors to display more information in more complex configurations than was possible in the roll format. While their work is dedicated to two early nonscriptural works, Grafton and Williams's observations regarding the usefulness of codices for reference and for comprehensiveness are relevant for understanding how Christians used the codex for the texts of both the Old Testament and the New Testament. The codex format made possible the assemblage of all the texts of Christian Scripture under one cover, though that did not take place regularly until the Middle Ages.[45] Perhaps more significantly, the codex format provided Christians with an apt medium for promoting their beliefs regarding the comprehensive and decisive work of the Triune God in history. The early Christians found the codex format an exceptionally useful instrument for bearing linguistic, referential witness to the action of the God of Israel through Jesus Christ and the Holy Spirit. The portability of the codex format allowed Christians to travel and transport these important documents conveniently.

John Barton has argued that the early Christians utilized codices for the texts that we know as the New Testament because they were more preoccupied with identifying and proclaiming significant recent events of Jesus Christ and the birth of the church than they were with interpreting or producing sacred scriptures. "For Christians as for Jews and, indeed, for pagans," Barton writes, "the idea of 'Scripture' inherently contained the idea of age and venerability."[46] Though the ancient Christians affirmed the venerability and authority of the ancient Jewish Scriptures, they treated the relatively new texts that we know as the New Testament as authoritative remarkably early.[47] While second century AD Christians quoted or alluded to the traditions of the texts we know as the New Testament as authoritative, and even did so with greater frequency than they cited the texts of the ancient Jewish Scriptures, they seldom did so in accordance with the norms for engaging the "scriptural texts" of their environment.[48] The Apostolic Fathers, for instance, were many times more likely to appeal to the traditions reflected in the texts of the New Testament as authoritative but seldom cited those traditions in conventional "scriptural" ways.[49] Scriptural introduction formulas seldom occur with early quotations of the content of New Testament texts.[50] Early Christians undoubtedly treated the texts that we know as the New Testament as witnesses and memory aids to events in history.[51] The use of codices confirms this practical bent. "One could hold," Barton writes,

> that Christians decided that they needed a distinctive form for their Scriptures, but it seems easier, in view of the extremely early date and the fact that elsewhere codices were only used for books of very *low* status, such as notebooks, to think that the original use for the Gospels was linked not to a perception of these works as holy books, 'Scripture', but to a sense that they were not exactly *books*, but memoranda or notes.[52]

The concrete codex form of these texts, at least at the beginning of their production and transmission, suggests that the value of the New Testament texts such as the Gospels for the early church was not intrinsic—though they were no doubt extremely important—but instead was, at least at first, mostly instrumental. The texts served as testimony mediating the words of Christ and the all-important events of his life.[53] I quote Barton at length:

> The first Christians had books about Jesus and his first disciples, and they used them as authoritative sources of information about the central events of salvation. *These events dwarfed, in their minds, anything in the holy books they had taken over from Judaism.* . . . [For] early Christian communities . . . the most important books were those that as yet were *not* 'Scripture'—the books which gave Christians access to the deeds and teachings of the Lord and of his authoritative first interpreters. These books were more important than '*Scripture*', and to

cite them as *graphē* might have diminished rather than enhanced them. . . . [These] books had a status greater than that of the Old Testament.[54]

Ignatius of Antioch bears witness to this disposition in his epistle to the Philadelphians:

> For I heard some people say, "If I do not find it in the archives, I do not believe it in the gospel." And when I say to them, "It is written," they answered me, "That is precisely the question." But for me, the "archives" are Jesus Christ, the unalterable archives are his cross and death and his resurrection and the faith that comes through him; by these things I want, through your prayers, to be justified (Ign. *Phld.* 8).[55]

Ignatius strikingly reveals his preference not for written records, or even for the oral word, but instead for the *actual events* of Christ's crucifixion, death, and resurrection and the faith that comes through him.[56] His emphasis on the actuality of God's work anticipates Irenaeus's subsequent focus on the economy of God's work in Christ and the Holy Spirit. The codex format made available and easily accessible the authoritative written testimony of the evangelists, apostles, *and* even the ancient Jewish prophets to that work. Their testimony was extremely important, of course, and it is unthinkable to suggest that the early Christians could have existed without their sacred texts.[57] But the referents, the *res*, of that testimony were more fundamental for them than were their texts. The actual saving and revelatory actions of the God of Israel who had raised Jesus Christ from the dead and poured out his Spirit on all flesh took precedence over and conditioned the early Christian reading of the ancient Jewish sacred texts.

Thus far I have focused almost exclusively on the early evidence of the texts that we know as the New Testament. The first Christian scriptures, though, were the ancient Jewish writings that contemporary Christians know as the Old Testament. As the copious citations of Old Testament texts in the New Testament demonstrate, the earliest Christians, of course, did affirm and appeal to the authority of the ancient Jewish Scriptures. At first, the only access they would have had to those texts would have been either through reading scrolls produced by Jewish scribes under the conventions of Jewish scribal practice or through their communal memory of those texts. Just as Christians treated the texts of the New Testament as instruments mediating testimony about events in history, so also they employed the ancient Jewish Scriptures as testimony to and confirmation of those recent events.[58] In fact, early Christians utilized collections of "proof text" quotations extracted from the ancient Jewish Scriptures, customarily called *testimonia*, as written tools for proving that Jesus Christ had fulfilled those ancient Scriptures.[59] While the earliest extant collections of Christian *testimonia* that we possess come from the third and fourth centuries AD, the characteristic citation of certain text forms in the New Testament and the Apostolic Fathers, and the existence of Jewish *testimonia* collections from Qumram, provides strong circumstantial evidence that Christians probably had such books very early.[60]

The earliest unequivocally Christian manuscripts of the ancient Jewish Scriptures are not in roll format; like the early manuscripts of the New Testament texts, Christians produced copies of the ancient Jewish Scriptures in codex form. The Christian use of that format for the ancient Jewish Scriptures would have been quite scandalous given the cultural conviction that such ancient and venerable works required a format reflecting their high status.[61] The minor post-Talmud tractate *Soferim* (ca. 8th c. AD) attests that the only appropriate format for the ancient Jewish Scriptures is the roll (1.1–6). Though it is late, *Soferim* probably reflects many of the scribal conventions of ancient Judaism.[62] The first Jewish Christians "took over" the texts of the ancient Jewish Scriptures from the synagogues to employ them in Christian worship.[63] The codex format of the ancient Jewish Scriptures within early Christianity indicates the instrumentality of those texts for the early church. As Frances Young summarizes:

> [In the] new Christian assemblies, it was not scrolls and reading which had primacy. The word written and read was testimony to something else, and the living and abiding voice of witness had greater authority. There was no reason why . . . this written testimony should not be recorded in notebooks so that reminders could be turned up more readily and carried about with less difficulty. . . . We are witnessing . . . not the gradual elevation of recent Christian books to the sacred status

of the Jewish scriptures, but rather the relativizing of those ancient scriptures. Certainly they retain an undeniable aura, both because of the respect accorded literature in the general culture of the Graeco-Roman world, and because of the specific legacy of their sacred place in Jewish tradition. *But they have become secondary to the Gospel of Christ.*[64]

The texts of both the ancient Jewish Scriptures and the new texts of distinctly Christian provenance served as instrumental witnesses pointing beyond themselves to the events of the work of the God of Israel in and through Jesus Christ and the Holy Spirit. A significant majority of the extant undoubtedly Christian manuscripts—of both nascent Testaments—are codices; that format was especially apt given the early Christian understanding of their instrumental purpose. In what follows I provide a brief overview of the distinctive characteristics of those instrumental written witnesses, mostly focusing on premodern manuscripts, in order to highlight the variability and instrumentality of the extant historical instantiations of the Christian Bible.

As I noted above, there are very few pandect codices among the early extant manuscripts of Christian Scripture.[65] The massive amount of materials required, the intrinsic physical limitations of those materials, and the cost of labor necessary to produce a complete pandect Bible would have made it almost impossible for most Christian communities to have one.[66] It is important to note that the freshness of the codex format meant that even *the possibility* of assembling all of the sacred books of Christianity into a single volume was itself novel in the early years of Christianity.[67] While many of the books of Christian Scripture present in contemporary canonical collections were authoritative from extremely early in Christian history, certain books were of disputed authority.[68] It would be impossible to produce a complete Bible before developments in codex technology made the *idea* of a complete Bible possible. And despite the extensive utilization of codex technology in the early church, the Christian "Bible," as I have already noted, still remained a physical "library" with somewhat flexible "boundaries" for most of its early history.[69]

In addition to manuscripts containing single books of the Bible, there are a number of part-Bible codices that contain multiple books among the extant textual artifacts of Christian Scripture.[70] By sometime in the second century AD, it is likely that more than one edition of the collected letters of Paul circulated among Christian communities.[71] There is also evidence that copies of the four canonical gospels, Matthew, Mark, Luke, and John, circulated together in a single codex in the second and third centuries.[72] The practice of producing and circulating these "incomplete" part-Bibles continued through the Middle Ages. A famous illumination in the Codex Amiatinus (ca. 700), one of the oldest extant pandect manuscripts of Christian Scripture, depicts Ezra recopying the books of the Law (see 4 Ezra 14.19–48) in front of an armarium, or bookcase, containing a nine-volume copy of the Christian Bible.[73]

Part-Bibles served a number of distinct purposes in premodern Christian communities and were produced and employed especially for liturgical use. Medieval scribes created highly ornate gospel collections, known as *Evangeliaria*, such as the Book of Kells, the Golden Gospels, and the Lindesfarne Gospels, for use in Christian worship.[74] The Psalter also regularly appeared as a single volume throughout the Middle Ages. Frans van Liere indicates that, in addition to the *Evangeliaria* and the Psalter manuscripts, we possess part-Bibles from the thirteenth and fourteenth centuries containing the respective collections of the Pentateuch, Hexateuch (Pentateuch plus Joshua), Heptateuch (Pentateuch plus Joshua and Judges), Octateuch (Pentateuch plus Joshua, Judges, and Ruth), Prophets, Wisdom books, a book of women (Ruth, Esther, Judith), Paul's writings, and the Catholic epistles (often with Acts; these were called *Praxapostolos*), respectively.[75] The practice of publishing part-Bibles continues even to the present day. Gideon's International, for instance, produces and distributes pocket "Bibles" containing only the New Testament, Psalms, and Proverbs.[76] The seven-volume St. John's Bible—a contemporary illuminated manuscript—follows the precedent set by premodern part-Bibles.[77]

While it is clear that written documents played an extremely important role in early Christian communities, scholars have relatively recently begun to give concentrated attention to the importance of considering the oral/aural dimensions of the ancient contexts in which the ancient scriptures of Judaism and Christianity were produced.[78] Many ancient readers, including Christians, had a distinct preference for testimony by word of mouth, or "the living voice" (ζώσης φωνῆς or, *viva vox*), over written testimony.[79] Papias of Heiropolis (ca. 70–135), for instance, states that he preferred the oral testimony of living disciples of Jesus to information written down in books (see Eusebius *Hist. eccl.* 3.39).[80] Written and oral traditions were complementary to and interpenetrated one another in ancient Judaism and Christianity.[81] Both religious communities exercised great care in transmitting their traditions via either memory or writing. They did so, though, "precisely because their contents were important— because of what they meant."[82] The media, whether oral or written, were instrumental to the message.

The ancient Jewish Scriptures/Old Testament bear witness to the importance of the public reading of Scripture in a number of places during Israel's history (See Deut 31.9–13; Josh 8.32–35; Jer 36; Neh 8–9, 13). Though the precise characteristics of the public reading of Scripture in first-century Judaism(s) are not completely clear, the earliest Christians undoubtedly inherited the practice of public recitation of Scripture from Jewish worship practices.[83] Luke reports that Jesus began his ministry by reading from the scroll of the prophet Isaiah in the synagogue at Nazareth (Luke 4.16–30). The earliest Christians read or heard the ancient Jewish Scriptures when they gathered in the temple and synagogue for prayer and teaching (Acts 2.46; 3.1; 5.42; 13.14–15; 15.21).[84] It is therefore not surprising to find Paul exhorting Timothy to "give attention to the public reading of scripture" (1 Tim 4.13).[85] The growth of the authority of the texts that we know as the New Testament is certainly related to their use in public worship. Paul writes that he expects his addressees to read his letters aloud to those gathered for worship (1 Thess 5.27; Col 4.16).

In the middle of the second century AD, Justin Martyr indicated that Christians in Rome read from "the memoirs of the apostles" (τά ἀπομνη-μόνευμα τῶν ἀποστόλων)—he is probably referring to one or more of the canonical Gospels and the book of Acts—and from the prophets— probably any and all of the ancient Jewish Scriptures—when they came together for worship on the first day of the week (1 *Apol.* 67.3).[86] The public/oral nature of these texts is inscribed into many of the manuscripts of the New Testament, which contain aids for public reading.[87] Of the 5,600-plus Greek New Testament manuscripts currently identified and cataloged, over 2,400 contain markings that indicate that they are lectionary texts.[88]

Ancient readers would regularly have read texts aloud, syllable by syllable.[89] The extant Greek manuscripts of the texts of the New Testament from the early centuries of Christian history were written *scriptio continua*, without spacing between words.[90] For that reason, in part, the individual texts comprising the manuscript history of the Christian Bible are seldom completely unadorned; most of them feature various "helps" for facilitating oral reading, cross-referencing, and ultimately understanding.[91] Neither the earliest manuscripts of the Old Testament nor those of the New Testament, though, had punctuation. Up until the eighth century, Greek writers seldom used punctuation, and only a few early New Testament manuscripts feature any form of punctuation.[92] The earliest extant Hebrew manuscripts of the ancient Jewish Scriptures, the Dead Sea Scrolls, lack the vowel markings and reading aids that appear in post-medieval copies of the Hebrew Bible.[93] The innovations in the text of the ancient Jewish Scriptures have their own complex history of development in the fifth through the seventh century and were standardized by the Masoretes, a group of Jewish scribes active in Tiberius in Palestine, between the seventh and tenth centuries.[94]

The versification and chapter divisions of contemporary Bibles are relatively recent additions, but many of the ancient manuscripts of Christian Scripture feature various extratextual markers for facilitating access and cross-referencing.[95] The chapter divisions of contemporary Bibles are extant for the first time in the work of Stephen Langton in the early thirteenth century, and the versification of our modern Bibles comes from Etienne Robert in 1534.[96] By approximately AD 200, though, Christian scribes were already using various markers to denote "sense-unit divisions" in manuscripts as an aid for readers.[97] Ancient manuscripts regularly include chapterlike divisions (κεφάλαια), and some gospel manuscripts include "chapter titles" (τίτλοι).[98] Many ancient manuscripts of parts of the Christian scriptures have line division markers (στίχοι) to facilitate reading and ease of access.[99] Manuscripts of the Gospels often contained an elaborate system of cross-referencing developed by Eusebius of Caesarea.[100] A number of later Greek manuscripts produced for liturgical use contain markers that indicate the beginning (ἀρχ, an abbreviation of ἀρχή) and ending (τέλ, an abbreviation of τέλος) of readings for worship gatherings.[101] The various markers and symbols discussed above made the already useful scriptures even more useful for liturgical recitation and study.

The extant manuscript artifacts of the Christian Bible prior to the invention of movable type, even in the most basic features of their technological shape, order, and presentation, exhibit tremendous variability. The use of printing technology for production of Christian Bibles "hides" the variety of its material history from contemporary readers. It also distances us from the distinctive features of the use and interpretation of Christian Scripture within premodern Christian communities. Candler has argued that the use of printing technology for the publication of Christian Scripture has had significant theological consequences.

> The invention of the printing press . . . makes possible the isolation and hypostasization of the biblical texts as the sole authority for Christian theology, as well as the abstraction of these texts from the way they are used in Christian worship and the continuing interpretive tradition. . . . [The] Bible [could then be understood] as a physical 'thing' whose spatial limits are quite clearly defined, a thing which is always to hand, easily accessible.[102]

The production of printed pandect Bibles makes it easier to overlook the variable history of Christian Scripture and its location within Christian worship and Christian practices. But that is only a tendency; it is entirely unnecessary for us to ignore the variable history of these material artifacts in their communities. We must attend to their history adequately, and acknowledge its variableness, if we are to articulate a faithful and responsible understanding of the nature and purpose of Scripture for our own time.

Despite the variability of the extant premodern manuscripts of Christian Scripture, some recurring key visual and technical characteristics are inscribed into them that indicate the unity of these texts in striking ways. From the earliest extant manuscripts of both the New Testament and the Old Testament until the invention of the printing press, Christian copyists passed on a tradition of specially marking keywords, customarily called *nomina sacra*, by abbreviating them by suspension—keeping only the first two letters—or by contraction—keeping the beginning and ending letters of words and by adding an overbar above their letters.[103] More than fifteen distinct *nomina sacra* exist in the early Greek manuscripts of the Christian scriptures, but the most prevalent ones are for God/Θεος ($\overline{\Theta C}$/ $\overline{\Theta Y}$), Christ/Χριστος ($\overline{XP}$/$\overline{XPC}$/$\overline{XC}$/$\overline{XY}$), Jesus/Ιησους ($\overline{IN}$/$\overline{INC}$/$\overline{IC}$/$\overline{IY}$), Lord/ Κυριος ($\overline{KC}$/$\overline{KY}$), cross/σταυρος ($\overline{CTC}$/$\overline{CTY}$), and Spirit/Πνευμα ($\overline{\Pi NA}$/ $\overline{\Pi NC}$).[104] Since five of those six (all except σταυρος) are appellations for the persons of the Triune God, Schuyler Brown has suggested that it is more appropriate to call them *nomina Dei*.[105] Other *nomina sacra* that regularly occur in early Christian manuscripts include the nouns Son/Υιος, David/ Δαυιδ, Mother/μητηρ, Father/Πατηρ, Israel/Ισραηλ, savior/σωτηρ, man/ ανθρωπος, Jerusalem/Ιερουσαλημ, heaven/ουρανος, the verb to crucify/ σταυροω, and the adjective spiritual/πνευματικος (when used in relation to the Holy Spirit).[106] The use of the *nomina sacra* is attested as early as the time of the composition of the Epistle of Barnabus (ca. AD 70–130), which includes a discussion of the numerical value of the nominative *nomen sacrum* for Jesus, $\overline{IN}$ (9.7–8).[107] The beginnings of this system of specialized markings cannot have originated any later than the first quarter of the second century AD, and some scholars have argued that the practice likely has its origins in the first century AD.[108]

The inscription of *nomina sacra* in Christian Scripture manuscripts may have its psychological origin in the early Jewish Christian practice of revering the personal name of God in the Hebrew Bible, יהוה (YHWH).[109] Many pre-Christian Jewish manuscripts, including those in Greek, render the divine name in square paleo-Hebrew script or substitute four dots (*tetrapuncta*) for the letters.[110] The *nomina sacra*, however, are a definitively and distinctively Christian innovation.[111] Whatever their precise origins, it seems almost certain that the practice is born out of Christian piety and served to reinforce it.[112] They are not restricted to the Greek manuscripts either; they occur in the early Latin, Coptic, Gothic, Slavonic, and Armenian translations of the Christian scriptures.[113] The practice of inscribing these *nomina sacra* in the texts of the early Christians not only unifies the diverse books that constituted sacred scripture for the earliest Christians and the texts of scriptures of both Testaments; it is a marker of the unity in diversity of the variable artifactual history of the manuscripts of Christian Scripture.[114] These diverse concrete texts of Christian Scripture have the same theological referents: they are fundamentally about the Triune God. While some of the *nomina sacra* are unequivocally *nomina*

Dei (Θεος, Χριστος, Ιησους, Κυριος, Πνευμα, Υιος, and Πατηρ), others connect directly to the person of Jesus Christ in his humanity (Δαυιδ, μητηρ, Ισραηλ, ανθρωπος, Ιερουσαλημ), and still others identify the work of Jesus Christ and the Holy Spirit (σταυρος, σταυροω, σωτηρ, ουρανος, πνευματικος). Tomas Bokedal and Colin Roberts have highlighted that the words abbreviated as *nomina sacra* in Christian Scripture are the keywords of the early kerygma about Christ, the rules of faith, and the later creeds.[115]

The use of these identifying markers also ties the texts of Christian Scripture to the other visual artifacts of nascent Christian culture; the *nomina sacra* feature prominently in premodern Christian art and architecture.[116] Their use in multiple media visually and psychologically links together Christian reading, confession, worship, and symbolic and artistic expressions of faith in a profound way. Their very visibility on the pages of Scripture would likely have had a profound effect on both literate and illiterate Christians in the ancient world. Jane Heath has helpfully situated the practice of the *nomina sacra* in the context of ancient attitudes towards the role of the mise-en-page for shaping the memory of the reader. "In Jewish, pagan, and Christian settings, often in similar ways," she writes, "an important purpose of reading was not merely to verbalize, but to memorize and internalize. In this process, contemplation of the text *ad res* (and not mere replication *verbaliter*) became significant."[117] The visual distinctiveness of the *nomina sacra* would have served to orient readers towards an overarching understanding of the *res* beyond the pages of Scripture.[118]

The mention of early Christian visual culture leads me to focus upon one final distinctive characteristic of the technology of the manuscripts throughout the history of Christian Scripture. Premodern Christian biblical manuscripts regularly feature symbolic and artistic adornments. Hurtado has noted that some very early manuscripts of the New Testament, including P66 (ca. AD 200), P45 (ca. AD 250), and P75 (ca. AD 175–225), feature staurograms—pictograms that depict Christ upon the cross by combining the Greek letters *tau* and *rho*: ⳨—within the *nomina sacra* for σταυρος and σταυροω.[119] The staurograms may be the earliest extant Christian representation of Christ's crucifixion and would have reminded readers of the founding event of Christian faith. Most early artistic adornment of Christian scriptural manuscripts was restricted to similarly modest symbols. As early as the sixth century AD, though, some manuscripts of the Gospels featured miniature illustrations of the evangelists or of scenes of the events of the New Testament.[120] Subsequent manuscripts received more and more extensive illumination. By the Middle Ages many biblical manuscripts were richly ornamented and featured elaborate and beautiful illustrations.[121] Such illumination both reflected the high esteem that readers held for the texts themselves and helped to reproduce such esteem in subsequent readers.[122]

Even prior to the incorporation of extensive illuminations on the very pages of Scripture manuscripts, though, the earliest Christians were already interpreting their scriptures through frescoes, sculptures, mosaics, architecture, and other visual media that depicted the scenes and characters of the texts. These believers freely expressed their understandings of Scripture artistically. That artwork, in turn, influenced their reading.[123] Robin Jensen draws attention to the "mutual dependence of verbal and visual modes of religious expression" in the early church.[124] Both word and image, though, served the same purposes. The symbolic and artistic dimensions of the manuscripts of Christian Scripture and the artistic and symbolic representations that Christians have produced under the influence of the words of Scripture have all characteristically served the instrumental purpose of mediating the meaning and actuality of the work of the Triune God in history. Both word and image rightly oriented readers and hearers, in mind, heart, and will, within reality.[125]

The Artifacts II: The Text and Language of Christian Scripture

The variability of the technology attested in the extant manuscripts of the Christian Bible is paralleled by the variability in the wording of the extant manuscripts we possess. Before a text, even the text of Christian Scripture, can be read, interpreted, and understood, it must be identified and determined. The question must be answered, what are *the precise words* of the Christian Bible? "In one sense," writes P. Kyle McCarter, "a text is an intangible entity. It is the wording of something written. The text is contained in the written work, but because it can be copied, the text is an independent thing, and when the work perishes, the text survives if it has been copied."[126] We do not, as is mostly well known, possess autographs of any of the books of either Testament. We are therefore dependent upon ancient manuscript copies for our knowledge of the textual content of Christian Scripture. This situation is both a blessing and a curse, McCarter notes, because the process of copying is "a source of both survival and corruption for a text; the very process that preserves the text also exposes it to danger."[127] More and better manuscript evidence for the texts of Christian and Jewish Scripture is available today than for any other ancient writing. No two premodern manuscripts in these textual traditions, however, are identical in their wording.

The diversity of readings or variants present within the textual history of the transmission of both Testaments is relatively unsurprising given the fact that they were copied again and again over hundreds of years by scribes of varied levels of skill.[128] Gamble provides an apt summary of the reasons for the characteristic lexical variability of ancient hand-copied texts:

> Errors of transcription are inevitable . . . given the various psychological and mechanical operations involved. A scribe's inadvertent departures from his exemplar tend to be typical. . . . Even in the most carefully transcribed manuscript there will be instances of omission, addition, transposition, and, of course, misspelling. Sometimes scribes made intentional changes in the text as they copied, undertaking to improve the language or to clarify the sense, assuming that they were rectifying the error of a previous scribe.[129]

The transmission history of Christian Scripture reflects the same kind of issues common in the premodern transmission of any text.

The question of the precise words of Christian Scripture can only be answered through painstaking investigations of fragmentary histories of multilingual manuscript evidence that spans centuries and several (often extinct) languages.[130] The modern discipline of textual criticism has developed in order to sort out the relationships between the various extant manuscripts of the Christian Bible.[131] Contemporary handbooks or textbooks on biblical exegesis characteristically emphasize the priority of textual criticism at the beginning of the exegetical process.[132] Though this discipline has developed extremely sophisticated tools and principles for examining the extant manuscript witnesses to the Christian scriptures and though we possess an abundance of manuscript witnesses for both Testaments, textual criticism is by no means an exact science. The fragmentary nature of the evidence, and the poor quality of much of it, makes analysis of the relationships between various texts quite challenging. Beyond these material challenges, the question of the actual goal of the process of textual criticism is itself philosophically and theologically challenging.

As David Parker notes with regard to the New Testament, "[What] we have is a mass of manuscripts, of which only about three hundred date from before AD 800. A mere thirty-four of these are older than AD 400, of which only four were at any time complete. All these differ, and *all at one time or another had authority as the known text.*"[133] Peter Gurry, on the basis of statistical comparisons of a few representative manuscript collections, has recently estimated that there are approximately 500,000 textual variants among the 5,600-plus extant Greek manuscripts of the New Testament![134] Beyond the Greek evidence, we possess quotations of the texts of the New Testament by premodern Christian thinkers and ancient translations of the New Testament in a variety of languages, including Syriac, Coptic, Armenian, Georgian, Ethiopic, Latin, Gothic, and Slavonic.[135] Many of the variants in these traditions are insignificant, but some discrepancies, including the absence of Mark 16.9–20 from the earliest versions of Mark and the absence of the narrative of the woman caught in adultery (John 7.53–8.11) from John's gospel, are more striking.[136] Other smaller variations have theological or liturgical significance, such as the absence of the trinitarian benediction in 1 John 5.7–8 from early versions and many variants present in the textual traditions of the Lord's Prayer (Matt 6.9–13; Luke 11.2–4).[137]

The vast majority of variant readings of the books of the New Testament likely arose in the earliest history of those texts.[138] Gamble notes that "the number of corruptions in the earliest manuscripts indicates that during the first several centuries these texts were widely circulated and frequently copied and that Christian books were not reproduced under highly controlled conditions."[139] That characteristic variability may have arisen not from carelessness but instead from the desire of the early Christians to disseminate these texts widely and quickly. As I noted above, the Christian communities held many if not most of the texts that we know as the New Testament to be authoritative extremely early (by the end of the first or beginning of the second century AD), but they were not entirely scrupulous in copying them; their content was far too important for them not to be disseminated in haste.[140] In his conclusion to a discussion on early Christian attitudes towards the New Testament text, Michael Kruger argues that the variability in the early manuscripts of the New Testament indicates that the "early Christians, as a whole, valued their texts as Scripture and did not view unbridled textual changes as acceptable, and, at the same time, some Christians changed the [New Testament] text and altered its wording (and sometimes in substantive ways)."[141]

The primary extant textual witnesses for the ancient Jewish Scriptures—which Christians know as the Old Testament—are the textual traditions of the Masoretes (7th–10th c. AD), pre-Samaritan and Samaritan textual traditions, the Hebrew, Aramaic, and Greek manuscripts from Qumran and the Judean desert (3rd c. BC–2nd c. AD), and ancient translations—the chief witnesses being the Greek versions.[142] The issues involved in understanding the lexical history of the Hebrew Bible/Old Testament are different from those involved in studying the New Testament because of the relative "standardization" of the Hebrew text by the Masoretes around the end of the first millennium AD.[143] Jewish scribes were generally quite meticulous in copying the texts of the Hebrew Bible.[144] Even so, there are considerable differences between the various textual traditions of the history of the textual transmission of the ancient Jewish Scriptures.[145] It is even misleading to speak of "the" Masoretic text because of the variations that occur in the textual witnesses from around the turn of the first millennium AD.[146] The evidence of the Dead Sea Scrolls, the Samaritan Pentateuch, and the ancient Greek translations forces us to recognize that the textual history of the ancient Jewish Scriptures is quite fluid. Ulrich writes that the text of the ancient Jewish Scriptures "was not a single static object but a pluriform and organically developing entity."[147]

Though textual criticism is a modern development, awareness of the inconsistencies in the textual traditions of the biblical books is not.[148] Around the middle of the second century AD Justin Martyr argued that recent Greek translations of the ancient Jewish Scriptures (perhaps those of Aquila, Theodotion, and Symmachus) had for anti-Christian theological purposes omitted key phrases that were found in the more ancient Greek translation of the Scriptures known as the Septuagint (see *Dial.* 71–73).[149]

Irenaeus shows his awareness of different textual traditions when he accepts a particular reading of the book of Revelation on the basis of its antiquity (*Haer.* 5.30.1). Origen, though, was the first Christian to extensively engage in text critical work.[150] He attempted to correct the texts of the manuscripts of the Gospels that he possessed (see *Comm. Matt.* 15.14, 16.19; *Comm. Jo.* 2.132, 6.204, 20.144) and prepared a massive text critical tool, known as the *Hexapla,* which set five textual traditions of the ancient Jewish Scriptures next to one another—a Hebrew tradition, a transliteration of that tradition into Greek, the LXX tradition, Aquila, Symmachus, and Theodotion—in order to determine their precise relationships to one another.[151] Jerome practiced textual criticism and retranslated most of the Christian scriptures from Hebrew (Old Testament) and Greek (New Testament) into Latin because of his frustration with the many variants present in the Old Latin manuscripts. Later medieval scholars and churchmen were also bothered by the textual variability of their copies of Scripture and set about the work of correcting them.[152]

Christians have characteristically undertaken text critical work in pursuit of the textual form of the lost autographs. Contemporary theorists of textual criticism have argued, however, on the basis of the available manuscript evidence, that it is no longer possible to assume that textual criticism can deliver the original contents of the lost autographs of the biblical books.[153] One major reason for this judgment, besides the fragmentary nature of the evidence, is that ancient people likely did not share our ideas of what an original text or final published version actually are.[154] We are now aware that a number of universally accepted books of the Bible were utilized in much different forms in antiquity than the forms they currently take.[155] To cite one example, the textual history of the book of Jeremiah presents a number of significant challenges.[156] We can read of some of the redactional processes "behind" the text of Jeremiah in the book itself (see Jer 36.4; 36.18, 36.27; 36.32).[157] Until the discovery of the Dead Sea Scrolls in the mid-twentieth century, the earliest extant Hebrew manuscripts of Jeremiah were those in the textual tradition of the Masoretes, which were produced around the turn of the first millenium AD.[158] The earliest Greek evidence of Jeremiah comes from the great Christian majuscule manuscripts Sinaiticus (4th c. AD), Vaticanus (4th c. AD), and Alexandrinus (5th c. AD). The Greek manuscripts, interestingly, are approximately one-sixth shorter than the later Masoretic manuscripts, and they exhibit a different organizational structure.[159] Ancestors of both the longer Masoretic traditions and the shorter Greek traditions are extant in the literature at Qumran.[160] Christians and Jews universally regard the book of Jeremiah as authoritative and inspired. But which copy is the "original" form of the book of Jeremiah?

The New Testament texts raise similar and different problems.[161] The book of Romans serves as a significant New Testament example. While all of the extant Greek manuscripts contain the entire letter, some omit the address (in Rom 1.7, 1.15), and there is significant indirect evidence that the letter may have circulated early on without some or all of the material of chapters 15 and 16.[162] Would a copy of Romans without the last two chapters still be a copy of Romans? The Gospel of Mark circulated with four separate endings, and the earliest versions lacked 16.9–20, yet most modern translations include those verses.[163] Why do they not eliminate them if "the original text" is the most fundamental goal of modern versions? If Matthew and Luke used Mark and another source, or if there is any literary dependence in the relationships between the synoptics, then can those two later texts really be considered "original"? Except for his habit of penning his final greetings in his own hand, Paul dictated his letters, and scribes exhibited a great deal of variability in the ways they took dictation. What was "original," Paul's exact spoken words or the exact words written by the scribe? Second Corinthians appears to be a composite of as many as five (!) different letters.[164] Which is the "original"? In the face of these questions, Eldon Epp judges that "the term 'original' has exploded into a complex and highly unmanageable multivalent entity."[165] Though many within the faith traditions of Judaism and Christianity have a felt need for determining a uniform ancient original, the evidence of the extant manuscript witnesses of Scripture indicates that our forebears who passed on the textual traditions of Scripture, even if they expressed and pursued high standards for textual uniformity, were not always able to maintain those standards and made peace, at least practically, with the variability of the texts they used and held authoritative.

The variability of languages represented in the early transmission of the scriptures poses further challenges for contemporary readers attempting to discern the text. Modern translations hide the original linguistic variability of the Christian scriptures.[166] One language, such as English, is used to render three: Hebrew, Aramaic, and Greek. Unlike contemporary Muslims, who have historically been extremely reluctant to translate the Qur'an into languages other than the Arabic of the original, and Jews, who must learn Hebrew in order to read from the Tanakh in religious ceremonies, Christians have always lived with and even embraced the situation of having a translated and translatable set(s) of authoritative scriptures.[167] The only access we have to most of the words of Christ, in fact, is likely through translation.[168] The processes involved in the translation of any written work from one language to another, though, require translators to make significant interpretive decisions. A famous Italian proverb expresses the risk of this necessity well: "Traduttore traditore" ([The] translator [is a] traitor).[169] Access to the abundant resources of the manuscript history of Christian and Jewish manuscripts allows us to examine and assess the interpretive decisions of Christian and Jewish communities in transmission *and* translation of what we possess as the Christian scriptures.

Christians faced multilingual challenges from the very beginnings of the church. The authors of the New Testament who accepted the authority of the ancient Jewish Scriptures did not restrict themselves to Hebrew manuscripts. In fact, a significant majority of the citations of the Old Testament extant in the texts of the New Testament are of Greek versions.[170] The evidence of the New Testament indicates a strong Christian preference for the Greek texts of the ancient Jewish Scriptures. As Lee Martin McDonald explains:

> The value attributed to the LXX in the early church cannot be overestimated. It was the *Christian* Bible. There was a strong belief in the early church that the LXX was an inspired translation that was superior to Hebrew. Indeed, when the Hebrew and the LXX differed, the later was preferred because the LXX translators who changed the Hebrew text were inspired by God to do so, which the apostles recognized by citing the LXX.[171]

I cannot give an extensive account of the ancient Greek versions of the Christian Old Testament, but it is important to note that they have their own complex histories.[172] Their textual complexity is evident in Origen's

Hex., which juxtaposed at least *four distinct* Greek Old Testament traditions.[173] The authors of the New Testament cited both Greek and Hebrew
traditions of the ancient Jewish Scriptures as if they possessed equal authority, even though the textual forms of those versions exhibited considerable differences from one another.[174]

As Christian communities gradually lost direct contact with their Jewish roots, beginning in some localities as early as the end of the first century, many lost contact with the Hebrew language altogether.[175] Of the
church fathers, aside from those in the Syriac tradition, probably only Origen and Jerome had any extensive engagement with the Hebrew texts of
the ancient Jewish Scriptures. Jerome's insistence that it was necessary
for Christians to defer to the *Hebraica ueritas* is a late innovation (see his
Epist. 18, 20, 36).[176] By preferring the Hebrew text tradition over the Greek,
Jerome makes a break with the ubiquitous early Christian preference for
the Greek translations of the Old Testament. A number of early Christians,
including Justin Martyr (*1 Apol.* 31.1–5; *Dial.* 71.1–2), Irenaeus (*Haer.*
3.21.2–4), Clement of Alexandria (*Strom.* 1.11.148–49), Eusebius of Caesarea (*Praep. ev.* 8.1–15.9), Hilary of Portiers (*Tr. Ps.* 2.3), John Chrysostum (*Hom. Gen.* 4.9; *Hom. Matt.* 5.4), and Augustine (*Civ.* 18.42–43) explicitly invoked or alluded to the legend recounted in the Letter of Aristeas
(ca. 3rd to 2nd c. BC)—which presented the Greek translation of the
Torah by seventy-two elders as miraculous—as support for the judgment
that the ancient Greek versions were truly inspired and should have a privileged place of authority for the church above the Hebrew text.[177]

The relative consistency of the textual traditions of both the Old Testament and New Testaments is certainly impressive and significant, but
reflection on such histories from the perspective of divine providence
demonstrates that the Triune God has not preserved for contemporary
or ancient Christian believers, or allowed such believers access to—with
certainty—the exact intricacies of the textual traditions of the Christian
scriptures. I contend that the fact that the Triune God has not preserved
the text—whether wholesale or merely in a single historical tradition—is
theologically instructive. The variable history of the wording of the texts of
the Christian Bible and their technological variability and adornment with
punctuation, place markers, reading markers, systems of cross-reference,
systems of abbreviation, and artistic beautification demonstrate that Chris-

tian communities have always sought to understand Scripture beyond the letters and words. These variable texts have always served as useful technical and artistic instruments to be performed and understood. The vast majority of the manuscripts of the Christian scriptures extant today serve as "the Word of God" for their respective communities, just as the ancient texts did, even though those texts differ from one another, sometimes significantly.

The Artifacts III: The Books and the Canon(s) of Christian Scripture

Uncertainty about the precise identity of the contents of the Christian Bible, of course, extends beyond questions concerning the continuity and discontinuity of the artifacts of Scripture, the variations in the textual histories of those artifacts, and the distinctive languages represented in those histories. The question of determining the actual distinct books that constitute the Christian scriptures also requires our attention. Karl Barth contends that theologians must raise the question of the precise scope and contents of the Christian scriptural canon in every age.[178] No universally recognized, definitively authoritative ecumenical church council has determined or recognized a final listing of the books of the Christian Bible.[179] Distinct contemporary Christian traditions, in fact, possess differing collections of biblical books in their authoritative Bibles.[180]

While an exhaustive history of the formation of these canons of Scripture is beyond the scope of the present work, a brief examination of this history will allow me to fill out my account of the variability of the material artifacts of Christian Scripture. Any purported understanding of the nature and purpose of Christian Scripture that cannot account for the historical processes involved in its canonization will prove inadequate. Thankfully, a number of scholars have provided extensive informative accounts of the historical processes of the canonization of Christian Scripture. I will make reference to and draw upon these studies in order to provide the basic historical judgments necessary for an adequate understanding of the historical development of notions of the boundaries of Christian Scripture.[181]

Before investigating the historical formation of the Christian biblical canons, though, we must define our terms. As McDonald notes, a lack of clarity concerning the meanings of the technical terminology employed in contemporary discussions of "canon" presents significant problems for achieving an adequate understanding of the history of Christian Scripture.

> The terms "canon," "canonical," "non-canonical," "biblical" or "non-biblical," "apocryphal," and "pseudepigraphal," even "Old Testament" and "New Testament," are often confusing when cited in contemporary investigations of ancient Jewish and Christian literature. *They are all anachronistic terms that later Christian communities used to describe literature that did or did not eventually find acceptance in the Hebrew and Christian Bibles.* Initially most of these writings, if not all of them, functioned as sacred literature in one or more Jewish or Christian religious communities.[182]

With reference to Scripture, the term "canon" has typically borne a great deal of semantic freight. "In its popular use today," McDonald writes, "canon speaks primarily of a closed collection of sacred Scriptures that Jews and Christians believe had their origins in God and are divinely inspired."[183] That popular usage, however, obscures the historical processes through which Christians came to recognize "the canon" of Christian Scripture. The word *canon* itself, as I explained in chapter 2, has a history prior to its employment as a cipher for a definitive listing of authoritative, accepted books.[184] As Barton indicates, while a number of early Christian lists of the books of Scripture exist from the second to the fifth century AD, Athanasius's *Ep. fest.* 39, written and delivered in AD 367, represents "the first unequivocal evidence for the use of the word to mean a fixed list of books."[185] Prior to that time, the word *canon* was used exclusively—at least in the extant texts we possess—to refer to the faith and practices of the Christian communities. For the church fathers, lists such as Athanasius's served to loosely rule or regulate Christian use of Scripture in worship and study.[186] Books accepted as canonical could serve Christian purposes. In fact, however, such lists were not determined and then employed to regulate Christian worship and study. McDonald writes that such lists, especially when produced by councils or regional synods, "acknowledged those books that had already obtained prominence from widespread usage among the various Christian churches in their areas."[187] There is, he states elsewhere, "no doubt that the individual documents that comprise a biblical canon functioned authoritatively as inspired sacred writings within a believing community *before* they were incorporated into a canonized fixed corpus."[188] Jewish and Christian communities *used* certain texts that they held to be authoritative and then *later* formalized their authoritative status and unification in specific lists. The lists themselves, however, provide ambiguous evidence for discerning "closures" of the canon.[189]

Because certain ancient Jewish texts—such as the Torah/Pentateuch, Prophets, and Psalms—and even emerging apostolic New Testament texts—such as Paul's letters to the churches and the four Gospels—had functional authority for Christians extremely early, it is potentially misleading to speak of canonization as a "process."[190] It seems best to contrast the "functional" or "core" canons of the early church with later lists that give the impression of the relative fixity of the contents of Scripture.[191] From the beginning of the Christian churches, Christians have possessed a "canon consciousness" centered on specific, almost universally accepted books, but they did not attempt to fix comprehensive lists of accepted books in any rigid sense until much later.[192] The evidence of the "fixed lists" of the early church—no two lists agree exhaustively—and of actual codices of Scripture that contain "noncanonical" works (Sinaiticus, Vaticanus, Alexandrinus, Claromantus, and many later manuscripts), and finally of the continued use of "noncanonical" books throughout Christian history, suggests that most Christians, at least before the Protestant Reformation, have not considered such "closures" to be absolute.[193] Martin Luther did not consider the texts he had received as absolutely fixed. In his translation of the New Testament he relocated Hebrews and James with Jude and Revelation at the end, marking them off as separate from those books that he considered definitely canonical.[194]

The earliest Christians possessed a functional canon of faith long before any individual or group of Christian believers set out to clearly define a fixed list of authoritative, inspired books. The κανών τῆς πίστεως/ *regula fidei* antedates all of the early Christian lists of authoritative books. As McDonald declares, "In the broadest definition of the term *canon*, neither the Israelites nor the Christians were ever without a canon or authoritative guide, that is to say, they always had *a story that enabled them to establish their identity and give life to their community*, even though they did not have a stabilized text of Scriptures in their earliest development."[195]

I have already offered an account of the emergence and development of the rule of faith in the early church and its function for Christian theological reflection through scriptural interpretation. As I discussed above, the rule of faith is arguably inscribed into the books of Scripture themselves in the *nomina sacra*. It is still necessary to briefly examine the historical vicissitudes of the "fixing" of Christian Scripture as a collection of authoritative books. As we have already seen, careful attention to the extant evidence of the Christian practice of Scripture is extremely complicated. The historical developments in the canonicity of Scripture are equally complicated, and this section attempts to both draw attention to these complications with regard to the "canon" of Christian Scripture and offer theological judgments regarding this history that must have a place in a responsible understanding of what it is precisely that the Triune God has given us in Christian Scripture.

The earliest Christians clearly accepted and endorsed the authority of the ancient Jewish Scriptures.[196] Some scholars have argued that Jesus and Paul had inherited a closed canon of Jewish Scripture, but such a suggestion, in my judgment, goes beyond the evidence, assuming theological positions about what must have happened and imposing them on the extant data.[197] Following his thorough investigation of the New Testament evidence, McDonald concludes that "[we] simply do not know what [Jesus's] biblical canon was."[198] Given the nature of the historical evidence, the precise identity, boundaries, and scope of the ancient Jewish Scriptures accepted by the earliest Christians are impossible to determine with absolute certainty.[199] The New Testament citations of the ancient Jewish Scriptures offer ambiguous evidence for discerning the books that the earliest Christians accepted as authoritative. Some Old Testament books in currently accepted Christian canons are cited nowhere in the New Testament (Jdgs; Ruth; Ezra; Esth; Obed; Zeph) or only sparingly (Josh, 1x; 1 Sam, 4x; 2 Kgs, 2x; Neh, 1x; Job, 3x).[200] Others, however, occur in abundance (Genesis, Exodus, Deuteronomy, the Psalms, and Isaiah are cited more than thirty times each, the latter two most frequently).[201] The New Testament authors also cited or alluded to other texts "outside" of traditional canonical boundaries (see Acts 17.28; 1 Cor 15.33; Tit 1.12–13; Heb 11.37; Jude 9, 14–15).[202] Sometimes they even cited texts as Scripture for which we have no extant evidence (Matt 2.23; Luke 24.46; John 7.38, 12.34; Eph 5.14; Jas

4.5). Though the ancient Jewish Scriptures clearly had functional authority as Scripture for the earliest Christians and though it is possible to identify with some probability the major works that constituted those scriptures, we are in the dark regarding the precise constitution and scope of the writings from which such citations are drawn.

The New Testament wording of the citations of the ancient Jewish Scriptures, as anyone who has perused the indices of Old Testament citations and allusions in the NA 28 or the UBS 5 can notice, frequently exhibits a great deal of variation from texts of known, extant manuscripts of the ancient Greek and Hebrew versions of the ancient Jewish Scriptures. The authors of the New Testament quoted freely from multiple text forms.[203] The earliest Christians made use of the variableness of the Hebrew and Greek texts they possessed, capitalizing on textual variants for specific, distinctly Christian purposes.[204] As noted above, it is possible that they utilized *testimonia* text traditions of the ancient Jewish Scriptures that are no longer extant in order to instruct their audiences.[205] The citations cannot give us evidence of the complete scope of the specific texts from which they originate either. The paucity of manuscript evidence from the early centuries of the Christian community, and the fact that much of the written materials that existed in such times has been lost to history completely, requires us to have a great deal of humility in any assessments of the text forms or scope of texts cited.[206]

The question of the precise books that were available to the earliest Christians is therefore a matter of uncertain conjecture. There are some hints, though, in ancient literature. In approximately AD 100, the Jewish historian Josephus wrote that the Jewish people possessed a collection of exactly 22 sacred scrolls, to match the number of letters in the Hebrew alphabet (*C. Ap.* 1.37–43), but he does not name the books that constituted that collection.[207] The book of Jubilees may also refer to an unspecified 22-book collection of scrolls (Jub. 2.23–24).[208] A number of later Jewish and Christian sources testify that there are 22 books in the ancient Jewish Scriptures, but "none of [those] lists . . . are the same in either Jewish or Christian sources.[209] A number of other ancient witnesses, on the other hand, including 4 Ezra 14.22–48 (ca. AD 100), Gos. Thom. 52 (ca. AD 100–140), the tractate B. Bat. 14b–15 (ca. AD 70–200), Victorinus (ca. AD 260), Jerome (ca. AD 390), and various texts of the Amoraim (3rd–6th c. AD), suggest that the Jewish people possessed a 24-book collection.[210] None of these witnesses, however, explicitly lists the names of the books of the ancient Jewish Scriptures/Old Testament until probably the second century AD.[211] Eva Mroczek has compellingly argued that we should not understand these numbers given by Josephus and 4 Ezra as quantitative; they "are typological, reflecting certain qualities, rather than quantities of precise and preexisting texts."[212]

B. Bat. 14b–15 is the earliest extant Jewish list of authoritative books of Scripture, and it lists the same twenty-four named books of the contemporary Tanakh.[213] Even if that list is contemporaneous with the writing of the New Testament, though, later rabbis disputed the authority of a number of books, including Ecclesiastes, Esther, Ezekiel, Proverbs, Ruth, and Song of Songs.[214] That list apparently did not exert much influence on early Christians either, "since they clearly depart from it and do not divide their Scriptures into the same groups."[215] No early Christian canon lists are identical to the contemporary Tanakh.

It was only around the late second/early third century AD that Christians began to exhibit a clear concern to precisely determine acceptable and unacceptable books. The earliest Christian lists of the books of the ancient Jewish Scriptures, by Melito of Sardis (ca. AD 180) and Origen (ca. AD 200) are provided by Eusebius of Caesarea (ca. AD 320–25).[216] Melito's list includes the names of the books that occur in the contemporary Protestant Old Testament except for Esther and Lamentations (*Hist. eccl.* 4.26.14, though the latter may have been included with Jer). Origen's list omits the book of the Twelve but includes the Epistle of Jeremiah (*Hist. eccl.* 6.25.2). While a number of other church fathers list the books of the ancient Jewish Scriptures, those lists "are broader than the Jewish Old Testament [*sic*] canon, and no two lists are identical."[217]

While the discordance of the canon lists of the early church exhibits that Christians continued to disagree over acceptable and unacceptable books even into the sixth century AD (and beyond), it seems clear that the earliest Christians received what Stephen Chapman has called a "core canon" of the Torah, Prophets, and Psalms (cf. Luke 24.44).[218] Michael Kruger's words concerning the New Testament canon in the early churches are apropos regarding the lack of universal agreement concerning books on the fringes of the canon of the ancient Jewish Scriptures: "We should not use lack of *agreement* over the edges of the canon as evidence for the lack of the *existence* of a canon."[219] The early Christians treated the core canon of the ancient Jewish Scriptures that they received in a distinctively Christian way, though.[220] And the core canon of the ancient Jewish Scriptures that the early Christians accepted was quickly supplemented with writings of the early church that exhibited and promoted their new perspective on Jesus Christ.[221]

As I stated above, Athanasius's *Ep. fest.* 39 (AD 367) is the earliest extant list of the 27 books of the New Testament accepted by almost all contemporary Christian communities.[222] Though a number of works in that collection were disputed for quite some time (Heb, 2 Pet, Jas, 2 Jn, 3 Jn, Rev), the early church possessed a functional core canon of New Testament books quite early.[223] As I noted above, the earliest Christians cherished both the words of Jesus Christ and the narrative testimonies of the apostles concerning his crucifixion and resurrection. Though this testimony was first oral (see 1 Cor 15.1–8), the New Testament writings, most if not all of which originated during the first century AD, exhibit an early Christian inclination towards writing.[224] The early Christians accepted the texts of the New Testament as functionally authoritative because of their deference to Christ's authority and to the authority of the apostles whom he had commissioned. Evidence of the early Christian deference to Jesus's authority, both his spoken words and his embodied actions, is present throughout the New Testament. Paul quotes Jesus or defers to Jesus's authority many times in his letters (1 Cor 7.10–11; 11.23–26; 2 Cor 12.9; 1 Tim 5.18; see also Acts 20.35), and other New Testament authors follow the same practice (see Jas 5.12; 2 Pet 3.2).[225] "The earliest *regula* (canon) for the Christian community," McDonald declares, "was Jesus himself."[226] Jesus had spoken and acted, and the earliest Christians returned to and reflected upon his words and actions again and again, including by recording those words and actions in the writings of the New Testament.

Even in the New Testament we can find judgments, if not reflecting, at least anticipating, the scriptural status of those writings.[227] While the authors of the New Testament texts refer to, and defer to, the authoritative "law and prophets," which serves as a merism for the entirety of the Jewish Scriptures, there is already evidence in the texts of the New Testament that the teachings of the apostles occupied a place of authority alongside those ancient Jewish Scriptures immediately. That ancient merism for the entirety of Scripture, "law and prophets," in fact, would eventually give way to a new one—the "prophets and apostles"—which is anticipated in the New Testament itself. The explicit connection of the "prophets and apostles" occurs in Luke 11.49; Ephesians 2.20, 3.5, 4.11; and 2 Peter 3.2, and that language eventually became a shorthand for describing Christian Scripture as a complete collection.[228] While that language undoubtedly first referred to the ancient Jewish Scriptures and to the teaching of the living apostles, it came to serve as a reference to the authoritative en-covenanted (ενδιάθηκον) writings of what we know as the respective Testaments during the second century AD.[229]

The author of 2 Peter already puts Paul's writings on par with the ancient Jewish Scriptures (2 Pet 3.15–16).[230] How did the apostles come to have authority on par with the prophets?[231] The impetus for this judgment came from the early Christian conviction of the fulfillment of God's work in Christ and the new Christian community.[232] Paul wrote that the message of that new event that he preached was "from God and not man" (Gal 1). In 1 Thessalonians (ca. AD 50), likely the earliest New Testament writing, Paul writes of the Thessalonians, "when you received the word of God that you heard from us, you accepted it not as a human word but as what it really is, God's word, which is also at work in you believers" (1 Thess 2.13). The New Testament documents reiterated, reflected, and quickly came to represent that Word, the proclamation of the work of the God of Israel in Jesus Christ, and so had a share in that authority.

Paul enjoined the recipients of his letters to read them aloud to the Christians gathered together (2 Cor 10.9; 1 Thess 5.27; Col 4.16).[233] That practice surely would have had a striking effect on those groups that customarily read from the ancient Jewish Scriptures when they gathered. The author of Hebrews uses the same language to describe his own work—it is a λόγου τῆς παρακλήσεως (13.22)—as he does to introduce a text from the ancient Jewish Scriptures (cf. 12.5, where he refers to Prov 3.11–12 as τῆς παρακλήσεως). Some in the early church held Paul's letters to be "weighty and strong" (1 Cor 10.10).[234] He stated that some of his letters had general relevance beyond their use for their original recipients (Col 4.16). Paul's writings, despite their particularity, began to circulate to places other than the locales of their original recipients very early. There is a good possibility, in fact, that both Romans and Ephesians circulated as general letters.[235] As I noted above, the technology of the codex made possible the gathering of disparate documents in an unprecedented way, and it is possible that most if not all of Paul's letters were gathered together in that new format and circulated before the end of the first century AD.[236] The fourfold gospel, as I have already indicated, likely circulated together quite early as well.[237]

The Apostolic Fathers, as I noted above, were far more likely to make reference to the content of the New Testament writings than they were to the ancient Jewish Scriptures.[238] *1 Clement* (ca. AD 96) exhibits an awareness of Romans, 1 Corinthians, and Hebrews and may have alluded to Matthew, Mark, Luke, John, Galatians, Ephesians, Philippians, Titus, 1 Peter, James, and Acts.[239] Clement also states that Paul wrote "with true inspiration" (*1 Clem* 47.3). There is substantive evidence that Ignatius of Antioch (ca. AD 110) knew of and accepted the authority of Romans, 1 Corinthians, Ephesians, Galatians, Philippians, and 1 and 2 Timothy.[240] Polycarp (ca. AD 110) states that he knew John personally (Eusebius *Eccl. hist.* 5.20.4) and expressed his admiration for the apostle Paul (*Phil.* 9.1). He appears to know of a collection of Paul's letters (*Phil.* 3.2), and his writings demonstrate his awareness of Romans, 1 Corinthians, Galatians, Ephesians, Philippians, and 1 and 2 Timothy, as well as 1 Peter, 1 John, Matthew, and John. He also cites Ephesians 4.26 as Scripture in *Pol. Phil.* 12.1.[241] Papias (ca. AD 125) probably knew of and accepted as authoritative Mark, Matthew, 1 John, 1 Peter, Revelation, and some of Paul's letters.[242] Barnabus (ca. AD 130) 4.14 cites the content of Matthew 22.14 as Scripture and appears to know of Matthew, Mark, Luke, Romans, 1 and 2 Peter, and Revelation.[243]

By the middle of the second century AD, Justin demonstrates an awareness of the traditions of the synoptic gospels and likely cites all three of them (see *Dial.* 100.1; 103.8; 105.5; 106.3–4; 107.1). On a number of occasions he may allude to passages in John as well (*Dial.* 63.2; 94.3; 106.1; 118.1; 135.6). He is also aware of and alludes to or cites Acts, Romans, 1 and 2 Corinthians, Galatians, Ephesians, Colossians, 2 Thessalonians, Titus, Hebrews, James, 1 Peter, 2 Peter, 1 John, and Revelation. The Muratorian Fragment, which may be the earliest list of New Testament books and is regularly dated to the late second century AD, includes most of the books of the New Testament. It does not include 1 and 2 Peter but does include Wisdom of Solomon and the Apocalypse of Peter.

Near the end of the second century AD, Melito, Irenaeus, Tertullian, and Clement of Alexandria bear witness to further developments in Christian "canon consciousness" with respect to the New Testament books. Melito associates the writings of the ancient Jewish Scriptures with the "old covenant" (Eusebius *Hist. eccl.* 4.26.14).[244] Clement uses the language "new covenant" to refer to the books of the apostles (*Strom.* 1.44.3; 3.17.3; 4.134.4; 5.85.1). Irenaeus famously insists on the exclusive authority of the fourfold gospels (*Haer.* 3.11.8) and demonstrates an awareness of some of Paul's letters, 1 John, and 1 Peter.[245] From the late first century through the end of the second, though, most of Paul's letters and probably all four canonical gospels (though Mark was not as favored as the others) already possessed functional authority in the Christian communities for whom we have evidence. Even though the later lists of canonical New Testament books frequently vary, most of the books consistently recur. The four Gospels, most of Paul's letters (with the possible exception of 1 and 2 Timothy and Titus), Acts, 1 Peter, Jude, and James were widely accepted, quoted, and utilized by most of the early Christian communities for which we have evidence.

Even so, the boundaries of acceptable books for some Christian communities remained unclear even after Athanasius's *Ep. fest.* 39.[246] Eucherius (mid-5th c. AD) does not list Galatians, 2 Thessalonians, Titus, Philemon, 2 and 3 John, and Jude as authoritative. Cassiodorus (ca. AD 551–62) does not include 2 and 3 John, 2 Peter, Jude, and Hebrews in his list of New Testament books. The extant major biblical manuscripts reflect differences in order and contents as well. Codex Sinaiticus (4th c. AD) includes Barnabus and the Shepard of Hermas. Vaticanus (4th c. AD) omits Paul's pastoral letters, Philemon, and Revelation. Alexandrinus (5th c. AD) includes the Psalms of Solomon and 1 and 2 Clement. Claromontanus (6th c. AD) omits Philippians, 1 and 2 Thessalonians, and Hebrews and includes Barnabus, the Shepard of Hermas, the Acts of Paul, and the Apocalypse of Peter.[247] As with the Old Testament evidence, we are faced with a lack of absolute consistency and clarity.

Beyond the ancient evidence, the fact that different contemporary Christian communions hold differing lists of canonical books poses another obstacle for understanding Christian Scripture today unless we are able to accept the possibility of multiple distinct canons as a matter of adiaphora. Trent (AD 1546) is the earliest "ecumenical" Christian council that determined an absolutely fixed list of texts.[248] Following Trent, the Reformed Protestant churches moved to precisely determine their own canons, and most removed the apocrypha completely from printed Bibles.[249] Both Trent and the Protestant rejection of apocryphal books were significant innovations, though certain figures and events, such as Jerome and some early regional synods, perhaps anticipated them. As Denis M. Farkasfalvy notes, "The books not included in the Jewish canon yet regarded as Scripture by various communities caused few and only minor disputes among the early Christian churches, and led to no schisms or confessional splits in the first fifteen hundred years."[250] Though Christians have often exhibited a desire to "close" the canon, such "closures" have never had their completely desired effects. Christians probably will continue to use the texts both within and outside their own respective canons that they find useful and will probably continue to ignore those in their canons that they find irrelevant or troubling.

SUMMARY AND CONCLUSION

The widespread availability of printed pandect Bibles today—despite the clear differences between translations and communal textual traditions—can lull many people into thinking that the Christian Bible has always had an adamantine solidity, stability, and completeness. Contact with the diverse, expansive, and incompletely documented and frequently misunderstood history of Christian Scripture, on the other hand, leaves many contemporary Christians—across denominational and traditional boundaries—perplexed and disoriented. Candler has shown that the invention of movable type and the subsequent production of printed Bibles, combined with the social and cultural changes of the Reformation, made possible an assumption of the static stability of the Christian scriptures that was previously unthinkable.[251] Awareness of the historical variegation of the actual material instantiations of Christian Scripture makes it impossible to exclusively locate the unity, authority, and divine origins and characteristics of Christian Scripture exclusively in any single historical instantiation of the text or in any single textual tradition of transmission.

The textual history of Christian Scripture raises a question of providence. Has the Triune God left the Christian churches, at any point in their history, in any particular location, with an insufficient Bible? I answer this question negatively. No. I affirm the judgment, expressed regularly by the authors of the New Testament, that God has provided the requisite gifts of grace, including these historically particular scriptures, that are sufficient for accomplishing God's creative and redemptive economic work (Rom 8, 12; 1 Cor 2; 12–14; Eph 4; Heb 2.4; 2 Pet 1.1–8). The judgment that God has done things in what appears to be a rather haphazard manner is not incompatible with the judgment that God has providentially ordered the history of Christian Scripture.[252] It is still possible to affirm the work of the Holy Spirit, not just in spite of the variable history of Christian Scripture, but through the very details of that history. "The Bible" is not imprisoned in the autographs, the LXX, the Codex Amiatinus, the MT, the *Textus Receptus*, the King James Version, the eclectic Greek New Testament, or any other particular translation or textual recension. "Early Christians," writes Eldon Epp, " . . . would have treated as 'canon' whatever text-form of a gospel or letter had reached them in the transmission process."[253] Christians can, and unconsciously do, follow their example in how we treat contemporary instantiations of the Christian scriptures. Most historical instantiations of "the Bible" have served their communities as the written Word of God. The Triune God has not made a mistake in delivering to us the Christian scriptures as we currently possess them, in all of their historical untidiness.[254]

While we might affirm that what the Triune God has given us is sufficient for God's purposes, we can only identify what God has given us in the seemingly arbitrary flux of historical changes in the texts. Attentive engagement with any particular instantiation of Christian Scripture invites us into a tangled web not just of the literary contexts of specific passages and the historical contexts of their origins, but into the manifold historical plurality of the extant texts of the scriptures themselves in all of their iterations. The textual history of the scriptures is a history of progress and decline like all human history. It is possible and reasonable, though, to affirm that the Holy Spirit has worked to not only initiate this history, but to direct it and sustain it. And we need not engage the texts of Scripture alone or atomistically. It is quite impossible to do so, and the exigency of responsibility requires contemporary readers to measure up to the particularities of the texts. The vast majority of the extant texts of Christian Scripture were produced by Christian communities for the edification of Christian communities. When we engage our contemporary Bibles, we defer to the authority of those Christians who have used and passed on those texts to us. All who read modern translations also implicitly defer to the authority of scholars who have done the work of textual criticism and translation necessary to make sense of the vast divergent resources of the manuscript traditions of Christian Scripture.

Near the very beginning of the magisterial *Summa Theologiae*, Thomas Aquinas famously argued that the Triune God, beyond using the written words of Scripture, was able to use the realities of history to which Scripture referred to instruct believers in Christian faith (*ST* I q.1, a.10, resp). In doing so, Thomas followed a precedent set by Augustine, who wrote that "the whole ordering of time was arranged by divine providence for our salvation" (*Doctr. chr.* 1.35.39). The Triune Lord of history orders all of the *res* of the history that is for pedagogical purposes. The *res* of the material histories of Scripture itself, and our awareness of and understanding of those histories, have unique and important places within that divine pedagogy. The texts of the Christian Bible have undoubtedly had a tumultuous (though not arbitrary) history. Yet that history does not prohibit them from serving the unique roles that they serve in the work of the Triune God in history. "The creatureliness of the text," Webster writes in *Holy Scripture*, "is not an inhibition of its role in the communicative self-presentation of God; and so the text does not have to assume divine properties as a protection against contingency."[255] The Triune God can and does utilize creaturely realities to communicate with humanity. "How would God give himself to man," after all, de Lubac inquires, "if he remained a stranger to him? And how would his Word penetrate him if it were not also to become a human word?"[256] The Triune God sets apart the Christian scriptures, in their very historicity, for unique purposes in God's communicative self-presentation.

The very writtenness of Scripture is not without significance for the pedagogical purposes of the Triune God. As I noted above, many early

Christians preferred the authority of the oral testimony of those associated with Christ over the testimonies represented by and manifest in the written texts of either the Old Testament or the New Testament. Paul, in fact, draws a sharp contrast between "the letter" that kills and the Spirit that gives life (2 Cor 3.6); his judgment of the danger of writing, whatever its specific import, reflects a perspective common in the ancient world that writing was intrinsically problematic.[257] Over three centuries before the coming of Christ, Socrates lamented that the invention and popularization of writing would have deleterious effects in Athenian culture and society. "It will atrophy people's memories," he says. "Trust in writing will make them remember things by relying on marks made by others, from outside themselves, not on their own inner resources, and so writing will make the things they have learnt disappear from their minds. [Writing] is a potion for jogging the memory, not for remembering" (*Phaedr.* 275a).[258] While we ought to give heed to the concerns of both Socrates and Paul, it is important to note that they do not identify consequences that necessarily follow from writing. Some might insist that the writtenness of Scripture will atrophy memory, or even that it will kill, but we can be on our guard against both of these possibilities.

The technologization of the words of Christian Scripture in certain forms and with certain reading and understanding aids is artificial in the technical sense of that adjective, to be sure. But this is not an intrinsic weakness of Scripture but its great advantage. Walter Ong identifies the artificiality of writing as its intrinsic value.

[To] say writing is artificial is not to condemn it but to praise it. Like other artificial creations and indeed more than any other, it is *utterly invaluable* and *indeed essential* for the realization of fuller, interior, human potentials. Technologies are not mere exterior aids but also *interior transformations of consciousness, and never more than when they affect the word. Such transformations can be uplifting. Writing heightens consciousness.* Alienation from a natural milieu can be good for us and indeed is in many ways essential for full human life. To live and to understand fully, we need not only proximity but also distance. This writing provides for consciousness as nothing else does.[259]

The writtenness of Christian Scripture, in its varied languages and shapes, and all the other technological innovations present in its history— the possibilities of the codex, the utility of systems of cross-reference and access, and the use of symbolic and artistic features—serve profound instrumental purposes. Even the variability of the textual tradition serves a higher purpose. Christians hold that these writings do not mediate merely human meanings. They are ultimately brought into being by the Triune God to serve as instruments in God's economic work of redemption. Such realities, in the limit, facilitate our self-transcendence by serving as conduits of our relationships with the Triune God and all that God has created and is redeeming.

CHAPTER SIX

Scripture in History II

The Intelligibility of Christian Scripture

> But as for you, continue in what you have learned and firmly believed,
> knowing from whom you learned it, and how from childhood you have
> known *the sacred writings that are able to instruct you for salvation through*
> *faith in Christ Jesus. All scripture is inspired by God* and is *useful* for teaching,
> for reproof, for correction, and for training in righteousness, so that everyone
> who belongs to God may be proficient, equipped for every good work.
>
> —2 Timothy 3.14–17

> [Whatever] was written in former days *was written for our instruction*,
> so that by steadfastness and by the encouragement of the scriptures we
> might have hope.
>
> —Romans 15.4

Because it is necessary to acknowledge the material variety of Christian
Scripture throughout its history, it is impossible, both for theological reasons and because of the exigencies of responsibility, to locate the unity of
Christian Scripture in some already-back-there-then or out-there-now-
real version or tradition of the Bible. But that judgment does not necessitate

that Christians abandon the judgments of the unity, authority, and truthfulness of Christian Scripture. The work of the Triune God in history is one. Despite our lack of understanding of the precise contours of the history that is, it is still one. Scripture, in all of its particularity, is a "participant" and an instrument within that singular history. Scripture is an instrument of the Triune God that bears witness to the unity of that divine economic work and that facilitates that work.

Besides holding specific doctrinal judgments about the nature and work of the Triune God—affirmed in the creed and examined in chapter 3—Christians have generally and characteristically affirmed specific doctrinal judgments about Scripture *itself*. In this work I assume and affirm the traditional doctrinal judgments that Christian Scripture is inspired by the Holy Spirit (2 Tim 3.14–17; 2 Pet 1.16–21), that Christian Scripture is the written Word of God that bears witness to and mediates the meaning of the Son of God Incarnate, Jesus Christ, in history (John 5.39), and, finally, that Christian Scripture is a useful instrument of the pedagogy of the Triune God in human history. It is impossible to understand these doctrinal affirmations, however, without properly locating them. Because it is a result of and facilitates the work of the "two hands of the Father," Scripture should be located in the contexts of the mission of the Holy Spirit and the mission of the Son of God respectively in the history that is. Clarifying the place of Scripture within the missions of the Son and the Holy Spirit will serve to help us understand its nature and purpose in that unified work.

The first of the three aforementioned doctrinal judgments concerning Scripture, the judgment that Scripture is inspired, has received a great deal of attention in contemporary examinations of the nature and purpose of Scripture.[1] The other two, that Scripture is the written Word of God and that it is useful in divine pedagogy, have also featured importantly in a number of studies.[2] A number of authors have proposed that the concurrence of Christ's divine and human natures can help us to understand the way in which Christian Scripture is both divine and human, but few recent works have examined how Scripture has functioned and can function as an instrument within and relative to the mission of Jesus Christ, the Son of God, in the history that is.[3]

The three major sections of this chapter locate Scripture in the work of the Triune God by examining the aforementioned three doctrines.

Scripture is inspired by the Holy Spirit, Scripture is the written Word of God that mediates the living Word of God, and Scripture is the preeminently useful instrument of divine teaching in the economic work of the Triune God. The first section examines the location of Scripture relative to the economic work of the Holy Spirit. The second examines the location of Scripture relative to the economic work of the Son of God. The third is an examination of the continuing purposes of Christian Scripture and its usefulness in the missions of both the Son and the Holy Spirit. None of these sections can stand on its own. To give thorough enough consideration of each respective question, I have sometimes had to divert my course to address questions that might fit better under other headings; the explanations of this chapter do not unfold in a strictly linear manner. This chapter, of course, must be read in light of the previous chapters.

In what follows I frequently draw on resources from Christian thought in the past to locate Christian Scripture in its divine contexts as an instrument in the missions of the Son of God and the Holy Spirit in history. Beyond drawing on these resources, however, I have found it necessary to respond to difficulties that historical consciousness poses for understanding Christian Scripture in its historical particularity. This chapter brings together a number of theological, philosophical, historical, and ethical judgments and hypotheses towards the end of providing an intelligent, reasonable, and responsible account of the intrinsic unity, authority, and truthfulness of Christian Scripture *in ipse.*

THE INSPIRATION OF SCRIPTURE: SCRIPTURE IN THE MISSION OF THE HOLY SPIRIT

The present account of the nature and purpose of Christian Scripture maintains the premodern Christian judgment that the Christian scriptures are inspired by the Holy Spirit (2 Tim 3.16; 1 Pet 1.20–21; see also 1 Clem. 45.2). No premodern Christian thinker, though, has left us a treatise on this specific theological doctrine.[4] The major New Testament texts cited above provide scant guidance on how we should understand this judgment.[5] Early Christians assumed that Scripture had come from God and so was useful (ὠφέλιμος, 2 Tim 3.16), and even essential, for Christian thought and life. The inspiration of Scripture was taken for granted within premodern Christian communities. The controversies over the loci of Christian authority since the Reformation, relatively recent rich discoveries of the manuscript traditions of Christian and Jewish Scripture, and the rise of historical-critical approaches to Scripture since the Enlightenment, however, have inspired a number of theologians, philosophers, and biblical scholars to consider in depth the precise meaning of the traditional Christian judgment that Scripture is inspired by the Holy Spirit.[6] Again, a thorough survey of such literature is beyond the scope of the present work. My goal instead is to raise and answer questions concerning the location and processes of the inspiration of Scripture in and relative to the contexts laid out in previous chapters. The three primary questions that I seek to address in the present section are the following: How does the inspiration of Scripture take place? Where and when is the inspiration of Scripture located? And, finally, how does the Holy Spirit's work in inspiration fit within the broader mission of the Holy Spirit?

Paul Achtemeier provides a very useful minimalist definition of the inspiration of Scripture that will serve as a point of departure for the position of the present work. "To say that the Bible is 'inspired,'" he writes,

> means at least that in some special way the literature of that book owes its origin to God himself and to the events behind which he has stood, which are reported in its pages, and that therefore the Bible occupies a central and irreplaceable position within the Christian faith. In a unique way our contact with the God of whom the Bible speaks is linked to the records of what that God has said and done in the past, which are contained in the Bible.[7]

A number of phrases in this definition require comment. The first is Achtemeier's use of the phrase "the Bible." "The Bible"—as Achtemeier knows and as I demonstrated in the previous chapter—does not exist as an already-out-there-now-real. "The Bible" only exists in the variable concrete manuscripts and printed copies that have been produced by human hands in human communities for human purposes throughout history. The variability of those concrete artifacts, in their technology, language, and scope, presents a potentially daunting challenge for the quest to understand the unity of Scripture and the unity of the Spirit's work in Scripture. I address this challenge below.

Scripture, Achtemeier notes, has "the God of whom the Bible speaks" as its origin. But who is this God? As we have already seen, Christian understandings of the identity, actions, and character of this God were on the move in the first few centuries of Christian faith. Such understandings developed through polemics, reflection on catechesis, and worship and prayer. In each of these endeavors the early Christians worked out their understanding of the Triune God through constant engagement with Scripture. While Scripture was clearly authoritative for the earliest Christians in both their polemical ventures and their more staid quests for understanding or catechesis, Christian communities did not begin to feel a pressing need to clearly delineate the boundaries of Christian Scripture of either Testament until the middle to the end of the second century at the earliest. But through their engagement with Scripture and their reflection on their experiences of God's revelatory work in Christ and through the Holy Spirit, the early Christians summarized their understanding of this God in the rule of faith. The rule of faith explicitly connected affirmations concerning the creative and redemptive work of the God of Jesus Christ. It also connected the work of the distinct persons, particularly the Son and the Holy Spirit, in the economy.

I have proposed the Niceno-Constantinopolitan Creed as an adequate representation of the achievements in understanding by the early church regarding the identity of "the God of whom the Bible speaks." I have also supplemented that doctrinal foundation with further hypothetical understandings of the intelligibility of the work of the Triune persons named in the creed. To reiterate what I have stated, the God of Scripture is the God revealed as Father, Son, and Holy Spirit. The Triune God has brought creation into being out of nothing, and sustains creation noncompetitively in creation's unfolding freedom. The Triune God has not created and abandoned his creation but has "entered into" creation in distinctive ways through the missions of the Son and the Holy Spirit. To judge that Scripture is inspired *by the Holy Spirit* is to make a statement about the relationship between the material texts of Christian Scripture in history and the work of the Holy Spirit who has entered into that history. The doctrine of the inspiration has its intelligibility in the broader context of the general work of the mission of the Holy Spirit. To reiterate what I have already affirmed, the economic work of the Triune God is one. The Spirit does not work independently of the Son and the Father in the unique work of inspiration.

Understandings of the causative nature of God's work with regard to Scripture are varied.[8] In chapter 3 I proposed, on the basis of the infinite qualitative distinction between God and creation, that the Triune God operates in all natural and created operations. "The omniscient and omnipotent cause of the whole universe," Lonergan writes, "does not operate blindly. He plans where men turn to probabilities. Nor does there come into existence, outside his planning, any agent that could interfere with his comprehensive design."[9] Such causative work, because it is the work of the Triune God, is not an extrinsic intervention into the emergent contingent realities of creation. The Triune God does not exercise agency in competition with created causes. That general divine operation includes the natural and voluntary movements behind, with, and before Christian Scripture. The judgment that Scripture is inspired, though, is more than a judgment about God's providential work in its initiation, production, transmission, dissemination, and interpretation. The Holy Spirit, in his mission, is concerned primarily with persons. The inanimate nature of Scripture, as marks on pages that are artifacts of human technology, will pose a unique challenge for understanding the intelligibility and location of the inspiration of Scripture unless we keep in mind the personal agencies involved. We are concerned to understand the agency of the Holy Spirit, the agencies of the authors— whether individual or communal—of the texts, and the agencies of subsequent readers and hearers of Scripture.

As I discussed above, theologians have often related the testimony of specific biblical authors concerning their compositions to the later determinations of the nature and extent of Christian Scripture. For instance, most who engage the questions of the nature and authority of Scripture offer interpretations, sometimes quite involved, of key passages such as 2 Peter 1.20–21 and 2 Timothy 3.16–17. Such exegetical or theological exercises serve the purpose of allowing Scripture to "speak for itself" regarding its own authority, divine inspiration, and authenticity. While I have already noted the philosophical problems with this strategy, brief examinations of each of these two key texts, followed by a brief examination of 2 Corinthians 3, will provide a means for discussing the location of the Holy Spirit's personal work of inspiration in the human authors of Scripture, in the texts themselves, and, finally, in those readers who receive and engage the texts in subsequent history.

I need to clarify something about my use of these particular passages. I hold that these New Testament passages reflect the beliefs of their authors and communities of reception concerning reality.[10] I also assume that none of these texts provides a technical account of the realities to which they refer.[11] The writings to which the respective authors of 2 Peter 1.20–21, 2 Timothy 3.16–17, and 2 Corinthians 3 referred were undoubtedly the ancient Jewish Scriptures.[12] Any judgment that these texts can refer—after being located within a pandect Bible and so textually relative to the rest of the texts of Christian Scripture—to the other canonically associated texts that we know as the New Testament depends upon a judgment of providence. The judgment that Scripture is inspired, Luke Timothy Johnson declares, does not rest "on the Bible's self-referential statements, but on the faith in Christians that through its very human and culturally conditioned words, God's word is also spoken and God's Spirit is at work."[13] To put it differently, we must remind ourselves that the judgment of the inspiration of Scripture is not a truth so objective as to get along without subjects; it is made in faith by the individuals and communities that receive Scripture. Readers and hearers make that judgment when they confess it with words, but readers and hearers make it incarnately when they read and hear Scripture expecting to receive an authoritative word from God.

In what follows, then, I do not provide an account of some specific, unique, and generalized process of divine action, named "inspiration," through which the Holy Spirit acted to create the specific texts of Christian Scripture. The material history of Scripture and the embodied use of Scripture in historical Christian communities both rule out of court any restrictive notion that the Holy Spirit moved to create these texts, and only these texts, by directly dictating, poetically influencing, or some other specific distinctive, mappable action of the Holy Spirit within or upon their human authors. Given the comprehensiveness and noncompetitive nature of divine causation in created history—including in the created history of Scripture itself—and given the plurality of genres represented in Christian Scripture—which themselves arise from and reflect a plurality of historically and culturally particular human purposes and psychological perspectives and which serve the singular purposes of the divine author—the search for a comprehensive model for the uniqueness of divine action relative to the historical creation of the particular texts of Christian Scripture is a quest for a foundation for Scripture's authority in dangerous neglect of its place within God's revelatory work.[14] *These* texts, including their particular histories, are the texts that Christians receive as the written Word of God. That is why they are unique. They are not unique because of some specific identifiable, generalized divine process called "inspiration" that they possess, bear, or reflect in contradistinction to all other books. Christians affirm that the Triune God is the authority behind, and so author of, these texts in their initiation, but we must also hold that God has served as a trustworthy and sufficient custodian of these texts, including their histories, in the providential guidance of their transmission and use in Christian communities. The texts, in their uniqueness of origin and transmission, serve as a providentially ordained, inexhaustible means of questions, understandings, judgments, and decisions willed by the Triune God for God's people.

2 Peter 1.20–21 is one of the key texts most frequently cited in discussions of the divine origins of Scripture.[15] "First of all you must understand this, that no prophecy of scripture is a matter of one's own interpretation," the Petrine author writes, "because no prophecy ever came by human will, but men and women moved by the Holy Spirit spoke from God." There is precious little in this text for articulating a full-blown theology of the mechanics or processes of the inspiration of Scripture. The syntax of the words connects the divine inspiration of the prophets with their *spoken* words, not with their writing after all. This is unsurprising given the emphasis on the authority of oral witnesses of the earliest Christians. The key judgment of the passage, though, is that the prophecy of the prophets came not from human but from divine initiative. The production of prophetic words, and so of Scripture itself, ultimately depends upon divine initiative exercised in and through human subjects. Farkasfalvy accordingly calls this "subjective" inspiration.[16] How, then, does the Holy Spirit act with respect to the human authors of Scripture?

Historically, Christian thinkers have often downplayed or left unnoticed the "human contribution" to the texts of Scripture, especially before the Enlightenment. In the early church, prophets—and prophetic authors of Scripture by extension—were regularly understood to be completely inert instruments of the divine work.[17] Premodern and contemporary theologians have suggested that Scripture is a product of the dictation of the Holy Spirit through completely passive human receptacles.[18] In this notion of inspiration, human authors are nothing more than pens, chisels, or musical instruments manipulated by the divine actor.[19] The position that God utilizes the human authors as a puppeteer manipulating puppets, however, is at odds with both the variable styles of the biblical writers and the material variability of Christian Scripture.[20] It also does not fit the affirmation of the noncompetitive relationship between divine and human freedom articulated in chapter 3 above.

How does the Holy Spirit move the authors of Scripture? The notion of divine concursus discussed above provides useful but not completely sufficient notional resources for answering this question. The divine initiative of the Spirit's work is effective in the voluntary, and so free, actions of the humans responsible for the composition of Scripture. "The divine cause," writes Farkasfalvy, "due to its transcendental character, does not reduce or restrict human freedom, but rather constitutes it; it neither diminishes human freedom nor is diminished by it."[21] The human authors of Scripture are thus "true authors" who freely make use of their own traditional, social, and cultural capital to express their own intentions under the initiative of the Holy Spirit.[22] It is necessary to contextualize the intentions of these human authors in an understanding of the intentions of the Holy Spirit, but first I must say more about differing notions of "authorship." Such comments are necessary because of the historical distance between premodern and contemporary notions of authorship.

The idea of the author as an autonomous individual who univocally determines the meaning of her writing and who exercises absolute rights of possession over that work is a decisively modern notion.[23] To the extent that we adopt such a notion of authority, we will prohibit ourselves from understanding the human authors of Scripture and their intentions and actions. Ancient notions of authorship were much less individualistic than our modern notions.[24] We do not know the identities of many of the human authors of Scripture. A number of texts of both Testaments are anonymous (Joshua, Judges, 1 and 2 Samuel, 1 and 2 Kings, 1 and 2 Chronicles, Job, Esther, Hebrews), and many others were likely originally anonymous (the Pentateuch, the Psalms, perhaps the Gospels).[25] "The Bible," writes William Schniedewind, " . . . shows a distressing disinterest in who wrote it."[26]

The texts we possess as Scripture are not merely the products of individual authors, as I noted above, but have come down to us through processes of redaction, transmission, correction, and even interpretive commentary; they are intrinsically communal.[27] Critical biblical scholarship has uncovered a number of key discoveries regarding the communal nature of the authorship of the texts comprising the Jewish and Christian canonical collections. The fact that the peoples of antiquity accepted pseudepigraphical works as authoritative and that many works of the Christian Bible were debated in the earliest church — or even were anonymous until declared definitively apostolic — demolishes any hopes that we will or could have absolute certitude regarding the exact identities of the individual human persons responsible for writing and transmitting these texts. Arguing for specific positions in debates about whether there are composite, redacted, or pseudonymous works in the Christian scriptures is beyond the scope of the present work.[28] I draw attention to developments in our understanding — or rather our recognition of our lack of understanding — of the human authorities responsible for producing Scripture because such developments have theological significance. They have a place in the actual history of Christian Scripture. Apparently, the Triune God has providentially chosen not to give us exhaustive knowledge of the precise human origins and vicissitudes of transmission of the written word.

Even if Christians are skeptical of scholarly reconstructions of the pluralistic origins of certain bodies of biblical literature — doubting the source-critical theories of the formation of the Pentateuch or the Gospels, for instance — it is still necessary to recognize and acknowledge the explicit testimony of numerous biblical authors to the communal dimensions of their works.[29] The following are only a few examples. Jeremiah, as I noted above, dictated the prophetic word he received to Baruch (see Jer 36). The apostle Paul wrote with a number of coauthors, including Sosthenes (1 Cor 1.1), Timothy (2 Cor 1.1; Phil 1.1; Col 1.1; 1 Thess 1.1; 2 Thess 1.1; Phlm 1), and Silvanus (1 Thess 1.1; 2 Thess 1.1). He also employed Tertius, and likely others, as amanuenses (Rom 16.22). Peter indicates that he wrote "by Silvanus" (1 Pet 5.12). There is clear evidence in the epilogue of John's gospel of the communal nature of the "final" versions of that text (see John 21.24–25).

A number of texts in Scripture indicate their dependence on previous works. Numbers refers to "the book of the wars of the Lord" (Nb 21.14). Both Joshua and 2 Samuel make reference to a lost book of Jasher (Josh 10.13; 2 Sam 1.18). The books of Kings depend upon previous literature (1 Kgs 15.31; 16.20; 2 Kgs 10.34; 13.8). Luke indicates that he has done research in written records regarding the life and teaching of Jesus (Luke 1.1–4). While some of the books of Scripture are spontaneous products of individuals caught up in ecstasy, most are not. The evidence of Qumran and of early manuscripts of the books of the Old Testament demonstrates that many of the texts of the Old Testament went through redactional processes on their way to their current forms in contemporary Bibles. As Achtemeier strikingly writes, "All of our biblical texts are . . . the products of interpretation of the will of God as that is illumined in a new time by earlier traditions."[30] All of those distinctive human authorial interpretations of the will of God, of course, are not self-referential. The authorial activity of the human persons involved in Scripture is directed towards the will of God and actions of God in actual history. The authorial activity of those who produced the scriptures is communal testimony to that work.

The Triune God acts providentially through all of the human activities involved in the production, dissemination, preservation, assemblage, and interpretation of the works constituting Christian Scripture. Inspiration, then, cannot be located *exclusively* in the processes of the Holy Spirit moving only the original authors to write.[31] The notion that each discrete text or book of Scripture has a singular "original author" is itself more than problematic. John Webster has suggested that it may be better to speak of the Holy Spirit's work of sanctifying these texts through the Spirit's work in the diverse human tradents of the Scriptures.[32] He writes that the Holy Spirit, "hallow[s] the creaturely process[es]" of the transmission of Scripture through human subjects.[33] The Spirit works not only in the initiation of the texts through the conduits of their authors, but in their subsequent history through their respective tradents. Webster's notion of the sanctification of the creaturely reality of Scripture provides a fitting transition for our discussion of the Spirit's work with reference to the actual words of the material *realia* produced by human tradents.

Historically, Christians have affirmed the authority of Scripture and its centrality for Christian life and thought on the supposition that the

scriptures *themselves,* and not merely their human authors, are θεόπνευστος, to use the vocabulary of another famous text often discussed in treatments of the authority of Christian Scripture (2 Tim 3.16).[34] The Vulgate
famously renders that word *divinus inspirata,* and most English translations render it "God-breathed."[35] As Daniel Arichea and Howard Hatton
note, that word, which occurs nowhere else in the New Testament, "has
perhaps produced more varieties of interpretation and generated more
controversy among Christians than any other term."[36] The author of 2
Timothy certainly does not offer a systematic explanation of what the
word means in the literary context of that passage.[37] The Pauline author
does note, of course, that those texts are "useful" (ὠφέλιμος) for "for teaching, for reproof, for correction, and for training in righteousness, so that
everyone who belongs to God may be proficient, equipped for every good
work" (2 Tim 3.17). I discuss the functional usefulness of Scripture at
greater length below.[38] For now, however, it is necessary to discuss the "objective" inspiration of the actual words of the texts of Christian Scripture.[39]

It is necessary to account for the precise work of the Spirit with respect
not only through the human agents of Scripture, but through the texts
themselves. Language concerning the action of the Holy Spirit "upon,"
"with," "through," and even "in" the text is useful, but it is necessary to exercise caution when employing such prepositional phrases. We must be
leery of the danger of positing "inspiration" as a static and discrete feature
back-there-then in history or out-there-now in the text today. The Holy
Spirit is not locked into the *realia* of Christian Scripture, as if revelation
was "frozen and canned in the canon."[40] As Webster cautions, despite
our affirmation of the inspired nature of the text itself, "no divine nature
or properties are to be predicated of Scripture; its substance is that of
a creaturely reality (even if it is a creaturely reality annexed to the self-
presentation of God); and its relation to God is instrumental."[41]

The judgment that Scripture is inspired is not merely a judgment
about God's past action with respect to Scripture; Christians generally
agree that the Holy Spirit continues to speak through Scripture even
today. "It is not only the sacred writers who were inspired one fine day," de
Lubac argues, "the sacred books themselves are and remain inspired."[42]
The inscription of Scripture codifies and freezes words; that codification
ensures, if conditions are correct, that the productions of the authors and

authorial communities will survive after the deaths of their human authors. "One of the most startling paradoxes inherent in writing," Ong declares, "is its close association with death."[43] The text of Scripture "stands written" in relative fixity.[44] Yet these texts, despite their remarkable solidity, if engaged attentively, attest everywhere the humanity of their authors, tradents, and communities of interpretation.[45] Recognition of the striking diversity and particularity of the texts of Scripture reinforces an awareness of their intrinsic human characteristics.

Just as the Spirit does not overwrite the freedom of the human authors and transmitters of Scripture, the Spirit does not distort or efface the once living humanity inscribed in the language of the texts. The Spirit takes up the linguistic, cultural, social, and generic features of the ancient authors and their communities, and the Spirit mediates divine meaning through those transient cultural forms. As I noted above, Scripture undoubtedly reflects the commonsense idioms of its original communities. Such human language is no hindrance to the Spirit's work, though. I discuss the Spirit's employment of human idioms at greater length in the next major section of this chapter. For now, however, it is necessary to discuss the work of the Spirit in those who take up the scriptures to read them. The affirmation of the inspiration of Scripture is, like all affirmations, one that takes place within and through the subjectivity of the one making it. Christian readers who make that affirmation hold that Scripture is an inspired gift given to us by God, and we have received the Spirit of God to understand that gift (1 Cor 2.14–16). The affirmation of the inspiration of Scripture depends upon the work of the Spirit in the affirming subject, whether individual or communal.

In a startling passage that reflects the early Christian conviction of the universal significance of the work of the God of Israel in Jesus Christ, the apostle Paul makes a distinction between "the letter [which] kills" and "the Spirit [which] gives life" (2 Cor 3.6).[46] In that same verse Paul declares that he and the Corinthians have been made ministers of a New Covenant of the Spirit's work that is connected to Jesus Christ.[47] A bit further on, Paul discusses Moses's reception of the Law on Sinai (Exod 34.1–4, 27–28) to contrast the perspective of those in Christ with those who read Scripture (Moses) without the Spirit.[48] A veil lies over their minds. "When one turns to the Lord," though, Paul writes, "the veil is removed" (2 Cor 3.16).

In Paul's understanding, the internal work of the Holy Spirit frees readers or hearers of Scripture to understand the spiritual realities to which the ancient Jewish Scriptures refer.[49]

It is impossible to understand and discern the influence of the Holy Spirit either in the human authorial actions of Scripture or in the texts as they stand written without actually engaging Scripture. "Words do not 'stand' on their own account. Whether they are spoken or written, their meaning is only fully realized within the context of life," Hans Georg Gadamer declares.[50] Yet that very engagement *entails our subjective involvement.* To read inspired Scripture as inspired requires of readers the recognition, and discernment, of the Holy Spirit's internal work in the subjective processes of reading and hearing. Post-Reformation Protestant and Catholic approaches to Scripture have regularly emphasized the necessity of the Spirit's internal work in the readers of Scripture.[51] Many of the church fathers had already expressed the importance of attending to the internal work of the Holy Spirit in readers of Scripture.[52]

The processes of identifying, understanding, and discerning the work of the Holy Spirit through the scriptural texts inspired by the Spirit can never take place except through the Spirit's congruent work within hearers, readers, and interpreters. "[The] same Spirit that guided all 'prophets and apostles' to understand, proclaim, and explain the mystery of Christ in their preaching and their writings," Farkasfalvy writes, " . . . continues his activity in the Church[,] . . . causing the faithful to believe and to understand the meaning of the writings of 'the Prophets and the Apostles.'"[53] Understanding the objective reality of the Spirit's work in the authors, texts, and words of Christian Scripture is always an achievement that takes place through the grace of the Holy Spirit *in subjects.* Even the ability to recognize and respond to Christian Scripture as Christian Scripture depends upon the antecedent work of the Holy Spirit in communities and individuals.

The objectivity of the inspiration of Scripture is a constitutive judgment of Christian faith. The discernment of the import of that judgment will always take place, though, through the alignment of the subjectivity of the reader or hearer with the work of the Holy Spirit in her. "Without the internal witness of the Holy Spirit," Achtemeier declares, "Scripture remains mute in its witness to truth."[54] It is only possible to "locate" the subjective and objective dimensions of the Holy Spirit's inspiring work in Scripture through our own subjective engagement with the texts, in all of their particularity, and through our own communal discernment of the Spirit's work in the authors of the texts, in the texts themselves, and in contemporary Christian communities.

Perhaps frustratingly, a complete view of the "how" and "when" of inspiration remains beyond our grasp for a number of reasons. The first reason is our incomplete and shifting understandings of the transmission history of the texts of Christian Scripture. If and when we discover more ancient scriptural manuscripts our understandings and judgments concerning the historical processes of the production, composition, and canonization of Christian Scripture will inevitably need to change. The undoubted loss of so much of the biblical *realia* in the fires of history necessarily puts a comprehensive understanding of the history of the inspiration of Scripture beyond our grasp. Restricting the Spirit's work to specific authors, communities, and text forms to the exclusion of others would be little more than theologically dangerous special pleading, especially for those who adopt the testimony of the authors of Scripture that the redemptive work of the God of Israel in Jesus Christ and through the Holy Spirit is universal in its orientation (Joel 2.28; Acts 1.8, 2.27; 1 Tim 2.3–4; 2 Pet 3.9) and that God's grace is sufficient for human beings in their weakness (2 Cor 12.9–10). The ostensible weakness of the material texts of Christian Scripture—which are necessarily mediated by human persons—is no impediment to the economic work of the Triune God through those texts.

There is another explicitly theological reason we cannot definitively locate the inspiring work of the Holy Spirit. The judgment that Scripture is a product of the Holy Spirit and a means of the work of the Holy Spirit is a judgment about a transcendent divine agent whose thoughts are not our thoughts and whose ways are not our ways (see Isa 55.8). In the Gospel of John, Jesus testifies to Nicodemus that "the Spirit blows where it wishes, and [we] hear his voice, but [we] do not know from whence he comes or where he is going" (John 3.8a).[55] The Spirit is and remains free through the Spirit's work of inspiration.[56] If the Spirit somehow "rests" on or in Scripture, the Spirit does so in the Spirit's characteristic way. And "when the Spirit rests," as Eugene Rogers puts it, "she is as static as water, as contained as oil, and as passive as fire. The Spirit rests like the wind."[57] Given the freedom and intrinsic mysteriousness of the work of the Holy Spirit, we should expect *not* to come to an exhaustive knowledge of every dimension of the inspiration of Scripture. We should also expect the unexpected when we engage Scripture. Any new and unexpected experiences of faith, hope, and love, and any new insights and critical judgments that we experience through reading, hearing, and meditating upon Scripture, and any new judgments of value that we experience through engaging the text—in any available disciplinary or spiritual methodologies— are in the end changes that take place in us as subjects according to the structures and norms of our subjectivity and according to the operation of God's grace in us.[58] The inspired scriptures are eminently useful for facilitating such changes, even if we cannot immediately recognize their effects. As Origen writes:

> There is a certain strength in Holy Scripture that may avail the reader, even without explanation if it is "inspired by divine influence and is useful," we ought to believe that it is useful even if we do not discern the usefulness. Doctors are accustomed at times to offer some food and at other times to give some drink that is prescribed, for example, to alleviate dimness of the eyes. Yet in consuming the food or in drinking, we do not perceive that it is useful and that it benefits the eye. But when one day passes, and another, and a third, the power of that food or drink, when conveyed to sight in its own time, through certain secret ways, little by little cleanses the faculty of seeing. Then at length we begin to understand that that food or drink benefited the eyes. Likewise, the same things regularly happen in other parts of the body. Therefore, we should also believe this about Holy Scripture, that it is useful and benefits the soul even if our perception at the present does not understand why. For, as we have said, both the good powers that assist us are refreshed by these discourses and are fed, and the hostile ones are made inert by these meditations and are driven away. (*Hom. Jes. Nav.* 20.2)[59]

Though a complete grasp of the precise location of inspiration eludes us, all is not lost. The human authors of Scripture have testified to the characteristic activities and purposes of the Holy Spirit in the economy of creation and redemption. The judgment that Scripture is inspired by the Holy Spirit, I contend, is only intelligible within an adequate understanding of what it is that the Holy Spirit characteristically has done, is doing, and will do in the economy of the Triune God. Scripture is an instrument of the economic mission of the Holy Spirit. I have already offered a brief account of the Spirit's missional work in chapter 3, but I will reiterate some of its key features presently.

The Holy Spirit, the authors of the New Testament testify, will flood our hearts with the love of God (Rom 5.5). The Spirit will take up residence in us such that our bodies become temples of the divine (1 Cor 6.19–20). Through the Spirit the Father and Son will dwell in us (John 14.23; 2 Cor 6.16–18; Eph 3.17; 1 John 3.24). The Spirit will convict us of sin (John 16.8). The Spirit will lead us into all truth (John 16.13). The fullness of truth, though, is not reducible to a set of propositions and abstractions; the fullness of truth is a person. "I am the way, the truth, and the life," Jesus declares according to the fourth evangelist, "no one comes to the Father expect through me" (John 14.6). The Spirit, because he is the Spirit of Christ, will testify to and lead us to Jesus Christ, the fullness of God's self-revelation in history (John 15.26).[60] The Spirit likewise testifies in us that we are sons and daughters of the God of Jesus Christ and coheirs with Jesus Christ (Gal 4.6–7; Rom 8.16). The Spirit intercedes on our behalf (Rom 8.26). The Spirit grants us gifts for service (1 Cor 12.1–7; cf. Isa 11.1–3), the Spirit will bear fruit in us (Gal 5.22–23), and the Spirit will grant us the mind of Christ (1 Cor 2.16).[61]

Where is the Spirit relative to Scripture? The Spirit moved the authors of Scripture to write as they did, and the Spirit works through the particularities of the authors, texts, and hearing and understanding communities of Christian Scripture to lead those communities to the fullness of the truth of the Son of God in whom the Father is reconciling all things (Eph 1.3–14, esp. 10). On the basis of testimony to the transformative work of the Triune God in human persons through their engagement with these texts, and on the basis of our own judgment that the Triune God has worked in us through these texts, it is only reasonable to return to them again and again expecting that such transformation is taking place and will take place, even when we do not understand or recognize that work in the immediacy of our reading and hearing.[62] Scripture is a participant in the history that God is redeeming in Christ, and the Holy Spirit works both before and through Scripture to testify to the truth of that work and to transform us for participation within it.

THE WRITTEN WORD OF GOD AND THE LIVING WORD: SCRIPTURE IN THE MISSION OF THE SON

As I have noted numerous times in the present work, I presume that engagement with Christian Scripture is a characteristic, if not constitutive, activity of Christian life within the economy of the work of the Triune God.[63] Because of the ubiquitous and trans-ecclesial emphasis on the authority and importance of Scripture in Christian history, many Christians and non-Christians have come to recognize and affirm Christians to be "a people of the Book."[64] This statement is potentially misleading, however.[65] On the contrary, de Lubac insists, Christians are not a people of the Book but a people of the Word.[66] The Word that was with God and was God in the beginning is not the written Word of Scripture but the living Word, the only begotten Son of the Father, who became incarnate in human history (John 1.1–18). God the Father has not sent a book to save the world but his Son. Even still, Christians hold the doctrinal judgment that Scripture is the written Word of God. I can begin to offer an explanation of the doctrine that Scripture is the written Word of God by reflecting on the relationship between that judgment and the judgment that Jesus Christ, the only Son of the Father, is the living Word of God.

Ong states well the problematic of the relationship between Jesus Christ as Word of God and Scripture as Word of God.

> In Christian teaching the Second Person of the One Godhead, who redeemed mankind from sin, is known not only as the Son but also as the Word of God. In this teaching, God the Father utters or speaks His Word, his Son. He does not inscribe him. The very Person of the Son is constituted as the Word of the Father. Yet Christian teaching also presents at its core the written word of God, the Bible, which, back of its human authors, has God as author as no other writing

does. In what way are the two senses of God's 'word' related to one another and to human beings in history? The question is more focused today than ever before.[67]

The way a Christian community understands the relationship between the written Word of Scripture and Jesus Christ will have a profound impact on its understanding and action in countless other areas. One of these realities is divine in nature, the other is not.[68] The present work takes the position that the written Word of Scripture, while it is of fundamental importance for Christian communities, is decisively subordinate to the living Word, the incarnate Son of God, Jesus Christ. Scripture is an instrument that mediates the meaning of the living Word, Jesus Christ. It is not possible for Christians to "search the Scriptures" responsibly and faithfully without coming to know and understand the living Word, Jesus Christ, to whom they bear witness (see John 5.39). There is no doubt that the knowledge of Jesus Christ is significantly, if not primarily, mediated by and even constrained by the scriptural testimony of the authors of the Old Testament and New Testament. Even so, to reverse the relationship by giving Scripture some quasi-hypostatic authority and priority that is separable from the authority of the Triune God is to put us at risk of idolatry.[69]

While Christians have had an invested interest in written texts from the very beginning (see 1 Cor 15.3), Christianity is not fundamentally a movement of textual hermeneutics.[70] The Christian community emerged as a distinctive response to actual *historical events* that its adherents held to be of utmost importance. The primary accent of Paul's testimony in 1 Corinthians 15.3–8 is not on the confirmation of Scripture itself but on the actual events of Christ's death and resurrection.[71] The Son of God had taken on flesh and dwelt among humanity, decisively revealing the Father (John 1.14; 18), in order to bring the creative and redemptive work of the Father to completion (Eph 1.10). As Barton puts it, "For the first Christians, what had happened in Christ was not an exegesis of Scripture, not even a strikingly original exegesis of Scripture, but a completely new, unprecedented and irreversible event in the external world."[72] For that reason, Farkasfalvy states that we "must not lose sight of the fact that the Christian Church neither came about as the product of literary activities, nor saw itself imprisoned by written words. The Christians' use of the sacred books of the Jews was governed by *a new understanding* which developed from their faith in Christ."[73]

The judgment of the absolute priority and authority of Christ is not opposed to but relativizes the priority and authority of Scripture. Scripture is an instrument of the Holy Spirit who mediates the meaning and even presence of the incarnate and still living Word of God, Jesus Christ of Nazareth in his bride the Christian Church and to the world. The meaning of Jesus Christ the Incarnate Son of God, which is the meaning of the Father through the Holy Spirit, is *die Sache*, that is, the content, of Christian Scripture. The meaning of Jesus Christ is not some abstract notion or concept, though; it is Christ himself in his incarnate meaning, encompassing his birth, life, words, death, resurrection, ascension, and *subsequent continuous lordship in the economy of redemption.*[74] Christian Scripture serves as an instrument of this meaning. The Holy Spirit who inspires Scripture—in the extensive sense articulated in the previous section of this chapter—intends to lead the readers and hearers of Scripture into all truth (John 14.26). That truth, though, is the truth of a person. The Spirit leads to the one, Jesus Christ, who is the "way, the truth, and the life" (John 14.6); he is the one who exegetes the Father (John 1.18).

The judgment that Christian Scripture is an instrument that leads readers to encounter and know Christ is not a new one in Christian tradition. It is present in the early Christian convictions concerning the self-revelation of the God of Israel that are attested in the New Testament itself. Christians have regularly held that Christian Scripture is itself divine revelation or serves as a medium or instrument of divine revelation.[75] But what is divine revelation? "Divine revelation," Lonergan writes, "is God's entry and his taking part in man's making of man. It is God's claim to have a say in the aims and purposes, the direction and development of human lives, human societies, human cultures, human history."[76] That generic definition, though, requires specification. How precisely does God "enter into" the human context, and how is Scripture related to that entry?[77]

In the recent past it was fashionable to speak of divine revelation in Christian Scripture as "progressive."[78] Advocates of that approach to Scripture trace through Scripture a gradual developmental process of the increasing enlightenment of its authors and communities from polytheism through henotheism and finally to ethical monotheism. That approach, while it has merit, especially in the resources it provides for discerning trajectories in the perspectives of the biblical authors and their communities, cannot adequately account for the explicit and somewhat shocking testimony of the authors of the New Testament to the radical newness of the thing that the God of Abraham, Isaac, and Jacob has done by sending his only begotten Son Jesus Christ and pouring out his Spirit on all flesh.[79]

The texts of the *New* Testament are punctuated with references to *the newness* of God's work in Christ.[80] In those texts we read of "new wine and wineskins" (Matt 9.17; Mark 2.22; Luke 5.37–39), a "new covenant" (Matt 26.28; Mark 14.25; Luke 22.20; 1 Cor 11.25; 2 Cor 3.6; Heb 8.8, 8.13, 9.15, 12.24; cf. Jer 31.31–34), a "new teaching" (Mark 1.27; Acts 17.19), a "new birth" (John 3.3; 3.7; 1 Pet 1.3, 1.23), a "new commandment" (John 13.34; 1 John 2.8), a "new creation" (2 Cor 5.17; Gal 6.15), a "new humanity" (Eph 2.15), a "new self" (Eph 4.24; Col 3.10), a "new and living way" (Heb 10.20), a "new heaven(s) and a new earth" (2 Pet 3.13; Rev 21.1), a "new name" (Rev 2.17; 3.12), a "new Jerusalem" (Rev 3.12; 21.2), a "new song" (Rev 5.9; 14.3), and a "newness of life" (Rom 6.4; cf. 7.6).

While the Christians of the New Testament had affirmed that God had spoken through many prophets in the past, they were convinced of the incomparable newness of the revelatory work of the God of Israel in Jesus Christ. "Long ago God spoke to our ancestors in many and various ways by the prophets," the author of Hebrews writes, "but in these last days he has spoken to us by a Son, *whom he appointed heir of all things, through whom he also created the worlds. He is the reflection of God's glory and the exact imprint of God's very being, and he sustains all things by his powerful word*" (Heb 1.1–3a).[81] The conviction of the apocalyptic nature of Christ's coming recurs frequently in the New Testament. "When the *fullness of time* had come," Paul writes to the Galatians, "God sent his Son, born of a woman, born under the law, in order to redeem those who were under the law, so that we might receive adoption as children. And because you are children, God has sent the Spirit of his Son into our hearts, crying, 'Abba! Father!'" (Gal 4.4–6). "[Christ]," writes the author of 1 Peter, "was destined before the foundation of the world, but was revealed at *the end of the ages* for your sake. Through him you have come to trust in God, who raised him from the dead and gave him glory, so that your faith and hope are set on God" (1 Pet 1.20–21; see also 1.10–12).[82]

The interruptive coming of the Son *reveals* God's plan for all times: "With all wisdom and insight he has *made known* to us the mystery of his will, according to his good pleasure that he set forth in Christ, as a plan for the fullness of time, to gather up all things in him, things in heaven and things on earth." (Eph 1.8b–10; see also 1.3–14; 2.13–22). In many other texts the authors of the New Testament express the judgment of the finality and universality of this work in different words (see Acts 2.1–36; Rom 1.1–5; 1 Cor 15.20–28; 2 Cor 5.17–21; 1 Thess 1.2–20; 1 John 1.1–4).[83] The judgment that the God of Israel had done something decisively new, revelatory, and redemptive through the coming of Jesus Christ of Nazareth represents a constitutive judgment of the earliest Christians. De Lubac has drawn attention to how this conviction is already present in 1 Thessalonians, the earliest New Testament book. In that book, he writes, "everything has reference to the person of Jesus, everything originates in the event of Jesus. Paul knows, with invincible certainty, that this event has overturned everything, that everything begins with it."[84] Irenaeus encapsulates this judgment well when he writes that Jesus Christ "has brought total newness by bringing himself" (*Haer.* 4.34.1).[85]

The communal Christian judgment of the incomparable newness and comprehensiveness of God's work in Christ *preceded* the writing of the earliest books of the New Testament and conditioned the way the authors of the New Testament read and used the ancient Jewish Scriptures. The early Christians thought the testimony of Scripture was not self-authenticating; the scriptures pointed not to themselves but to Jesus Christ. He is the center of the Christian understanding of the history that is. This judgment has significant implications for how Christians should read Scripture. "With Christ being both the peak and the fullness of this history," Farkasfalvy writes, "one needs to ask of every part of Scripture how it refers to Christ."[86] The New Testament Christians insisted, on the basis of their collective memories of Jesus's own authority and his own treatment of the ancient Jewish Scriptures (Matt 5.17–48, 7.29, 22.37–40; Mark 1.22, 2.23–27; Luke 4.32, 24.25–27; John 5.39), that those scriptures could only be rightly understood through the definitive authoritative and revelatory teaching and work of Jesus Christ.[87] Following the recognition of the major works of the New Testament as Scripture in the second century at the latest, the early Christians read both Testaments as witnesses that had Christ as their central referent. Each Testament served as testimony, prophetic and apostolic, to the incomparable revelatory and redemptive work of the God of Israel in Jesus Christ and through the Holy Spirit. The church, which Paul regularly calls the Body of Christ, was a community of "citizens with the saints and also members of the household of God, built upon the foundation of the apostles and prophets, with Christ Jesus himself as the cornerstone" (Eph 2.19b–20). Their approach to Scripture manifested their commitment to the authoritative exegesis of Christ in his words and in his deeds. They held that the scriptures, and their authors, were instruments testifying to this work; the work itself is their referent. The work itself was of fundamental and universal significance.[88]

Such an approach is anything but neutral. It even makes some contemporary Christians uncomfortable. John Goldingay, for instance, has recently argued that Christians should not read the Old Testament in Christocentric ways. "While I do not see much danger in an autonomous First Testament," he writes, "I see much danger in the narrowing down of the First Testament's agenda to that of a Christian tradition that is itself narrower even than that of the New Testament. Christocentric interpretation makes it harder for the Scriptures to confront us when we need to be confronted."[89] While I appreciate Goldingay's candor and find much of value in his work, I find this particular statement, and his overall argument in *Do We Need the New Testament?*, problematic in a number of respects.

First and foremost, I am not sure what kind of Christocentric hermeneutic he has in mind, but I cannot conceive of one that prevents the Triune God from confronting us through Scripture when we need to be confronted. Belief in Jesus Christ as the Incarnate Son of God and acceptance of his authority go hand in hand.[90] Jesus, after all, cannot be separated from his teaching and example. Jesus exhorts his disciples, "Be perfect as your heavenly Father is perfect" (Matt 5.48; see also Matt 19.21). Jesus makes absolute demands on them: "If any want to become my followers, let them deny themselves and take up their cross and follow me" (Mark 8.34; Matt 16.24; Luke 9.23). Jesus states that the greatest commandment is to love God with the entirety of one's being and to love one's neighbor as oneself (Matt 22.37–40; Mark 12.28–34). He commands his disciples to love even their enemies (Matt 5.44; Luke 6.27; 6.35). The New Testament authors believed that Jesus embodies and reflects perfection, both the perfection of God and the perfection of humanity (See Col 1.19, 2.9; Heb 1.3; 2.10; 4.15; 5.9; 7.8; 10.14). His hearers testified that he "taught as one who had authority" (Matt 7.29). His question to the disciples is implicitly a question to us: "who do you say that I am?" (Mark 8.29; Matt 16.15). We must decide what to do with him. Is he not challenging enough? Is his teaching not confrontational enough?

Goldingay also poses too sharp a distinction between the God of Israel and the Son of God, Jesus Christ. Goldingay argues that we should read the First Testament—his preferred name for the ancient Jewish Scriptures/Old Testament—theocentrically and not Christocentrically.[91] He also admits that he confesses the creed "without any mental reservations" on a weekly basis.[92] Is not a Christocentric reading theocentric, since Jesus is "God from God, Light from Light, true God from true God"?[93] Despite his affirmation of the divinity of Jesus, Goldingay consistently downplays the significance and shockingness of this constitutive Christian judgment. He suggests that the incarnation is like meeting someone for dinner with whom he has only spoken over the phone.[94] He writes that "the New Testament is new in the way that Isaiah was new or that Genesis was new over Exodus."[95] He also separates the Christological content of the New Testament from its other emphases such as ecclesiology and ethics.[96] Is not the Christian community the Body of Christ? Is not "the way" of Christian discipleship, with all of its moral demands, the imitation of and participation in the work of the one who is "the way, the truth, and the life" (John 14.6)?

Finally, Goldingay consistently utilizes language that attributes agency to Scripture. The subtitle of the book is *Letting the Old Testament Speak for Itself*.[97] As I noted above, it is risky to uncritically attribute agency to the text of Scripture. As text itself, and even as uninterpreted words, Scripture does not confront us, speak, or say anything. The God to whom Scripture bears witness does confront us and speak to us through the words of Scripture. But we can only understand the human and divine address inscribed in Scripture by consciously and conscientiously engaging the texts ourselves. The agents responsible for the production, transmission, and dissemination of Scripture can and do address us, but they only do so when we hear the words of Scripture read, when we take them up ourselves, or when we remember them and meditate upon them. Having a

hermeneutical framework, as I have argued elsewhere, is absolutely necessary for hearing. We have the choice between affirming and taking responsibility for our framework or for giving it no thought. Goldingay has
clearly taken responsibility for his framework, and his framework is sophisticated and informed, but I find it problematic to the extent that it
downplays the significance of the definitive and new work of the God of
Israel in Jesus Christ. To the extent that he downplays that newness, he
prohibits himself from measuring up to the shocking claims of the authors of the New Testament concerning Jesus Christ himself and concerning the ultimate purpose of the texts of the Old Testament.

Goldingay does present a number of useful insights and injunctions
for responsible Christian engagement with Scripture. In fact, he regularly
draws attention to the complications involved in Christian discernment
of the moral import of Scripture in helpful ways. He highlights how
"Christian" reading strategies have been utilized in support of injustice.[98]
The response to irresponsible and unjust theological readings, though, is
not to reject Christological and trinitarian reading strategies but to first
repudiate such irresponsible and unjust reading strategies and then return to Scripture with humility and contrition in expectation that the Triune God who has spoken to Israel but speaks definitively through his Son
and the Holy Spirit will transform us and conform us to his will. That will
is the mysterious reconciliation of all things in Christ (Eph 1.8–10). Paul
regularly states that Christian believers are "in Christ," or are "the body of
Christ" (Rom 6.11; 7.4; 8.11; 12.4–5; 1 Cor 1.30; 12.12–27; 2 Cor 5.17–19;
Gal 3.26–28; 5.6; Eph 1.4–13; 1.23; 2.5–13; 4.4; 4.12–16; 5.30; Phil 2.5–11;
Col 1.18–24; 2.19; 3.15; see also 1 Pet 3.16). The participation of the
church in Christ will feature in and facilitate the reconciliation of all
things in Christ. As I indicated above, that reconciliation will not take
place through violence but through our conformity to the just and mysterious Law of the Cross, which is the summit of God's progressive revelation of God's own benevolent love for humanity most clearly manifest in
Jesus's own passion.[99]

Neither the creed nor systematic theological reflection is a replacement for Scripture. And there is no doubt that Christological and trinitarian reading strategies pose significant risks. Christians have at times flat-
tened out the witnesses of both the Old Testament and the New Testament

in their desire to find a theologically univocal and completely tidy inscripturated Word from God.[100] Christians have invoked the treatment of the Old Testament by Jesus and Paul as authorization for promoting anti-Judaism.[101] Christians have summoned Scripture as an authoritative divine sanction for committing all kinds of other atrocities.[102] There is no necessary correlation, however, between the employment of Christological, trinitarian, and creedal reading strategies and such results.

The position on Scripture that I am advocating entails a commitment to the *res* of the gospel of Jesus Christ, who became man in order to make humanity divine, which relativizes all other concerns that Christians bring to Scripture.[103] I hold this position on the basis of what I take to be a straightforward reading and appropriation of the judgments of the authors of the New Testament in texts such as John 5.39, Luke 24.44–47, and many others. Scripture is useful for instruction and formation in this faith in Christ (2 Tim 3.15). Christians never engage it, however, apart from their own subjective horizons constituted by values, judgments, and understandings. Such subjective dispositions and thoughts must be "taken captive unto Christ" (2 Cor 10.5). The reading of Scripture well, then, has as its goal the transformation of our entire being to take our horizons of value, judgment, understanding, and experience captive to Christ.

"In some sort Christ," de Lubac writes, "took Scripture into his own hands, and he has filled it with himself through the mysteries of his Incarnation, Passion, and Resurrection."[104] "Christ," he states elsewhere, "is book enough for all."[105] The written Word of God is an instrument that can mediate the meaning of the living Word of God, Jesus Christ, the only begotten Son of the Father. Scripture can only facilitate this work—which is its divine intention and for which it is extremely useful—however, in those who are being transformed by the internal work of the Triune God to bear the image of Christ in greater and greater degrees (2 Cor 3.18). It is necessary to explore the possibilities of this mediation in a differentiated way, and it is to that task that I proceed.

While Christians characteristically defer to Jesus Christ the Son of God as the highest authority in the economy of redemption (Matt 28.18–20), Christ taught that the ancient Jewish Scriptures were truthful witnesses to his Father. Jesus Christ is unintelligible apart from "the oracles of God" (Rom 3.1–2), which were entrusted to Israel. Even after the

Christian communities became almost exclusively Gentile in their ethnic makeup, it was therefore still necessary for them to retain the ancient Jewish Scriptures and to submit to the authority of those texts. As noted above, Christians do not read the ancient Jewish Scriptures apart from an awareness of the fundamental newness of the work of the God of Israel in Jesus Christ; they do not read these except in deference to the one who took those texts up and fulfilled them (Matt 5.17–20). Christians have historically held that *both* the Old Testament and the New Testament are witnesses to the incarnation, life, teaching, death, resurrection, and ascension of Christ and stand together in Christian Scripture.[106] The task of understanding the relationship of the two Testaments has proven extremely complicated throughout Christian history. De Lubac states:

> Nothing is more wonderful, in the reality of things, than the way the two Testaments hinge on one another. But neither is there anything trickier than the accurate perception of such a fact. Christian Tradition has been meditating on this for two thousand years and will go on doing so. It will go on, from one age to another, finding in it the mainspring of a solution for the most contemporary and seemingly unknown problems.[107]

It is important to recall that neither the witness of the ancient Jewish Scriptures/Old Testament nor the witness of the texts of the early Christian community is sufficient in itself. The *Testaments* are both *testimony*, prophetic and apostolic, pointing beyond themselves to the reality and actuality of the work of the One who called Israel, sent his Son, and has poured out his Spirit on all flesh.

From as early as perhaps the epistle to the Ephesians, the new Christian community held as authoritative the teachings of the prophets and apostles, a twofold designation that corresponds to the later two-Testament Christian Bible. In his reflections on the unity of the Jewish and Gentile peoples achieved through the work of Jesus Christ, the author of that epistle declares to his audience, "You are no longer strangers and aliens, but you are citizens with the saints and also members of the household of God, built upon the foundation of the apostles and prophets, with Christ Jesus himself as the cornerstone. In him the whole structure is joined together and grows into a holy temple in the Lord; in whom you also are built together spiritually into a dwelling-place for God" (Eph 2.19–22). Before Christians could hold two distinct, concrete, written Testaments as authoritative, they characteristically spoke of two dispensations or covenants (διαθήκη). As de Lubac writes:

> What we call nowadays the Old and New Testaments is not primarily a book. It is a twofold event, a twofold "covenant," a twofold dispensation which unfolds in development through the ages, and which is fixed, one might suppose, by no written account. When the Fathers said that God was its author—the one and only author of the Old and New Testaments—they did not liken him merely, nor indeed primarily, to a writer, but saw in him the founder, the lawgiver, the institutor of these two "instruments" of salvation, these two economies, two dispensations which are described in the Scriptures and which divide between them the history of the world.[108]

At first this twofold foundation, as Barton has shown, and as I have discussed above, functioned in a very complex way.[109] While the Christian communities treated texts of the ancient Jewish Scriptures in scriptural ways, the written apostolic witnesses—which would later become the New Testament—functioned not "as holy texts but records of living memory. They [were thought to be] corrigible in the light of fresh information, and especially of eyewitness testimony or reliable reporting of it."[110] The early Christians treated the ancient Jewish Scriptures as authoritative support for their proclamation of the definitive coming of Christ. They utilized the ancient Jewish Scriptures, through "the twofold law of analogy and contrast," in order to magnify their proclamation of the definitive coming of Christ.[111] They found Christ everywhere in the ancient scriptures.[112]

After the regular recognition of a two-covenanted division of writings, Christians were more likely to treat the texts of both Testaments in scriptural ways. The New Testament, though, because it attested the content of the Gospel, took priority for them. "The Spirit of Christ cannot lead further than Christ," de Lubac states. And so "the New Testament will never date; it is of its very nature the 'Testament that never grows old,' the last Testament, *novissimum Testamentum*."[113] It was actually not the text of the

New Testament but instead the reality of Jesus Christ himself, including his body the church, that held their attention and ordered their thought.

But Christians have traditionally held, as I argued earlier, that the economic work of the Triune God in history is one. That economic work which Jesus Christ makes most fully manifest, and fulfills in his authoritative action, is nevertheless the continuation of the antecedent work of Father, Son, and Holy Spirit through Israel and even from the foundations of creation. Jesus Christ takes up and reassembles and reorients the institutions of the written Old Covenant. But in his fulfillment of the first covenant, the Son does not abrogate the nascent completeness of that covenant; there is already in the ancient Jewish Scriptures testimony to the universal scope of God's reign (Gen 12; Isa 49.6), the integral value of all human persons and the divine favor for the disenfranchised, vulnerable, and alien (Deut 10.12–18; Micah 6.6–8), and the telos of created human life, individual and social, in the love of God and neighbor (Deut 6.5 and Lev 19.18) ultimately extending even to the love of enemies which returns good for evil (Exod 23.4–5; Prov 25.21–22).[114] Christ embodies all of these purposes in his incarnate meaning and shows these to be the unified emphases of the divine revelation given to Israel for the sake of the world.[115]

As de Lubac has shown through his historical work on premodern scriptural exegesis, the earliest Christian exegetes understood Scripture as a comprehensive and unified whole that encompassed the entire history of the world.

> The Bible, which contains the revelation of salvation, *contains too, in its own way, the history of the world.* In order to understand it, it is not enough to take note of the factual details it recounts, but there must also be an awareness of *its concern for universality,* in spite of its partial, schematic and sometimes paradoxical mode of expression. It was in this way that the Bible was read by the Fathers of the Church. From Irenaeus to Augustine, by way of Clement of Alexandria and Eusebius, *they all found in it a treatise on the history of the world.*[116]

The organizational structure of the various books in contemporary Christian Bibles, as I noted in chapter 2, reflects the ubiquitous traditional theological conviction that the Christian Bible contains or reflects a comprehensive theological account of history. From the creation of the world and beginning of human history in Genesis 1–3 through the eschatological consummation of all things in Revelation, the actual physical order of the books of Christian Scripture exhibits this Christian theological depiction of history. Even the placement of the writing prophets— from Isaiah through Malachi, and including Daniel—at the end of the Protestant Old Testament represents a theological judgment about the shape of history in Christ; these texts point forward to and are fulfilled in the coming of Christ and the establishment of the New Covenant.[117]

In truth, in fact, as I noted above, Scripture and the rule of faith are both expressions of "one and the same norm[,] . . . the transmitted Christian truth itself."[118] This truth is the truth of the economic work of the Triune God. The Triune God referred to in the rule of faith and attested in the scriptures of the Old and New Testaments, though, is absolutely sovereign and transcendent. This God's ways are not our ways and thoughts are not our thoughts (Isa 55.8). Engaging Scripture with the intentions of coming to know this God is a risky endeavor. The question concerning the content of the Christian scriptures "is a dangerous question."[119] Recent evangelical interpreters have insisted that Scripture addresses every question that contemporary readers could put to it.[120] Yet the otherness of the God of Scripture calls our frivolous questioning, and so our judgments, values, and priorities, into question. "The question, What is within the Bible? has a mortifying way of converting itself into the opposing question," Barth writes. "Well, what are you looking for, and who are you, pray, who make bold to look?"[121] We encounter a "strange new world" in Christian Scripture, the world of the Most High God. "If we wish to come to grips with [it]," Barth writes, " . . . we must dare to reach far beyond ourselves."[122]

The mission of the Son of God is to reveal the love of the Father for all humanity, and the Holy Spirit mediates to us an understanding of that mystery by granting us the mind of Christ (1 Cor 2.16). Fundamentally that mystery is the mystery of Christ's passion. The wisdom of God "is Christ crucified, a stumbling block to Jews and foolishness to Gentiles" (1 Cor 1.23). It is regularly foolishness to Christians, who would prefer that we not have to align our attitudes and our lives with Christ's. While Christ's work on behalf of the world is his own and is absolute, believers in Christ are called to participate in that work, even to the point of suffering with Christ. "For those who want to save their life will lose it, and those who lose their life for my sake will find it" (Matt 16.25; see also Col 1.24). Christians share in the foolishness of that lot. The cross, for Christians, stands over the whole world. The cross "communicates to us, along with the experience of Love, the knowledge of its conditions."[123] Scripture itself and Christian life are unified in Christ's passion.

While the fact of Christ is at the center of Scripture and while that fact is the ordering reality of the economic work of the Triune God in history, that central reality is attested by an anthology of diverse literature including historical and mythopoetic narratives, genealogies, letters, apocalypses, poetry, prophetic oracles, hymns, aphorisms, chronicles, treatises, legal codes, and dozens of other subforms.[124] "[The] Bible is itself a wonder," William Brown states, "wondrously full of all kinds of discourse."[125] The Triune God both intends and communicates through this manifold diversity of literary forms. To many contemporary readers, the particularity, peculiarity, and even dissonance of the human words and perspectives represented in Scripture seem to be irreconcilable with any unified theological perspective, let alone the overarching Christian theology of history articulated in the early church that I have attempted to retrieve. John J. Collins reflects the hard-won judgment of modern historical criticism when he writes that "the internal pluralism of the Bible, both theological and ethical, has been established beyond dispute."[126] Collins's judgment is unassailable from a merely human perspective. As I noted above, because the Holy Spirit operates as a transcendent cause in the inspiration of Scripture, the Spirit does not manipulate or compete with the human perspectives of its authors. There are as many human perspectives, then, in Scripture as there are human authors. There is no singular "biblical perspective" or "biblical worldview." The unified divine perspective that Christians seek through their engagement with Scripture, the mystery of the creative and redemptive work of the Triune God, is only available through what can seem to be the dissonance of the particular words of the texts.

"What is impossible for mortals is possible for God" (Luke 18.27). It is possible to think of the plurality and polysemy of Scripture not as a hindrance, however, but as a philosophical and spiritual aid. The plurality of Scripture, de Lubac argues, "is indispensable to the equilibrium and vitality of Christian thought . . . because it conveys a consciousness of the transcendence of faith."[127] The diversity of Scripture, Farkasfalvy states, "[demands] that unity be regarded as an ongoing task."[128] "Like gold," Ephraim Radner writes, "whose very 'filings' are precious, the scattered pieces of Scripture are each of enormous value, and demand some kind of synthesis. This, however, takes place in the hearer's memory, as the whole Scripture ... is stored up and entered into by the Christian."[129] Because the highest task of engagement with Christian Scripture is the recognition of and understanding of the mystery of the Triune God, it will never be complete this side of the eschaton. *Si finisti, Deus non est* (Augustine *Serm.* 53.12). Because the Triune God is a transcendent cause, an exhaustive knowledge of God's work in history, even through an inspired resource such as Scripture, will always be beyond the finite capacities of human interpreters, even those illumined by the Holy Spirit. The mystery of the reconciliation of all things in Christ does not cease being a mystery even after we can advance to nuanced understandings and judgments regarding that work. Because such understanding takes place under the conditions of our finitude, retrospective—and even prospective—understanding of the concrete events "behind" the texts or in the histories of the texts cannot be univocally grasped or expressed exhaustively in language; the work of adequately measuring up to the merely human social, cultural, personal, and communal dimensions of the texts of Scripture has no final terrestrial terminus.

The concrete form of pandect Bibles already brings the disparate written words of Scripture together under one cover. We can only achieve the unity of the disparate human words, perspectives, and horizons of Scripture, though, through our own processes of reasoning and critical reflection in our own actual engagement with the scriptures. The subjectivity of such engagement, as I stated above, is unavoidable.[130] The attempt to achieve the unity of Scripture through the employment of harmonizing strategies reflects a commitment to a specific set of expectations for Scripture and forms of reasoning that may actually manifest a partial refusal of the transformative work intended by the Holy Spirit. That approach rightly acknowledges the truthfulness of Scripture, but it fails to acknowledge that its truthfulness nevertheless is mediated by the historical particularity—technological, linguistic, symbolic, conceptual—of its human authors. Such reasoning cannot therefore recognize and accommodate the intelligibility of the actual texts of Scripture in their historicity.[131] It is also a rationalistic refusal of the divine object of Scripture, the Triune God. Such modern rationalism has parallels in the rationalism of "monarchians," "arians," and other early heretics who attempted to resolve and collapse the mysteries of the Trinity and the hypostatic union. To take such an approach is to refuse to admit the presence of mystery in theology, and consequently to refuse to countenance and measure up to the transcendent God to whom Scripture bears witness. "The text," though, writes Ben Meyer, "is an initiation into mystery."[132]

The refusal of some historical critics to raise questions concerning the transcendent referents of Scripture also makes manifest an unnecessary subjective commitment that cannot respect or respond to the transcendent and transformative intentions of the divine cause of Christian Scripture. A comprehensive and closed naturalism or historicism disallows even the possibility of such transcendence. But that move is philosophically unwarranted and represents a refusal to countenance the possibilities of supernatural knowledge assumed and presented by the authors of Scripture. The present account assumes that Scripture can and does have its unity in Christ, who mediates the transcendent meaning of God the Father through the further mediating work of the Holy Spirit in human persons, but such an approach necessarily leaves open more questions than it closes. The ongoing task of grasping the unity of Scripture can only take place in adequate horizons of understanding and judgment. No one human perspective, save Jesus's own, is adequate to the reality of the transcendence of the Triune God.[133] No human perspective, save Jesus's own, is adequate to the mystery of the economic work of the Triune God. For us, discernment of this mystery will always take place through ongoing human subjective activity as it is transformed and conformed to Christ (1 Cor 2.16; 2 Cor 5.18–21) through the mediation of Scripture and prayer.[134] The subjectivity of the ongoing processes of scriptural interpretation does not entail a vicious and circular subjectivism, though. Christians engage the text out of the conviction that the God to whom it bears witness will transform us so that we can come to possess a "subjectivity correlative to the [written] Word of God."[135]

The language of the creeds provides a confessional way to talk about the actuality of the work of the Triune God in history, and the language of systematic theology provides a technical and self-appropriated way to speak about the actuality of the work of the Triune God in history. But the language of Scripture stands as inspired, variegated, commonsensical, plurivocal, artistic, and anthological language about the actuality of the work of the Triune God in history. The dramatic scriptural forms retain their significance, importance, and authority even after the developments of confessional and systematic resources. The language of Christian Scripture is nontechnical and reflects the diverse, communal common sense of its authors and original audiences. As Seán McEvenue indicates:

> The Bible is not written in either a theoretic or scientific mode of thought. It does not define terms, or use them univocally, or proceed according to rigid systems of logic, or by way of controlled experiment. The norms which govern writers of the Bible are norms of tradition, commonsense truth, literary form, aesthetic satisfaction, rhetorical effectiveness, and so forth.[136]

As such, much of the language of Scripture is unassuming. Both Origen and Augustine noticed the humble nature of the language of Scripture.[137] Origen stated that neither the solecisms of Scripture nor its lowliness of style, however, were impediments to its value for communicating the realities to which it refers (see *Philoc.* 4.1–2; 8.1–3; 15.1–20). The weakness of the language was fitting because it would not distract readers from their quest to encounter the God to whom Scripture bears witness through their hearing, reading, study, and meditation. In his preface to his translation of the Old Testament, Martin Luther exhorts his readers:

> I beg and really caution every pious Christian not to be offended by the simplicity of the language and stories frequently encountered there, but fully realize that, however simple they may seem, these are the very words, works, judgments, and deeds of the majesty, power, and wisdom of the most high God. . . . Therefore dismiss your own opinions and feelings and think of the Scriptures as the loftiest and noblest of holy things, the richest of mines which can never be sufficiently explored, in order that you may find that divine wisdom which God here lays before you in such simple guise as to quench all

pride. Here you will find the swaddling clothes and the manger in which Christ lies. . . . Simple and lowly are these clothes, but dear is the treasure, Christ, who lies in them.[138]

Johann Georg Hamann expresses this judgment beautifully and compellingly in his first Hellenistic Letter:

> It is part of the unity of the divine revelation that the Spirit of God, through the man's pen belonging to the holy men whom it has led, humbled itself and made itself of no majesty, just as the Son of God did through the form of a servant, and as the whole creation is a work of the highest humility.[139]

Within the view of divine providence I have provided in this work, the humility of Scripture is not a coincidental accident of history but is itself divinely intended and so has an integral place within the purposes of the Triune God.[140] Origen states that "every letter, no matter how strange, which is written in the oracles of God, does its work" (*Philoc.* 10.1).[141] Christians have returned again and again to these texts not primarily because of their literary brilliance, though a number of passages and texts of both Testaments are certainly arresting, profound, and beautifully structured, but because *these* words, precisely in their unique particularity, are eminently useful as a divine means of comfort, instruction, confrontation, and transformation (2 Tim 3.16–17). Through their humility, they exemplify preeminently the choice of the God to whom they bear witness of "what is foolish in the world to shame the wise; [of] . . . what is weak in the world to shame the strong; [of] . . . what is low and despised in the world, things that are not, to reduce to nothing things that are, so that no one might boast in the presence of God" (1 Cor 1.27–28). It is therefore unsurprising that the early fathers expected to encounter enigmas and even stumbling blocks in the human language of Scripture.[142]

The early Christians certainly took with utmost seriousness the testimony of the authors of Scripture regarding the importance of the very words of Scripture (Deut 4.2, 12.32; Matt 5.18, 24.35; Luke 21.33; Rev 22.19).[143] It is important to note, however, that despite the high esteem in which premodern Christians held even the smallest details of Scripture, they did not performatively treat the language of Scripture as either absolutely univocal or absolutely inviolable.[144] This is understandable given the fact that they held the realities that the language of Scripture mediates to be of greater relative importance than the written words or texts themselves.[145] "However important words may be—and they are extremely important—," writes Hefling, "what they refer to is more important still."[146] Whatever the precise meaning of those passages indicating the inviolable nature of the words of Scripture in their original settings, then, they plainly cannot serve as justification for the stolid judgment that Christian Scripture cannot be translated out of its original languages or mediated by fallible human copyists. Otherwise the authors of the New Testament, who more often than not relied on the Greek translations of the Old Testament, would themselves have erred! As the discussion of the material *realia* of Christian Scripture in chapter 5 demonstrates, the unity of Scripture cannot be "found" exclusively in some already-back-there-then perfect version of the text. No such version has ever existed in a single spatio-temporal location, after all, and even if one did it would be largely unusable—because of its trilingual nature—to almost every Christian community that has ever existed.

The unity of Scripture, instead, is located in its creation and maintenance, reference, and purpose within the economic work of the Triune God. The reality of the economy of creation and redemption is one. The reality of created non-divine being *in se* is one. The history that is, is one. God is reconciling all things in that history in Christ. The only access any human person has to that reality, though, is through that person's own horizon of interests, understandings, judgments, and values. Engagement with the inspired language and inspired history of Scripture is a constitutive means through which the Holy Spirit works in Christian believers to grant them horizons correlative to the written Word of God.[147] Christians hear, read, meditate on, and study Scripture, and through that engagement the Holy Spirit—who caused the words to be written in the first place—works within then, transforming them to understand "what is truly God's." "Those who are spiritual discern all things," Paul writes, "and they are themselves subject to no one else's scrutiny. 'For who has known the mind of the Lord so as to instruct him?' But we have the mind of Christ" (1 Cor 2.11, 15–16).

The Christian scriptures find their center in Jesus Christ, the Son of God, and serve as prophetic and apostolic testimony to the work that he has done in history in his incarnation, teaching, death, resurrection, ascension, and continued presence in the church through the Holy Spirit. The actual work of articulating precisely *how* the Christian scriptures generally, in all their historical variegation and internal diversity, both have mediated and can continue to mediate the entry of the divine meaning of the Triune God into history in the incarnation of the Son of God remains beyond the scope of the present work.[148] In a sense, the absolutely transcendent object of Scripture makes its comprehensive understanding infinitely beyond the scope of *any* work. It is a matter of faith and existential commitment to adopt the position of the current work. As Frederick Crowe puts it succinctly, "The Scriptures, even when they are badly translated, even when they are read with ignorance of the biblical mentality, may still mediate to us the Lord Jesus and the saving facts of his life, death, and resurrection."[149] The judgment that Scripture is authored by the Spirit of God and is useful for instructing us concerning Christ's work, precisely in the diversity of its material instantiations and the diversity of its internal witness, is a judgment of Christian faith that is not justifiable under any secular criteria of rationality. Still, though, as Joseph Lienhard has written, "there are some sorts of knowledge that can only follow commitment, love, and risk."[150]

Because the meaning that Scripture mediates is the fullness of God's self-revelation in the Son of God, our understanding of it, because its object is the Triune God, will never be complete this side of the eschatological consummation of God's recapitulation of all things in Jesus Christ. The entire task of understanding remains ever before us, and all attentive, intelligent, reasonable, responsible, and ultimately loving engagement with Scripture will bear fruit in us. But for now we will continue to "see in a mirror, dimly, but then we will see face to face." To paraphrase the apostle Paul, in this life we know only in part; then we will know fully, even as we have been fully known (1 Cor 13.12). While I have already addressed the purpose or telos of Scripture in brief a number of times above, it is finally necessary to write more about the specific functions of Christian Scripture in the economic work of the Triune God on the way towards seeing God face-to-face.

THE USEFULNESS OF SCRIPTURE: INSTRUMENT OF TRANSFORMATIVE DIVINE PEDAGOGY

As I noted in the introduction to this work and in chapter 4, many of the church fathers insisted that the Triune God had given Scripture to Christian believers as a pedagogical aid for accomplishing God's redemptive purposes.[151] The recovery and adaptation of that judgment today could prove extremely useful for understanding the nature and purpose of Scripture. The present work holds that Scripture is an eminently useful instrument for mediating both the meaning and actuality of the economic work of the Triune God. Authoritative support for this position already appears in the texts of the New Testament themselves.[152] The apostle Paul explicitly states that the ancient Jewish law is a pedagogue in Galatians (Gal 3.24–26; see also Rom 3–6). For Christians, Christian Scripture in both Testaments is a more comprehensive pedagogue than the ancient Torah. In 1 Corinthians Paul states that the events of Israel's wanderings in Sinai "happened to them to serve as an example, *and they were written down to instruct us,* on whom the end of ages have come" (1 Cor 10.11; see also 9.10–11).[153] Near the end of his letter to the Romans, Paul writes that "whatever was written in former days *was written for our instruction,* so that by steadfastness and by the encouragement of the scriptures we might have hope" (Rom 15.4).

In 2 Timothy 3.14–17, as I noted above, the Pauline author emphasizes the usefulness (ὠφέλιμος) of Scripture "for teaching, for reproof, for correction, and for training in righteousness, so that everyone who belongs to God may be proficient, equipped for every good work" (2 Tim 3.16b–17). While many recent accounts of the nature and purpose of Scripture utilize this text to emphasize the divine origins of Scripture and the inspired nature of the Bible, because it is God-breathed (θεόπνευστος), the accent of the passage, given the flow of the author's argument, seems to be more on the usefulness of these writings for instilling and aiding believers in their faith.[154] "The sacred writings," in the words of the previous verse, " . . . are able (τὰ δυνάμενά) to instruct you for salvation through faith in Jesus Christ" (2 Tim 3.15). Many premodern Christian authorities accordingly invoked this text to insist on the eminent *usefulness* of Scripture within the transformative work of God in history.[155] The approach of connecting the divine initiative behind and with Scripture to its usefulness for mediating the work of God in history follows the wording and emphasis of the language of the passage quite well. While the three aforementioned Pauline texts (1 Cor 10.11; Rom 15.4; 2 Tim 3.14–17) have the ancient Jewish Scriptures later known to Christians as the Old Testament as their referents, New Testament authors sometimes drew attention to the pedagogical and transformative purposes of their own writings (see Luke 1.1–4; John 20.30–31; 1 John 5.13). Premodern interpreters regularly invoked the words of each of these texts to emphasize the usefulness of all Scripture for both teaching and transforming its readers.[156]

Irenaeus insisted that the entire economy of creation and redemption served as divine pedagogy (see *Haer.* 4.38–39).[157] Though he does not say so explicitly, he would undoubtedly have insisted that Sacred Scripture itself played a significant role in that pedagogy. In chapter 2 I already gestured to the pedagogical function of scriptural exegesis for both Origen and Augustine. That judgment appears regularly in their writings. In one of his homilies on John's gospel, for example, Origen states that God has given Scripture to the world "to the service of the soul" (*Comm. Jo.* 10.174).[158] "The whole Scripture is the one, perfect, harmonious instrument of God," he writes elsewhere, "blending the different notes, for those who wish to learn, into one song of salvation" (*Philoc.* 6.2).

To cite a more elaborate example, in book 13 of the *Confessions* Augustine gives an extended figural interpretation of the creation of the firmament in Genesis 1.7 to highlight the pedagogical purpose of Scripture.[159] Augustine identifies Scripture as "the vault" that conceals the truths that God is teaching him and his community.

> Moreover, you alone, our God, have made for us a vault overhead in giving us your divine scripture. The sky will one day be rolled up like a book, but for the present it is stretched out above us like the skin of a tent, for your divine scripture has attained an even nobler authority now that the mortal writers through whom you provided it for us have died. And you know, Lord, you know how you clothed human beings in skins when they became mortal in consequence of their sin. That is why you are said to have stretched out the vault that is your book, stretched out like the skin of a tent those words of yours so free

from discord, which you have canopied over us through the ministry of mortal men. The authority inherent in your revelation, which they have passed on to us, is by their very death spread more widely over all the world below, for in their lifetime it had not been raised so high or extended so far. (*Conf.* 13.15.16)[160]

Augustine states that the "other waters" above the vault, which are "immortal and immune to decay," are the angels. Such spiritual creatures behold the face of the Triune God without ceasing and therefore have no need of the scriptures (13.15.18). Because humans do not see God face-to-face, however, they must constantly look up into the vault of Scripture "there to recognize the mercy which manifests you in time, you who have created time" (13.15.18). "These things you teach us," Augustine concludes, "with consummate wisdom in your book, which is the vault you provide for us, O our God, so that they may all become plain to us through contemplation of your wonders. Still, though, we must discern them through signs, and transient phases, and passing days and years" (13.18.23).

Such references could be multiplied. Origen and Augustine represent key witnesses to the ubiquitous judgment of the church fathers that Scripture was a means of the divine teaching of the Triune God that facilitated the deifying transformation of its readers and hearers.[161] As Ayres summarizes, for the fathers,

> the scriptures are a providentially ordered resource for the shaping and reformation of the Christian's imagination and desire. The reformation of imagination and desire is a reformation of the human soul—the soul that finds its mission and true end as the *imago Dei* within the body of Christ. The human person finds this mission and true end through a creedally normed meditation on the text of scripture within the church. Understanding scripture's place in the economy of salvation is inseparable from understanding the place of the soul in the triune soteriological action.[162]

As I argued above, it is possible to affirm the divine origins, revelatory nature, and functional authority of Scripture today, and Augustine and Origen, among others, provide useful heuristics and images for understanding those doctrinal judgments. Our own setting, though, requires us to recognize the historical diversity of concrete instantiations of Scripture, and the necessity of engaging that history with an awareness of and attention to the plurality of the distinct concrete instantiations of Scripture throughout its history. To read any modern translation is to be in contact with countless decisions and judgments concerning the antecedent history of the technology, words, language, and scope of Christian Scripture.

I articulated an understanding of the doctrinal judgment that Scripture mediates the revelation of the Triune God and the intelligibility of God's redemptive work through the Son and the Holy Spirit in the previous two sections of this chapter. The present section concludes this chapter with an explanation of the doctrine that Scripture is a useful instrument of the Triune God for mediating the intelligibility of that work and facilitating that ongoing work in the readers, hearers, and interpreters of Christian Scripture. Scripture is a servant of that work even in its manifold and variegated creatureliness.[163] The final telos of Christian Scripture is not the mediation of a singular "Biblical worldview" or "biblical culture." The purpose of Christian Scripture is instead the transformation of readers, through the work of the Holy Spirit, so that they have the mind of Christ and so know and love the Triune God and everything the Triune God loves.

In this work I have maintained that the authors of Scripture mediate their judgments and beliefs through the written texts of Christian Scripture. I affirm the doctrinal judgment that Scripture is useful for teaching (πρὸς διδασκαλίαν; 2 Tim 3.16). I have therefore marshaled and ordered a number of texts of Scripture, particularly from the New Testament, as specific beliefs and judgments that I take to be constitutive within a Christian understanding of the economic work of the Triune God. I have consciously chosen specific scriptural judgments over others. I have also invoked a rule of faith, the Niceno-Constantinopolitan Creed, and have supplemented the judgments of that rule with hypotheses for understanding. Readers will have to decide whether my choices are intelligent, reasonable, responsible, and faithful from their own perspective and within their own lights. If any reader does find my responses of value, though, and if she finds my presentation of the biblical data persuasive, her understanding of that data will change. She will better measure up to the text— and its history—which "stands written."[164] Perhaps her specific judgments and values will change. Any change in her understanding and judgments, though, is a change in *her*.[165] Through attentive, intelligent, reasonable, responsible, and faithful engagement with Scripture, the reading subject will find herself changed to measure up to the technological, linguistic, and intelligible content of Scripture.

Christian faith has intelligible content. Scripture inscribes the judgments of its human authors, moved by the Holy Spirit, concerning the realities of Christian faith. Scripture is technology for manifesting the content of Christian faith. For much of Christian history, believers have, recognizing the Spirit's work, privileged certain documents as authoritative written witnesses to that content. Scripture indeed refers to historical, psychological, and theological realities, and it mediates judgments about the actuality and characteristics of the work of God, Father, Son, and Holy Spirit, which are constitutive judgments of Christian faith. Beyond mediating the historical events of the economic work of the Triune God, however, and the faith of its authors and tradents, the manifold generic variety of Scripture touches the differentiated aspirations and possibilities of human consciousness and so serves to advance God's transformative work in readers. In divine providence, the Lord of history has worked so that believers would not be without a written witness to his work. The witness itself is aptly varied to address all readers and hearers in their own locations. The Triune God has utilized fallible and finite human persons to transmit this precious message. The message itself, though, is not fallible. The power and grace of God are sufficient for us in our weakness (2 Cor 12.9–10). It is fitting that the written technological witnesses to this power and grace of Christian Scripture are themselves fragile and simple.

Scripture does not bear witness to itself but instead to God. The divine *res* of Scripture are its true end and purpose. The language of Scripture *does* mediate historical and doctrinal truths. The reality to which Scripture refers, though, is not a set of discrete, logically or conceptually related propositions of doctrine. The reality to which Scripture refers is the recapitulation of all things in Jesus Christ in the history that is. *Every* teaching and doctrine of Christian faith has this reality as its referent. This reality is a divine mystery. It is the gift of God's self to humanity through the cross of Christ and sending of the Holy Spirit. "It is already a first abstraction," writes de Lubac, ". . . to separate completely the gift and the revelation of the gift, the redemptive action and the knowledge of redemption, the mystery as act and the mystery as proposed to faith. It is a second abstraction to separate from this total revelation . . . certain particular truths, enunciated in separate propositions, which will concern respectively the Trinity, the incarnate Word, baptism, grace, and so on."[166]

De Lubac states that such abstractions are necessary given the constitution of our created minds. We cannot help but naturally raise questions. We cannot help but understand the unity of the work of an infinite God through our finite and discursive minds.[167] We must, however, take care to remember that "in Jesus Christ all has been both given and revealed to us at one stroke; and that, in consequence, all the explanations to come, whatever might be their tenor and whatever might be their mode, will never be anything but coins in more distinct parts of a treasure already possessed in its entirety; that all was already really, actually contained in a higher state of awareness and not only in 'principles' and 'premises.'"[168]

What the Triune God proposes to us through Scripture has intelligible content, but the good news of the redemptive work of the Triune God is more fundamentally a call to us. The entry of divine meaning into human history in the person of Jesus Christ and the mission of the Holy Spirit requires a response. The Holy Scriptures, after all, are able to instruct us for faith in Jesus Christ (2 Tim 3.15). At Pentecost, Luke testifies that Peter preached the message of the crucifixion and resurrection of the Lord of Glory, foretold by the prophets, which was fulfilled in their own time. The people were cut to the heart and responded in faith (see Acts 2.14–42). That is the appropriate response to the work of the Holy Spirit in the exposition of Scripture. Engagement with Scripture is a means through which God addresses and so transforms us.

> Revelation, in fact, is at the same time a call: the call to the Kingdom, which is not open to men without a "conversion," . . . an inner transformation and, as it were, a recasting not only of will but of being itself. Then the entrance into another existence is produced. It is a new creation, which resounds in one's entire awareness: it upsets the original equilibrium, it modifies the orientation of it, it opens up unsuspected depths in it. Eyes open anew on a new world. The community of life allows the giving of new meaning, its whole meaning to the divine object of faith.[169]

The ultimate end of Scripture, in the missions of the Son of God and Holy Spirit in history, is the ongoing process of conversion in those who engage it. The study of Scripture provides a means through which Christians can be "transformed by the renewing of [their] minds, so that [they] may discern what is the will of God—what is good and acceptable and perfect" (Rom 12.2b).

Scripture does not merely mediate judgments about things that have taken place in the past or about the doctrinal truths of Christianity. That is only part of its purpose. Scripture, like all literature, is an invitation to encounter. "Literature," writes John Topel, "invites the reader into its world and asks for a commitment to that world. In so doing, it works the transformation of the reader's experience, imagination, understanding, and action."[170] Scripture is a privileged literature for the Christian community because Christians have historically discerned the Triune God calling them through it towards Godself. De Lubac explains, "All that Scripture recounts has indeed happened in history, but the account that is given does not contain the whole purpose of Scripture in itself. This purpose still needs to be accomplished and is actually accomplished in us each day."[171] "Exegesis is a kind of 'exercise,'" he writes elsewhere, "through which the believer's mind progresses."[172] Christian engagement with Scripture facilitates the Holy Spirit's work of transforming the believer spiritually, morally, and intellectually, conforming her to the likeness and form of Jesus Christ who reveals the Father through the Holy Spirit.

The ultimate telos of engagement with Scripture is encounter with the transcendent God who is Father, Son, and Holy Spirit. Such an encounter reorients the horizons of the reading and hearing communities of Scripture towards transcendent values. Those in Christ set their minds on "heavenly things" (see Col 3.1–4, 12–17). "For the Spirit," Paul writes elsewhere, "searches everything, even the depths of God" (1 Cor 2.10). The indwelling of the Holy Spirit radically reorients Christians' focus and direction towards the transcendent Lord of the universe. I described this momentous transformation in chapter 4 as religious conversion. It is the reception of the love of God flooding our hearts (Rom 5.5), so that we are able to return that love to God with "all of our heart, soul, strength, and mind" (Mark 12.30). Christians return to the texts of Scripture again and again to be "trained in righteousness" (2 Tim 3.16), which is the very righteousness of the Triune God.

But the love of God that floods the hearts of Christian believers entails a love of all that God has created. It is impossible to love with God's love if one does not love *all* that God loves (1 John 4.7–12). The dual end or purpose of Scripture, the *finis* of the law of God (Rom 13.8; 1 Tim 1.5), is this love of God and neighbor (Matt 22.37–40). "So if it seems to you that you have understood the divine Scriptures, or any part of them," Augustine declares, "in such a way that by this understanding you do not build up this twin love of God and neighbor, *then you have not yet understood them*" (*Doctr. chr.* 1.26.40). The purpose of reading, studying, meditating upon, remembering, and hearing Scripture is this ongoing divine work in the Christian believer. It is impossible to understand Scripture in any adequate measure if the reader stops short of these divine intentions. Scripture has as its purpose the transformation not only of our minds, but of our wills; such transformation entails new possibilities for new action in the world. God frees us to love all who God loves and all that God loves. And we act in accordance with that change.

"The Christian gospel is an invitation to *metanoia*, to change," writes M. Shawn Copeland, "the standard against which that change is measured is the life of Jesus Christ."[173] The experience of the Holy Spirit's work conforms the Christian believer to the form of Christ through giving her the mind of Christ. That divine work transforms readers so they are able, like God, to love even their enemies (Rom 5.10). Engagement with Scripture is a means of grace oriented towards that end. Scripture, as inspired by and used instrumentally by the Holy Spirit, represents an especially apt resource for the Christian believer's growth in the fruit of the Spirit, "love, joy, peace, patience, kindness, generosity, gentleness, faithfulness, and self-control" (Gal 5.22).

Even the stumbling blocks of the history of Scripture have roles in the transformative pedagogy of the Triune God. Critical biblical scholars, for all of their tremendous work, must recognize in humility the historical gaps in our knowledge of the ancient worlds in which Scripture was first written and transmitted. The recognition that Scripture, though written through the movement of the Holy Spirit, has nevertheless—and necessarily—been mediated in human language and by human hands, minds, lips, and ears throughout Christian history requires a measure of humility in all Christians; we must admit both our dependence upon faith in the providence and wisdom of the Triune God for acting in such ways and our dependence upon the countless believers—and even scholars—who have handed on these texts before us so that we could possess and read and hear Scripture today.

As they return to the Sacred Page again and again the Spirit conforms those who read to the image of Jesus Christ. The transforming work of the Triune God in Christian believers through Scripture thus entails ongoing moral transformation. The processes of reading, hearing, studying, meditating upon, memorizing, and reciting Scripture reorient believers towards God, and that reorientation transforms their priorities and values to align with the priorities and values that God reveals are God's own.

Engagement with Scripture can also induce changes in the philosophical horizons of those who study it. The achievement of being able to recognize the plurality of human perspectives in Scripture can be an invitation for one to take responsibility for one's own perspective. That achievement can help one to reflect on why and how the language of Scripture and the realities attested in Scripture should have a place in informing one's own perspective. Recognition of the historical distance between the world(s) of Scripture and the contemporary world can be an invitation for readers to make explicit an awareness of the historicity of human language and culture. The modern discipline of historical scholarship is built upon the recognition and thematization of historical consciousness. Historians, including those whose life work involves the study of the texts of the Christian Bible, operate within a scholarly differentiation of consciousness through which they are able to selectively study and hypothesize about social, cultural, and religious developments in the past. Because of the legitimacy of such questions and answers about the past, McEvenue notes, "the rejection of scholarship cannot be tolerated once scholarship has become a cultural possibility."[174] Biblical scholarship cannot be ignored because it raises, and sometimes answers, actual authentic questions about the origins and intelligibility of the Christian scriptures as the human artifacts that they are. "The questions remain important and valid," Young writes, "even if we are unsure of the answers."[175] The exigencies of attentiveness, intelligence, reasonableness, and responsibility require that such questions be asked and answered to the best of our abilities.[176] But questions about the historical particularity of the authors, audiences, and cultures of Christian Scripture are not the only questions we can ask about the text. In fact, authentic engagement with Christian Scripture is a divine means through which further questions of commitment and response occur in and to readers, hearers, and interpreters of these texts.

The recognition that those who engage Scripture, both historically and in the present, employ diverse culturally conditioned forms of reasoning in order to make sense of it can serve to help one become aware of the ways in which one's own education, family histories, political allegiances, and faith traditions have formed one's own questions. The fact that reading always takes place in cultural circumstances, coupled with the judgment that the Triune God addresses or intends to address and speak to all people in all cultures, requires the concomitant judgment that authentic readings are possible precisely from and within the particularity of specific cultures.[177] The work of sorting out faithful and responsible interpretations that reflect and promote the redemptive economic work of the Triune God and those that oppose it remains an ongoing task for the global and historical body of Christ. The recognition of the differences in the kinds of language that are employed in Scripture, in the creeds, and in systematic theology, respectively, can serve as an invitation for individuals to consider the possibilities that the specialization of languages provides for understanding and making judgments about divine and created being and for expressing those judgments in forms of commonsense language, the specifications of technical language, and symbolic and artist representations.

In each of these ways, engagement with Scripture can facilitate a process of self-appropriation, whereby readers recognize what it is that they know about and through Scripture, how and why that knowledge is actually knowledge, and, finally, what it is that they know when they are in possession of that knowledge. It is not possible to approach Scripture from nowhere, but it is not necessary for readers to remain in ignorance of where they stand when they are engaging it. "Everybody has his filter," writes de Lubac, "which he takes about with him, through which, from the indefinite mass of facts, he gathers in those suited to confirm his prejudices. And the same fact again, passing through different filters, is revealed in different aspects, so as to confirm the most diverse opinions. It has always been so, it always will be so in this world. Rare, very rare are those who check their filter."[178]

Authentic engagement with Scripture can provoke readers and hearers to check their filters and so serves as a performative means of spiritual, moral, and philosophical renewal. Scripture is thus an apt instrument for enabling its readers to undergo religious, moral, and intellectual conversion. While concrete history demonstrates that such conversions do not automatically or of necessity follow from engagement with Scripture, Scripture both reflects the influence of such conversions and, when engaged authentically, leads to such conversions. The kinds of attention, intelligence, critical reflection, and deliberation that Scripture requires of its readers and hearers impel individual and communal readers towards the self-transcendence that is both natural to them as human beings and is supernaturally possible for them through the grace of God healing and elevating their whole selves.[179]

Christian Scripture is an instrument of the Holy Spirit and Son of God, and its purpose is to facilitate the transformation of its readers for their participation in the recapitulation of all things in Christ. It is the Holy Spirit's broad, historically multifaceted work in inspiring Scripture—in the loci of its authors, the worlds it projects, and its interpreting communities—that has affected and will continue to affect the manifestation and actualization of the work of the Son in history. As Paul writes, "No one can say 'Jesus is Lord' except by the Holy Spirit" (1 Cor 12.3b). The Christian church, the Body of Christ, participates in this work through the continuing missions of the Son and Holy Spirit in history. The church takes up and reads Scripture again and again to discern the will of God, to be convicted of the sins of her members, and grow "to maturity, to the measure of the full stature of Christ" (Eph 4.13b).

Christian Scripture is a potentially dangerous instrument, however. Because Christian believers recognize it as an instrument of the Triune God, it possesses a profound symbolic authority.[180] And some readers and hearers have mistakenly construed its authority in demonic and idolatrous ways. Scripture has proven itself useful as an instrument for the work of the Triune God in history, but it has tragically also proven to be a useful instrument of violence and oppression.[181] To use Scripture in the latter way, however, is to reject the authority of the Son of God Incarnate, Jesus Christ, to whom Scripture testifies. The authority that Jesus Christ exercises in his incarnation, life, teaching, death, resurrection, ascension, and lordship over all of creation is self-sacrificial; it is kenotic.[182] Jesus declared to his disciples, "You know that the rulers of the Gentiles lord it over them, and their great ones are tyrants over them. *Whoever wishes to be great among you must be your servant, and whoever wishes to be first among you must be your slave*; just as the Son of Man came not to be served but to serve, and to give his life a ransom for many" (Matt 20.25–26). Paul writes that Christians should have the same mind-set "that was in Christ Jesus, who, though he was in the form of God, did not regard equality with God as something to be exploited, but emptied himself, taking the form of a slave, being born in human likeness. And being found in human form, he humbled himself and became obedient to the point of death—even death on a cross" (Phil 2.6–11).[183] The humility of Christ is the measure of all exercises of human authority, including those that appeal to and utilize Christian Scripture. Those who utilize Christian Scripture authoritatively must take caution; for Christ testifies that everyone will give an account for every careless word uttered (Matt 12.36; see also Rom 14.10–12). Given the high responsibility of speaking for the Triune God, James cautions that not many should become teachers, because those who do will be judged more harshly (Jas 3.1).

As a textual and linguistic artifact Christian Scripture does not impose itself on readers *in ipse* because it is not an agent. "The Word of God," on the other hand, "is living and active, sharper than any two-edged sword, piercing until it divides soul from spirit, joints from marrow; it is able to judge the thoughts and intentions of the heart" (Heb 4.12). The written Word of God mediates this living Word of God in the processes of attentive, intelligent, reasonable, responsible, and faithful Christian use and interpretation of Scripture. A Christian reading of Scripture thus requires a posture of openness and vulnerability. Scripture is useful for correction and rebuke (2 Tim 3.16). The Christian reader must be self-critical above all else. Christian reading requires one to have experienced the Holy Spirit's internal work, refashioning the inner person in conformity with Christ. It requires one to have an openness to mystery, to transcendence, to perplexity, and to suffering. To participate in the economic work of the Triune God, one must lay down any desire to control God or God's authority. One must become as Christ. It is possible to read Scripture in willful ignorance and blindness, utilizing it to promote our selfish desires. To turn Scripture from its purpose towards such selfish ends, though, is to reject an invaluable treasure and to shirk the authority of the Triune God to whom it bears witness. Those trained for the kingdom of heaven, however, are able to draw out of this treasure "what is new and what is old" (Matt 13.52b).

SUMMARY AND CONCLUSION

The unity, authority, and truthfulness of Christian Scripture can only be "found" or discovered in a nuanced understanding of its production, reference, and purpose within the unified work of the Triune God in history. Christian readers remain committed to the judgment that the Triune God is reconciling all things in history, but they also realize that the full fruition of that work has not yet come to pass. The Christian scriptures are a privileged, divinely sanctioned instrument in that singular history, and their language bears witness to and mediates that history. Even so, the Christian scriptures bear the distinctive influences of their specific human authors throughout. There is no univocal and singular "biblical horizon," "biblical worldview," or "biblical perspective" already-out-there-now "in" or "behind" the text. As I have shown in chapter 5, there is no already-back-there-then Christian Bible either. But Christians throughout history have always been able to sufficiently discern—through the illuminating internal work of the Holy Spirit—the contours of the economic work of the Triune God *through their own historically diverse instantiations of Christian Scripture.* The historical diversity of Scripture, even the diversity of its material *realia*, has a place in its transformative and educative purposes.

Augustine already recognized and affirmed this judgment in the fifth century AD. As is well known, Augustine followed most of the antecedent church fathers in affirming the authority of the Greek translations of the ancient Jewish Scriptures.[184] But Augustine had also recognized and lamented the variations in the old Latin translations of the Greek Old Testament (see *Doctr. chr.* 2.11.16; also *Ep.* 71, 82). His older contemporary, Jerome, as I noted above, was also troubled by those discrepancies. Jerome sought to address such variations by creating a new Latin translation, the famous Vulgate, from the ancient Hebrew texts.[185] Augustine and Jerome corresponded about the practical and theological implications of Jerome's project around the beginning of the fifth century.[186] At first, Augustine staunchly opposed Jerome's endeavor. Augustine requested that Jerome instead focus solely on translating from the ancient Greek versions of the Old Testament, which Jerome had already done for the book of Job (see *Ep.* 28, ca. 394 or 395 AD). Later, Augustine expressed concern that Jerome's translation from the Hebrew would have disastrous pastoral effects in the churches. Augustine argued that Jerome was severing an important tie between Greek-speaking Christians and Latin-speaking Christians. Augustine also reported an incident where the congregation at Oea almost rioted when Jerome's version of Jonah was read aloud because it contradicted the congregation's previously accepted Latin translation of the Greek (*Ep.* 71, ca. 403 AD).[187]

Near the end of his life, however, Augustine had a change of mind and heart. In his magnum opus *The City of God*, Augustine strikingly affirmed the authority and inspiration of *both* the Hebrew and Greek traditions of the ancient Jewish Scriptures, *even while—and because—those traditions contained contradictory language.*[188] As he put it a few years before his death (ca. 425 AD):

> For the very same Spirit that was at work in the prophets when they uttered their messages was at work also in the seventy scholars when they translated them. And the Spirit could have said something else as well, with divine authority, as if the prophet had said both things because it was the same Spirit that said both. The Spirit could have said the same thing in a different way, so that even the words were not the same, the same meaning would still shine through to those who properly understood them. He could also have omitted something, so that it might be shown in this way too that the task of translation was achieved not by the servile labor of a human bond-servant of words, but by the power of God which filled and directed the mind of the translator. . . . Hence even I, in my small measure, follow the footsteps of the apostles, because they themselves quoted prophetic testimonies from both sources, from the Hebrew and the Septuagint; and I have assumed both sources should be employed as authoritative, since both are one, and both are inspired by God. (*Civ.* 18.43–44)[189]

Augustine was able to make this affirmation because of his conviction of the instrumental purpose of Scripture in the work of the Triune God in history itself. All of the dimensions of Scripture, including the stumbling blocks of its content and its providentially guided material history, had a role in its purpose for transforming its readers. While Augustine explicitly states that the Hebrew and Greek versions are inspired, he implicitly accepts the authority of the Latin translations of those texts as well. Antecedent and subsequent Christians have followed his practice by expecting to encounter and be transformed by the Spirit of God through reading, hearing, and meditating on their own *distinct* historical instantiations of Christian Scripture. That is not to say that all versions are equally "inspired" in a rigid sense.[190] The historicity of difference in the texts, though, like the transcendent referents of the texts themselves, always leads readers *beyond* those texts *towards* the actual work of the Triune God in history itself. That is the normative intention and work of the Holy Spirit. The texts of Christian Scripture are therefore "self-consuming artifacts" orchestrated by the Holy Spirit to impel their readers beyond Scripture to the reality of the economic work of the Triune God.[191] The distinct particular words in their varied material instantiations are of unique value and play their distinctive roles in the redemptive pedagogy of the Triune God.

A recently published evangelical book has the subtitle *Moving Beyond the Bible to Theology*.[192] In truth, however, we are always beyond the Bible. The ongoing and inescapable work of hearing, reading, interpreting, and understanding Scripture always takes us beyond the original words and original intentions of any of its particular human authors. And yet Christians are also never beyond Sacred Scripture.[193] The work of discerning the precise histories of the texts of Scripture, the work of discerning the intelligibility of the histories that the language of Scripture mediates, and the work of discerning the singular overarching economic work of the Triune God are ongoing tasks with intrinsically anagogic and centrifugal orientations. Christians will continually return to the texts of Christian Scripture to grow in their understanding of these realities. "[The] interpretation of Scripture is indefinite, being as it is in the image of the infinity of its Author," de Lubac writes. "It is like a great poem, with a pedagogical intent, whose inexhaustible significance leads us to the pure heights of the summit of contemplation."[194] In a remarkable paradox, Christians are always beyond Scripture and yet, at least in their mortal lives, will never be beyond Scripture.

Conclusion

That Christian Scripture is truthful, unified, and authoritative for Christian faith, thought, and praxis is non-negotiable within the horizon of Christian faith. It is a constitutive judgment of the present work. But making that judgment is one thing, and understanding what it could possibly mean is another. How Scripture has actually functioned authoritatively in Christian history has depended upon the specific judgments and decisions of the Christian communities in which particular historical instantiations of Scripture—whether specific technological forms, text forms, translations, or canonical collections—have been accepted, read, studied, interpreted, and otherwise used. Whatever "it" is in the concrete, its authority and meaning depend upon its use, and its use has varied throughout Christian history and is enormously varied in contemporary Christian communities. Unless we are willing to accept the current situation of interpretive cacophony by either ignoring it—which is what many Christian groups and leaders seem most comfortable doing—or downplaying the significance of the irreducible historical plurality of forms and interpretation and dismissing that plurality with defensive apologetics, we must find another way to responsibly understand the unity of Scripture even in its past and present historical variegation.

In this work I have articulated a systematic theology of the Christian Bible as a resource for meeting that need to help contemporary believers navigate the current situations of Christian Scripture in the academy and in ecclesial communities. As I noted in the introduction, the present work is only *a* systematic theology of the Christian Bible. It represents one attempt to grapple with the extant historical data of Christian Scripture, the histories of its use and interpretation, and traditional doctrinal judgments about Scripture itself. The approach of the present work depends upon ancient precedents. As I showed in the second chapter, the Christians of the NT period and of the period before any "closures" of either Testament already read and used the Scriptures—first the ancient Jewish Scriptures and then the texts of the Christian NT—with reference to and through a horizon of judgments and understandings of the economic work of the God of Israel through Jesus Christ and the Holy Spirit. Such judgments were held with consistency in the early Christian communities; but Christian understandings of those judgments and Christian understandings of the implications of those judgments were on the move. Irenaeus, Origen, and Augustine bear witness to the impulses towards clarity and specification in Christian reflection on the work of the Triune God. Their utilizations of the rule of faith as a hermeneutical framework for engaging Scripture demonstrate their shared concern to locate Scripture within Christian beliefs about the economic work of the God attested in those texts.

The use of the rule of faith by those particular fathers provided a point of reference for the present position on the nature and purpose of Christian Scripture. Both their willingness to read Scripture through the rule of faith and their willingness to reflect on the implications of the rule for making judgments about the actual economic work of God set an example for the present work. In chapter 3, then, I proposed the Nicene Creed as a rule of faith that provided an ecclesially received set of judgments concerning the divine context or location of Christian Scripture. Following the example of Irenaeus, Origen, and Augustine, I sought to explore the implications of the rule by supplementing it with further judgments and heuristics for understanding the precise doctrinal content of the creed. I utilized contemporary and traditional resources to articulate a theological position on the relationship between divine and human freedom and causation, and then utilized various testimonies from the authors of Scripture, particularly the NT, to reflect on the precise contours of the redemptive missions of the Son of God and the Holy Spirit in history.

That chapter provided a set of categories, doctrines, and heuristics for identifying the general divine context of Christian Scripture.

But Christian Scripture is still a product of specific human individuals and communities. In chapter 4, then, I provided an account of human nature and human history for locating Christian Scripture within the self-transcending reflection and expression of human beings in history. I began that chapter by reappropriating the premodern Christian judgment that Scripture is useful as divine pedagogy for transforming human persons. From that point of departure I utilized contemporary and historical resources to develop a philosophical and theological anthropology as the distinctively human context of Christian Scripture.

After a brief interlude on the instrumental nature of Scripture near the beginning of chapter 5, the rest of that chapter provided an overview and theological evaluation of the technological forms, transmission, lexical and translational components, and scope of Christian Scripture throughout its history. I concluded that chapter by noting that the Triune God has continually used the diversity and apparent incongruities of the histories of Scripture to encounter and transform readers and hearers in accordance with God's redemptive purposes. No single material instantiation of Scripture can be removed from these overarching histories and set against any other instantiation as more pure or more completely Scripture. Any responsible engagement with Scripture today requires an acknowledgment of the historical diversity of Christian Scripture. Such an acknowledgment serves the transformative intentions of the God who inspires Scripture in interpreting subjects who must both recognize and measure up to that plurality.

The Triune God does not give us Christian Scripture, however, only to confront us with the historicity of all human language and human culture. The fundamental purpose for which God gives humanity Christian Scripture is the transformation of the understanding and praxis of those who read, hear, and mediate upon it in accordance with God's unified overarching redemptive purposes. In chapter 6, therefore, I provided an account of the unity and authority of Scripture by explicitly locating the doctrinal judgment of the inspiration of Scripture within my earlier account of the mission of the Holy Spirit and by locating the judgment that Scripture is the written Word of God relative to the earlier account of the mission of the Son of God in history. Christian Scripture is unified because the intentions of the Holy Spirit and the Son of God are unified in the history that is. But despite the nascent completeness of the work of the Triune God in the work of the Son of God in his incarnation, teaching, crucifixion, death, resurrection, and ascension, and despite the nascent completeness of the work of the Holy Spirit at Pentecost and in the hearts of historical Christian believers, the Triune God is still, in a great mystery, reconciling all things in Christ (Eph 1.10). I concluded chapter 6 by articulating an account of the doctrinal judgment that Christian Scripture serves as an eminently useful instrument of the ongoing work of the Son and Holy Spirit. It can serve as such an instrument because its particular words eminently mediate the meaning of that work and because the Holy Spirit continues to transform the readers and hearers of Scripture who return to the written word of God again and again.

The Triune God has not given us Scripture as it is for the sole purpose that we should believe specific things. God has given us Scripture as it is for the purpose that we should do specific things. Now, believing is certainly a kind of doing, and so what we believe is extremely important. But believing is only a part of doing. The level of decision is the highest level of conscious human activity. It is at this level where we locate ourselves within our traditions, and it is at this level that we come to discern and articulate our fundamental judgments and values. What could possibly provide an adequate perspective for making such decisions about transcendent truth and goodness? It would take divine wisdom to make such decisions. Yet Christians profess, following the judgment of the apostle Paul, that the Spirit of God dwells in us giving us the mind of Christ (1 Cor 2.16). The mind of Christ is the meaning of Christ whose form is manifest in his incarnation, teaching, life, death, resurrection, and ascension. It is our transformation into this form, this self-sacrificing love that reconciles person to person, community to community, and all humanity to the Triune God, that represents the authoritative rule for human life. It is the relative promotion of this form that is the paradigm against which all engagement with Scripture will be eschatologically measured and towards which engagement with Scripture normatively tends. Christian Scripture is the primary linguistic instrument that the Triune God has given to the world through which God continues to facilitate such transformation in communities and interpreters.

Why, then, if we already have knowledge of this plan of cosmos, history, and human restoration, the *res* to which Scripture bears witness, do we need to return to Scripture again and again? Near the end of book 1 of *Doctr. chr.*, Augustine makes a shocking, perhaps rhetorically excessive, declaration: "People supported by faith, hope, and charity, and retaining a firm grip on them, have no need of the Scriptures except for instructing others. And so there are many who live by these three even in the desert without books" (1.39.43). For Augustine it is—at least theoretically—possible for Christians to get along without Scripture. But most of us cannot do without it. And even those of us who are committed in faith continually come up short of such ideals. While we are able to understand and participate in the work of the Triune God in history through grace, such participation is, metaphysically speaking, not necessary. It is a free and so precarious participation in and cooperation with God's work and so requires prayer, focus, and even ascetic praxis. Ongoing engagement with Scripture is a constitutive part of that regimen of discipline. In his commentary on Romans, Origen writes:

> [Our] mind is renewed through training in wisdom and meditation upon the Word of God, and the spiritual interpretation of his law. And to the extent that it makes daily progress by reading the Scriptures, to the extent that its understanding goes deeper, to that extent it becomes continuously new and daily new. I do not know if anyone can be renewed who is lazy in respect to the Holy Scriptures and training in spiritual understanding, by which it becomes possible not only to understand what has been written, but also to explain more clearly and to reveal more carefully. (*Comm. Rom.* 9.1.12)[1]

Any individuals and communities who are not yet able to bear witness completely to the reconciling, self-sacrificial work of the Triune God on behalf of the world in their own embodied concreteness, in word and deed, can return to Scripture again and again to grow in their faith, hope, and especially love. Scripture is an eminently useful instrument for such transformative work in human persons. As symbols give rise to thought, so the language of Scripture gives rise to reflection in readers and hearers.[2] The experience of Scripture gives rise to wonder and to questions, and such questions bring readers into contact with the diverse worlds of meaning behind, of, and in front of the texts of Christian Scripture. But all such worlds, for Christian readers, are centered on and find their right place relative to Jesus Christ who is the fullness of the self-revelation of the Tri-une God in the economy of creation and redemption. The Christian reader thus takes all thoughts captive unto Christ (2 Cor 10.5), even those thoughts that emerge through her engagement with Scripture. As man Christ sets a standard for the translation of divine meaning into human in-tersubjectivity, language, and symbol. But though the Triune God speaks a clear Word to us through Christ's visible work, because Christ's meaning is divine we ought not expect to arrive at complete knowledge of this Truth in this life. Even though we can fruitfully advance in our understanding of these mysteries, they do not cease being mysteries. We continue to see as through a mirror darkly (1 Cor 13.12). As Augustine declares, "If you have finished, it is not God."[3] Human understandings of Scripture, in its his-torical, ethical, cultural, social, and religious dimensions, will always take place within our completely human anagogic and centrifugally expand-ing personal horizons.

The words of Christian Scripture truthfully and usefully mediate the reality, the *res* or *Sache*, of the recapitulation of all things in Christ. The systematic theology of Christian Scripture that I have articulated in the present work is therefore a transcendently open heuristic. It is a matter of faith to accept the doctrines affirmed in the present work. It is a matter of ongoing growing human understanding, illuminated by the Holy Spirit dwelling within, that allows us to advance in our grasp of these truths in our concrete experience, understanding, judgment, and decisions. Such choices, affirmations, and understandings, of course, have their own broader con-text within the recapitulation of all things in Christ (Eph 1.10). And the material and intelligent *res* of Scripture are God-breathed and eminently useful instruments for that creative and redemptive work which the Tri-une God is accomplishing through his two hands, Son and Spirit, in our midst and on our behalf.

NOTES

CHAPTER ONE

Scripture at the Level of Our Times

1. I use the language "Christian Bible," "Christian Scripture(s)," "Bible," and "scriptures" interchangeably. For consistency, I utilize the singular "Scripture"—capitalizing it to designate the religious/theological significance of the Christian Bible for Christians—most often. The use of such terms is, however, contested. A recent conference (2010) at the University of Koblentz-Landau drew attention to the plurality of perspectives regarding the scope, contents, and details of the referents of the noun *Bible* and adjective *biblical*. See the published proceedings in Finsterbusch and Lange, *What Is Bible?* I write from a Christian perspective and so I understand these terms to refer to a Christian canonical collection of writings. Even so, the question of the scope and shape of the canon is itself contested. There is no already-out-there-now-real Christian Bible to which this language could be applied univocally. Karl Barth notes that the question of canonical scope can and must be asked at all times. See Barth, *CD*: 1.2, 476–481. I address these difficulties directly in chapters 5 and 6.

2. Sokolowski, *The God of Faith and Reason*, 119. The context of the phrase is worth quoting in full: "How are we to read the Bible? Whether we read it privately, or with others, or for others, how are we to make our own what is written in the scriptures? A theological question arises today in the reading of Scripture because of what we might call an embarrassment of riches; there is so much historical and philological information, so many parallels in other literary traditions, and so many distinctions to be made in the body of the text itself, between original and modified formulations, between authentic words and attributed speeches, between passages coming from different hands and reflecting different theologies, that the sense of the Bible as one book becomes questioned in a way it was never questioned before. Furthermore, it is often said that we no longer live in the 'world' the Bible talks about, that the world defined by the Bible, and taken for granted by it, is not congruent with ours."

The words *premodern*, *modern*, and *postmodern* bear a wide range of associations in contemporary philosophy, theology, biblical studies, and other disciplines. I use the terms descriptively and do not intend value judgments in my use of any of the three. I use the term "premodern," for instance, to refer to works and figures that antedate the epochal shifts in the Western world of the scientific revolution of the seventeenth and eighteenth centuries and the Enlightenment.

3. Many specific proposals classifiable as either primarily historical, primarily contextual, or primarily theological in focus also address questions that fall under the purview of the other approaches. For example, by engaging questions of NT historical criticism, theological questions about revelation and inspiration, and the relevance of contextual methodologies for drawing upon the perspectives of the New Testament as a resource for women, Sandra Schneiders's *The Revelatory Text* crosses the "boundaries" of the typology. See also Gorman, *Scripture and Its Interpretation*.

4. Useful studies that focus explicitly on these philosophical emphases and their impacts on Christian use of Scripture include Broggi, *Sacred Language, Sacred World*; Jeanrond, *Text and Interpretation*; Jeanrond, *Theological Hermeneutics*; Smith, *The Fall of Interpretation*; Thiselton, *New Horizons in Hermeneutics*; Thiselton, *The Two Horizons*; Vanhoozer, *Is There a Meaning*; Westphal, *Whose Community?*

5. T. J. Lang uses the term "historical consciousness" to identify the "totalizing reconception of history and ecclesial identity that enabled [the early] Christians to imagine themselves as simultaneously new to the world in terms of revelation and yet also ancient with respect to God's eternal plan" (Lang, *Mystery and the Making*, 6). I discuss the same phenomenon Lang investigates in chapters 2, 3, and 6. To be clear, however, I use the terms "historical consciousness" and "historical mindedness" to refer to awareness of and thematization of the temporal, social, and cultural locatedness of all human meaning.

6. "We are always somewhere (socially, culturally, historically, linguistically) and never nowhere when we interpret." Westphal, *Whose Community?*, 35. For explanation, see also Lonergan, *MIT*, 325 (CWL 14, 302).

7. Direct engagement with their works is beyond the scope of the present project. For helpful historical overviews of developments in modern philosophical hermeneutics, see Grondin, *Introduction to Philosophical Hermeneutics*; Thiselton, *Hermeneutics*.

8. It is a worthy endeavor to study any of these particular figures to discern the intelligibility of their own philosophical work. The present work, however, incorporates their insights about reality, understanding, and language through the mediation of Bernard Lonergan's philosophical work. I find in Lonergan's work a resource for both affirming the contributions of such figures and maintaining the judgment that human knowledge is possible.

9. Bernard Lonergan said this to Sebastian Moore in the 1950s; see Moore, "For Bernard Lonergan," 13. See also Lonergan, "*Existenz* and *Aggiornamento*," 226. I attempt to address these challenges directly in chapters 4 through 6. For two recent helpful treatments of the theological problems historical consciousness raises for scriptural interpretation, see Fulford, *Divine Eloquence*; Rae, *History and Hermeneutics*.

10. Rehearsing the history of such discoveries and evaluating their particular significance is beyond the scope of the present project. A helpful general overview can be found in Wegner, *The Journey from Texts to Translations*. For more focused studies, see Collins, *The Dead Sea Scrolls*; Ulrich, *The Dead Sea Scrolls*; Blumell and Wayment, *Christian Oxyrhynchus*; Luijendijk, *Greetings in the Lord*; Parker, *Codex Sinaiticus*.

11. It would, of course, be impossible to make note of all the significant developments and works in critical biblical scholarship from the past two hundred years. The classic approaches are form, source, tradition historical, and redaction criticism(s); and newer approaches include social-scientific, canonical, rhetorical, and reception criticism(s), narrative, semiotic, and intertextual approaches. For helpful summaries of these various approaches, see McKenzie and Haynes, *To Each Its Own Meaning*; McKenzie and Kaltner, *New Meanings for Ancient Texts*. For historical surveys of the developments of such approaches with respect to the OT, see Sæbø, *Hebrew Bible/Old Testament*; and Smend, *From Astruc to Zimmerli*. On historical criticism of the NT, see Neill and Wright, *The Interpretation of the New Testament*; Baird, *History of New Testament Research*. For examinations of theological, philosophical, religious, social, and cultural developments in the modern Western world that made possible the rise of historical-critical approaches, see Frei, *The Eclipse of Biblical Narrative*; Hauser and Watson, *A History*; Legaspi, *The Death of Scripture*; Sheehan, *The Enlightenment Bible*.

12. For recent defenses of historical criticism by a Catholic and a Protestant, respectively, see Fitzmyer, *The Interpretation of Scripture*; Harrisville, *Pandora's Box Opened*.

13. So Lonergan, *MIT*, 276 (CWL 14, 258). For discussion, see Gordon, "Scripture as Truth."

14. Seminal works include, among others, Alter, *The Art of Biblical Narrative*; and Rhoads, Dewey, and Michie, *Mark as Story*. For introductions, see Alter and Kermode, *The Literary Guide to the Bible*; Powell, *What Is Narrative Criticism?*; Resseguie, *Narrative Criticism*. For a helpful assessment of the literary nature of Scripture from a distinctly Catholic perspective, see Boyle, *Sacred and Secular Scriptures*.

15. Again, even a brief survey or annotated bibliography of relevant works would be enormous. I am reluctant to even identify "representative" examples of works of these contextual approaches to Scripture given their laudable focus on the particularity of the interpretive praxis of specific communities. For thorough discussion of these issues, note especially Schüssler Fiorenza, *Democratizing Biblical Studies*; De La Torre, *Reading the Bible*; Sugirtharajah, *Exploring Postcolonial Biblical Criticism*. For a thoughtful response to the influx in biblical scholarship of contextual methodologies from the perspective of a sympathetic but committed historical critic, see Collins, *The Bible after Babel*.

16. For an extremely helpful account of how a historical critic has recognized and affirmed the critiques of contextual approaches as legitimate, see Patte, *Ethics of Biblical Interpretation*.

17. For discussion, see Fowl, *Theological Interpretation of Scripture*, ix; Gordon, "On the (Relative) Authenticity." A comprehensive bibliography of these studies would be enormous. Especially notable recent publishing endeavors include the *Journal of Theological Interpretation* (2007–), *Ex Auditu* (1985–), and *Letter & Spirit* (2005–); commentary series such as *The Ancient Christian Commentary on Scripture* (Downers Grove, IL: InterVarsity Press, 1998–), *Belief: A Theological Commentary on the Bible* (Louisville, KY: Westminster John Knox Press, 2010–), *The Brazos Theological Commentary on the Bible* (Grand Rapids, MI: Brazos Press, 2006–), *The Church's Bible* (Grand Rapids, MI: Eerdmans, 2003–), *T & T Clark International Theological Commentary* (New York: T & T Clark, 2016–), the *Two Horizons New Testament Commentary* (Grand Rapids, MI: Eerdmans, 2005–), and the *Two Horizons Old Testament Commentary* (Grand Rapids, MI: Eerdmans, 2008–); theological dictionaries, including Vanhoozer et al., *The Dictionary for the Theological Interpretation of the Bible*; and McKim, *The Dictionary of Major Biblical Interpreters*; and book series such as the University of Notre Dame Press's *Reading the Scriptures*, Baker Academic's *Studies in Theological Interpretation*, and Eisenbrauns' *Journal for Theological Interpretation Supplement Series*. For two extremely helpful monograph introductions to theological interpretation, see Treier, *Introducing Theological Interpretation*; Billings, *The Word of God for the People of God*. See also Fowl, *The Theological Interpretation of Scripture*; Bartholomew and Thomas, *A Manifesto for Theological Interpretation*.

18. Fowl, *Engaging Scripture*, 8.

19. See, e.g., Andrews, *Hermeneutics and the Church*; Fulford, *Divine Eloquence*; Sarisky, *Scriptural Interpretation*.

20. See Byassee, *Praise Seeking Understanding*; Crawford, *Cyril of Alexandria's Trinitarian Theology*; Ramage, *Dark Passages*; Tapie, *Aquinas on Israel*.

21. This is a challenging question, and the present work cannot answer it completely. In the final chapter of this work I argue that Scripture serves as a means of divine pedagogy through which readers and reading communities are transformed to understand and reflect the form and values of Jesus Christ personally, culturally, socially, and vitally. The various approaches are successful to the extent that they enable and facilitate such transformation and human self-transcendence; the latter has its telos in increasing communion with the Triune God. In a subsequent monograph I intend to elaborate on the implications of this judgment; for now, however, the present work confines itself to an investigation of the nature and purpose of Scripture. That later work will explicate the norms and structures of Christian interpretation of Scripture in the light of the present position on what Scripture actually is in its created and redemptive contexts.

22. Hebrew Bible scholarship has had similar mixed impacts in Jewish religious praxis.

23. This literature overlaps significantly with the new studies in theological interpretation. See, e.g., Adam et al., *Reading Scripture*; Breck, *Scripture in Tradi-*

tion; Hagan, *The Bible in the Churches*; Kimbrough, *Orthodox and Wesleyan Scriptural Understanding*; Lienhard, *The Bible, the Church, and Authority*; Okoye, *Scripture in the Church*. See also the Pontifical Biblical Commission's *The Interpretation of the Bible*.

24. See the collection of essays in Ford and Pecknold, *The Promise of Scriptural Reasoning*. This volume represents the fruit of ten years of interreligious dialogue by Jewish, Muslim, and Christian scholars centered on engagement with the holy books of each tradition.

25. See Smart, *The Strange Silence*. For a recent, faith-filled engagement with Scripture that incorporates the insights of historical criticism from a United Methodist minister, see Hamilton, *Making Sense of the Bible*. For a millennial approach from an ordained Cooperative Baptist, see Myers, *Making Love with Scripture*. For a theologically sophisticated treatment by an Episcopal New Testament scholar, see Martin, *Biblical Truths*.

26. Martin, *Pedagogy of the Bible*.

27. Smith, *The Bible Made Impossible*. For other incisive and helpful examinations of these "high views," see Smith, *The Fall of Interpretation*; and Allert, *A High View of Scripture?*

28. It is ironic that anti-traditional evangelical groups have produced so many distinct traditions of interpretation that the evangelical publisher Zondervan has created the Counterpoints series, comprising at least 28 volumes, each of which places two to six different perspectives on specific doctrines next to one another.

29. The differing theological and practical approaches of various ecclesial groups to the use and interpretation of Scripture, particularly differences in how they understand the relationship between biblical authority and ecclesial authority, create unique ecumenical problems. See Geoffrey Wainwright's useful examination of these problems in "Towards an Ecumenical Hermeneutic."

30. Prothero, *Religious Literacy*. See also Gallup, *Surveying the Religious Landscape*. For anecdotal—but damning—evidence of the pervasiveness of biblical illiteracy in America, see twitter.com/biblestdntssay.

31. Peter Enns argues that such biblical illiteracy in evangelicalism has been ironically aided by specific evangelical construals of the authority of Scripture. See Enns, *The Bible Tells Me So*.

32. See Barth, *The Word of God*, 28–50.

33. The shock of this historical distance is exacerbated by the popularization and sensationalization of the results of the historical study of Scripture—and sometimes by the exaggerations of its implications for Christian faith—by authors such as Bart Ehrman. The influence of "historical" fiction such as *The Da Vinci Code* in popular culture has also brought about more confusion concerning the nature and purposes of Christian Scripture in Christian faith.

34. For a variety of useful attempts to address these problems in different ways, see Collins, *Does the Bible Justify Violence?*; Creech, *Violence in Scripture*; Nugent,

The Politics of Yahweh; Siebert, *Disturbing Divine Behavior*; Siebert, *The Violence of Scripture*; Sparks, *Sacred Word*; Weems, *Battered Love*.

35. See Trible, *Texts of Terror*. For treatments of the effective history of difficult texts in controversies over slavery in the United States before the Civil War and the genocidal activities of the conquistadors in the settlement of the New World, see respectively Noll, *The Civil War*; Stannard, *American Holocaust*, 196–246.

36. See Avalos, *The End of Biblical Studies*. The question of how the text does, or does not, "approve" of such violence is a challenging one. I will argue presently that even putting things in such a manner is problematic. The text is not an agent that could "approve of" or "disapprove of" its "contents." The more significant question is whether or not, and if so, how, the God attested in Christian Scripture approves of such violence. For extremely helpful discussion of the issues, see Siebert, *Disturbing Divine Behavior*; Siebert, *The Violence of Scripture*.

37. Martin, "The Necessity of a Theology of Scripture," 83; emphasis in original. See also Hefling, "On Understanding Salvation History," 221.

38. Swain, *Trinity, Revelation, and Reading*, 4.

39. Thiselton, "The Future of Biblical Interpretation," 19.

40. I have much more to write on "systematic theology" below. Lonergan borrows the phrase "the level of the times" from José Ortega y Gasset. See Lonergan, "The Original Preface," 4.

41. For two recent works that focus explicitly on historic Christian positions on the nature and purpose of Scripture, see Holcomb, *Christian Theologies of Scripture*; Baker and Mourachian, *What Is the Bible?*

42. See Lonergan, *MIT*, 335–53 (CWL 14, 310–26).

43. The next chapter is an exception to this statement. I offer a reason for that digression below.

44. As Lonergan notes, systematics must proceed, as much as possible, in the *ordo doctrinae*, or order of teaching. In a systematic treatise the theologian "postpones solutions that presuppose other solutions. He begins with the issue whose solution does not presuppose the solution of other issues." Lonergan, *MIT*, 346 (CWL 14, 319). See below.

45. No definitive and complete biography of Lonergan has been written yet. For helpful orientations to his life and work, see Crowe, *Lonergan*; Mathews, *Lonergan's Quest*.

46. One need only refer to the works he prepared on Christology, trinitarian theology, grace, and theological method to confirm his scriptural learning. See Lonergan, *The Ontological and Psychological Constitution of Christ*; Lonergan, *The Incarnate Word*; Lonergan, *The Redemption*; Lonergan, *The Triune God: Doctrines*; Lonergan, *The Triune God: Systematics*; Lonergan, *Early Latin Theology*; and Lonergan, *Early Works in Theological Method 1–3*. For discussion, see Gordon, "The Truthfulness of Scripture."

47. For monograph-length studies, see Bernier, *Aposynagōgos and the Historical Jesus*; Bernier, *Quest for the Historical Jesus*; Laughlin, *Jesus and the Cross*; Mc-

Evenue, *Interpretation and Bible*; McEvenue, *Interpreting the Pentateuch*; Meyer, *The Aims of Jesus*; Meyer, *Christus Faber*; Meyer, *The Church in Three Tenses*; Meyer, *Critical Realism and the New Testament*; Meyer, *Reality and Illusion*; Ryan, *The Role of the Synagogue*; Shillington, *Reading the Sacred Text*; Barbara Stafford, "Bernard Lonergan and New Testament Interpretation."

For essays and articles, see McEvenue, "Old Testament, Scripture or Theology?"; McEvenue, "Scholarship's Impenetrable Wall"; McEvenue, "Theological Doctrines"; Meyer, "The Challenges of Text"; Meyer, "The Primacy of Consent"; Meyer, "A Tricky Business." Through the work of Meyer, Lonergan's critical realism has significantly influenced N. T. Wright, James D. G. Dunn, and Scot McKnight.

48. See Crowe, "The Power of the Scriptures"; Crowe, *Theology of the Christian Word*; Drilling, "Preaching: A Mutual Self-Mediation"; Gordon, "On the (Relative) Authenticity"; Gordon, "The Truthfulness of Scripture"; Kelly, "Dimensions of Meaning: Theology and Exegesis"; Ormerod, *Method, Meaning, and Revelation*; Rosenberg, "The Drama of Scripture"; Topel, "Faith, Exegesis, and Theology"; Topel, "What Does Systematic Theology Say."

49. See the next two sections of this chapter.

50. Lonergan, *MIT*, 25 (CWL 14, 26).

51. See Lonergan, *MIT*, 265 (CWL 14, 248).

52. For more thorough treatments of this seemingly simple yet profound judgment, see Lonergan, *Insight*, chs. 1–11, esp. 11; Lonergan, *Understanding and Being*; Lonergan, "The Subject," in *ASC*, 69–86 (CWL 13, 60–75). I provide an articulation of human nature that depends heavily on Lonergan's position in chapter 4.

53. The question of how such a grand claim can accommodate the legitimate postmodern emphases on historicity and subjectivity is not insignificant. Is this not an aporia? There are a number of ways to address the question. One way is to invite an interlocutor protesting the claim to argue against it. He will find himself invoking his own experiences, understandings, and judgments to bring them to bear against the position Lonergan articulates. He might argue that we should not call such "things" experience, understanding, judgment, but the fact that he makes such an appeal cannot be in doubt. For an account of this approach, see Meyer, "The Philosophical Crusher." Another way to address the claim is by adopting a strategy of out-narration. R. J. Snell has brought Lonergan's work into dialogue with Richard Rorty to argue that Lonergan's position on subjectivity and objectivity affirms the legitimacy of authentic aspects of Rorty's pragmatic approach to historicity and linguistics while not succumbing to the relativism that seems to follow from a thoroughgoing adoption of Rorty's arguments. Lonergan thus reveals himself to be the actual "integral postmodern" thinker through this dialogue. See Snell, *Through a Glass Darkly*. See also Lawrence, "Lonergan's Postmodern Subject."

54. For an invaluable account of how Lonergan's position accounts for the postmodern insights regarding the subjectivity of human understanding and provides resources for moving beyond relativism, see Snell, *Through a Glass Darkly*.

55. See, e.g., the essays in the ironically titled *Looking at Lonergan's Method* (ed. Corcoran). Lonergan's *Method* has sometimes been critiqued for a lack of theological specificity. See, e.g., Rahner, "Some Critical Thoughts," 194–96. As Crowe notes, however, "Critics who call his method *a priori*, devised without reference to actual theology, do so surely in close to total disregard of that quarter of a century [when he lectured on trinitarian theology, Christology, and theology of grace]." Crowe, *Lonergan*, 80.

56. This terseness can be attributed, in part, to the fact that Lonergan's health was poor and he was uncertain how much life he had left. He had lung cancer and had to have one of his lungs removed in 1965.

57. Lonergan's collected works will eventually total 25 volumes. See CWL. Robert Doran has joked that if Lonergan's works were lost and rediscovered hundreds or thousands of years from now, it is conceivable that scholars who discovered them would judge that his *Insight* and *Method in Theology* were written by at least two different authors.

58. See *MIT*, 7, 7n2 (CWL 14, 11, 11n4).

59. In addition to those studies listed in notes 45 and 46 above, the following studies, among others, have also influenced the present work: Burrell, *Aquinas: God and Action*; Burrell, *Towards a Jewish-Christian-Muslim Theology*; Tracy and Grant, *A Short History of the Interpretation of the Bible*; Tracy, *Plurality and Ambiguity*; Crowe, *Christ and History*; Crowe, *Lonergan and the Level of Our Time*; Crowe, *Theology of the Christian Word*; Doran, *Theology and the Dialectics of History*; Doran, *What Is Systematic Theology?*

60. David Burrell has suggested that Lonergan emphasized collaboration more than he actually practiced it. See Wright, *Postliberal Theology and the Church Catholic*, 87. Nevertheless, Lonergan's works bear witness to the fact that he practiced a hermeneutic of charity in his engagement with other thinkers.

61. This will include, of course, the theologian's critical appropriation of judgments of the authors who wrote the documents that we know as the Old and New Testaments. Christians have generally, if not universally, understood Scripture as containing judgments that subsequent interpreters must necessarily hold in order to identify themselves as Christians.

62. The conventional name is ironic; Henri de Lubac thought it was misleading. Since so much of his work was directed towards helping the Roman Catholic Church recover the riches of its past, particularly the heritage of the church fathers and early medieval doctors, calling de Lubac's work "new" is quite strange. See de Lubac, *At the Service*, 361.

63. For a concise expression, in de Lubac's own words, of the goals and purposes of such recovery work, see de Lubac, *Paradoxes of Faith*, 57–58.

64. I have discussed the significance of de Lubac's work on Christian exegetical praxis in Gordon, "*Ressourcement* Anti-Semitism?"; Gordon, "Treasures Old and New." For de Lubac's own account of his life and work, see de Lubac, *At the*

Service. For a helpful summary of de Lubac's life and the key themes of his writings, see Voderholzer, *Meet Henri de Lubac.* See also Grummett, *De Lubac.* Georges Chantraine began a multivolume biography of de Lubac, but his work was cut short by his untimely death. See Chantraine, *Henri de Lubac: De la naissance à la démobilisation, 1896–1919;* Chantraine, *Henri de Lubac: Les années de formation, 1919–1929.* Marie-Gabrielle Lemaire has recently finished the work Chantraine had done on the later years of de Lubac's life. See Chantraine and Lemaire, *Henri de Lubac: Concile et après-Concile, 1960–1991.* On the key themes of de Lubac's work, see Hillebert, *T & T Clark Companion to Henri de Lubac.*

65. See Gordon, "*Ressourcement* Anti-Semitism?," 614–16.

66. See Gordon, "*Ressourcement* Anti-Semitism?," 616.

67. Monograph-length studies and dissertations and theses include D'Ambrosio, "Henri de Lubac and the Recovery"; von Esbroeck, *Herméneutique, structuralisme, et exégèse;* Flipper, *Between Apocalypse and Eschaton;* Gordon, "Treasures Old and New"; Gracias, "The Spiritual Sense of Scripture According to Henri de Lubac"; Hollon, *Everything Is Sacred;* Storer, *Reading Scripture to Hear God;* Voderholzer, *Die Einheit der Schrift;* Wood, *Spiritual Exegesis and the Church.*

Shorter studies include Ayres, "The Soul and the Reading of Scripture"; Bertoldi, "Henri de Lubac on *Dei Verbum*"; Certeau, "Exégèse, théologie et spiritualité"; D'Ambrosio, "Henri de Lubac and the Critique"; Fédou, "Histoire et l'esprit"; Lemaire, "Brève étude sur l'intelligence spirituelle"; Gordon, "*Ressourcement* Anti-Semitism?"; Guillett, "Le sens de l'écriture"; Hughes, "The Fourfold Sense"; Hughes, "The Spiritual Interpretation of Scripture"; Moscicke, "The Theological Presuppositions"; Moullins-Beaufort, "Henri de Lubac"; Murphy, "Henri De Lubac's Mystical Tropology"; Pesce, "Un 'bruit absurde'?"; de la Potterie, "Le sens spirituel de l'Écriture"; Storer, "Theological Interpretation"; Voderholzer, "Dogma and History"; Wright, "The Literal Sense of Scripture."

68. See below on the relationships between doctrines and systematic theology.

69. See de Lubac, *At the Service,* 144–45.

70. "Such achievement has a permanence of its own. It can be improved upon. It can be inserted in larger and richer contexts. But unless its substance is incorporated in subsequent work, the subsequent work will be a substantially poorer affair." *MIT,* 352 (CWL 14, 325).

71. As Hugo Meynell puts it, "There is a danger, with any thinker supposed by anyone to be of importance, that those who take some account of her thought will polarize into one group that simply repeats her ideas in her own terminology, and another which rejects them without sufficiently careful consideration." Meynell, "Taking A(nother) Look at Lonergan's Method," 475. I hope I have avoided the former error with regard to my dependence on both Lonergan and de Lubac.

72. Though this work could be understood as either Lonerganian or de Lubacian, its intention is more general. In an interview that took place during a conference devoted to his work, Lonergan had the following to say: "The word *Lonerganian* has

come up in recent days. In a sense there's no such thing. Because what I'm asking people is to discover themselves and be themselves. They can arrive at conclusions different from mine on the basis of what they find in themselves." Lonergan, "An Interview," 213. I am aware of the irony of appealing to Lonergan's words to argue that my project should not be understood as Lonerganian. For what follows, though, I take full responsibility. In *Paradoxes of Faith*, de Lubac declares, "The theologian should give the testimony of a theologian. His testimony is not superior to others, but it is his, the one he will be held to account for, the one he must give in order to be faithful, the one that no other can give in his place." De Lubac, *Paradoxes*, 37. What follows is my own testimony.

73. *Living and Active* is a revision of Work's PhD dissertation at Duke University. Particular merits of Work's monograph include its broad and deep reading in Christian tradition, its trinitarian focus and structure, and its useful discussion of the controversies over the validity of icons in the Eastern Churches as a tool for evaluating the contested place of Scripture in contemporary Christian experience. Scott Swain also covers similar territory in his *Trinity, Revelation, and Reading*. I regret that I have been unable to read Denis Farkasfalvy's *A Theology of the Christian Bible*, which is not yet in print.

74. Work, *Living and Active*, 2.

75. See Work, *Living and Active*, 8–9.

76. Work's monograph will certainly advance the understanding of any curious and committed reader. Another feature of the present study that differentiates it from Work's is my much more extensive and sustained account of the material *realia* of Christian Scripture in chapter 5.

77. For a recent helpful defense of systematic theology, see Sarah Coakley's account of *théologie totale* in her *God, Sexuality, and the Self*, 33–65.

78. One notable historical theologian contends, "The best way to define the fundamental rhetorical purpose of modern Catholic Systematic theology is 'the attempt to articulate Christianity in terms and concepts which non-believing intellectual elites can find reasonable.' Or, more practically, 'To talk to the establishment of non-believing intelligentsia in terms which they can credit, understand and find respectable.'" Barnes, "Ebion at the Barricades," 515. Barnes ("Ebion at the Barricades," 516) argues that the demythologization and so effective rejection of Scripture as an idiom for theological reflection and the treatment of other premodern texts such as those of the church fathers and the creeds as "blank slates" which are no longer intrinsically meaningful (518) are also constitutive features of modern Catholic systematics. My own project takes such accusations seriously and includes an implicit response to them; since this is not a dialectical work, however, I leave the discernment of my response to the reader. In the aforementioned article, Barnes claims that "systematicians interweave different narratives with no sense of the contradictions between these narratives and their different historical genealogies. Philosophies are treated as though their constitutive concepts are modular

and parts can be mixed and matched freely at the initiative of the theologian" (518). While I am not by trade a "historical theologian," I recognize the need for and difficulty of understanding Christian tradition historically; I am also aware of both the risk and the temptation of sloppily appropriating historical figures and ideas without due respect for their nestedness in history. Historical sloppiness, though, is not an intrinsic feature of systematic theology. *Quod gratis asseritur, gratis negatur.* I should also note that my primary interlocutors take stances towards history that I judge to be wholly harmonious with Barnes's laudable emphasis on the need to attend carefully to the particularities of specific historical movements and figures. See esp. Lonergan, "Philosophy and Theology," 204–6 (CWL 13, 173–74); de Lubac, *HS*, 450–52.

79. On these risks, see Sugirtharajah, "Complacencies and Cul-de-Sacs," 22–36. For an acknowledgment of and response to such risks in systematic theology, see Schüssler Fiorenza, "Systematic Theology," 50–64.

80. On description and explanation, see Wittgenstein, *Philosophical Investigations*, §109: "Und wir dürfen keinerlei Theorie aufstellen. Es darf nichts Hypothetishes in unsern Betrachtungen sein. Alle Erklärun muß fort, und nur Beschreibung an ihre Stelle treten" (And we may not advance any kind of theory. There must not be anything hypothetical in our considerations. All explanation must disappear, and description alone must take its place).

81. On the anti-systematic disposition of contemporary continental philosophy, see Simpson, "Between God and Metaphysics," 358–61; the work of Jacques Derrida in literary theory and the work of Gilles Deleuze in fundamental ontology represent two salient examples of this tendency. The work of Katherine Keller represents a formidable theological example of such thinking as well.

82. See Fowl, "Texts Don't Have Ideologies." Fowl might disagree with this particular appropriation of his work, but I simply want to emphasize the fact that methodologies, at least in the abstract, are inert. *Methodologists*, on the other hand, like authors, redactors, interpreters, and canonizers, do have motives and ideologies.

83. See Lonergan, *MIT*, 335–53 (CWL 14, 310–26).

84. For Lonergan, systematics is only *one* of eight functional specialties; I discuss these below. In systematics the theologian attempts to understand "the religious realities affirmed by doctrines." *MIT*, 349 (CWL 14, 322). It is important to note that Lonergan understands doctrine generally as any affirmation or judgment deemed to be a constitutive aspect of Christian faith. The principle doctrines, for Lonergan, are those which are dogmatically defined.

85. Lonergan, *The Triune God: Systematics*, 15–17. As de Lubac notes, "Christianity is not an object that we can hold in our hand: it is a mystery before which we are always ignorant and uninitiated." De Lubac, *Paradoxes of Faith*, 43.

86. Lonergan, *The Triune God: Systematics*, 17.

87. I thank Neil Ormerod for asking me to offer this clarification here.

88. See Lonergan, *Insight*; *MIT*, 3–99 (CWL 14, 7–95).

89. Lonergan, *MIT*, 350 (CWL 14, 323).

90. Lonergan, *MIT*, 350 (CWL 14, 323). I will invoke both the Nicene Creed and Scripture as providing constitutive Christian judgments about reality.

91. See chapter 3 below.

92. I discuss the nature of such religious conversion in chapter 4 below.

93. Lonergan, *MIT*, 351 (CWL 14, 323).

94. Lonergan, *MIT*, 351 (CWL 14, 324).

95. Obviously, it is not Lonergan's understanding of systematics exactly; it is my understanding of Lonergan's presentation of his understanding of systematic theology. My work depends, if not in every point in most, on thinking through what a systematics of the nature and purpose of Christian Scripture would require in light of Lonergan's chapter on systematics in Lonergan, *MIT*, 335–53 (CWL 14, 310–26); and Lonergan, *The Triune God: Systematics*, 6–123. It also depends on my appropriation of the work Robert Doran has done to explain and advance Lonergan's position on systematics. See Doran, "Envisioning a Systematic Theology"; Doran, "The Starting Point of Systematic Theology"; Doran, "System and History"; Doran, *Theology and the Dialectics of History*; Doran, *The Trinity in History*, vol. 1; Doran, *What Is Systematic Theology?*

96. In what follows, as I have already noted, I draw on the work of both Lonergan and de Lubac. Both were theologians committed to and well versed in Christian tradition; I will also draw extensively on other premodern, modern, and contemporary thinkers.

97. I am not suggesting that they did articulate or should have articulated this shared subjective constitution as I have done here.

98. On how Lonergan affirms the continuity of Christian faith, see *MIT*, 351–52 (CWL 14, 324–25). He illustrates the possibility of authentic developments with reference to Aquinas's achievements in trinitarian theology and grace: "Such achievement has a permanence of its own. It can be improved upon. It can be inserted into larger and richer contexts. But unless its substance is incorporated in subsequent work, the subsequent work will be a substantially poorer affair." Lonergan, *MIT*, 352 (CWL 14, 325). Lonergan's position on minor and major authenticity also allows for the fact that not all developments in a tradition will be authentic: "There is the minor authenticity or unauthenticity of the subject with respect to the tradition that nourishes him. There is the major authenticity that justifies or condemns the tradition itself. In the first case there is passed a judgment on subjects. In the second case history, and, ultimately, divine providence pass judgment on traditions." Lonergan, *MIT*, 80 (CWL 14, 77).

99. See Lonergan, *MIT*, xi (CWL 14, 3).

100. Functional specialization is not field or subject specialization akin to any concrete division of labor within the theological academy. It is not, for instance, akin to the common field division present at Marquette University, where I completed my PhD. The department there is divided into three specializations (each of

which has a number of further divisions): Judaism and Christianity in Antiquity, Historical Theology, and Systematic Theology and Ethics, respectively. As Lonergan writes, "One can justify field specialization by urging that the relevant data are too extensive to be investigated by a single mind. One can defend subject specialization on the ground that the matter is too broad to be taught successfully by a single professor. But functional specialization is essentially not a distinction of specialists but a distinction of specialties. It arises, not to divide the same sort of task among many hands, but to distinguish different tasks and to prevent them from being confused." Lonergan, *MIT*, 136 (CWL 14, 131).

101. Lonergan, "An Interview," 211.

102. I note again, systematics cannot be undertaken well if it does not attend to the historicity of human meaning. To be fully responsible in pursuing systematic theology, the theologian must attentively, intelligently, and reasonably study the tradition. She must exhibit the same responsibility in her use of secondary works of history and exegesis.

103. Lonergan, *MIT*, 267 (CWL 14, 250).

104. Lonergan, *MIT*, 149–51 (CWL 14, 141–44).

105. Lonergan, *MIT*, 153–73 (CWL 14, 145–63).

106. See Lonergan, *MIT*, 185 (CWL 14, 173).

107. Lonergan frequently referred to W. F. H. Albright's ability to determine the time period of a piece of potsherd from the Levant simply by touching it with his hands as an example of the fruit of such historical investigation. See Lonergan, *Early Works in Theological Method I*, 101.

108. See Lonergan, *MIT*, 175–234 (CWL 14, 164–219).

109. For an extremely helpful articulation of how Lonergan's work on history and interpretation can aid historical-critical biblical scholarship, see Meyer, *Reality and Illusion*, 5–39.

110. Lonergan, *MIT*, 235–66 (CWL 14, 250–74).

111. Lonergan, *MIT*, 246 (CWL 14, 231).

112. The precise matter of discerning authentic developments and distinguishing them from inauthentic developments is a necessarily sensitive process. As a faithful Roman Catholic theologian, Lonergan holds that the magisterium represents the final court of appeal for determining authentic and inauthentic developments. He writes, for instance, that "the church's teaching alone is determinative of the meaning of revealed truth and of sacred dogmas." Lonergan, *The Triune God: Systematics*, 59.

113. Lonergan, *MIT*, 267–93 (CWL 14, 250–74).

114. In my judgment, Robert Doran has convincingly argued that by treating both the conversions and the derivation of categories, the functional specialty of foundations does too much. He proposes dividing it into two specialties, horizons and categories. "Horizons" would refer to a functional specialty outside of the other eight dedicated to the operations involved in "the ongoing articulation of the

structure of the concrete universal that is the normative subject." "Categories" would designate the operations involved in deriving the general and special categories. See Doran, *The Trinity in History*, 112–15; quotation on 113. I examine these conversions in much greater depth in chapters 4 and 6.

115. The "Law of the Cross" is the just and mysterious law revealed in Jesus Christ's sacrificial death on the cross. The cross constitutes and reveals the redemptive activity of the Triune God on behalf of God's creation. We participate in this activity, and its form is the measure of human authenticity in history. As Doran explains, "The solution to the problem of evil is not available on the basis of human resources alone, but must be a divinely originated solution, a matter of human collaboration with the divine partner in our search for direction in the movement of life. The inner form of that collaboration lies in the pattern adopted by the divine measure of all human integrity become flesh in our history. That inner form is represented in the Deutero-Isaian symbolic or mythic vision of redemptive suffering, but myth becomes history in the incarnation of the Word, of the measure, and that incarnation of the measure is obedience unto death, even death on a cross, that this measure assumed as the catalytic agency through which a new law would be established on earth. Conformity to the cross of the divine measure become human flesh is the summit of the process of self-transcendence under the conditions of a human history shot through with the surd of evil and sin." Doran, *Theology and the Dialectics of History*, 113. I discuss this law in chapters 3 and 6.

116. Lonergan, *MIT*, 295–333 (CWL 14, 275–309).

117. See Lonergan, *MIT*, 350 (CWL 14, 309).

118. Doran, *What Is Systematic Theology?*, 8.

119. Lonergan, *MIT*, 335–53 (CWL 14, 310–28).

120. Lonergan, *MIT*, 338 (CWL 14, 311). See also Doran, *What Is Systematic Theology?*, 9.

121. Lonergan, *MIT*, 355–68 (CWL 14, 327–39).

122. Lonergan, *MIT*, 362 (CWL 14, 333).

123. This work concomitantly assumes that Christian engagement with Scripture is also in the service of the conversion and transformation of individuals and communities. I will have much more to say about this when I discuss the telos of Scripture in history in chapter 6.

124. While a historical account of the development of trinitarian theology in the early Church would proceed diachronically, taking care to highlight, as best as possible, each significant step forward and each step backward in the movement of Christian reflection between the 1st century and the present, a systematic theology of trinitarian theology would begin with the most general specific achievements of those developments. For examples of Lonergan's own attempts at these two approaches with respect to trinitarian theology, see Lonergan, *The Triune God: Doctrines* and *The Triune God: Systematics*, respectively. These were worked out prior to his insight of the functional specialties. For a more recent exemplary

study of the vicissitudes of trinitarian theology in the fourth century, see Ayres, *Nicaea and Its Legacy.*

125. See Lonergan, *The Triune God: Systematics,* 61–63.

126. Lonergan, *The Triune God: Systematics,* 63.

127. Though systematics usually offers an account of the doctrines of Christian faith of the major Christian confessions, i.e., the Creeds, such traditional resources provide only scant evidence of the distinctive beliefs of Christians regarding Scripture. The Nicene Creed, which I discuss below, only contains two relevant judgments: Jesus Christ "rose again in accordance with the Scriptures," and the Holy Spirit "has spoken through the Prophets." No major ecumenical council has offered precise and technical reflection on the nature and purpose of Scripture. Nevertheless, Christians have universally held that Scripture (1) comes from God; (2) is, in some sense, God's address to humanity; and (3) is useful for God's work in us. These are the three major doctrinal judgments explained in chapter 6 below.

128. This is not to say, of course, that I affirm the truthfulness of every definition given for each term.

129. For two helpful evangelical accounts that dwell on these terms and others, see Swain, *Trinity, Revelation, and Reading,* 61–93; Vanhoozer, "Holy Scripture," 30–56. For a classic reformed account, see Berkouwer, *Holy Scripture.*

130. Lonergan, *The Triune God: Systematics,* 19, 55.

131. Peterson, *Eat This Book,* 55.

132. See chapters 2 and 5 in particular.

133. The argument that Scripture is *autopistis,* or self-authenticating, is articulated by John Calvin and is a key feature in Protestant scholasticism and contemporary Reformed theology. See Calvin, *Institutes of the Christian Religion,* I.6–9. If pressed, though, I take the risk of assuming that Calvin would not make Scripture into a self or an agent. For variations of the argument that Scripture is "self-authenticating," that "it" testifies to its own nature and authority, see Grudem, "Scripture's Self-Attestation," 19–59.

134. Dale Martin has emphatically made this point a number of times in print. See Martin, *Pedagogy of the Bible,* 30–31; Martin, *Sex and the Single Savior,* 1–16; Martin, *Biblical Truths,* 57, 95–96.

135. Hefling, *Why Doctrines?,* 138.

136. Martin, "The Necessity of a Theology of Scripture," 91.

137. Lonergan, *Insight,* 605. Martin similarly speaks of "spots" on the page. See Martin, *Pedagogy of the Bible,* 35. There is a further historical and theological question—raised by textual criticism, translation, and canonization—that complicates the issue further with respect to Scripture. What are the precise "marks" or "spots" "out there"? I address this complicated question in chapter 5.

138. See Schjedal, "Faces: A Cindy Sherman Retrospective," 84–85. I thank Eric Vanden Eykel for directing me to this review.

139. The failure to ask such questions can have consequences beyond theological ones; for a striking—though extreme—example, see the real-world political, economic, and social impacts of the work of the Green family, owners of Hobby Lobby, to create the Museum of the Bible. See Moss and Baden, *Bible Nation*.

140. Such statements are unsurprising given the preference for the oral and aural word in the ancient world. There are, of course, countless other examples in the literature of early Christianity. A search of γραφὴ λέγει in the *Thesaurus Linguae Graecae* turned up nine loci in the works of Clement of Alexandria, seven in the works of Justin Martyr (and Pseudo-Justin), one in Theophilus's *Autol.*, four in the works of Gregory of Nyssa, five in the works of Eusebius of Caesarea, three in the works of Epiphanius, seven in the works of Athanasius, three in the works of Basil of Caesarea, and dozens of others.

141. If not for these examples, and if I had any authority to do so, I would call for a moratorium on the phrase, "The Bible says . . ."

142. There are countless other examples. It is interesting that God is never, to my knowledge, depicted as writing Scripture directly in the Christian Bible (though YHWH does inscribe the Tablets of the Law, see Exod 32.18, 34.1).

143. Modern convictions about the absurdity, or impossibility, of divine action in history, or convictions concerning the impossibility of coming to true general judgments about the structure, direction, or purpose of the history, would of course prevent one from being able to recognize Christian Scripture as a witness to and instrument within the economic work of the Triune God. It is unnecessary and philosophically irresponsible, however, to refuse to countenance questions concerning such possibilities on the basis of an axiomatic positivism. The refusal to ask and answer questions of transcendence and divine action is an extrascientific philosophical judgment that we need not make. For an illuminating discussion of the poverty of such philosophical assumptions, see Balthasar, *Epilogue*, 19–22. For a powerful and beautiful philosophical metaphysic that welcomes, invites, and explores such questions, see the work of William Desmond, especially his *God and the Between*. For an introduction to his theological philosophy, see Gordon and Long, "'Way(s) to God.'"

144. Scripture is virtually but not necessarily indispensable because the Triune God can do and has (historically) done God's redemptive work without reference to or use of Scripture.

145. Jenson, *Canon and Creed*, 79.

146. That articulation will regularly appeal to Scripture, of course, which mediates the work of the Triune God truthfully. Articulations of Christian faith in that truth—confessions—are already present in the New Testament itself; see the epigraphs at the beginning of chapter 2.

147. See *Haer.* 1.10.1; *Princ.* pref.; and *Doctr. chr.* 1.3.1. I discuss these examples in the next chapter.

CHAPTER TWO. Historical Precedents

1. I use the word *general* deliberately. All recent Christian pandect Bibles, to my knowledge, begin with Genesis and end with Revelation. Different Christian communities have different canons, though, and those canons have different internal orders. For a comparison of the orders of contemporary and historic Christian canons, see McDonald, *The Biblical Canon*, 439–51.

2. This is evident when one compares the structure of the Jewish Tanakh with Christian orderings of the OT. The former ends with the Writings, while the latter ends—in most Protestant and Catholic Bibles—with the prophets (including Daniel) in anticipation of the coming of Christ or in Mainline Protestant Bibles with the Apocrypha, which function as a historical bridge between the time of the prophets and the New Testament.

3. I discuss the theological significance of the material history of Scripture in much greater detail in chapter 5. On pandects, and their rarity in early Christian communities, see Gamble, *Books and Readers*, 80; Grafton and Williams, *Christianity and the Transformation of the Book*, 57–58, 135–36. Even in the early medieval period, as late as the twelfth century, before the books had "been gathered together in a definitive canon, which conferred a kind of visible and material unity on the Bible," the Christian scriptures were more a library than a single book. De Lubac, *ME*, 1.247.

4. As Hugh Pyper rightly notes, it is not necessary for a religious or theological text to begin with an account of beginnings. See "The Beginnings of the Bible," 35–44. It is also not necessary for one to end with the end. That the scriptures of Christianity do both is quite significant. De Lubac, citing copious ancient sources, demonstrates that Christianity's account of the scheme of divine redemption in history, beginning with creation and ending with the last things, was decisively novel in the ancient world. See *Catholicism*, 137–216.

5. Contemporary literature on the diversity of perspectives in Scripture unsurprisingly is extensive. For two helpful collections of essays, see Freyne and van Wolde, *The Many Voices of the Bible*; Barton and Wolter, *Die Einheit der Schrift*. See also Dunn, *Unity and Diversity in the New Testament*. For a fascinating theological account of the diversity of perspectives in the OT, see Brueggemann's *Theology of the Old Testament*.

6. On "pervasive interpretive pluralism," see Smith, *The Bible Made Impossible*, 54. William Abraham has suggested that such an epistemological and criteriological approach to Scripture is unsustainable. Instead, he proposes a more general return to the canonical inheritance of the early church—including its canons of scripture, doctrine, saints, church fathers, theologians, liturgy, bishops, councils, regulations, icons, etc.—as a basis for contemporary theological reflection. I agree with Abraham's general program of seeking to responsibly appropriate the heritage of the (patristic) church to renew theological thought and praxis today. Such

renewal, however, will not reject all epistemological criteria. The transcendental criteria of authentic subjectivity, which I would argue are operative in Abraham's own attentive, intelligent, reasonable, and responsible proposals, must replace conceptual criteria. For Abraham's approach, see his *Canon and Criterion* and the subsequent literature his work has inspired, such as Abraham, Vickers, and Van Kirk, *Canonical Theism*. On the specific canons that Abraham identifies as the canonical heritage of the church, see Abraham, "Canonical Theism," 2.

7. Lonergan, *MIT*, 236 (CWL 14, 221–22).

8. D. H. Williams puts it as follows: "What the church believed was canonical long before that belief took written, codified forms. In fact, the earliest canons or norms of the preaching and defending of the early tradition served as the standard for the canonization of texts." Williams, *Evangelicals and Tradition*, 27. Williams, while basically correct, states things too strongly in my estimation. As the diversity of the New Testament attests, the churches' early beliefs were not entirely uniform. They were not a static deposit of "already-out-there-now-real" beliefs. They certainly developed as Christians responded to challenges and came to broader understanding of the implications of their judgments. Williams's suggestion of their criteriological use for determining the canon also seens inflated. As John Barton argues, "It is very doubtful whether inherent merit was a major factor in determining canonicity. . . . In reality, things seem to work the other way about: certain books are of (apparently) unimpeachable apostolic or prophetic authorship; therefore they are regarded as 'holy Scripture'; and therefore they are read in ways which cause them to yield a helpful and edifying message." Barton, *Oracles of God*, 139. The ancient scriptures that we know as the OT, as Christopher Seitz has rightly noted, were not accepted on the basis of their apostolicity, catholicity, or orthodoxy; these books were with the church from the very beginning. See Seitz, *The Character of Christian Scripture*.

9. For an excellent analysis of the significance of this fact for Christian understanding of the OT, see Seitz, *The Character of Christian Scripture*, 191–203. In this work Seitz is concerned to demonstrate the continuing validity of the Old Testament *as* Christian Scripture. The OT is inextricable from Christian faith. Seitz shows that the fathers who made exegetical arguments prior to the emergence of the New Testament assumed the relevance and sufficiency of the Jewish scriptures for proving Christ. Nevertheless, Paul does not say, "If Christ's resurrection cannot be discovered in the scriptures our faith is in vain." While Paul might have held that judgment, he actually declares that "if Christ is not risen our faith is in vain" (1 Cor 15.14, 17). As will become clear in this chapter my focus is primarily on Christian judgments about the extratextual realities to which Scripture bears witness. Christian judgments about the relationship between the OT scriptures and Christ are not insignificant for our understanding of reality but are of secondary importance for our current focus. Their relationship is explored explicitly in chapter 6.

10. For the data, see Gallagher and Meade, *The Biblical Canon Lists*. The dynamics of the process of the canonization of both Testaments are extremely convoluted. I discuss the implications of these processes for our understanding of the nature of Scripture in much greater depth in chapter 5.

11. Voderholzer, *Meet Henri de Lubac*, 172.

12. Lewis Ayres's measured judgments on the continuity and unity of Christian teaching, its development, and the historiographical task are helpful here: "For Christians working with a theology of the Triune God's maintenance and guidance of the Church surely we should no more expect to be able to trace the paths of that continuity with certainty than we expect to be able to locate the history of grace in the Church with certainty. I do not mean that we cannot conceive of the Church being able to judge the appropriate structure of a faith resulting from development, but that there are good theological reasons (let alone historical ones) for supposing that we will not always find it possible to follow the steps by means of which the Spirit guided the expression of the Apostles' faith until it emerged into pro-Nicene theology. Christian theologians, I suggest, find themselves negotiating a narrow path. On the one hand, they must attempt to narrate the continuity of their core beliefs with those of the apostles. . . . But, on the other hand, the path by which the Spirit leads occurs under the ultimate agency of the Spirit. . . . [T]he narratives that we attempt will always ultimately fail this side of the *eschaton*. Thus the Christian historian may go astray both by thinking that no such continuity is possible and by thinking that she or he has it within their power to prove that continuity: there is a complex negotiation here that cannot easily be summarized." Ayres, *Nicaea and Its Legacy*, 427–28.

13. *Canon* is the English translation or transliteration of the Greek κανών. *Regula* is the roughly equivalent term in Latin. Both can be appositely translated as "rule." See below for further discussion of these terms. For a useful overview of the "rule of faith/truth" in the early church, see Ferguson, *The Rule of Faith*. For a more thorough investigation, see the published version of Heinz Ohme's *Habilitationsschrift: Kanon ekklesiastikos*. Other helpful examinations of the phenomenon include Blowers, "The 'Regula Fidei'"; and Osborn, "Reason and the Rule of Faith." See also the essays in Rombs and Hwang, *Tradition and the Rule of Faith*. As Osborn helpfully warns, "The rule of faith, like many theological simplicities, is surrounded by an historical jungle which obscures its exact place and by a liturgical jungle which obscures its exact use." Osborn, "Reason and the Rule," 42. For a helpful and measured historical account of the landmark developments bridging the biblical confessions and the second-century expressions of the rule, see Bokedal, "The Rule of Faith: Tracing Its Origins."

14. For evaluative treatments of the relationship of the various iterations of the rule to patristic interpretation of Scripture, see Blocher, "The Analogy of Faith"; Grech, "The *Regula Fidei*"; Lienhard, *The Bible, the Church, and Authority*, 42–58; McDonald, *The Formation of the Biblical Canon*, 2:117–21; O'Keefe and Reno,

Sanctified Vision, 114–39; Williams, *Tradition, Scripture, and Interpretation*, 67–79; Young, *Biblical Exegesis*, 17–21. See also González, "The Rule of Faith."

15. See Billings, *The Word of God for the People of God*, 17–30; Driver, "Childs and the Canon or Rule of Faith"; Finn, "Reflections on the Rule of Faith"; Gavrilyuk, "Scripture and the *Regula Fidei*"; Swain, *Trinity, Revelation, and Reading*, 106–18; Treier, *Theological Interpretation of Christian Scripture*, 57–78; Wall, "Reading the Bible from Within our Traditions"; Seitz, *The Character of Christian Scripture*, 191–203; Young, *Virtuoso Theology*, 45–65.

16. Meyer, *The Aims of Jesus*, 60.

17. See note 36 below.

18. See Bokedal, "The Rule of Faith," passim.

19. I note again: understanding(s) and judgment(s) have technical meaning in the present work; see chapter 4.

20. See Rudolf Bultmann's famous essay, "Is Exegesis without Presuppositions Possible?"

21. Long, "Sources as Canons," 229. In a footnote Long differentiates between an unexpressed "canon-in-general" and one clearly articulated—one might say "objectified"—such as those provided by Irenaeus, Origen, and Augustine, which I investigate below. While the former is necessary for interpretation, the latter is, strictly speaking, not necessary. I will argue that while we need not provide such canons, we must do so if we are to interpret Scripture intelligently, critically, responsibly, and faithfully. See Long, "Sources as Canons," 248n16.

22. Lonergan puts it nicely: "The fulfillment that is being in love with God is not the product of our knowledge and choice. It is God's gift.... So far from resulting from our knowledge and choice, it dismantles and abolishes the horizon within which our knowing and choosing went on, and it sets up a new horizon within which the love of God transvalues our values and the eyes of that love transform our knowing." Lonergan, "The Response of the Jesuit as Priest and Apostle in the Modern World," *ASC*, 172 (CWL 13, 145–46).

23. Ben F. Meyer identifies three elements that a biblically responsible hermeneutics must incorporate today: "first, the claims of the biblical text, that is the primacy of its intended sense; second, the claims of human authenticity, ... [;] third, the claims of Christian authenticity, that is ... the intelligibility and cohesiveness of salvation and of the scriptures that attest it in hope and in celebration." Meyer, "The Primacy of the Intended Sense of Texts," 115. The present chapter is primarily concerned with the third element; chapter 4 is concerned with the second element, and chapters 5 and 6 address the first element.

24. As J. Todd Billings notes, many Christians from bibliocentric traditions have raised the question when encountering self-critical theological hermeneutics, "Why should I think about my theological presuppositions in approaching scripture? Shouldn't I just get my theology *from* Scripture?" Billings, *The Word of God for the People of God*, xii. The answer is that our inescapable historicity necessarily will

influence our interpretation. It is better to advert to and take responsibility for our horizon than to pretend it does not exist. See the excursus, "What Does the Bible 'Say'?," in chapter 1 above.

25. Paddison, *Scripture*, 1; emphasis in original. Fowl also argues that Scripture finds its proper place within God's desires for creation: "If one has a grasp of what God's ultimate desires for us are and how Scripture fits into God's plans ultimately to bring those desires to fruition, then theological interpretation of Scripture will need to be closely tied both to our proper end in God, that is, God's ultimate desires for us, and Scripture's role in bringing us to that end." Fowl, *Theological Interpretation of Scripture*, xi.

26. Lonergan, *MIT*, 175 (CWL 14, 164).

27. As Robert Doran notes, this is the most appropriate starting point for systematic theology today. See Doran, *What Is Systematic Theology?*, 152–53.

28. See Hefling, "On Understanding Salvation History," 249.

29. "The church cannot simply opt out of modernity's critical pathos; we may not be of the world, but we are in it, and all in it are now critics. The question has to be 'Following *what* critical theory, and penetrating *whose* agenda, should the church read its Scripture?'" Jenson, *Canon and Creed*, 81.

30. As John Rogerson puts it, "The study of the Bible has always been critical, in the sense that scholars have used a knowledge of languages other than Hebrew and Greek as well as philosophical and scientific knowledge about the world and human growth and development in their interpretation of biblical passages." Rogerson, "Preface," 165.

31. See again, Westphal, *Whose Community?*, 35.

32. See again, Fowl, *Engaging Scripture*, 8.

33. The judgments and understanding of God's action and work in history are judgments of special categories, and the judgments of the structure of subjectivity and the structure of history are general categories. As noted in chapter 1, theology shares general categories with other disciplines. Special categories are unique to theology itself.

34. Recall the distinction between "doctrines," or the specific beliefs of the Christian community, and "systematics" or the intelligibility of those beliefs, as explained in chapter 1.

35. See Lonergan, "The Origins of Christian Realism (1961)"; Lonergan, "The Origins of Christian Realism (1972)"; Lonergan, *The Triune God: Doctrines*, 28–255; Lonergan, *MIT*, 302–26 (CWL 14, 282–302). For further discussion, see chapter 4 below; Crowe, *Theology of the Christian Word*; Gordon, "The Truthfulness of Scripture."

36. See also Rom 1.1–4; 8.34; 1 Cor 8.6; Phil 2.5–11; Col 1.15–20; 1 Tim 3.16. Other examples occur in the non-Pauline literature, e.g., 1 Pet 3.18–19, 21b–22. The sermons in the book of Acts also have generic and structural similarities with these confessions; see Acts 2, 3, 10, 13, and 17. It is beyond the scope of this chapter

to demonstrate the precise generic features of these texts or to demonstrate decisively that they are definitively liturgical, hymnic, or confessional statements that
existed and were liturgically performed prior to their inclusion in these letters.
What is important is to note that these likely liturgical expressions summarized the
shared convictions of their authors and the communities they addressed regarding
the intelligibility (at least from a commonsense or symbolic perspective) of God's
work in their midst in Jesus Christ and the Holy Spirit. See Meyer, *The Aims of
Jesus*, 60–69. For a recent analysis of potential confessional material in the apostle
Paul's writings, see Sumney, *Steward of God's Mysteries*. For specific discussions of
Phil 2.6–11 and Col 1.15–20, respectively, see Martin, *A Hymn of Christ*; Gordley,
The Colossian Hymn in Context. For an extended argument that (nearly) the whole
of the NT has liturgical origins and intentions, see Farkasfalvy, *Inspiration and In-
terpretation*, 63–87.

37. Young, *The Making of the Creeds*, 8.

38. Young, *The Making of the Creeds*, 13.

39. Meyer notes, however, that at least Phil 2.5–11 may already anticipate the
later use of theoretical language to clarify Christian confession: "Certain of its words
(e.g., *morphē*, 'form') smack of 'terminology'; more important, the inescapable mo-
tifs of pre-existence and incarnation and the terms in which the divinity of Christ
is described create the impression of a lyric flowering from the soil of speculation."
Meyer, *The Aims of Jesus*, 65. I would add to Meyer's judgment regarding Phil 2 the
further judgment that the language of both the prologue of Hebrews and the prologue of John's Gospel are already on the way towards the specialization of technical language. On the latter, Jonathan Bernier, following Lonergan, notes that in
"John's Gospel we find the vanguard of what will from the second century onward
become a common preoccupation among early Christian writers, namely the effort
to make systematic sense of the emergent Christian doctrine of God within the vocabulary of Hellenic thought." Bernier, *The Quest for the Historical Jesus*, 155. See
Lonergan, *The Triune God: Doctrines*, 30–55.

40. I explore the significance of this fact in much greater depth in chapter 6.

41. Lonergan, *MIT*, 295 (CWL 14, 276). For a distinctively Lonerganian account of the development of "the original message," see Crowe, *Theology of the
Christian Word*.

42. See the literature cited in notes 13–15 above.

43. For the sake of convenience, I refer to all such confessions as simply "the
rule" in the singular. As we will see, there are many expressions of the rule—so
many that it is difficult to affirm their precise unity from a strictly linguistic perspective.

44. Bokedal, "The Rule of Faith," 233.

45. For extensive discussion of the ancient use of κανών, see McDonald, *The
Biblical Canon*, 38–55. As Bokedal notes, Philo of Alexandria's use of this language
may anticipate the critical dimension of later Christian usage: "In Philo of Alexan-

dria (c. 15/10 BC–AD 50), the expression 'canon of truth' is used to mark out limits over against the sophists (*Leg.* 3, 233) and against mythologizing. To Philo, the canon (or canons) of truth can refer to the basic norm(s) and the truth of the Jewish faith: The Torah as God's revelation and the divine truth." Bokedal, "The Rule of Faith," 237.

46. Osborn ("Reason and Rule," 40–42) and Bokedal ("The Rule of Faith: Tracing Its Origins," 236–37) helpfully assemble the pertinent pre-Christian uses of κανών.

47. See Osborn, "Reason and Rule," 40–42.

48. For a discussion of Paul's usage of κανόνι in 2 Cor, see Hutson, "The Cross as Canon," 51.

49. On the influence of these texts on formulations of the rule of faith in the second-century churches, see Farmer, "Galatians and the Second-Century Development of the *Regula Fidei*."

50. See Grech, "The *Regula Fidei*," 590.

51. See Farmer, "Galatians and the Second-Century Development of the *Regula Fidei*," 145.

52. "No scholar today," writes Tomas Bokedal, "subscribes to the widespread medieval view, hinted at already by Rufinus (ca. AD 345–410), that each of the apostles made his personal contribution to the Apostles' Creed ("each contributing the clause he judged fitting"). It is still sensible, however, to reflect on the possible historical kernel of the strong insistence of apostolic origins, not only concerning the fixed creed(s), but prior to that, with regard to the closely related Rule of Faith." Bokedal, "The Rule of Faith," 239. For a useful account of the legend that the Apostles' Creed originated with the twelve apostles, see de Lubac, *The Christian Faith*, 19–53. Though the account is apocryphal, de Lubac shows that the content of the creed is consonant with the teaching of the apostles.

53. For references and discussion, see Ferguson, *The Rule of Faith*, 3, 16–17.

54. On the two-clause and three-clause forms, see Bokedal, "The Rule of Faith," 234, 244–48. On 1 Cor 8.6, see Hurtado, *Lord Jesus Christ*, 123–26.

55. See Farmer, "Galatians and the Second-Century Development of the *Regula Fidei*," 145. For an extremely helpful recent investigation of theological understandings of creation in the early church, see Blowers, *Drama of the Divine Economy*. For a study of the creation theologies of Justin, Irenaeus, Tertullian, and Origen, see Norris, *God and World*.

56. For summary of the key components of the rule, see Bokedal, "The Rule of Faith," 238–39.

57. See Bokedal, "The Rule of Faith," 247–48.

58. Young, *The Making of the Creeds*, 12.

59. Blowers, "The *Regula Fidei*," 202.

60. See Bokedal, "The Rule of Faith," 234n5.

61. See Young, *The Making of the Creeds*, 6.

62. The rule is not, as we have already seen, trinitarian in every case. For other early witnesses that tie trinitarian confessions to baptism, see Eph 4.4–6; Did. 7.1; and Justin Martyr *1 Apol.* 61. Note also the iconic trinitarian character of Jesus's baptism in the synoptic gospels (Mark 1.9–11; Matt 3.13–17; Luke 3.21–22). Some scholars have suggested, on the basis of citations of a shorter text of Matt 28 that only includes "in the name of Jesus" by Eusebius of Caesarea, that the trinitarian formula is not original to Matthew's gospel. For a summary of scholarly discussion of the Eusebian evidence, see Green, "Matthew 28.19, Eusebius, and the *lex orandi*." For further discussion of the relationship between baptismal confessions, the rule, and creeds, see Stewart, "'The Rule of Truth . . . which He Received through Baptism.'"

63. Young, *Biblical Exegesis*, 290.

64. Young, *Biblical Exegesis*, 19.

65. Young, *Biblical Exegesis*, 21.

66. See Young, *The Making of the Creeds.*

67. Tertullian is another early significant witness to the rule. See his *Praescr.* 13; *Virg.* 1.3; and *Prax.* 2.1–2. For translations, see Ferguson, *The Rule of Faith,* 6–8. For discussion, see Countryman, "Tertullian and the *Regula Fidei*"; Ferguson, *The Rule of Faith,* 21–24; Osborn, *Tertullian,* 37–39. Clement of Alexandria made reference to the rule but does not clearly delineate its contents. See *Strom.* 1.1.15; 6.15; 6.18.165; 7.15–16. For discussion, see Ferguson, *The Rule of Faith,* 21; Osborn, *Clement of Alexandria,* 172–75.

68. I do not intend to suggest any sort of literary dependence or direct historical influence or development from Irenaeus through Origen to Augustine. In my presentation of their unique employments of the concept of the rule I hope to highlight how it functioned for each of them. I also have no intention of suggesting that other figures who employ the rule are unimportant.

69. The actual title is Ἔλεγχος καὶ ἀνατροπὴ τῆς ψευδωνύμου γνώσεως; see the prefaces to books 2, 4, and 5. We know of the shorter title from Eusebius's *Hist. eccl.* 3.23.3. For focused examinations of Irenaeus's employment of the rule, see Behr, *Irenaeus of Lyons: Identifying Christianity,* 79–84, 110–18; Bingham, "The Bishop in the Mirror"; Ferguson, "The Rule of Truth and Irenaean Rhetoric"; Lanne, "'La Regle de la Verite'"; MacDonald, "Israel and the Old Testament Story"; Osborn, *Irenaeus of Lyons,* 143–61; Pagels, "Irenaeus, the 'Canon of Truth,' and the 'Gospel of John'"; Stewart, "The Rule of Truth."

70. He provides summaries of Christian beliefs in this work in a number of other passages without using the term.

71. English translations of book 1 are taken from *St. Irenaeus of Lyons Against the Heresies* (trans. and ann. Dominic J. Unger, rev. John J. Dillon). Unger and Dillon have provided a helpful introduction and overview in pages 1–20 of that work. Books 2 and 3 have appeared in English translation in the same series as volumes 65 (2012; also edited by Unger and Dillon, it has an introduction by Michael Slusser) and 64 (2012; edited by Unger with an introduction and further revisions

by M. C. Steenberg). The standard critical edition of the entire work is in the series Sources chrétiennes (vols. 100, 151, 152, 210, 211, 263, 264, 293, 294).

72. Irenaeus's iterations of the rule, however, are not exclusively trinitarian. To use such language is potentially anachronistic as well. To be sure, Irenaeus does not possess the technical language of later trinitarian theology. Tertullian is the ostensible inventor of the Latin term *trinitas* (see *De pud.* 21.16; *Prax.* 8).

73. Young, *Biblical Exegesis*, 290. Jeffrey Bingham argues that the rule represents Irenaeus's exposition of his self-understanding. See Bingham, "The Bishop in the Mirror." See also Loewe, *Lex Crucis*, 6.

74. So Young: "It was the contribution of Irenaeus to make [the community's emerging sense of identity] explicit, claiming the public tradition of the Church over against private teaching, eschewing speculation yet articulating beyond the existing tradition the *first systematic account of Christian theology* and the first biblical canon which explicitly related old and new scriptures." Young, *Biblical Exegesis*, 290; emphasis mine. Paul L. Allen states that "there is evidence to support the claim that Irenaeus is the first truly systematic theologian of the church." Allen, *Theological Method*, 51. See also Osborn, "Reason and the Rule," 43.

75. For extremely useful reflection on Irenaeus's orderliness in an "oral narrative" and not "analytical philosophical" mode, see Loewe, *Lex Crucis*, 18.

76. The title is regularly translated as *Demonstration of the Apostolic Preaching.*

77. Bokedal cites Polycrates's employment of the rule in the Quartodecian controversy as another example of the nonpolemical employment of the rule. See Bokedal, "The Rule of Faith," 237.

78. See Osborn, *Irenaeus of Lyons*, 145n17.

79. Young, *Virtuoso Theology*, 52.

80. Young, *Virtuoso Theology*, 48. Theodore Zahn thought that the rule was identical with a baptismal creed. See Zahn, "Glaubensregel und Taufbekenntnis in der alten Kirche." While it was likely connected to baptismal creeds (see *Haer.* 1.9.4), Zahn's proposal has major problems. For discussion, see Armstrong, "From the κανὼν τῆς ἀληθείας to the κανὼν τῶν γραφῶν."

81. The most famous example of this rhetoric is the Vincentian canon, of Vincent of Lérins (d. ca. 450). Vincent holds that the true catholic faith is "what has been believed everywhere, always, and by all." *Commonitorium* 2. I hold that Christian faith maintains consistency, integrity, and truthfulness, but its actual unity is not to be identified with any single univocal, historical, and culturally bounded expression. Its unity and truth are never apprehended apart from human understanding, and our understanding is itself historically conditioned. This provides an ongoing exigency for attentiveness, intelligence, reasonableness, responsibility, and faithfulness. For further reflection, see chapter 4 below.

82. This language is an adaptation of Lonergan's words regarding naive realist epistemology; the naive realist equates reality with sensation and so holds that truth is an already-out-there-now-real. See Lonergan, *Insight*, 276–79; Lonergan, *MIT*,

263 (CWL 14, 246). For further discussion of the preferable position of critical realism, see chapter 4 below.

83. See de Lubac, *The Christian Faith*, 19–53.

84. As Dillon and Unger note, Irenaeus's iteration of the rule in *Haer.* 1.10.1
contains allusions to Ex 20.11; Ps 145; Acts 4.24; 14.5; John 1.14; Luke 9.51; Eph 1.6;
1 Pt 1.8; Matt 16.27; Eph 1.10; Col 1.15; Eph 1.9; Phil 2.10–11; Rom 2.5; Matt 18.8;
25.41; Eph 6.12; Tit 1.8; John 14.15; 15.10; 15.27; 2 Tim 2.10; 1 Pt 5.10; and Acts
4.32. See *St. Irenaeus of Lyons Against the Heresies*, 183n1–186n24.

85. Bokedal, "The Rule of Faith," 235. See *Haer.* 2.28.1. See also Brox, *Offenbarung: Gnosis und gnostiker Mythos bei Irenaus von Lyon*, 105–12. As Unger and
Dillon summarize: "[Brox] holds that the rule of Truth is in Irenaeus not a Creed,
but is the entire faith believed and preached by the Church. It is *ipse veritas.*" *St. Irenaeus Against the Heresies*, 1:182n23.

86. On the narrative character of the rule, see Blowers, "The *Regula Fidei.*"

87. Translation from Irenaeus, *On the Apostolic Preaching*, 41.

88. For Irenaeus, the rule "is the content of scripture," writes Brevard Childs,
"but [is] not identical with the Bible; rather, it is *that to which scripture points.* . . .
Irenaeus did not see the rule-of-faith as the church's 'construal' of the Bible, but
rather as *the objective truth of the Apostolic Faith*, which has been publically revealed
and not concealed in a secret gnosis." Childs, *Biblical Theology of the Old and New
Testaments*, 32; emphasis mine.

89. For thorough discussion of Thomas Aquinas's understanding of the unity
of the work of the Triune God and of appropriation, see Emery, *The Trinitarian
Theology of St. Thomas Aquinas*, 349–59.

90. On the Son and Holy Spirit as "hands" of the Father, see *Haer.* 4.pref. 4,
4.20.1, 5.1.3.

91. For a thorough overview of Irenaeus on recapitulation, see Osborn, *Irenaeus of Lyons*, 117–40.

92. Irenaeus's reflections on the Trinity in his expositions of the rule are
largely centered, to risk an anachronism, on the economic work of the Father, Son,
and Spirit. In *Prax.*, Tertullian, by contrast, invokes a rule to discuss the unity and
distinction of the Father, Son, and Spirit in the immanent Trinity. See *Prax.* 8–9.
Tertullian's explicit mentions of the rule of faith, however, all focus on the economic work of the Father, Son, and Holy Spirit. See *Praescr.* 13; *Virg.* 1; and *Prax.* 2.

93. For discussion, see Stewart, "The Rule of Truth."

94. "How was such a complex body of literature, even in translation, to be
made accessible to aural recipients for whom this was foreign and unknown, who
had no prior acquaintance with the plots, characters, heroes, contexts? How would
they 'follow' a text, presumably read piecemeal according to some lectionary system? How would they retain a sense of direction and overview as each extract was
heard? . . . The 'hypothesis' of scripture had to be articulated to enable its 'hearing.'"
Young, *Biblical Exegesis*, 17–18. So also Barton, *Holy Writings, Sacred Text*, 51–53.

95. Young, *Virtuoso Theology*, 47.

96. Later we will see that Augustine explicitly states that the rule is derived from Scripture in *Doctr. chr.* 3.2.2. For contemporary repetition of this judgment, see Billings, *The Word of God*, 21; Daley, "In Many and Various Ways," 18; Fowl, *Theological Interpretation of Scripture*, 29–30.

97. For a helpful treatment of the relationship between the development of the rule and the recognition of the scriptural canon(s), see Armstrong, "From the κανὼν τῆς ἀληθείας to the κανὼν τῶν γραφῶν," 30–47.

98. Irenaeus famously argues for the validity and authority of the four canonical gospels alone (see *Haer.* 3.11.8). It is, of course, at this point impossible to know exactly which text forms Irenaeus had. For discussion of the books Irenaeus held as authoritative Scripture, see Grant, *Irenaeus of Lyons*, 21–29; Eric Osborn, *Irenaeus of Lyons*, 178–82.

99. See Young, *Virtuoso Theology*, 48; Norris, "The Insufficiency of Scripture."

100. Emphasis mine. Even for Irenaeus the rule is an internal principle in the reader of Scripture. Both Origen and Augustine will spell out the implications of the subjectivity of the rule at much greater length than Irenaeus. See below for discussion. In chapter 4 I note how such articulations are objectifications of fundamental beliefs of a specific subject that constitute her horizon of meaning and value.

101. Farkasfalvy, *Inspiration & Interpretation*, 117.

102. While Origen has sometimes been cast as the arch-heretic of the church fathers in Christian historiography, his works have received a much more favorable and historically responsible assessment in the twentieth and twenty-first centuries. The careful examinations of his work by Henri de Lubac, Henri Crouzel, and Jean Danielou in the middle of the twentieth century provided a platform for reevaluating his legacy and contributions. See de Lubac, *History and Spirit*; Danielou, *Origène*; Crouzel, *Origène*. For a more recent assessment of Origen's significance indebted to these earlier works, see Heine, *Origen*. For a recent helpful account of Origen's rehabilitation, see Siecienski, "(Re) Defining the Boundaries of Orthodoxy." For description of the historic case against Origen and a defense of his ecclesiastical bona fides, see de Lubac, *History and Spirit*, 15–102; de Lubac, "Dispute about the Salvation of Origen." On the history of "the Origenist controversy," see Clark, *The Origenist Controversy*.

103. De Lubac, *ME*, 1:151. For de Lubac's historical discussion of the origins of the fourfold sense and Origen's key place in its development, see de Lubac, *ME*, 1:117–59. Elsewhere de Lubac writes that "it is not an exaggeration to say that Origen's influence on the establishment of the doctrine of the fourfold sense, like his influence on all western hermeneutics and exegesis, was determinant. No other influence was the equal of his" (de Lubac, *ME*, 1:154). Origen's understanding of the nature of Scripture and its purpose in particular have received a great deal of attention in recent attempts to understand and evaluate his work. Notable works, in addition to de Lubac's *History and Spirit*, include Lauro, *The Soul and Spirit of Scripture*;

Hanson, *Allegory and Event*; Martens, *Origen and Scripture*; Neuschäfer, *Origenes als Philologe*; Torjesen, *Hermeneutical Procedure and Theological Method*; Trigg, *Origen*; Vogt, *Origenes als Exeget*. For a comprehensive bibliography, see Martens, *Origen and Scripture*, 255–71.

104. It is not the first Christian work with the title. Clement of Alexandria states that he wrote a work with the same title, but no copies of it have survived. See Clement of Alexandria, *Strom.* 3.13.1; 3.21.1. English translations of *Princ.* come from Origen, *On First Principles* (trans. Herbert Butterworth). For a critical edition, see Origen, *Traité des principes*.

105. For his other employments of the rule, see his *Comm. Jo.* 8.9–15, 32.15–16; *Comm. Matt.* 61.1–11; *Comm. Rom.* 5.1; *Fr. 1 Cor.*; *Cels.* 5.8. For discussion of these, see Outler, "Origen and the *Regula Fidei*," 136–38. For more thorough accounts of Origen's employment of the rule, see de Lubac, *History and Spirit*, 60–76; Hanson, *Origen's Doctrine of Tradition*, 91–126; Martens, *Origen and Scripture*, 127–31. A comprehensive account of Origen's hermeneutics would require attention to his employment of the rule in the above-mentioned loci, to his other explicit reflections on hermeneutics in other locations in his extant works, and finally to his exegetical praxis itself. Others have done fruitful work towards these ends. Martens, *Origen and Scripture*, deserves special mention.

106. For discussion of the dates of the work, see Butterworth, "Translator's Introduction," vi–ix; Heine, *Origen*, 83–84, 104, 124–26, 130.

107. For discussion, see Daley, "Origen's *De Principiis*"; see also Lies, *Origenes' "Peri archon."* Heine writes that *Princ.* "is a kind of first attempt at systematic theology." Heine, *Origen*, 83. For others who suggest that Origen's *Princ.* is a systematic work, or that Origen is a systematic theologian, see Fiorenza, "Systematic Theology: Tasks and Methods," 7–8; Jenson, *Canon and Creed*, 118; McClendon, *Systematic Theology: Ethics*, 42–44.

108. Heine, *Origen*, 130.

109. As Heine rightly notes, it is easy to detect Origen's implicit and explicit responses to differences of opinion present in the church of his day. See Heine, *Origen*, 130–31. Even so, while these concerns likely provided Origen with the primary impetus for the work, its structure and generality suggests a more universal intention. As Heine rightly judges, the work represents "Origen's effort to pull together his understanding of the major doctrines of the Christian faith." See Heine, *Origen*, 130.

110. See, e.g., Martens, *Origen and Scripture*, 20–21.

111. "Rufinus," Albert Outler writes, "errs grossly on the side of orthodoxy. [The concepts of the rule of faith] occur in the Latin translations with a frequency out of all proportion to similar references in the Greek originals. This is a suspicious contrast and suggests inevitably that a great many of the Latin phrases are nothing more than pious asides interpolated by Rufinus at points he felt appropriate." Outler, "Origen and the *Regula Fidei*," 135.

112. For learned discussion of Origen's trinitarian theology in its historical context, see Waers, "Monarchianism and Origen's Early Trinitarian Theology."

113. Outler, "Origen and the *Regula Fidei.*"

114. Farmer, "Galatians and the Second Century Development of the *Regula Fidei*," 146.

115. Outler, "Origen and the *Regula Fidei*," 141.

116. Outler, "Origen and the *Regula Fidei*," 140–41.

117. "To Origen, the consensus of the belief of the church, based on the Scriptures and the oral tradition, was of paramount importance, his obvious intention was to use it everywhere as a norm for his teaching." Outler, "Origen and the *Regula Fidei*," 140–41.

118. Outler, "Origen and the *Regula Fidei*," 141.

119. He reiterates the antiquity and apostolicity of the rule later in the same work. Those who follow the methods he lays out for the interpretation of Scripture "keep to the rule of the heavenly church of Jesus Christ through the succession of the apostles." *Princ.* 4.2.2.

120. Heine, *Origen*, 143.

121. See Martens, *Origen and Scripture*, 210–11.

122. See Martens, *Origen and Scripture*, passim.

123. Martens, *Origen and Scripture*, 25–87. Martens draws attention to the fact that Origen has extremely lofty expectations for interpreters.

124. See Martens, *Origen and Scripture*, 89–106.

125. I discuss the usefulness of Scripture in much greater depth in chapter 6. For orientation to this principle of patristic exegesis, see Sheridan, "The Concept of 'Useful' in Patristic Exegesis"; Sheridan, *Language for God in Patristic Tradition*, 226–29.

126. See Origen, *Homilies on Genesis and Exodus* (trans. Heine), 275–76. For a list of extant locations in Origen's work where he invokes the authority of Paul as providing an example of spiritual interpretation that we are to follow, see Martens, *Origen and Scripture*, 158n100.

127. See Martens, "Revisiting the Allegory/Typology Distinction," for a survey of the literature on Origen's literal and nonliteral exegesis.

128. Martens, *Origen and Scripture*.

129. Martens, *Origen and Scripture*, 246.

130. For a critical edition of the Latin text of *Doctr. chr.*, see *De Doctrina Christiana Libri Quattuor*. All English translations of *Doctr. chr.* are taken from Augustine, *Teaching Christianity* (trans. Hill). On the reception of this work, see the essays in Arnold and Bright, *De Doctrina Christiana*; and Pollmann and Vessey, *Augustine and the Disciplines*.

131. *Doctr. chr.* could profitably be used in contemporary university or seminary courses on theological exegesis, theological method, and even homiletics. Randy Rosenberg told me that he has used it in a course on theological method. While the work bears the marks of its historical context, its generality gives it classical value. I should note here the importance of attending to Augustine's actual exegetical practices and his other hermeneutical reflections for a comprehensive understanding of

his approach to Scripture. A full exploration of these other areas, of course, is far beyond the scope of the present work. For a helpful orientation to Augustine's exegeses and hermeneutics, see Williams, "Hermeneutics and Reading Scripture." For more thorough investigations, see esp. Andrews, *Hermeneutics and the Church*; Bright, *Augustine and the Bible*; Byassee, *Praise Seeking Understanding*; Cameron, *Christ Meets Me Everywhere*; Pollman, *Doctrina Christiana*; Stock, *Augustine the Reader*; Toom, *Thought Clothed with Sound*.

132. For more thorough discussions of the date and circumstances of the work, see Kannengiesser, "The Interrupted," 3–6; Bright, "Biblical Ambiguity in African Exegesis," 25–32; and esp. Kannengiesser and Bright, *A Conflict of Christian Hermeneutics*.

133. Hill proposes AD 397 as the *terminus ante quem* for the early part of the work because Augustine did not mention Ambrose in 2.40.61. See Hill, *Teaching Christianity*, 168n126. Augustine writes in the *Retractiones*, "When I found the books on *Teaching Christianity* incomplete, I preferred to complete them, rather than to leave them as they were and pass on to revising other works" (2.4). Quoted from Hill, *Teaching Christianity*, 98. Theories of why Augustine stopped writing are manifold. For a brief summary and bibliographic references, see Andrews, *Hermeneutics and the Church*, 235n4. Augustine continues to develop his hermeneutical reflections in both the *Confessiones* (ca. 397–401; see esp. books 10–13) and *Contra Faustum* (ca. 397–398), two works that may have overlapped the end of his composition of *Doctr. chr.* 1–3.24.35. Gaetano Lettieri, in fact, argues that *Confessiones* 11–13 function as "La nouva Doctrina Christiana." See *L'altro Agostino*, 177–89.

134. See, e.g., his letter to Jerome, *Epistle 9*, in which he requests that Jerome make translations of biblical commentaries (particularly those of Origen) so that Augustine can prepare himself for the exigencies of being "a leading expositor of Scripture." Kannengieser, "The Interrupted," 4.

135. See van Fleteren, "St. Augustine, Neoplatonism, and the Liberal Arts," for an assessment of how Augustine's training in the liberal arts, particularly his encounters with Neoplatonism, influenced his writing of *Doctr. chr.* While van Fleteren perhaps overstates his case regarding the influence of Neoplatonic thought on Augustine at this time in his career, Augustine does mention the value of certain works of the *Platonici* (3.40.60) for the understanding of Scripture. That being said, any influence of the *Platonici* should only be seen as *utilis*, and "becomes little enough if it is compared with the knowledge of the divine scriptures" (3.42.63). For a more balanced account of Augustine's debt to ancient learning in *Doctr. chr.*, see Toom, *Thought Clothed with Sound*, 19–26, 111–56.

136. See Kannengiesser, "The Interrupted," 3–13.

137. Augustine had recently begun to turn his attention to scriptural exegesis. For a thorough and nuanced study of Latin exegesis of Paul's epistles prior to Augustine, see Stephen Andrew Cooper, Introduction to *Marius Victorinus' Commentary on Galatians*, 4–249, esp. 183–249; For discussion of Augustine's dependence

on this tradition of commentators, see Plummer, "Introduction," 6–59. On Augustine's engagement with philosophy, see Toom, *Thought Clothed with Sound*, 27–64.

138. Green, "Introduction," ix; notes that *Doctr. chr.* bears "faint echoes of controversies which loomed large in Augustine's career." Augustine's treatment of polygamy and other conventions of Old Testament culture in 3.20.31–3.23.33, which his Manichee contemporaries found repugnant, is one such echo. For Augustine's discussion of the customs and morals of the OT and scriptural interpretation directed against the Manichees, see *Gen. Man.* 1.19.30; 1.20.31; 1.22.33–34; and 2.7.8 (ca. AD 388/389); *Mor. Manich.* 9.14–15; 16.26; and 29.59 (ca. AD 389/391); *Util. cred.* 3.5–9 (AD 391); and *Faust.* 4.1–2; 6.1–10; 8.1–2; and 10.1–3 (ca. AD 397–98).

139. Pollmann, "Augustine's Hermeneutics as a Universal Discipline!?," 209–12. For a more thorough treatment, see part 4 of Pollmann's habilitation thesis, *Doctrina Christiana*, 66–244. For more discussion of the genre of the work, see Toom, *Thought Clothed with Sound*, 71–74, 71n26. Andrews, *Hermeneutics and the Church*, 23–39, helpfully divides the many scholarly proposals of *Doctr. chr.*'s genre into four categories (while offering nuanced treatments of different representatives he groups together): (1) handbook of hermeneutics; (2) handbook of rhetoric; (3) charter for the formation of Christian culture; and (4) handbook for preachers. He writes his own work from the presupposition that "the whole of *Doc.* is an eclectic hermeneutics, even one that is universal in scope, while attempting to maintain [the] insight that the work begs to be read, at least initially, by practicing preachers, who, at the time of composition, would have consisted primarily of ordained clergy." Andrews, *Hermeneutics and the Church*, 41.

140. So Pollmann, "Augustine's Hermeneutics as a Universal Discipline!?," 209. On the significance of Augustine finishing the work, see also Andrews, *Hermeneutics and the Church*, 15.

141. For helpful treatments of Augustine's understanding of and employment of the rule of faith, see Lifton, "The Rule of Faith in Augustine"; Ayres "Augustine on the Rule of Faith"; Rombs, "*Unum Deum . . . Mundi Conditorem*"; and esp. Dawidowski, "*Regula Fidei* in Augustine."

142. See, e.g., *Doctr. chr.* 1.5.5. Augustine's articulation of the persons is closer to the Athanasian rule here than to the rules that focus on the economic activity of the persons.

143. See Liftin, "The Rule of Faith in Augustine," 88–89. For a reconstruction of the content of Augustine's baptismal creed, see Liftin, "The Rule of Faith in Augustine," 88n10.

144. On the ecclesial dimensions of the rule for Augustine, see Dawidowski, "*Regula Fidei* in Augustine," 284–89; Liftin, "The Rule of Faith in Augustine," 89, 92–95.

145. See Ayres, "Augustine on the Rule of Faith," 34, 36.

146. See Rombs, "*Unum Deum . . . Mundi Conditorem*."

147. See Liftin, "The Rule of Faith in Augustine," 96.

148. In *Doctr. chr.* Augustine only names two of the traditional Latin rhetorical *partes*. See Quintillian, *Inst.* 3.1.1.

149. Cicero defines *inventio* as *excogitatio* in *De inventione rhetoria* 1.9, which Toom renders "discovery." See Toom, *Thought Clothed with Sound*, 83n71.

150. See Andrews, *Hermeneutics and the Church*, 92–104.

151. Ayres, "Augustine on the Rule of Faith," 36. Augustine's own education in rhetoric and moral psychology provides him with the means for developing the rule in new ways. "Once Christians had begun to develop precise creedal definitions of their faith in the late fourth century and once those definitions were understood to represent the 'mind' of Scripture read by the appropriately formed Christian," Ayres writes, "then the notion of the *regula fidei* no longer needed to stand as the only prophylactic against 'private' or 'heretical' interpretation. The *regula* could now take on new senses and be used with a new fluidity. Similarly, developing engagements with rhetorical, moral and educational theory provided opportunities for the *regula fidei* to acquire new significations. . . . [N]ew polemical contexts and the development of creedal formulations has meant that a wider range of beliefs and principles are now identified with the rule." Ayres "Augustine on the Rule of Faith," 33, 44.

152. Irenaeus, as we have seen, does not follow through on the potential systematic relevance of the rule as thoroughly as Origen.

153. Certain contemporary threats, no doubt, do bear interesting resemblances to these earlier historical challenges. See O'Regan, *Gnostic Return in Modernity*.

154. Origen and Augustine advert to the historicity of the OT in a sporadic way, for instance, when they note the ancientness of certain customs and religious observances of the peoples of the OT. Origen acknowledges the ancientness of the customs of the OT in *Cels.* Augustine's understanding of the historicity of the OT is especially evident in *Faust.*

CHAPTER THREE. The Location of Scripture I

1. See the works cited in note 15 in chapter 2.

2. It is obviously impossible for any single person to have an adequate grasp of all the authentic developments of Christian tradition. I am not claiming to possess such knowledge or suggesting that the achievement of such knowledge will be necessary for an adequate understanding of the nature and purpose of Christian Scripture. The constructive approach I am proposing, I reiterate, represents only one attempt to articulate an adequate systematic theology of the nature and purpose of Christian Scripture at the level of our time. I propose this attempt on the basis of my own research in Christian tradition(s), personal reflection, and discussion and dialogue in the theological communities in which I have been formed. Readers will have to determine, to the best of their own abilities, the value, responsibility, reasonableness, and intelligibility of my work.

3. I discuss the historicity of meaning and historical consciousness directly in chapters 4 and 6. For an exceptional historical overview of the developments, particularly in the nineteenth century, that led to the full recognition of the historical locatedness of doctrines and their development, see Chadwick, *From Bossuet to Newman*. On Vincent's own nuanced account of historical development, see Guarino, *Vincent of Lérins*, 14–42.

4. Lonergan writes, "To change . . . meanings is to change . . . reality. . . . [Changing] the meaning changes the reality because the meaning is constitutive of the reality." Lonergan, "The Analogy of Meaning," 203.

5. Some explanation of the development of doctrine is required here. Perhaps it would be better, however, to speak of the development of the understanding of doctrine than of the development of doctrine itself. If doctrines are specific theological judgments about reality that express the faith of the Christian community, such judgments, if truly constitutive, cannot develop as judgments (though the language through which these judgments were expressed certainly did develop and change). They are, however, liable to refinement in understanding and expression. Systematic expressions—which I will discuss in greater depth presently—represent the terminus of such refinement. The present reflections are occasioned by de Lubac's excellent essay "The Problem of the Development of Dogma." In that essay, he declares that "in Jesus Christ all has been both given and revealed to us at one stroke; and that, in consequence, all the explanations to come, whatever might be their tenor and whatever might be their mode, will never be anything but coins in more distinct parts of a treasure already possessed in its entirety." De Lubac, "The Problem of the Development of Dogma," 275. These "explanations to come" express the developing understanding of the church. The entire content of dogma, for de Lubac, is the judgment that the mystery of Jesus Christ is the fullness of the Triune God's self-revelation in history. See de Lubac, "The Problem of the Development of Dogma," 274. Charles Hefling provides a complementary explanation of the development of doctrine. The starting question should be, he states, "how it is *possible* that Christian doctrine has changed. If the Christian message is indeed the word of God, a communication of specific meaning and not just a symbolic reflection on the general religiousness of the human race; if it is a 'revelation,' to use a much debated theological term, how can human minds develop it? How can they improve, so to speak, on God? *The answer, I would say, is that they do not. What improves is themselves. The evidence for developments in Christian doctrine is evidence for developments in the thinking, understanding, and judging of the Christian community.*" Hefling, *Why Doctrines?*, 110; emphasis mine. I discuss this judgment regarding the content and scope of revelation in much greater depth in chapter 6.

6. Ayres, *Nicaea and Its Legacy*, 423.

7. I discuss the universal human impulse towards understanding at length in chapter 4.

8. See Blowers, "The *Regula Fidei* and the Narrative Character of Early Christian Faith."

9. Blowers, "The *Regula Fidei* and the Narrative Character of Early Christian Faith," 202.

10. Blowers, "The *Regula Fidei* and the Narrative Character of Early Christian Faith," 209.

11. For a critical examination of treatments of the rule that emphasize its narratival dimensions, see MacDonald, "Israel and the Old Testament Story."

12. Hefling, "On Understanding Salvation History," 228.

13. Doran indicates that teaching on revelation and redemption are two such doctrines: "In many instances the meaning of some of the mysteries of faith is perhaps permanently best expressed in categories that are symbolic, aesthetic, dramatic, narrative. Even if a technical explanation is possible in, for example, metaphysical terms, nonetheless the value of aesthetic, dramatic, and narrative theologies of the same mysteries is unmistakable." Doran, *What Is Systematic Theology?*, 14. Hefling corroborates this judgment; see "On Understanding Salvation History," 228n16. Hefling also rightly rules out a "pure datum" approach to revelation that would locate God's action only in "already-back-there-then-events," which are objectively prior to subjective human mediation and so are more stable. Such an approach rests on the judgment that knowledge results from taking a good look. See Hefling, "On Understanding Salvation History," 229–30. For an extended argument on the usefulness and aptness of artistic forms for expressing Christian truth—and their complementarity with technical metaphysical language—that utilizes the work of Hans Urs von Balthasar as an example and guide, see Carpenter, *Theo-Poetics*.

14. For a thorough and helpful articulation of the context, content, and consequences of Arius's teaching, see Williams, *Arius: Heresy and Tradition*.

15. Young, *Biblical Exegesis*, 34.

16. See Athanasius, *Inc.* 54.

17. "For the Word of God became man, and He who is God's Son became the Son of man to this end, [that man,] having been united with the Word of God and receiving adoption, might become a son of God. Certainly, in no other way could we have received imperishability and immortality unless we had been united with imperishability and immortality. But how could we be united with imperishability and immortality unless imperishability and immortality had first become what we are, in order that the perishable might be swallowed up by imperishability, and the mortal by immortality, that we might receive the adoption of sons?" *Haer.* 3.19.1.

18. Young, "The 'Mind' of Scripture."

19. Young, *Biblical Exegesis*, 35.

20. For two excellent and provocative treatments of the presence of such reflection in the language of the NT itself, see Bates, *The Birth of the Trinity*; Hill, *Paul and the Trinity*.

21. Young, *Biblical Exegesis*, 35. As Ayres notes, "It is a pre-Nicene understanding of the *regula fidei* that has captured the interest of many seeking to appropriate

early Christian exegesis. This concern, however, frequently seems to circumvent the growing awareness in the fourth and fifth centuries that shifts in the public life of the Church and the Trinitarian controversies themselves *rendered necessary more precise doctrinal formulations*: modern Christians wishing to remain classical Trinitarians avoid such formulae only by way of romanticism." Ayres, *Nicaea and Its Legacy*, 420; emphasis mine.

22. The apostle Paul may use technical, specialized language in his letters. If he does so, though, he does not do so often, and he never explicitly defines his terms. Ben Meyer notes the possible presence of technical language in Phil 2.5–11 (see Meyer, *The Aims of Jesus*, 65), and I would identify some of the titles given Christ in Heb 1.1–4 as technical as well. I explain the judgment that the language of Scripture is commonsense language further in chapters 4 and 6. See also Gordon, "The Truthfulness of Scripture"; Gordon, "On the (Relative) Authenticity."

23. Lonergan, *The Triune God: Doctrines*, 209.

24. See Lonergan, "The Origins of Christian Realism (1961)"; Lonergan, "The Origins of Christian Realism," in *ASC*, 239–62 (CWL 13, 202–20). He treats its unfolding in the early centuries of Christianity in *The Triune God: Doctrines*.

25. Lonergan, *MIT*, 319 (CWL 14, 297).

26. Lonergan, "The Origins of Christian Realism (1961)," 89; emphasis mine. As William Brown puts it, "Poetry is not well suited for settling heated theological debates." Brown, *Sacred Sense*, 56.

27. For Lonergan's discussion of Clement of Alexandria, who he takes to be a key witness to this tendency, see Lonergan, *MIT*, 296, 307, 319, 329, 344 (CWL 14, 276, 286, 297, 305, 318); Lonergan, *The Triune God: Doctrines*, 211–33. For a recent work that corroborates Lonergan's judgments about Clement's understanding of the referential nature of language for God, see Hägg, *Clement of Alexandria*.

28. David Yeago offers a partially complementary account of the achievement of the *homoousios* in "The New Testament and Nicene Dogma." As he writes, "We cannot concretely perform an act of judgment without employing some particular, contingent verbal and conceptual resources; judgment-making *is* an operation performed with words and concepts. At the same time, however, the same judgment can be rendered in [a] variety of conceptual terms, all of which may be informative about a particular judgment's force and implications. The possibility of valid alternative verbal/conceptual renderings of the identical judgment accounts for the fact that we ourselves often do not realize the full implications of the judgments we pass: only *some* of their implications are ever unpacked in the particular renderings we have given them" (93).

29. Recall the discussion in chapter 1.

30. Paddison, "The Authority of Scripture and the Triune God," 456.

31. See Paddison, "The Authority"; Paddison, *Scripture*; Treier, "In the End, God"; Work, *Living and Active*. See also Webster, *Holy Scripture*. In the realm of New Testament scholarship, N. T. Wright has argued persuasively that the authority

of Scripture must be understood under the broader consideration of the authority of the God to whom Scripture gives witness. See Wright, *Scripture and the Authority of God.* I return to the argument that Scripture functions as an instrument mediating the authority of the Triune God in chapter 6.

32. For an extended argument against proposals that either ignore the necessity of mediation in scriptural interpretation or argue that it is intrinsically violent, see Smith, *The Fall of Interpretation.* Smith argues that we should not understand the necessity of subjective mediation as unfortunate or a problem to be solved but as a fact that reflects the goodness of God's creation. While the second edition of Smith's work proposes some helpful suggestions for affirming the value of mediation and the importance of reading Scripture communally and with reference to Christian tradition, I think that attention to and investigation of possible norms for subjective mediation would further bolster his already strong work. Not all subjective mediation is equal. Smith, of course, recognizes the truth of that judgment.

33. This version of the creed is the English translation of the Latin recension found in the most recent version of Denzinger's *Enchiridion symbolorum;* see Hünermann et al., *Compendium of Creeds,* *150. I have included the *filioque* clause in brackets because of its lateness. Even the creeds cannot stand as already-back-there-then-reals but are located in specific historical contexts in the vicissitudes of social and cultural discourse in specific times and places.

34. Blowers, *Drama of the Divine Economy,* 1.

35. See Tanner, *God and Creation in Christian Theology.* I do not intend to suggest that the understandings of divine and human freedom and activity that I articulate here can be "found" in Irenaeus, Augustine, Anselm, Aquinas, or any other particular Christian thinker, or that my own articulation should be taken as the terminus of a uniform and distinctly traceable process of historical development. Tanner herself cautions against understanding her work as a historical treatment of these doctrinal themes. The affirmations do undoubtedly have their own histories. In *Creation and the God of Abraham,* Ernan McMullin and Janet M. Soskice have offered useful treatments of the historical foundations of the doctrine of God's creation ex nihilo in Jewish and Christian thought. See McMullin, "Creation *ex nihilo*"; and Soskice, "*Creatio ex nihilo*"; see also May, *Creatio ex nihilo.* Burrell gives attention to the place of such judgments in Christian, Jewish, and Islamic theology in his *Freedom and Creation in Three Traditions.*

36. Young, *Virtuoso Theology,* 57.

37. It is important to note here, of course, that Irenaeus declares explicitly that *the Father* is simple; he does not use this language for the Son or the Holy Spirit. From early on the adherence of the fathers to the judgment of divine simplicity ruled out the possibility of understanding the anthropomorphic and anthropopathic depictions of God of the OT in a univocal way. Andrew Radde-Gallwitz argues that the judgment of divine simplicity was a hermeneutical tool utilized to identify specific actors/characters of the texts of Scripture as early as the time of Marcion. See Radde-Gallwitz, *Basil of Caesarea,* 20–37.

38. For a discussion of Origen's understanding and employment of divine simplicity, see Radde-Gallwitz, *Basil of Caesarea*, 59–66.

39. For a discussion of Augustine's understanding of the distinction between creator and creation and his adherence to the doctrine of *creatio ex nihilo*, see Torchia, *Creatio Ex Nihilo*.

40. See Radde-Gallwitz, *Basil of Caesarea,* for a historical treatment of the early Christian understanding of the distinction between divine and created natures. For an extremely valuable overview of the philosophical and theological antecedents of these positions and the ways they affected Christian engagement with Scripture, see Sheridan, *Language for God in Patristic Tradition.*

41. See the locus classicus in *ST* I. qq 2–26. Thomas appropriated, refined, and transformed the philosophy of Aristotle, mediated by Maimonides, to arrive at his articulation in the *ST.* His thought and language were rejoinders not to the anthropomorphic deities of the pagans or the celestial hierarchies of the Gnostics but to the emanationist schemes of Neoplatonism wherein material reality emanated from the One. For discussion, see Burrell, *Freedom and Creation in Three Traditions.*

42. For discussion of this loss in modern and postmodern theological reflection, see Tanner, *God and Creation,* 120–62; Vanhoozer, *Remythologizing Theology,* 81–138; see also Duby, *Divine Simplicity;* Long, *The Perfectly Simple Triune God.*

43. Meyer, *The Church in Three Tenses,* 2–3.

44. For another recent presentation of the judgments of classical theism in the context of a discussion of Scripture, see Martin, *Biblical Truths,* 111–68. For two recent theological endeavors that use Lonergan's work on divine and human freedom as the basis for treatments of theology of the atonement and grace theology, see Laughlin, *Jesus and the Cross,* 34–96; Cone, *An Ocean Vast of Blessing,* 1–27.

45. Ormerod and Crysdale, *Creator God,* 45.

46. Sokolowski, *The God of Faith and Reason,* 122.

47. Burrell, "The Act of Creation with Its Theological Consequences," 45. Burrell has written extensively on creation and divine freedom elsewhere. See especially his *Aquinas: God and Action; Freedom and Creation in Three Traditions; Faith and Freedom;* and *Towards a Jewish, Christian, Muslim Theology.*

48. Sokolowski, *The God of Faith and Reason,* 122.

49. For a useful articulation of the way such a "participatory" understanding of history provides resources for understanding God's action in Scripture, see Levering, *Participatory Biblical Exegesis.*

50. Aside from the already mentioned works of Burrell, Sokolowski, and Tanner, see the following: Hart, *The Beauty of the Infinite;* McFarland, *From Nothing;* Weinandy, *Does God Suffer?*

51. As McFarland argues, the most convincing proof of the aptness of the argument of *creatio ex nihilo* is living out the implications of its dogmatic function: "In teaching creation from nothing, Christians affirm that in all things God is acting for creatures' good. This does *not* entail the belief that everything that happens is good, but rather that if 'God so loved the world that he gave his only Son' (John

3.16), then we may be confident that in all things God is working to overcome evil. In the face of the myriad threats to creaturely well-being, there is nothing self-evident about this belief, and Christians therefore have no grounds for looking down on those who do not share it. If they wish to persuade others of its truth, they need to act in ways that display their trust in God's creative work, striving to honor the integrity of all creatures in the conviction that no creature exists except as God gives it being: sustaining, empowering, and guiding it to the end that God intends for it. And if asked why God does this, their answer must be clear: it is simply and solely because God sees every creature as good. There is no other reason, no other motive, no other factor in play. Nothing." McFarland, *Out of Nothing*, 188–89; emphasis in original.

52. Sokolowski, *The God of Faith and Reason*, 33.

53. Sokolowski, *The God of Faith and Reason*, 34. See *ST* I, q. 45, a. 3, ad 1.

54. Sokolowski, *The God of Faith and Reason*, 34.

55. Sokolowski, *The God of Faith and Reason*, 34.

56. Sokolowski, *The God of Faith and Reason*, 122.

57. See Harnack, *History of Dogma*, vol. 1; Harnack, *What Is Christianity?* For a recent critique of Harnack's position, see Gavrilyuk, "Harnack's Hellenized Christianity or Florovsky's 'Sacred Hellenism.'"

58. For a creative and compelling examination of a couple of key OT texts that anticipate the distinction, see the first five essays in Anderson, *Christian Doctrine and the Old Testament*, 3–94.

59. Sokolowski, *The God of Faith and Reason*, 123.

60. Sokolowski, *The God of Faith and Reason*, 123.

61. Kevin Vanhoozer affirms this possibility in his *Remythologizing*, 93–94. Lonergan also does so in his presentation of divine and human freedom and grace in *De scientia atque voluntate Dei*, which he presents as an explanation of the intelligibility of the following scriptural texts: Luke 17.10; Sir 15.14; Rom 8.28–29; 9.18; 1 Tim 2.1–4; 2 Tim 4.2; Rom 10.14; Hos 13.9; Rom 11.33–36. See Lonergan, "God's Knowledge and Will," 411.

62. On systematic meaning, see Lonergan, *MIT*, 304 (CWL 14, 283).

63. Lonergan, *MIT*, 319 (CWL 14, 297). Lonergan frequently refers to Clement of Alexandria's rejection of anthropomorphic language for God in the *Stromateis* as an example of the development of systematic meaning. See Lonergan, *MIT*, 307, 319, 329, 344–45 (CWL 14, 276, 286, 305, 318–19); Lonergan, "Exegesis and Dogma," 148–49. See also Gordon, "The Truthfulness of Scripture."

64. The most famous text adduced as evidence for creation out of nothing is 2 Mac 7.28; I leave it out because the book in which it occurs is not canonical for all Christian groups. For discussion of the other mentioned passages and the exegetical difficulties with affirming the doctrine of *creatio ex nihilo*, see McFarland, *From Nothing*, 2–5, 21–24. For a profound and carefully argued alternative to *creatio ex nihilo* via theologically rich engagement with the evidence of the Hebrew scriptures, see Levenson, *Creation and the Persistence of Evil*.

65. So also the judgment in the creed and Scripture that God is the creator of all things "visible and invisible" (Col 1.16; see also Heb 11.3).

66. Burrell, *Freedom and Creation in Three Traditions*, 10; emphasis in original.

67. See also 1 Sam 15.29; Mal 3.6; Titus 1.2; Heb 6.18. See Sheridan, *Language for God in Patristic Tradition*, 27–44. Sheridan simultaneously notes that despite this distinction, God still teaches humanity "as a Father teaches a child" (see Dt 8.5). I give concentrated attention to such divine teaching in chapters 4 and 6.

68. For a helpful recent discussion and response to these challenges, see Moberly, *Old Testament Theology*, 107–43.

69. For further discussion of the three following possibilities, see Robinette, "The Difference Nothing Makes," 527–28.

70. The theologians associated with "open theism" and "process theology" characteristically reject judgments that God is simple. For examples of the former, see Pinnock, *Most Moved Mover*; Boyd, *God of the Possible*. For an introduction to process theology, see Epperly, *Process Theology*. For an argument against divine simplicity from an analytic theologian, see Mullins, "Simply Impossible: A Case against Divine Simplicity." For an argument by an OT scholar, see Freitheim, *The Suffering of God*. Ormerod and Crysdale provide a robust—in my judgment compelling—alternative to process perspectives by articulating an understanding of an evolving and emergent creation within the constraints of classical understandings of the distinction between God and creation and divine sovereignty. See Ormerod and Crysdale, *Creator God: Evolving World*.

71. See the essays in Feldman, *Judaism and Hellenism Reconsidered*.

72. For discussion of the pagan confusion regarding the personal interest of the God of Christian (and Jewish) faith in humanity in the early history of Christianity, see Hurtado, *Destroyer of the gods*, 63–66.

73. As Sokolowski has pointed out, though the church fathers articulate their understandings of divine nature in conversation with Greco-Roman thought, the judgment of "the distinction" is a Jewish-Christian contribution: "The gods of pagan religion and the first principles of pagan philosophers are gods and principles *for* the world and they could not be without the world. Although the best, most powerful, and most favored parts of the whole, they remain only parts. Without the world, they could not be gods. They are not distinguished from the world, from the whole of things, in the way the biblical divinity is." See *The God of Faith and Reason*, x; emphasis in original.

74. Soskice, "*Creatio ex nihilo*," 38.

75. Anderson, *Christian Doctrine and the Old Testament*, 58.

76. See Robinette, "The Difference Nothing Makes," 528.

77. We can, however, see those expressions as evidence of a divine pedagogy of condescension. See below, and Sheridan, *Language for God*; Dreyfus, "Divine Condescendence (Synkatabasis) as a Hermeneutic Principle."

78. I discuss this distinction in the use of language and the nature of the biblical language itself in chapters 4 and 6.

79. Sokolowski's articulation, of course, is a completely contemporary one.

80. Robinette, "The Difference Nothing Makes," 548; emphasis mine.

81. See Sheridan, *Language for God in Patristic Tradition*. Sheridan astutely draws attention to the aforementioned patristic use of Num 23.19, "God is not as man to be deceived nor as the son of man to be threatened," and Deut 1.31, "As a man he takes on the manners of his son," as hermeneutical principles. The quotations come from English translations of Origen's citations. The fathers employed these texts to argue for the ontological distinction between God and the world *and* to affirm that God nevertheless used created causes to teach humanity. See Sheridan, *Language for God in Patristic Tradition*, 27–44. I provide a contemporary account of the place of Scripture in divine pedagogy in chapter 6.

82. See Dreyfus, "Divine Condescendence." As he summarizes, "God has placed himself within man's reach by using human language in Scripture, as well as in becoming Man for him through the Incarnation." Dreyfus, "Divine Condescendence," 77.

83. The variegation of such language is no argument against its truthfulness. But its truthfulness lies not in its univocity but in its evocative capacities.

84. Again, see Lonergan, *The Triune God: Doctrines*, 209; for further discussion, see Gordon, "The Truthfulness of Scripture."

85. The incarnation and the work of the Holy Spirit are of course exceptions to this rule. I return to this judgment briefly in the discussion of the historical causality of the missions of the Son and Spirit in history below.

86. "Deus operatur in omni operante naturae et voluntatis." Lonergan, "On God and Secondary Causes," 53. This essay is a critical review of Iglasias, *De Deo in operatione vel voluntatis operante*. In his early career Lonergan treated the questions of providence, human and divine freedom, and grace extensively in his historical work on Thomas's understanding of these topics in *Grace and Freedom*. Lonergan taught on these topics a number of times as well, and his most extensive discussions of them can be found in "The Supernatural Order (*De ente supernaturali*)" and "God's Knowledge and Will (*De scientia atque voluntate Dei*)," published in *Early Latin Theology*, 53–255 and 257–411, respectively.

87. On the Athanasian rule, see Lonergan, *The Triune God: Doctrines*, 171–99. See also Lonergan, "The Dehellenization of Dogma," in *ASC*, 22–23 (CWL 13, 21–22).

88. Lonergan, "On God and Secondary Causes," 56–57.

89. For a much more thorough discussion, see the seldom studied treatment in Lonergan, "God's Knowledge and Will," 256–411.

90. Hefling, "On Understanding Salvation History," 232. The incarnation, however, is the one notable exception to this judgment. See Hefling, "On Understanding Salvation History," 232n19. We should note here that sin, properly speaking, is a culpable failure of operation. God does not directly will such participation in non-being but indirectly wills it through creating and sustaining the world that

does exist. See Lonergan, "God's Knowledge and Will," 303–9, 343–53. See chapters 4 and 6 below for further discussion.

91. Hefling, "On Understanding Salvation History," 232n19. The created external term of the mission of the Spirit is also an instance of God's causal efficacy in creation.

92. To clarify, the missions do not bring about change in God but only in creatures. I discuss this at greater length below. Levering states this clearly in a recent work: "The procession of the Son coming forth from the Father is not combined with a second procession in which the Father sends the Son into the world. Rather, there is only one procession constitutive of the Son, but the Son is nevertheless rightly said to be 'sent' into the world because the procession has two terms: the Son's eternal subsistence and his temporal subsistence as Jesus Christ. The visible mission of the Son is not a change in the Son, but a change that occurs on the side of the creature that is united to the Son in the incarnation. Likewise, the mission of the Holy Spirit is not a second procession of the Holy Spirit but a temporal 'term' whereby creatures are sanctified by the Holy Spirit. Sanctifying grace makes the Holy Spirit present to creatures in this way." Levering, *Engaging the Doctrine of Revelation*, 40–41.

93. John Webster concurs with this starting point. In *Holy Scripture*, he writes that "Holy Scripture is dogmatically explicated in terms of its role in God's self-communication, that is, the acts of Father, Son, and Spirit which establish and maintain that saving fellowship with mankind in which God makes himself known to us and by us." Webster, *Holy Scripture*, 8. See also Swain, *Trinity, Revelation, and Reading*, 4–8.

94. For helpful overviews of contemporary trinitarian theologies, see Hunt, *Trinity*; Emery, *The Trinity*. See also Levering and Emery, *Oxford Handbook on the Trinity*.

95. In general, the present understanding of trinitarian theology takes its bearings from the trinitarian reflections of Augustine, Aquinas, Lonergan, and Doran. On the relationships between the differences and similarities of these accounts, see Doran, *The Trinity in History*, 168–75. See also Doran, *What Is Systematic Theology*, 78–79, 144–46, on genetic sequences in systematic theology.

96. See Rahner, *The Trinity*, 10, 22. Along with Karl Barth, Rahner helped twentieth-century Christian theology recover a lost focus on the significance of the Triunity of the God of Scripture. For discussion of Rahner's and Barth's efforts and their influence on subsequent trinitarian theologies, see Collins, *The Trinity*, 103–9; Baik, *The Holy Trinity*, 1–21. As is clear from Baik's study, there are multiple ways of understanding Rahner's axiom. For an appreciative and critical investigation of Rahner's *Grundaxiom*, see Sanders, *The Image of the Immanent Trinity*.

97. The missions of the Son of God and the Holy Spirit in creation are the processions of the Son and Spirit in the inner life of God plus the created "external" terms of the humanity of the Son of God and the graces of the Spirit's work in

history. For two technical accounts of these judgments, see Lonergan, *The Triune God: Systematics*; Doran, *The Trinity in History: Volume 1*. The Triune God does not become "entangled" in creation through the missions, but the missions instead manifest or reveal that eternal life truly in a manner appropriate to the reception of created beings. Through this revelatory work, we are able to understand *that* the Triune God is but not *what* the Triune God is *en se*. Our analogical and imperfect knowledge of the Triune God is adequate, yet remains created.

98. For two different but complementary accounts of the historical developments of Christian reflection on the Trinity, see Lonergan, *The Triune God: Doctrines*, 29–56; Behr, *The Way to Nicaea*. The section of Lonergan's collected works just cited appeared under almost exactly the same title as Behr's work in 1976. See Lonergan, *The Way to Nicea*.

99. See Crowe, *Christ and History*, 174.

100. "The three persons act together, not by the juxtaposition or the superimposition of three different actions, but in one same action, because the three persons act by the same power and in virtue of their one divine nature." Emery, *The Trinity*, 162.

101. De Lubac, *Catholicism*, 141. While it is true that the scope of the saving work of the Triune God is not restricted to God's work on behalf of, in, and through human persons and human communities, given the intrinsically human dimension of Scripture I will restrict my focus to God's saving work among human persons and communities.

102. The language of "two hands," as we have seen above, is Irenaeus's. On appropriation, see Emery, *The Trinity*, 161–68.

103. Lonergan, "Mission and the Spirit," in *ATC*, 26 (CWL 16, 25). Lonergan's phrase gives a traditional taxis of the missions of the Son and the Holy Spirit, with the mission of the Spirit succeeding that of the Son—completed through the Son's incarnate work—at Pentecost. In what follows I will complicate this taxis slightly.

104. For a complementary account of God's self-communication from a Reformed Evangelical perspective that focuses on the biblical theme of the covenant, see Swain, *Trinity, Revelation, and Reading*, esp. 35–60.

105. "It is not that God cannot make lesser creatures easily enough, but he finds greater creatures a bit more difficult, and finally finds it impossible to make a creature with the same nature as himself. It is not a question of difficulty. When we say that God could not make a creature with the same nature as himself, we are saying the same sort of thing as when we say he couldn't make a square circle. God couldn't make a square circle, not because he is not powerful enough, but because a square circle is a contradiction, something that couldn't be made; the phrase 'square circle' is a self-cancelling one, it could not be the name of anything. In the same way, a creature which is by nature divine is a contradiction; it is a creature which is uncreated, and the phrase 'uncreated creature' could not be the name of anything." McCabe, *Faith within Reason*, 20–21.

106. "Strictly speaking," Hefling writes, "God does not participate in human history, but history may participate in the being of God. That being so, no distinction can be drawn which separates an existential realm, in which God can act, from a natural realm in which things happen on their own, because 'what occurs' and 'what God understands and wills to occur' are different names for the same thing: the single, emergently probable, actually existing universe. The only legitimate distinction is one drawn within that universe, and in the last resort it can only be a distinction between that which participates in God as One and that which also participates in God as Three." Hefling, "On Understanding Salvation History," 232.

107. McCabe, *Faith within Reason*, 21. For McCabe's extended—and winsome—discussion of this new order, see his *The New Creation*.

108. As Lonergan puts it, rather tersely, "About the year 1230 Philip the Chancellor completed a discovery that in the next forty years released a whole series of developments. The discovery was a distinction between two entitatively disproportionate orders: grace was above nature; faith was above reason; charity was above human good will; merit before God was above the good opinion of one's neighbors. This distinction and organization made it possible (1) to discuss the nature of grace without discussing liberty, (2) to discuss the nature of liberty without discussing grace, and (3) to work out the relation between grace and liberty." *MIT*, 310 (CWL 14, 288–89). Lonergan footnotes his own work, *Grace and Freedom*, for a fuller account of this historical development. See Lonergan, *Grace and Freedom*, 3–20. For Lonergan's systematic treatise on the supernatural order, see Lonergan, "*De ente supernaturali*/The Supernatural Order."

109. Thankfully, restricting our focus to the actual history of what the Triune God has done permits us to forgo any forays into the ocean of literature on the natural and supernatural that has appeared since Henri de Lubac's seminal work, *Surnaturel*. For a comparison of Lonergan's account of the supernatural with de Lubac's, see Maloney, "De Lubac and Lonergan on the Supernatural." For helpful overviews of the literature on the supernatural, see Bonino, *Surnaturel*.

110. I treat our natural and supernatural capacities as human persons in depth in chapter 4.

111. See Lonergan, *Grace and Freedom*, 49–58.

112. Doran has recently pointed out the way that beginning with the missions in trinitarian theology provides an opportunity to understand and articulate the missions of the Son and the Holy Spirit by returning to the biblical witness. See Doran, "A New Project in Systematic Theology," 248.

113. Again, see Lonergan, *The Triune God: Doctrines*, 28–255, on the development of trinitarian doctrine.

114. For two accounts of the significance of the relational language of the NT, and even OT authors, with regard to the persons of the Trinity in early Christian reflection, see Hill, *Paul and the Trinity*; Bates, *The Birth of the Trinity*, respectively.

115. I offer an explanation of this judgment in chapter 6.

116. See Gordon, "'The Incomprehensible Someone.'"

117. Lonergan, *Method in Theology*, 105. De Lubac concurs: "The Spirit is in truth the first of the gifts which come to us from the redemption accomplished by Christ." De Lubac, *The Christian Faith*, 122. See John 7.39.

118. For an extremely helpful overview of historical Christian teaching regarding the Holy Spirit, see Congar, *I Believe in the Holy Spirit*. For an excellent recent pneumatology that draws on ancient resources, see Rogers, *After the Spirit*.

119. Since I have already affirmed the coequality of the Holy Spirit with the Son and the Father, I will not give further attention to this aspect of the creed.

120. See de Lubac, *The Christian Faith*, 137, 203–6.

121. For a helpful discussion of the unity of the work of the persons, see Emery, *The Trinity*, 164.

122. See Gordon, "'The Incomprehensible Someone,'" 42–45.

123. See Doran, *The Trinity in History*, 65–82.

124. Doran, *The Trinity in History*, 78. I discuss the intelligibility of Christ's revelatory work in greater depth below and explore the specific role of Scripture in mediating this revelation in chapter 6. Doran also states that the Son has an invisible mission that is potentially universal. "The knowledge born of religious love, the faith that constitutes the word emanating from the gift of God's love, the ineffable judgment of value that proceeds from the gift," he writes, "is a created participation in the eternal Word, and so represents the external term of the invisible mission of the divine Word." Doran, *The Trinity in History*, xi. Such universal faith, however, as a judgment of value, would temporally follow upon the reception of the love of God flooding our hearts through the Holy Spirit.

125. For discussion of patristic reflection on this clause of the creed, see de Lubac, *The Christian Faith*, 119–23.

126. "The prophets" was used—in juxtaposition to "apostles"—as a designation for the entirety of the OT testimony—whether written or oral—even in the texts of the NT (see Eph 2.19; 3.5). I discuss the significance of this at length in chapters 5 and 6.

127. For further discussion, see chapter 6.

128. Lonergan, "Supplementary Notes on Sanctifying Grace," 581. Lonergan cites a number of NT texts in support of each of these points.

129. As Lonergan notes, the NT provides "evidence on the language and the beliefs that were current" in the NT churches. See Lonergan, "Christology Today: Methodological Reflections," in *ATC*, 81 (CWL 16, 77). The texts are fundamentally testimonies of beliefs; such testimonies included constitutive beliefs about historical events and their meaning. Richard Bauckham makes this point with regard to the Gospels in nuanced and compelling ways in his *Jesus and the Eyewitnesses*, 5–6, and passim.

130. Though faith may more properly result from the invisible mission of the Son. "The 'universal teacher' [Thomas Aquinas] has said that the whole content of

the truth of Christian faith can be reduced to the dogma of the trinitarian God and the dogma that man participates in the life of God through Christ." Pieper, *Faith, Hope, Love*, 83.

131. Doran, *The Trinity in History*, 55.

132. See Lonergan, "Transition from a Classicist World-View to Historical Mindedness," *ASC*, 7–9 (CWL 13, 8–10); Lonergan, *The Redemption*. For discussion, see Crowe, *Christ and History*, 127–28; Hefling, "Lonergan's *Cur Deus Homo*"; Volk, "Lonergan on the Historical Causality of Christ"; Loewe, *Lex Crucis*.

133. See Gorman, *Inhabiting the Cruciform God*.

134. In the immanent Trinity, the Son is spoken and does not speak. In the economic Trinity, the Son speaks the Father. Jesus Christ, in speaking the Father, is thus the person who participates economically in paternity. See Doran, *The Trinity in History*, 85, 97, 137.

135. "La substance du Nouveau Testament, c'est le Mystère du Christ. Or ce Mystère est tout d'abord un grand Fait: c'est ce qu'on peut appeler, pour faire court, le Fait rédempteur, ou le Fait du Christ. C'est le Fait de son incarnation, de sa vie terrestre, de sa mort, de sa résurrection et de son ascension. Il est aussi le Fait de l'Église, qui n'est pas séparable du Christ, étant son Épouse et son « Corps ». C'est le Fait mystérieux, ou le Mystère effectif des noces du Verbe avec l'Humanité." De Lubac, *EM*, 2:2.111.

136. Irenaeus, Clement of Alexandria, Ephrem the Syrian, Gregory Nazianzus, Augustine, Cyril of Alexandria, Maximus the Confessor, and others also adhere to the judgment of this "exchange formula." For references and discussion, see Russell, *The Doctrine of Deification*, 106, 108, 125, 169, 199, 215, 268, 278, 295, 322, 337; Gordon, "Deifying Adoption as Impetus for Moral Transformation," 198. The apostle Paul perhaps anticipates the "exchange formula" in 2 Cor 8.9: "For you know the generous act of our Lord Jesus Christ, that though he was rich, yet for your sakes he became poor, so that by his poverty you might become rich."

137. For a brilliant and concise explanation and defense of divine impassibility, see Hart, "No Shadow of Turning: On Divine Impassibility." See also Weinandy, *Does God Suffer?* For a theologically sophisticated proposal affirming the possibility of God suffering, see Jenson, *Systematic Theology: The Triune God*. For a salutary argument in favor of the paradoxical position that the impassible God suffered in the flesh, see Gavrilyuk, "God's Impassible Suffering in the Flesh." Gavrilyuk argues that "God is neither eternally indifferent to suffering, nor eternally overcome by it. Rather, there is eternal victory over suffering in God, manifest most fully through the cross and resurrection." Gavrilyuk, "God's Impassible Suffering in the Flesh," 131.

138. For Lonergan, revelation is God entering into "man's making of man." See Lonergan, "Theology in Its New Context," in *ASC*, 61–62 (CWL 13, 54–55). Lonergan's noninclusive language was customary for his time.

139. For a more thorough explanation of this change, see Hefling, "Lonergan's *Cur Deus Homo*."

140. For an exceptional summary of how Christ's work changes the possibilities of human relationships with the Triune God, see Weinandy, "God and Human Suffering," 113–14.

141. Doran, *The Trinity in History*, 96. See also Hefling, "Revelation and/as Insight"; Hefling, "Another Perhaps Permanently Valid Achievement."

142. Again, see the works cited in note 121 above.

143. And what belongs to the Son is not his own but the Father's (John 7.16).

144. See Schlesinger, *Missa Est: A Missional Liturgical Ecclesiology*, for an ecclesiology developed from the perspective of mission that makes special mention of the relationship between the mission of the church and the missions of the Son and Holy Spirit.

145. Webster, *Holy Scripture*, 8.

146. Again, I must note that the present account does not aspire to absolute finality and comprehensiveness; a full systematic theology at the level of our times, Doran has argued, would be a multivolume, collaborative endeavor that articulates the interrelations between the following topics: God, Trinity, Invisible-Missions-Holy Spirit-Grace, Revelation, Creation, Incarnation, Anthropology/Nature, Sin (Original, Personal, and Social), Social Grace, Redemption, Resurrection, Sacraments, Church, Praxis, Eschatology/Reign of God. Doran, "A New Project in Systematic Theology," 243–59.

147. Young, *Virtuoso Theology*, 56. J. Todd Billings concurs on the necessity of a framework: "If Scripture is to be taught and preached in the church, a rule of faith will come into play whether we like it or not. There is no escaping a map with at least broad outlines of who God is and who we as human beings are." *The Word of God*, 25.

148. We can also not, for the same reasons, posit an already-back-there-then-real tradition or an "already out there now final magisterial pronouncement" as the final court(s) of appeal for determining the effective authority of the Triune God in history. I have yet to be convinced of the responsibility and usefulness of making an appeal to a living magisterium, somehow insulated from the historicity of human meaning, as a final court of appeal. Judgments about the indefectibility of the church and its teaching authority within that indefectibility, in my judgment, could much more easily and reasonably be located within eschatological considerations than located rigidly and unequivocally in *specific* magisterial judgments in history (which themselves rely on the acceptance of the judgment *that* this particular magisterium can and does make such judgments when such-and-such considerations are met). In the eschatological judgment of the indefectibility of the church that I hold, the gates of Hell *will not finally* prevail over the church, and what the Triune God does in the economy is sufficient to guarantee this, even with our finite, mediated, flawed knowledge of and participation in such work.

149. See Greene-McCreight, "Literal Sense"; Frei, "'The Literal Reading' of Biblical Narrative"; Rogers, "How the Virtues of the Interpreter Presuppose and Perfect Hermeneutics."

150. Lonergan, *Insight*, 605.

151. I review the testimonies of some specific human authors of Scripture regarding its purpose and intelligibility in chapter 6. I must note that the testimony of the authors of 2 Tim 3.16–17, 2 Pet 1.21, Heb 4.12, and others cannot be recognized as simply, univocally, and naively referring to the Christian Bible. To reiterate what I have stated a number of times before, there was no Christian Bible with two Testaments, and probably no absolutely definitive set of Jewish Scriptures recognized universally in all the early Christian communities, during the first century when the authors of these passages wrote. If we are to understand these texts as referring to the two-Testament Christian Bible with which we are familiar, we must do so through an account of divine action—that is, of providence—that can articulate how God utilizes earlier texts to "refer" to a later body of canonical Scripture. Again, such an account will necessarily express a human understanding of these judgments about divine activity. For the human interpreter and her community, such an account will express how such texts are potentially intelligible within later horizons of understanding in a way that does justice to the historicity of the texts and the historicity of the Christian Bible itself. I return to this judgment in our discussion of the relationship between the historicity of the Christian Bible and the theological judgment of its inspiration in chapter 6.

152. For Lonergan on the impossibility of demonstrating the mysteries of Christian faith, see *The Triune God: Systematics*, 151–53, 207–13.

153. Lonergan, *MIT*, 268 (CWL 14, 251–52).

154. Young, *Virtuoso Theology*, 56.

CHAPTER FOUR. The Location of Scripture II

1. Lonergan, "Philosophy and Theology," in *ASC*, 205 (CWL 13, 173).

2. Lonergan, "Aquinas Today: Tradition and Innovation," in *ATC*, 35–54, at 51 (CWL 16, 34–51, at 50).

3. Wilfred Cantwell Smith uses this phrase in *What Is Scripture?*, 18, 183, 203. In this text, as its subtitle, *A Comparative Approach*, suggests, Smith has in mind not only the texts of the Christian Bible, but all of the texts held sacred in the religious traditions of the world.

4. For two general introductions to the judgment of the usefulness of Scripture for transformation of the reader/interpreter/hearer, especially in premodern exegesis, see Ayres, "Patristic and Medieval Theologies of Scripture"; Stroumsa, "The New Self." See also Boersma, *Scripture as Real Presence*, 42–43, 71–72, 114–15, 131–58, 251, 263–72. For more thorough examinations of specific premodern interpreters, see Becker, *Fear of God and the Beginning of Knowledge*; Blowers, *Exegesis and Spiritual Pedagogy*; Boersma, *Embodiment and Virtue*; Cain, *The Letters of Jerome*; Candler, "St. Thomas Aquinas"; Candler, *Theology, Rhetoric, and Manuduction*; Fulford, *Divine Eloquence*; Kovacs, "Divine Pedagogy"; Harkins,

Reading and the Work of Restoration; Martens, *Adrian's Introduction to the Divine Scriptures*; Martens, *Origen and Scripture*; Dawson, *Christian Figural Reading*; Hicks, *Trinity, Economy, and Scripture*; Rorem, *Biblical and Liturgical Symbols*; Rorem, *Pseudo-Dionysius*; Rylaarsdam, *John Chrysostom on Divine Pedagogy*; Sarisky, *Scriptural Interpretation*; Stock, *Augustine the Reader*; and Andrews, *Hermeneutics and the Church*; on the Syriac tradition at Nisibis, Maximus the Confessor, Gregory of Nyssa, Jerome, Thomas Aquinas, Gregory Nazianzus, Clement of Alexandria, Hugh of St. Victor, Adrian of Antioch, Origen of Alexandria, Didymus the Blind, Pseudo-Dionysius, John Chrysostum, Basil of Caesarea, and Augustine of Hippo, respectively. By grouping these fine studies together I do not intend to blur the historical and theological differences of the figures treated in each of them. Each premodern figure, however, clearly shares the judgment that engagement with and study of Scripture is a means of the transforming work of God in its interpreters, though each figure—and each modern expositor—expresses her or his understanding of what that judgment entails in particular ways.

5. This judgment, while it was often justified by appeal to specific scriptural texts and has its earliest roots in apostolic Christian praxis—as the above-cited NT texts exhibit—undoubtedly received further support through the Christian appropriation of Greco-Roman philosophical traditions, which can be best understood, Pierre Hadot argues, as diverse programs for moral and spiritual formation in reason. See Hadot, *Philosophy as a Way of Life*, 126–44, 264–76; *What Is Ancient Philosophy?*, 237–53. On the influence of Greco-Roman philosophical and rhetorical resources in early Christian biblical exegesis, see Ayres, "Irenaeus vs. the Valentinians"; Eden, *Hermeneutics and the Rhetorical Tradition*, 41–63; Stroumsa, *The Scriptural Universe*; Young, *Biblical Exegesis*, 49–118; Young, "The Rhetorical Schools," 182–99.

6. See, e.g., Irenaeus, *Epid.* 46; Origen, *Hom. Gen.* 7.1, 13.3; *Comm. Jo* 10.174; *Cels.* 4.44; and Augustine, *Conf.* 13.15.16–3.16.19.

7. Ayres, "The Soul," 176. See also Boersma, *Scripture as Real Presence*, 158. For de Lubac's discussion of this theme, see especially the conclusion of *HS*, 450–507; and *ME*, 2 passim.

8. Ayres, "The Soul and the Reading of Scripture," 174. A full-scale articulation of the fourfold sense and its possible relevance for contemporary engagement with Scripture is beyond the scope of the present work. Such an endeavor, however, could serve as a useful traditional foundation for a systematic theology of scriptural interpretation at the level of our times. In a subsequent volume I plan to provide such an account and transposition in light of the positions on the Triune God, the distinctive constitution of human persons and communities, the historicity of human meaning, and the nature and purpose of Scripture that I have articulated in the present work. For now I can only indicate that this future work will relate the fourfold "senses" to specific human drives and capacities for historical/literary, theological, moral, and spiritual understanding of the scriptures. I will argue that Scripture—in and even through its human historicity—both bears witness to and

is a means of facilitating the kinds of differentiations of consciousness and conversions constitutive of attentive, intelligent, reasonable, responsible Christian discipleship at the level of our times. The Triune God has given Scripture to the Christian community and to the world for these purposes, and it is an eminently (and constitutively) useful instrument in the work of the Triune God in history.

9. De Lubac's "Tripartite Anthropology" (in *Theology in History*, 117–200) is his most extensive discussion of the notion of the soul in premodern Christian thought. Ayres provides a helpful summary of his intentions in this lengthy essay. "De Lubac's concern," Ayres notes, ". . . is to suggest that accounts of the soul must reflect the *aporia* which follows from our need to acknowledge that in its depths the soul always has as gift the ability to contemplate the divine and receive the presence of Son and Spirit." Ayres, "The Soul," 184.

10. Ayres, "The Soul," 184.

11. See Ayres, "The Soul," 176–80.

12. Ayres, "The Soul," 178.

13. See chapter 3.

14. The references from the previous two sentences come from Ayres, "The Soul," 177n6. *Psychē* occurs over one hundred times in the NT. While it is probably impossible to decisively prove the influence of technical Hellenistic psychologies on any of these passages, or the relevance of Greek psychological notions for understanding them, their authors cannot have been wholly removed from such traditions of development. The very presence of this terminology in the authoritative texts that would become the NT and in the LXX proved decisive for later Greek Christian reflection on anthropology. If the Triune God had intended to preserve Christian faith in a pure Hebraic mind-set, it is certainly strange that the advent of the incarnation took place in the extremely Hellenized milieu of first-century Israel and that its primary literary attestation—and the language of its authoritative ancient scriptures, at least in their citations in the NT—were mostly Greek. For surveys of the influence of Greek translations of the ancient Jewish scriptures/OT in first-century Christianity, see Jobes and Silva, *Invitation to the Septuagint*; Law, *When God Spoke Greek*.

15. Ayres, "The Soul," 178.

16. "The context of late Hellenistic and early Imperial philosophical and religious writing," Ayres writes, " . . . sustained a highly diverse discussion about the sort of reality that soul is (material or immaterial), the many ways in which it may be understood to relate to the body and the many ways in which one can conceive of the relationship between the rational power of the soul and the 'passions.'" Ayres, "The Soul," 178.

17. A number of works have given attention to various facets of Christian appropriation of Greek philosophical reflection on human nature. See, e.g., Jaeger, *Early Christianity and Greek Paideia*; Pelikan, *Christianity and Classical Culture*, 120–35, 280–326; Pelikan, *The Emergence of the Catholic Tradition (100–600)*, 278–331; Russell, *The Doctrine of Deification*; A. N. Williams, *The Divine Sense*.

18. See Augustine's famous description of the value of pagan learning in *Doctr. chr.* 2.40.60–2.41.62.

19. For a helpful historical investigation of Origen's theological anthropology and the impact of scriptural exegesis on the Christian soul, see Martens, *Origen and Scripture*, 94–106; for a historically astute account of Basil of Caesarea's notion of the soul and the impact of engagement with Scripture on the soul, see Sarisky, *Scriptural Interpretation*, 35–70.

20. For a historical treatment of how subsequent Christian interpreters understood this verse, see de Lubac, "Tripartite Anthropology."

21. Stendahl, "The Apostle Paul and the Introspective Conscience of the West."

22. Even so, "no one would accuse Paul of lacking a robust sense of himself," as Susan Eastman has recently noted, "whether or not he had a 'theory of the self.'" Eastman, *Paul and the Person*, 13.

23. That doing so was not Paul's primary focus does not entail the further judgment that Paul was completely unconcerned with reflection on human consciousness and conscience. It follows that Paul did any such reflection, of course, utilizing the particular resources he had in his day. For a fascinating recent investigation of Paul's sense of anthropology in conversation with ancient Stoic and contemporary psychological and scientific resources, see Eastman, *Paul and the Person*.

24. Stendahl, "The Apostle Paul and the Introspective Conscience of the West," 204.

25. This is not to say, however, that Paul and the other authors of Scripture did not give any attention whatsoever to human interiority. For two helpful investigations of interiority in Scripture that stay close to the texts, see Crowe, *Theology of the Christian Word*, 127–32; Keener, *The Mind of the Spirit*. See also Eastman, *Paul and the Person*.

26. The "New Perspective on Paul," of course, is not monolithic. See the work of E. P. Sanders, James D. G. Dunn, and N. T. Wright. For a useful introduction to the scholarship on the "New Perspective," see Dunn, *The New Perspective on Paul*, esp. 1–98.

27. In his oft-cited article on biblical theology, Stendahl argues that our historical distance from the contexts of Scripture forces us to make a clear distinction between seeking what a text "meant"—the text's original import in the particularities of its ancient context—and its subsequent "meaning"—the ways that later authors appropriated it for theological purposes. Stendahl insists that the only way for Scripture to be relevant is for Scripture scholars to pursue the former task of seeking what the texts "meant"—which he calls the descriptive task—as far as is possible as a check against our propensity to attempt to make Scripture reinforce our already existing presuppositions and biases. See Stendahl, "Biblical Theology, Contemporary." While neglect of the historical difference between the worlds of Scripture and the contemporary world is irresponsible, it would be overly hasty to suggest that such neglect *makes it impossible* for God to act in the ways God desires

to act in human communities and persons through their relatively uninformed reading, hearing, and meditation upon Scripture. Augustine's insistence that love of God and neighbor is the true *finis* of scriptural interpretation provides a broader perspective for evaluating ahistorical readings. For Augustine humble but mistaken assessments of "authorial intention" are not culpably evil if they facilitate and manifest the love of God and neighbor. See *Doctr. chr.* 1.36.40; *Conf.* 12.18.27.

The judgment that the texts contain a single meaning is a red herring as well. Certainly it is possible to raise and answer questions about the intentions of the authors of Scripture, and the failure to do so is irresponsible. But the answers to those questions must remain hypothetical and ought not be identified exhaustively with "the meaning" of the text under consideration. There are a host of other legitimate questions that have occurred and will continue to occur to Christian readers when we read and hear these texts, and many of them are worth pursuing.

28. To the problem of the historicity of perspectives, Lonergan argues that archaism and anachronism are two of three possible approaches to understanding the authority of tradition: "[Archaism] denies the fact of historical change, or it claims that men should not have changed. It insists that the Gospel be preached in every age as it was preached in Antioch and Ephesus, in Corinth and Rome. It refuses to answer the questions that arise, not within the context of the New Testament, but on the later soil of Greco-Roman culture, or in medieval Paris, or at Trent, or at Vatican I or II. A second solution is anachronism. It answers the questions, but it does not know about history. It assures everyone that these answers are already in the doctrines of the New Testament, that if they are not there explicitly, they are there implicitly." "Besides archaism and anachronism," however, Lonergan writes, "there are development and aberration. Both development and aberration answer the questions of the day within their proper context. But development answers them in the light of revelation and under the guidance of the Holy Spirit. Aberration fails to do so in one or more respects." Lonergan, "Philosophy and Theology," 198–99.

29. Pierre Hadot argues that the theoretical reflection practiced in the various Greco-Roman philosophical schools provided distinctive modes or ways of life that highlighted or emphasized the importance of different human characteristics and capacities. These philosophies emerged from and served as reflective constraints upon their adherents' concrete lives. See Hadot, *Philosophy as a Way of Life.*

30. This judgment, of course, presumes other judgments about the relationship between language and reality and about the possibility of both understanding and communicating the distinctive features and intelligible structures that make human knowledge and communication possible. I discuss these judgments at greater length below.

31. The present account of human nature draws explicitly and exclusively upon Western and (mostly) Christian perspectives, not because there are not authentic advances in the understanding of human persons in non-Western perspectives, but instead because I am best acquainted with Western notions of human personhood.

32. See Ayres, "The Soul," 182. Darren Sarisky utilizes Basil of Caesarea's notion of the soul to challenge modern, immanentist notions of personhood. See Sarisky, *Scriptural Interpretation*, 50.

33. The latter task is, I think, what Ayres (and de Lubac) is actually after. Ayres tellingly writes that de Lubac "captures with remarkable precision the key common themes of the pre-modern traditions for which he is trying to create a voice within modern Catholic debate." Ayres, "The Soul," 180. Recovery and understanding of "key common themes" are the goals of the work of retrieval.

34. Ayres, "The Soul," 178–79.

35. Ayres, "The Soul," 181.

36. Ayres, "The Soul," 180–81.

37. As de Lubac cautions, "[The] Christian idea of man, however, has not been delivered, complete, in some formula that can be analyzed for our purposes. While implied in concrete examples in the sources of revelation, in the Church's attitude, in the teachings of her doctors and in the spontaneous reactions of her saints, it has never appeared in a discernable, complete form in itself." De Lubac, *The Drama of Atheist Humanism*, 400–401. I have no pretentions that what I offer below instantiates such a "complete form in itself"; it will only be a hypothesis on the way towards such a total explanation.

38. I assume that this telos is the objective of a natural desire, and that God's fulfillment of the desire is supernatural and gratuitous. Since my goal is to focus on the economy of the creative and redemptive work of the Triune God, I will not discuss the question whether the natural desire requires God to grant our supernatural end and so impinges upon God's freedom. It is more fruitful, especially for the present project, to focus not on what is impossible and possible within the constraints of divine and human freedom but instead on what we can say about the actuality of the revelatory and redemptive work of the Triune God. For a recent excellent treatment of the natural desire to see God, see Rosenberg, *The Givenness of Desire*.

39. For a theological account of Scripture that draws on a premodern source to "restore a sense of the end" of human persons for a contemporary theological account of Scripture, see Sarisky's work on Basil of Caesarea and Stanley Hauerwas in *Scriptural Interpretation*, 37–70, 140–58, 205–11.

40. I will leave speculation as to the form and character of postdeath formation to other thinkers more competent than myself. As noted in the previous chapter, my focus is on the place of Scripture in *this* economy of God's creative and redemptive work.

41. See Ayres, *Nicaea and Its Legacy*, 284–85, 298–99, 322.

42. Though he maintained a high regard for Aristotle throughout his life, Lonergan argued that viewing his works as timeless achievements denuded them of their enduring classical value. Authentic contemporary faithfulness to the creative, synthetic, and erudite genius of Aristotle would both respect and appreciate the significance of his achievements and simultaneously inspire us to seek to collabora-

tively do for our own time what he did for his. Lonergan is much more explicit on this need with regard to Aristotle's great theological interpreter, Thomas Aquinas. Lonergan himself spent almost a decade of his life "reaching up to the mind of St. Thomas." Lonergan, *Insight*, 769. Through his vast knowledge of Scripture, the church fathers, and Aristotle, Thomas was able to articulate an understanding of Christian faith of enduring significance. He has unsurprisingly been portrayed as the be-all and end-all of Christian theological reflection. Leo XIII's commendation of Thomas's work in *Aeterni Patris*, and the resulting "Thomism(s)" of the twentieth century, bears witness to the historical fact of the lionization of "Thomas's" thought. Such an approach to Thomas, however, risks dehistoricizing Thomas's achievement. "To follow Aquinas today," writes Lonergan, "is not to repeat Aquinas today, but to do for the twentieth century what Aquinas did for the thirteenth" (Lonergan, "Theology and Man's Future," in *ASC*, 138 [CWL 13, 117]). The same holds true of Aristotle, or Augustine, or any other significant thinker in history.

43. Aristotle's understanding of the soul has indeed impressed many contemporary philosophers and psychologists. Michael Durant, for instance, notes that *De anima* "is not solely a work of interest to those who study the problems of ancient philosophy, but has a valuable contribution to make to contemporary philosophy and indeed, in one aspect at least, to contemporary science." Durant, "Preface," vii. For a strongly dissenting perspective, however, see Burnyeat, "Is an Aristotelian Philosophy of Mind Still Credible (A Draft)," 15–26.

44. English translation from Aristotle, *On the Soul*, 69. See also *De an.* 2.4 (415b9–415b10).

45. See *De an.* 2.3 (414b20–414b29). Lonergan argues that Aristotle's achievement is a systematic extension of Socrates's pursuit of *omni et soli* definitions. See Lonergan, "The Origins of Christian Realism [1972]," 252 (CWL 13, 213).

46. This is not to deny that Aristotle's use of these terms bears witness to his own developing understanding of the realities to which these terms refer. Aristotle undoubtedly does not employ these terms univocally or in a technical sense each and every time. He defines and utilizes a number of other technical terms throughout the work as well. See, e.g., his clarification of the definitions of "cause" (*aitia*) and "first principle" (*archē*) in 2.4 (415b9–415b29) and his discussion of how he utilizes "potentiality" (*dynameōs*) and "actuality" (*entelecheia*) in his discussion of sensation and the sensed in 2.5 (417a22–418a6).

47. English translation from Aristotle, *Posterior Analytics Topica*, 30. Lonergan cites or alludes to this passage frequently when he discusses Aristotle's ideal of science and its difference from the modern ideal of empirical science.

48. Lonergan, "The Future of Thomism," in *ASC*, 47 (CWL 13, 43). Lonergan notes that Aristotle does ultimately ground this notion of science in the constitution of the soul in its "intuitions" of first principles. These first principles, however, modern science sees only as "insights" that are subject to verification. See Lonergan, "Horizons and Transpositions," 422–25.

49. "Magnificently," Lonergan writes in *Method*, "[Aristotle] represented an early stage of human development—the emergence of systematic meaning." *MIT*, 310 (CWL 14, 289).

50. See Lonergan, *MIT*, 311 (CWL 14, 289–90); and especially Lonergan, "Method: Trend and Variations," in *ATC*, 13–22 (CWL 16, 10–20).

51. Later in his career, Lonergan argued that Aristotle could not be blamed for his lesser imitators' irresponsible adherence to the ideal of necessary knowledge of causes of the *Posterior Analytics*. See Lonergan, "Second Lecture: Religious Knowledge," in *ATC*, 136 (CWL 16, 131).

52. Lonergan, "The Future of Thomism," in *ASC*, 48 (CWL 13, 43).

53. Lonergan, "The Subject," in *ASC*, 72 (CWL 13, 62).

54. Lonergan, "The Subject," in *ASC*, 72 (CWL 13, 62). Lonergan's use of the phrase "primitive cultures" here is unfortunate. He is no advocate of some modern narrative of the march of modern man out of the dark ages of the superstitious tradition of savage primitives. He is well aware of the evils of modern culture manifest in the brutalities of industrialism, jingoism, modern warfare, eugenics, genocide, etc. He is equally aware of the authentic cultural achievements of non-Western premodern cultures and traditions. His language in this quotation, however, does not reflect how such awareness should impact responsible discussion of the histories of human cultures.

55. See Lonergan, "Transition from a Classicist World-View," in *ASC*, 3 (CWL 13, 5).

56. See Lonergan, "Transition from a Classicist World-View," in *ASC*, 3 (CWL 13, 4–5).

57. See Lonergan, "Transition from a Classicist World-View," in *ASC*, 5–6 (CWL 13, 6–7). It is possible, though, to read Aristotle (and Aquinas) as preoccupied not with the ideal of necessity but instead with wisdom. See Lonergan, "Horizons and Transpositions," 424.

58. Hector, to be sure, notes that not all metaphysics are equally distorting. See Hector, *Theology without Metaphysics*, 2–3. I follow Lonergan in his promotion of a "non-necessitarian" metaphysics. See Lonergan, *Insight*, 410–55. Before the question of what being or the real is can be answered, we must ask and answer two prior questions. Adequate answers to the questions, What am I doing when I am knowing? and Why is doing that knowing?, must precede an answer to the question of metaphysics, What do I know when I do that? See Lonergan, *Insight*, passim; Lonergan, "Theories of Inquiry," in *ASC*, 37 (CWL 13, 35).

59. The hypothetical is "an instance of the logical that has some likelihood of being relevant to an understanding of the data of sense or of consciousness." Lonergan, "Insight Revisited," in *ASC*, 274 (CWL 13, 230).

60. Lonergan, "Theology in Its New Context," in *ASC*, 61 (CWL 13, 53–54).

61. For brief autobiographical remarks on his personal development prior to and subsequent to *Insight*, see Lonergan, "Insight Revisited," in *ASC*, 263–78 (CWL

13, 221–33). For a helpful and concise account of Lonergan's notion of the subject, see Doran, *Theology and the Dialectics of History*, 19–41. For a history of Lonergan's intellectual development through *Insight*, see Mathews, *Lonergan's Quest*; for Lonergan's development subsequent to *Insight*, see Whelan, *Redeeming History*.

62. Strictly speaking, the proof or disproof of this thesis will depend upon its usefulness as a generalized heuristic for identifying the constituents of human nature. Individual readers will have to judge its relative success or failure on the basis of their discernment of its adequacy or inadequacy to their own experience and understanding of their capacities as persons.

63. See Lonergan, "The Subject," in *ASC*, 80 (CWL 13, 69). Elsewhere Lonergan refers to this as the level of responsibility or conscience at which we achieve or fail to achieve moral self-transcendence. See Lonergan, "Self-Transcendence: Intellectual, Moral, Religious," 318, 322–25.

64. See Lonergan, *MIT*, 9 (CWL 14, 13).

65. See Lonergan, *MIT*, 105, 278, 282, 327, 340 (CWL 14, 101, 261, 265, 304, 315); Lonergan, "Natural Knowledge of God," in *ASC*, 129 (CWL 13, 109).

66. Chrétien, *Under the Gaze of the Bible*, ix.

67. As I have noted elsewhere, I intend to write a monograph that will articulate a hermeneutic for scriptural interpretation on the basis of the account of the nature and purpose of Scripture in the present work. The thesis of that work will be that Scripture is the preeminent linguistic witness to and means through which such self-transcendence is possible in human history.

68. As noted above, I do not intend to abandon the achievements of metaphysical accounts of the soul but instead focus on the normativity of the processes that made such achievements as Aristotle's possible. Lonergan emphasizes the continuity of his own position with a metaphysical notion of the soul, and I hope my own position reflects the influence of such achievements as well. "I do not mean that the metaphysical notion of the soul and of its properties is to be dropped," Lonergan states, "any more than I mean that logic is to be dropped. But I urge the necessity of self-appropriation of the subject, of coming to know at first hand oneself and one's own operations both as a believer and a theologian." Lonergan, "The Future of Thomism," *ASC*, 51 (CWL 13, 46).

69. This list is adapted from Lonergan, *MIT*, 6 (CWL 14, 10).

70. As we saw above, Aristotle indicates that an understanding of the soul is the most valuable kind of knowledge one could possess. See *De an.* 402a1–402a5.

71. As Charles Taylor helpfully indicates, the language and conception of "inwardness" and "outwardness" and their application to questions of human nature are modern developments with their own contingent histories. The relevance, usefulness, and objectivity of such conceptions and language is not self-evident in every human culture, historic or present. I use the language with Taylor's caution in mind. See Taylor, *Sources of the Self*, 111–207. Even with this caution in mind, however, Taylor affirms that there is some truth "in the idea that people always are

selves, that they distinguish inside from outside in all cultures? In one sense, there no doubt is. The really difficult thing is distinguishing the human universals from the historical constellations and not eliding the second into the first so that our particular way seems somehow inescapable for humans as such, as we are always tempted to do." Taylor, *Sources of the Self*, 112.

72. Lonergan calls this heightened self-awareness and self-possession "appropriation of one's own rational self-consciousness," or "self-appropriation." His primary goal in *Insight* is to facilitate such self-appropriation for his readers. See *Insight*, 11–24. He notes that self-appropriation is not easy and often can only come through a lengthy and bloody process. Constraints of time and space obviously prohibit the reproduction of the pedagogical arguments of *Insight* through which Lonergan attempts to help bring about that process in his readers. I direct readers interested in utilizing Lonergan's work to undertake that process to *Insight*, Lonergan's more terse account in *MIT*, 3–25 (CWL 14, 7–27), and Joseph Flanagan's helpful work *Quest for Self-Knowledge*. See also Tekippe, *Bernard Lonergan*.

73. The word is "misleading inasmuch as it suggests an inward inspection. Inward inspection is just myth. Its origin lies in the mistaken analogy that all cognitional events are to be conceived on the analogy of ocular vision." Lonergan, *MIT*, 8 (CWL 14, 12).

74. Lonergan, *MIT*, 8 (CWL 14, 12).

75. So Lonergan, who writes in a footnote in *Method in Theology*, "I am offering only a summary, . . . the summary can do no more than present a general idea. . . . [T]he process of self-appropriation occurs only slowly, and, usually, only through a struggle with some such book as *Insight*." Lonergan, *MIT*, 7n2 (CWL 14, 11n4).

76. See Lonergan, "The Human Good," 349.

77. Note the qualifier "adult," which I discuss in greater depth below.

78. Lonergan, *MIT*, 9 (CWL 14, 13); original emphasis.

79. On the metaphor "levels," see Lonergan, *MIT*, 9–10 (CWL 14, 13).

80. Lonergan, "The Subject," in *ASC*, 81 (CWL 13, 70).

81. See Lonergan, *MIT*, 13–14n4 (CWL 14, 17n11).

82. "The universe of proportionate being" is the existing, non-necessary universe that exists. See Lonergan, *Insight*, 533–34, 674–80.

83. See Lonergan, "The Subject," in *ASC*, 81n13 (CWL 13, 70n14).

84. For an introduction to the scholastic theory of the transcendentals, see Garcia, "The Transcendentals in the Middle Ages."

85. See Lonergan, "Horizons," 22; Lonergan, "Natural Knowledge of God," in *ASC*, 128 (CWL 13, 108).

86. For a brilliant account of the dependence of human rationality and moral agency on our embodiment and on our dependence upon others, see McIntyre, *Dependent Rational Animals*. The absence of the following "levels" of consciousness in disabled people—if that could even be proven—would by no means indicate that such individuals would be subhuman or lack human nature in any way.

87. On this point, see Lonergan, "Theories of Inquiry," in *ASC*, 35–36 (CWL 13, 33–34). For a brilliant and nuanced account of the dependence of consciousness upon physical, chemical, and biological substrates, its irreducibility to such substrates, and finally the higher intelligibilities of human consciousness that emerge from such substrates, see Helminiak, *Brain, Consciousness, and God*. See Crysdale and Ormerod, *Creator God, Evolving World*, 103–24, esp. 107–9; Humphreys, *Soul Dust*; Murphy, *Bodies and Souls*; Murphy, "Reductionism and Emergence"; Sokolowski, *Christian Faith and Human Understanding*, 151–64. For a general challenge to the extrascientific reductionism regnant in significant portions of the scientific community, see Cartwright, *The Dappled World*.

88. On emergence, see Lonergan, *Insight*, 144–50.

89. McIntyre, *Dependent Rational Animals*.

90. For the child, intersubjective interaction with adults is antecedent to the emergence of the child's interiority/self-consciousness; the latter depends upon the former. As Susan Eastman helpfully states, "Interaction itself motivates imitation and the further cognitive and emotional developments that follow, through a reciprocal mimetic interplay between adult and child." Eastman, *Paul and the Person*, 67.

91. I discuss this distinction in much greater depth below. On the distinction between the data of consciousness and the data of sense, see Lonergan, *Insight*, 299.

92. See Lonergan, "Self-Transcendence: Intellectual, Moral, Religious," 319–20; Lonergan, "Reality, Myth, Symbol," 387.

93. See Lonergan, "Reality, Myth, Symbol," 385. Lonergan speaks of the world mediated by meaning and motivated by belief frequently in his later works. See Lonergan, "The World Mediated by Meaning," 107–18; Lonergan, "Response of a Jesuit as Priest and Apostle," 169; Lonergan, *MIT*, 262–65 (CWL 14, 245–48); Lonergan, "Sacralization and Secularization," 278; Lonergan, "Self-Transcendence: Intellectual, Moral, Religious," 327–28; Lonergan, "The Human Good," 335, 339, 345; Lonergan, "Questionaire on Philosophy: Response," 363, 370, 371; and Lonergan, "Reality, Myth, Symbol," 385, 387, 389. He discusses the "world mediated by meaning" in depth without addressing how it is "motivated by value" as early as 1963 in Lonergan, "The Analogy of Meaning." See also Lonergan, *MIT*, 28–32, 76–95, 302–5 (CWL 14, 29–33, 74–91, 282–84). I will return to the topic of mediation and "the world mediated by meaning" in much greater depth below.

94. Crysdale and Ormerod, *Creator God*, 103. Later they quote Eric Fromm, "Man is the only animal for whom his own existence is a problem he has to solve and from which he cannot escape." See Crysdale and Ormerod, *Creator God, Evolving World*, 104; originally from Fromm, *Man for Himself*, 40.

95. Lonergan, *MIT*, 9 (CWL 14, 13).

96. See Lonergan, "Horizons," 10–29; Lonergan, "Merging Horizons: System, Common Sense, Scholarship"; and Lonergan, "Horizons and Transpositions."

97. Lonergan, "Horizons," 11.

98. Lonergan, "Horizons," 11.

99. See Lonergan, *MIT*, 57–99 (CWL 14, 55–95); I discuss this distinction in much greater depth below.

100. In fact, experimental psychologists have demonstrated that unself-conscious bodily mimesis is antecedent to self-awareness in infants. As Eastman summarizes, "Infants have an innate propensity for interpersonal connection long before the development of language or the capacity for abstract thought.... [P]arent and child act in concert with one another in an interpersonal dance at the very beginning of human development." Eastman, *Paul and the Person*, 66–67; see also 63–84.

101. Lonergan examines the famous story of Archimedes, who discovered how to determine whether King Heiro's crown was made of gold entirely or not by submerging it in water, to examine and explain the characteristics of insight in intellectual experience. See Lonergan, *Insight*, 27–31.

102. For examples that show the process and fruits of the intellectual level of consciousness in mathematics and physics, see Lonergan, *Insight*, 57–195.

103. "Jetzt weiß ich weiter." See Wittgenstein, *Philosophical Investigations*, § 151, 154, 155, 179, 181, 323, at 65e, 66e, 67e, 78e–79e, 112e. To be sure, Wittgenstein thinks that "mental processes are just strange" (Seelische Vorgänge sind eben merkwürdig). Wittgenstein, *Philosophical Investigations*, § 363 at 122g/122e. He refuses to speculate on the contents and structure of such an inner conscious activity. He is always concerned with the practical import of understanding and not with its constitution as an inner process. So he writes elsewhere, concerning the example of understanding how to play chess: "What would we reply to someone who told us that with him understanding was an inner process?—What would we reply to him if he said that with him knowing how to play chess was an inner process?—We'd say that when we want to know if he can play chess, we aren't interested in anything that goes on inside him. And if he retorts that this is in fact just what we are interested in, that is, in whether he can play chess then we should have to draw his attention to the criteria which would demonstrate his ability, and on the other hand to the criteria for 'inner states.'" Wittgenstein, *Philosophical Investigations*, § *36, at 190e. While I find his emphasis on the fruit of understanding exceptionally helpful, I find his refusal to examine mental acts potentially obfuscating. His reticence to investigate such acts may stem from his distaste for psychology, which he inherited from Frege. For helpful discussion of the relationship between Lonergan's understanding of understanding and Wittgenstein's, see Beards, " *Übersicht* as Oversight"; Fitzpatrick, "Descartes under Fire"; Meynell, "Doubts about Wittgenstein's Influence"; Meynell, "Lonergan, Wittgenstein, and Where Language Hooks onto the World."

104. Lonergan, *Insight*, 196. For much more extensive discussion of common-sense intelligence, see Lonergan, *Insight*, 196–269. Later in *Insight* Lonergan gives the following useful definition of common sense: "Common sense is that vague name given to the unknown source of a large and floating population of elementary judgments which everyone makes, everyone relies on, and almost everyone regards as obvious and indisputable" (314).

105. On "forms of life," or *Lebensformen*, see Wittgenstein, *Philosophical Investigations*, § 19, 23, at 11e, 15e.

106. Lonergan, "Self-Transcendence: Intellectual, Moral, Religious," 317. See also Lonergan, "Faith and Beliefs," 34.

107. Hefling, *Why Doctrines?*, 2.

108. There are at least two possible ways to understand objects, or the objective. With Immanuel Kant we could understand the object as that which stands against us (*Gegenstand*) which we can only gape at and never reach. For a Kantian, the phenomenal is out there and the noumenal in here, and never the twain shall meet. A second understanding of objects is possible, however. It is possible to understand an object as that which is "intended in questions" and understood in true insights. For a brief Lonerganian rejoinder to Kant, see Lonergan, "Natural Knowledge of God," in *ASC*, 121–24 (CWL 13, 103–5). For Lonergan's more extensive critiques of Kant, see Lonergan, *Insight*, 362–66, 438–40; and Lonergan, *Understanding and Being*, 156–80. For a thorough exposition of the relationship between Lonergan's positions on knowledge and Kant's by a recognized scholar of both Kant and Lonergan, see Sala, *Lonergan and Kant*.

109. Lonergan refers to this position on epistemology as "naïve realism." See Lonergan, *MIT*, 263–64, 341 (CWL 14, 247, 316). See also Lonergan, *Insight*, 437, 529, 598, 647.

110. There are, of course, countless instances of human knowledge not typically mediated through language, hypothesis, or concept. Know-how is still human knowledge. The kind of know-how involved in actually playing soccer, painting a masterpiece, playing the piano, or countless other human activities is a kinesthetic knowledge which resists objectification in language. It is performative knowledge. The kinds of insights and judgments—such performance does still entail insight and judgment—that enable such know-how elude objectification in hypothesis or language.

111. Lonergan, "Theories of Inquiry," *ASC*, 36 (CWL 13, 34).

112. Again, see the earlier discussion of Wittgenstein.

113. Lonergan argues that we reach true judgments when we achieve, through reflective insight, a grasp of the virtually unconditioned. It is a hypothesis whose conditions are fulfilled. Lonergan gives a thorough account of the level of judgment and the processes and requirements of judgments in *Insight*, 296–340.

114. Lonergan, "Self-Transcendence: Intellectual, Moral, Religious," 317.

115. Lonergan, "The World Mediated by Meaning," 109.

116. Lonergan, "Cognitional Structure," 219.

117. Lonergan, "Self-Transcendence: Intellectual, Moral, Religious," 315.

118. Our judgments of value, just like our insights and judgments of what is the case, are not infallible. I discuss the unique criteria of authenticity at the level of decision and action below.

119. Lonergan, *MIT*, 292 (CWL 14, 273).

120. Lonergan, "Cognitional Structure," 213.

121. Lonergan calls this dynamic drive "vertical finality." See Lonergan, "Mission and the Spirit," 24.

122. Lonergan, *MIT*, 13 (CWL 14, 16).

123. See Lonergan, "Horizons," 13.

124. For a recent lucid account of the relevance of this judgment for historical investigation of the texts of the New Testament, see Bernier, *The Quest for the Historical Jesus*, passim, but esp. 159–63.

125. De Lubac, "The Problem of the Development of Dogma," 275.

126. Lonergan makes this explicit of his own account of human subjectivity in *Method in Theology*: "Clearly it [the present account of human nature] is not transcultural inasmuch as it is explicitly formulated. *But it is transcultural in the realities to which the formulation refers, for these realities are not the product of any culture but, on the contrary, the principles that produce cultures, preserve them, and develop them.* Moreover, since it is to these realities we refer when we speak of homo sapiens, it follows that these realities are transcultural with respect to truly human cultures." Lonergan, *MIT*, 282 (CWL 14, 264); emphasis mine. Lonergan's own technical account of the capacities of human persons and their intrinsic interrelations is, of course, bounded by the limitations of its idiom. It is therefore subject to modification and even correction through subsequent advances in understanding and through the development of new linguistic tools for objectifying the processes and operations of consciousness. But the very fact that such advances are possible and that they take place—and do so in conformity with the subjective capacities and exigencies Lonergan has disentangled and objectified—suggests the permanence of Lonergan's achievement. As noted above, our consciousness operates within but cannot be reduced to its biological basis in the metabolic and sensitive capacities characteristic of human life. Its full reach is also contingent upon the "normal" unfolding of personal development on an individual-by-individual basis. I discuss specific impediments to such development in greater depth below.

127. Lonergan, "Theology in Its New Context," in *ASC*, 61–62 (CWL 13, 54). Lonergan is alluding to Ps 19.1.

128. For Lonergan's discussion of the symbolic dimension of human nature, see Lonergan, "First Lecture: Religious Experience," in *ATC*, 115 (CWL 16, 111); Lonergan, "Second Lecture: Religious Knowledge," in *ATC*, 141 (CWL 16, 128); and Lonergan, "Third Lecture: The Ongoing Genesis of Methods," in *ATC*, 161–62 (CWL 16, 155–56).

129. Certain animals, such as dolphins and chimpanzees, among others, have highly sophisticated "languages" for communication. Certain others communicate in seemingly miraculous ways, as evidenced in the integrity and beauty of the coordinated movements of herds of mammals and flocks of birds. Even so, there are no dolphin libraries, chimpanzee universities, gazelle scriptoria, or macaw-produced historical treatises. I risk venturing the judgment that none of those animals is cur-

rently or ever will be able to read these words. For lucid discussion of the distinctions and similarities between human and nonhuman animals regarding language, see McIntyre, *Dependent Rational Animals*, 12–79.

130. As Hefling notes, "Noticing what we have no words for is unlikely but not impossible." Hefling, *Why Doctrines?*, 12.

131. It would take us too far afield to research, analyze, and evaluate these contemporary studies. Moreover, to the extent that these studies maintain behaviorist and positivist conceptions of human nature, sorting the gold from the dross would prove an extremely involved endeavor.

132. Lonergan is well aware of this fact, and adverts to the linguistic nestedness of his account of human subjectivity in *MIT*: "The explicit formulation of the method is historically conditioned and can be expected to be corrected, modified, complemented as the sciences continue to advance and reflection on them improves. What is transcultural is the reality to which such formulation refers, and that *reality is transcultural because it is not the product of any culture but rather the principle that begets and develops cultures* that flourish, as it also is the principle that is violated when cultures crumble and decay" (Lonergan, *MIT*, 283 [CWL 14, 265]); emphasis mine. In this quotation, Lonergan refers not to the specialized method that theology employs but to the "transcendental method," or "generalized empirical method," that undergirds all specialized methods of human knowing. See Lonergan, *MIT*, 13–25 (CWL 14, 17–27), for Lonergan's discussion of transcendental method and its functions. On "generalized empirical method," see Lonergan, *Insight*, 95–96, 268–96.

133. In his own work Lonergan drew extensively on the work of the educational psychologist Jean Piaget to make this point. For Lonergan's appropriation of Piaget, see Lonergan, *MIT*, 27–29 (CWL 14, 28–31); Lonergan, "The Human Good," 334–36. See Piaget, *The Origins of Intelligence*.

134. For Plato on the acquisition of the forms through anamnesis, see *Meno* 80a–86c and *Phaed.* 73c–78b. For Augustine's account of his acquisition of language, see *Conf.* 1.6.8, 1.8.13. Lonergan utilizes "trial and error" to identify what Piaget has more technically labeled assimilation, adjustment, and grouping; see Lonergan, "The Human Good," 335; Piaget, *The Psychology of Intelligence*, 8–10, 40–52. For a non-Lonerganian account of language acquisition that draws on Piaget, see Erneling, *Understanding Language Acquisition*.

135. Piaget labels this the "sensorimotor stage." See Piaget, *The Origin of Intelligence*, 21–262.

136. For Piaget's thorough discussion of this development, see Piaget, *The Origin of Intelligence*. For helpful discussion of the prelinguistic nature of questions, see Byrne, *The Ethics of Discernment*, 38–41.

137. On intersubjectivity, see Lonergan, *MIT*, 57–59, 60–61 (CWL 14, 56–57, 58–59). For a complementary discussion of language acquisition that highlights the importance of intersubjectivity for those processes, see Sokolowski, *Phenomenology of the Human Person*, 58–67.

138. See note 93 above for references.

139. Lonergan, "The Human Good," 335.

140. Lonergan, "The Human Good," 335.

141. Lonergan, *MIT*, 71 (CWL 14, 68–69). He goes on to state that "grammar almost gives us Aristotle's categories of substance, quantity, quality, relation, action, passion, place, time, posture, habit, while Aristotle's logic and theory of science are deeply rooted in the grammatical function of predication."

142. See Lonergan, *MIT*, 70 (CWL 14, 67). Lonergan writes that meaning itself achieves its greatest liberation in language.

143. See Austin, *How to Do Things with Words*.

144. Lonergan, *MIT*, 28 (CWL 14, 29).

145. See Lonergan, *MIT*, 76–77 (CWL 14, 74–75).

146. See Lonergan, "Theology in Its New Context," in *ASC*, 62 (CWL 13, 54).

147. I discuss this judgment in much greater depth in chapter 6 in the section on the place of Scripture in the mission of the Son of God in history.

148. See Lonergan, *MIT*, 41–47 (CWL 14, 42–47).

149. Lonergan, *MIT*, 41.

150. See Lonergan, *MIT*, 42–43 (CWL 14, 43–44); Lonergan, "Method: Trend and Variations," 14–15.

151. Lonergan, *MIT*, 43 (CWL 14, 44).

152. Experts, to be sure, are not infallible. They are beholden to the same exigencies of self-transcendence as nonexperts. They are prone to the same kinds of errors too, and their expertise may contribute to a sort of delusion of omnicompetence in fields or disciplines different from their own. I discuss this at greater length below.

153. See Lonergan, "The Transition from a Classicist World-View," in *ASC*, 1–9 (CWL 13, 3–10).

154. Doran, *What Is Systematic Theology?*, 144.

155. Lonergan first broaches the subject of classicism in his published works in "*Existenz* and *Aggiornamento*," 228. This essay appeared in print in 1965. He had already spoken of classicism, however, as early as 1949. See *Collection*, CWL 4, 307t. Lonergan treats classicism extensively in the essays that appear in *ASC*, especially "The Transition from a Classicist World-View," 1–9 (CWL 13, 3–10).

156. Lonergan, "Theology and Man's Future," in *ASC*, 141 (CWL 13, 119).

157. I use the masculine pronoun here intentionally.

158. See Lonergan, "Belief: Today's Issue," in *ASC*, 92 (CWL 13, 79); Lonergan, "The Absence of God in Modern Culture," in *ASC*, 101 (CWL 13, 86); and Lonergan, "The Future of Christianity," in *ASC*, 161 (CWL 13, 119).

159. See Young, *Biblical Exegesis*. While Young writes independently of an awareness of Lonergan's notion of classicism (as far as I can tell), her argument that Christian exegetical praxis underwrote the early church's formation of a "totalizing discourse enshrining an encompassing worldview or ideology" (Young, *Biblical Exegesis*, 257) identifies the classicist impulse present in early Christianity.

160. See Lonergan, "Belief: Today's Issue," 92 (CWL 13, 79). Lonergan calls the contemporary notion of culture "modern," but I think that term may be an obstacle to understanding what he is trying to explain. Many early modern thinkers, in their emphasis on replacing traditional authorities with empirically grounded and/or rationally rigorous attempts to rethink previous positions, were still beholden to the classicist ideal of certain stable knowledge. On this tendency in rationalism, see Lonergan, "The Subject," in *ASC*, 72 (CWL 13, 62–63). To risk an oversimplification, in the Enlightenment, the intelligibility of change was first conceived mechanistically and only later as statistically intelligible. The mechanistic notion of change maintains the classicist ideal of sure and certain knowledge. On mechanistic and statistical conceptions of change and on emergence, see Lonergan, *Insight*, 102–7, 146–51. The renewal of a classicist notion of culture, besides its inadequacy to the reality of cultural plurality in the concrete, could not be reinstated without a return to the decisively modern colonialism or imperialism it underwrote. As Lonergan writes, the "classicist would feel it was perfectly legitimate for him to impose his culture on others. For he conceives culture normatively, and he conceives his own to be the norm." *MIT*, 363 (CWL 14, 334).

161. Martin, *Biblical Truths*, 216.

162. "Modern culture conceives itself empirically and concretely. It is the culture that recognizes cultural variation, difference, development, breakdown, that investigates each of the many cultures of mankind, that studies their histories, that seeks to understand what the classicist would tend to write off as strange or uncultivated or barbaric." Lonergan, "The Future of Christianity," in *ASC*, 161 (CWL 13, 137).

163. I address this challenge in the next two chapters.

164. Origen and Augustine had already recognized and emphasized the usefulness and limitations of language. As Origen writes in *Princ.*, "Let everyone, then, who cares for truth, care little about names and words, for different kinds of speech are customary in different nations. Let him be more anxious about the fact signified than about the words by which it is signified, and particularly in questions of such difficulty and importance as these" (4.3.15). Augustine recurrently treats the instrumental nature of language and its slipperiness and limitations throughout *Doctr. chr.* See especially his discussion of the sign character of language in book 1 and the entirety of book 3, which is devoted to ambiguous linguistic signs in Scripture.

165. Lonergan, "Self-Transcendence: Intellectual, Moral, Religious," 320. See also Lonergan, "The World Mediated by Meaning," 109; Lonergan, *MIT*, 77 (CWL 14, 75); Lonergan, "The Origins of Christian Realism [1972]," in *ASC*, 241 (CWL 13, 204).

166. For further reflection on art and symbol, see Lonergan, *MIT*, 61–69 (CWL 14, 59–67); Lonergan, *Topics in Education*, CWL 10, 208–32. Randy Rosenberg has provided a cogent argument that Lonergan's discussion of art in *Topics* provides a useful heuristic for understanding premodern symbolic or allegorical interpretation of Scripture. See Rosenberg, "The Drama of Scripture," 126–48.

167. See Snell and Cone, *Authentic Cosmopolitanism*. For another recent work that has highlighted the importance of desire in theological reflection, see Smith, *Desiring the Kingdom*.

168. Lonergan, *MIT*, 30 (CWL 14, 32).

169. Lonergan, *MIT*, 31 (CWL 14, 32); emphasis mine.

170. Lonergan, *MIT*, 30 (CWL 14, 32). See also Lonergan, "An Interview," in *ASC*, 220–23 (CWL 13, 186–88).

171. Lonergan, *MIT*, 31 (CWL 14, 32).

172. The testimony of the synoptic gospels concerning Christ's prayer to the Father in the Garden of Gethsemane illustrates an instance when the truly good—the possibility or even inevitability of Christ's imminent death—was disagreeable at the level of personal preference (see Mark 14.32–36; Matt 26.36–42; Luke 22.41–44).

173. Lonergan, *MIT*, 31–32 (CWL 14, 32–33). For a remarkable and learned exposition of the scale of values and the structure of human history, see Doran, *Theology and the Dialectics of History*.

174. Lonergan, *MIT*, 32 (CWL 14, 33).

175. Fowl, *Theological Interpretation of Scripture*, 45.

176. Fowl, *Theological Interpretation of Scripture*, 45.

177. Lonergan, "Self-Transcendence: Intellectual, Moral, Religious," 315.

178. Sarisky draws on the work of Charles Taylor (particularly Taylor's *Sources of the Self*) to emphasize the importance of recognizing the dramatic character of human living in his recent work on scriptural interpretation and Christian formation. See Sarisky, *Scriptural Interpretation*, 42.

179. Lonergan, "Self-Transcendence: Intellectual, Moral, Religious," 314.

180. Lonergan, "Self-Transcendence: Intellectual, Moral, Religious," 315.

181. Lonergan, "Self-Transcendence: Intellectual, Moral, Religious," 315.

182. See Lonergan, *Insight*, 251.

183. It is also possible that our psychic or dramatic conditioning can keep us from asking relevant questions or having relevant insights. Such dramatic bias is almost entirely outside of our conscious control. On dramatic bias and its remedy in psychic conversion, see Doran, *Theology and the Dialectics of History*, 33, 42–63.

184. See Lonergan, *Insight*, 244–47.

185. Lonergan, *Insight*, 245.

186. Lonergan, *Insight*, 247–50.

187. Lonergan, "The Absence of God in Modern Culture," in *ASC*, 102 (CWL 13, 87). Such structures and organizations, history has taught us, however, are subject to development and breakdown as much as they are subject to such cyclical recurrence.

188. For a thorough accounting of these dynamics, see Doran, *Theology and the Dialectics of History*.

189. See Lonergan, *Insight*, 248–49. Doran has identified this social dialectic, the "dialectic of community," as one of three major dialectics identifiable in the

processes of historical development and regression. See Doran, *Theology and the Dialectics of History*, 355–472.

190. See Lonergan, *Insight*, 249.

191. See Lonergan's stark and honest discussion in *MIT*, 80 (CWL 14, 77).

192. Lonergan, *MIT*, 80 (CWL 14, 77).

193. See Lonergan, *Insight*, 250–67.

194. Lonergan, *Insight*, 251.

195. Traditionally, certain construals of the inerrancy of Scripture have kept Christian thinkers from arguing that the human intentions of the authors of Scripture could themselves be sinful. Kenton Sparks has recently offered a robust challenge to that judgment, however. See Sparks, *Sacred Word, Broken Word*.

196. For a number of disturbing examples, see Siebert, *The Violence of Scripture*. The refusal to recognize the historicity or historical locatedness of the language and cultures of Scripture may represent a manifestation of general bias.

197. Fowl, *Theological Interpretation of Scripture*, 44.

198. For more on religious conversion, see Lonergan, "Self-Transcendence: Intellectual, Moral, Religious," 325–29; for Lonergan's earlier discussion of sanctifying grace as *sanans et elevans*, which he would later identify with religious conversion, see Lonergan, "De ente supernaturali/The Supernatural Order."

199. Lonergan, "Natural Knowledge of God," in *ASC*, 129 (CWL 13, 110).

200. Lonergan, "Self-Transcendence: Intellectual, Moral, Religious," 326.

201. Snell and Cone, *Authentic Cosmopolitanism*, 107.

202. Lonergan, "Self-Transcendence: Intellectual, Moral, Religious," 326.

203. The experience of that acceptance transforms our nonintentional psyche, too, in what Doran has described as psychic conversion. In addition to the data of our intentional, spiritual consciousness, there are also data of consciousness in the nonintentional flow of our conscious experience. As Doran writes, "The habitual orientation of our intelligence and affectivity exercises a censorship over the emergence into consciousness of the images that are the psychic representation and conscious integration of an underlying neural manifold. But that censorship can be either constructive or repressive" (Doran, *Theology and the Dialectics of History*, 59–60). Psychic conversion is the liberation of the psyche from repressive to constructive censorship. It is a reorientation away from dysfunctional unadverted self-deception towards openness to previously painful truths. For more, see Doran, *Theology and the Dialectics of History*, 42–63. I intend to discuss the implications of psychic conversion for engagement with Scripture in a future monograph. See note 8 above and notes 149, 154, and 180 in chapter 6 for descriptions of that project.

204. Lonergan often discussed moral conversion prior to his discussion of religious conversion but argued that the concrete religious conversion more often preceded moral conversion. For an excellent account of the relationship between moral and religious conversion in Lonergan's work, see Cone, "Transforming Desire."

205. Lonergan, "Faith and Beliefs," 38–39.

206. On the Law of the Cross, see note 132 in chapter 3.

207. See Lonergan, *MIT*, 273–76 (CWL 14, 256–58).

208. Lonergan, *MIT*, 274 (CWL 14, 257). The achievements of historical criticism and historical-grammatical biblical exegesis reflect the fruits of scholarly differentiated consciousness. I return to the significance of these developments for engagement with Scripture in chapter 6.

209. See Lonergan, *MIT*, 273 (CWL 14, 256).

210. Lonergan, "Horizons and Transpositions," 419.

211. Though many of the texts of Scripture, of course, had oral "lives" prior to the time they were committed to writing. The texts also "live on" apart from their material instantiations in the memories of individuals and communities; they also "live" in being recited. I discuss this point at greater length in the next chapter.

CHAPTER FIVE. Scripture in History I

1. On the larger (81-book) canon of the Tewahedo Ethiopian Church, see Cowley, "The Biblical Canon."

2. The reader may recognize that each respective question—of material realities, of agents of production, of formal intelligibility, and of purpose—is roughly parallel to Aristotle's material, efficient (and instrumental), formal, and final causes. At an earlier stage of my reflection on the structure of this work I planned on utilizing Aristotle's causes as a heuristic for organizing the material for this chapter and chapter 6. I discovered shortly thereafter that there is a long tradition of utilizing Aristotle's understanding of causation, especially the relationship between efficient causality and instrumental causality, to understand Scripture. For discussion, see Achtemeier, *Inspiration and Authority*, 11–15; Froelich, *Sensing the Scriptures*, 40; Froelich, "Interpretation of the Old Testament," 522–24; Minnis, *Medieval Theory of Authorship*; Vawter, *Biblical Inspiration*, 43–75.

3. See Gordon, "St. Thomas Aquinas"; Reinhardt, "Thomas Aquinas as Interpreter of Scripture."

4. The translation of Bar 4.1 comes from Aquinas, "The Inaugural Lectures," 5. For an examination of this text and of the genre of the resumption *principia*, see Gordon, "St. Thomas Aquinas." For English translation of this sermon, see Aquinas, "The Inaugural Lectures," 5–17.

5. See Gordon, "St. Thomas Aquinas," 261–68.

6. For discussion of the premodern judgments that constituted such "high" views of scripture, see Allert, *A High View of Scripture?*

7. Ceslas Spicq notes that Thomas uses the *correctoria* of Hugh of St. Victor, but Thomas did not engage in textual criticism himself as we understand it. See Spicq, *Esquisse d'une histoire*, 165–72. Frans van Liere argues that modern text-critical scholarship has "its roots in the traditions of biblical criticism of the Middle Ages." *An Introduction*, 15.

8. And we do not know, for instance, if Thomas gestured to a particular copy of the book as he stated, "Hic est liber mandatorum Dei!" Mark Johnson has suggested, in personal conversation, that Thomas might have gestured just as easily towards a lectionary copy of the Bible as to a pandect containing both Testaments.

9. Earlier figures such as Melito of Sardis (ca. AD 180) and Origen (ca. AD 220–30) do not list it among the ancient Jewish scriptures. Athanasius (AD 367), Cyril of Jerusalem (AD 350), and Epiphanius (ca. AD 374–77) include it in lists of canonical books. It appears in the major majescules Vaticanus (4th c. AD) and Alexandrinus (5th c. AD) but not Sinaiticus (4th c. AD), though sections of that manuscript are missing after Lamentations and before Joel. It does not appear in most Western lists around the same period. Hilary of Portiers lists the Epistle of Jeremiah but not Baruch (ca. AD 350–65). Neither Jerome nor Augustine judges it canonical, though they may have thought it was included with Jeremiah. For discussion and evaluation of these ancient sources, see McDonald, *The Biblical Canon*, 200–206, 439–42. For a thorough examination of the textual history of Baruch, see Adams, *Baruch and the Epistle to Jeremiah*, 1–32.

10. For discussion, see Adams, *Baruch and the Epistle of Jeremiah*, 2–3, 8; Bogaert, "Le livre de Baruch"; Mukenge, "Les Particularités des Témoins Latins de Baruch."

11. For discussion of scholarly proposals on the dating and provenance of the work, see Adams, *Baruch and the Epistle to Jeremiah*, 4–6.

12. See Adams, *Baruch and the Epistle to Jeremiah*, 3.

13. As Adams writes: "The location of wisdom is notably different in Baruch, which claims that wisdom is exclusively to be found in Israel. Not only do the other nations lack wisdom, they are unable to find it no matter how hard they look. Conversely, Israel has been given wisdom by God through the Torah. Wisdom, as embodied by Torah, is God's unique gift to the people of Israel and functions in such a way as to differentiate Israel from all other nations. Although other nations might possess people of intellect, they are still lacking wisdom, as wisdom can come only from God, and God has given a record of it only to Israel. It is this exclusivity that exemplifies Baruch's unique literary perspective: hypostatised wisdom is conceived of as embodied in Torah, Israel's unique gift and privilege from God (cf. Deut 4.6–8)." Adams, *Baruch and the Epistle to Jeremiah*, 115.

14. In Vaticanus, that verse reads as follows: "αὕτη ἡ βίβλος τῶν προσταγμάτων τοῦ θεοῦ καὶ ὁ νόμος ὁ ὑπάρχων εἰς τὸν αἰῶνα." See Adams, *Baruch and the Epistle to Jeremiah*, 42.

15. The Latin text of Thomas's Bible would likely have had *prudentia* (see 3.9, 3.14, 3.23 in the Clementine Vulgate) or *sapientia* (see 3.12, 3.23, 3.28), both feminine. This peculiar and unwarranted change demonstrates the kind of slippage that has taken place in the transmission of all texts of antiquity. For penetrating discussion of such slippage and its possible impacts on theological reflection, see David Bentley Hart's astute comments on the Latin translation of Rom 5.12 in Hart, *The New Testament*, 296–97.

16. There is no doubt that Thomas's world, particularly thirteenth-century Paris, was remarkably diverse culturally. Nevertheless, contemporary historians know more about the diversity of Thomas's world than he did.

17. On the contrast between Thomas's philosophical presuppositions and those necessary for adequately understanding and evaluating historical change and the variability of cultures, see Lonergan, "Aquinas Today: Tradition and Innovation."

18. See, e.g., Avalos, *The End of Biblical Studies*, 339–42.

19. For extensive and insightful discussion of the location of Scripture in these communal churchly contexts in the first few centuries of Christian history, see Young, *Biblical Exegesis*, 217–247; see also Stroumsa, *The Scriptural Universe*, 10–28. For poignant comments on the historical value and reverence given the text, see Charles Hefling, *Why Doctrines?*, 117–19.

20. The epigraphs of the next chapter serve as explicit testimony that the authors of Scripture recognized the ancient Jewish Scriptures as having such usefulness and intended their own writings to have such usefulness.

21. The *Cambridge History of the Bible* and *New Cambridge History of the Bible* are exemplary starting points for investigating the material history of the Christian Bible. See Ackroyd and Evans, *The Cambridge History of the Bible*; Lampe, *The Cambridge History of the Bible*; Greenslade, *The Cambridge History of the Bible*; Paget and Schaper, *The New Cambridge History of the Bible*; Marsden and Matter, *The New Cambridge History of the Bible*; Cameron, *The New Cambridge History of the Bible*; and Riches, *The New Cambridge History of the Bible*. Other important works include Boynton and Reilly, *The Practice of the Bible in the Middle Ages*; Carr, *Writing on the Tablet of the Heart*; Gamble, *Books and Readers*; Grafton and Williams, *Christianity and the Transformation of the Book*; Hurtado, *The Earliest Christian Artifacts*; Piazzoni with Manzari, *The Bible*; Roberts and Skeat, *The Birth of the Codex*; Schniedewind, *How the Bible Became a Book*; Stroumsa, *The Scriptural Universe*; Turner, *Typology of the Early Codex*; Van der Toorn, *Scribal Culture*; van Liere, *An Introduction*. See also Siker, *Liquid Scripture*, for a recent examination of the significance and impacts of digital technologies for engaging Scripture.

22. *Manuscript* comes from the Latin *manu* (by hand) *scriptus* (past participle of *scribere* "to write"). The history of ancient scribal practices is fascinating, but to do it justice would take us too far afield. For extensive discussion, though, see Carr, *Writing on the Tablet of the Heart*; Rollston, *Writing and Literacy*; Haines-Eitzen, *Guardians of Letters*; Reynolds and Wilson, *Scribes and Scholars*; Römer and Davies, *Writing the Bible*.

23. My own students, many of whom are actually well acquainted with the content of Scripture, are often baffled and disturbed when I point them to the footnotes in their personal Bibles that indicate that the ending of Mark (16.9–20) and the ordeal of the suspected adulteress (John 7.53–8.11) do not appear in many of the earliest and most important manuscripts of Mark and John. Biblical illiteracy extends beyond a lack of awareness of the content of Scripture; very few are aware

of what Scripture actually is and has been. For discussion, see Ehrman and Wallace, "The Textual Reliability."

24. The word is Greek in origin—from *pan* (all) *dektēs* (receiver)—and originally referred to Byzantine legal texts that were comprehensive in nature. See van Liere, *An Introduction*, 25.

25. "In fact," he continues, "the word 'Bible' itself indicates as much: our English term comes from what was originally a Greek plural, *ta biblía* ('the books')— this is how the Greek-speaking Jews of Alexandria in ancient times referred to Judaism's sacred library." While Kugel's statements have the Tanakh as their referent, his judgment is true of the Christian scriptures as well. Kugel, *How to Read the Bible*, 6.

26. See van Liere, *An Introduction*, 26. For helpful discussion of the significance of Cassiodorus's innovations and achievements in the history of the transmission of the Bible, see Gamble, *Books and Readers*, 198–202. In *ME*, de Lubac marshals a number of eleventh- and twelfth-century witnesses to the practice of calling Christian Scripture a "sacred library" or "heavenly library." De Lubac identifies references to the Bible as a library as late as the time of Peter Abelard (1079–1142) and Albricius (ca. 1209). See de Lubac, *ME*, 1:247, 1:443nn92–94.

27. Gamble, *Books and Readers*, 80. "Indeed" he writes, "there are no examples from the pre-Constantinian period of manuscripts containing even a complete New Testament, whose scope was still indeterminate." Gamble holds that the "Bibles" that Constantine commissioned Eusebius of Caesarea to produce were not likely pandects because they were to be quickly produced and portable. Gamble, *Books and Readers*, 79–80.

28. See Gamble, *Books and Readers*, 80.

29. See Light, "The Bible and the Individual," 228–246; van Liere, *An Introduction*, 10, 20, 25, 56.

30. Boynton and Reilly, "Orientation for the Reader," 1–2. So also Frans van Liere, who writes, "The modern conception of the Bible, as a single volume of portable size containing all of the Old and New Testaments, is essentially a medieval invention." *An Introduction*, 3. He dates their invention to the third decade of the thirteenth century (20).

31. So van Liere, *An Introduction*, 25.

32. Grafton and Williams, *Christianity and the Transformation of the Book*, 12.

33. For discussion of the production of papyrus, see Gamble, *Books and Readers*, 44–46; for discussion of the production of parchment/vellum, see Gamble, *Books and Readers*, 46. See also Roberts and Skeat, *The Birth of the Codex*, 5–10. On rolls/scrolls in antiquity, see Johnson, *Bookrolls and Scribes*.

34. The word *codex* comes from the Latin *caudex*, meaning "block of wood." See Gamble, *Books and Readers*, 50. For more thorough discussion of this historical development, see Roberts and Skeat, *The Birth of the Codex*; Gamble, *Books and Readers*, 42–81; Turner, *Typology of the Codex*. Gamble notes that the earliest

explicit mention of a parchment codex in Greek literature is found in Paul's words to Timothy in 2 Tim 4.13: "When you come, bring the cloak that I left with Carpus at Troas, also the books (τὰ βιβλία), and above all the parchments (τὰς μεμβράνας)." Gamble holds that if he meant to refer to parchment scrolls, Paul would have used the readily available, standard word διφθέραι instead of τὰς μεμβράνας. See Gamble, *Books and Readers*, 50, 64.

35. Gamble, *Books and Readers*, 49. Prior to the third century AD, Gamble notes, more than 98 percent of extant Greek books are rolls. Extant Christian books, especially Scripture, on the contrary, are almost exclusively codices from the start. Gamble, *Books and Readers*, 49. "Christian scholars like Origen and Jerome," writes Frances Young, "reverted to the roll for their literary works, thus confirming the peculiarity of Christian custom." Young, *Biblical Exegesis*, 14. Guy Stroumsa captures the bizarreness of the Christian adoption of the codex by calling Christianity "a religion of the paperback." Stroumsa, *The Scriptural Universe*, 21. Stroumsa's judgment is provocative but calls for qualification. While it is probably true that Christian preference for the codex demonstrates a predilection against textual elitism—at least in part—in religious praxis, the early Christians nevertheless took the authority of both the ancient Jesus scriptures and those more recent apostolic texts with utmost seriousness.

36. See Gamble, *Books and Readers*, 49–54.

37. See McDonald, *The Formation of the Biblical Canon*, 1:294–95.

38. The DSS (3rd c. BC–1st c. AD), for instance, are exclusively rolls. On the production and characteristics of those manuscripts, see Tov, *Scribal Practices*. On the history of the transmission of the Hebrew Bible via scrolls/rolls (*megilla*), see the brief discussion and bibliography in Tov, *Textual Criticism*, 191–95; and Resnick, "The Codex." Resnick argues that Christians utilized codices for their copies of Old Testament texts to set them apart from the practices of first-century Jews. It seems likely, however, that the Christian preference for the codex must have some roots in first-century AD Jewish practices given the Jewish origins of Christianity. Saul Lieberman suggests that the disciples of Jesus probably followed the proto-rabbinic and rabbinic practice of copying oral law on πίνακες and thereafter adopted that format for their scriptures. See Lieberman, *Hellenism in Jewish Palestine*, 203–8.

39. For a thorough study of the extant evidence from the second through fourth centuries, see Hurtado, *The Earliest Christian Artifacts*.

40. Gamble, *Books and Readers*, 63. See also Roberts and Skeat, *The Birth of the Codex*, 50–51. The latter provide a critical evaluation of the practicality of the codex for Christians and argue that such practical considerations cannot exhaustively account for the Christian preference for this unique format. See also Hurtado, *Destroyer of the gods*, 135.

41. See Gamble, *Books and Readers*, 54–55; Roberts and Skeat, *The Birth of the Codex*, 45–46.

42. Gamble, *Books and Readers*, 55; Roberts and Skeat, *The Birth of the Codex*, 47–48. Martial comments that the portability of the codex is its chief advantage (*Epigrams* 1.2).

43. So Epp, "The Codex and Literacy."

44. Grafton and Williams, *Christianity and the Transformation of the Book*, 12.

45. I discuss the theological significance of this possibility below.

46. Barton, *Holy Writings, Sacred Texts*, 65.

47. See Barton, *Holy Writings, Sacred Texts*, 64–68.

48. Such quotations and allusions to the content of the New Testament texts *may* be citations from literary texts, but it is always possible that they may be remembered oral tradition.

49. See Barton, *Holy Writings, Sacred Texts*, 18–19. Barton draws on Franz Stulhofer's statistical study of citations in the Apostolic Fathers. See Stulhofer, *Der Gebrauch der Bibel von Jesus vis Euseb*. In many cases, it is important to note, they may have cited orally transmitted versions of the content of the texts that would become the New Testament.

50. Such as "It is written," "Scripture says," "God says," "The Holy Spirit says," etc.

51. So also Hart, who puts it well by contrasting the HB/OT texts and the NT texts: "Whereas the Jewish Bible represents the concentrated literary genius of an ancient and amazingly rich culture—mythic, epic, lyric, historical, and visionary, in texts assembled over many centuries then judiciously synthesized, redacted, and polished—the Christian New Testament is a somewhat unsystematically compiled and pragmatically edited compendium of 'important documentation': writings from the first generations of witnesses to the new faith, the oldest ambassadors to us from the apostolic and post-apostolic ages, consisting in quickly limned stories, theological discourses, and even a bit of historically impenetrable occasional writing." Hart, *The New Testament*, xxi.

52. Barton, *Holy Writings, Sacred Texts*, 88; emphasis in original. This conviction would perhaps explain why Tatian felt free to disassemble and reassemble the different parts of the (pre)canonical fourfold gospel in his *Diatessaron*. See Barton, *Holy Writings, Sacred Texts*, 48. McDonald raises the provocative and suggestive question, "Would he have taken such liberties with the Gospels if he had considered them to be Sacred Scripture and therefore inviolable?" McDonald, *The Biblical Canon*, 32.

53. I revisit this point below at greater length. For discussion, see Barton, *Holy Writings, Sacred Texts*, 17–19, 63–105.

54. Barton, *Holy Writings, Sacred Texts*, 67–68; emphasis mine.

55. Translation from Holmes, *The Apostolic Fathers*, 243.

56. I discuss the oral dimensions of books in antiquity below.

57. On their distinctive "bookishness," see Hurtado, *Destroyer of the gods*, 105–41.

58. See Barton, *Holy Writings, Sacred Text*, 75–79. A few of the key early Christian works that exhibit this strategy are Justin Martyr's *Dialogue with Trypho*, the epistle of Barnabus, and Melito of Sardis's *On the Pascha*.

59. See Albl, "*And Scripture Cannot Be Broken*"; Albl, "Introduction" and "Commentary."

60. DSS 4QTestimonium and 4QFlorilegium are evidence that some Jews made use of such collections prior to the birth of Christianity. See Gamble, *Books and Readers*, 27. Gamble states that there is "at least a strong circumstantial probability that collections of testimonies were current in the early church and should be reckoned among the lost items of the earliest Christian literature." See Gamble, *Books and Readers*, 27. Barton suggests that "there is not much doubt that for some Christian communities books of *testimonia* were more or less 'canonical.'" Barton, *Holy Writing, Sacred Text*, 52.

61. See Roberts, "Books in the Greco-Roman World," 61; see also Young, *Biblical Exegesis*, 13–16.

62. There is, however, one exception, but it is a very late development; it was permissible to copy the entirety of the Tanakh in a single codex (see *Sof.* 3.6). For brief discussion of the history and contents of this post-Talmud document, see Tov, *Textual Criticism*, 195. Tov, in *Scribal Practices*, frequently comments on the relationship between the directives for Jewish scribal praxis in *Soferim* and the actual material evidence of the DSS.

63. Farkasfalvy, *Inspiration and Interpretation*, 21. Though cf. Jenson's helpful qualifications of this language in *Canon and Creed*, 14.

64. Young, *Biblical Exegesis*, 15; emphasis mine.

65. The earliest extant pandects, Codex Sinaiticus and Codex Vaticanus, are from the fourth century AD. Neither of them is identical in contents to any modern Bible.

66. For discussion, see Metzger and Ehrman, *The Text of the New Testament*, 26.

67. It is therefore historically impossible that the autographs of all the books of Christian Scripture—in any historically accepted canonical collection—were gathered together in one single codex at any point in time. Such a codex would be mostly useless to any historically extant Christian community as well given its trilingual nature.

68. Near the beginning of the fourth century AD, Eusebius of Caesarea, for instance, notes—citing Clement of Alexandria—the existence of three different categories of books for the early church: ομολογούμενος (accepted), νόθος (spurious), and ἀντιλεγόμενα (disputed). See *Hist. eccl.* 6.13.6; 6.14.1. I give further attention to the historical processes and problems of canonization below. For a helpful recent summary and analysis, see Bovon, "Beyond the Canonical."

69. McDonald also makes this point in *The Formation of the Biblical Canon*, 1:294.

70. See Gamble, *Books and Readers*, 67. For fascinating discussion of the partitions of the early manuscripts, see Trobisch, *The First Edition*.

71. See Gamble, *Books and Readers*, 59–61; Gamble, *The New Testament Canon*, 35–46. The earliest manuscript collection containing most of the epistles of Paul (the Pastorals were probably absent; Hebrews is included), P46, is regularly dated to ca. AD 175–225. For a thorough analysis of the state of the question regarding the dating of early New Testament manuscripts, which depends largely on the analysis of specific paleographic handwriting styles, see Orsini and Clarysse, "Early New Testament Manuscripts." Hurtado identifies a number of other papyri that may originally have existed as editions of Paul. See Hurtado, *The Earliest Christian Artifacts*, 38–39. Marcion famously had a specific collection of Paul's letters. For further discussion, see Parker, *An Introduction*, 251.

72. Hurtado identifies P45 (ca. AD 250), which originally contained the four canonical Gospels and Acts, as the earliest extant evidence of the circulation of a Gospels book. See Hurtado, *The Earliest Christian Artifacts*, 35–38. See also Parker, *An Introduction*, 312–15. T. C. Skeat, however, argues that P4, P64, and P67, dated to approximately AD 200, *may* be the earliest evidence of a gospel codex. See Skeat, "The Oldest Manuscript." Though cf. Head, "Is P4, P64, and P67 the Oldest Manuscript of the Gospels?"

73. It appears in Codex Amiatinus I, fol. 4r/5r. See van Liere, *An Introduction*, 6; and the cover of Grafton and Williams, *Christianity and the Transformation of the Book*. For discussion of this illumination, see van Liere, *An Introduction*, 27; Ramirez, "*Sub culmine gazas*."

74. See van Liere, *An Introduction*, 28; Backhouse, *The Lindesfarne Gospels*.

75. See van Liere, *An Introduction*, 25–30. Elsewhere van Liere states that "most medieval biblical codices consist of partial Bibles . . . or individual Bible books." Van Liere, "The Latin Bible," 96.

76. Founded by three Christian businessmen in 1899, Gideons International has distributed over two billion Bibles and/or New Testaments. They note that this format fulfills their primary goal of introducing people to Jesus Christ. See www.gideons.ca/help/faqs.aspx. See also Howsam and McClaren, "Producing the Text," 77–79. Ignatius Press also publishes part-Bibles containing the New Testament and the Psalms and the Gospels, respectively.

77. See Calderhead, *Illuminating the Word*.

78. For discussion of the relation between oral and written testimony in early Christianity, see Bokedal, *The Formation of the Christian Biblical Canon*, 157–93; Kelber, *The Oral and Written Gospel*; Dunn, *The Oral Gospel Tradition*; Eve, *Behind the Gospels*; Hurtado, "Oral Fixation"; Rodriguez, *Oral Tradition*. See also Elder, "New Testament Media Criticism."

79. See Alexander, "The Living Voice."

80. As Jonathan Bernier notes, the primary thrust of this passage is that Papias prefers firsthand testimony. But he nevertheless embraces oral testimony. See Bernier, *The Quest for the Historical Jesus*, 134n25. Bernier cites Gamble, *Books and Readers*, 30–31. For further discussion of Papias, see Bauckham, *Jesus and the Eyewitnesses*, 12–38. For an introduction to the coexistence and interrelation of oral

and written testimony, and the frequent preference for oral testimony, in early Christianity, see Achtemeier, "*Omne Verbum Sonat.*"

81. The most striking example of the presence of ongoing oral tradition in early Christianity is the the *agrapha*, unwritten sayings of Jesus that circulated orally. The New Testament authors had already cited sayings of Jesus that are not directly identifiable with any statements in the written texts of the Gospels (Acts 20.35; 1 Cor 7.10–11; 9.14; 2 Cor 12.8–9; James 5.12). The early church fathers carried on that practice prior to, and even after, the relative stabilization of the four-fold written Gospels of the New Testament in the second century AD. For discussion see McDonald, *The Biblical Canon*, 253–55, 282–84.

82. Barton, *Holy Writings, Sacred Texts*, 107.

83. For discussion, see Ryan, *The Role of the Synagogue*; see also Hurtado, *Destroyer of the gods*, 109–11; Rouwhorst, "The Bible in Liturgy," 822–42, esp. 824–27; Olszowy-Schlanger, "The Hebrew Bible," 24–25.

84. In this, of course, they were following Jewish precedents. Hurtado draws attention to the evidence for these Jewish reading practices in two first-century texts, by Josephus (*C. Ap.* 2.175) and Philo (*Somn.* 2.127). See Hurtado, *Destroyer of the gods*, 110; Ryan, *The Role of the Synagogue*.

85. Many scholars argue that Paul could not have written the Pastoral Epistles. See my discussions of pseudepigraphy in the next chapter.

86. For discussion of the referents of "the memoirs of the apostles and the prophets," see Bokedal, *The Formation of the Christian Biblical Canon*, 263; Hurtado, *Destroyer of the gods*, 106.

87. See Hurtado, *Destroyer of the gods*, 108–9. I discuss these aids immediately below.

88. See Osburn, "The Greek Lectionaries of the New Testament"; Metzger and Ehrman, *The Text of the New Testament*, 48–49.

89. On *scriptio continua*, see Metzger and Ehrman, *The Text of the New Testament*, 22. Augustine bears witness to the strangeness of silent reading in *Conf.* 6.3, though it was certainly not absent in antiquity. For discussion, see Balogh, "*Vocens Paginarum*," 84–109, 202–40. For evidence of silent reading in antiquity, see Gavrilov, "Techniques of Reading in Classical Antiquity," 56–73; Burnyeat, "A Postscript on Silent Reading"; Knox, "Silent Reading in Antiquity."

90. For discussion, see Gamble, *Books and Readers*, 48, 203–4.

91. See Metzger and Ehrman, *The Text of the New Testament*, 33–46.

92. See Metzger and Ehrman, *The Text of the New Testament*, 26, 41.

93. On the history of the Hebrew of the ancient Jewish Scriptures/Old Testament, see Sáenz-Badillos, *A History of the Hebrew Language*, passim but esp. 76–111.

94. See Olszowy-Schlanger, "The Hebrew Bible," 22–23; Brotzman and Tully, *Old Testament Textual Criticism*, 50–60; Sáenz-Badillos, *A History of the Hebrew Language*, 77–79; Ulrich, "The Old Testament Text and Its Transmission," 83–104.

95. For reading aids in the Greek New Testament, see Metzger and Ehrman, *The Text of the New Testament*, 33–47; for reading aids in the traditions of the Hebrew Bible, see Tov, *Textual Criticism*, 195–205. On the special features of the Masoretic texts, see Tov, *Textual Criticism*, 23–73.

96. On Stephen Langton's contribution, see van Liere, *An Introduction*, 43. On Etienne Robert's, see van Liere, *An Introduction*, 45.

97. So Hurtado, *The Earliest Christian Artifacts*, 181.

98. See Metzger and Ehrman, *The Text of the New Testament*, 34–35. Beyond these, Eusebius of Caesarea created an elaborate set of "Canon Tables" for indicating parallel passages in the four Gospels. These regularly appear in manuscripts of the Gospels from the fourth century through 1000! See van Liere, *An Introduction*, 106; Metzger and Ehrman, *The Text of the New Testament*, 38–39.

99. See Metzger and Ehrman, *The Text of the New Testament*, 25–26; Lang, "Schreiben nach Mass."

100. For discussion of the Eusebian Canons, see Watson, *The Fourfold Gospel*, 101–24.

101. See Metzger and Ehrman, *The Text of the New Testament*, 46–47.

102. Candler, *Theology, Rhetoric, Manuduction*, 15.

103. The term *nomina sacra* was coined by Ludwig Traube in his monograph *Nomina sacra*. For investigations of the *nomina sacra* since Traube, see Bokedal, *The Formation and Significance of the Christian Biblical Canon*, 83–123; Brown, "Concerning the Origin of the *Nomina Sacra*"; Charlesworth, "Consensus Standardization in the Systematic Approach to *nomina sacra*"; Comfort, *Encountering the Manuscripts*, 199–253; Estes, "Reading for the Spirit of the Text"; Haines-Eitzen, *Guardians of Letters*, 91–94; Heath, "*Nomina sacra* and *Sacra memoria*"; Hurtado, "The Origin of the *Nomina Sacra*"; Hurtado, *The Earliest Christian Artifacts*, 95–134; Paap, *Nomina Sacra in the Greek Papyri*. For examples, see the photographs and transcriptions in Comfort and Barrett, *The Complete Text*.

104. The last abbreviation in each set is the genitive form of the respective *nomen sacrum*; all others are nominative forms. According to Tomas Bokedal, the six forms above occur in 89% (Πνευμα), 95% (σταυρος), 99% (Κυριος), or 100% (the others) of the extant possible occurrences of each respective word in 74 manuscripts dated between the second and fourth century. See Bokedal, "Notes on the *Nomina Sacra*."

105. Brown, "Concerning the Origin of the *Nomina Sacra*."

106. There are others, but these fifteen became somewhat standardized by the Byzantine period. See Hurtado, *The Earliest Christian Artifacts*, 97. Elsewhere Hurtado notes that the variableness of the evidence of the *nomina sacra* in early Christian manuscripts does not permit the judgment that the early church developed a rigid and strictly regulated system of *nomina sacra*. See Hurtado, *The Earliest Christian Artifacts*, 128. On the variableness of the practice, especially early, see Estes, "Reading for the Spirit"; Haines-Eitzen, *Guardians of Letters*, 91–94. On more rare *nomina sacra*, see Bokedal, "Notes on the *Nomina Sacra*," 265.

107. For discussion, see Bokedal, *The Formation and Significance of the Christian Biblical Canon*, 106; Hurtado, *Earliest Christian Artifacts*, 114.

108. See Bokedal, "Notes on the *Nomina Sacra*," 263; Hurtado, "The Origin of the *Nomina Sacra*," 659–60. For an argument of a pre–AD 70 origin, see Roberts, *Manuscript, Society, and Belief*, 36, 46. Jane Heath has made a fascinating argument that the apostle Paul himself employed them in Galatians 3.1. See Heath, "*Nomina sacra* and *Sacra memoria*," 544–46.

109. See Bokedal, *The Formation and Significance of the Christian Biblical Canon*, 98; Hurtado, *The Earliest Christian Artifacts*, 101–5.

110. For discussion, see Roberts, *Manuscript, Society, and Belief*, 28–35; Tov, *Scribal Practices*, 19, 205–8, 224–31.

111. There are a few instances of *nomina sacra* in unmistakably Jewish contexts, but they are late. See Edwards, "A *Nomen Sacrum* in the Sardis Synagogue"; Tuckett, "'Nomina Sacra' Yes and No?," 433–35.

112. See Bokedal, *The Formation and Significance of the Christian Biblical Canon*, 85; Hurtado, *The Earliest Christian Artifacts*, 120; Hurtado, "Manuscripts and the Sociology of Early Christian Reading," 62; Wicker, "Pre-Constantinian *Nomina sacra*," 53. Cf., though, Tuckett, "'Nomina Sacra' Yes and No?"

113. See Comfort, *Encountering the Manuscripts*, 367n1; Hurtado, *Earliest Christian Artifacts*, 96n4; Kruger, *The Question of Canon*, 101n137; Paap, *Nomina Sacra*, 120. On *nomina sacra* in Latin manuscripts, see Bischoff, *Latin Paleography*, 152–54; Haughton, *The Latin New Testament*, 22, 52, 80, 109, 128, 147, 189, 191–92; Turner, "The *Nomina Sacra*." On the Coptic *nomina sacra*, see Luijendijk, *Forbidden Oracles*, 44, 68, 105n1. On the Gothic evidence, see Falluomini, *The Gothic Version*, 21, 45, 27, 63–64. On the Slavonic evidence, see Gillet, "Note sur les *nomina sacra*," 105–7; Still, "*Nomina Sacra.*"

114. On *nomina sacra* in manuscripts of Old Testament books, see Comfort, *Encountering the Manuscripts*, 202, 210–11, 214, 231, 250.

115. "Besides the suitable designation 'embryonic creed,' we could also speak of the *nomina sacra* as an important link bridging the potential structural, theological, and narrative gap between the Scriptures and the second-century oral kerygma, the developing *regula fidei*." Bokedal, *The Formation and Significance of the Christian Biblical Canon*, 116. The phrase "embryonic creed" comes from Roberts, *Manuscript, Society, and Belief*, 46.

116. For discussion of their employment in other literature and media in early Christianity, see Wicker, "Pre-Constantinian *Nomina sacra*."

117. Heath, "*Nomina sacra* and *Sacra memoria*," 547.

118. Heath suggests, in a discussion of Irenaeus's employment of the rule of faith, that the *nomina sacra* would have the visual effect of directing readers towards the ὑποθέσεις of Scripture. See Heath, "*Nomina sacra and Sacra memoria*," 533–35.

119. For discussion, see Hurtado, *The Earliest Christian Artifacts*, 135–54; for a photograph of an example from P75, see Hurtado, *The Earliest Christian Artifacts*, 236–37.

120. Metzger and Ehrman, *The Text of the New Testament*, 43–44.

121. For discussion and examples, see de Hamel, *A History of Illuminated Manuscripts*; Fingernagel and Gastberger, *In The Beginning Was the Word*; van Liere, *An Introduction*, 237–60; McKendrick and Doyle, *Bible Manuscripts*.

122. See Hefling, *Why Doctrines?*, 117–18.

123. See Jensen, *Understanding Early Christian Art*, 64–92.

124. Jensen, *Understanding Early Christian Art*, 3.

125. Mark Edwards notes that though the plastic arts flourished in early Christianity, at least after the time of Constantine, they were always subservient to and of less authority than the written word. See Edwards, *Image, Word, and God*, 189–92.

126. McCarter, *Textual Criticism*, 12.

127. McCarter, *Textual Criticism*, 12.

128. The fact that these texts were translated into numerous languages further complicates the textual history of Christian Scripture. I discuss the theological significance of the translatability of Scripture below.

129. Gamble, *Books and Readers*, 71.

130. I discuss the variableness of the languages represented in the history of Christian Scripture below. On the fragmentary nature of the evidence, the New Testament textual critic David Parker writes, "Given the tiny number of manuscripts to have survived from antiquity, our theories can be no more than provisional attempts to understand these fragments of the textual tradition." Parker, *An Introduction*, 348.

131. Standard monographs include Brotzman and Tully, *Old Testament Textual Criticism*; Ehrman and Holmes, *The Text of the New Testament in Contemporary Research*; McCarter, *Textual Criticism*; Metzger and Ehrman, *The Text of the New Testament*; Parker, *An Introduction*; Tov, *Textual Criticism of the Hebrew Bible*. There is also a journal devoted to text critical studies: *TC: A Journal of Biblical Textual Criticism*.

132. For examples across the theological and ecclesial spectrum, see Blomberg and Markley, *A Handbook of New Testament Exegesis*, 1–36; Bock and Fanning, *Interpreting the New Testament Text*, 33–56; Duvall and Hays, *Grasping God's Word*, 24–26; Fee, *New Testament Exegesis*, 59–70; Gorman, *Elements of Biblical Exegesis*, 39; Hays and Holladay, *Biblical Exegesis*, 34–52; Windham, *New Testament Greek*, 15–61.

133. Parker, "Scripture Is Tradition," 12; emphasis mine. For the earliest evidence, from before the fourth century AD, see Comfort and Barrett, *The Complete Text*.

134. Gurry, "The Number of Variants." Gurry bases his study upon an analysis of the text critical work of Bruce Morrill, Matthew Solomon, and Tommy Wassermann on John 18, Philemon, and Jude respectively. His article includes an excellent survey of earlier estimates in text critical scholarship and he gives an incisive critique of those estimates.

135. For discussion of the evidence of the translations, see Metzger, *The Early Versions*; and the essays on versions in Ehrman and Holmes, *The Text of the New*

Testament. The latter also contains essays by Gordon D. Fee and Roderic L. Mullin on the Greek fathers, H. A. G. Houghton on the Latin fathers, and Sebastian Brock on the Syriac fathers.

136. For discussion, see Metzger, *A Textual Commentary*, 102–7 (Mark 16.9–20), 187–90 (John 7.53–8.11). The *pericope adulterae* is inserted after Luke 21.38 in a number of manuscripts; see Metzger, *A Textual Commentary*, 147.

137. See Metzger, *A Textual Commentary*, 13–14 (Matt 6.9–13), 130–32 (Luke 11.2–4), 647–51 (1 John 5.7–8).

138. See Gamble, *Books and Readers*, 74.

139. Gamble, *Books and Readers*, 74.

140. See Barton, *Holy Writings, Sacred Texts*, 68; Gamble, *Books and Readers*, 74.

141. Kruger, "Early Christian Attitudes," 79.

142. For an overview of the extant ancient manuscripts in the textual traditions of the Hebrew Bible, see Tov, *Textual Criticism*, 23–154.

143. The idea that there is a standardized Hebrew text has received frequent criticism in recent years. See Tov, *Textual Criticism*, 174–90; Ulrich, *The Dead Sea Scrolls*, 1–28.

144. Gamble contrasts the textual transmission of the New Testament with Jewish practices: "In the case of early Christian books . . . [t]here is a level of contingency in the transcription of scriptural texts that cannot be reconciled with the rigorous stipulations governing the production of Jewish scriptural books." Gamble, *Books and Readers*, 78.

145. See Tov, *Textual Criticism*, 1–4.

146. Tov clarifies that "the term Masoretic Text is imprecise . . . for [the MT] is not attested in any one single source. Rather, [the MT] is an abstract unit reflected in various sources that differ from one another in many details." Tov, *Textual Criticism*, 24–25.

147. Ulrich, *The Dead Sea Scrolls*, 2. "The evidence from Qumran," he writes, "indicates that the two processes of textual formation and textual transmission repeatedly overlapped for extensive periods of time" (2). For discussion of the theological significance of this discovery, see Harkins, "Theological Attitudes toward the Scriptural Text," 505–10. See also Mroczek, *The Literary Imagination*.

148. See Farkasfalvy, *Inspiration and Interpretation*, 59n8. For discussions of the textual criticism of the fathers and medievals, see, respectively, Metzger, "The Practice of Textual Criticism"; van Liere, *An Introduction*, 98–102.

149. Justin is alluding to the legend of the translation of the Pentateuch that is described in the Letter of Aristeas (2nd c. BC). He appears to be unaware that the letter only describes the translation of the Torah/Pentateuch; it does not refer to the translation of (any of) the prophets.

150. See Martens, *Origen and Scripture*, 42–48.

151. The references come from Martens, *Origin and Scripture*, 43n8. On the Hexapla, see Martens, *Origin and Scripture*, 44–48; Grafton and Williams, *Christianity and the Transformation of the Book*, 86–132.

152. See van Liere, *An Introduction*, 14–15, 98–102.

153. For discussion of the elusiveness of the "original text," see Epp, "The Multivalence of the Term 'Original Text'"; Metzger and Ehrman, *The Text of the New Testament*, 272–74; McDonald, *The Formation of the Biblical Canon*, 2:208–12; Tov, *Textual Criticism*, 161–69; Ulrich, *The Dead Sea Scrolls*, 1–28.

154. See Larsen, "Accidental Publication."

155. For a recent article that addresses the data on the textual variability of the book of Daniel in antiquity, see Portier-Young, "Three Books of Daniel."

156. For discussion, see Blenkinsopp, *A History of Prophecy in Israel*, 130–35; Tov, *Textual Criticism*, 286–94; Ulrich, *The Dead Sea Scrolls*, 141–50.

157. The original of (part of) that book, after all, was burned (see Jer 36.27–32)!

158. For descriptions of these manuscripts, see Würthwein, *The Text of the Old Testament*, 35–37.

159. Tov, *Textual Criticism*, 287. The Greek texts lack approximately 2,700 words found in the Hebrew of the Masoretic text. See Würthwein, *The Text of the Old Testament*, 53.

160. See Tov, *Textual Criticism*, 287; Ulrich, *The Dead Sea Scrolls*, 141–50.

161. For discussion, see Epp, "The Multivalence of the Term 'Original Text'"; Metzger and Ehrman, *The Text of the New Testament*, 272–74.

162. For concise discussions, see Metzger, *A Textual Commentary*, 447, 470–73; Fitzmyer, *Romans*, 48–51. For more extensive discussion, see Gamble, *The Textual History*; Lampe, "Zur Textgeschichte des Römerbriefes."

163. For discussion, see Metzger, *A Textual Commentary*, 102–7.

164. See Brown, *An Introduction*, 548–51.

165. Epp, "The Multivalence of the Term 'Original Text,'" 591.

166. See Hart's helpful reflections on such stylistic flattening in NT translations in Hart, *The New Testament*, xv, xxi, xxiii.

167. For a historical investigation of the history of the translation of Christian Scripture, see Metzger, *The Text in Translation*. On the reluctance of Muslims to translate the Qur'an, which derives from the explicit internal identification of the revelatory nature of the Qur'an with its expression in Arabic, see Q Yusef 12.2; Q ar-Ra'd 13.37; Q Ta-Ha 20.113; Q az-Zumar 39.28; Q Fussilat 41.2–3; Q ash-Shura 42.7; and Q az-Zuhruf 43.3. For discussion see Bobzin, "Translations of the Qur'ān." See also Stroumsa, *The Scriptural Universe*, 18.

168. Most scholars believe Jesus spoke Aramaic and possibly Hebrew (see Mark 5.41; 7.34; 14.36; 15.34; Matt 5.18; 5.22; 6.24; John 20.16). Cf., however, Gleaves, *Did Jesus Speak Greek?*

169. The plural form, *traduttori traditori*, occurs in Giusti, *Proverbi toscani*, 238. The Italian follows the Latin "Omnis traductor traditor." For winsome and poignant reflections on the traitorous process of translating Scripture, see Hart, "Through a Gloss, Darkly"; Hart, *The New Testament*, xiii–xxxv. See also Peterson, *Eat This Book*, 119–76 (Peterson quotes the proverb on 170).

170. In 2007, McDonald wrote that the Greek versions are used in more than 90% of the New Testament references to the OT. See McDonald, *The Biblical Canon*, 35. Since then, he has increased his evaluation to 94%. See McDonald, *The Origin of the Bible*, 83. For the evidence, Archer and Chirichigno, *Old Testament Quotations*. The fact that he has offered differing percentages hints at the convoluted nature of determining the vorlage of translated texts in antiquity.

171. McDonald, *The Biblical Canon*, 123; emphasis in original. For general studies of the textual history of the Greek versions of the ancient Jewish Scriptures, see Jobes and Silva, *Invitation to the Septuagint*. For extensive analysis of the high estimation of the ancient Greek versions of the OT by the early Christian communities, see Hengel, *The Septuagint as Christian Scripture*; Law, *When God Spoke Greek*; Müller, *The First Bible of the Church*.

172. For useful orientation, see Lamarche, "The Septuagint."

173. See Grafton and Williams, *Christianity and the Transformation of the Book*, 86–132. The authors note that some books of Scripture, particularly poetic ones, may have had as many as seven Greek versions represented in the Hexapla. See Grafton and Williams, *Christianity and the Transformation of the Book*, 89.

174. See McLay, "The Use of the Septuagint," 237–40.

175. The Syriac Christian communities are a notable exception. For discussion, see Marcos, "Teodoreto de Ciro y la lengua hebrea"; and Van Rompay, "The East (3): Syria and Mesopotamia," 366–69.

176. For two recent assessments of Jerome's engagement with Scripture that include helpful discussion of his preference for the Hebrew of the OT, see Cain, *The Letters of Jerome*, 43–67, esp. 53–67; Graves, *Jerome's Hebrew Philology*, 1–11. For a critical evaluation of his facility with the Hebrew language, see Rebenich, "The '*Vir Triliguis*.'"

177. For a recent examination of the Letter of Aristeas, see De Crom, "The Letter of Aristeas." For discussion of the importance of Let. Aris. in the early church, see Müller, *The First Bible of the Church*, 68–78.

178. Barth, *CD*, I.2.476–81.

179. The "best" candidates would be the regional Synods of Laodicea (AD 363) and Hippo/Carthage (AD 393/397) in the fourth century or Trent in the sixteenth.

180. For comparison of contemporary canonical collections, see McDonald, *The Biblical Canon*, 443–44.

181. There are a number of excellent works treating this history. Pride of place must go to the works of Lee Martin McDonald. I have extensively cited McDonald, *The Biblical Canon*, but McDonald's magnum opus appeared in print too late for me to make reference to all of the new insights of that work in my arguments. See McDonald, *The Formation of the Biblical Canon*, 2 vols. Other important recent works include Allert, *A High View of Scripture?*; Barton, *Holy Writings, Sacred Text*; Bokedal, *The Formation of the Christian Biblical Canon*; Bruce, *The Canon of Scripture*; von Campenhausen, *The Formation of the Christian Bible*; Carr,

The Formation of the Hebrew Bible; Evans and Tov, *Exploring the Origins of the Bible*; Gamble, *The New Testament Canon*; Lim, *The Formation of the Jewish Canon*; McDonald and Sanders, *The Canon Debate*; Metzger, *The Canon of the New Testament*; Mroczek, *The Literary Imagination*; Sanders, *Torah and Canon*; van der Toorn, *Scribal Culture*; and Ulrich, *The Dead Sea Scrolls*.

182. McDonald, "What Do We Mean by Canon?," 8; emphasis mine. Ulrich also gives extensive attention to the meaning of these terms. See Ulrich, *The Dead Sea Scrolls*, 265–79.

183. McDonald, *The Biblical Canon*, 38.

184. See chapter 2 for my brief discussion of the historical meanings of the word prior to its use for designating a closed list of scriptural books.

185. Barton, *Holy Writings, Sacred Text*, 10. Athanasius uses the verbal form *kanonizomenōn*. For discussion of this letter, see McDonald, *The Biblical Canon*, 202–3; Brakke, "Canon Formation." According to McDonald the word *canon* has only been used to designate lists of authoritative literary works regularly since David Ruhnken did so in his *Historia critica oratorum Graecorum*, published in 1768. See McDonald, *The Biblical Canon*, 51.

186. I write "loosely," because even those premodern Christians who defined the boundaries of authoritative Scripture precisely continued to use books not included in their own lists. See McDonald, *The Biblical Canon*, 105–11, 216.

187. McDonald, *The Biblical Canon*, 209.

188. McDonald, *The Biblical Canon*, 49; emphasis in original. Later he writes, "[The] Church councils of the fourth and fifth centuries acknowledged those books that had already obtained prominence from widespread usage among the various Christian churches in their areas. Church council decisions reflect what the communities *recognized*, and they subsequently authorized this recognition for the church. If any decisions were made by church councils in such matters, it was only in regard to the books *on the fringe* of collections that had already obtained widespread recognition in the majority of the churches. These decisions came only at the end of a long process of recognition in the churches, and they were not unilateral decisions issued from the top of an organization. In other words, *church councils did not create biblical canons*, but rather reflect the state of affairs in such matters in their geographical location." McDonald, *The Biblical Canon*, 209; emphasis in original.

189. For the data, see Gallagher and Meade, *The Biblical Canon Lists*.

190. So McDonald, *The Biblical Canon*, 57. For discussion of the difference between attending to the functional authority of texts and defining their boundaries, see Barton, *Holy Writings, Sacred Text*, 1–32.

191. I get the notion of a "core" canon from Stephen B. Chapman's work. See Chapman, "The Old Testament Canon."

192. As Hurtado notes, their "bookishness" itself is innovative in the context of the religious traditions of antiquity. See Hurtado, *Destroyer of the gods*, 105–41. See also Stroumsa, *The Scriptural Universe*.

193. For the evidence of the lists, see McDonald, *The Biblical Canon*, 439–51; Gallagher and Meade, *The Biblical Canon Lists*. For striking comments on the continuing influence of both NT and OT pseudepigrapha and apocrypha in the medieval churches, see van Liere, *Introduction to the Medieval Bible*, 64–66, 69–71.

194. See Luther, *Luther's Works*, 35:395–99; Luther, *The Luther Bible of 1534.*

195. McDonald, *The Biblical Canon*, 56; emphasis mine.

196. Actual physical texts known to us as the "OT," the "Hebrew Bible," or the "first scriptures," and known to the authors of (what would become) the NT as the "Law and Prophets/Prophets and Law/Moses and Prophets," were with the earliest Christian believers from the very beginning. See Matt 5.17; 7.12; 11.13; 22.40; Luke 16.16; 16.29; 16.31; 24.27; John 1.45; Acts 13.5; 24.14; 26.22; 28.23; Rom 3.21. See also the references to the "Law of Moses, Prophets, and Psalms" (Luke 24.44), "the Prophets/Prophet" (Matt 2.23; 25.56; Mark 1.2; Luke 1.70; 18.31; 24.25; John 6.45; Acts 3.18; 3.21–25; 7.42–52; 10.43; 13.27; 13.40; 15.15, 26.27; Rom 1.2; 1 Thess 5.20; Heb 1.1; Jas 5.10; 1 Pet 1.10; 2 Pet 3.2; Rev 10.7), simply "the Law," (Matt 5.18; 12.5; 15.6; 22.36; 23.23; Luke 2.22–39; 10.26; 16.17; John 7.19; 7.23; 7.49; 7.51; 8.5; 8.17; 10.34; 12.34; 15.25; 18.31; Acts 5.34; 6.13; 7.53; 13.39; 15.5; 18.13–15; 21.20; 21.24; 22.3; 22.12; 23.3, 29; 25.8; Rom 2.12–27; 3.19–31; 4.13–16; 5.13; 5.20; 6.14–15; 7; 8; 9.4; 9.31; 10.5; 13.8–10; 1 Cor 9.8–9; 9.20–21; 14.21; 14.34; Gal 2.16–21; 3; 4; 5.3–4; 5.14; 5.18; 6.13; Eph 2.15; Phil 3.5–9; 1 Tim 1.7–9; Heb 7.5; 7.12; 7.19; 7.28; 8.4; 9.19; 9.22; 10.1; 10.8; Jas 1.25, 2.8–12; 4.11), or "the scriptures/writings" (Matt 21.42; 22.29; 26.54; 26.56; Mark 12.10; 12.24; 14.49; 15.27; Luke 4.21; 22.37; 24.27; 24.32; 24.45; John 2.22; 5.39; 7.38; 7.42; 10.35; 13.18; 17.12; 19.24; 19.28; 19.36–37; 20.9; Acts 1.16; 8.32; 8.35; 17.2; 17.11; 18.24; 18.28; Rom 1.2; 4.3; 9.17; 10.11; 11.2; 15.4; 1 Cor 15.3–15; 2 Cor 4.13; Gal 3.8; 3.22; 4.30; 1 Tim 4.13; 5.18; 2 Tim 3.16; Jas 2.8; 2.23; 4.5; 1 Pet 2.6; 2 Pet 1.20; 3.16). Even so, it is impossible to definitively delineate their contents, and it is necessary to advert to the fact that many of the above texts may refer to orally transmitted versions of the law, prophets, and other Jewish writings and therefore not necessarily to specific written documents. In recent years a number of significant and helpful studies have appeared that treat the question of the use of ancient Jewish Scriptures in the texts that would become the NT. What is more certain is that the words, ideas, and images of these antecedent texts—whatever their precise scope—served as the matrices of said believers' understandings of Jesus of Nazareth and the new community he inaugurated, and the early Christian assemblage of these words and images in all likelihood has its origins in Jesus's own teaching. I will investigate and seek to offer an adequate understanding of these judgments and their significance for the present work below. For extensive study and bibliography, see Beale and Carson, *Commentary on the New Testament Use of the Old Testament*. See also Hays, *The Conversion of the Imagination*; Hays, *Echoes of Scripture in the Gospels*; Hays, *Echoes of Scripture in the Letters of Paul*; Hays, *Reading Backwards*; Longenecker, *Biblical Exegesis in the Apostolic Period*; Mitchell, *Paul, the Corinthians, and the Birth of Christian Hermeneutics*; Moyise, *Jesus and Scripture*;

Moyise, *Paul and Scripture*; Moyise, *The Later New Testament Writings*; Porter, *Sacred Tradition*; Watson, *Paul and the Hermeneutics of Faith*.

197. A full-scale investigation of the developments in the functional canonization of the Hebrew Scriptures/OT prior to the NT era is beyond the scope of the present work. For a thorough investigation of the extant textual data from both Jewish and Christian sources, see McDonald, *The Biblical Canon*, 114–240. Other important works include Carr, *The Formation of the Hebrew Bible*; Lim, *Formation of the Jewish Canon*; Sanders, *Torah and Canon*; van der Toorn, *Scribal Culture*. For an extensive argument (which is not persuasive in my opinion but still has a great deal of value) that the first Jewish Christians inherited a finalized set of books, see Beckwith, *The Old Testament Canon*. For a compelling argument against positing a "finalized" canon of the HB/OT during the NT era, see Mroczek, *The Literary Imagination*.

198. McDonald, *The Biblical Canon*, 194.

199. For a relatively comprehensive demonstration of this assertion, see McDonald, *The Formation of the Biblical Canon*, vol. 1.

200. See the appendixes in the UBS 5/NA 28 and Bratcher, *Old Testament Quotations*, 81–88.

201. These texts are from the OT "core canon" of the early churches.

202. McDonald has compiled a list of 549 potential NT allusions to works outside of the Protestant OT. Most are to books customarily labeled "apocryphal" or "deuterocanonical" (Tobit, Wisdom of Solomon, Sirach, Judith, Baruch, 1–4 Maccabees, Bel and the Dragon, Susanna, 4 Esdras) and are present in the larger canonical collections of the Roman Catholic and Eastern Orthodox Churches. A significant number, though, are references to works customarily deemed "pseudepigraphal" (1 Enoch, Testaments of the Twelve Patriarchs, Jubilees, Psalms of Solomon, Assumption of Moses). See McDonald, *The Biblical Canon*, 454–64.

203. See McLay, "The Use of the Septuagint."

204. The most famous example of this is the Christian use of the LXX of Isa 7.14 (see Matt 1.18–25; Ignatius *Eph.* 18.2–19.1; Justin *Dial.* 71.3) as a prophecy of the virgin birth of Jesus Christ. For discussion, see Law, *When God Spoke Greek*, 5, 96–97, 116.

205. To cite one example, in Eph 4.8 Paul appears to quote from Ps 68.18, but the wording does not match any extant witness to that text in Hebrew or Greek. Paul either cites a no longer extant text or modifies Ps 68.18 for his specific purposes. For discussion, see Thielman, "Ephesians," 821–22. As I discussed above, some early Christians probably used collections of OT texts, or *testimonia*, as proof-text resources for polemical purposes. One of the key reasons for this hypothesis is the evidence that regularly appearing Christian quotations of certain OT texts do not match any otherwise extant text-forms of the ancient Greek or Hebrew text forms. Cf. though, McDonald, who writes that "the NT writers . . . took many liberties in citing the OT, sometimes even altering the passages they cited (e.g., Ps 94.11 in 1 Cor 3.19–20; Ps 68.18 in Eph 4.8; and Ps 8.4–6 in Heb 2.6–8)."

McDonald, *The Biblical Canon*, 207. See also Meyer's striking comments in *The Church in Three Tenses*, 26–27.

206. The evidence available to us is remarkable, given the wear and tear such documents would have experienced and given that the destruction of books was one of the primary means by which Diocletian attempted to suppress the influence of Christian communities. That we possess, at least relatively, so much ancient material also displays the high esteem that Christians and Jews had for their scriptures. See Gamble, *Books and Readers*, 132, 141, 145–50, 160.

207. See McDonald, *The Biblical Canon*, 151–58.

208. The earliest manuscripts of the text from Qumram do not have the pericope in question, and it is not entirely clear that the later form is actually a reference to books of Scripture. See McDonald, *The Biblical Canon*, 158–60.

209. McDonald, *The Biblical Canon*, 169.

210. See McDonald, *The Biblical Canon*, 160–65.

211. McDonald, *The Biblical Canon*, 150–70; see also Gallagher and Meade, *The Biblical Canon Lists*, 57.

212. Mroczek, *The Literary Imagination*, 171.

213. Roger Beckwith creatively argues that it must be dated to the second century BC. See Beckwith, *The Old Testament Canon*. For a thorough critique of Beckwith's position, see McLay, "The Use of the Septuagint," 226–32.

214. See McDonald, *The Biblical Canon*, 164–65, 176–77.

215. McDonald, *The Biblical Canon*, 165. On the same page McDonald notes its limited influence within Judaism as well; it originated in Babylon, not Israel, and it was not included in the Mishnah. See also McDonald, *The Biblical Canon*, 223.

216. The dates are from McDonald, *The Biblical Canon*.

217. McDonald, *The Biblical Canon*, 221. For the canon lists of Melito, Origen, Athanasius, Cyril of Jerusalem, Epiphanius (who gives three different lists), Gregory Nazianzus, Amphilochius, Hilary, Jerome (who gives two different lists), Rufinus, Augustine, the Council of Carthage, and Sinaiticus, Vaticanus, and Alexandrinus, see McDonald, *The Biblical Canon*, 439–42. See also Gallagher and Meade, *The Biblical Canon Lists*.

218. See Chapman, "The Old Testament Canon," 137. This division roughly aligns with the three sections of the Tanakh: the Torah, Neviim, and Kethuvim.

219. Kruger, *The Question of the Canon*, 163; emphasis in original.

220. I discuss their unique exegetical maneuvers below.

221. For much more thorough historical studies of the developments pertinent to the canonicity of the NT books, see Gamble, *The New Testament Canon*; Kruger, *Question of the Canon*; Metzger, *The Canon of the New Testament*. For two explicitly theological accounts of these processes, see Farkasfalvy, *Inspiration and Interpretation*, 25–51; Jensen, *Canon and Creed*, 33–42.

222. The Syrian Orthodox Church uses the 22-book NT canon of the Peshitta, which lacks 2 Peter, 2 John, 3 John, James, and Revelation in their liturgy.

223. For evidence of the "fuzziness" of the boundaries of the NT canon, see the lists of NT books and records of manuscript evidence in McDonald, *The Biblical Canon*, 445–51; Gallagher and Meade, *The Biblical Canon Lists*.

224. For helpful evaluations of the early Christian willingness to write authoritative works, even though there was a preference for oral testimony, see Kruger, *The Question of the Canon*, 79–118; Hurtado, *Destroyer of the gods*, 105–41.

225. On Paul's awareness of Jesus traditions, see Meyer, *The Aims of Jesus*, 74–75. See also esp. Dungan, *The Sayings of Jesus*; Batten and Kloppenborg, *James, 1 & 2 Peter, and Early Jesus Traditions*. For a list of parallels between phrases in the Catholic epistles and Jesus's words, see McDonald, *The Biblical Canon*, 254–55n39.

226. McDonald, *The Biblical Canon*, 245.

227. For an extremely helpful account along these lines, see Kruger, *The Question of Canon*.

228. It may depend on the earlier formulations in Rom 1.1–2, 1 Pet. 1.10–12, and Jude 17. See the later use of the two terms in Ign. *Phld.* 5.2, For discussion, see Farkasfalvy, *Inspiration and Interpretation*, 91–94; Farkasfalvy, "Prophets and Apostles."

229. See below on Melito, Irenaeus, Tertullian, and Clement of Alexandria.

230. The authorship and dating of 2 Peter are disputed both in contemporary scholarship and in the ancient church. Eusebius, for instance, did not accept its authority as "encovenanted" (ενδιαθηκον) and labeled it a disputed (αντιλεγομενων) writing (*Hist. eccl.* 3.3.1–4). On the history of the reception of 2 Peter in the early churches, see Grünstäudl and Nicklas, "Searching for Evidence," 220–28.

231. In the NT "Prophets" can serve as a synecdoche for the whole OT. See note 186 above.

232. I have already discussed this at length in chapter 2. I return to it again when I discuss the relationship between the authority of Jesus Christ and the authority of Scripture in chapter 6.

233. The author of the Revelation of John also expected his work to be read aloud (Rev 1.3).

234. This is likely due to both their content and their length, which was often much greater than other typical Greco-Roman letters. See Hurtado, *Destroyer of the gods*, 120–21.

235. There are extant manuscripts of both letters that lack the addressees. See Metzger, *A Textual Commentary*, 446–47, 532. On the possibility that an alternative edition of Romans circulated among the early Christian communities, see the references in note 162 above.

236. Marcion possessed a collection of Paul's letters, and other second-century figures make reference to such collections. See Gamble, *The New Testament Canon*, 36–46; Trobisch, *Paul's Letter Collection*. On the possible importance of the use of the codex for "canon consciousness" in the early church, see Kraft, "The Codex and Canon Consciousness."

237. See the discussion of Gospel codices above.

238. They may have been referring to oral traditions, though. See Young, *Jesus Tradition*. For a thorough and careful argument that the best explanation for a number of NT allusions and citations in the Apostolic Fathers is literary dependence, see Kruger, *The Question of the Canon*, 176–202. See also Gregory and Tuckett, *The Reception of the New Testament*. For a list of allusions to and citations of NT texts by the Apostlic Fathers, see McDonald, *The Biblical Canon*, 255n41, 256n43, 269nn69–71. For the data in the rest of this paragraph, I have utilized the indexes in Holmes, *The Apostolic Fathers*.

239. See Kruger, *Question of the Canon*, 197–99.

240. See Kruger, *Question of the Canon*, 189–93.

241. See Kruger, *Question of the Canon*, 193–97.

242. Kruger, *Question of the Canon*, 182–87.

243. Kruger, *Question of the Canon*, 187–89.

244. The language of covenants, of course, occurs in the NT texts themselves. See 1 Cor 11.25; 2 Cor 3.6; Heb 8.8 (cf. Heb 7.22; 10.16; 10.29; 12.24). It has its roots in Jer 31.31–34.

245. He also quotes from the Shepard of Hermas as if it is Scripture; see *Haer.* 4.20.2.

246. Again, see Gallagher and Meade, *The Biblical Canon Lists*.

247. See McDonald, *The Biblical Canon*, 382–451.

248. Martin Chemnitz criticized Trent sharply for this closure. As Peter Nafzger summarizes, he argued that "the church does not have the authority to change the historical record. The exact boundaries of the canon were never firmly settled in the early church." See Nafzger, *"These Are Written,"* 19.

249. See Nafzger, *"These Are Written,"* 19. Interestingly, Lutherans did not follow these trends immediately. They first followed the example set by Luther, who had relegated the authority of certain books, most famously James, to a secondary status. The Book of Concord (1580), for instance, still lists books as *homoleguomena* (accepted) and *antilegoumena* (disputed). See Nafzger, *"These Are Written,"* 19–20. Luther separated Hebrews, James, Jude, and Revelation from the books of the NT in his translation of the NT.

250. Farkasfalvy, *Inspiration and Interpretation*, 22.

251. Candler, *Theology, Rhetoric, Manuduction*, 14–18.

252. Ayres makes a similar point with reference to the historical study of theological reflection in the early church. "Attention to the complexity of history," he writes, "especially in light of modern historicism is not incompatible with belief in the Spirit's shaping of that history." Ayres, *Nicaea and Its Legacy*, 428.

253. Epp, "The Multivalence of the Term 'Original Text,'" 585. He goes on to say: "Just as each of the 5,300 Greek New Testament manuscripts and the perhaps 9,000 versional manuscripts is an 'original,' so each of these thousands of manuscripts likely was considered 'canonical' when used in the worship and teaching of individual churches—and yet no two are exactly alike. Consequently, each collec-

tion or 'canon' of early Christian writings during the centuries long process of canonization was likewise different, whether in the writings it included and excluded or—more likely—in the detailed content of those writings as represented in their respective manuscripts, with their varying textual readings" (586). Comfort and Barrett make similar statements about the earliest extant fragments of the NT. Those texts *were* Scripture for their original recipients. Comfort and Barrett, *The Complete Text*, 13.

254. In a sense, this judgment is a commitment to a position that *could be* labeled inerrancy. But I find much of the literature applying the term "inerrancy" to Christian Scripture extremely problematic. I prefer the language "trustworthiness." See Moberly, *The Bible*, 186–87. For evaluation of inerrantist positions, see Achtemeier, *Inspiration and Authority*, 45–63. See also the helpful reflections in Enns, *Inspiration and Incarnation*, ix–xi, 165–80. In my estimation, Farkasfalvy's words concerning God's economic word are apropos for thinking about divine intentions with respect to the humanity of Scripture: "God chose to descend into the realm of human imperfection, where the light of truth is sparse and must exist in the penumbra of partial knowledge mixed with partial ignorance." Farkasfalvy, *Inspiration and Interpretation*, 188. For another illuminating argument that historically and concretely distinct versions of the text can serve as inspired Scripture for their respective communities of reception, see Martin, *Biblical Truths*, 71–85. For a recent nuanced articulation of the possibility of affirming scriptural inerrancy that accounts for the particularity of Scripture (he calls it an "inerrancy of the cross"), see Vanhoozer, "Augustinian Inerrancy."

255. Webster, *Holy Scripture*, 24. The quotation comes from Webster's discussion of the merits of calling Scripture a "servant" of God's action. Webster indicates that the source of the language of servanthood is Berkouwer, *Holy Scripture*.

256. De Lubac, "The Light of Christ," 206.

257. I discuss this important passage at greater length in the next chapter. It is slightly ironic that Paul *writes* about the danger of writing.

258. Plato, *Phaedrus* (trans. Waterfield), 69.

259. Ong, *Orality and Literacy*, 81; emphasis mine. For a similar judgment with regard to the utility of the written Gospels, see Bernier, *The Quest for the Historical Jesus*, 141–42.

CHAPTER SIX. Scripture in History II

1. The presence of the word *inspiration* in the titles of a number of recent works illustrates this judgment. See Achtemeier, *Inspiration and Authority*; Enns, *Inspiration and Incarnation*; Farkasfalvy, *Inspiration and Interpretation*; Graves, *The Inspiration and Interpretation*; and Law, *Inspiration of the Scriptures*. See also the Pontifical Biblical Commission's recent document *The Inspiration and Truth of Sacred Scripture*.

2. See, e.g., Billings, *The Word of God for the People of God*; Boersma, *Scripture as Real Presence*; Nafzger, *"These Are Written"*; Sargent, *Written for Our Learning*; Sparks, *God's Word in Human Words*.

3. Michael Gorman articulates the "Chalcedonian (or Incarnational) Principle" as the first of eight principles for guiding theological interpretation with Scripture. See Gorman, *Elements of Biblical Exegesis*, 149. For some thoughtful articulations of the judgment that we can fruitfully understand the human and divine dimensions of Scripture by analogy with the divine and human natures of the person of Christ, see Braaten, "A Chalcedonian Hermeneutic," 18–22; Enns, *Inspiration and Incarnation*; Farkasfalvy, *Inspiration and Interpretation*, 188–90, 219–21; Gorman, *Elements of Biblical Exegesis*, 148–50; Sparks, *Sacred Word, Broken Word*, 23–29; Work, *Living and Active*, 23–27. De Lubac showed how Origen had already assumed the usefulness of this analogy; see *HS*, 385–426. For a pointed warning against the dangers inherent in this approach, though, see Webster, *Holy Scripture*, 22–23. For a stimulating and learned constructive approach that more strongly connects the written word with the living Word, see Radner, *Time and the Word*, passim but esp. 100–104. This quotation (emphasis in original) is from 104: "Is there a scriptural 'type'? (or better, 'antitype'?) Christ Jesus! But Scripture is not 'less' of Jesus; it is Christ displayed in this form as antitypical artifact, of which the Scriptures are indeed the type, at any given time, of his very life. Even this is too limited: they *are* Christ among us." While Radner's study has much to commend it, he emphasizes the connection between the living Word and the written Word too strongly in my judgment.

4. As Denis Farkasfalvy and David Law have noticed. See Farkasfalvy, *Inspiration and Interpretation*, 203; Law, *Inspiration of the Scriptures*, 41.

5. I examine the two NT texts, along with 2 Cor 3, below.

6. See Abraham, *The Divine Inspiration of Holy Scripture*; Achtemeier, *Inspiration and Authority*; Burtchaell, *Catholic Theories of Biblical Inspiration*; Enns, *Inspiration and Incarnation*; Farkasfalvy, *Inspiration and Interpretation*; Farkasfalvy, "How to Renew the Theology of Biblical Inspiration?"; Gnuse, *The Authority of the Bible*; Graves, *The Inspiration and Interpretation*; Law, *Inspiration of the Scriptures*; Rahner, *Inspiration in the Bible*; Marshall, *Biblical Inspiration*; Pontifical Biblical Commission, *The Inspiration and Truth of Sacred Scripture*; Preus, *The Inspiration of Scripture*; Schökel, *The Inspired Word*; Vawter, *Biblical Inspiration*.

7. Achtemeier, *Inspiration and Authority*, 8.

8. For a recent work that provides a typology of divine action relative to Scripture, see Bowald, *Rendering the Word*.

9. Lonergan, "Mission and the Spirit," in *ATC*, 25 (CWL 16, 24).

10. Lonergan, "Christology Today," in *ATC*, 81 (CWL 16, 77).

11. I discuss the nontechnical nature of the language of Scripture in the section below.

12. And those ancient Scriptures, as I noted above, were themselves not "closed" in the first century.

13. Johnson, *The First and Second Letters to Timothy*, 423.

14. So John Webster helpfully notes that "inspiration is not foundational but derivative, a corollary of the self-presence of God which takes form through the providential ordering and sanctification of creaturely auxiliaries." Webster, *Holy Scripture*, 32.

15. For discussion of this passage, see Farkasfalvy, *Inspiration and Interpretation*, 54–57; Vawter, *Biblical Inspiration*, 13; Webster, *Holy Scripture*, 36–39.

16. See Farkasfalvy, *Inspiration and Interpretation*, 56, 202.

17. For more thorough treatments of the prophetic model, see Achtemeier, *Inspiration and Authority*, 16–19, 80–90; Farkasfalvy, *Inspiration and Interpretation*, 148–50; Graves, *The Inspiration and Interpretation*, 70–74; Vawter, *Biblical Inspiration*, 8–17.

18. For discussion of premodern dictation approaches, see Achtemeier, *Inspiration and Authority*, 18–19. For a thoroughgoing critique of recent dictation proposals, see Abraham, *The Divine Inspiration*, 28–38.

19. The metaphors come from Farkasfalvy, *Inspiration and Interpretation*, 136.

20. Such notions, writes Abraham, "are insufficient to cope with the emergence and results of inductive historical judgment." Abraham, *Divine Inspiration*, 27.

21. Farkasfalvy, *Inspiration and Interpretation*, 182.

22. The language of "true authors" comes from *Dei Verbum* § 3. For discussion, see Farkasfalvy, *Inspiration and Interpretation*, 178–85.

23. See Bennett, *The Author*, passim but esp. 29–71.

24. For a recent discussion, see Schniedewind, *How the Bible Became a Book*, 6–12.

25. Though many scholars argue that the Gospels were originally anonymous, Farkasfalvy notes that the attribution of gospels to Mark and Luke instead of to other major apostolic figures suggests their authenticity. For discussion of the traditions of attribution, see Farkasfalvy, *Inspiration and Interpretation*, 29–30. See also the helpful remarks in Bernier, *The Quest for the Historical Jesus*, 128–29n4; Watson, *The Fourfold Gospel*, 1–20.

26. Schniedewind, *How the Bible Became a Book*, 9.

27. For theological evaluations of the work of the Spirit through these processes, see Achtemeier, *Inspiration and Authority*, 122–26; Farkasfalvy, *Inspiration and Interpretation*, 183–85, 217–19, 232.

28. For contrasting positions on the implications of pseudonymity for scriptural authority, see Clark, "The Problem of Pseudonymity"; Carson, "Pseudonymity and Pseudepigraphy." On Christian attitudes towards pseudepigraphy in early Christianity, see Reed, "Pseudeipigraphy, Authorship, and the Reception of 'the Bible' in Late Antiquity." See also Meade, *Pseudonymity and Canon*.

29. I am referring to the documentary hypothesis concerning the origins of the Pentateuch and the synoptic problem concerning the relationship between the gospels of Mark, Matthew, and Luke. One legitimate reason for critically evaluating the various paradigms proposed for understanding the composition of these texts

is the fact that such hypothetical constructions are on the move. For recent discussions of the *status quaestiones* of the documentary hypothesis and the synoptic problem, see Baden, *The Composition of the Pentateuch*; Tuckett et al., *New Studies in the Synoptic Problem*.

30. Achtemeier, *Inspiration and Authority*, 76. On the repurposing of traditions in Scripture, see Fishbane, "Revelation and Tradition"; Kugel, *In Potiphar's House*; Kugel, *Traditions of the Bible*.

31. So Achtemeier, *Inspiration and Authority*, 64–73.

32. Webster, *Holy Scripture*, 17–30.

33. Webster, *Holy Scripture*, 17.

34. The context of the passage is Paul's exhortation for Timothy to remain true to the *sure traditions* he has received from Paul in contrast to the unstable and inauthentic teaching of false teachers (2 Tim 3.5). For discussion, see Johnson, *The First and Second Letters to Timothy*, 416–26.

35. See also 1 Clem. 45.2; 53.1.

36. Arichea and Hatton, *A Handbook on Paul's Letters to Timothy and to Titus*, 235.

37. I do not assume that Paul either did or did not author 2 Timothy. I do not assume that Peter did or did not author 2 Peter. What follows does not depend upon whether the traditional ascriptions of authorship hold. The position on the authority and inspiration of Scripture of the present work is relevant whether my readers find arguments for traditional authorship or pseudepigraphical authorship more persuasive. For recent discussion, see Porter and Fewster, *Paul and Pseudepigraphy*. My own judgment, in nuce, is that Paul's clear employment of amanuenses in his other letters and the likelihood that Paul himself developed are good reasons for maintaining the traditional judgments of attribution, but I consider that judgment to be a matter of adiaphora.

38. On the emphasis of the passage on the functional usefulness of Scripture, see Achtemeier, *Inspiration and Authority*, 93–94; Johnson, *The Letters of First and Second Timothy*, 423.

39. See Farkasfalvy, *Inspiration and Interpretation*, 54, 56. For a discussion of theories of inspiration focused on the words of Scripture specifically, see Law, *Inspiration of the Scriptures*, 47–98.

40. Kirster Stendahl, quoted in Hefling, *Why Doctrines?*, 143.

41. Webster, *Holy Scripture*, 23. See also Farkasfalvy, *Inspiration and Interpretation*, 219–20. Cf. though, the judgment of de Lubac, who writes that "the Spirit immured himself in [Scripture], as it were, He lives in it. His breath has always animated it.... It is full of the Spirit." De Lubac, *ME*, 1:82.

42. De Lubac, *ME*, 1:81.

43. Ong, *Orality and Literacy*, 80.

44. See Bokedal, *The Formation and Significance*, 198, 232, 241, 366. Bokedal gets this phrase from Gadamer, *The Relevance of the Beautiful*, 109–11, 142.

45. Ong writes that the death of the letter is not the end, however: "The paradox lies in the fact that the deadness of the text, its removal from the living human lifeworld, its rigid visual fixity, assures its endurance and its potential for being resurrected into limitless living contexts by a potentially infinite number of living readers." Ong, *Orality and Literacy*, 80. And Christians, to be sure, hold characteristic perspectives on the lack of finality in death. The Spirit capably breathes life into ostensibly "dead" texts. I discuss this below.

46. For a recent set of essays on this passage and its reception, particularly in the early church, see Fiddes and Bader, *The Spirit and the Letter*; see also Cover, *Lifting the Veil*.

47. The language of the "new covenant" and Paul's discussion of inner transformation of the heart undoubtedly have their roots in his reflection on the tradition he has received concerning Jesus's eucharistic words. See 1 Cor 11.23–26; Jer 31.31–34; Ezek 11.16–23; 36.24–32. See also Stockhausen, *Moses' Veil*, 42–54.

48. Paul has very strong words here concerning the "blindness" of those of his own flesh and blood who have not turned to the Lord Jesus Christ. But there are tensions in Paul's presentation of "Judaism" and the Jewish people (see Rom 3.1–2; 9.1–5; 11.2). For discussion of the thorny challenges Paul's words pose for Christian theological reflection today, see Gager, "Paul, the Apostle of Judaism," 56–76. See also Soulen, *The God of Israel*.

49. For more extensive discussion of the work of the Holy Spirit in individual and communal readers and hearers, see Achtemeier, *Inspiration and Authority*, 116–26; Bovell, "All Scripture Is Hermeneutically God-Breathed."

50. Gadamer, *The Relevance of the Beautiful*, 132.

51. See, e.g., Calvin, *Institutes*, 1.7.4–1.7.5.

52. For discussion and citations, see Graves, *The Inspiration and Interpretation*, 43–48.

53. Farkasfalvy, *Inspiration and Interpretation*, 113.

54. Achtemeier, *Inspiration and Authority*, 123.

55. My translation. The Greek reads: "Τὸ πνεῦμα ὅπου θέλει πνεῖ καὶ τὴν φωνὴν αὐτοῦ ἀκούεις, ἀλλ᾽ οὐκ οἶδας πόθεν ἔρχεται καὶ ποῦ ὑπάγει."

56. See Jenson, "The Religious Power of Scripture," 94.

57. Rogers, *After the Spirit*, 71. Given his salutary focus on the characteristic affinity of the Holy Spirit for material realities (oil, water, bread, etc.), I am surprised that Rogers does not treat the Spirit's work of "resting" upon the material texts of Christian Scripture in *After the Spirit*.

58. See the position on human nature in chapter 4.

59. Origen, *Homilies on Joshua* (trans. White and Bruce), 177–78.

60. I discuss this judgment at greater length in the next section.

61. I should note that in citing these diverse texts I do not intend to suggest that their distinct human authors in their distinct original historically particular circumstances shared a uniform understanding of the Holy Spirit as a third person

of the Trinity. I do nevertheless affirm that they were talking about divine activity and purposes and that the similarities of their languages and conceptions of such dynamic divine activity coupled with the later technical specifications of Trinitarian doctrine and a conviction of the providence of God allow one to bring these texts together as references to the mysterious work of the third person of the Trinity. For an illuminating discussion of the historical challenges regarding talk about matters of the Holy Spirit in Scripture, see Martin, *Biblical Truths*, 221–61.

62. For winsome reflections on the persistent return of believers to these texts, see Jenson, "The Religious Power of Scripture."

63. I do hold, with Augustine, that it is *possible*, even in this terrestrial life, for believers to have no need of Scripture. He writes in *Doctr. chr.* that "people supported by faith, hope, and charity, and retaining a firm grip on them, have no need of the scriptures except for instructing others" (1.39.43). Though this is *possible*, and would be a work of the grace of the Triune God if ever actual (Matt 19.26), certainly it has seldom happened in history, if at all. Some have argued, from Jesus's statement recorded in Matt 24.35 and Luke 21.33 (from Matt: "Heaven and earth will pass away, but my words (pl. λόγοι μου) will not pass away") that the Bible itself possesses some quasi-eternality. Such a judgment cannot stand in the light of the historical evidence of the material *realia* of Scripture, and if uncritically accepted could easily direct Christian attention away from God.

64. The phrase, interestingly, is first attested in the Qur'an (see Q an-Nisa 4.153; 4.159–60; 4.171; Q al-'Ankabut 29.46), where it is used to refer to both Jews and Christians. For discussion of these texts, see Barton, *People of the Book?*, 1–2; Jeffrey, *People of the Book*, xi–xx.

65. Though Hurtado rightly notes that "bookishness" has been a key distinguishing feature of Christian faith and praxis since the beginning. See Hurtado, *Destroyer of the gods*, 105–41. See also Bernier, *The Quest for the Historical Jesus*, 141.

66. See de Lubac, *ME*, 3:146.

67. Ong, *Orality and Literacy*, 175–76.

68. It is of course impossible to come to unmediated experiences, understandings, and judgments concerning the Son of God himself (except perhaps in mystical experiences, but such experiences would be by definition inscrutable and incommunicable). It is also true that Scripture should authoritatively constrain our perspectives on Jesus, the only Son of the Father. But not all mediated understandings of the Son and the Son's work are equally faithful, responsible, and intelligent. As James Cone has recently written, "The cross can heal and hurt; it can be empowering and liberating but also enslaving and oppressive" (Cone, *The Cross and the Lynching Tree*, xix). For a selection of illuminating, faithful, and responsible mediations of the Son and the Son's work, I recommend Cone's *The Cross and the Lynching Tree*; Laughlin, *Jesus and the Cross*; Loewe, *The College Student's Introduction*; Loewe, *Lex Crucis*; Lonergan, *The Incarnate Word*; Lonergan, *The Redemption*; Rutledge, *The Crucifixion*.

69. As noted above, Ephraim Radner strongly emphasizes the connection and continuity of the written Word and the living Word. See his *Time and the Word*. Boersma, however, cautions that we should be sure to qualify that we are only using incarnation language of Scripture in an analogical sense. Boersma, *Scripture as Real Presence*, 113n28.

70. John Barton and James Barr critique Paul Ricoeur for statements that he makes to this effect. See Barton, *People of the Book?*, 7; Barr, *Holy Scripture*, 70; Ricoeur, *Essays in Biblical Interpretation*, 51.

71. "[The] motif of scriptural testimony," writes Meyer, "is not the primary theme but a qualifier; the primary thematic accent falls on 'he died for our sins' and 'he was raised on the third day.'" Meyer, *The Aims of Jesus*, 62.

72. Barton, *People of the Book?*, 7.

73. Farkasfalvy, *Inspiration and Interpretation*, 9; emphasis mine.

74. It is the meaning of "the event" or "the fact" of Christ, as de Lubac notes. See de Lubac, *ME*, 2:104–5; de Lubac, *EM*, 2.2:106–23. On incarnate meaning, see chapter 4 above.

75. For fuller treatments of the nature of divine revelation, see Abraham, *Crossing the Threshold*; Dulles, *Models of Revelation*; Fackre, *The Doctrine of Revelation*; Gunton, *A Brief Theology of Revelation*; Levering, *Engaging the Doctrine of Revelation*; Wahlberg, *Revelation as Testimony*.

76. Lonergan, "Theology in Its New Context," in *ASC*, 61–62 (CWL 13, 54). For a thorough study of Lonergan's understanding of divine revelation, see Ormerod, *Method, Meaning, and Revelation*.

77. The spatial and temporal aspects of such language are problematic in themselves. It is not as though the creator is "outside" of creation. We live and move and have our being in the Triune God (Acts 17). And God is nearer to us than we can imagine (Ps 139). Nevertheless, the incarnation and all of its effects are decisively new *in created history*.

78. For a survey of some characteristic tenets of "progressive revelation" approaches, see Davies, *The Immoral Bible*, 22–43. For two classic nuanced and valuable treatments of progressive revelation, see Albright, *From the Stone-Age to Christianity*; Dodd, *The Authority of the Bible*. For a more recent evaluation of Israel's progressive apprehension of YHWH in the OT, see Gnuse, *No Other Gods*.

79. "The history of revelation also offers the spectacle of discontinuity that has no equal." De Lubac, *ME*, 1:234. See also de Lubac, *ME*, 234–41; de Lubac, *ME*, 2:98–106. For analysis of the historical permutations of early Christian reflection on this "newness," from the time of Paul's letters through the second century, see Lang, *Mystery and the Making*.

80. While my focus will be on the NT texts in what follows, the authors of the NT documents were clearly adopting and claiming the testimony of Israel's prophets to the future work of the God of Israel on behalf of his people and the world. See Isa 42.9–21; 48.6; 65.17; Jer 31.31–34; Ezek 11.19; 18.31; 36.26. For a recent examination of these texts, see Leene, *Newness in Old Testament Prophecy*.

81. The emphasis is mine here and in the following texts.

82. For an excellent recent treatment of the significance of the apocalyptic invasion of the Son, see Rutledge, *The Crucifixion*.

83. Readers schooled in NT criticism will recognize the clear distinctions between the various perspectives that I have cited in these key verses. Nevertheless, the unity of their conviction that the God of Israel has done something of universal importance and uniqueness in Christ is quite striking.

84. De Lubac, *More Paradoxes*, 17.

85. "Omnen novitatem attulit, semetipsum afferens." The translation is mine. De Lubac is fond of this passage and regularly quotes it. See de Lubac, "The Light of Christ," 207, 218; de Lubac, *HS*, 507.

86. Farkasfalvy, *Inspiration and Interpretation*, 112.

87. See de Lubac, *HS*, 465–66. At the very least, the early Christians thought that Jesus had referred the scriptures to himself. It would be quite remarkable, even stretching the boundaries of credulity, if they produced such associations in complete independence from Christ's own use of Scripture. "What extraordinary witnesses," de Lubac writes, "capable of inventing, each on his own, such things that, for long centuries, were destined to overturn minds and hearts, to fulfill the tradition of Israel by seeming to destroy it, to introduce into the old civilization a spiritual leaven that would transform it completely—and all agreeing to attribute everything to someone else, to that very Jesus they all considered, across the diversity of their intentions, to be the unique Master and Lord: they were themselves the authors of this unparalleled Newness, which as they show us despite themselves and by so many signs, they had so poorly understood!" De Lubac, *More Paradoxes*, 26. See de Lubac's penetrating reflections on the NT witness and the presuppositions of historical criticism in de Lubac, *More Paradoxes*, 11–38. For an excellent presentation of the historical evidence for this supposition by a historical critic, see Meyer, *Christus Faber*, 59–80. See also Meyer, *The Aims of Jesus*, 74–75; Hays, *Echoes of Scripture in the Gospels*, 5.

88. For a learned and penetrating account of the distinctiveness of their praxis, see Kreider, *The Patient Ferment*.

89. Goldingay, *Do We Need the New Testament?*, 165.

90. Goldingay affirms his belief in the incarnation in *Do We Need the New Testament?*, 21.

91. See Goldingay, *Do We Need the New Testament?*, 160–65.

92. Goldingay, *Do We Need the New Testament?*, 169. Since Goldingay is an Episcopal priest, I assume he means the Niceno-Constantinopolitan Creed. Elsewhere he expresses more tentativeness in his estimation of the creeds: "I have questions about the common forms of the Christian grand narrative that leap straight from creation to Jesus, as Christian creeds do, or that comprise only creation, fall, redemption, in Christ and the second coming. These involve gross oversimplification." Goldingay, *Do We Need the New Testament?*, 88.

93. Goldingay is correct to state that the creed is not Scripture and that the rule of faith "enables us to see things that are there [in Scripture]; it does not determine what is allowed to be there." See Goldingay, *Do We Need the New Testament?*, 169, 173. I find his comments on the origins and value of the rule and the creeds extremely problematic, though. He states that the creed is "a human formula" and that it is "not part of the New Testament." He also writes that trinitarian theology "appeals to Westerners because we are desperate to become more relational." Is Scripture not also human language? Do the pre-NT confessions not express judgments about reality taken up by the creeds? Trinitarian theology is not appealing to me because it is relational; it is appealing to me because I have been baptized into the name of the Father, the Son, and the Holy Spirit, and I am interested in having some idea what in the world that might mean, and finally because I have done—and continue to do—the hard work of seeking to understand what that confession means by studying the advances in understanding of brothers and sisters in Christ concerning the meaning and significance of that confession.

94. Goldingay, *Do We Need the New Testament?*, 21.

95. Goldingay, *Do We Need the New Testament?*, 31.

96. See Goldingay, *Do We Need the New Testament?*, 161. He notes that the NT "uses the First Testament for insight on the church, the ministry, mission, the world, and so on." What is the church if not the Body of Christ? What is ministry if not our participation in Christ's ministry of reconciliation? What is mission if not the mission given by Christ to his disciples? And is the world not created through Christ?

97. While Goldingay has confirmed that he was not responsible for the title—his preferred epithet for the OT is the "First Testament"—he nevertheless utilizes the colloquial language of the agency of Scripture that I find slightly irresponsible. See Andrew Lewis, "Symposium Introduction," https://syndicatetheology.com/symposium/do-we-need-the-new-testament/.

98. See Goldingay, *Do We Need the New Testament?*, 144–56.

99. So Doran: "This ultimate meaning of history in the Law of the Cross is at the heart of the revelation that is gradually communicated by God through the history of the biblical literature, a revelation that finds its principal site in the beatific knowledge of Jesus of Nazareth." Doran, *The Trinity in History*, 98. For examinations of Paul's teaching on Christian participation in the mission of God through cruciform imitation of Christ by Christian believers, see Gorman, *Inhabiting the Cruciform God*; Gorman, *Becoming the Gospel*.

100. Meyer argues that this tendency is evident in the allegorism of many early church fathers. See Meyer, *Reality and Illusion*, 178–81.

101. For examinations of this history, see Cohen, *Living Letters of the Law*; Dahan, *The Christian Polemic*; Hirshman, *A Rivalry of Genius*; Simon, *Verus Israel*; Wilken, *John Chrysostom*; Wilken, *Judaism and the Early Christian Mind*. For an extremely useful analysis of Thomas Aquinas's treatment of the relationship between

Judaism and Christianity with relevance for contemporary theological reflection on the perils of Christian interpretation, see Tapie, *Aquinas on Israel and the Church*. See also Soulen, *The God of Israel*. David Tracy astutely writes, "There is no reason why any Christian today should not challenge the portrait of the Jews in John's Gospel and elsewhere in the New Testament. One may do so, moreover, not only on the basis of more accurate historical information about the Johannine communities and first-century Judaism, nor even on the basis of the frightening effects of these anti-Judaic texts in Christian anti-Semitism, but on the basis of the fundamental envisionment of all reality in Jesus Christ in John's own Gospel." Grant and Tracy, *A Short History*, 183–84.

102. See Siebert, *The Violence of Scripture*.

103. Ben Meyer argues that such an approach is the most pressing need for contemporary scriptural hermeneutics: "The task of New Testament hermeneutics . . . is sublated by the Christian missionary task: to open, to keep open, or to re-open access to the gospel; to remove the blocks that stop the flow of meaning and extinguish the light of truth." Meyer, *Reality and Illusion*, xi. "The revelatory event," writes Tracy, "must be allowed to judge the textual witnesses to the event." Grant and Tracy, *A Short History*, 183.

104. De Lubac, *Catholicism*, 181.

105. De Lubac, *ME*, 3:145. "The parchment of the Book henceforth is his flesh; what has been written down is his divinity." De Lubac, *ME*, 3.143. For fuller treatments of de Lubac on the fullness of God's self-revelation in Christ, see *HS*, 433–34, 448, 465–68; *ME*, 1:234–41; *ME*, 2:98–107; *ME* 3:140–45; de Lubac, "The Light of Christ."

106. For studies that focus upon the relationship between the two Testaments, see Baker, *Two Testaments*; Barr, *Old and New in Interpretation*; Beauchamp, *La Loi de Dieu*; Beauchamp, *L'un et l'autre testament: 1. Essai de lecture*; Beauchamp, *L'un et l'autre testament: 2. Accomplir les écritures*; Childs, *Biblical Theology*; Coppens, *Les harmonies des deux Testaments*; McDonald, *Metaphysics and the God of Israel*; Seitz, *The Character of Christian Scripture*; Seitz, *Figured Out*.

107. De Lubac, *Paradoxes*, 145–46. For de Lubac's most extended treatment of the relationship between the OT and NT, see de Lubac, *ME*, 1:225–68.

108. De Lubac, *Catholicism*, 169.

109. See Barton, *Holy Writings, Sacred Text*, passim but esp. 63–105.

110. Barton, *Holy Writings, Sacred Text*, 79. See also Watson, *The Fourfold Gospel*, 9–15, 140–41. This insight offers an explanation for the justification of inserting additions in the texts of the Gospels (see Mark 16.9–20; John 7.53–11).

111. De Lubac, *HS*, 433.

112. For explorations of the theological use of the OT in the early church, see Boersma, *Scripture as Real Presence*; Cameron, *Christ Meets Me Everywhere*; Heine, *Reading the Old Testament*; Reno and O'Keefe, *Sanctified Vision*.

113. De Lubac, *Catholicism*, 171.

114. For a discussion of the universality of God's reign in the expression of the OT authors, see Anderson, *Christian Doctrine and the Old Testament*, 147. I identify this universality as one key characteristic of de Lubac's promotion of spiritual exegesis in Gordon, "*Ressourcement* Anti-Semitism?"

115. Goldingay argues that Jesus embodies God's desire to sacrifice himself for his people, a desire already expressed in the First Testament. See Goldingay, *Do We Need the New Testament?*, 153.

116. De Lubac, *Catholicism*, 165; emphasis mine. A number of subsequent detailed studies have corroborated de Lubac's judgment that many if not most premodern figures saw in Scripture an overarching narrative of the divine economy from creation to redemption. See Behr, *Identifying Christianity*, 90–103; Young, *Biblical Exegesis*, 43–45, 143, 151, 168, 181; Levering, "Linear and Participatory History"; Harris, "The Bible and the Meaning of History."

117. In contrast, the Tanakh concludes not with the Neviim but with the Kethuvim.

118. Bokedal, *The Formation of the Christian Biblical Canon*, 169.

119. Barth, *The Word of God*, 32.

120. For discussion, see Smith, *The Bible Made Impossible*, 8–11.

121. Barth, *The Word of God*, 32.

122. Barth, *The Word of God*, 33.

123. De Lubac, "The Light of Christ," 211n21.

124. As Rowan Williams puts it, "The diversity of the Bible is as great as if you had within the same two covers, for example, Shakespeare's sonnets, the law reports of 1910, the introduction to Kant's *Critique of Pure Reason*, the letters of St Anselm and a fragment of *The Canterbury Tales. All within the same two covers.*" Williams, *Being Christian*, 24–25; emphasis in original.

125. Brown, *Sacred Sense*, 11.

126. Collins, *The Bible after Babel*, 160–61.

127. De Lubac, *ME*, 1:32. On the premodern embrace of this dimension of Scripture, see Graves, *The Inspiration and Interpretation*, 48–55.

128. Farkasfalvy, *Inspiration and Interpretation*, 106.

129. Radner, *Time and the Word*, 225. Radner suggests that the breadth of the lectionary readings provides the material occasion, in Christian worship, supplying the particular filings of this synthesis. The point remains, however, whether we have the lectionary readings in mind or any other reading and hearing of Christian Scripture by Christian believers.

130. For an extended argument to this effect, see Smith, *The Fall of Interpretation.*

131. Achtemeier does not mince words: "The . . . displacement of the biblical witness by critical reason is at work every time a conservative author tries to 'prove' that a narrative of some miraculous activity is 'true' by arguing that it could have come about by natural causes of which we have analogies. . . . An appeal to an

errorless autograph of Scripture to account for errors and discrepancies in our copies of the Bible is a further example of allowing reason to stand in judgment over Scripture." Achtemeier, *Inspiration and Authority*, 58–59.

132. Meyer, "Primacy of the Intended Sense of Texts," 46. For further discussion, see Meyer, *Reality and Illusion*, 179–81. See also Moberly, *The Bible*, 189.

133. See Hefling, "Another Perhaps Permanently Valid Achievement"; Hefling, "Revelation and/as Insight."

134. See Lonergan, "The Mediation of Christ in Prayer"; Crowe, "The Power of the Scriptures."

135. See Meyer, *Reality and Illusion*, 174–96.

136. McEvenue, "Theological Doctrines and the Old Testament," 136–37. See also McEvenue, *Interpreting the Pentateuch*, 152–53; Rutledge, *The Crucifixion*, esp. 6–7, 146, 210–12.

137. See Origen, *Princ.* 4.1.7; Augustine, *Conf.* 3.5.9; 12.27.37.

138. Luther, "Preface to the Old Testament," 98.

139. Hamann, "Cloverleaf of Hellenistic Letters (1762)," 39. Note the trinitarian shape of kenosis in Hamann's reference to the work of God. I am grateful to David Hart for pointing me to Hamann's reflections on the humility of Scripture. See also Hamann, "Biblische Betrachtungen eines Christen." For discussion, see Alexander, *Johann Georg Hamann*, 25–36; Lindner, "Johann Georg Hamann."

140. When considered in its historical context relative to other faith traditions, Stroumsa notes that the demotic—as opposed to hieratic—language of the NT in particular reflects "a revolutionary attitude to scriptural language, now meant to be accessible to all, even to those with a very modest level of literacy." Stroumsa, *The Scriptural Universe*, 18.

141. Origen, *The Philocalia of Origen*, 52.

142. The conviction of the enigmatic nature of divine communication already occurs in Scripture; see Ps 78.2; John 2.19; 16.25; 2 Pet 3.16–17. On the early Christian conviction of the inscrutability of Scripture, see Graves, *The Inspiration and Interpretation*, 61–64; Origen, *Philoc.* 1.10; 10.1; 18.14.

143. For discussion, see Graves, *The Inspiration and Interpretation*, 22–26; Law, *Inspiration of the Scriptures*, 67–69.

144. For discussion, see McDonald, *The Biblical Canon*, 198.

145. See Origen, *Princ.* 4.3.15 and Augustine's discussion of *res* and *signa* in *Doctr. chr.* 1.

146. Hefling, *Why Doctrines?*, 2.

147. Again, see Meyer, *Reality and Illusion*, 174–96.

148. As I noted in chapter 4 (note 8), in a subsequent monograph I intend to provide an answer to this question through a transposing of the medieval fourfold sense of Scripture in light of the categories and judgments of subjectivity and conversion laid out in that chapter.

149. Crowe, "The Power of the Scriptures," 292.

150. Lienhard, *The Bible, the Church, and Authority*, 7. See also Lonergan, *MIT*, 115 (CWL 14, 111–12).

151. See chapter 1, note 4, and the introduction to chapter 4.

152. The arguments of the present section depend upon the structures and possibilities of human nature that I laid out in chapter 4.

153. Numerous church fathers invoke this passage in particular, alongside Gal 4.21–31; 1 Cor 9.9–10; 2 Cor 3; and Eph 5.31–32, as a justification for detecting "spiritual" (also referred to as allegorical, figural, tropological, or anagogical) senses of the OT. Such spiritual reading had a constitutive place in the spiritual transformation of the interpreter. See, e.g., Origen, *Cels.* 4.49–50; *Philoc.* passim. Adequate examination and evaluation of these spiritual reading approaches and their potential value as resources for contemporary engagement with Scripture would take us beyond the scope of the present work, but I plan to attempt such a task in a future major project. That project will offer an account of the ways in which Scripture both reflects and effects certain transformations and differentiations of consciousness in readers and hearers; it will explain how Scripture is divine pedagogy, in Ben Meyer's words, how it brings about "subjectivity correlative to the [written] Word of God." See Meyer, *Reality and Illusion*, 174–96.

For orientation to the spiritual senses, see de Lubac, *ME*, 2:83–226. For articles evaluating the possibility of utilizing premodern exegetical or hermeneutical praxis today, see Daley, "Christ, the Church, and the Shape of Scripture"; Daley, "Is Patristic Exegesis Still Usable?"; Steinmetz, "The Superiority of Pre-Critical Exegesis"; Treier, "The Superiority of Pre-Critical Exegesis: *Sic et Non*"; and Wilken, "In Defense of Allegory." For recent efforts to reappropriate the premodern senses for Christian scriptural interpretation today, see Boersma, *Scripture as Real Presence*; Froelich, *Sensing the Scriptures*; Radner, *Time and the Word*.

154. See Johnson, *The First and Second Letters to Timothy*, 420, 423. For a recent example of an evangelical account that invokes 2 Tim 3.14–17 and 2 Pet 1.20–21 to articulate an ontology of Scripture, see Hamilton, "Still *Sola Scriptura*." For pointed critiques of "biblicist" approaches to the ontology of scripture such as Hamilton's, see Smith, *The Bible Made Impossible*; Enns, *The Bible Tells Me So*.

155. For useful introductions to how the church fathers understood the usefulness of Scripture with citations of specific examples, see Graves, *The Inspiration and Interpretation*, 17–41; Sheridan, "The Concept of 'Useful.'" For a discussion of Augustine's understanding of the instrumentality of Scripture that contrasts Augustine's approach with some contemporary works focused on Scripture's ontology, see Andrews, *Hermeneutics and the Church*, 6–8.

156. See, e.g., Origen, *Comm. Jo.* 10.174; *Comm. Rom.* 8.6.5; 9.1.9–9.1.12; 10.6.10–10.6.11; *Hom. Judic.* 2.3; 2.5; *Hom. Jes. Nav.* 3.1; 5.2; 13.1; 20.2; *Philoc.*

1.13–1.16; 10.1. For a contemporary study that takes John 20.30–31 as a basis for articulating a theology of Scripture focused on its instrumental purpose, see Nafzger, *"These Are Written."*

157. For discussion, see Loewe, *Lex Crucis*, 24–31, 40–42.

158. Just prior to this passage, Origen makes reference to 1 Cor 2.11–15 to emphasize that readers of Scripture are only able to understand it through their possession of "the mind of Christ" (10.173). The translation is from *Commentary on the Gospel According to John* (trans. Heine), 294–95. In 10.174 Origen is alluding to the statement of the author of the Gospel of John concerning his specific intentions in John 20.30–31.

159. In *Doctr. chr.*, Ayres notes, Augustine "gloss[es the creed] as a plan not only of cosmos and history but also of human restoration." Ayres, "Augustine on the Rule of Faith," 37. Elsewhere in the same article Ayres writes that the rule of faith "is both the drama of Christ's descent and ascent and the faith and hope through which one's attention is drawn to and in the ascending Christ" (40). Brian Stock also expresses this judgment concisely in his thorough study on Augustine's positions on reading. For Augustine, Stock demonstrates, "the reading of Scripture is the key element in the pursuit of wisdom, the *amor* or *studium sapientiae.*" Stock, *Augustine the Reader*, 9.

160. English translation taken from *The Confessions* (trans. Boulding), 353–54. Augustine continues his figural interpretation of "the vault" through 13.18.23.

161. See the list of premodern studies in chapter 4, note 4.

162. Ayres, "The Soul and the Reading of Scripture," 189. Ayres presents this judgment as a possible tenth thesis to add to the nine proposed in Davis and Hays, "Nine Theses on the Interpretation of Scripture," 1–5.

163. For a complementary but different account of the instrumentality of Scripture for mediating the saving work of the Triune God, see Webster, *Holy Scripture*, 5–41.

164. As Bokedal notes; see note 45 above.

165. Again, such changes will take place in accord with the norms of subjectivity given in chapter 4.

166. De Lubac, "The Problem of the Development of Dogma," 274.

167. Again, chapter 4 articulates an account of human nature as a heuristic for identifying the intelligible structures that undergird such discursive learning and transformation in us.

168. De Lubac, "The Problem of the Development of Dogma," 275.

169. De Lubac, "The Problem of the Development of Dogma," 275.

170. Topel, "Faith, Exegesis, and Theology," 342. So also Boersma: "As we read Scripture, we come to understand ourselves in the process—and, of course, vice versa: as we come to understand ourselves better, we become better equipped to read Scripture." Boersma, *Scripture as Real Presence*, 114.

171. De Lubac, *ME*, 1:227.

172. "*L'exégèse est de la sorte un 'exercice', grâce auquel l'esprit du croyant progresse.*" De Lubac, *EM*, 2.2:86; translation mine.

173. Copeland, *Enfleshing Freedom*, 6.

174. McEvenue, *Interpreting the Pentateuch*, 28. For two apologies for this judgment, see Fitzmyer, *The Interpretation of Scripture*; Harrisville, *Pandora's Box Opened.*

175. Young, *Virtuoso Theology*, 18.

176. It is not necessary for all who read Scripture to become scholars, but the massive amount of historical data relevant to the origins of Christian faith and the publication of that data in works of history written in a nonspecialist idiom—and even the production and dissemination of fictional works such as *The Da Vinci Code*—require some response from a faith perspective.

177. This compact judgment reflects my assent to the legitimacy of "so-called" contextual reading strategies (all reading, after all, is contextual). But such reading strategies find their own legitimate place within the historic Christian community's discernment of the actual redemptive and transformative work of the Triune God in history.

178. De Lubac, *Paradoxes of Faith*, 102.

179. As I have noted (chapter 4, note 8; notes 149 and 154 above), in my next major project I intend to demonstrate how Scripture both reflects the fruit of the conversions—intellectual, moral, and religious—and serves as an instrument that facilitates such conversions *and* the differentiations of consciousness entailed in both scholarship and contextual reading strategies. That work will bring together the Lonerganian reflection on anthropology with a consideration of the ancient fourfold sense of Scripture recovered by de Lubac to appropriate and transform the historical/literal, allegorical/theological, moral/tropological, and anagogical/spiritual senses of Scripture for the level of our own times.

180. For discussion of the "status" authority of Scripture, see Cosgrove, *Appealing to Scripture*, 9–11.

181. See Siebert, *The Violence of Scripture*; and the works listed in its bibliography.

182. For a brilliant discussion of the kenotic dimensions of Christ's lordship, see Copeland, *Enfleshing Freedom*, 63–65.

183. For discussion on the import of this passage for Christian spirituality, see Gorman, "A New Translation."

184. For his own words, at least early in his career, see *Doctr. chr.* 2.15.22. See also my discussion of the Greek versions in the previous chapter. Richard Hays cites Augustine as an ancient and venerable authority for affirming the authority of the ancient Greek translations and reinstating them in Christian worship today. See Hays, *Reading Backwards*, 106–7. Augustine's mature position, as I show presently, however, is nuanced and makes space for the authority of both the Hebrew and Greek versions of the OT.

185. For Jerome's conviction that the Greek versions were flawed, see his preface to his translation of Joshua.

186. The texts are collected and translated in White, *The Correspondence*. Unsurprisingly, their communication was hindered by a number of concrete historical complications in the transmission of the letters. For discussion, see White, *The Correspondence*, 35–42; Kotzé, "Augustine, Jerome, and the Septuagint."

187. The controversy was likely over Jerome's translation of the plant that God caused to grow over Jonah (see Jon 4.6). The version(s) translated from Greek had the equivalent of the English "gourd," while Jerome rendered the Hebrew as the equivalent of "ivy." See Jerome, *Ep.* 112.

188. For a contemporary articulation of a similar position, see Jenson, *Canon and Creed*, 53–55, 61–62. For a helpful analysis of the general reluctance to speak of contradictions in Scripture, see Moberly, *Old Testament Theology*, 111–16, 232–33.

189. From Augustine, *Concerning the City of God* (trans. Bettenson), 821–23. See also *Doctr. chr.* 4.7.15. He may anticipate this later judgment in *Doctr. chr.* 2.17.

190. For an interesting proposal that all versions approved by Roman Catholic ecclesial synods—what he calls Canon tokens—are the words of Scripture, see Griffiths, "Which Are the Words." He concludes that "the meanings of all versions taken together constitute to the meaning of Scripture; and apparent semantic conflicts among the versions should be considered an opportunity for exegesis rather than a problem for it, just as is the case for prima facie conflicts of meaning within a particular version." Griffiths, "Which Are the Words," 718.

191. The phrase is Stanley Fish's; see his *Self-Consuming Artifacts*. Richard Hays uses it to describe the book of Hebrews in "Here We Have No Lasting City."

192. Kaiser et al., *Four Views on Moving beyond the Bible to Theology*. See also Marshall, Vanhoozer, and Porter, *Beyond the Bible*.

193. As de Lubac writes, "When we are faced with a very great text, a very profound one, never can we maintain that the interpretation we give of it—even if it is very accurate, the most accurate, if need be, the only accurate one—coincides exactly with its author's thought. The fact is, the text and the interpretation are not of the same order; they do not develop at the same level, and therefore they cannot overlay one another. The former expresses spontaneous, synthetic, 'prospective,' in some fashion, creative knowledge. The latter, which is a commentary, is of the reflective and analytical order. In a sense, the commentary, if it is at all penetrating, always goes farther than the text, since it makes what it finds there explicit; and if it does not in fact go farther, it is of no use, since no light would then be shed by it on the text. But in another and more important sense, the text, by its concrete richness, always overflows the commentary, and never does the commentary dispense us from going back to the text. There is virtually infinity in it." De Lubac, *Paradoxes*, 109. See also Boersma, *Scripture as Real Presence*, 19.

194. De Lubac, *ME*, 1:77. Hart and Radner argue that this truth makes possible or even requires allegorical or figural reading. See Hart, *The Beauty of the Infinite*, 284n143; Radner, *Time and the Word*, 89.

Conclusion

    1. Origen, *Commentary on the Epistle to the Romans,* 196.

    2. See Ricoeur, *The Symbolism of Evil,* 237, 347–57; Lonergan, *MIT,* 313 (CWL 14, 291); Lonergan, *Insight,* 483.

    3. "Si finisti, Deus non est." *Sermo* 53.12.

BIBLIOGRAPHY

Abraham, William J. *Canon and Criterion in Christian Theology: From the Fathers to Feminism*. New York: Oxford University Press, 1998.

———. "Canonical Theism: Thirty Theses." In *Canonical Theism: A Proposal for Theology and the Church*, edited by William J. Abraham, Jason E. Vickers, and Natalie B. Van Kirk, 1–7. Grand Rapids, MI: Eerdmans, 2008.

———. *Crossing the Threshold of Divine Revelation*. Grand Rapids, MI: Eerdmans, 2006.

———. *The Divine Inspiration of Holy Scripture*. New York: Oxford University Press, 1981.

Abraham, William J., Jason E. Vickers, and Natalie B. Van Kirk, eds. *Canonical Theism: A Proposal for Theology and the Church*. Grand Rapids, MI: Eerdmans, 2008.

Achtemeier, Paul J. *Inspiration and Authority: Nature and Function of Christian Scripture*. Grand Rapids, MI: Baker Academic, 2010.

———. "*Omne Verbum Sonat*: The New Testament and the Oral Environment of Late Western Antiquity." *Journal of Biblical Literature* 109, no. 1 (1990): 3–27.

Ackroyd P. R., and C. F. Evans, eds. *The Cambridge History of the Bible: From the Beginnings to Jerome*. New York: Cambridge University Press, 1975.

Adam, A. K. M. "Authors, Readers, Hermeneutics." In *Reading Scripture with the Church: Toward a Hermeneutic for Theological Interpretation*, edited by A. K. M. Adam, Stephen E. Fowl, Kevin J. Vanhoozer, and Francis Watson, 119–24. Grand Rapids, MI: Baker, 2006.

———. "Integral and Differential Hermeneutics." In *The Meanings We Choose: Hermeneutical Ethics, Indeterminacy, and the Conflict of Interpretations*, edited by Charles Cosgrove, 24–38. New York: T & T Clark, 2004.

———. *What Is Postmodern Biblical Criticism?* Minneapolis: Fortress, 1995.

Adam, A. K. M., Stephen E. Fowl, Kevin J. Vanhoozer, and Francis Watson. *Reading Scripture with the Church: Toward a Hermeneutic for Theological Interpretation*. Grand Rapids, MI: Baker, 2006.

Adams, Sean E. *Baruch and the Epistle to Jeremiah: A Commentary Based on the Texts of Codex Vaticanus*. Boston: Brill, 2014.

Adler, Mortimer, and Charles Van Doren. *How to Read a Book: The Classic Guide to Intelligent Reading*. Rev. and Updated. New York: Touchstone, 1972.

Albl, Martin C. *"And Scripture Cannot Be Broken": The Form and Function of the Early Christian Testimonia Collections.* Boston: Brill, 1999.

————. Introduction and commentary in *Pseudo-Gregory: Testimonies against the Jews.* Translated with Introduction and Notes by Martin C. Albl. Atlanta, GA: Society of Biblical Literature, 2014.

Albright, William Foxwell. *From the Stone-Age to Christianity: Monotheism and the Historical Process.* Baltimore, MD: Johns Hopkins University Press, 1940.

Alexander, Loveday. "The Living Voice: Skepticism towards the Written Word in Early Christian and in Greco-Roman Texts." In *The Bible in Three Dimensions,* edited by David J. A. Clines, Stephen E. Fowl, Stanley E. Porter, 221–47. Sheffield: Sheffield Academic Press, 1990.

Alexander, W. M. *Johann Georg Hamann: Philosophy and Faith.* The Hague: Martinus Nijhoff, 1966.

Allen, Paul L. *Theological Method: A Guide for the Perplexed.* New York: T & T Clark, 2012.

Allert, Craig D. *A High View of Scripture? The Authority of the Bible and the Formation of the New Testament Canon.* Grand Rapids, MI: Baker Academic, 2007.

Alter, Robert. *The Art of Biblical Narrative.* 2nd ed. New York: Basic Books, 2011.

Alter, Robert, and Frank Kermode. *The Literary Guide to the Bible.* Cambridge, MA: Belknap Press of Harvard University Press, 1987.

Anderson, Gary A. *Christian Doctrine and the Old Testament: Theology in the Service of Biblical Exegesis.* Grand Rapids, MI: Baker, 2017.

Andrews, James A. *Hermeneutics and the Church: In Dialogue with Augustine.* Notre Dame, IN: University of Notre Dame Press, 2012.

Archer, Gleason L., and Gregory Chirichigno. *Old Testament Quotations in the New Testament.* Chicago: Moody Press, 1983.

Arichea, Daniel C., and Howard A. Hatton. *A Handbook on Paul's Letters to Timothy and to Titus.* New York: United Bible Societies, 1995.

Aristotle. *On the Soul, Parva Naturalia, On Breath.* Translated by W. S. Hett. Loeb Classical Library 288. Cambridge, MA: Harvard University Press, 1957.

————. *Posterior Analytics Topica.* Translated by Hugh Tedrennick and E. S. Forster. Loeb Classical Library 391. Cambridge, MA: Harvard University Press, 1960.

Armstrong, Jonathan J. "From the κανὼν τῆς ἀληθείας to the κανὼν τῶν γραφῶν: The Rule of Faith and the New Testament Canon." In *Tradition and the Rule of Faith in the Early Church: Essays in Honor of Joseph T. Lienhard, S.J.,* edited by Ronnie J. Rombs and Alexander Y. Hwang, 30–47. Washington, DC: Catholic University of America Press, 2010.

Arnold, Duane W. H., and Pamela Bright, eds. *De Doctrina Christiana: A Classic of Western Culture.* Notre Dame, IN: University of Notre Dame Press, 1995.

Augustine. *Concerning the City of God against the Pagans.* Translated by Henry Bettenson. Introduction by C. R. Evans. New York: Penguin, 2003.

——. *The Confessions.* Translated by Maria Boulding. The Works of Saint Augustine: A Translation for the 21st Century. Vol. I/1. Hyde Park, NY: New City Press, 1997.

——. *De doctrina christiana libri quattuor.* Edited by William McAllen Green. Corpus Scriptorum Ecclesiasticorum Latinorum v. 80. Vindobonae: Hoelder-Pichler-Tempsky, 1963.

——. *Teaching Christianity (De Doctrina Christiana).* Edited by John E Rotelle. Translated by Edmund Hill. The Works of Saint Augustine: A Translation for the 21st Century. Vol. I/11. Hyde Park, NY: New City Press, 1996.

Austin, John L. *How to Do Things with Words.* 2nd ed. New York: Oxford University Press, 1975.

Avalos, Hector. *The End of Biblical Studies.* Amherst, NY: Prometheus, 2007.

——. *Slavery, Abolitionism, and the Ethics of Biblical Scholarship.* Sheffield: Sheffield Phoenix, 2011.

Ayres, Lewis. "Augustine on the Rule of Faith: Rhetoric, Christology, and the Foundation of Christian Thinking." *Augustinian Studies* 36, no. 1 (2005): 33–49.

——. "Irenaeus vs. the Valentinians: Toward a Rethinking of Patristic Exegetical Origins." *Journal of Early Christian Studies* 23, no. 2 (2015): 153–87.

——. *Nicaea and Its Legacy: An Approach to Fourth Century Trinitarian Theology.* New York: Oxford University Press, 2004.

——. "Patristic and Medieval Theologies of Scripture." In *Christian Theologies of Scripture: A Comparative Introduction,* edited by Justin S. Holcomb, 11–20. New York: New York University Press, 2006.

——. "The Soul and the Reading of Scripture: A Note on Henri de Lubac." *Scottish Journal of Theology* 61, no. 2 (2008): 173–90.

Ayres, Lewis, and Stephen Fowl. "(Mis)reading the Face of God: The Interpretation of the Bible in the Church." *Theological Studies* 60 (1999): 513–28.

Baden, Joel S. *The Composition of the Pentateuch: Renewing the Documentary Hypothesis.* New Haven, CT: Yale University Press, 2012.

Baik, Chung-Hyun. *The Holy Trinity—God for God and God for Us: Seven Positions on the Immanent-Economic Trinity Relation in Contemporary Trinitarian Theology.* Eugene, OR: Pickwick, 2011.

Baird, William. *History of New Testament Research.* 3 vols. Minneapolis, MN: Fortress, 1992–2013.

Baker, David L. *Two Testaments, One Bible: The Theological Relationship between the Old and New Testaments.* 3rd ed. Downers Grove, IL: InterVarsity, 2010.

Baker, Matthew, and Mark Mourachian, eds. *What Is the Bible? The Patristic Doctrine of Scripture.* Minneapolis, MN: Fortress, 2016.

Balogh, Josef. "*Vocens Paginarum*: Beiträge zur Geschichte des lauten Lesens und Schreibens." *Philologus* 82 (1927): 84–109, 202–40.

Balthasar, Hans Urs von. *Epilogue.* Translated by Edward T. Oakes. San Francisco, CA: Ignatius, 2004.

Barnes, Michel René. "Ebion at the Barricades: Moral Narrative and Post-Christian Catholic Theology." *Modern Theology* 26 no. 4 (2010): 511–48.

Barr, James. *Holy Scripture: Canon, Authority, Criticism.* New York: Oxford University Press, 1983.

———. *Old and New in Interpretation: A Study of the Two Testaments.* London: SCM, 1966.

Barth, Karl. *The Church Dogmatics: 1.2; The Doctrine of the Word of God.* Edited by Geoffrey Bromiley and T. F. Torrance. Translated by G. T. Thompson and Harold Knight. New York: T & T Clark, 2004.

———. *The Epistle to the Romans.* Translated by Edwyn C. Hoskins. Oxford: Oxford University Press, 1968.

———. *Die Kirchliche Dogmatik I: Die Lehre vom Worte Gottes 2.* Zollikon-Zurich: Evangelischer Verlag, 1938.

———. *The Word of God and the Word of Man.* Translated by Douglas Horton. New York: Harper & Row, 1957.

Bartholomew, Craig G., ed. *Canon and Biblical Interpretation.* Grand Rapids, MI: Zondervan, 2006.

Bartholomew, Craig G., and Heath A. Thomas, eds. *A Manifesto for Theological Interpretation.* Grand Rapids, MI: Baker Academic, 2016.

Barton, John. *Holy Writings, Sacred Text: The Canon in Early Christianity.* Louisville, KY: Westminster John Knox, 1998.

———. *Oracles of God: Perceptions of Ancient Prophecy in Israel after the Exile.* New York: Oxford University Press, 1988.

———. *People of the Book? The Authority of the Bible in Christianity.* Louisville, KY: Westminster John Knox, 1988.

Barton, John, and Michael Wolter, eds. *Die Einheit der Schrift und die Vielfalt des Kanons (The Unity of Scripture and the Diversity of the Canon).* New York: Walter de Gruyter, 2003.

Bates, Matthew W. *The Birth of the Trinity: Jesus, God, and Spirit in New Testament & Early Christian Interpretations of the Old Testament.* New York: Oxford University Press, 2015.

Batten, Alicia J., and John Kloppenborg. *James, 1 & 2 Peter, and Early Jesus Traditions.* New York: Bloomsbury, 2015.

Bauckham, Richard. *Jesus and the Eyewitnesses: The Gospels as Eyewitness Testimony.* 2nd ed. Grand Rapids, MI: Eerdmans, 2017.

Beards, Andrew. "*Übersicht* as Oversight: Problems in Wittgenstein's Later Philosophy." In *Insight and Analysis: Essays in Applying Lonergan's Thought,* 63–77. New York: Continuum, 2010.

Beauchamp, Paul. *La Loi de Dieu.* Paris: Editions du Seuil, 1999.

———. *L'un et l'autre testament: 1. Essai de lecture.* Paris: Editions du Seuil, 1976.

———. *L'un et l'autre testament: 2. Accomplir les Écritures.* Paris: Editions du Seuil, 1990.

Béchard, Dean P., ed. and trans. *The Scripture Documents: An Anthology of Official Catholic Teachings.* Collegeville, MN: Liturgical Press, 2002.

Becker, Adam H. *Fear of God and the Beginning of Knowledge: The School of Nisibis and Christian Scholastic Culture.* Philadelphia: University of Pennsylvania Press, 2006.

Beckwith, Roger. *The Old Testament Canon of the New Testament Church and Its Background in Early Judaism.* Grand Rapids, MI: Eerdmans, 1985.

Behr, John. *Irenaeus of Lyons: Identifying Christianity.* New York: Oxford University Press, 2013.

———. *The Way to Nicaea.* Crestwood, NY: St. Vladimir's Seminary, 2001.

Bennett, Andrew. *The Author.* New York: Routledge, 2005.

Berkouwer, G. C. *Holy Scripture.* Grand Rapids, MI: Eerdmans, 1975.

Bernier, Jonathan. *Aposynagōgos and the Historical Jesus in John: Rethinking the Historicity of the Johannine Expulsion Passages.* Boston: Brill, 2013.

———. *Quest for the Historical Jesus after the Demise of Authenticity: Toward a Critical-Realist Philosophy of History in Jesus Studies.* New York: T & T Clark, 2016.

Bertoldi, Francesco. "Henri de Lubac on *Dei Verbum.*" Translated by Mandy Murphy. *Communio* 17 (1990): 88–94.

Billings, J. Todd. *The Word of God for the People of God: An Entryway to the Theological Interpretation of Scripture.* Grand Rapids, MI: Eerdmans, 2010.

Bingham, Jeffrey. "The Bishop in the Mirror: Scripture and Irenaeus's Self-Understanding in *Adversus Haereses* Book One." In *Tradition and the Rule of Faith in the Early Church: Essays in Honor of Joseph T. Lienhard, S.J.,* edited by Ronnie J. Rombs and Alexander Y. Hwang, 48–67. Washington, DC: Catholic University of America Press, 2010.

Bischoff, Bernard. *Latin Paleography: Antiquity and the Middle Ages.* New York: Cambridge University Press, 1990.

Blenkinsopp, Joseph. *A History of Prophecy in Israel.* Rev. and enlarged. Louisville, KY: Westminster John Knox, 1996.

Blocher, Henri. "The Analogy of Faith in the Study of Scripture." *Scottish Bulletin of Evangelical Theology* 5 (1987): 17–38.

Blomberg, Craig L., and Jennifer Foutz Markley. *A Handbook of New Testament Exegesis.* Grand Rapids, MI: Baker Academic, 2006.

Blowers, Paul. *Drama of the Divine Economy: Creator and Creation in Early Christian Theology and Piety.* New York: Oxford University Press, 2012.

———. *Exegesis and Spiritual Pedagogy in Maximus the Confessor: An Investigation of the Questiones ad Thalassium.* Notre Dame, IN: University of Notre Dame Press, 1991.

———. "The '*Regula Fidei*' and the Narrative Character of the Early Christian Faith." *Pro Ecclesia* 6, no. 2 (1997): 199–228.

Blumell, Lincoln H., and Thomas A. Wayment, eds. *Christian Oxyrhynchus: Texts, Documents, and Sources.* Waco, TX: Baylor University Press, 2015.

Bobzin, Hartmut. "Translations of the Qur'ān." In *The Encyclopedia of the Qur'ān*, vol. 5, 340–58, edited by Jane Dammen McAuliffe. Leiden: Brill, 2006.

Bock, Darrell L., and Buist M. Fanning. *Interpreting the New Testament Text: Introduction to the Art and Science of Exegesis.* Wheaton, IL: Crossway, 2006.

Boersma, Hans. *Embodiment and Virtue in Gregory of Nyssa: An Anagogical Approach.* New York: Oxford University Press, 2013.

———. *Scripture as Real Presence: Sacramental Exegesis in the Early Church.* Grand Rapids, MI: Baker Academic, 2017.

Bogaert, Pierre-Maurice. "Le livre de Baruch dans les manuscrits de la Bible latine: Disparition et reintegration." *Revue bénédictine* 115 (2005): 286–342.

Bokedal, Tomas. *The Formation of the Christian Biblical Canon: A Study in Text, Ritual, and Interpretation.* New York: T & T Clark, 2014.

———. "Notes on the *Nomina Sacra* and Biblical Interpretation." In *Beyond Biblical Theologies*, edited by Heinrich Assel, Stefan Beyerle, and Christfried Böttrich, 263–95. Tübingen: Mohr Siebeck, 2012.

———. "The Rule of Faith: Tracing Its Origins." *Journal of Theological Interpretation* 7, no. 2 (2013): 233–55.

Bonhoeffer, Dietrich. *Reflections on the Bible: Human Word and Word of God.* Translated by M. Eugene Boring. Peabody, MA: Hendricksen, 2004.

Bonino, Serge-Thomas, ed. *Surnatural: A Controversy at the Heart of Twentieth-Century Thomistic Thought.* Washington, DC: Catholic University of America Press, 2007.

Bovell, Carlos R. "All Scripture Is Hermeneutically God-Breathed." In *Biblical Inspiration and the Authority of Scripture*, edited by Carlos R. Bovell, 3–26. Eugene, OR: Wipf & Stock, 2015.

Bovon, François. "Beyond the Canonical and the Apocryphal Books, the Presence of a Third Category: The Books Useful for the Soul." *Harvard Theological Review* 105, no. 2 (2012): 125–37.

Bowald, Mark Alan. *Rendering the Word in Theological Hermeneutics: Mapping Divine and Human Agency.* Aldershot: Ashgate, 2007.

Boyd, Gregory. *God of the Possible: A Biblical Introduction to the Open View of God.* Grand Rapids, MI: Baker, 2000.

Boyle, Nicholas. *Sacred and Secular Scriptures: A Catholic Approach to Sacred Literature.* Notre Dame, IN: University of Notre Dame Press, 2004.

Boynton, Susan, and Diane J. Reilly, eds. *The Practice of the Bible in the Middle Ages: Production, Reception, and Performance in Western Christianity.* New York: Columbia University Press, 2011.

Braaten, Carl. "A Chalcedonian Hermeneutic." *Pro Ecclesia* 3, no. 1 (1994): 18–22.

Brakke, David. "Canon Formation and Social Conflict in Fourth-Century Egypt: Athanasius of Alexandria's Thirty-Ninth Festal Letter." *Harvard Theological Review* 87 (1994): 395–419.

Bratcher, Robert G. *Old Testament Quotations in the New Testament.* 3rd ed. New York: United Bible Societies, 1987.

Breck, John. *Scripture in Tradition: The Bible and Its Interpretation in the Orthodox Church.* Crestwood, NY: St. Vladimir's Seminary, 2001.

Bright, Pamela, ed. *Augustine and the Bible.* Notre Dame, IN: University of Notre Dame Press, 1999.

———. "Biblical Ambiguity in African Exegesis." In *De Doctrina Christiana: A Classic of Western Culture,* edited by Duane W. H. Arnold and Pamela Bright, 25–32. Notre Dame, IN: University of Notre Dame Press, 1995.

Broggi, Joshua. *Sacred Language, Sacred World: The Unity of Scriptural and Philosophical Hermeneutics.* New York: T & T Clark, 2015.

Brotzman, Ellis R., and Eric J. Tully. *Old Testament Textual Criticism: A Practical Introduction.* 2nd ed. Grand Rapids, MI: Baker Academic, 2016.

Brown, Raymond E. *An Introduction to the New Testament.* New York: Doubleday, 1997.

Brown, Schuyler. "Concerning the Origin of the *Nomina Sacra.*" *Studia Papyrologica* (1970): 7–19.

———. *Text and Psyche: Experiencing Scripture Today.* New York: Continuum, 1998.

Brown, William P. *Sacred Sense: Discovering the Wonder of God's Word and World.* Grand Rapids, MI: Eerdmans, 2015.

———, ed. *Engaging Biblical Authority: Perspectives on the Bible as Scripture.* Louisville, KY: Westminster John Knox, 2007.

Brox, Norbert. *Offenbarung: Gnosis und gnostiker Mythos bei Irenaus von Lyon: Zur Charakteristik der Systeme.* Munich: A. Pustet, 1966.

Bruce, F. F. *The Canon of Scripture.* Downers Grove, IL: InterVarsity, 1988.

Brueggemann, Walter. *Theology of the Old Testament: Testimony, Dispute, Advocacy.* Minneapolis, MN: Fortress, 1997.

Brueggemann, Walter, William C. Placher, and Brian K. Blount. *Struggling with Scripture.* Louisville, KY: Westminster John Knox, 2002.

Bultmann, Rudolf. "Is Exegesis without Presuppositions Possible?" In *The Hermeneutics Reader: Texts of the German Tradition from the Enlightenment to the Present,* edited by Kurt Mueller-Vollmer, 242–47. New York: Continuum, 1989.

Burnyeat, M. F. "Is an Aristotelian Philosophy of Mind Still Credible (A Draft)." In *Essays on Aristotle's "De Anima,"* edited by Martha C. Nussbaum and Amelie Oksenberg Rorty, 15–26. Oxford: Clarendon, 1992.

———. "A Postscript on Silent Reading." *Classical Quarterly* 47, no. 1 (1997): 74–76.

Burrell, David B. "The Act of Creation with Its Theological Consequences." In *Creation and the God of Abraham,* edited by David B. Burrell, Carlo Cogliatti, Janet M. Soskice, and William R. Stoeger, 40–52. New York: Cambridge University Press, 2010.

———. *Aquinas: God and Action.* Notre Dame, IN: University of Notre Dame Press, 1979.

———. *Faith and Freedom: An Interfaith Perspective.* Malden, MA: Wiley-Blackwell, 2004.

————. *Freedom and Creation in Three Traditions.* Notre Dame, IN: University of Notre Dame Press, 1993.

————. *Friendship and Ways to Truth.* Notre Dame, IN: University of Notre Dame Press, 2000.

————. *Towards a Jewish-Christian-Muslim Theology.* Malden, MA: Wiley-Blackwell, 2011.

Burtchaell, James T. *Catholic Theories of Biblical Inspiration since 1810: A Review and Critique.* Cambridge: Cambridge University Press, 1969.

Byassee, Jason. *Praise Seeking Understanding: Reading the Psalms with Augustine.* Grand Rapids, MI: Eerdmans, 2007.

Byrne, Patrick H. *The Ethics of Discernment: Lonergan's Foundations for Ethics.* Toronto: University of Toronto Press, 2016.

Cain, Andrew. *The Letters of Jerome: Asceticism, Exegesis, and the Construction of Christian Authority in Late Antiquity.* New York: Oxford University Press, 2009.

Calderhead, Christopher. *Illuminating the Word: The Making of the Saint John's Bible.* 2nd ed. Collegeville, MN: Liturgical Press, 2015.

Calvin, John. *Institutes of the Christian Religion.* Translated by Henry Beveridge. Peabody, MA: Hendrickson, 2008.

Cameron, Euan, ed. *The New Cambridge History of the Bible: From 1450 to 1750.* New York: Cambridge University Press, 2016.

Cameron, Michael. *Christ Meets Me Everywhere: Augustine's Early Figurative Exegesis.* New York: Oxford University Press, 2012.

Campenhausen, Hans von. *The Formation of the Christian Bible.* Philadelphia, PA: Augsberg Fortress, 1977.

Candler, Peter M. "St. Thomas Aquinas." In *Christian Theologies of Scripture: A Comparative Introduction,* edited by Justin S. Holcomb, 60–80. New York: New York University Press, 2006.

————. *Theology, Rhetoric, and Manuduction, or Reading Scripture Together on the Path to God.* Grand Rapids, MI: Eerdmans, 2006.

Carpenter, Anne M. *Theo-Poetics: Hans Urs von Balthasar and the Risk of Art and Being.* Notre Dame, IN: University of Notre Dame Press, 2015.

Carr, David M. *The Formation of the Hebrew Bible: A New Reconsideration.* New York: Oxford University Press, 2011.

————. *Writing on the Tablet of the Heart: The Origins of Scripture and Literature.* New York: Oxford University Press, 2008.

Carson, Donald A. "Pseudonymity and Pseudepigraphy." In *Dictionary of New Testament Background,* edited by Craig A. Evans and Stanley E. Porter, 857–64. Downers Grove, IL: InterVarsity, 2000.

Carson, Donald A., and Gregory K. Beale, eds. *Commentary on the New Testament Use of the Old Testament.* Grand Rapids, MI: Baker Academic, 2007.

Cartwright, Nancy. *The Dappled World: A Study of the Boundaries of Science.* New York: Cambridge University Press, 1999.

Certeau, Michel de. "Exégèse, théologie et spirtualité." *Revue d'ascetique et de mystique* 36 (1960): 357–71.

Chadwick, Owen. *From Bossuet to Newman.* 2nd ed. New York: Cambridge University Press, 1987.

Chantraine, Georges. *Henri de Lubac: De la naissance à la démobilisation, 1896–1919.* Paris: Cerf, 2007.

———. *Henri de Lubac: Les années de formation, 1919–1929.* Paris: Cerf, 2009.

Chantraine, Georges, and Marie-Gabrielle Lemaire. *Henri de Lubac: Concile et après-Concile, 1960–1991.* Paris: Cerf, 2013.

Chapman, Stephen B. "The Old Testament Canon and Its Authority for the Christian Church." *Ex Auditu* (2003): 125–48.

Charlesworth, S. D. "Consensus Standardization in the Systematic Approach to *nomina sacra* in Second- and Third-Century Gospel Manuscripts." *Aegyptus* 86 (2006): 37–68.

Childs, Brevard. *Biblical Theology of the Old and New Testaments: Theological Reflection on the Christian Bible.* Minneapolis, MN: Fortress, 1993.

Chrétien, Jean-Louis. *Under the Gaze of the Bible.* Translated by John Marson Dunaway. New York: Fordham University Press, 2015.

Clark, Elizabeth A. *The Origenist Controversy: The Cultural Construction of an Early Christian Debate.* Princeton, NJ: Princeton University Press, 1992.

Clark, Kent D. "The Problem of Pseudonymity in Biblical Literature and Its Implications for Canon Formation." In *The Canon Debate*, edited by Lee Martin McDonald and James A. Sanders, 440–68. Peabody, MA: Hendrickson, 2002.

Coakley, Sarah. *God, Sexuality, and the Self: An Essay "On the Trinity."* New York: Cambridge University Press, 2013.

Coelho, Ivo. *Hermeneutics and Method: The "Universal Viewpoint" in Bernard Lonergan.* Toronto: University of Toronto Press, 2001.

Cohen, Jeremy. *Living Letters of the Law: Ideas of the Jew in Medieval Christianity.* Berkeley: University of California Press, 1999.

Collins, John J. *The Bible after Babel: Historical Criticism in a Postmodern Age.* Grand Rapids, MI: Eerdmans, 2005.

———. *The Dead Sea Scrolls: A Biography.* Princeton, NJ: Princeton University Press, 2012.

———. *Does the Bible Justify Violence?* Minneapolis, MN: Fortress, 2004.

Collins, Paul M. *The Trinity: A Guide for the Perplexed.* New York: T & T Clark, 2008.

Comfort, Philip. *Encountering the Manuscripts: An Introduction to New Testament Paleography and Textual Criticism.* Nashville, TN: Broadman & Holman, 2005.

Comfort, Philip W., and David P. Barrett. *The Complete Text of the Earliest New Testament Greek Manuscripts.* Grand Rapids, MI: Baker, 1999.

Cone, James H. *The Cross and the Lynching Tree.* Maryknoll, NY: Orbis, 2011.

Cone, Steven D. *An Ocean Vast of Blessing: A Theology of Grace.* Eugene, OR: Cascade, 2014.

————. "Transforming Desire: The Relation of Religious Conversion and Moral Conversion in the Later Writings of Bernard Lonergan." PhD dissertation, Boston College, 2009.

Congar, Yves. *I Believe in the Holy Spirit*. Translated by Geoffrey Chapman. New York: Crossroad, 1997.

Cooper, Stephen Andrew. Introduction to *Marius Victorinus' Commentary on Galatians: Introduction, Translation, and Notes*. Translated by Stephen Andrew Cooper. New York: Oxford University Press, 2005.

Copeland, M. Shawn. *Enfleshing Freedom: Body, Race, and Being*. Minneapolis, MN: Fortress, 2010.

Coppens, Joseph. *Les harmonies des deux Testaments: Essai sur les divers sens des Écritures et sur l'unité de la révélation*. Tournai-Paris: Casterman, 1949.

Cosgrove, Charles. *Appealing to Scripture in Moral Debate: Five Hermeneutical Rules*. Grand Rapids, MI: Eerdmans, 2002.

Countryman, L. William. "Tertullian and the *Regula Fidei*." *Second Century* 2, no. 4 (1982): 208–27.

Cover, Michael. *Lifting the Veil: 2 Corinthians 3:7–18 in Light of Jewish Homiletic and Commentary Traditions*. Boston: Walter de Gruyter, 2015.

Cowley, R. W. "The Biblical Canon of the Ethiopian Orthodox Church Today." *Ostkirchliche Studien* 23 (1974): 318–23.

Crawford, Matthew R. *Cyril of Alexandria's Trinitarian Theology of Scripture*. New York: Oxford University Press, 2014.

Creech, Jerome D. *Violence in Scripture*. Louisville, KY: Westminster John Knox, 2013.

Crouzel, Henri. *Origène*. Paris: Lethielleux, 1985.

Crowe, Frederick E. *Christ and History: The Christology of Bernard Lonergan from 1935–1982*. Toronto: Novalis, 2005.

————. *Lonergan*. Collegeville, MN: Liturgical Press, 1992.

————. "The Power of the Scriptures: An Attempt at Analysis." In *Lonergan and the Level of Our Time*, edited by Frederick E. Crowe and Michael Vertin, 279–93. Toronto: University of Toronto Press, 2010.

————. *Theology of the Christian Word: A Study in History*. New York: Paulist, 1978.

Crowe, Frederick E., and Michael Vertin, eds. *Lonergan and the Level of Our Time*. Toronto: University of Toronto Press, 2010.

Crysdale, Cynthia, and Neil Ormerod. *Creator God, Evolving World*. Minneapolis, MN: Fortress, 2013.

Dahan, Gilbert. *The Christian Polemic against Jews in the Middle Ages*. Translated by Jody Gladding. Notre Dame, IN: University of Notre Dame Press, 1998.

Daley, Brian E. "Christ, the Church, and the Shape of Scripture: What We Can Learn from Patristic Exegesis." In *From Judaism to Christianity: Tradition and Transition*, edited by Patricia Walters, 267–88. Leiden: Brill, 2010.

————. "In Many and Various Ways." In *Heaven on Earth? Theological Interpretation in Ecumenical Dialogue*, edited by Hans Boersma and Matthew Levering, 13–33. Malden, MA: Wiley-Blackwell, 2013.

———. "Is Patristic Exegesis Still Usable? Some Reflections on Early Christian Interpretation of the Psalms." In *The Art of Reading Scripture*, edited by Ellen F. Davis and Richard B. Hays, 69–88. Grand Rapids, MI: Eerdmans, 2003.

———. "Origen's *De Principiis*: A Guide to the Principles of Christian Scriptural Interpretation." *In Nova et Vetera: Patristic Studies in Honor of Thomas Patrick Halton*, edited by John Petruccione, 3–21. Washington, DC: Catholic University of America Press, 1998.

D'Ambrosio, Marcellino. "Henri de Lubac and the Critique of Scientific Exegesis." *Communio* 19 (Fall 1992): 365–88.

———. "Henri de Lubac and the Recovery of the Traditional Hermeneutic." PhD dissertation, Catholic University of America, 1991.

Danielou, Jean. *Origène*. Paris: Association André Robert, 1986.

Davies, Eryl W. *The Immoral Bible: Approaches to Biblical Ethics*. New York: T & T Clark, 2010.

Dawidowski, Wieslaw. "*Regula Fidei* in Augustine: Its Use and Function." *Augustinian Studies* 35, no. 2 (2004): 253–99.

Dawson, John David. *Allegorical Readers and Cultural Revision in Ancient Alexandria*. Berkeley: University of California Press, 1992.

———. *Christian Figural Reading and the Fashioning of Identity*. Berkeley: University of California Press, 2001.

De Crom, Dries. "The Letter of Aristeas and the Authority of the Septuagint." *Journal for the Study of the Pseudepigrapha* 17, no. 2 (2008): 141–60.

de Lubac, Henri. *At the Service of the Church: Henri de Lubac Reflects on the Circumstances That Occasioned His Writings*. Translated by Anne Elizabeth Englund. San Francisco: Ignatius, 1993.

———. *Catholicism: Christ and the Common Destiny of Mankind*. Translated by Lancelot Sheppard. San Francisco: Ignatius, 1988.

———. *Catholicisme: Les aspects sociaux du dogme*. Œuvres complètes 7. Paris: Cerf, 2003.

———. "Christian Explanation of Our Times." In *Theology in History*, 440–56. Translated by Anne Englund Nash. San Francisco: Ignatius, 1996.

———. *The Christian Faith*. Translated by Richard Arnandez. San Francisco: Ignatius, 1986.

———. *The Drama of Atheist Humanism*. Translated by Edith M. Riley, Anne Englund Nash, and Marc Sebanc. San Francisco: Ignatius, 1995.

———. *Exégèse médiévale: Les quatre sens de l'Écriture*. Coll. Théologie 41, 42, 59. Paris: Aubier-Montaigne, 1959, 1961, 1964.

———. "Hellenistic Allegory and Christian Allegory." In *Theological Fragments*, 165–96. Translated by Rebecca Howell Balinski. San Francisco: Ignatius, 1989.

———. *Histoire et esprit: L'Intelligence de l'Écriture d'après Origène* (+ 5 articles). Edited by Michel Fédou. Œuvres complètes 16. Paris: Éditions du Cerf, 2002.

———. *History and Spirit: The Understanding of Scripture According to Origen*. Translated by Anne Englund Nash. San Francisco: Ignatius, 2007.

————. "Internal Causes of the Weakening and Disappearance of the Sense of the Sacred." In *Theology in History*, 223–40. Translated by Anne Englund Nash. San Francisco: Ignatius, 1996.

————. "The Light of Christ." In *Theology in History*, 201–20. Translated by Anne Englund Nash. San Francisco: Ignatius, 1996.

————. *Medieval Exegesis: The Four Senses of Scripture.* Vol. 1. Translated by Marc Sebanc. Grand Rapids, MI: Eerdmans, 1998.

————. *Medieval Exegesis: The Four Senses of Scripture.* Vol. 2. Translated by E. M. Macierowski. Grand Rapids, MI: Eerdmans, 2000.

————. *Medieval Exegesis: The Four Senses of Scripture.* Vol. 3. Translated by E. M. Macierowski. Grand Rapids, MI: Eerdmans, 2009.

————. *Memoire sur l'occasion de mes écrits.* Namur: Culture et Verité, 1989.

————. *More Paradoxes.* [No translator named.] San Francisco: Ignatius, 2002.

————. "Mysticism and Mystery." In *Theological Fragments*, 35–69. Translated by Rebecca Howell Balinski. San Francisco: Ignatius, 1989.

————. "A New Religious 'Front.'" In *Theology in History*, 457–87. Translated by Anne Englund Nash. San Francisco: Ignatius, 1996.

————. "On an Old Distich: The Doctrine of the Fourfold Sense of Scripture." In *Theological Fragments*, 109–27. Translated by Rebecca Howell Balinski. San Francisco: Ignatius, 1989.

————. *Paradoxes of Faith.* Translated by Paulie Simon, Sadie Kreilkamp, and Ernest Beaumount. San Francisco: Ignatius, 1987.

————. *La postérité spirituelle de Joachim de Flore.* 2 vols. Paris: Lethielleux, 1979, 1983.

————. "The Problem of the Development of Dogma." In *Theology in History*, 248–80. Translated by Anne Englund Nash. San Francisco: Ignatius, 1996.

————. *Résistance chrétienne au Nazisme.* Preface, Introductions, and Notes by Renée Bédarida. *Oeurves complètes* 34. Paris: Cerf, 2006.

————. "Révélation divine." In *Révélation divine–Affrontements mystiques–Athéisme et sens de l'homme*, 34–231. Œuvres complètes 6. Paris: Cerf, 2006.

————. *Scripture in the Tradition.* Translated by Luke O'Neill. New York: Crossroad, 2000.

————. *A Theologian Speaks.* Los Angeles: Twin Circle, 1985.

————. "The Theological Foundation of the Missions." In *Theology in History*, 367–427. Translated by Anne Englund Nash. San Francisco: Ignatius, 1996.

————. "Typology and Allegory." In *Theological Fragments*, 129–64. Translated by Rebecca Howell Balinski. San Francisco: Ignatius, 1989.

Desmond, William. *God and the Between.* Malden, MA: Wiley-Blackwell, 2008.

Dodd, C. H. *The Authority of the Bible.* New York: Harper, 1958.

Doran, Robert M. "Envisioning a Systematic Theology." *Lonergan Workshop* 20 (2008): 105–26.

————. "A New Project in Systematic Theology." *Theological Studies* 76, no. 2 (2015): 243–59.

———. "The Starting Point of Systematic Theology." *Theological Studies* 67, no. 4 (2006): 750–76.

———. "System and History: The Challenge to Catholic Theology." *Theological Studies* 60, no. 4 (1999): 652–78.

———. *Theology and the Dialectics of History.* Toronto: University of Toronto Press, 1990.

———. *The Trinity in History,* vol. 1: *Missions and Processions.* Toronto: University of Toronto Press, 2013.

———. *What Is Systematic Theology?* Toronto: University of Toronto Press, 2005.

Dreyfus, François. "Divine Condescendence (*Synkatabasis*) as a Hermeneutic Principle of the Old Testament in Jewish and Christian Tradition." *Immanuel* 19 (1984–85): 74–86.

Drilling, Peter. "Preaching: A Mutual Self-Mediation of the Word of God, a Preacher, and a Congregation." *Lonergan Workshop* 7 (1988): 85–114.

Driver, Daniel R. "Childs and the Canon or Rule of Faith." In *The Bible as Christian Scripture: The Work of Brevard H. Childs,* edited by Robert C. Kashow, Kent Harold Richards, and Christopher R. Seitz, 243–78. Atlanta, GA: Society of Biblical Literature, 2013.

Duby, Stephen J. *Divine Simplicity: A Dogmatic Account.* New York: T & T Clark, 2016.

Dulles, Avery. *Models of Revelation.* Maryknoll, NY: Orbis, 1992.

Dungan, David L. *The Sayings of Jesus in the Churches of Paul: The Use of the Synoptic Tradition in Early Church Life.* Philadelphia: Fortress, 1971.

Dunn, James D. G. *Jesus Remembered.* Vol. 1 of Christianity in the Making. Grand Rapids, MI: Eerdmans, 2003.

———. *The New Perspective on Paul.* Rev. ed. Grand Rapids, MI: Eerdmans, 2008.

———. *The Oral Gospel Tradition.* Grand Rapids, MI: Eerdmans, 2013.

———. *Unity and Diversity in the New Testament: An Inquiry into the Character of Earliest Christianity.* 2nd ed. London: SCM, 1990.

Durant, Michael. "Preface." In *Aristotle's "De Anima" in Focus,* edited by Michael Durant, vii–viii. New York: Routledge, 1993.

Duvall, J. Scott, and J. Daniel Hays. *Grasping God's Word: A Hands-On Approach to Reading, Interpreting, and Applying the Bible.* 3rd ed. Grand Rapids, MI: Zondervan, 2012.

Eastman, Susan Grove. *Paul and the Person: Reframing Paul's Anthropology.* Grand Rapids, MI: Eerdmans, 2017.

Eden, Kathy. *Hermeneutics and the Rhetorical Tradition: Chapters in the Ancient Legacy and Its Humanist Reception.* New Haven, CT: Yale University Press, 1997.

Edwards, James R. "A *Nomen Sacrum* in the Sardis Synagogue." *Journal of Biblical Literature* 128, no. 4 (2009): 813–21.

Edwards, Mark. *Image, Word, and God in Early Christian Centuries.* Burlington, VT: Ashgate, 2013.

Ehrman, Bart D., and Michael W. Holmes, eds. *The Text of the New Testament in Contemporary Research: Essays on the Status Quaestionis.* 2nd ed. Boston: Brill, 2013.

Ehrman, Bart D., and Daniel E. Wallace. "The Textual Reliability of the New Testament: A Dialogue." In *The Reliability of the New Testament: Bart D. Ehrman and Daniel B. Wallace in Dialogue,* edited by Robert B. Stewart, 13–60. Minneapolis, MN: Fortress, 2011.

Elder, Nicholas. "New Testament Media Criticism." *Currents in Biblical Research* 15, no. 3 (2017): 315–37.

Emery, Gilles. *The Trinitarian Theology of St. Thomas Aquinas.* Translated by Francesca Aran Murphy. New York: Oxford University Press, 2009.

———. *The Trinity: An Introduction to Catholic Doctrine on the Triune God.* Translated by Matthew Levering. Washington, DC: Catholic University of America Press, 2011.

Enns, Peter. *The Bible Tells Me So: Why Defending Scripture Has Made Us Unable to Read It.* San Francisco, CA: HarperCollins, 2014.

———. *Inspiration and Incarnation: Evangelicals and the Problem of the Old Testament.* 2nd ed. Grand Rapids, MI: Eerdmans, 2015.

Epp, Eldon Jay. "The Codex and Literacy in Early Christianity and at Oxyrhynchus: Issues Raised by Harry Y. Gamble's *Books and Readers in the Early Church.*" In *Perspectives on New Testament Textual Criticism: Collected Essays, 1962–2004,* 521–50. Boston: Brill, 2005.

———. "The Multivalence of the Term 'Original Text.'" In *Perspectives on New Testament Textual Criticism: Collected Essays, 1962–2004,* 551–94. Boston: Brill, 2005.

Epperly, Bruce G. *Process Theology: A Guide for the Perplexed.* New York: T & T Clark, 2011.

Erneling, Christian E. *Understanding Language Acquisition: The Framework of Learning.* Albany: SUNY Press, 1993.

Esbroeck, Michel von. *Herméneutique, structuralisme, et exégèse: Essai de logique kérygmatique.* Paris: Desclée, 1968.

Estes, Joel D. "Reading for the Spirit of the Text: *Nomina sacra* and πνευμα Language in P46." *New Testament Studies* 61, no. 4 (2015): 566–94.

Evans, Craig A., and Emmanuel Tov, eds. *Exploring the Origins of the Bible: Canon Formation in Historical, Literary, and Theological Perspective.* Grand Rapids, MI: Baker Academic, 2008.

Eve, Eric. *Behind the Gospels: Understanding the Oral Tradition.* Minneapolis, MN: Fortress, 2014.

Fackre, Gabriel J. *The Doctrine of Revelation: A Narrative Interpretation.* Grand Rapids, MI: Eerdmans, 1997.

Falluomini, Carla. *The Gothic Version of the Gospels and Pauline Epistles: Cultural Background, Transmission, and Character.* Boston: Walter de Gruyter, 2015.

Farkasfalvy, Denis M. "The Case for Spiritual Exegesis." *Communio* 10, no. 4 (1983): 332–50.

———. "How to Renew the Theology of Biblical Inspiration?" *Nova et Vetera* 4 (2006): 231–54.

―――. *Inspiration and Interpretation: A Theological Introduction to Sacred Scripture*. Washington, DC: Catholic University of America Press, 2010.

―――. "Prophets and Apostles: The Conjunction of the Two Terms before Irenaeus." In *Texts and Testaments*, edited by E. W. March, 109–34. San Antonio, TX: Trinity University Press, 1980.

―――. *A Theology of the Christian Bible: Revelation-Inspiration-Canon*. Washington, DC: Catholic University of America Press, 2018.

Farmer, William. "Galatians and the Second-Century Development of the *Regula Fidei*." *Second Century* 4, no. 3 (1984): 143–70.

Fédou, Michel. "Histoire et l'esprit: Les travaux du père de Lubac sur l'interprétation de l'Ecriture et leurs apports a la théologie contemporaine." In *Henri de Lubac: La rencontre au cœur de l'Eglise*, edited by Jean-Dominique Durand, 253–66. Paris: Cerf, 2006.

Fee, Gordon D. *New Testament Exegesis: A Handbook for Students and Pastors*. 3rd ed. Louisville, KY: Westminster John Knox, 2002.

Feldman, Louis H. *Judaism and Hellenism Reconsidered*. Leiden: Brill, 2006.

Ferguson, C. L. "The Rule of Truth and Irenaean Rhetoric in Book 1 of *Against Heresies*." *Vetus Christiana* 55 (2001): 356–75.

Ferguson, Everett. *The Rule of Faith: A Guide*. Eugene, OR: Cascade, 2015.

Fiddes, Paul S., and Günter Bader, eds. *The Spirit and the Letter: A Tradition and a Reversal*. New York: T & T Clark, 2013.

Fingernagel, Andres, and Christian Gastberger, eds. *In the Beginning Was the Word: The Power and Glory of Illuminated Bibles*. Köln: Taschen, 2003.

Finn, Leonard G. "Reflections on the Rule of Faith." In *The Bible as Christian Scripture: The Work of Brevard H. Childs*, edited by Robert C. Kashow, Kent Harold Richards, and Christopher R. Seitz, 221–42. Atlanta, GA: Society of Biblical Literature, 2013.

Finsterbusch, Karin, and Armin Lange, eds. *What Is Bible?* Leuven: Peeters, 2012.

Fish, Stanley E. *Is There a Text in This Class? The Authority of Interpretive Communities*. Cambridge, MA: Harvard University Press, 1980.

―――. *Self-Consuming Artifacts: The Experience of Seventeenth-Century Literature*. Berkeley: University of California Press, 1972.

Fishbane, Michael A. "Revelation and Tradition: Aspects of Inner-Biblical Exegesis." *Journal of Biblical Literature* 99 (1980) 343–61.

Fitzmyer, Joseph A. *The Interpretation of Scripture: In Defense of the Historical-Critical Method*. New York: Paulist, 2008.

―――. *Romans: A New Translation with Introduction and Commentary*. New York: Doubleday, 1993.

Fitzpatrick, Joseph. "Descartes under Fire: Lonergan and Wittgenstein." In *Philosophical Encounters: Lonergan at the Analytical Tradition*, 105–46. Toronto: University of Toronto Press, 2005.

Flanagan, Joseph. *Quest for Self-Knowledge: An Essay in Lonergan's Philosophy*. Toronto: University of Toronto Press, 1997.

Fleteren, Frederick van. "St. Augustine, Neoplatonism, and the Liberal Arts: The Background to *De Doctrina Christiana.*" In *De Doctrina Christiana: A Classic of Western Culture*, edited by Duane W. H. Arnold and Pamela Bright, 14–24. Notre Dame, IN: University of Notre Dame Press, 1995.

Flipper, Joseph. *Between Apocalypse and Eschaton: History and Eternity in Henri de Lubac.* Minneapolis, MN: Fortress, 2015.

Ford, David F., and Chad Pecknold, eds. *The Promise of Scriptural Reasoning.* Malden, MA: Wiley-Blackwell, 2006.

Fowl, Stephen. *Engaging Scripture: A Model for Theological Interpretation.* Eugene, OR: Wipf & Stock, 1998.

———. "The Ethics of Interpretation, or What's Left over after the Elimination of Meaning." In *The Bible in Three Dimensions*, edited by D. J. A. Clines, S. E. Fowl, and S. E. Porter, 379–98. Sheffield: JSOT, 1990.

———. "Further Thoughts on Theological Interpretation." In *Reading Scripture with the Church: Toward a Hermeneutic for Theological Interpretation*, edited by A. K. M. Adam, Stephen E. Fowl, Kevin J. Vanhoozer, and Francis Watson, 125–30. Grand Rapids, MI: Baker, 2006.

———. "The Importance of a Multivoiced Literal Sense of Scripture: The Example of Thomas Aquinas." In *Reading Scripture with the Church: Toward a Hermeneutic for Theological Interpretation*, edited by A. K. M. Adam, Stephen E. Fowl, Kevin J. Vanhoozer, and Francis Watson, 25–50. Grand Rapids, MI: Baker, 2006.

———. "Texts Don't Have Ideologies." *Biblical Interpretation* 3, no. 1 (1995): 1–31.

———. *Theological Interpretation of Scripture.* Eugene, OR: Cascade, 2009.

———, ed. *The Theological Interpretation of Scripture: Classic and Contemporary Readings.* Malden, MA: Blackwell, 1997.

Fowl, Stephen, and L. Gregory Jones. *Reading in Communion: Scripture and Ethics in Christian Life.* Eugene, OR: Wipf & Stock, 1998.

Frei, Hans. *The Eclipse of Biblical Narrative: A Study in Eighteenth and Nineteenth Century Hermeneutics.* New Haven, CT: Yale University Press, 1974.

———. "The 'Literal Reading' of Biblical Narrative in the Christian Tradition: Does It Stretch or Will It Break?" In *The Bible and the Narrative Tradition*, edited by Frank McConnell, 36–77. New York: Oxford University Press, 1986.

Freitheim, Terrence. *The Suffering of God: An Old Testament Perspective.* Minneapolis, MN: Fortress, 1984.

Freyne, Seán, and Ellen van Wolde, eds. *The Many Voices of the Bible.* London: SCM, 2002.

Froelich, Karlfried. "Interpretation of the Old Testament in the High Middle Ages." In *Hebrew Bible/Old Testament: The History of Its Interpretation*, vol. 1: *From Beginnings to the Middle Ages (until 1300)*, part 2: *The Middle Ages*, edited by Magne Sæbø, 496–558. Göttingen: Vanderhoeck & Ruprecht, 2000.

———. *Sensing the Scriptures: Aminadab's Chariot and the Predicament of Biblical Interpretation.* Grand Rapids, MI: Eerdmans, 2014.

Fromm, Eric. *Man for Himself: An Inquiry into the Psychology of Ethics*. New York: Routledge, 2013.

Fulford, Ben. *Divine Eloquence and Human Transformation: Rethinking Scripture and History through Gregory of Nazianzus and Hans Frei*. Minneapolis, MN: Fortress, 2013.

Gabrielle-Lemaire, Marie. "Brève étude sur l'intelligence spirituelle de l'Écriture, selon Henri de Lubac." *Bulletin de l'Association internationale Cardinal Henri de Lubac* 10 (2010): 101–10.

Gadamer, Hans Georg. *Hermeneutics, Religion, and Ethics*. Translated by Joel Weinsheimer. New Haven, CT: Yale University Press, 1999.

———. *Philosophical Hermeneutics*. Translated and edited by David E. Linge. Berkeley: University of California Press, 1977.

———. *The Relevance of the Beautiful and Other Essays*. Edited by Robert Bernasconi. Translated by Nicholas Walker. New York: Cambridge University Press, 1986.

———. *Truth and Method*. 2nd ed. Edited and Translated by J. Weinsheimer and D. Marshall. New York: Continuum, 1998.

———. *Warheit und Methode: Grundzüge einer philosophischen Hermeneutik*. Tübingen: Mohr, 1960.

Gager, John. "Paul, the Apostle of Judaism." In *Jesus, Judaism, and Christian Antisemitism: Reading the New Testament after the Holocaust*, edited by Paula Fredriksen and Adele Reinhartz, 56–76. Louisville, KY: Westminster John Knox, 2002.

Gallagher, Edmon L., and John D. Meade. *The Biblical Canon Lists from Early Christianity: Texts and Analysis*. New York: Oxford University Press, 2018.

Gallup, George. *Surveying the Religious Landscape: Trends in U.S. Beliefs*. Harrisburg, PA: Morehouse, 1999.

Gamble, Harry Y. *Books and Readers in the Early Church: A History of Early Christian Texts*. New Haven, CT: Yale University Press, 1995.

———. *The New Testament Canon: Its Making and Meaning*. Philadelphia, PA: Fortress, 1985.

———. *The Textual History of the Letter to the Romans: A Study in Textual and Literary Criticism*. Grand Rapids, MI: Eerdmans, 1977.

Garcia, Jorge. "The Transcendentals in the Middle Ages: An Introduction." *Topoi: An International Review of Philosophy* 11, no. 2 (1992): 113–20.

Gavrilov, A. K. "Techniques of Reading in Classical Antiquity." *Classical Quarterly* 47, no. 1 (1997): 56–73.

Gavrilyuk, Paul L. "God's Impassible Suffering in the Flesh: The Promise of Paradoxical Christology." In *Divine Impassibility and the Mystery of Human Suffering*, edited by James F. Keating and Thomas Joseph White, 127–49. Grand Rapids, MI: Eerdmans, 2009.

———. "Harnack's Hellenized Christianity or Florovsky's 'Sacred Hellenism': Questioning Two Metanarratives of Early Christian Engagement with Late Antique Culture." *St. Vladimir's Theological Quarterly* 54, no. 3–4 (2010): 323–44.

———. "Scripture and the *Regula Fidei*: Two Interlocking Components of the Canonical Heritage." In *Canonical Theism: A Proposal for Theology and the Church*, edited by William J. Abraham, Jason E. Vickers, and Natalie B. Van Kirk, 27–42. Grand Rapids, MI: Eerdmans, 2008.

Gillet, Louis. "Note sur les *nomina sacra* en paléoslave-ecclésiatique." *Revue bénédictine* 35 (1923): 105–7.

Giusti, Giuseppe, ed. *Proverbi toscani*. Pisa: Pacini, 1873.

Gleaves, G. Scott. *Did Jesus Speak Greek? The Emerging Evidence of Greek Dominance in First-Century Palestine*. Cambridge: James Clarke and Co., 2014.

Gnuse, Robert K. *The Authority of the Bible: Theories of Inspiration, Revelation, and the Canon of Scripture*. Mahwah, NY: Paulist, 1985.

———. *No Other Gods: Emergent Monotheism in Israel*. Sheffield: Sheffield Academic, 1997.

Goldingay, John. *Do We Need the New Testament? Letting the Old Testament Speak for Itself*. Downers Grove, IL: InterVarsity, 2015.

Gordley, Matthew E. *The Colossian Hymn in Context: An Exegesis in Light of Jewish and Greco-Roman Hymnic and Epistolary Conventions*. Tübingen: Mohr Siebeck, 2007.

Gordon, Joseph K. "Deifying Adoption as Impetus for Moral Transformation: Augustine's Sermons on the Christological Ethics of Godhood." *Stone Campbell Journal* 16, no. 2 (2013): 193–206.

———. "The 'Incomprehensible Someone': Hans Urs von Balthasar on the Mission of the Holy Spirit for a Contemporary Theology of History." In *Theology in the Present Age: Essays in Honor of John D. Castelein*, edited by Christopher Ben Simpson and Steven Cone, 29–51. Eugene, OR: Pickwick, 2013.

———. "On the (Relative) Authenticity of Theological Interpretation of Scripture." *Lonergan Review* 9, no. 1 (2018): 78–102.

———. "*Ressourcement* Anti-Semitism? Addressing an Obstacle to Henri de Lubac's Proposed Renewal of Premodern Christian Spiritual Exegesis." *Theological Studies* 78, no. 3 (2017): 614–33.

———. "St. Thomas Aquinas 'Rightly Dividing the Word of Truth': The Historical and Theological Contours of Thomas's *Principia*." *Nova et Vetera* 14, no. 1 (2016): 245–70.

———. "The Subject, Scripture, and Theological Interpretation." October 2012. Published in Proceedings of Lonergan on the Edge: A Graduate Student Conference Inspired by the Thought of Bernard J. F. Lonergan, S.J., Marquette University, Milwaukee, WI, September 2012. www.lonerganresource.com /conference.php?12.

———. "Treasures Old and New: Henri de Lubac on Revelation, History, and Christian Hermeneutics." Master of Divinity thesis, Lincoln Christian Seminary, 2011.

———. "The Truthfulness of Scripture: Bernard Lonergan's Contribution and Challenges for Protestants." *Method: A Journal of Lonergan Studies* 6, no. 2 (2015): 35–55.

Gordon, Joseph K., and D. Stephen Long. "'Way(s) to God': William Desmond's Theological Philosophy." In *Desmond and Theology: The Donation of William Desmond to Theology*, edited by Christopher Ben Simpson and Brendon Sammon, 139–64. Notre Dame, IN: University of Notre Dame Press, 2017.

Gorman, Michael J. *Becoming the Gospel: Paul, Participation, and Mission.* Grand Rapids, MI: Eerdmans, 2015.

———. *Elements of Biblical Exegesis: A Basic Guide for Students and Ministers.* Rev. and expanded ed. Grand Rapids, MI: Baker Academic, 2010.

———. *Inhabiting the Cruciform God: Kenosis, Justification, and Theosis in Paul's Narrative Soteriology.* Grand Rapids, MI: Eerdmans, 2009.

———. "A New Translation of Philippians 2:5 and Its Significance for Paul's Theology and Spirituality." In *Conception, Reception, and the Spirit: Essays in Honor of Andrew T. Lincoln*, edited by J. Gordon McConville and Lloyd K. Pietersen, 104–21. Eugene, OR: Cascade, 2015.

———, ed. *Scripture and Its Interpretation: A Global, Ecumenical Introduction to the Bible.* Grand Rapids, MI: Baker Academic, 2017.

Gracias, Agnacio. "The Spiritual Sense of Scripture According to Henri de Lubac." STD thesis, Pontifical Gregorian University Press, 1975.

Grafton, Anthony, and Megan Williams. *Christianity and the Transformation of the Book: Origen, Eusebius, and the Library of Caesarea.* Cambridge, MA: Belknap Press of Harvard University Press, 2006.

Grant, Robert M. *Irenaeus of Lyons.* New York: Routledge, 1997.

Grant, Robert M., and David Tracy. *A Short History of the Interpretation of the Bible.* 2nd ed. Philadelphia: Fortress, 1984.

Graves, Michael. *The Inspiration and Interpretation of Scripture: What the Early Church Can Teach Us.* Grand Rapids, MI: Eerdmans, 2014.

———. *Jerome's Hebrew Philology: A Study Based on His Commentary on Jeremiah.* Boston: Brill, 2007.

Grech, Prosper S. "The *Regula Fidei* as a Hermeneutical Principle in Patristic Exegesis." In *The Interpretation of the Bible: The International Symposium in Slovenia*, edited by Jože Krašovec, 589–601. Sheffield: Sheffield Academic, 1998.

Green, H. Benedict. "Matthew 28.19, Eusebius, and the *lex orandi*." In *The Making of Orthodoxy: Essays in Honour of Henry Chadwick*, edited by Rowan Williams, 124–41. New York: Cambridge University Press, 1989.

Green, Joel B. *Seized by Truth: Reading the Bible as Sacred Scripture.* Nashville, TN: Abingdon, 2007.

Greene-McCreight, Kathryn. "Literal Sense." In *Dictionary for the Theological Interpretation of the Bible*, edited by Keven Vanhoozer, Craig Bartholomew, Daniel Treier, and N. T. Wright, 455–56. Grand Rapids, MI: Baker Academic, 2005.

Greenslade, S. L., ed. *The Cambridge History of the Bible: The West from the Reformation to the Present Day.* New York: Cambridge University Press, 1975.

Gregory, Andrew, and Christopher M. Tuckett, eds. *The Reception of the New Testament in the Apostolic Fathers.* Oxford: Oxford University Press, 2005.

Griffiths, Paul. "Which Are the Words of Scripture?" *Theological Studies* 72 (2011): 703–22.

Grondin, Jean. *Introduction to Philosophical Hermeneutics*. Translated by Joel Weinsheimer. New Haven, CT: Yale University Press, 1997.

Grudem, Wayne. "Scripture's Self-Attestation and the Problem of Formulating a Doctrine of Scripture." In *Scripture and the Truth*, edited by Donald A. Carson and J. D. Woodbridge, 19–59. Grand Rapids, MI: Baker, 1992.

Grumett, David. *De Lubac: A Guide for the Perplexed*. New York: T & T Clark, 2007.

Grünstäudl, Wolfgang, and Tobias Nicklas. "Searching for Evidence: The History of Reception of the Epistles of Jude and 2 Peter." In *Reading 1–2 Peter and Jude: A Resource for Students*, edited by Troy W. Martin and Eric F. Mason, 215–28. Atlanta, GA: Society of Biblical Literature, 2014.

Guarino, Thomas G. *Vincent of Lérins and the Development of Doctrine*. Grand Rapids, MI: Baker Academic, 2013.

Guillett, Jacques. "Le sens de l'écriture: Exégèses d'autrefois, recherches d'aujourd'hui." *Recherches de science religieuse* 80 (1992): 359–72.

Gunsalus González, Catherine. "The Rule of Faith: The Early Church's Source of Unity and Diversity." In *Many Voices, One God: Being Faithful in a Pluralistic World*, edited by Walter Brueggemann and George Stroup, 95–106. Louisville, KY: Westminster John Knox, 1998.

Gunton, Colin. *A Brief Theology of Revelation*. New York: T & T Clark, 1995.

Gurry, Peter J. "The Number of Variants in the Greek New Testament: A Proposed Estimate." *New Testament Studies* 62, no. 1 (2016): 91–121.

Hadot, Pierre. *Philosophy as a Way of Life*. Edited and Introduction by Arnold I. Davidson. Translated by Michael Chase. Malden, MA: Blackwell, 1995.

———. *What Is Ancient Philosophy?* Translated by Michael Chase. Cambridge, MA: Belknap Press of Harvard University Press, 2004.

Hagan, Kenneth, ed. *The Bible in the Churches: How Various Christians Interpret the Scriptures*. 3rd ed. Milwaukee, WI: Marquette University Press, 1995.

Hägg, Henny Fiskå. *Clement of Alexandria and the Beginnings of Christian Apophaticism*. New York: Oxford University Press, 2006.

Haines-Eitzen, Kim. *Guardians of Letters: Literacy, Power, and the Transmitters of Early Christian Literature*. New York: Oxford University Press, 2000.

Hamann, Johann Georg. "Biblische Betrachtungen eine Christen." In *Londoner Schriften*, edited by Oswald Bayer and Bernd Weißenborn, 65–104. Munich: C. H. Beck, 1993.

———. "Cloverleaf of Hellenistic Letters (1762)." In *Writings on Philosophy and Language*, translated and edited by Kenneth Hayes, 33–59. New York: Cambridge University Press, 2007.

Hamel, Christopher de. *A History of Illuminated Manuscripts*. 2nd ed. London: Phaidon, 1997.

Hamilton, Adam. *Making Sense of the Bible: Rediscovering the Power of Scripture Today*. San Francisco, CA: HarperOne, 2014.

Hamilton, James M. "Still *Sola Scriptura*: An Evangelical Perspective on Scripture." In *The Sacred Text: Excavating the Texts, Exploring the Interpretations, and Engaging the Theologies of the Christian Scriptures*, edited by Michael Bird and Michael Pahl, 215–40. Piscataway, NJ: Gorgias Press, 2010.

Hanson, R. C. P. *Allegory and Event: A Study of the Sources and Significance of Origen's Interpretation of Scripture.* London: SCM, 1959.

———. *Origen's Doctrine of Tradition.* London: SPCK, 1954.

Harkins, Angela K. "Theological Attitudes toward the Scriptural Text: Lessons from the Qumran and Syriac Exegetical Traditions." *Theological Studies* 67 (2006): 498–516.

Harkins, Franklin T. *Reading and the Work of Restoration: History and Theology in the Work of Hugh of St. Victor.* Toronto: Pontifical Institute of Medieval Studies, 2009.

Harnack, Adolf von. *History of Dogma.* Vol. 1. Translation by Neil Buchanan. New York: Russell & Russell, 1958.

———. *What Is Christianity?* Translated by Thomas Bailey Saunders. Philadelphia: Fortress, 1986.

Harris, Jennifer A. "The Bible and the Meaning of History in the Middle Ages." In *The Practice of the Bible in the Middle Ages*, edited by Susan Boynton and Diane J. Reilly, 84–104. New York: Columbia University Press, 2011.

Harrisville, Roy A. *Pandora's Box Opened: An Examination and Defense of Historical-Critical Method and Its Master Practitioners.* Grand Rapids, MI: Eerdmans, 2014.

Hart, David Bentley. *Atheist Delusions: The Christian Revolution and Its Fashionable Enemies.* New Haven, CT: Yale University Press, 2009.

———. *The Beauty of the Infinite: The Aesthetics of Christian Truth.* Grand Rapids, MI: Eerdmans, 2003.

———. *The Experience of God: Being, Consciousness, Bliss.* New Haven, CT: Yale University Press, 2013.

———. *The New Testament: A Translation.* New Haven, CT: Yale University Press, 2017.

———. "No Shadow of Turning: On Divine Impassibility." *Pro Ecclesia* 11, no. 2 (2002): 184–206.

———. "Through a Gloss, Darkly." *First Things* 225 (August–September 2012): 72, 71.

Hauerwas, Stanley. *Unleashing the Scripture: Freeing the Bible from Captivity to America.* Nashville, TN: Abingdon, 1993.

Haughton, H. A. G. *The Latin New Testament: A Guide to Its Early History, Texts, and Manuscripts.* New York: Oxford University Press, 2016.

Hauser, Alan J., and Duane F. Watson, eds. *A History of Biblical Interpretation*, vol. 3: *The Enlightenment through the Nineteenth Century.* Grand Rapids, MI: Eerdmans, 2017.

Hays, John H., and Carl R. Holladay. *Biblical Exegesis: A Beginners Handbook.* Louisville, KY: Westminster John Knox, 2007.

Hays, Richard B. *The Conversion of the Imagination: Paul as Interpreter of Israel's Scripture.* Grand Rapids, MI: Eerdmans, 2005.

———. *Echoes of Scripture in the Gospels.* Waco, TX: Baylor University Press, 2016.

———. *Echoes of Scripture in the Letters of Paul.* New Haven, CT: Yale University Press, 1993.

———. "'Here We Have No Lasting City': New Covenantalism in Hebrews." In *The Epistle to the Hebrews and Christian Theology,* edited by Richard Bauckham, Daniel Driver, Trevor Hart, and Nathan MacDonald, 151–73. Grand Rapids, MI: Eerdmans, 2009.

———. *The Moral Vision of the New Testament: A Contemporary Introduction to New Testament Ethics.* San Francisco: Harper San Francisco, 1996.

———. *Reading Backwards: Figural Christology and the Fourfold Gospel Witness.* Waco, TX: Baylor University Press, 2014.

Head, Peter M. "Is P4, P64, and P67 the Oldest Manuscript of the Gospels? A Response to T. C. Skeat." *New Testament Studies* 51, no. 3 (2005): 450–57.

Heath, Jane. "*Nomina sacra* and *Sacra memoria* before the Monastic Age." *Journal of Theological Studies* 61, no. 2 (2010): 516–49.

Hector, Kevin. *Theology without Metaphysics: God, Language, and the Spirit of Recognition.* New York: Cambridge University Press, 2011.

Hefling, Charles. "Another Perhaps Permanently Valid Achievement: Lonergan on Christ's Self-Knowledge." *Lonergan Workshop* 20 (2008): 127–64.

———. "Lonergan's *Cur Deus Homo*: Revisiting the 'Law of the Cross.'" In *Meaning and History in Systematic Theology: Essays in Honor of Robert M. Doran, S.J.,* edited by John Dadosky, 145–66. Milwaukee, WI: Marquette University Press, 2009.

———. "On Understanding Salvation History." In *Lonergan's Hermeneutics: Its Development and Application,* edited by Ben F. Meyer and Seán McEvenue, 221–75. Washington, DC: Catholic University of America Press, 1989.

———. "Revelation and/as Insight." In *The Importance of Insight: Essays in Honor of Michael Vertin,* edited by John Liptay and David Liptay, 97–115. Toronto: University of Toronto Press, 2007.

———. *Why Doctrines?* 2nd ed. Boston: Lonergan Institute at Boston College, 2000.

Heine, Ronald E. *Origen: Scholarship in the Service of the Church.* New York: Oxford University Press, 2010.

———. *Reading the Old Testament with the Early Church: Exploring the Formation of Early Christian Thought.* Grand Rapids, MI: Baker Academic, 2007.

Helminiak, Daniel A. *Brain, Consciousness, and God: A Lonerganian Integration.* Albany: SUNY Press, 2015.

Hengel, Martin. *The Septuagint as Christian Scripture: Its Prehistory and the Problem of Its Canon.* Translated by E. M. Biddle. Edinburgh: T & T Clark, 2002.

Hicks, Jonathan Douglas. *Trinity, Economy, and Scripture: Recovering Didymus the Blind.* Winona Lake, IN: Eisenbrauns, 2015.

Hill, Wesley. *Paul and the Trinity: Persons, Relations, and the Pauline Letters.* Grand Rapids, MI: Eerdmans, 2015.

Hillebert, Jordan, ed. *T & T Clark Companion to Henri de Lubac.* New York: Bloomsbury T & T Clark, 2017.

Hirshman, Marc G. *A Rivalry of Genius: Jewish and Christian Biblical Interpretation in Late Antiquity.* Albany: SUNY Press.

Holcomb, Justin S., ed. *Christian Theologies of Scripture: A Comparative Introduction.* New York: New York University Press, 2006.

Hollon, Bryan G. *Everything Is Sacred: Spiritual Exegesis in the Political Theology of Henri de Lubac.* Eugene, OR: Cascade, 2009.

Holmes, Michael, trans. and ed. *The Apostolic Fathers: Greek Texts and English Translations.* 3rd ed. Grand Rapids, MI: Baker Academic, 2007.

Howsam, Leslie, and Scott McClaren. "Producing the Text: Production and Distribution of Popular Editions of the Bible." In *The New Cambridge History of the Bible:* vol. 4: *From 1750 to the Present,* edited by John Riches, 49–82. New York: Cambridge University Press, 2015.

Hughes, Kevin L. "The Fourfold Sense: De Lubac, Blondel, and Contemporary Theology." *Heythrop Journal* 42 (2001): 451–62.

———. "The Spiritual Interpretation of Scripture." In *T & T Clark Companion to Henri de Lubac,* edited by Jordan Hillebert, 205–24. New York: Bloomsbury T & T Clark, 2017.

Humphreys, Nicholas. *Soul Dust: The Magic of Consciousness.* Princeton, NJ: Princeton University Press, 2012.

Hünermann, Peter, Robert Fastiggi, and Anne Englund Nashm, eds. *Enchiridion symbolorum definitionum et declarationum de rebus fidei et morum (Compendium of Creeds, Definitions, and Declarations on Matters of Faith and Morals).* 43rd ed. San Francisco: Ignatius, 2012.

Hunt, Anne. *Trinity: Nexus of the Mysteries of Christian Faith.* Maryknoll, NY: Orbis, 2005.

Hurtado, Larry W. *Destroyer of the gods: Early Christian Distinctiveness in the Roman World.* Waco, TX: Baylor University Press, 2016.

———. *The Earliest Christian Artifacts: Manuscripts and Christian Origins.* Grand Rapids, MI: Eerdmans, 2006.

———. *Lord Jesus Christ: Devotion to Jesus in Earliest Christianity.* Grand Rapids, MI: Eerdmans, 2003.

———. "Manuscripts and the Sociology of Early Christian Reading." In *The Early Text of the New Testament,* edited by Charles E. Hill and Michael J. Kruger, 49–62. New York: Oxford University Press, 2014.

———. "Oral Fixation and New Testament Studies? 'Orality,' 'Performance,' and Reading Texts in Early Christianity." *New Testament Studies* 60, no. 3 (2014): 321–40.

———. "The Origin of the *Nomina Sacra*: A Proposal." *Journal of Biblical Literature* 117, no. 4 (1998): 655–73.

Hutson, Christopher R. "The Cross as Canon: Galatians 6.16." *Leaven* 12, no. 1 (2004): 49–53.

Irenaeus of Lyons. *Contre les hérésies*. Translated and edited by Adelin Rousseau, Louis Doutreleau, Bertrand Hemmerdinger, and Charles Mercier. Sources chrétiennes 100, 152, 153, 210, 211, 263, 264, 293, 294. Paris: Cerf, 1969–2008.

———. *On the Apostolic Preaching*. Translated and Introduction by John Behr. Crestwood, NY: St. Vladimir's Seminary, 1997.

———. *St. Irenaeus of Lyons Against the Heresies*. Book I. Translated and Annotated by Dominic J. Unger. Revised by John J. Dillon. Ancient Christian Writers 55. New York: Paulist, 1992.

———. *St. Irenaeus of Lyons Against the Heresies*. Book II. Translated and Annotated by Dominic J. Unger. Revised by John J. Dillon. Introduction by Michael Slusser. Ancient Christian Writers 65. New York: Paulist, 2012.

———. *St. Irenaeus of Lyons Against the Heresies*. Book III. Translated and Annotated by Dominic J. Unger. Revised by Irenaeus M. C. Steenberg. Ancient Christian Writers 64. New York: Paulist, 2012.

Jacobs, Alan. *A Theology of Reading: A Hermeneutics of Love*. Cambridge, MA: Westview, 2001.

Jaeger, Werner. *Early Christianity and Greek Paideia*. Cambridge, MA: Belknap Press of Harvard University Press, 1961.

Jeanrond, Werner. *Text and Interpretation as Categories of Theological Thinking*. Translated by Thomas Wilson. New York: Crossroad, 1988.

———. *Theological Hermeneutics: Development and Significance*. London: SCM, 1994.

Jeffrey, David Lyle. *People of the Book: Christian Identity and Literary Culture*. Grand Rapids, MI: Eerdmans, 1996.

Jensen, Robin M. *Understanding Early Christian Art*. New York: Routledge, 2000.

Jenson, Robert. *Canon and Creed*. Louisville, KY: Westminster John Knox, 2010.

———. "The Religious Power of Scripture." *Scottish Journal of Theology* 52, no. 1 (1999): 89–105.

———. *Systematic Theology: The Triune God*. Vol. 1. New York: Oxford University Press, 1999.

Jobes, Karen H., and Moisés Silva. *Invitation to the Septuagint*. 2nd ed. Grand Rapids, MI: Baker Academic, 2015.

Johnson, Luke Timothy. *The First and Second Letters to Timothy*. New York: Doubleday, 2001.

———. *Scripture and Discernment: Decision Making in the Church*. Rev. and expanded ed. Nashville, TN: Abingdon, 1996.

Johnson, William A. *Bookrolls and Scribes in Oxyrhynchus*. Toronto: University of Toronto Press, 2004.

Kaiser, Walter C., Daniel M. Doriani, Kevin J. Vanhoozer, and William J. Webb. *Four Views on Moving beyond the Bible to Theology*. Grand Rapids, MI: Zondervan, 2009.

Kannengiesser, Charles. "The Interrupted *De Doctrina Christiana*." In *De Doctrina Christiana: A Classic of Western Culture*, edited by Duane W. H. Arnold and Pamela Bright, 3–6. Notre Dame, IN: University of Notre Dame Press, 1995.

Kannengiesser, Charles, and Pamela Bright. *A Conflict of Christian Hermeneutics in Roman Africa: Tyconius and Augustine*. Berkeley, CA: Center for Hermeneutical Studies, 1989.

Keener, Craig. *The Mind of the Spirit: Paul's Approach to Transformed Thinking*. Grand Rapids, MI: Baker Academic, 2016.

Kelber, Werner. *The Oral and Written Gospel: The Hermeneutics of Speaking and Writing in the Synoptic Tradition, Mark, Paul, and Q*. Bloomington: Indiana University Press, 1997.

Kelly, Anthony J. "Dimensions of Meaning: Theology and Exegesis." In *Transcending Boundaries: Contemporary Readings of the New Testament: Essays in Honor of Francis J. Maloney*, 41–55. Rome: Liberia Ateneo Salesiano, 2005.

Kelsey, David. *The Uses of Scripture in Recent Theology*. Philadelphia: Fortress, 1975.

Kerr, Fergus. "Objections to Lonergan's Method." *New Blackfriars* 56 (1975): 305–16.

———. *Theology after Wittgenstein*. 2nd ed. London: SPCK, 1997.

Kimbrough, S. T., Jr., ed. *Orthodox and Wesleyan Scriptural Understanding and Practice*. Crestwood, NY: St. Vladimir's Seminary, 2006.

Knox, Bernard M. W. "Silent Reading in Antiquity." *Greek, Roman, and Byzantine Studies* 9 (1968): 421–35.

Kotzé, Annemaré. "Augustine, Jerome, and the Septuagint." In *Septuagint and Reception*, edited by Johann Cook, 245–60. Boston: Brill, 2009.

Kovacs, Judith L. "Divine Pedagogy and the Gnostic Teacher according to Clement of Alexandria." *Journal of Early Christian Studies* 9, no. 1 (2001): 3–25.

Kraft, Robert A. "The Codex and Canon Consciousness." In *The Canon Debate*, edited by Lee Martin McDonald and James Sanders, 229–33. Peabody, MA: Hendrickson, 2002.

Kreider, Alan. *The Patient Ferment of the Early Church*. Grand Rapids, MI: Baker Academic, 2016.

Kruger, Michael J. "Early Christian Attitudes toward the Reproduction of Texts." In *The Early Text of the New Testament*, edited by Charles E. Hill and Michael J. Kruger, 63–80. New York: Oxford University Press, 2012.

———. *The Question of Canon: Challenging the Status Quo in the New Testament Debate*. Downers Grove, IL: IVP Academic, 2013.

Kugel, James L. *How to Read the Bible: A Guide to Scripture, Then and Now*. New York: Free Press, 2008.

———. *In Potiphar's House: The Interpretive Life of Biblical Texts*. New York: HarperCollins, 1990.

———. *Traditions of the Bible: A Guide to the Bible as It Was at the Start of the Common Era*. Cambridge, MA: Harvard University Press, 1998.

Lamarche, Paul. "The Septuagint: Bible of the Earliest Christians." In *The Bible in Greek Christian Antiquity*, edited and Translated by Paul Blowers, 15–33. Notre Dame, IN: University of Notre Dame Press, 1997.

Lamb, William. *Scripture: A Guide for the Perplexed*. New York: Bloomsbury T & T Clark, 2013.

Lampe, G. W. H., ed. *The Cambridge History of the Bible: The West from the Fathers to the Reformation*. New York: Cambridge University Press, 1975.

Lampe, Peter. "Zur Textgeschichte des Römerbriefes." *Novum Testamentum* 27, no. 3 (1985): 273–77.

Lang, Friedrich G. "Schreiben nach Mass: Zur Stichometrie in der antiken Literatur." *Novum Testamentum* 41, no. 1 (1999): 40–57.

Lang, T. J. *Mystery and the Making of a Christian Historical Consciousness: From Paul to the Second Century*. Boston: Walter de Gruyter, 2015.

Lanne, E. "'La Regle de la Verite': Aux sources d'une expression de saint Irenee." In *Lex orandi lex credendi: Miscellanea in onore di P. Cipriano Vagaggine*, edited by G. J. Bekes and G. Farnedi, 57–70. Rome: Anselmiana, 1980.

Larsen, Matthew. "Accidental Publication, Unfinished Texts and the Traditional Goals of New Testament Textual Criticism." *Journal of Biblical Literature* 39 (2017): 363–87.

Laughlin, Peter. *Jesus and the Cross: Necessity, Atonement, Meaning*. Eugene, OR: Pickwick; Cambridge: James Clarke & Co, 2014.

Lauro, Elizabeth Dively. *The Soul and Spirit of Scripture within Origen's Exegesis*. Boston: Brill, 2005.

Law, David R. *Inspiration of the Scriptures*. New York: Continuum, 2001.

Law, Timothy Michael. *When God Spoke Greek: The Septuagint and the Making of the Christian Bible*. New York: Oxford University Press, 2013.

Lawrence, Frederick. "Lonergan's Postmodern Subject: Neither Neoscholastic Substance nor Cartesian Ego." In *Lonergan and Contemporary Continental Thought: In Deference to the Other*, edited by Jim Kanaris and Mark Doorley, 107–20. Albany: SUNY Press, 2004.

Legaspi, Michael. *The Death of Scripture and the Rise of Biblical Studies*. Oxford: Oxford University Press, 2010.

———. "Whatever Happened to Historical Criticism?" *Journal of Religion and Society* 9 (2007): 1–11.

Lettieri, Gaetano. *L'altro Agostino: Ermeneutica e retorica della grazia dalla crisi alla metamorfosi del De Doctrina Christiana*. Brescia: Morcelliana, 2001.

Levenson, Jon. *Creation and the Persistence of Evil: The Jewish Drama of Divine Omnipotence*. San Francisco, CA: Harper & Row, 1988.

Levering, Matthew. *Engaging the Doctrine of Revelation: The Mediation of the Gospel through Church and Scripture*. Grand Rapids, MI: Baker Academic, 2014.

————. "Linear and Participatory History: Augustine's City of God." *Journal of Theological Interpretation* 5, no. 2 (2011): 175–96.

————. *Participatory Biblical Exegesis: A Theology of Biblical Interpretation.* Notre Dame, IN: University of Notre Dame Press, 2008.

————. *Scripture and Metaphysics: Aquinas and the Renewal of Trinitarian Theology.* Malden, MA: Blackwell, 2004.

Levering, Matthew, and Gilles Emery, eds. *Oxford Handbook on the Trinity.* New York: Oxford University Press, 2014.

Lieberman, Saul. *Hellenism in Jewish Palestine: Studies in the Literary Transmission, Beliefs and Manners of Palestine in the I Century B.C.E.–IV Century C.E.* 2nd ed. Philadelphia: Mauriel Jacobs, 1962.

Lienhard, Joseph T. *The Bible, the Church, and Authority: The Canon of the Christian Bible in History and Theology.* Collegeville, MN: Michael Glazier, 1995.

Liere, Franz van. *An Introduction to the Medieval Bible.* New York: Cambridge University Press, 2014.

————. "The Latin Bible, ca. 900 to the Council of Trent, 1546." In *The New Cambridge History of the Bible: From 600 to 1450,* edited by Richard Marsden and E. Ann Matter, 93–109. New York: Cambridge University Press, 2012.

Lies, Lothar. *Origenes' "Peri archon": Eine undogmatische Dogmatik: Einführung und Erläuterung.* Darmstadt: Wissenschaftliche Buchgesellschaft, 1992.

Lifton, Bryan M. "The Rule of Faith in Augustine." *Pro Ecclesia* 14, no. 1 (2005): 85–101.

Light, Laura. "The Bible and the Individual: The Thirteenth-Century Paris Bible." In *The Practice of the Bible in the Middle Ages: Production, Reception, and Performance in Western Christianity,* edited by Susan Boynton and Diane J. Reilly, 228–46. New York: Columbia University Press, 2011.

Lim, Timothy K. *The Formation of the Jewish Canon.* New Haven, CT: Yale University Press, 2013.

Lindner, Helgo. "Johann Georg Hamann on Bible and Revelation." *Evangelical Review of Theology* 2, no. 1 (1978): 113–23.

Loewe, William P. *The College Student's Introduction to Christology.* Collegeville, MN: Michael Glazier, 1996.

————. *Lex Crucis: Soteriology and the Stages of Meaning.* Minneapolis, MN: Fortress, 2015.

Lonergan, Bernard. "The Analogy of Meaning." In *Philosophical and Theological Papers, 1958–1964,* edited by Robert C. Croken, Frederick E. Crowe, and Robert M. Doran, 183–213. Collected Works of Bernard Lonergan 6. Toronto: University of Toronto Press, 1996.

————. "Aquinas Today: Tradition and Innovation." In *A Third Collection: Papers by Bernard J. F. Lonergan, S.J.,* edited by Frederick E. Crowe, 35–54. New York: Paulist, 1985.

———. "Christ as Subject: A Reply." In *Collection*, edited by Frederick E. Crowe and Robert M. Doran, 153–84. Collected Works of Bernard Lonergan 4. Toronto: University of Toronto Press, 1988.

———. "Christology Today: Methodological Reflections." In *A Third Collection: Papers by Bernard J. F. Lonergan, S.J.*, edited by Frederick E. Crowe, 74–99. New York: Paulist, 1985.

———. "Cognitional Structure." In *Collection*, edited by Frederick E. Crowe and Robert M. Doran, 205–21. Collected Works of Bernard Lonergan 4. Toronto: University of Toronto Press, 1988.

———. "The Dehellenization of Dogma." In *A Second Collection: Papers by Bernard J. F. Lonergan, S.J.*, edited by William Ryan and Bernard Tyrrell, 11–32. Toronto: University of Toronto Press, 1996.

———. "Dimensions of Meaning." In *Collection*, edited by Frederick E. Crowe and Robert M. Doran, 232–45. Collected Works of Bernard Lonergan 4. Toronto: University of Toronto Press, 1988.

———. "Doctrinal Pluralism." In *Philosophical and Theological Papers, 1965–1980*, edited by Robert C. Croken and Robert M. Doran, 70–104. Collected Works of Bernard Lonergan 17. Toronto: University of Toronto Press, 2004.

———. *Early Latin Theology*. Edited by Robert M. Doran and H. Daniel Monsour. Translated by Michael Shields. Collected Works of Bernard Lonergan 19. Toronto: University of Toronto Press, 2011.

———. *Early Works in Theological Method I*. Edited by Robert M. Doran and Robert C. Croken. Collected Works of Bernard Lonergan 22. Toronto: University of Toronto Press, 2010.

———. "Exegesis and Dogma." In *Philosophical and Theological Papers, 1958–1964*, edited by Robert C. Croken, Frederick Crowe, and Robert M. Doran, 142–59. Collected Works of Bernard Lonergan 6. Toronto: University of Toronto Press, 1996.

———. "*Existenz* and *Aggiornamento*." In *Collection*, edited by Frederick E. Crowe and Robert M. Doran, 222–31. Collected Works of Bernard Lonergan 4. Toronto: University of Toronto Press, 1988.

———. "Faith and Beliefs." In *Philosophical and Theological Papers, 1965–1980*, edited by Robert C. Croken and Robert M. Doran, 30–48. Collected Works of Bernard Lonergan 17. Toronto: University of Toronto Press, 2004.

———. "Finality, Love, Marriage." In *Collection*, edited by Frederick E. Crowe and Robert M. Doran, 17–52. Collected Works of Bernard Lonergan 4. Toronto: University of Toronto Press, 1988.

———. "First Lecture: Religious Experience." In *Third Collection: Papers by Bernard J. F. Lonergan, S.J.*, edited by Frederick E. Crowe, 115–28. New York: Paulist, 1985.

———. "The Functional Specialty 'Systematics,'" in *Philosophical and Theological Papers, 1965–1980*, edited by Robert C. Croken and Robert M. Doran, 172–98. Collected Works of Bernard Lonergan 17. Toronto: University of Toronto Press, 2004.

——. "The Future of Christianity." In *A Second Collection: Papers by Bernard J. F. Lonergan, S.J.*, edited by William Ryan and Bernard Tyrrell, 149–63. Toronto: University of Toronto Press, 1996.

——. "The Future of Thomism." In *A Second Collection: Papers by Bernard J. F. Lonergan, S.J.*, edited by William Ryan and Bernard Tyrrell, 43–53. Toronto: University of Toronto Press, 1996.

——. "God's Knowledge and Will." In *Early Latin Theology*, edited by Robert M. Doran and H. Daniel Monsour, 257–411. Translated by Michael Shields. Collected Works of Bernard Lonergan 19. Toronto: University of Toronto Press, 2011.

——. *Grace and Freedom: Operative Grace in the Thought of St Thomas Aquinas.* Edited by Frederick E. Crowe and Robert M. Doran. Collected Works of Bernard Lonergan 1. Toronto: University of Toronto Press, 2000.

——. "Horizons." In *Philosophical and Theological Papers, 1965–1980*, edited by Robert C. Croken and Robert M. Doran, 10–29. Collected Works of Bernard Lonergan 17. Toronto: University of Toronto Press, 2004.

——. "Horizons and Transpositions." In *Philosophical and Theological Papers 1965–1980*, edited by Robert C. Croken and Robert M. Doran, 409–32. Collected Works of Bernard Lonergan 17. Toronto: University of Toronto Press, 2004.

——. "The Human Good." In *Philosophical and Theological Papers, 1965–1980*, edited by Robert C. Croken and Robert M. Doran, 332–51. Collected Works of Bernard Lonergan 17. Toronto: University of Toronto Press, 2004.

——. *Insight: A Study of Human Understanding.* Edited by Frederick E. Crowe and Robert M. Doran. Collected Works of Bernard Lonergan 3. Toronto: University of Toronto Press, 1992.

——. "Insight Revisited." In *A Second Collection: Papers by Bernard J. F. Lonergan, S.J.*, edited by William Ryan and Bernard Tyrrell, 263–78. Toronto: University of Toronto Press, 1996.

——. "An Interview with Fr. Bernard Lonergan, S.J." In *A Second Collection: Papers by Bernard J.F. Lonergan, S.J.*, edited by William Ryan and Bernard Tyrrell, 209–30. Toronto: University of Toronto Press, 1996.

——. "Is It Real." In *Philosophical and Theological Papers 1965–1980*, edited by Robert C. Croken and Robert M. Doran, 119–39. Collected Works of Bernard Lonergan 17. Toronto: University of Toronto Press, 2004.

——. "The Mediation of Christ in Prayer." In *Philosophical and Theological Papers 1958–1965*, edited by Robert C. Croken, Frederick E. Crowe, and Robert M. Doran, 160–82. Collected Works of Bernard Lonergan 6. Toronto: University of Toronto Press, 1996.

——. "Merging Horizons: System, Common Sense, Scholarship." In *Philosophical and Theological Papers 1965–1980*, edited by Robert C. Croken and Robert M. Doran, 49–69. Collected Works of Bernard Lonergan 17. Toronto: University of Toronto Press, 2004.

———. "Method: Trend and Variations." In *A Third Collection: Papers by Bernard J. F. Lonergan, S.J.*, edited by Frederick E. Crowe, 13–22. New York: Paulist, 1985.

———. "Method in Catholic Theology." In *Philosophical and Theological Papers, 1958–1964*, edited by Robert C. Croken, Frederick E. Crowe, and Robert M. Doran, 29–53. Collected Works of Bernard Lonergan 6. Toronto: University of Toronto Press, 1996.

———. *Method in Theology*. 2nd ed. Toronto: University of Toronto Press, 1996.

———. *Method in Theology*. Edited by Robert M. Doran and John D. Dadosky. Collected Works of Bernard Lonergan 14. Toronto: University of Toronto Press, 2017.

———. "Mission and the Spirit." In *A Third Collection: Papers by Bernard J. F. Lonergan, S.J.*, edited by Frederick E. Crowe, 23–34. New York: Paulist, 1985.

———. "The Natural Desire to See God." In *Collection*, edited by Frederick E. Crowe and Robert M. Doran, 81–91. Collected Works of Bernard Lonergan 4. Toronto: University of Toronto Press, 1988.

———. "Natural Knowledge of God." In *A Second Collection: Papers by Bernard J. F. Lonergan, S.J.*, edited by William Ryan and Bernard Tyrrell, 117–33. Toronto: University of Toronto Press, 1996.

———. "Natural Right and Historical Mindedness." In *Third Collection: Papers by Bernard J. F. Lonergan, S.J.*, edited by Frederick E. Crowe, 169–83. New York: Paulist, 1985.

———. "A New Pastoral Theology." In *Philosophical and Theological Papers, 1965–1980*, edited by Robert C. Croken and Robert M. Doran, 221–39. Collected Works of Bernard Lonergan 17. Toronto: University of Toronto Press, 2004.

———. "The Notion of Sacrifice." In *Early Latin Theology*, edited by Robert M. Doran and H. Daniel Monsour, 3–51. Translated by Michael Shields. Collected Works of Bernard Lonergan 19. Toronto: University of Toronto Press, 2011.

———. "On God and Secondary Causes." In *Collection*, edited by Frederick E. Crowe and Robert M. Doran, 53–65. Collected Works of Bernard Lonergan 4. Toronto: University of Toronto Press, 1988.

———. *The Ontological and Psychological Constitution of Christ*. Translated by Michael Shields. Collected Works of Bernard Lonergan 7. Toronto: University of Toronto Press, 2002.

———. "The Original Preface of Insight." *Method: Journal of Lonergan Studies* 3, no. 1 (1985): 3–8.

———. "The Origins of Christian Realism (1961)." In *Philosophical and Theological Papers, 1958–1964*, edited by Robert C. Croken, Frederick E. Crowe, and Robert M. Doran, 80–93. Collected Works of Bernard Lonergan 6. Toronto: University of Toronto Press, 1996.

———. "The Origins of Christian Realism (1972)." In *A Second Collection: Papers by Bernard J. F. Lonergan, S.J.*, edited by William Ryan and Bernard Tyrrell, 239–62. Toronto: University of Toronto Press, 1996.

————. "Philosophy and Theology." In *A Second Collection: Papers by Bernard J. F. Lonergan, S.J.*, edited by William Ryan and Bernard Tyrrell, 193–208. Toronto: University of Toronto Press, 1996.

————. "Philosophy, God and Theology: Lecture I: Philosophy of God." In *Philosophical and Theological Papers, 1965–1980*, edited by Robert C. Croken and Robert M. Doran, 162–78. Collected Works of Bernard Lonergan 17. Toronto: University of Toronto Press, 2004.

————. "Prolegomena to the Study of the Emerging Religious Consciousness of Our Time." In *Third Collection: Papers by Bernard J. F. Lonergan, S.J.*, edited by Frederick E. Crowe, 55–73. New York: Paulist, 1985.

————. "Questionnaire on Philosophy: Response." In *Philosophical and Theological Papers 1965–1980*, edited by Robert C. Croken and Robert M. Doran, 352–83. Collected Works of Bernard Lonergan 17. Toronto: University of Toronto Press, 2004.

————. "Reality, Myth, Symbol." In *Philosophical and Theological Papers, 1965–1980*, edited by Robert C. Croken and Robert M. Doran, 384–90. Collected Works of Bernard Lonergan 17. Toronto: University of Toronto Press, 2004.

————. "The Response of the Jesuit as Priest and Apostle in the Modern World." In *A Second Collection: Papers by Bernard J. F. Lonergan, S.J.*, edited by William Ryan and Bernard Tyrrell, 165–88. Toronto: University of Toronto Press, 1996.

————. "Sacralization and Secularization." In *Philosophical and Theological Papers, 1965–1980*, edited by Robert C. Croken and Robert M. Doran, 259–81. Collected Works of Bernard Lonergan 17. Toronto: University of Toronto Press, 2004.

————. "*De scientia atque voluntate Dei.*" In *Early Latin Theology*, edited by Robert M. Doran and H. Daniel Monsour, 257–411. Collected Works of Bernard Lonergan 19. Toronto: University of Toronto Press, 2011.

————. *A Second Collection.* Edited by Robert M. Doran and John D. Dadosky. Collected Works of Bernard Lonergan 13. Toronto: University of Toronto Press, 2016.

————. "Second Lecture: Religious Knowledge." In *A Third Collection: Papers by Bernard J. F. Lonergan, S.J.*, edited by Frederick E. Crowe, 129–45. New York: Paulist, 1985.

————. "Self-Transcendence: Intellectual, Moral, Religious." In *Philosophical and Theological Papers, 1965–1980*, edited by Robert C. Croken and Robert M. Doran, 313–31. Collected Works of Bernard Lonergan 17. Toronto: University of Toronto Press, 2004.

————. "The Subject." In *A Second Collection: Papers by Bernard J. F. Lonergan, S.J.*, edited by William Ryan and Bernard Tyrrell, 69–86. Toronto: University of Toronto Press, 1996.

————. "The Supernatural Order." In *Early Latin Theology*, edited by Robert M. Doran and H. Daniel Monsour, 562–665. Translated by Michael Shields. Collected Works of Bernard Lonergan 19. Toronto: University of Toronto Press, 2011.

————. "Supplementary Notes on Sanctifying Grace." In *Early Latin Theology*, edited by Robert M. Doran and H. Daniel Monsour, 53–255. Translated by Michael Shields. Collected Works of Bernard Lonergan 19. Toronto: University of Toronto Press, 2011.

————. "Theology and Man's Future." In *A Second Collection: Papers by Bernard J. F. Lonergan, S.J.*, edited by William Ryan and Bernard Tyrrell, 135–48. Toronto: University of Toronto Press, 1996.

————. "Theology as Christian Phenomenon." In *Philosophical and Theological Papers, 1958–1964*, edited by Robert C. Croken, Frederick E. Crowe, and Robert M. Doran, 244–72. Collected Works of Bernard Lonergan 6. Toronto: University of Toronto Press, 1996.

————. "Theology in Its New Context." In *A Second Collection: Papers by Bernard J. F. Lonergan, S.J.*, edited by William Ryan and Bernard Tyrrell, 55–67. Toronto: University of Toronto Press, 1996.

————. "Theories of Inquiry: Responses to a Symposium." In *A Second Collection: Papers by Bernard J.F. Lonergan, S.J.*, edited by William Ryan and Bernard Tyrrell, 33–42. Toronto: University of Toronto Press, 1996.

————. *A Third Collection*. Edited by Robert M. Doran and John D. Dadosky. Collected Works of Bernard Lonergan 16. Toronto: University of Toronto Press, 2017.

————. "Time and Meaning." In *Philosophical and Theological Papers, 1958–1964*, edited by Robert C. Croken, Frederick E. Crowe, and Robert M. Doran, 94–121. Collected Works of Bernard Lonergan 6. Toronto: University of Toronto Press, 1996.

————. *Topics in Education: The Cincinnati Lectures of 1959 on the Philosophy of Education*. Edited by Robert M. Doran and Frederick E. Crowe. Collected Works of Bernard Lonergan 10. Toronto: University of Toronto Press, 1993.

————. "The Transition from a Classicist World-View to Historical-Mindedness." In *A Second Collection: Papers by Bernard J. F. Lonergan, S.J.*, edited by William Ryan and Bernard Tyrrell, 1–9. Toronto: University of Toronto Press, 1996.

————. *The Triune God: Doctrines*. Edited by Robert M. Doran and H. Daniel Monsour. Translated by Michael Shields. Collected Works of Bernard Lonergan 11. Toronto: University of Toronto Press, 2009.

————. *The Triune God: Systematics*. Edited by Robert M. Doran and H. Daniel Monsour. Translated by Michael Shields. Collected Works of Bernard Lonergan 12. Toronto: University of Toronto Press, 2007.

————. *Understanding and Being: The Halifax Lectures on "Insight."* Edited by Elizabeth Morelli and Mark Morelli. 2nd ed., revised by Frederick E. Crowe et al. Collected Works of Bernard Lonergan 5. Toronto: University of Toronto Press, 1990.

————. *Verbum: Word and Idea in Aquinas*. Edited by Frederick E. Crowe and Robert M. Doran. Collected Works of Bernard Lonergan 2. Toronto: University of Toronto Press, 1997.

————. *The Way to Nicea: The Dialectical Development of Trinitarian Theology.* Translated by Conn O'Donovan. Philadelphia: Westminster, 1976.

————. "What Are Judgments of Value?" In *Philosophical and Theological Papers, 1965–1980*, edited by Robert C. Croken and Robert M. Doran, 149–56. Collected Works of Bernard Lonergan 17. Toronto: University of Toronto Press, 2004.

————. "The World Mediated by Meaning." In *Philosophical and Theological Papers, 1965–1980*, 107–118. Edited by Robert C. Croken and Robert M. Doran. Collected Works of Bernard Lonergan 17. Toronto: University of Toronto Press, 2004.

Long, D. Stephen. *The Perfectly Simple Triune God: Aquinas and His Legacy.* Minneapolis, MN: Fortress, 2016.

————. "Sources as Canons: The Question of Canonical Coherence." *Modern Theology* 28, no. 2 (2012): 229–51.

Longenecker, Richard. *Biblical Exegesis in the Apostolic Period.* 2nd ed. Grand Rapids, MI: Eerdmans, 1999.

Luijendijk, AnneMarie. *Forbidden Oracles? The Gospel of the Lots of Mary.* Tübingen: Mohr Siebeck, 2014.

————. *Greetings in the Lord: Early Christians and the Oxyrhynchus Papyri.* Cambridge, MA: Harvard University Press, 2007.

Luther, Martin. *The Luther Bible of 1534.* Introduction by Stephan Füssel. 3 vols. Köln: Taschen, 2016.

————. *Luther's Works.* Edited by Jaroslav Pelikan and Helmutt T. Lehmann. 55 vols. Philadelphia: Muhlenberg, 1957–86.

————. "Preface to the Old Testament." In *Martin Luther's Basic Theological Writings*, 97–106. Edited by Timothy F. Lull and William R. Russell. 3rd ed. Minneapolis, MN: Fortress, 2012.

MacDonald, Nathan. "Israel and the Old Testament Story in Irenaeus's Presentation of the Rule of Faith." *Journal of Theological Interpretation* 3, no. 2 (2009): 281–98.

MacDonald, Neil B. *Karl Barth and the Strange New World of the Bible: Barth, Wittgenstein, and the Metadilemmas of the Enlightenment.* Waynesboro, GA: Paternoster, 2000.

Maloney, Raymond. "De Lubac and Lonergan on the Supernatural." *Theological Studies* 69, no. 3 (2008): 509–27.

Marcos, Natalio Fernández. "Teodoreto de Ciro y la lengua hebrea." *Henoch* 9 (1987): 39–54.

Marsden, Richard, and E. Ann Matter, eds. *The New Cambridge History of the Bible: From 600 to 1450.* New York: Cambridge University Press, 2012.

Marshall, I. Howard. *Biblical Inspiration.* Grand Rapids, MI: Eerdmans, 1982.

Marshall, I. Howard, Kevin J. Vanhoozer, and Stanley E. Porter. *Beyond the Bible: Moving from Scripture to Theology.* Grand Rapids, MI: Baker Academic, 2004.

Martens, Peter, ed. *Adrian's Introduction to the Divine Scriptures: An Antiochene Handbook for Scriptural Interpretation.* New York: Oxford University Press, 2017.

————. *Origen and Scripture: The Contours of the Exegetical Life.* New York: Oxford University Press, 2012.

————. "Revisiting the Allegory/Typology Distinction: The Case of Origen." *Journal of Early Christian Studies* 16, no. 3 (Fall 2008): 283–317.

Martin, Dale B. *Biblical Truths: The Meaning of Scripture in the Twenty-First Century.* New Haven, CT: Yale University Press, 2017.

————. "The Necessity of a Theology of Scripture." In *The Reliability of the New Testament: Bart D. Ehrman and Daniel B. Wallace in Dialogue,* edited by Robert B. Stewart, 81–94. Minneapolis, MN: Fortress, 2011.

————. *Pedagogy of the Bible: An Analysis and Proposal.* Louisville, KY: Westminster John Knox, 2008.

————. *Sex and the Single Savior: Gender and Sexuality in Biblical Interpretation.* Louisville, KY: Westminster John Knox, 2006.

Martin, Ralph P. *A Hymn of Christ: Philippians 2:5–11 in Recent Interpretation & in the Setting of Early Christian Worship.* Downers Grove, IL: InterVarsity, 1997.

Mathews, William. *Lonergan's Quest: A Study of Desire in the Authoring of Insight.* Toronto: University of Toronto Press, 2005.

May, Gerhard. *Creatio ex nihilo: The Doctrine of "Creation out of Nothing" in Early Christian Thought.* Translated by A. S. Worrall. Edinburgh: T & T Clark, 1994.

McCabe, Herbert. *Faith within Reason.* New York: Continuum, 2007.

————. *The New Creation.* New York: Continuum, 2010.

McCarter, P. Kyle. *Textual Criticism: Recovering the Text of the Hebrew Bible.* Philadelphia: Fortress, 1986.

McClendon, James W. *Systematic Theology: Ethics.* Nashville, TN: Abingdon, 1986.

McDonald, Lee Martin. *The Biblical Canon: Its Origin, Transmission, and Authority.* Updated and rev. 3rd ed. Grand Rapids, MI: Baker Academic, 2007.

————. *The Formation of the Biblical Canon:* Vol. I: *The Old Testament: Its Authority and Canonicity.* New York: Bloomsbury T & T Clark, 2017.

————. *The Formation of the Biblical Canon:* Vol. II: *The New Testament: Its Authority and Canonicity.* New York: Bloomsbury T & T Clark, 2017.

————. *The Origin of the Bible: A Guide for the Perplexed.* New York: T & T Clark, 2011.

————. "What Do We Mean by Canon? Ancient and Modern Questions." In *Jewish and Christian Scriptures: The Function of "Canonical" and Non-Canonical Religious Texts,* edited by James H. Charlesworth and Lee Martin McDonald, 8–40. New York: T & T Clark, 2010.

McDonald, Lee Martin, and James A. Sanders, eds. *The Canon Debate.* Peabody, MA: Hendrickson, 2002.

McEvenue, Seán. *Interpretation and Bible: Essays on Truth in Literature.* Collegeville, MN: Liturgical Press, 1994.

————. *Interpreting the Pentateuch.* Collegeville, MN: Liturgical Press, 1990.

————. "Old Testament, Scripture or Theology?" *Interpretation: A Journal of Bible and Theology* 35, no. 3 (1981): 229–42.

————. "Scholarship's Impenetrable Wall." *Lonergan Workshop* 16 (2000): 121–38.

————. "Theological Doctrines and the Old Testament: Lonergan's Contribution." In *Lonergan's Hermeneutics: Its Development and Applications,* edited by Ben F. Meyer and Seán E. McEvenue, 133–54. Washington, DC: Catholic University of America Press, 1989.

McEvenue, Seán, and Ben F. Meyer, eds. *Lonergan's Hermeneutics: Its Development and Application.* Washington, DC: Catholic University of America Press, 1989.

McFarland, Ian. *From Nothing: A Theology of Creation.* Minneapolis, MN: Fortress, 2014.

McIntyre, Alasdair. *Dependent Rational Animals: Why Human Beings Need the Virtues.* Chicago: Open Court, 1999.

McKendrick, Scot, and Kathleen Doyle. *Bible Manuscripts: 1400 Years of Scribes and Scripture.* London: British Library, 2007.

McKenzie, Steven L., and Stephen R. Haynes, eds. *To Each Its Own Meaning: Biblical Criticisms and their Application.* Rev. and expanded ed. Louisville, KY: Westminster John Knox, 1999.

McKenzie, Steven L., and John Kaltner, eds. *New Meanings for Ancient Texts: Recent Approaches to Biblical Criticisms and their Applications.* Louisville, KY: Westminster John Knox, 2013.

McKim, Donald, ed. *The Dictionary of Major Biblical Interpreters.* Downers Grove, IL: InterVarsity, 2007.

McLay, R. Timothy. "The Use of the Septuagint in the New Testament." In *The Biblical Canon: Its Origin, Transmission, and Authority,* ed. Lee Martin McDonald, 224–40. Grand Rapids, MI: Baker Academic, 2007.

McMullin, Ernan. "Creation *ex nihilo*: Early History." In *Creation and the God of Abraham,* edited by David B. Burrell, Carlo Cogliatti, Janet M. Soskice, and William R. Stoeger, 11–23. New York: Cambridge University Press, 2010.

Meade, David. *Pseudonymity and Canon: An Investigation into the Relationship of Authorship and Authority in Jewish and Earliest Christian Tradition.* Tübingen: Mohr Siebeck, 1986.

Metzger, Bruce M. *The Canon of the New Testament: Its Origin, Development, and Significance.* New York: Oxford University Press, 1997.

————. *The Early Versions of the New Testament: Their Origin, Transmission, and Limitations.* New York: Oxford University Press, 1977.

————. "The Practice of Textual Criticism among the Church Fathers." *Studia Patristica* 12, 340–49. Edited by Elizabeth A. Livingstone. Oxford: Oxford University Press, 1975.

————. *The Text in Translation: Ancient and English Versions.* Grand Rapids, MI: Baker Academic, 2001.

———. *A Textual Commentary on the Greek New Testament*. 2nd ed. Stuttgart: Deutsche Bibelgesellschaft, 1994.

Metzger, Bruce M., and Bart D. Ehrman. *The Text of the New Testament: Its Transmission, Corruption, and Restoration*. 4th ed. New York: Oxford University Press, 2005.

Meyer, Ben F. *The Aims of Jesus*. San Jose, CA: Pickwick, 2002.

———. "The Challenges of Text and Reader to the Historical-Critical Method." *Concilium* 1 (1991): 3–12.

———. *Christus Faber: The Master Builder and the House of God*. Allison Park, PA: Pickwick, 1992.

———. *The Church in Three Tenses*. Garden City, NY: Doubleday, 1971.

———. *Critical Realism and the New Testament*. Allison Park, PA: Pickwick, 1989.

———. "The Philosophical Crusher." *First Things* (April 1991): 9–11.

———. "The Primacy of Consent and the Uses of Suspicion." *Ex Auditu* 2 (1987): 7–18.

———. *Reality and Illusion in New Testament Scholarship: A Primer in Critical Realist Hermeneutics*. Collegeville, MN: Liturgical Press, 1994.

———. "A Tricky Business: Ascribing New Meaning to Old Texts." *Gregorianum* 71, no. 4(1990): 743–61.

Meynell, Hugo. "Doubts about Wittgenstein's Influence." *Philosophy* 57 (1982): 251–60.

———. "Lonergan, Wittgenstein, and Where Language Hooks onto the World." In *Creativity and Method: Studies in Honor of Bernard Lonergan*, edited by Matthew Lamb, 369–81. Milwaukee: Marquette University Press, 1981.

———. "Taking A(nother) Look at Lonergan's Method." *New Blackfriars* 90 no. 1028 (2009): 474–500.

Minnis, A. J. *Medieval Theory of Authorship*. 2nd ed. Philadelphia: University of Pennsylvania Press, 1988.

Mitchell, Margaret. "Patristic Rhetoric on Trial: Origen and Eustathius Put 1 Kingdoms 28 on Trial." In *The "Belly-Myther" of Endor: Interpretations of 1 Kingdoms 28 in the Early Church*, edited by Rowan A. Greer and Margaret Mary Mitchell, lxxxv–cxxiii. Atlanta, GA: Society of Biblical Literature, 2006.

———. *Paul, the Corinthians, and the Birth of Christian Hermeneutics*. New York: Cambridge University Press, 2010.

Moberly, R. W. L. *The Bible in a Disenchanted Age: The Enduring Possibility of Christian Faith*. Grand Rapids, MI: Baker Academic, 2018.

———. *Old Testament Theology: Reading the Hebrew Bible as Christian Scripture*. Grand Rapids, MI: Baker Academic, 2013.

Moore, Sebastian. "For Bernard Lonergan." *Compass: A Jesuit Journal* 2 (1985): 12–13.

Moscicke, Hans. "The Theological Presuppositions of Ancient Christian Exegesis: G. K. Beale and Henri de Lubac in Conversation." *Journal of Theological Interpretation* 10, no. 1 (2016): 125–44.

Moss, Candida R., and Joel S. Baden. *Bible Nation: The United States of Hobby Lobby.* Princeton, NJ: Princeton University Press, 2017.

Moullins-Beaufort, Eric. "Henri de Lubac: Reader of *Dei Verbum.*" *Communio* 28 (2001): 669–93.

Moyise, Steve. *Jesus and Scripture: Studying the New Testament Use of the Old Testament.* Grand Rapids, MI: Baker Academic, 2011.

———. *The Later New Testament Writings and Scripture: The Old Testament in Acts, Hebrews, the Catholic Epistles and Revelation.* Grand Rapids, MI: Baker Academic, 2012.

———. *Paul and Scripture: Studying the New Testament Use of the Old Testament.* Grand Rapids, MI: Baker Academic, 2010.

Mroczek, Eva. *The Literary Imagination in Jewish Antiquity.* New York: Oxford University Press, 2016.

Mukenge, Kabasele. "Les Particularités des Témoins Latins de Baruch: Etude d'un phénomène de réception scripturaire." *Revue biblique* 107 (2000): 24–41.

Müller, Mogens. *The First Bible of the Church: A Plea for the Septuagint.* Sheffield: Sheffield Academic, 1996.

Mullins, Ryan T. "Simply Impossible: A Case against Divine Simplicity." *Journal of Reformed Theology* 7 (2013): 181–203.

Murphy, Nancey. *Bodies and Souls, or Spirited Bodies?* New York: Cambridge University Press, 2006.

———. "Reductionism and Emergence: A Critical Perspective." In *Human Identity at the Intersection of Science, Technology, and Religion,* edited by Christopher C. Knight and Nancey C. Murphy, 67–79. Surrey: Ashgate, 2010.

Murphy, William F., Jr. "Henri de Lubac's Mystical Tropology." *Communio* 27 (2000): 171–201.

Myers, Jacob D. *Making Love with Scripture: Why the Bible Doesn't Mean How You Think It Does.* Minneapolis, MN: Fortress, 2015.

Nafzger, Peter H. *"These Are Written": Toward a Cruciform Theology of Scripture.* Eugene, OR: Pickwick, 2013.

Neill, Stephen, and N. T. Wright. *The Interpretation of the New Testament, 1861–1986.* New York: Oxford University Press, 1988.

Neuschäfer, Bernard. *Origenes als Philologe.* 2 vols. Basel: Friedrich Reinhard, 1987.

Noll, Mark. *The Civil War as a Theological Crisis.* Chapel Hill: University of North Carolina Press, 2006.

Norris Jr., Richard A. *God and World in Early Christian Theology.* New York: Seabury, 1965.

———. "The Insufficiency of Scripture: *Adversus haereses* 2 and the Role of Scripture in Irenaeus's Anti-Gnostic Polemic." In *Reading in Christian Communities: Essays on Interpretation in the Early Church,* edited by Charles A. Bobertz and David Brakke, 63–79. Notre Dame, IN: University of Notre Dame Press, 2002.

Nugent, John. *The Politics of Yahweh: John Howard Yoder, the Old Testament, and the People of God.* Eugene, OR: Wipf & Stock, 2011.

Ohme, Heinz. *Kanon ekklesiastikos: Die Bedeutung des altkirchlichen Kanonbegriffs.* New York: Walter de Gruyter, 1998.

O'Keefe, John, and R. R. Reno. *Sanctified Vision: An Introduction to Early Christian Exegesis of the Bible.* Baltimore, MD: Johns Hopkins University Press, 2005.

Okoye, James Chukwuma. *Scripture in the Church: The Synod on the Word of God.* Collegeville, MN: Michael Glazier, 2011.

Olszowy-Schlanger, Judith. "The Hebrew Bible." In *The New Cambridge History of the Bible:* Vol. 2: *From 600–1450,* edited by Richard Marsden and E. Ann Matter, 19–40. New York: Cambridge University Press, 2012.

Ong, Walter. *Orality and Literacy: The Technologizing of the Word 30th Anniversary Edition.* New York: Routledge, 2012.

O'Regan, Cyril. *Gnostic Return in Modernity.* Albany: SUNY Press, 2001.

Origen. *Commentary on the Epistle to the Romans.* Translated by Thomas P. Scheck. Washington, DC: Catholic University of America Press, 2002.

———. *Commentary on the Gospel According to John: Books 1–10.* Translated by Ronald Heine. Washington, DC: Catholic University of America Press, 1989.

———. *Contra Celsum.* Translated with an Introduction and Notes by Henry Chadwick. New York: Cambridge University Press, 1953.

———. *Homilies on Genesis and Exodus.* Translated by Ronald E. Heine. Washington, DC: Catholic University of America Press, 1982.

———. *Homilies on Joshua.* Translated by Cynthia White and Barbara J. Bruce. Washington, DC: Catholic University of America Press, 2002.

———. *On First Principles.* Translated by Herbert Butterworth. Foreword by John Cavadini. Introduction by Henri de Lubac. Notre Dame, IN: Ave Maria, 2013.

———. *The Philocalia of Origen.* Translated by George Lewis. Edinburgh: T & T Clark, 1911.

———. *Traité des principes.* Translated and edited by Henri Crouzel and Manlio Simonetti. Sources chrétiennes 252, 253, 268, 269, 312. Paris: Cerf, 1978–80.

Ormerod, Neil. *Method, Meaning, and Revelation: The Meaning and Function of Revelation in Bernard Lonergan's Method in Theology.* Lanham, MD: University Press of America, 2000.

Orsini, Pasquale, and Willy Clarysse. "Early New Testament Manuscripts and Their Dates: A Critique of Theological Paleography." *Ephemerides Theologicae Lovanienses* 88, no. 4 (2012): 443–74.

Osborn, Eric S. *Clement of Alexandria.* New York: Cambridge University Press, 2005.

———. *Irenaeus of Lyons.* New York: Cambridge University Press, 2001.

———. "Reason and the Rule of Faith in the Second Century." In *The Making of Orthodoxy: Essays in Honor of Henry Chadwick,* edited by Rowan Williams, 40–62. New York: Cambridge University Press, 1989.

———. *Tertullian: First Theologian of the West.* New York: Cambridge University Press, 1997.

Osburn, Carroll. "The Greek Lectionaries of the New Testament." In *The Text of the New Testament in Contemporary Research: Essays on the Status Quaestionis*, edited by Bart D. Ehrman and Michael W. Holmes, 93–114. 2nd ed. Boston: Brill, 2013.

Paap, Anton H. *Nomina Sacra in the Greek Papyri of the First Five Centuries AD: The Sources and Some Deductions*. Boston: Brill, 1959.

Paddison, Angus. "The Authority of Scripture and the Triune God." *International Journal of Systematic Theology* 13, no. 4 (2011): 448–62.

———. *Scripture: A Very Theological Proposal*. New York: Bloomsbury T & T Clark, 2009.

Pagels, Elaine. "Irenaeus, the 'Canon of Truth,' and the 'Gospel of John': 'Making a Difference' through Hermeneutics and Ritual." *Vetus Christiana* 56, no. 4 (2002): 339–71.

Paget, James Carolton, and Joachim Schaper, eds. *The New Cambridge History of the Bible: From the Beginnings to 600*. New York: Cambridge University Press, 2013.

Pambrun, James R. "Revelation and Interiority: The Contribution of Frederick E. Crowe, S.J." *Theological Studies* 67 (2006): 320–44.

Parker, David C. *An Introduction to the New Testament Manuscripts and Their Texts*. New York: Cambridge University Press, 2008.

———. *Codex Sinaiticus: The Story of the World's Oldest Bible*. Peabody, MA: Hendrickson, 2010.

———. "Scripture Is Tradition." *Theology* 94, no. 11 (1991): 11–17.

Patte, Daniel. *Ethics of Biblical Interpretation: A Reevaluation*. Louisville, KY: Westminster John Knox, 1995.

———. "Scriptural Criticism as a Practice of Biblical Studies: Conceiving a Commentary on Romans." In *The Meanings We Choose: Hermeneutical Ethics, Indeterminacy, and the Conflict of Interpretations*, edited by Charles Cosgrove, 62–80. New York: T & T Clark, 2004.

Pelikan, Jaroslav. *Christianity and Classical Culture: The Metamorphosis of Natural Theology in the Christian Encounter with Hellenism*. New Haven, CT: Yale University Press, 1993.

———. *The Emergence of the Catholic Tradition (100–600)*. Chicago: University of Chicago Press, 1971.

———. *Whose Bible Is It? A Short History of the Scriptures*. New York: Penguin Books, 2005.

Pesce, Mauro. "Un 'bruit absurde'? Henri de Lubac di fronte alla distinzione tra esegesi storica e esegesi spirituale." *Annali di storia dell'esegesi* 10, no. 2 (1993): 301–53.

Peterson, Eugene. *Eat This Book: A Conversation on the Art of Spiritual Reading*. Grand Rapids, MI: Eerdmans, 2006.

Piaget, Jean. *The Origin of Intelligence in the Child*. Translated by Margaret Cook. New York: Routledge, 1953.

————. *The Psychology of Intelligence*. Translated by Malcom Piercy and D. E. Berlyne. New York: Routledge, 2003.

Piazzoni, Embrogio M., with Francesca Manzari, eds. *The Bible: From Late Antiquity to the Renaissance: Writings and Images from the Vatican Library*. Collegeville, MN: Liturgical Press, 2017.

Pieper, Joseph. *Faith, Hope, Love*. Translated by Richard and Clara Winston. San Francisco: Ignatius, 1997.

Pinnock, Clark. *Most Moved Mover: A Theology of God's Openness*. Grand Rapids, MI: Baker Academic, 2001.

Plato. *Phaedrus*. Translated by Robin Waterfield. New York: Oxford University Press, 2003.

Plummer, Eric Antone. Introduction to *Augustine's Commentary on Galatians*. Translated by Eric Antone Plumer. New York: Oxford University Press, 2003.

Pollmann, Karla. "Augustine's Hermeneutics as a Universal Discipline!?" In *Augustine and the Disciplines: From Cassiciacum to Confessions*, edited by Karla Pollmann and Mark Vessey, 206–31. New York: Oxford University Press, 2005.

————. *Doctrina Christiana: Untersuchungen zu den Anfängen der Christlichen Hermeneutik unter besonderer Berücksichtigung von Augustinus, De Doctrina Christiana*. Paradosis 41. Freiburg: Universitätsverlag, 1996.

Pollmann, Karla, and Mark Vessey, eds. *Augustine and the Disciplines from Cassiciacum to Confessions*. New York: Oxford University Press, 2005.

Pontifical Biblical Commission. *The Inspiration and Truth of Sacred Scripture*. Collegeville, MN: Liturgical Press, 2014.

————. *The Interpretation of the Bible in the Church*. Vatican City: Libreria Editrice Vaticana; Washington, DC: United States Catholic Conference, 1993.

Porter, Stanley E. *Sacred Tradition in the New Testament: Tracing Old Testament Themes in the Gospels and Epistles*. Grand Rapids, MI: Baker Academic, 2016.

Porter, Stanley E., and Gregory P. Fewster, eds. *Paul and Pseudepigraphy*. Boston: Brill, 2013.

Porter, Stanley E., and Matthew R. Malcolm, eds. *The Future of Biblical Interpretation: Responsible Plurality in Biblical Hermeneutics*. Downers Grove, IL: InterVarsity, 2013.

Portier-Young, Anathea. "Three Books of Daniel: Plurality and Fluidity among the Ancient Versions." *Interpretation: A Journal of Preaching and Teaching* 71, no. 2 (2017): 143–53.

Potterie, Ignace de la. "Le sens spirituel de l'Écriture." *Gregorianum* 78, no. 4 (1997): 627–45.

Powell, Mark Alan. *What Is Narrative Criticism?* Minneapolis, MN: Fortress, 1991.

Preus, Robert. *The Inspiration of Scripture: A Study of the Theology of the Seventeenth Century Lutheran Dogmaticians*. Edinburgh: Oliver and Boyd, 1957.

Prothero, Stephen. *Religious Literacy: What Every American Needs to Know—And Doesn't*. San Francisco: HarperCollins, 2007.

Pyper, Hugh. *The Unchained Bible: Cultural Appropriations of Biblical Texts*. New York: T & T Clark, 2012.

Quesnell, Quentin. "Mutual Misunderstanding: The Dialectic of Contemporary Hermeneutics." In *Lonergan's Hermeneutics: Its Development and Application*, edited by Seán E. McEvenue and Ben F. Meyer, 19–37. Washington, DC: Catholic University of America Press, 1989.

———. "Theological Method on Scripture as Source." In *Foundations of Theology: Papers from the International Lonergan Conference 1970*, edited by Philip McShane, vol. 1, 162–93. Notre Dame, IN: University of Notre Dame Press, 1972.

Radde-Gallwitz, Andrew. *Basil of Caesarea, Gregory of Nyssa, and the Transformation of Divine Simplicity*. New York: Oxford University Press, 2009.

Radner, Ephraim. *Time and the Word: Figural Reading of the Christian Scriptures*. Grand Rapids, MI: Eerdmans, 2016.

Rae, Murray. *History and Hermeneutics*. New York: T & T Clark, 2005.

Rahner, Karl. *Inspiration in the Bible*. Translated by Charles H. Henkey. Edinburgh: Nelson, 1961.

———. "Some Critical Thoughts on 'Functional Specialization.'" In *Foundations of Theology*, edited by Philip McShane, 194–96. Notre Dame, IN: University of Notre Dame Press, 1970.

———. *The Trinity*. Translated by Joseph Donceel. New York: Burns & Oats, 2001.

Ramage, Matthew J. *Dark Passages of the Bible: Engaging Scripture with Benedict XVI and St. Thomas Aquinas*. Washington, DC: Catholic University of America Press, 2013.

Ramirez, Janina. "*Sub culmine gazas*: The Iconography of the Armarium on the Ezra Page of the Codex Amiatinus." *Gesta* 48, no. 1 (2009): 1–18.

Rebenich, Stefan. "The '*Vir Triliguis*' and the '*Hebraica Veritas*.'" *Vigiliae Christianae* 47, no. 1 (1993): 50–77.

Reed, Annette Yoshiko. "Pseudeipigraphy, Authorship, and the Reception of 'the Bible' in Late Antiquity." In *The Reception and Interpretation of the Bible in Late Antiquity: Proceedings of the Montréal Colloquium in Honour of Charles Kannengiesser, 11–13 October 2006*, edited by Lorenzo DiTommaso and Lucian Tercescu, 467–90. Leiden: Brill, 2008.

Reinhardt, Elisabeth. "Thomas Aquinas as Interpreter of Scripture in Light of His Inauguration Lectures." In *Reading Sacred Scripture with Thomas Aquinas: Hermeneutical Tools, Theological Questions, and New Perspectives*, edited by Piotr Roszak and Jörgen Vijgen, 71–90. Turnhout: Brepols, 2015.

Rende, Michael. *Lonergan on Conversion: The Development of a Notion*. New York: University Press of America, 1991.

Reno, R. R., and John O'Keefe. *Sanctified Vision: An Introduction to Early Christian Exegesis of the Bible*. Baltimore, MD: Johns Hopkins University Press, 2005.

Resnick, Irven M. "The Codex in Early Jewish and Christian Communities." *Journal of Religious History* 17 (1992): 1–17.

Resseguie, James L. *Narrative Criticism and the New Testament: An Introduction.* Grand Rapids, MI: Baker Academic, 2005.

Reynolds, L. D., and Nigel Guy Wilson. *Scribes and Scholars: A Guide to the Transmission of Greek and Latin Literature.* 4th ed. Oxford: Oxford University Press, 2013.

Rhoads, David, Johanna Dewey, and James Michie. *Mark as Story: An Introduction to the Narrative of a Gospel.* 3rd ed. Minneapolis, MN: Fortress, 2012.

Riches, John, ed. *The New Cambridge History of the Bible: From 1750 to the Present.* New York: Cambridge University Press, 2015.

Ricoeur, Paul. *Le conflit des interprétations: Essais d'herméneutique.* Paris: Editions du Seuil, 1969.

———. *Essays on Biblical Interpretation.* Philadelphia: Fortress, 1980.

———. *Hermeneutics and the Human Sciences: Essays on Language, Action, and Interpretation.* Translated by John B. Thompson. New York: Cambridge University Press, 1981.

———. *The Symbolism of Evil.* Translated by Emerson Buchanan. Boston: Beacon, 1969.

Roberts, C. H. "Books in the Greco-Roman World and in the New Testament." In *The Cambridge History of the Bible*, edited by P. R. Ackroyd and C. F. Evans, 48–66. New York: Cambridge University Press, 1970.

———. *Manuscript, Society, and Belief in Early Christian Egypt.* New York: Oxford University Press, 1979.

Roberts, C. H., and T. C. Skeat. *The Birth of the Codex.* New York: Oxford University Press, 1987.

Robinette, Brian. "The Difference Nothing Makes: *Creatio Ex Nihilo*, Resurrection, and Divine Gratuity." *Theological Studies* 72 (2011): 525–557.

Rodriguez, Rafael. *Oral Tradition and the New Testament: A Guide for the Perplexed.* New York: T & T Clark, 2014.

Rogers, Eugene F. *After the Spirit: A Constructive Pneumatology from Resources outside the Modern West.* Grand Rapids, MI: Eerdmans, 2005.

———. "How the Virtues of the Interpreter Presuppose and Perfect Hermeneutics: The Case of Thomas Aquinas." *Journal of Religion* 76, no. 1 (1996): 64–81.

Rogerson, John. Preface to *The Oxford Illustrated History of the Bible*, edited by John Rogerson, 164–65. New York: Oxford University Press, 2001.

Rollston, Chris A. *Writing and Literacy in the World of Ancient Israel: Epigraphic Evidence from the Iron Age.* Atlanta, GA: Society of Biblical Literature, 2010.

Rombs, Ronnie J. "*Unum Deum . . . Mundi Conditorem*: Implications of the Rule of Faith in Augustine's Understanding of Time and History." In *Tradition and the Rule of Faith in the Early Church: Essays in Honor of Joseph T. Lienhard, S.J.*, edited by Ronnie J. Rombs and Alexander Y. Hwang, 232–50. Washington, DC: Catholic University of America Press, 2010.

Rombs, Ronnie J., and Alexander Y. Hwang, eds. *Tradition and the Rule of Faith in the Early Church: Essays in Honor of Joseph T. Lienhard, S.J.* Washington, DC: Catholic University of America Press, 2010.

Römer, Thomas, and Philip R. Davies. *Writing the Bible: Scribes, Scribalism and Script*. New York: Routledge, 2016.

Rorem, Paul. *Biblical and Liturgical Symbols within the Pseudo-Dionysian Synthesis*. Toronto: Pontifical Institute of Medieval Studies, 1984.

———. *Pseudo-Dionysius: A Commentary on the Texts and an Introduction to Their Influence*. New York: Oxford University Press, 1993.

Rosenberg, Randall. "The Drama of Scripture: Reading Patristic Biblical Hermeneutics through Lonergan's Reflections on Art." *Logos: A Journal of Catholic Thought and Culture* 11, no. 2 (2008): 126–48.

———. *The Givenness of Desire: Concrete Subjectivity and the Natural Desire to See God*. Toronto: University of Toronto Press, 2017.

Rouwhorst, Gerard. "The Bible in Liturgy." In *The New Cambridge History of the Bible: From the Beginnings to 600*, edited by James Carolton Paget and Joachim Schaper, 822–42. New York: Cambridge University Press, 2013.

Russell, Norman K. *The Doctrine of Deification in the Greek Patristic Tradition*. New York: Oxford University Press, 2004.

Rutledge, Fleming. *The Crucifixion*. Grand Rapids, MI: Eerdmans, 2015.

Ryan, Jordan J. *The Role of the Synagogue in the Aims of Jesus*. Minneapolis, MN: Fortress, 2017.

Rylaarsdam, David. *John Chrysostom on Divine Pedagogy: The Coherence of His Theology and Preaching*. Oxford: Oxford University Press, 2014.

Sæbø, Magne, ed., *Hebrew Bible/Old Testament: The History of Its Interpretation*. 3 vols. Göttingen: Vandenhoeck & Ruprecht, 1996–2013.

Sáenz-Badillos, Angel. *A History of the Hebrew Language*. Translated by John Elwolde. New York: Cambridge University Press, 1996.

Sala, Giovanni B. *Lonergan and Kant: Five Essays on Human Knowledge*. Translated by Joseph Spoerl. Edited by Robert M. Doran. Toronto: University of Toronto Press, 1994.

Sanders, Fred. *The Image of the Immanent Trinity: Rahner's Rule and the Theological Interpretation of Scripture*. New York: Peter Lang, 2005.

Sanders, James A. *Torah and Canon*. 2nd ed. Eugene, OR: Cascade, 2005.

Sargent, Benjamin. *Written for Our Learning: The Single Meaning of Scripture in Christian Theology*. Eugene, OR: Cascade, 2016.

Sarisky, Darren. "Exegesis and Participation." *Journal of Theological Interpretation* 3, no. 2 (2009): 299–306.

———. *Scriptural Interpretation: A Theological Exploration*. Malden, MA: Wiley-Blackwell, 2012.

Schjedal, Peter. "Faces: A Cindy Sherman Retrospective." *New Yorker*, March 5, 2012, 84–85.

Schleiermacher, Friedrich. *Hermeneutics and Criticism and Other Writings*. Edited by Andrew Bowie. New York: Cambridge University Press, 1998.

Schlesinger, Eugene. *Missa Est: A Missional Liturgical Ecclesiology*. Minneapolis, MN: Fortress, 2017.

Schneiders, Sandra. *The Revelatory Text: Interpreting the New Testament as Sacred Scripture.* 2nd ed. Collegeville, MN: Liturgical Press, 1999.

Schniedewind, William N. *How the Bible Became a Book: The Textualization of Ancient Israel.* New York: Cambridge University Press, 2005.

Schökel, Luis Alonso. *The Inspired Word: Scripture in the Light of Language and Literature.* London: Burns & Oats, 1967.

Schüssler Fiorenza, Elisabeth. *Democratizing Biblical Studies: Toward an Emancipatory Educational Space.* Louisville, KY: Westminster John Knox, 2009.

———. "The Ethics of Biblical Interpretation: Decentering Biblical Scholarship." In *Reading the Bible in the Global Village,* 109–26. Atlanta, GA: Society of Biblical Literature, 2000.

Schüssler Fiorenza, Francis. "Systematic Theology: Tasks and Methods." In *Systematic Theology: Roman Catholic Perspectives,* edited by Francis Schüssler Fiorenza and John P. Galvin, 1–78. 2nd ed. Minneapolis, MN: Fortress, 2011.

The Scripture Project. "Nine Theses on the Interpretation of Scripture." In *The Art of Reading Scripture,* edited by Ellen F. Davis and Richard B. Hays, 1–5. Grand Rapids, MI: Eerdmans, 2003.

Seitz, Christopher. *The Character of Christian Scripture: The Significance of a Two-Testament Bible.* Grand Rapids, MI: Eerdmans, 2011.

———. *Figured Out: Typology and Providence in Christian Scripture.* Louisville, KY: Westminster John Knox, 2001.

Sheehan, Jonathan. *The Enlightenment Bible: Translation, Scholarship, Culture.* Princeton, NJ: Princeton University Press, 2005.

Sheridan, Mark. "The Concept of 'Useful' in Patristic Exegesis." In *Studia Patristica* 39, edited by Frances Young, Mark Edwards, and Paul Parvis, 253–57. Leuven: Peeters, 2006.

———. *Language for God in Patristic Tradition: Wrestling with Biblical Anthropomorphism.* Foreword by Thomas Oden. Downers Grove, IL: InterVarsity, 2015.

Shillington, V. George. *Reading the Sacred Text: An Introduction to Biblical Studies.* New York: T & T Clark, 2002.

Siebert, Eric A. *Disturbing Divine Behavior: Troubling Old Testament Images of God.* Minneapolis, MN: Fortress, 2009.

———. *The Violence of Scripture: Overcoming the Old Testament's Troubling Legacy.* Minneapolis, MN: Fortress, 2012.

Siecienski, A. Edward. "(Re)Defining the Boundaries of Orthodoxy: The Rule of Faith and the Twentieth Century Rehabilitation of Origen." In *Tradition and the Rule of Faith in the Early Church: Essays in Honor of Joseph T. Lienhard, S.J.,* edited by Ronnie J. Rombs and Alexander Y. Hwang, 286–307. Washington, DC: Catholic University of America Press, 2010.

Siker, Jeffrey S. *Liquid Scripture: The Bible in a Digital World.* Minneapolis, MN: Fortress, 2017.

Simon, Marcel. *Verus Israel: A Study of the Relations between Christians and Jews in the Roman Empire (135–425).* Translated by H. McKeating. Oxford: Oxford University Press, 1986.

Simpson, Christopher Ben. "Between God and Metaphysics: An Interview with William Desmond." *Radical Orthodoxy: Theology, Philosophy, Politics* 1, nos. 1 and 2 (2012): 357–73.

Skeat, T. C. "The Oldest Manuscript of the Four Gospels?" *New Testament Studies* 43 (1997): 1–34.

Smart, James D. *The Strange Silence of the Bible in the Church: A Study in Hermeneutics.* Philadelphia: Westminster, 1970.

Smend, Rudolf. *From Astruc to Zimmerli: Old Testament Scholarship in Three Centuries.* Translated by Margaret Kohl. Tübingen: Mohr Siebeck, 2007.

Smith, Christian. *The Bible Made Impossible: Why Biblicism Is Not a Truly Evangelical Reading of Scripture.* Grand Rapids, MI: Eerdmans, 2011.

Smith, James K. A. *Desiring the Kingdom: Worship, Worldview, and Cultural Formation.* Grand Rapids, MI: Baker Academic, 2009.

———. *The Fall of Interpretation: Philosophical Foundations for a Creational Hermeneutic.* 2nd ed. Grand Rapids, MI: Baker Academic, 2012.

Smith, Wilfred Cantwell. *What is Scripture? A Comparative Approach.* Minneapolis, MN: Fortress, 1993.

Snell, R. J. *Through a Glass Darkly: Bernard Lonergan & Richard Rorty on Knowing without a God's-Eye View.* Milwaukee, WI: Marquette University Press, 2006.

Snell, R. J., and Steven D. Cone. *Authentic Cosmopolitanism: Love, Sin, and Grace in the Christian University.* Eugene, OR: Pickwick, 2013.

Sokolowski, Robert. *Christian Faith and Human Understanding: Studies on the Eucharist, Trinity, and Human Person.* Washington, DC: Catholic University of America Press, 2006.

———. *The God of Faith and Reason.* 2nd ed. Washington, DC: Catholic University of America Press, 1995.

———. *Phenomenology of the Human Person.* New York: Cambridge University Press, 2008.

Soskice, Janet M. "*Creatio ex nihilo*: Its Jewish and Christian Foundations." In *Creation and the God of Abraham*, edited by David B. Burrell, Carlo Cogliatti, Janet M. Soskice, and William R. Stoeger, 24–39. New York: Cambridge University Press, 2010.

Soulen, Kendall. *The God of Israel and Christian Theology.* Minneapolis, MN: Fortress, 1996.

Sparks, Kenton. *God's Word in Human Words: An Evangelical Appropriation of Critical Biblical Scholarship.* Grand Rapids, MI: Baker, 2008.

———. *Sacred Word, Broken Word: Biblical Authority and the Dark Side of Scripture.* Grand Rapids, MI: Eerdmans, 2012.

Spicq, Ceslas. *Esquisse d'une histoire de l'exegese latine au moyen age.* Paris: J. Vrin, 1944.

Stafford, Barbara. "Bernard Lonergan and New Testament Interpretation." PhD dissertation, University of Nottingham, 2008.

Stannard, David E. *American Holocaust: Columbus and the Conquest of the New World.* New York: Oxford University Press, 1993.

Stebbins, J. Michael. *The Divine Initiative: Grace, World-Order, and Human Freedom in the Early Writings of Bernard Lonergan.* Toronto: University of Toronto Press, 1996.

Steinmetz, David C. "The Superiority of Pre-critical Exegesis." In *The Theological Interpretation of Scripture: Classic and Contemporary Readings,* edited by Stephen E. Fowl, 26–38. Malden, MA: Blackwell, 1997.

Stendahl, Krister. "The Apostle Paul and the Introspective Conscience of the West." *Harvard Theological Review* 56, no. 3 (1963): 199–215.

———. "The Bible as Classic and the Bible as Scripture." *Journal of Biblical Literature* 103 (1984): 3–10.

———. "Biblical Theology, Contemporary." In *The Interpreter's Dictionary of the Bible,* edited by George Arthur Buttrick, vol. 1: 418–32. Nashville, TN: Abingdon, 1962.

Stewart, Alistair. "'The Rule of Truth . . . which He Received through Baptism' (*Haer.* 1.9.4): Catechesis, Ritual, and Exegesis in Irenaeus's Gaul." In *Irenaeus: Life, Scripture, Legacy,* edited by Paul Foster and Sarah Parvis, 151–58. Minneapolis, MN: Fortress, 2012.

Still, Ute. *"Nomina Sacra" im Altkirchenslavischen: bis zum 11. Jahrhundert.* Munich: W. Fink, 1972.

Stock, Brian. *Augustine the Reader: Meditation, Self-Knowledge, and the Ethics of Interpretation.* Cambridge, MA: Harvard University Press, 1996.

Stockhausen, Carol Kern. *Moses' Veil and the Glory of the New Covenant: The Exegetical Substructure of II Cor 3,1–4, 6.* Rome: Editrice Pontificio Istituto Biblico, 1989.

Storer, Kevin. *Reading Scripture to Hear God: Kevin Vanhoozer and Henri de Lubac on God's Use of Scripture in the Economy of Redemption.* Eugene, OR: Wipf & Stock, 2014.

———. "Theological Interpretation and the Spiritual Sense of Scripture: Henri de Lubac's Retrieval of a Christological Hermeneutic of Presence." *Journal of Theological Interpretation* 7, no. 1 (2013): 79–96.

Stroumsa, Guy G. "The New Self and Reading Practices in Late Antique Christianity." *Church History and Religious Culture* 95 (2015): 1–18.

———. *The Scriptural Universe of Ancient Christianity.* Cambridge, MA: Harvard University Press, 2016.

Stuhhofer, Franz. *Der Gebrauch der Bibel von Jesus bis Euseb: Eine statistische Untersuchungen zur Kanongeschichte.* Wuppertal: R. Brockhaus, 1988.

Sugirtharajah, R. S. "Complacencies and Cul-de-Sacs: Christian Theologies and Colonialism." In *Postcolonial Theologies: Divinity and Empire,* edited by

Catherine Keller, Michael Nauser, and Mayra Rivera, 22–36. St. Louis, MO: Chalice, 2004.

———. *Exploring Postcolonial Biblical Criticism: History, Method, Practice.* Malden, MA: Wiley-Blackwell, 2012.

Sumney, Jerry L. *Steward of God's Mysteries: Paul and Early Church Tradition.* Grand Rapids, MI: Eerdmans, 2017.

Swain, Scott. *Trinity, Revelation, and Reading: A Theological Introduction to the Bible and Its Interpretation.* New York: T & T Clark, 2011.

Tanner, Kathryn. *God and Creation in Christian Theology: Tyranny or Empowerment?* Minneapolis, MN: Fortress, 1998.

———. "Theology and the Plain Sense." In *Scriptural Authority and Narrative Interpretation,* edited by Garrett Green, 59–78. Philadelphia: Fortress, 1987.

Tapie, Matthew A. *Aquinas on Israel and the Church: The Question of Supersessionism in the Theology of Thomas Aquinas.* Eugene, OR: Pickwick, 2014.

Taylor, Charles. *Sources of the Self: The Making of Modern Identity.* Cambridge, MA: Harvard University Press, 1989.

Teevan, Donna. *Lonergan, Hermeneutics, & Theological Method.* Milwaukee, WI: Marquette University Press, 2005.

Tekippe, Terry J. *Bernard Lonergan: An Introductory Guide to Insight.* New York: Paulist, 2003.

Thielman, Frank S. "Ephesians." In *Commentary on the New Testament Use of the Old Testament,* edited by Gregory. K. Beale and Donald A. Carson, 813–34. Grand Rapids, MI: Baker Academic, 2007.

Thiselton, Anthony. "The Future of Biblical Interpretation and Responsible Plurality in Hermeneutics." In *The Future of Biblical Interpretation: Responsible Plurality in Biblical Hermeneutics,* edited by Stanley E. Porter and Matthew R. Malcolm, 11–28. Downers Grove, IL: IVP Academic, 2013.

———. *Hermeneutics: An Introduction.* Grand Rapids, MI: Eerdmans, 2009.

———. *New Horizons in Hermeneutics.* Grand Rapids, MI: Zondervan, 1992.

———. *The Two Horizons: New Testament and Philosophical Description with Reference to the Work of Heidegger, Bultmann, Gadamer, and Wittgenstein.* Grand Rapids, MI: Eerdmans, 1980.

Thomas Aquinas. "The Inaugural Lectures." In *Thomas Aquinas, Selected Writings,* 5–17. Edited and Translated with an Introduction by Ralph McInerny. Harmondsworth: Penguin, 1998.

Toom, Tarmo. *Thought Clothed with Sound: Augustine's Christological Hermeneutics in De Doctrina Christiana.* Bern: Peter Lang, 2002.

Topel, John. "Faith, Exegesis, and Theology." *Irish Theological Quarterly* 69 (2004): 337–48.

———. "What Does Systematic Theology Say to New Testament Interpretation?" In *Theology and Sacred Scripture,* edited by Carol J. Dempsey and William P. Loewe, 105–24. Maryknoll, NY: Orbis, 2001.

Torchia, N. Joseph. *Creatio Ex Nihilo and the Theology of St. Augustine: The Anti-Manichaean Polemic and Beyond.* New York: Peter Lang, 1999.

Torjesen, Karen Jo. *Hermeneutical Procedure and Theological Method in Origen's Exegesis.* New York: Walter de Gruyter, 1986.

Torre, Miguel De La. *Reading the Bible from the Margins.* Maryknoll, NY: Orbis, 2002.

Tov, Emanuel. *Scribal Practices and Approaches Reflected in the Texts Found in the Judean Desert.* Boston: Brill, 2004.

———. *Textual Criticism of the Hebrew Bible.* 3rd ed. rev. and expanded. Minneapolis, MN: Fortress, 2012.

Tracy, David. *The Analogical Imagination: Christian Theology and the Culture of Pluralism.* New York: Crossroad, 1981.

———. *Blessed Rage for Order: The New Pluralism in Theology.* New York: Seabury, 1975.

———. *Plurality and Ambiguity: Hermeneutics, Religion, Hope.* San Francisco: Harper & Row, 1987.

Traube, Ludwig. *Nomina sacra: Versuch einer Geschichte der christlichen Kürzung.* Munich: Beck, 1907.

Treier, Daniel J. *Introducing Theological Interpretation of Scripture: Recovering a Christian Practice.* Grand Rapids, MI: Baker Academic, 2008.

———. "In the End, God: The Proper Focus of Theological Exegesis." *Princeton Theological Review* 14, no. 1 (2008): 7–12.

———. "The Superiority of Pre-Critical Exegesis: *Sic et Non.*" *Trinity Journal* 24, no. 1 (2003): 77–103.

———. "What Is Theological Interpretation? An Ecclesiological Reduction." *International Journal of Systematic Theology* 12, no. 2 (2010): 144–61.

Trible, Phillis. *Texts of Terror: Literary-Feminist Readings of Biblical Narratives.* London: SCM, 2003.

Trigg, Joseph. *Origen: The Bible and Philosophy in the Third-Century Church.* Atlanta, GA: John Knox, 1983.

Trobisch, David. *The First Edition of the New Testament.* New York: Oxford University Press, 2000.

———. *Paul's Letter Collection: Tracing the Origins.* Minneapolis, MN: Fortress, 1994.

Tuckett, Christopher M. "'*Nomina Sacra*' Yes and No?" In *The Biblical Canons,* edited by J. M. Auwers and H. J. de Jonge, 431–58. Leuven: Leuven University Press, 2003.

Tuckett, Cristopher M., Paul Foster, Andrew F. Gregory, John S. Kloppenborg, and Jozef Verheyden, eds. *New Studies in the Synoptic Problem.* Leuven: Peeters, 2011.

Turner, C. H. "The *Nomina Sacra* in Early Latin Christian MSS." *Studi e Testi* 40 (1924): 62–74.

Turner, Eric G. *Typology of the Early Codex.* Philadelphia: University of Pennsylvania Press, 1975.

Ulrich, Eugene. *The Dead Sea Scrolls and the Developmental Composition of the Bible.* Boston: Brill, 2015.

———. "The Old Testament Text and Its Transmission." In *The New Cambridge History of the Bible: From the Beginnings to 600*, edited by James Carolton Paget and Joachim Schaper, 83–104. New York: Cambridge University Press, 2013.

Van der Toorn, Karel. *Scribal Culture and the Making of the Hebrew Bible.* Cambridge, MA: Harvard University Press, 2009.

Vanhoozer, Kevin J. "Augustinian Inerrancy: Literary Meaning, Literal Truth, and Literate Interpretation in the Economy of Divine Discourse." In *Biblical Inerrancy: Five Views*, edited by James R. A. Merrick and Stephen M. Garrett, 199–235. Grand Rapids, MI: Zondervan, 2013.

———. *The Drama of Doctrine: A Canonical Linguistic Approach to Christian Theology.* Louisville, KY: Westminster John Knox, 2005.

———. "Holy Scripture." In *Christian Dogmatics: Reformed Theology for the Church Catholic*, edited by Michael Allen and Scott Swain, 30–56. Grand Rapids, MI: Baker Academic, 2017.

———. *Is There a Meaning in This Text? The Bible, the Reader and the Morality of Literary Knowledge.* Tenth Anniversary Edition. Grand Rapids, MI: Zondervan, 2008.

———. *Remythologizing Theology: Divine Action, Passion, and Authorship.* Cambridge: Cambridge University Press, 2010.

Vanhoozer, Kevin, Craig G. Bartholomew, Daniel J. Treier, and N. T. Wright, eds. *Dictionary for the Theological Interpretation of the Bible.* Grand Rapids, MI: Baker, 2005.

Van Rompay, Lucas. "The East (3): Syria and Mesopotamia." In *The Oxford Handbook of Early Christian Studies*, edited by Susan Ashbrook Harvey and David G. Hunter, 365–88. New York: Oxford University Press, 2008.

Vawter, Bruce. *Biblical Inspiration.* Philadelphia: Westminster, 1972.

Voderholzer, Rudolf. "Dogma and History: Henri de Lubac and the Retrieval of Historicity as a Key to Theological Renewal." Translated by Adrian Walker. *Communio* 28, no. 4 (2001): 648–68.

———. *Die Einheit der Schrift und ihr geistiger Sinn: Der Beitrag Henri de Lubac zur Erforschung von Geschichte und Systematik christlicher Bibelhermeneutik.* Freiburg: Johannes Verlag Einsiedeln, 1998.

———. *Meet Henri de Lubac.* Translated by Michael J. Miller. San Francisco: Ignatius, 2008.

Vogt, Hermann Josef. *Origenes als Exeget.* Paderborn: Schöningh, 1999.

Volk, John. "Lonergan on the Historical Causality of Christ: An Interpretation of 'The Redemption': A Supplement to *De Verbo Incarnato*." PhD dissertation, Marquette University, 2010.

Waers, Stephen. "Monarchianism and Origen's Early Trinitarian Theology." PhD dissertation, Marquette University, 2016.

Wahlberg, Mats. *Revelation as Testimony: A Philosophical Theological Study*. Grand Rapids, MI: Eerdmans, 2014.

Wainwright, Geoffrey. "Towards an Ecumenical Hermeneutic: How Can All Christians Read the Scriptures Together?" *Gregorianum* 76, no. 4 (1995): 639–62.

Wall, Robert. "Reading the Bible from within our Traditions: The 'Rule of Faith' in Theological Hermeneutics." In *Between Two Horizons: Spanning New Testament Studies and Systematic Theology*, edited by Joel B. Green and Max Turner, 88–107. Grand Rapids, MI: Eerdmans, 2000.

Watson, Francis. "Are There Still Four Gospels? A Study in Theological Hermeneutics." In *Reading Scripture with the Church: Toward a Hermeneutic for Theological Interpretation*, edited by A. K. M. Adam, Stephen E. Fowl, Kevin J. Vanhoozer, and Francis Watson, 95–116. Grand Rapids, MI: Baker, 2006.

———. *The Fourfold Gospel: A Theological Reading of the New Testament Portraits of Jesus*. Grand Rapids, MI: Baker Academic, 2016.

———. "Hermeneutics and the Doctrine of Scripture: Why They Need Each Other." *International Journal of Systematic Theology* 12, no. 2 (2010): 118–43.

———. *Paul and the Hermeneutics of Faith*. 2nd ed. New York: T & T Clark, 2016.

———. "Toward a Resolution Yet to Be Revealed." In *Reading Scripture with the Church: Toward a Hermeneutic for Theological Interpretation*, edited by A. K. M. Adam, Stephen E. Fowl, Kevin J. Vanhoozer, and Francis Watson, 143–48. Grand Rapids, MI: Baker, 2006.

Webster, John. *Holy Scripture: A Dogmatic Sketch*. New York: Cambridge University Press, 2003.

Weems, Renita. *Battered Love: Marriage, Sex, and Violence in the Hebrew Prophets*. Minneapolis, MN: Fortress, 1995.

Wegner, Paul. *The Journey from Texts to Translations: The Origin and Development of the Bible*. Grand Rapids, MI: Baker Academic, 2004.

Weinandy, Thomas G. *Does God Suffer?* Notre Dame, IN: University of Notre Dame Press, 2000.

———. "God and Human Suffering: His Act of Creation and His Acts in History." In *Divine Impassibility and the Mystery of Human Suffering*, edited by James F. Keating and Thomas Joseph White, 99–116. Grand Rapids, MI: Eerdmans, 2009.

Westphal, Merold. *Whose Community? Which Interpretation? Philosophical Hermeneutics for the Church*. Grand Rapids, MI: Baker Academic, 2009.

Whelan, Gerard. *Redeeming History: Social Concern in Bernard Lonergan and Robert Doran*. Rome: Gregorian and Biblical Press, 2013.

White, Carolinne, trans. and notes. *The Correspondence (394–419) between Jerome and Augustine of Hippo*. Lewiston, NY: Edwin Mellen, 1990.

Wicker, James R. "Pre-Constantinian *Nomina sacra* in a Mosaic and Church Graffiti." *Southwest Journal of Theology* 52, no. 1 (2009): 52–72.

Wilken, Robert L. "In Defense of Allegory." In *Theology and Scriptural Imagination*, edited by L. Gregory Jones and James J. Buckley, 35–50. Malden, MA: Blackwell, 1998.

———. *John Chrysostum and the Jews: Rhetoric and Reality in the Late 4th Century*. Eugene, OR: Wipf & Stock, 2004.

———. *Judaism and the Early Christian Mind: A Study of Cyril of Alexandria's Exegesis and Theology*. Eugene, OR: Wipf & Stock, 2004.

Williams, A. N. *The Divine Sense: The Intellect in Patristic Theology*. New York: Cambridge University Press, 2007.

Williams, Daniel H. *Evangelicals and Tradition: The Formative Influences of the Early Church*. Grand Rapids, MI: Baker Academic, 2005.

———. *Tradition, Scripture, and Interpretation: A Sourcebook of the Ancient Church*. Grand Rapids, MI: Baker Academic, 2006.

Williams, David. *Receiving the Bible in Faith*. Washington, DC: Catholic University of America Press, 2004.

Williams, Rowan. *Arius: Heresy and Tradition*. 2nd ed. Grand Rapids, MI: Eerdmans, 2002.

———. *Being Christian: Baptism, Bible, Eucharist, Prayer*. Grand Rapids, MI: Eerdmans, 2014.

Williams, Thomas. "Hermeneutics and Reading Scripture." In *The Cambridge Companion to Augustine*, edited by David Vincent Meconi and Eleonore Stump, 311–28. 2nd ed. Cambridge: Cambridge University Press, 2014.

Windham, Neal. *New Testament Greek for Preachers and Teachers: Five Areas of Application*. Lanham, MD: University Press of America, 1991.

Wittgenstein, Ludwig. *Philosophical Investigations*. Translated by G. E. M. Anscombe, P. M. S. Hacker, and Joachim Shulte. Rev. 4th ed. Malden, MA: Wiley-Blackwell, 2009.

Wood, Susan. *Spiritual Exegesis and the Church in the Theology of Henri de Lubac*. Eugene, OR: Wipf & Stock, 2010.

Work, Telford. *Living and Active: Scripture in the Economy of Salvation*. Grand Rapids, MI: Eerdmans, 2002.

Wright, John, ed. *Postliberal Theology and the Church Catholic: Conversations with George Lindbeck, David Burrell, and Stanley Hauerwas*. Grand Rapids, MI: Baker Academic, 2012.

Wright, N. T. "Introduction for the New Edition." In *The Aims of Jesus*, 9a–91, by Ben F. Meyer. 2nd ed. San Jose, CA: Pickwick, 2002.

———. *The New Testament and the People of God*. Minneapolis, MN: Fortress, 1992.

———. *Scripture and the Authority of God: How to Read the Bible Today*. San Francisco: HarperCollins, 2011.

Wright IV, William M. "The Literal Sense of Scripture According to Henri de Lubac: Insights from Patristic Exegesis of the Transfiguration." *Modern Theology* 28, no. 2 (2012): 252–77.

Würthwein, Ernst. *The Text of the Old Testament: An Introduction to the Biblia Hebraica.* Translated by Erroll F. Rhodes. 2nd ed. Grand Rapids, MI: Eerdmans, 1995.

Yeago, David A. "The New Testament and Nicene Dogma." In *The Theological Interpretation of Scripture: Classic and Contemporary Readings,* edited by Stephen E. Fowl, 87–100. Malden, MA: Wiley-Blackwell, 1997.

Yeo, Khiok-khng. "Culture and Intersubjectivity as Criteria for Negotiating Meanings in Cross-Cultural Interpretations." In *The Meanings We Choose: Hermeneutical Ethics, Indeterminacy, and the Conflict of Interpretations,* edited by Charles Cosgrove, 81–100. New York: T & T Clark, 2004.

Young, Frances M. *Biblical Exegesis and the Formation of Christian Culture.* Peabody, MA: Hendrickson, 2002.

———. *The Making of the Creeds.* London: SCM, 1991.

———. "The 'Mind' of Scripture: Theological Readings of the Bible in the Fathers." *International Journal of Systematic Theology* 7, no. 2 (2005): 126–41.

———. "The Rhetorical Schools and Their Influence on Patristic Exegesis." In *The Making of Orthodoxy: Essays in Honour of Henry Chadwick,* edited by Rowan Williams, 182–99. Cambridge: Cambridge University Press, 1989.

———. *Virtuoso Theology: The Bible and Interpretation.* Eugene, OR: Wipf & Stock, 1993, 2002.

Young, Stephen E. *Jesus Tradition in the Apostolic Fathers.* Tübingen: Mohr Siebeck, 2011.

Zahn, Theodore. "Glaubensregel und Taufbekenntnis in der alten Kirche." In *Skizzen aus dem Leben der alten Kirche,* 138–70. 3rd ed. Leipzig: Deichert, 1908.

GENERAL INDEX

Achtemeier, Paul, 214–15, 221, 224, 365n131
Adler, Mortimer, 1
aggiornamento, 121
agrapha, 342n81
allegory. *See* exegesis/interpretation of Scripture
already-out-there-now/already-back-there-then, 71, 79, 109, 169, 171, 211, 214, 246, 260, 261n1, 293n82, 302n13, 304n33, 314n148
Anderson, Gary, 91
anti-semitism/anti-judaism, 236, 363–64n101
Arichea, Daniel, 222
Aristotle, 44, 77, 124–27, 129, 132
Athanasius, 36, 39, 76, 78, 105, 140, 196, 201, 204, 302n16
Augustine, 194, 207, 242, 249–50, 255, 260, 261, 267
    and Jerome, 260–61
    on language acquisition, 147
    and Manicheans, 299n138
    and the rule of faith, 61–65
    and Septuagint/LXX, 260–61
author/authorship
    anonymous of biblical books, 219
    composite of biblical books, 220–21
    contemporary views of, 219
    premodern views of, 221–22
    relationship between human and divine, 218–20

autographs. *See* manuscripts
Ayres, Lewis, 65, 116–18, 119, 120, 121–22, 250, 287n12, 300n151

Baba Batra, 199, 200
Balthasar, Hans Urs von, 99–100
Barth, Karl, 108, 195, 240, 269n1, 309n96
Barton, John, 176–78, 196, 229, 238, 286n8
Baruch, 169, 170
bias
    general, 158
    group, 157, 159
    individual, 157, 159
Bible. *See* Scripture
Blowers, Paul, 45, 73, 83
Bokedal, Thomas, 44, 51, 186, 290n45, 291n52, 293n77, 343n104
Brown, William, 241
Burrell, David, vii, 86, 89

Candler, Peter, 184, 205
canon
    "canon consciousness," 197, 204
    and Church councils, 195, 205
    closures of, 196–97
    and codices, 180
    core, 197, 200
    encovenanted, 202, 204, 238
    and fixed lists, 196–97
    functional, 197

SCRIPTURAL INDEX

JOSEPH K. GORDON

is associate professor of theology at Johnson University.

CPSIA information can be obtained
at www.ICGtesting.com
Printed in the USA
LVHW090005190319
611110LV00004B/40/P